AF327429

ABANDONED WRECKS

ABANDONED WRECKS

CHRIS McNAB

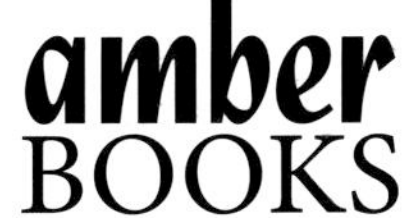
amber
BOOKS

Published by
Amber Books Ltd
74–77 White Lion Street
London
N1 9PF
United Kingdom
www.amberbooks.co.uk
Appstore: itunes.com/apps/amberbooksltd
Facebook: www.facebook.com/amberbooks
Twitter: @amberbooks

ISBN: 978-1-78274-520-4

Project Editor: Sarah Uttridge
Designer: Keren Harragan
Picture Research: Terry Forshaw

Printed in China

Contents

Introduction

T ime, as we all come to realize but often struggle to accept, is the ultimate power over our lives. Silently, and with infinite patience, the inexorable passage of time changes all, from our physical appearance and health to the contours of mountain ranges. Very visibly, it also transforms the inventions of human ingenuity. The wrecks that are featured in this book – be they cars, trucks, ships, tanks, bicycles, trains, aircraft – provide a mute testimony to time's persistence

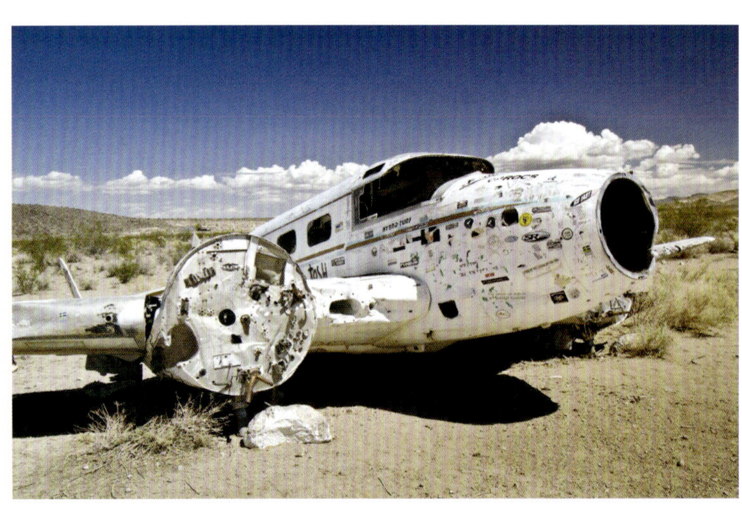

and effect. The fascination with such wrecks is entirely human. Abandoned or derelict vehicles are historical, engineering and indeed human monuments, gravestones reminding us of past achievements and passing cultural signs. Many of the wrecks displayed here speak of intense and sometimes fatal human drama – especially those vehicles destroyed in conflict. Others have a gentler message, reminding us of daily lives and regular events, and with all the poignancy of old family photos. Such is the power of the wreck, speaking to us about the vitality of the past while warning us of the inevitability of the future.

ABOVE:
A wrecked twin-prop commercial aircraft in the Nevada Desert, United States, both of its engines shorn from their mounts.
RIGHT:
HMAS *Brisbane*, an Australian guided missile destroyer sunk as a dive attraction in 2005.

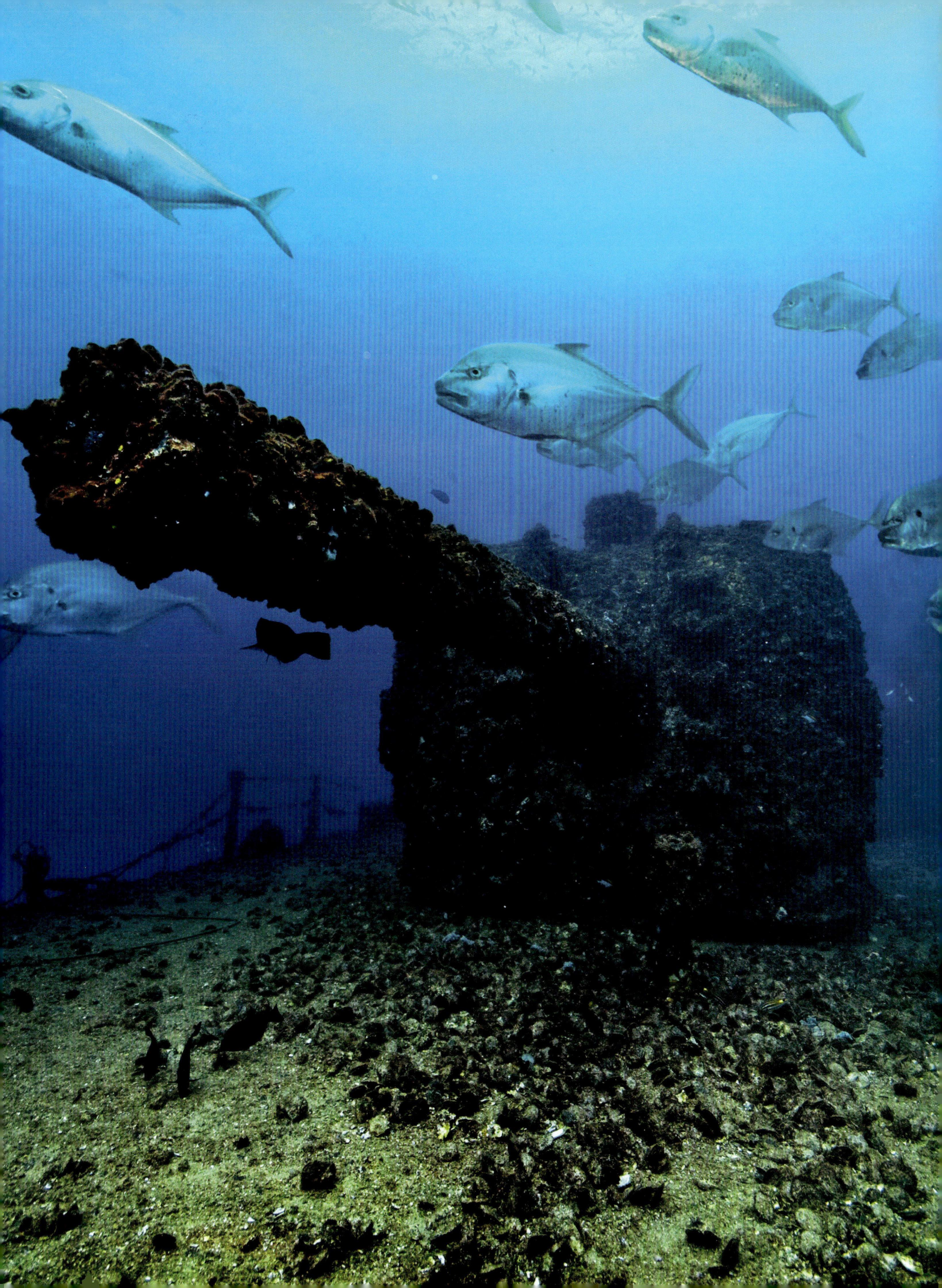

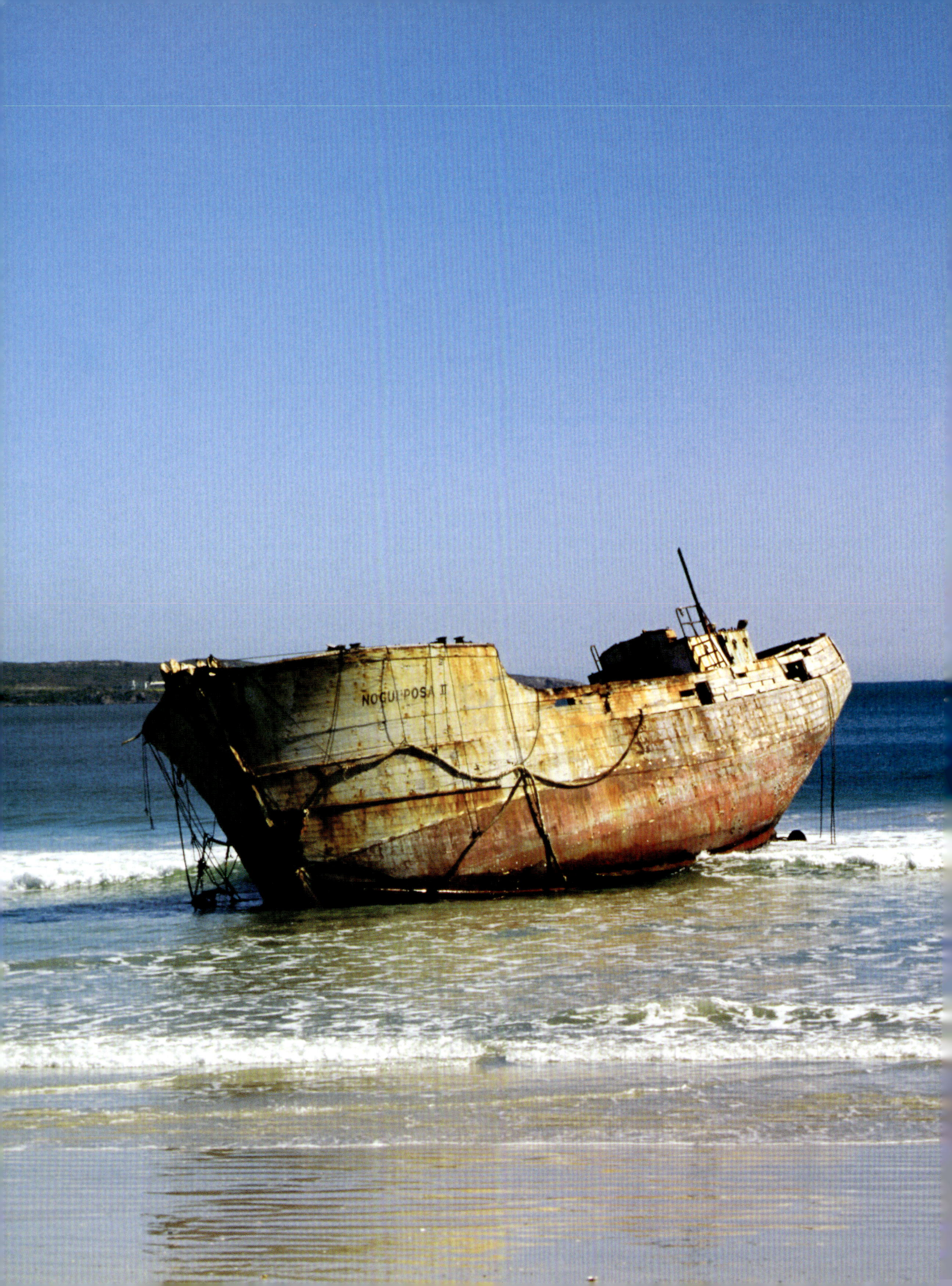
NOGUEPOSA II

Ships

There is something unnerving about almost any shipwreck. With shipwrecks there is the reminder that once a vessel loses its buoyancy, either through a breach of the hull or through grounding, it is instantly transformed into a massive dead weight of metal and wood. Shipwrecks tell us that working vessels are only temporarily defying the laws of entropy and decay. At the same time, shipwrecks are undeniably fascinating. Larger vessels are intricate spaces, the hull and superstructure consisting of labyrinthine corridors and numerous rooms both large and small, once thrumming with life and activity. The thought of being able to move weightlessly through these now dark and silent spaces, in the company of only marine life and the ghosts of the past, is a compelling attraction behind the wreck-diving industry. Some of the wrecks that feature in this chapter are globally famous – the *Titanic* is the chief example. Many others, however, represent the less glamorous side of life at sea – commercial cargo ships, whaling vessels, fishing boats – or are military specimens, some of them veterans of conflicts in waters very distant from home. Looking at any shipwreck, however, regardless of scale or historical period, there is always the sense that each has its own story. Exploring the wreck, even just imaginatively, feels as if it will reveal the secrets of the occupants who once stood on the breezy salt-blown decks or in the noisy spaces below.

Cape Town Beach, Cape Peninsula, South Africa
A beached merchant vessel sits in the surf on a South African beach, battered by time and tides. Wrecked ships can form a persistent environmental hazard, especially through the prolonged leakage of engine oil plus any hazardous on-board materials. Ideally, such vessels should be recovered and scrapped.

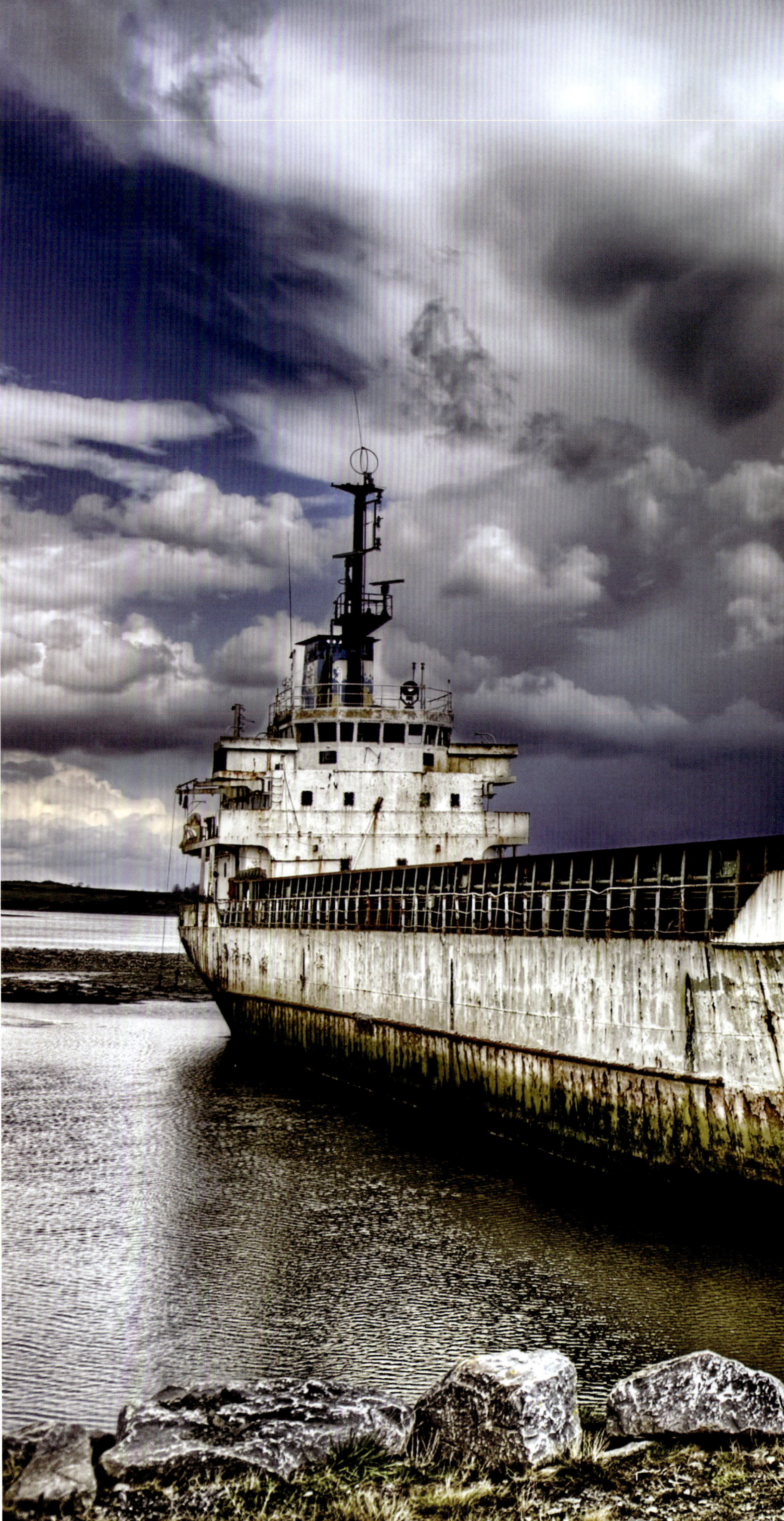

River Shannon, Ireland
This logistics ship has been left
to rust away at a quayside on
the River Shannon in Ireland.
Although modern ships are
naturally built to resist the rusting
effects of seawater, without regular
maintenance the integrity of the
hull will quickly be compromised.

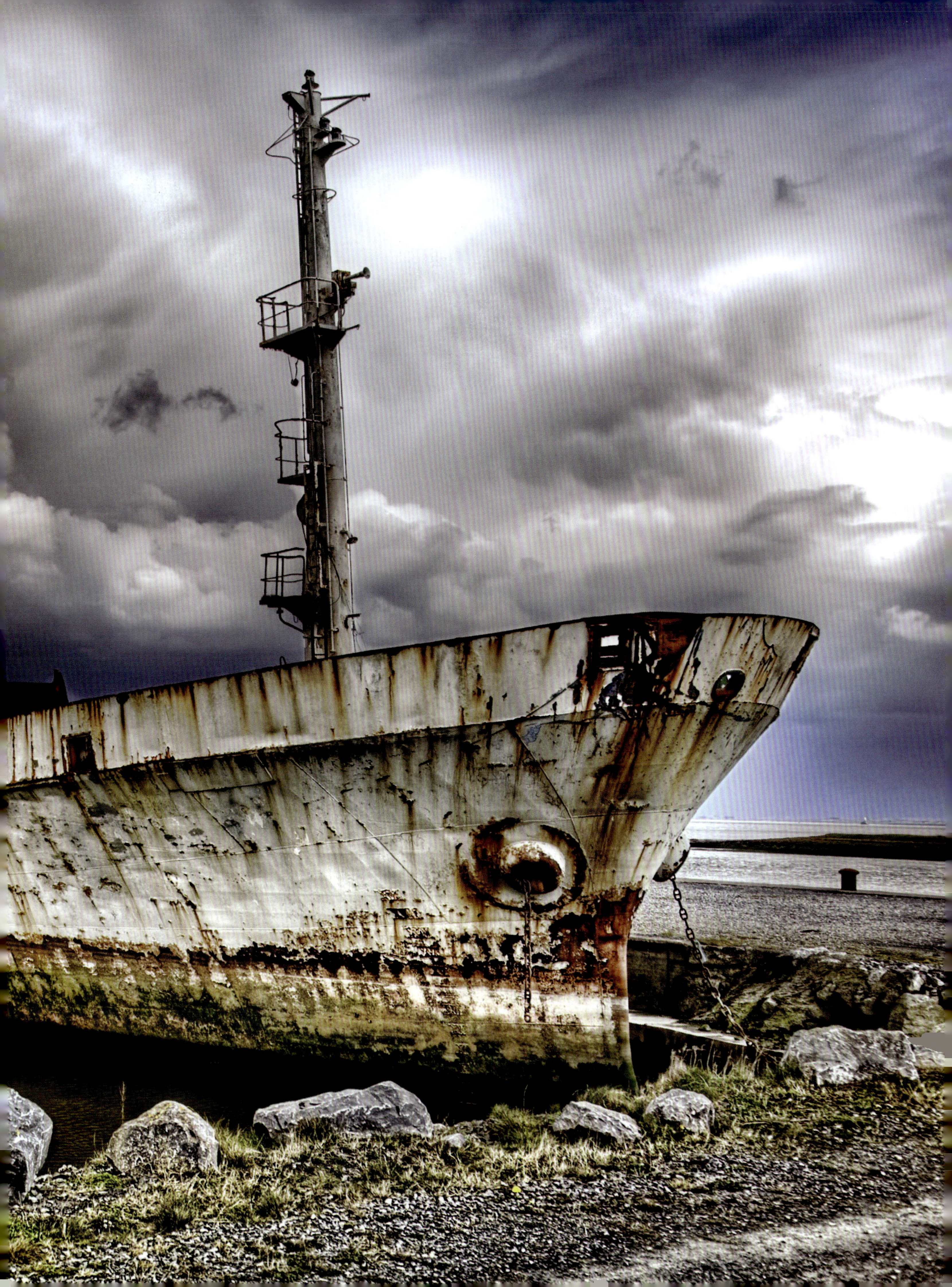

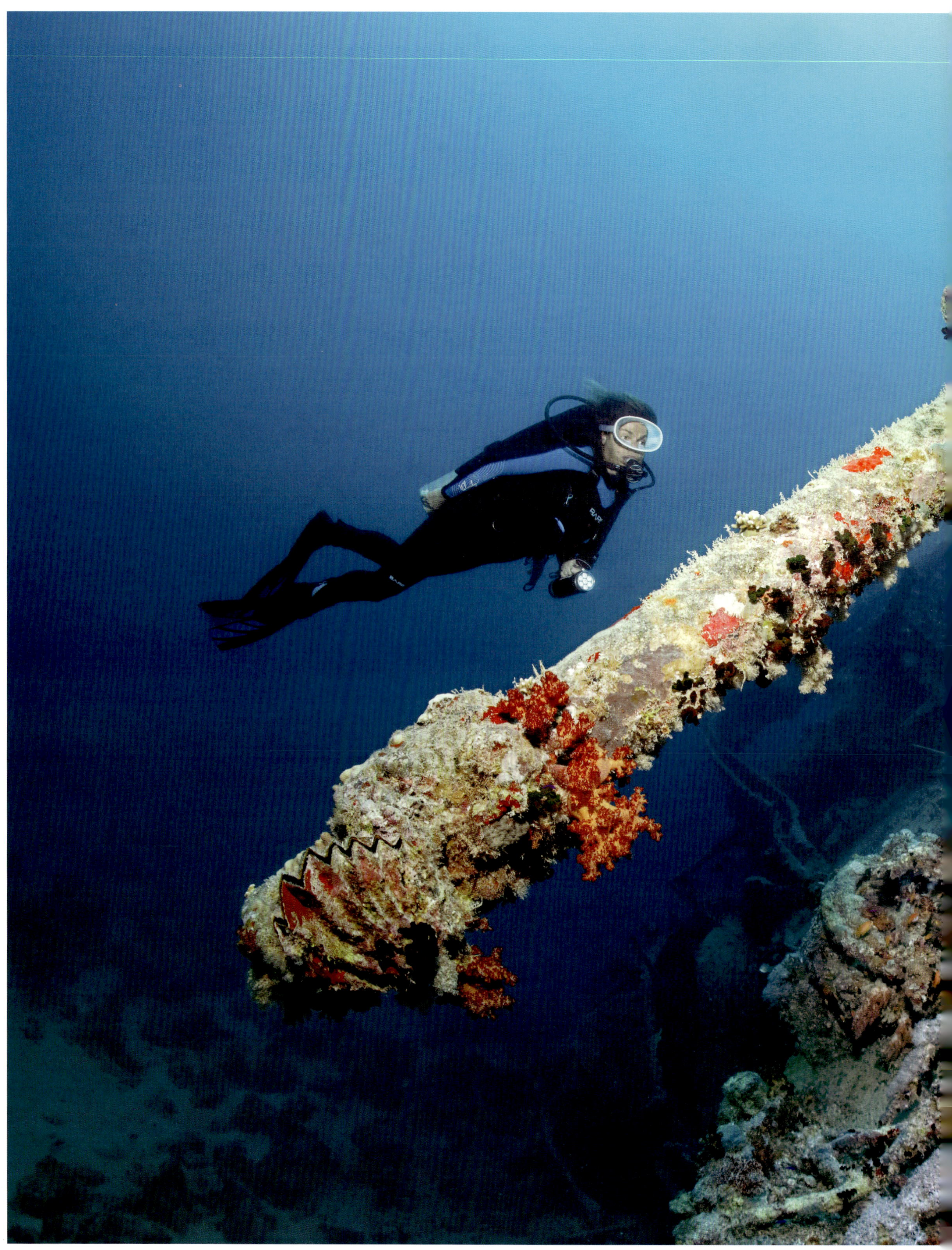

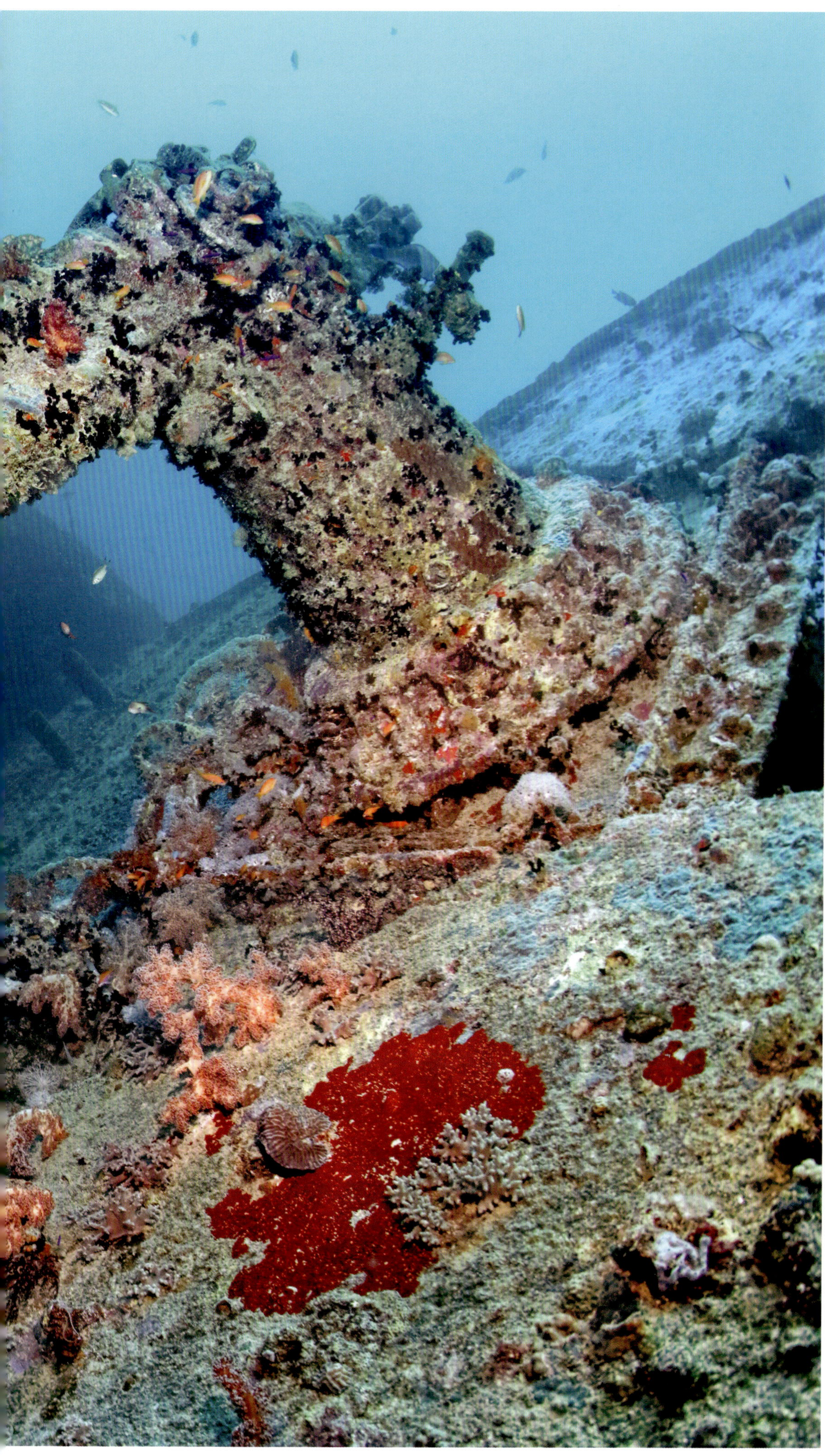

SS *Thistlegorm*, Red Sea, Shaab Ali, Sinai Peninsula, Egypt
A diver investigates the coral-encrusted deck gun of the SS *Thistlegorm*, a merchant ship packed with equipment and sunk by German air attack on 6 October 1941. The deck gun would have been used for light defence against submarines or small surface vessels, but could have done little to fight off an air assault.

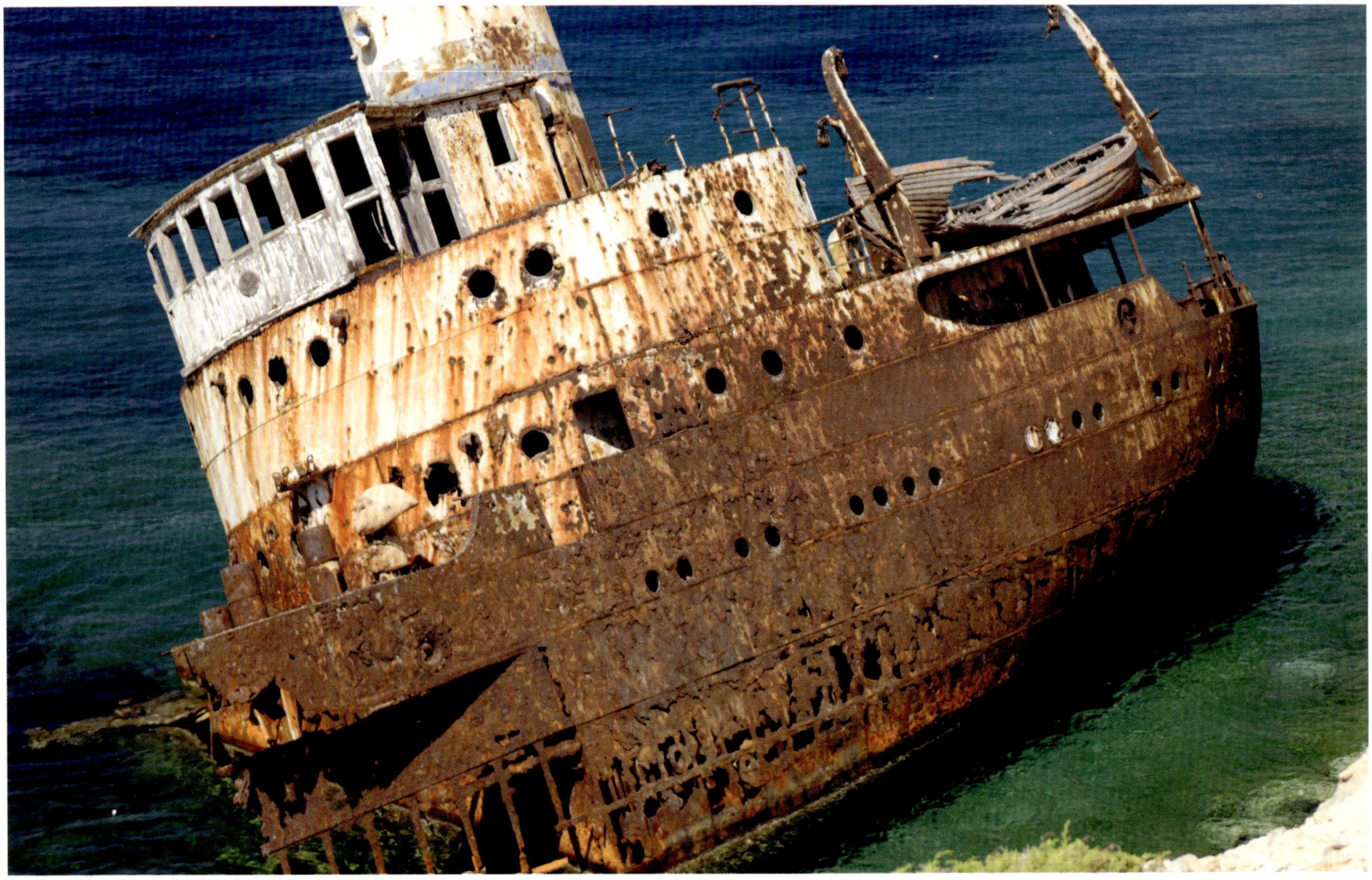

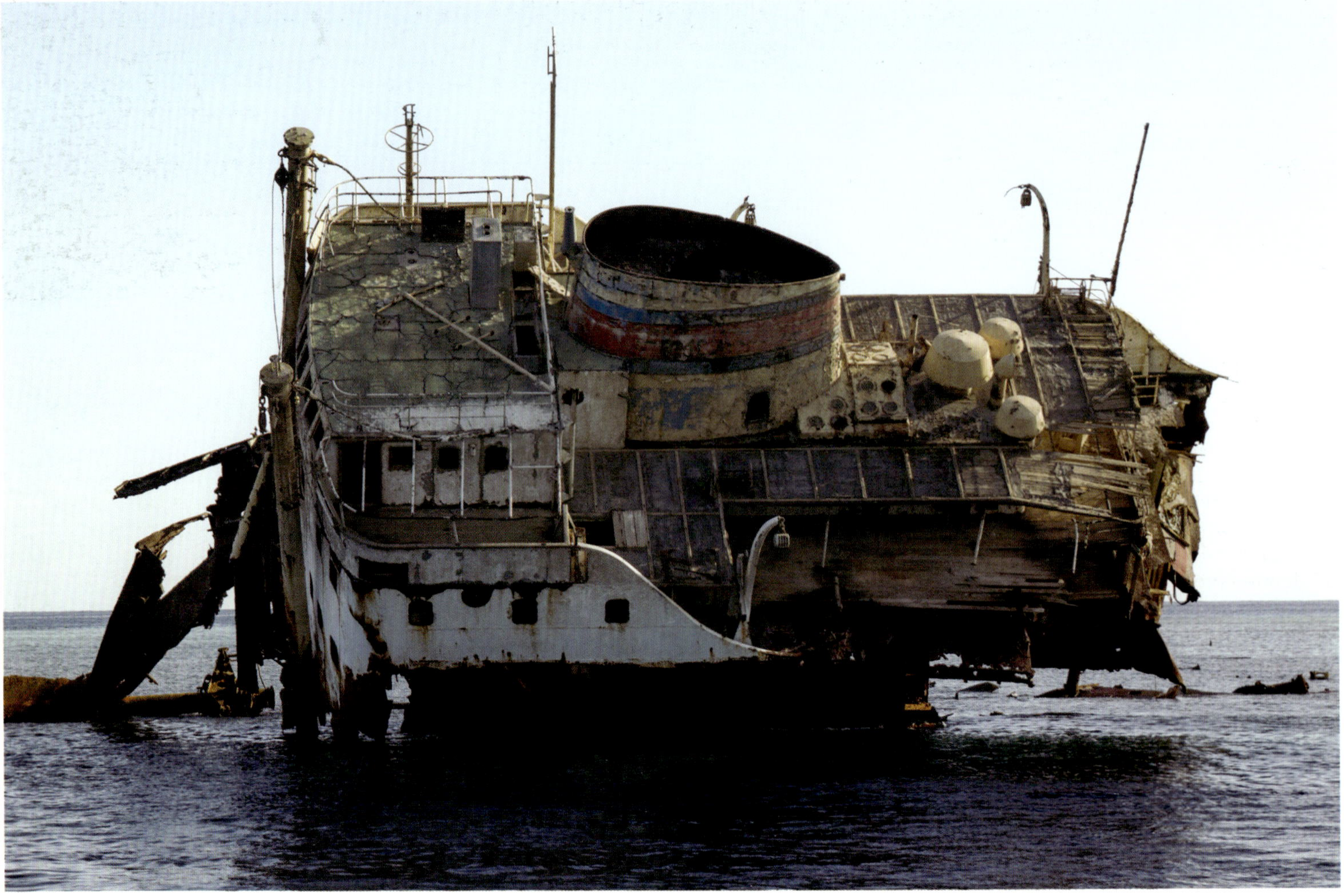

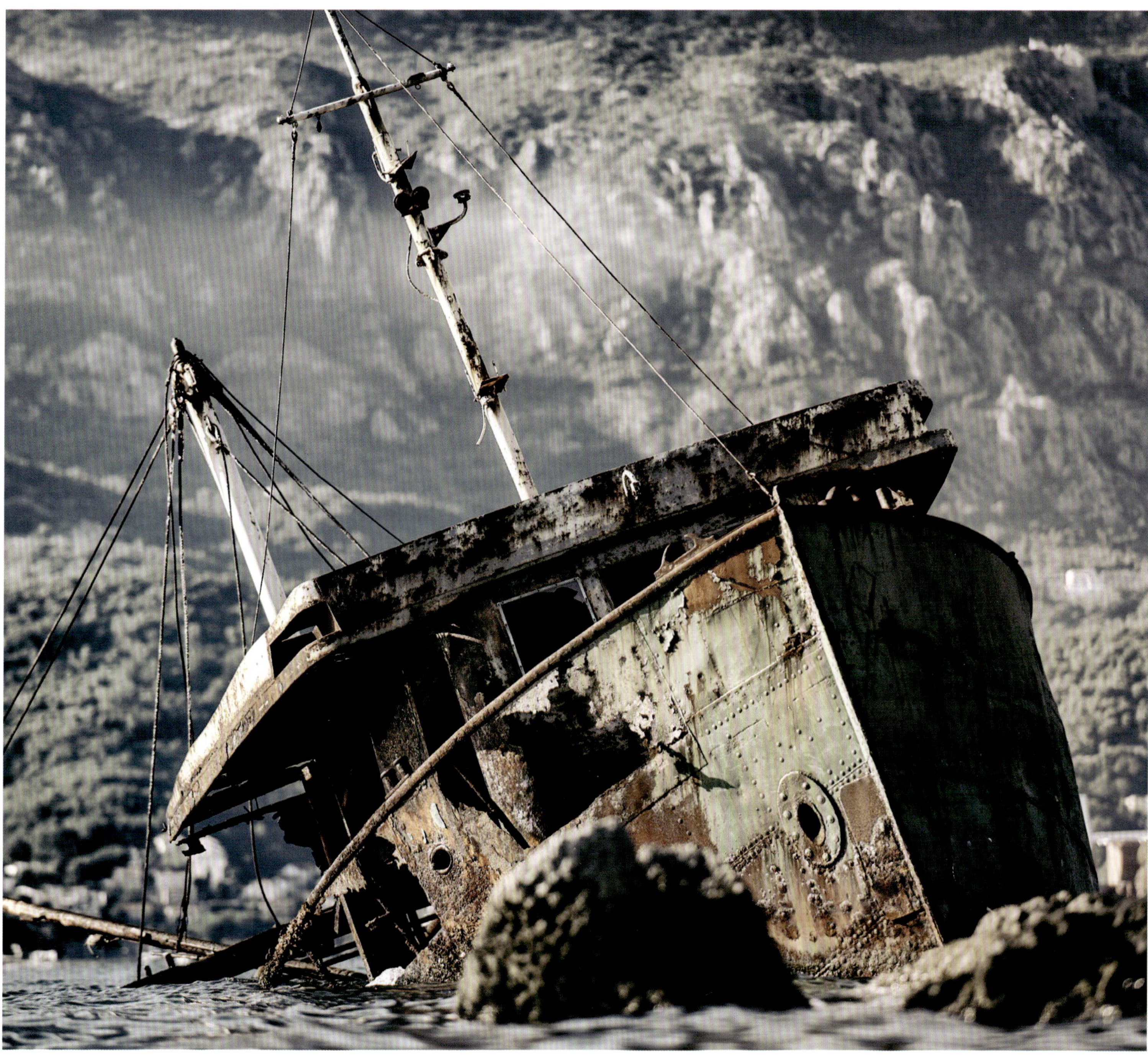

Amorgos Island, Cyclades Islands, Greece
This ship, stuck on the rugged and picturesque coastline of Amorgos Island in Greece, was wrecked in February 1980 when its captain attempted to find somewhere to shelter the craft from stormy seas. High waves drove the vessel in against the rocks, where it was destroyed. It has featured in several movies and documentaries.

***Loullia*, Straits of Tiran, Red Sea**
Despite the enormous resilience of sea-going vessels, if left as wrecks long enough the sea will devour even the sturdiest structures. Little remains of the *Loullia*, a motor bulk carrier that ran aground in the Straits of Tiran in September 1981, except for the derelict bridge structure, the ship's funnel (still displaying its colours) and the rusted outline of the hull.

Rose, Montenegro
Hundreds of small fishing boats are lost globally each year to accident or disrepair, such as this one off the Montenegrin coast. Fishing fleets have also suffered from global commercial conditions, particularly regarding the depletion of fish stocks and the inability of small independent boats to compete with the large fishing companies.

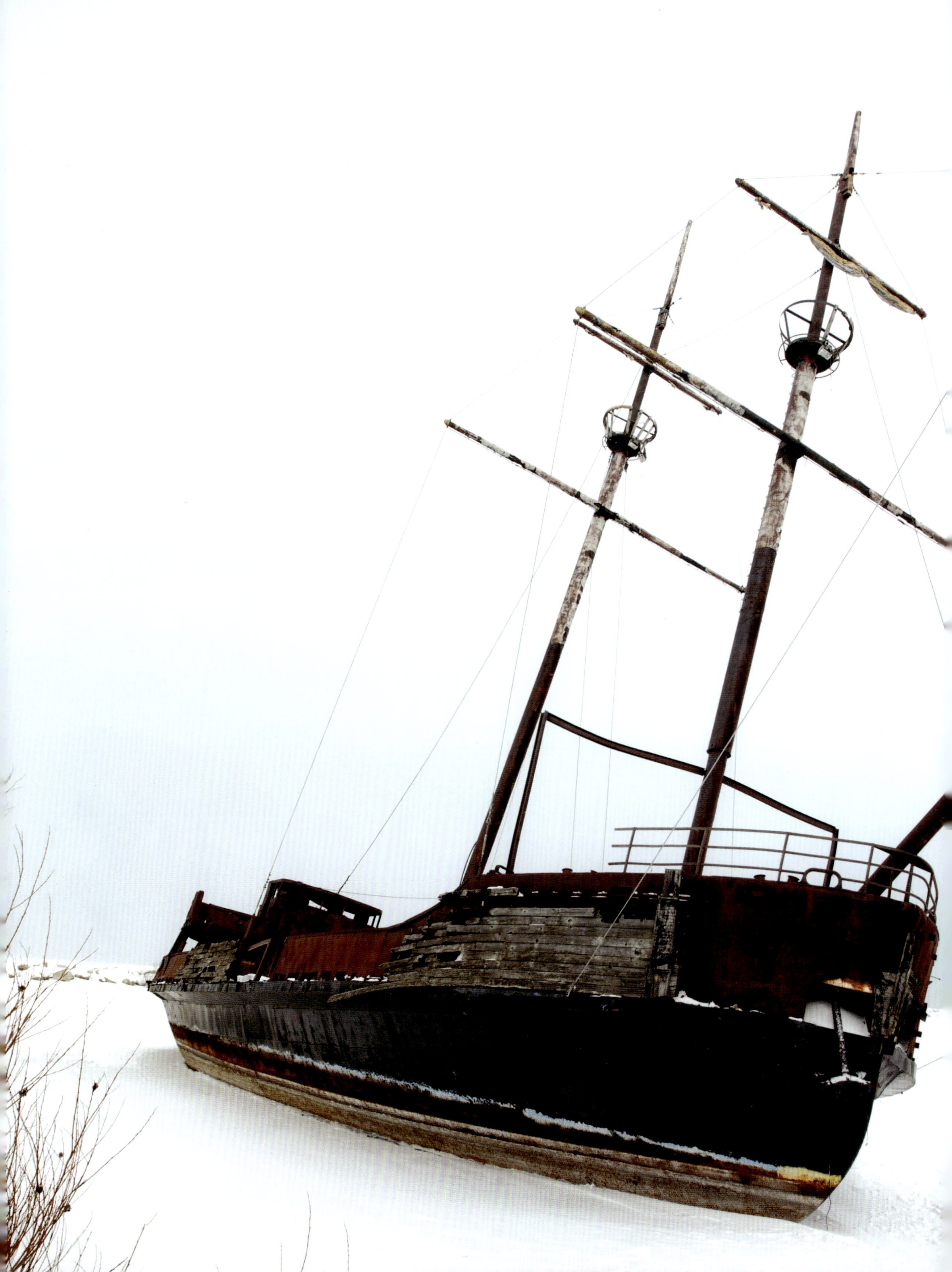

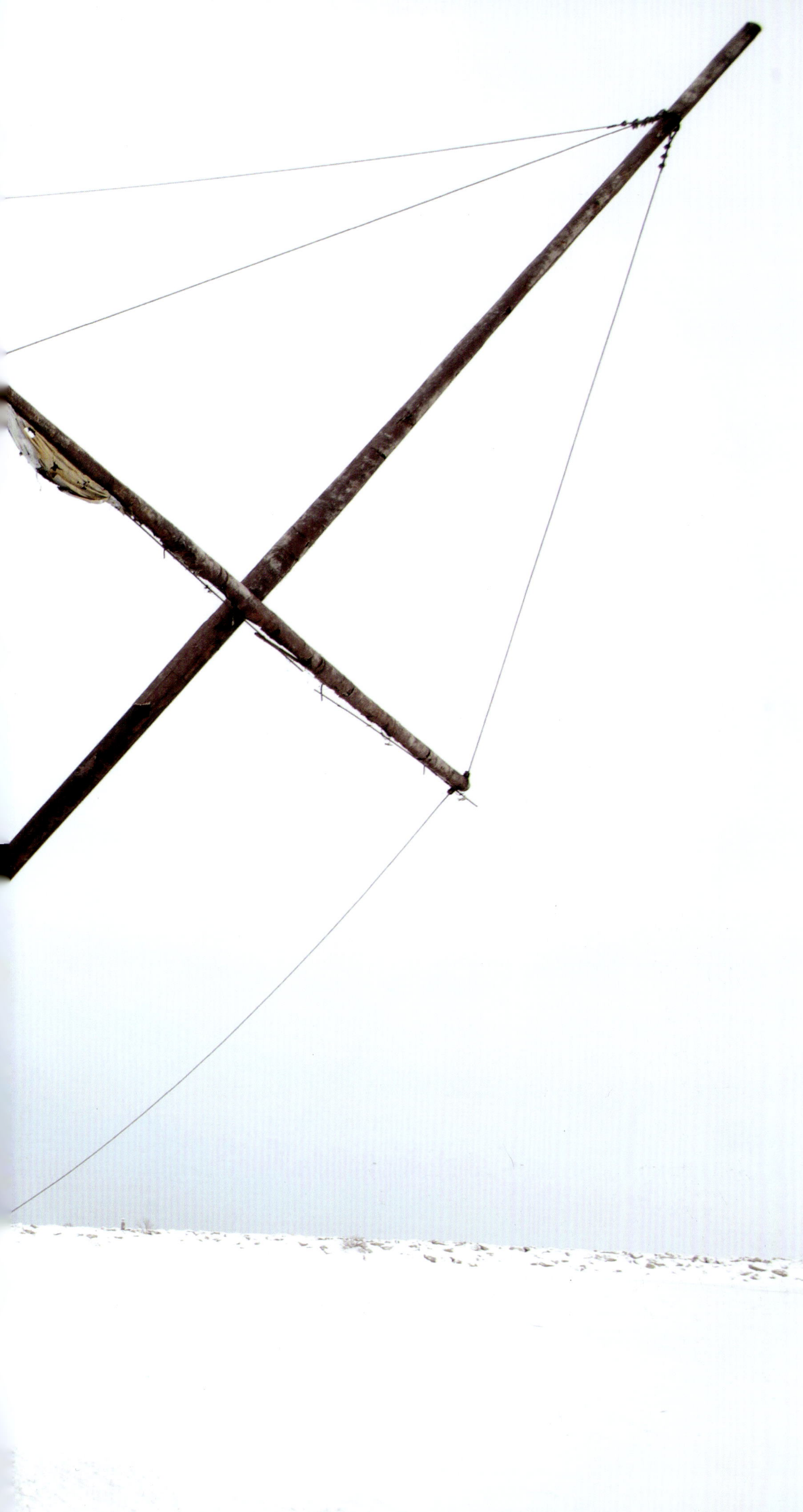

La Grande Hermine, Jordan Harbour, Lake Ontario, Canada
La Grande Hermine (The Big Weasel) was built in Quebec in 1914, designed as a replica of a ship used by French explorer Jacques Cartier to sail up the St Lawrence River in the 16th century. The vessel went through numerous commercial purposes over its lifetime, including being used as a floating restaurant and a Halloween party ship, but was eventually abandoned for financial reasons in the 1990s.

Landévennec, Brittany, France
These vessels are some of the
many civilian and military ships
kept at this maritime graveyard in
Brittany. Defunct military vessels,
even those of a bygone era, can
still contain secrets relating to
design and combat capability, so
such graveyards help to control
their disposal.

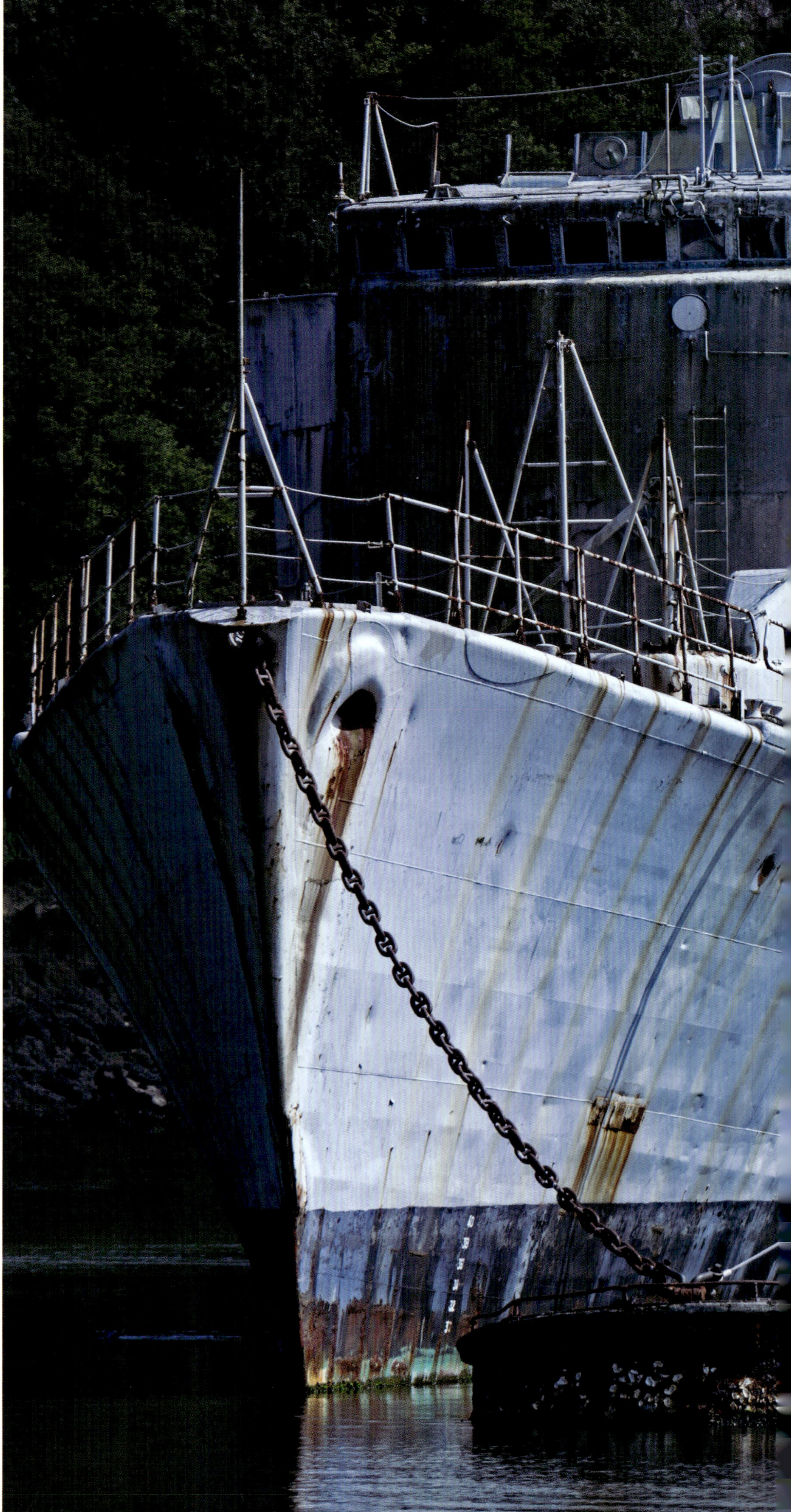

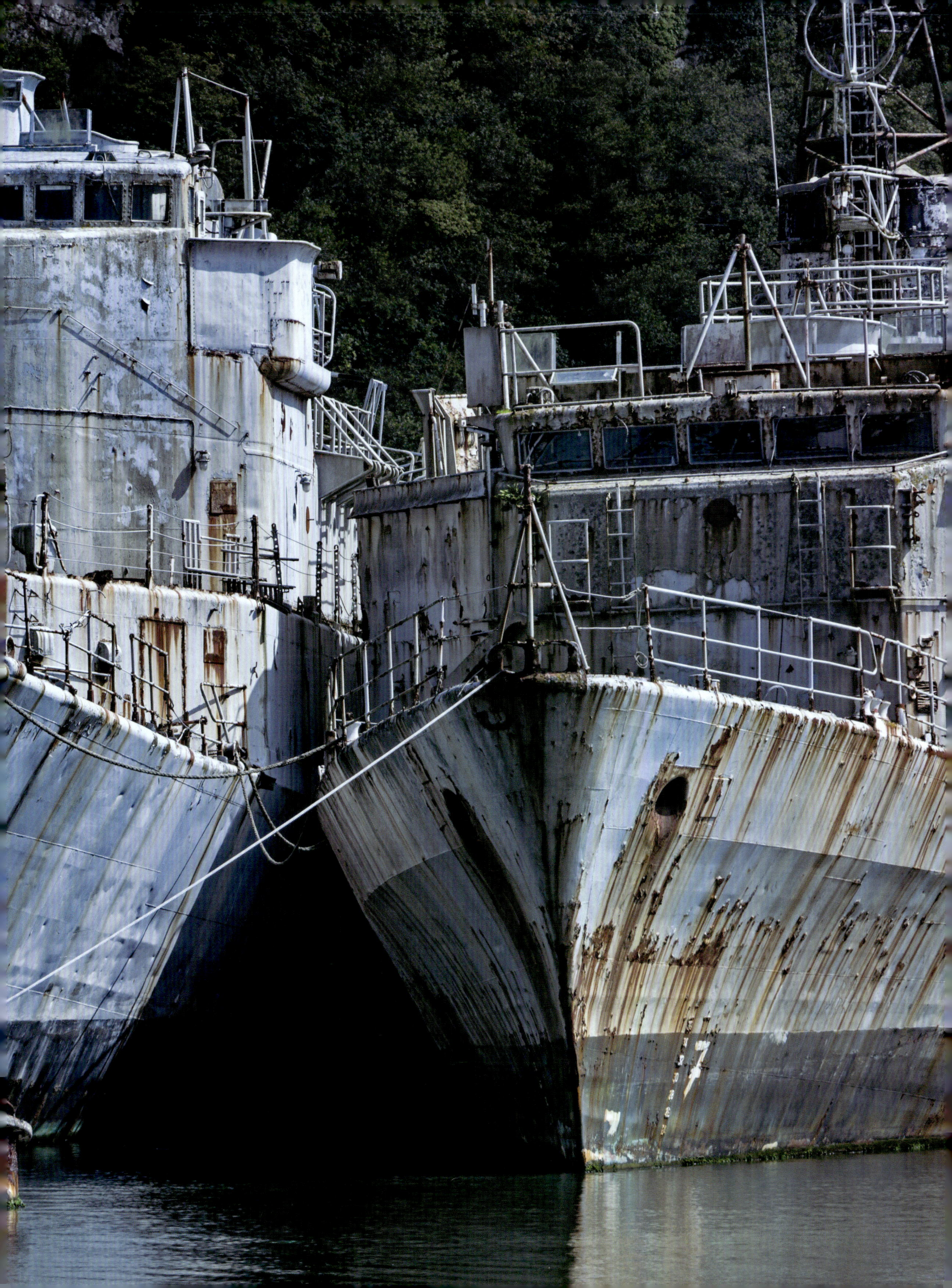

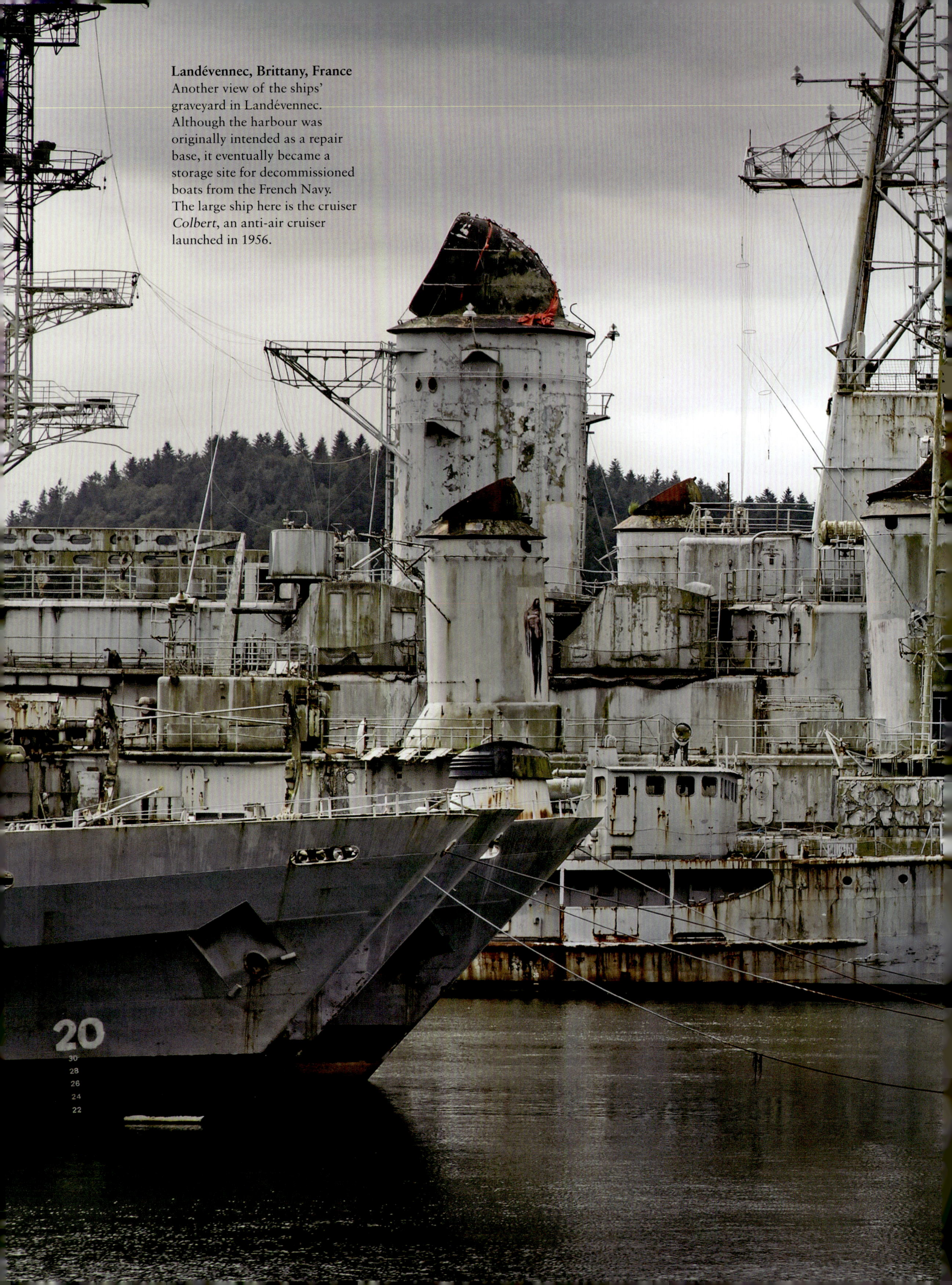

Landévennec, Brittany, France
Another view of the ships' graveyard in Landévennec. Although the harbour was originally intended as a repair base, it eventually became a storage site for decommissioned boats from the French Navy. The large ship here is the cruiser *Colbert*, an anti-air cruiser launched in 1956.

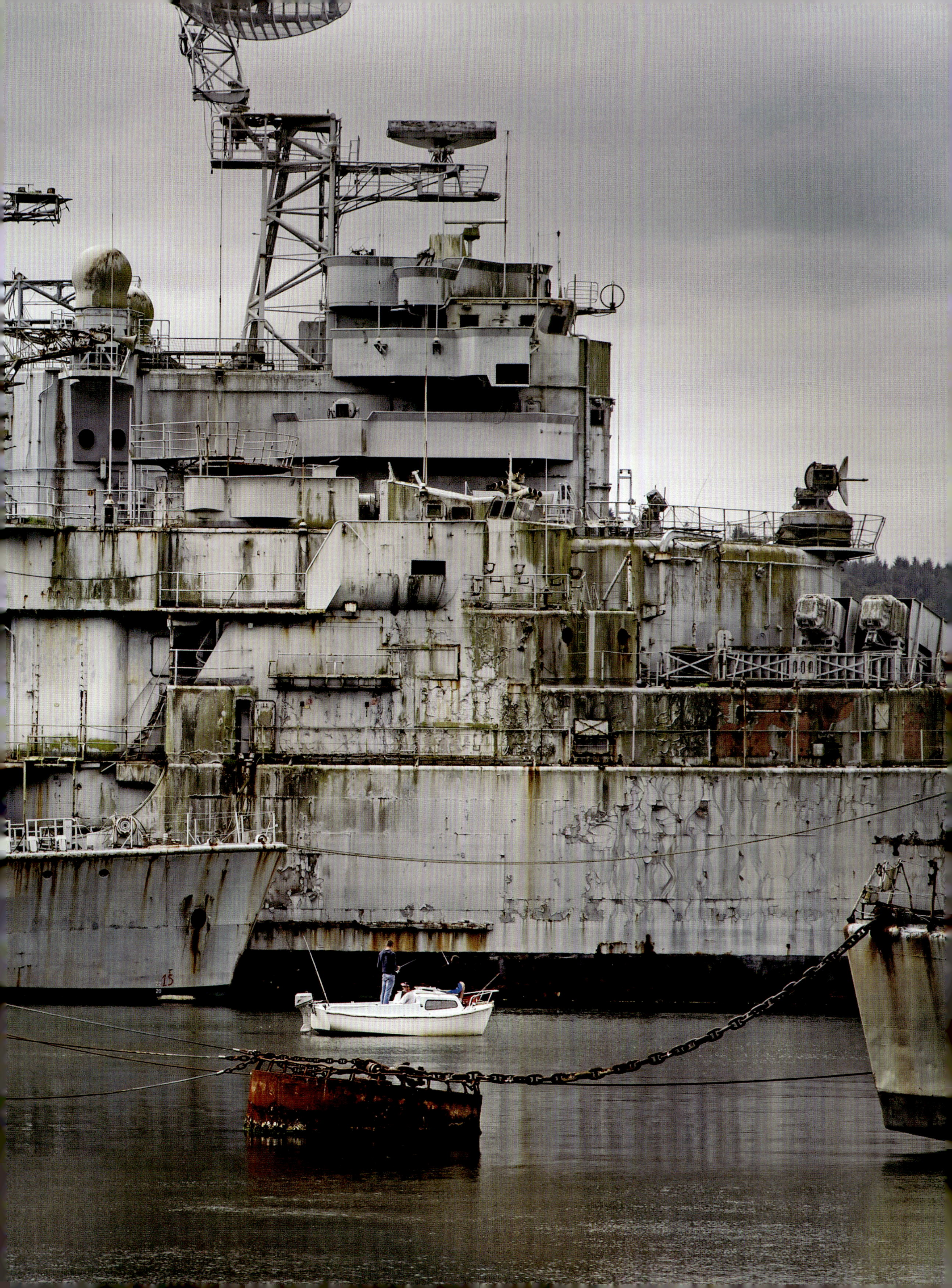

Aida, El Ikhwa Islands, Red Sea, Egypt

Bathed in blue subterranean light, the wreck of the *Aida* lies in the Red Sea off Egypt. *Aida*, launched in 1911, was originally built as a lighthouse/buoy tender for the Egyptian Ports and Lighthouses Administration at the Loire shipyard in Western France. Used as a troop carrier during World War II, she was sunk by air attack on 8 October 1941.

Semiramis, Andros Island, Cyclades Islands, Greece

This wreck is that of the Brazilian cargo ship *Semiramis*, which was wrecked while under tow in 1996. The ship had actually been laid up after fire damage in 1990.

Klein Curaçao, Caribbean Sea

The Caribbean, although a beautiful and often tranquil part of the world, has a weather system and geology frequently hazardous to shipping. Here we see a large bulk carrier wrecked on the beach of Klein Curaçao.

Chittagong, Bangladesh

Bangladeshi shipbreakers are transferred by launches to a defunct cruise ship at a yard near Chittagong in April 2005. Scrapped ships end up beached along the coast at high tide, where the hulls are cut into metal plates for projects such as houses, roads and bridges, or used as raw material by steel mills.

Bay of Ensenada, Mexico

Wildlife can quickly adjust to the presence of a familiar shipwreck. In this photograph we see a group of sea lions resting on the deck of an abandoned tourist ship in the Bay of Ensenada, home to a major civilian port and a naval base.

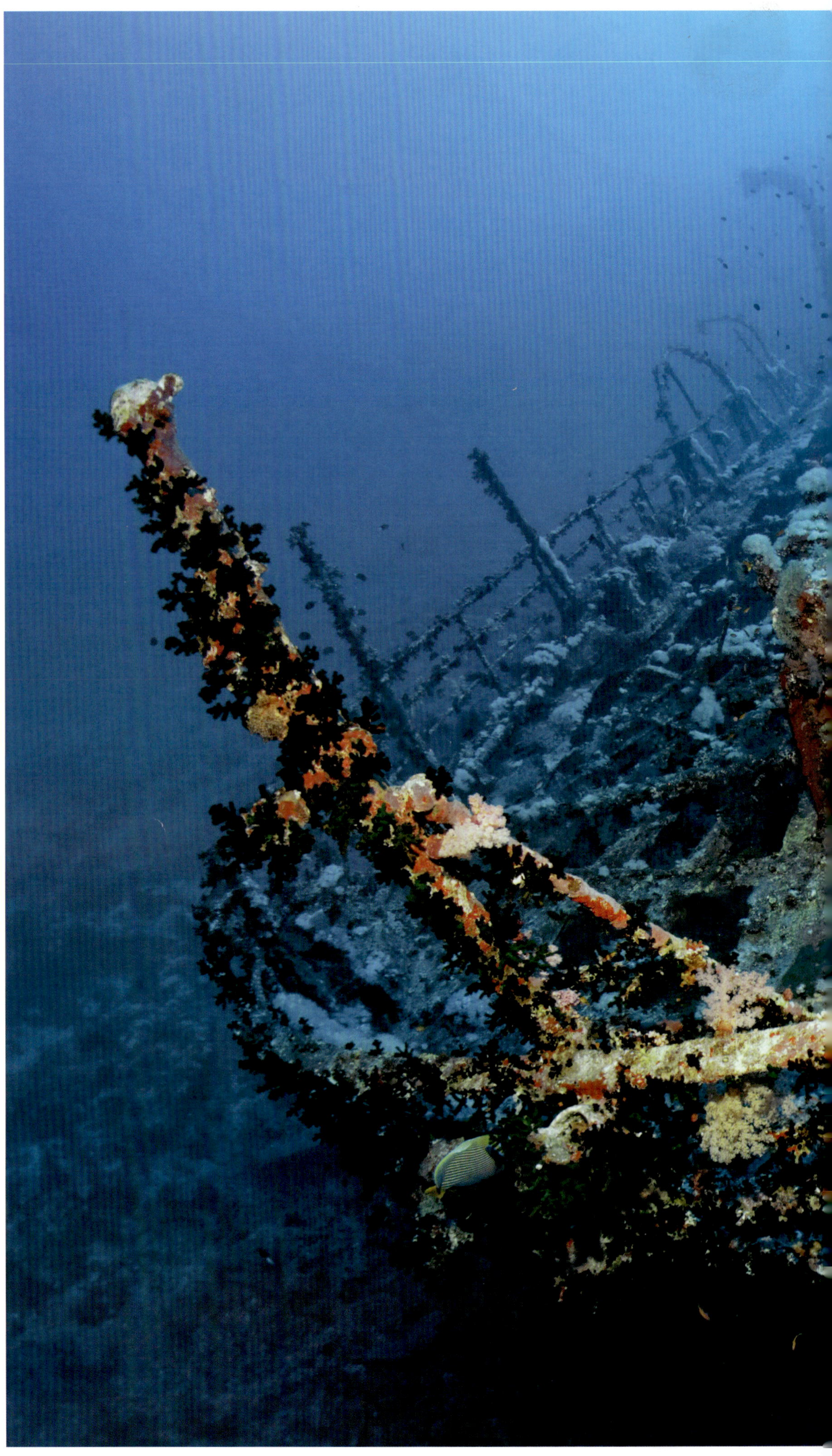

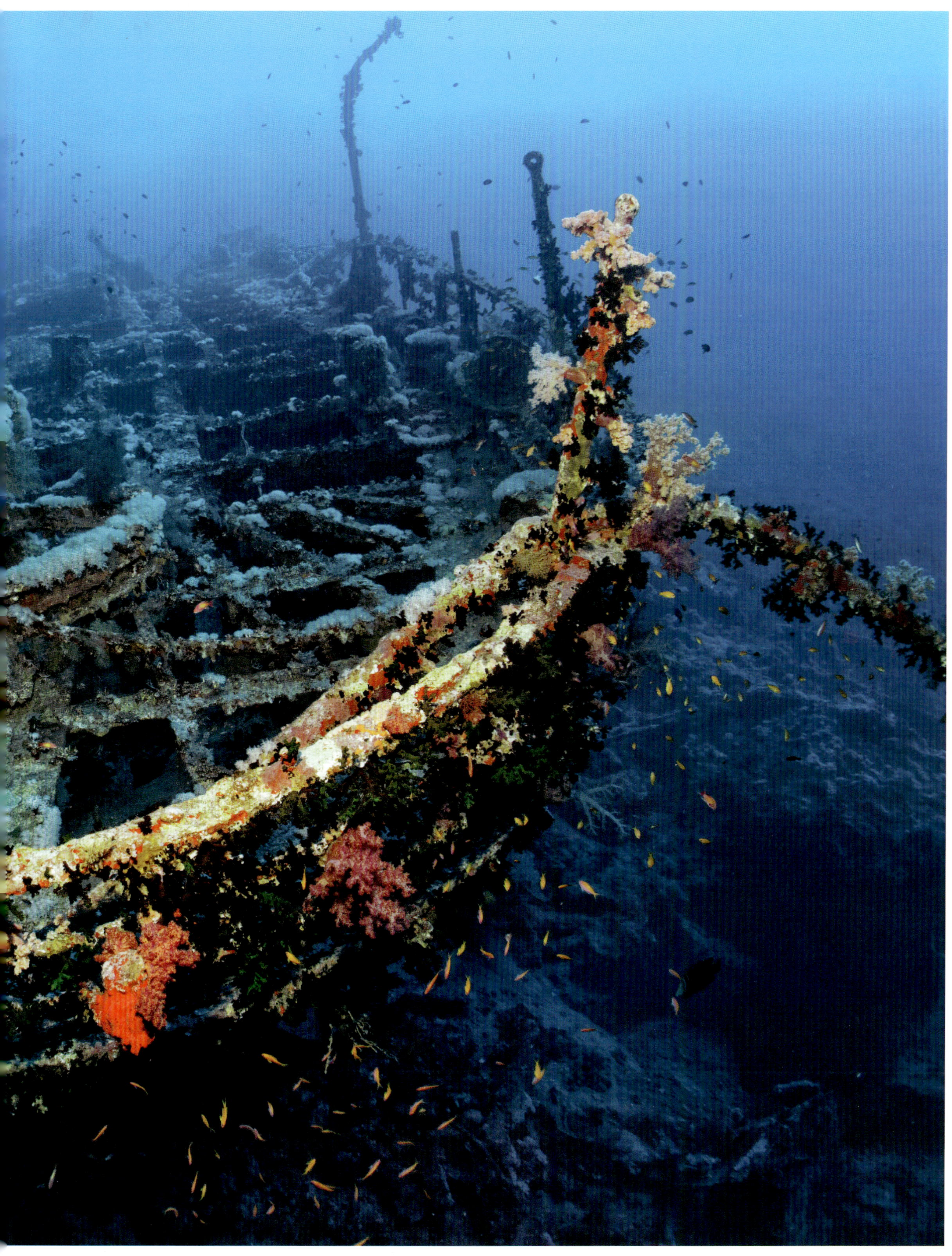

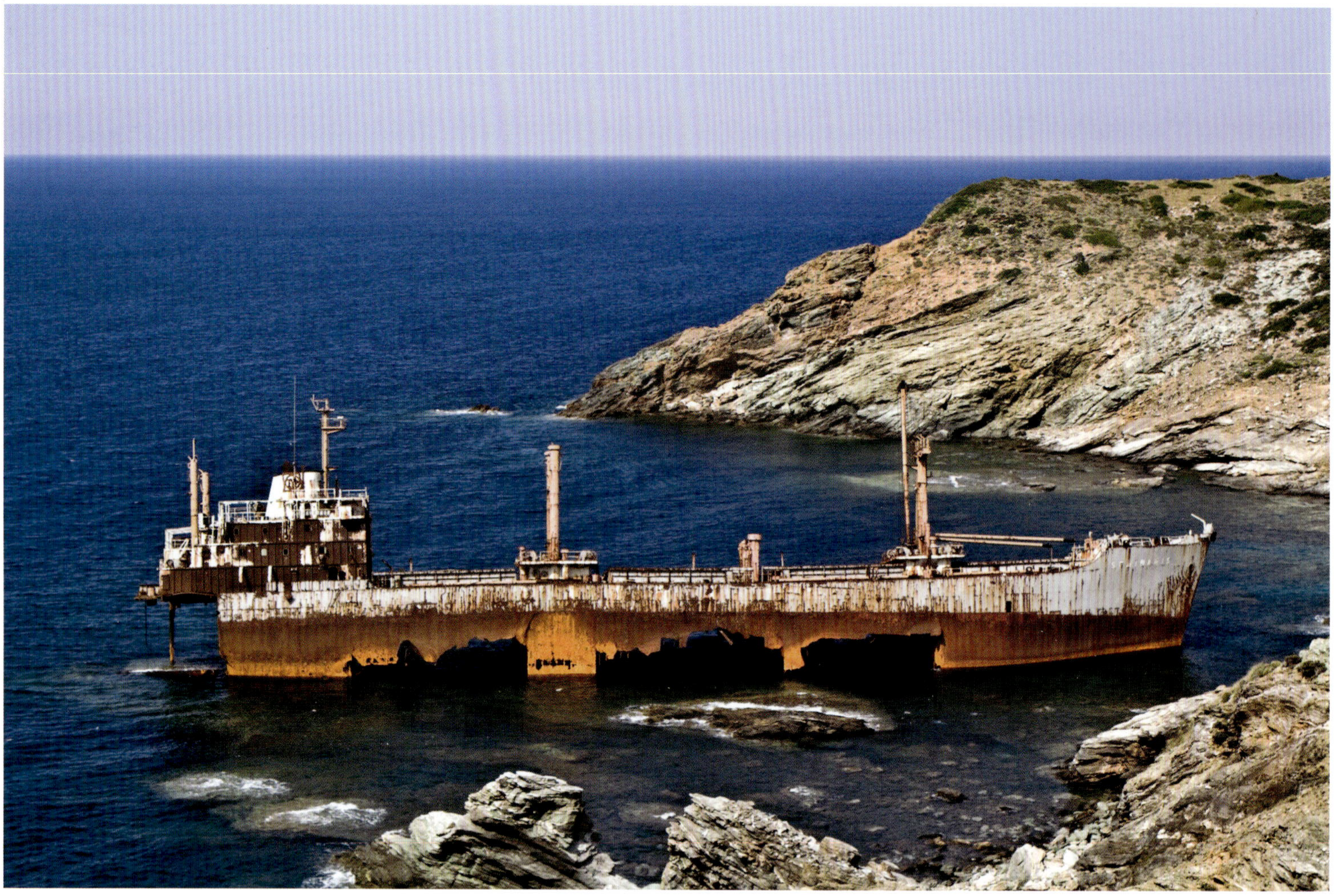

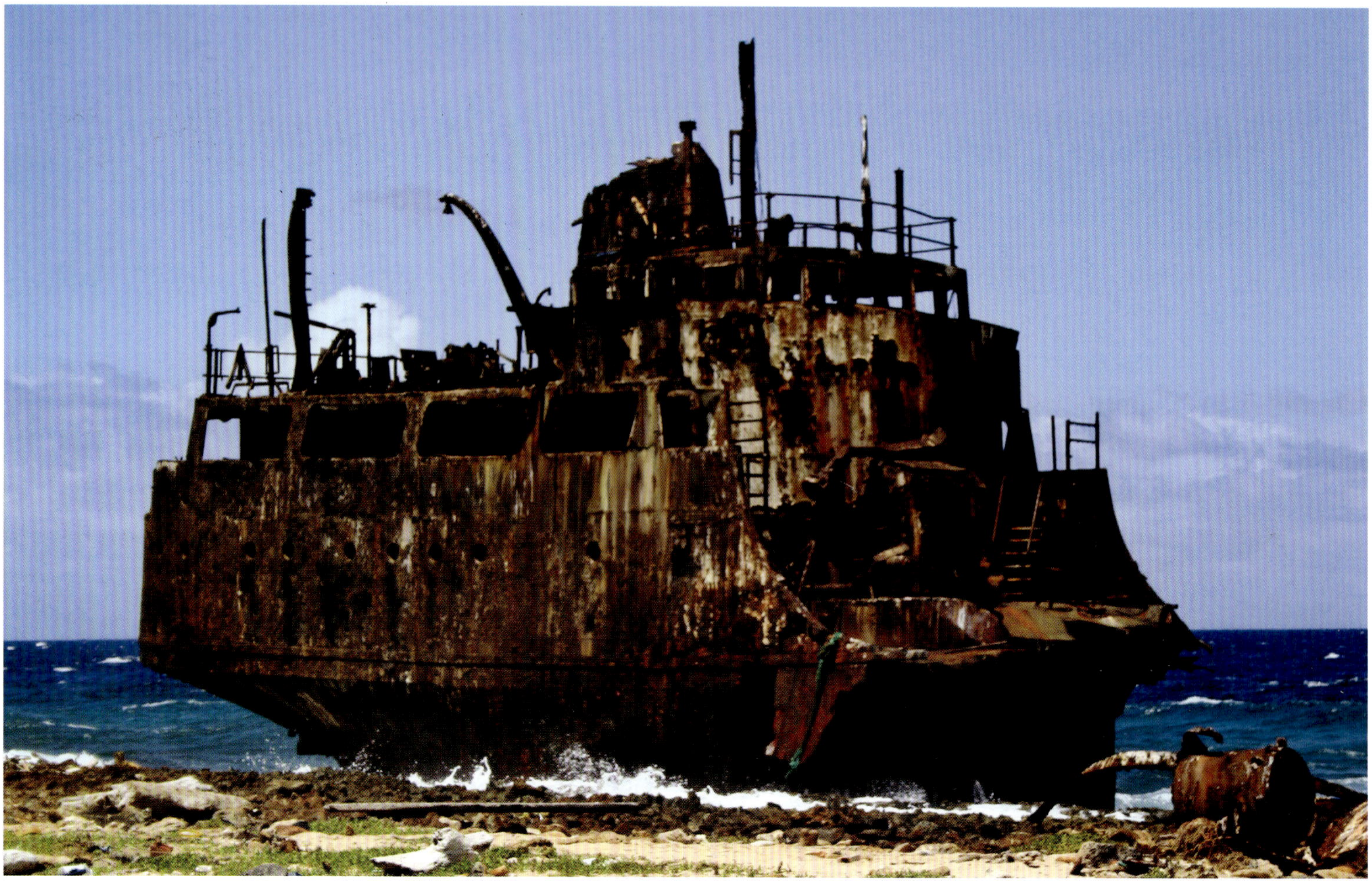

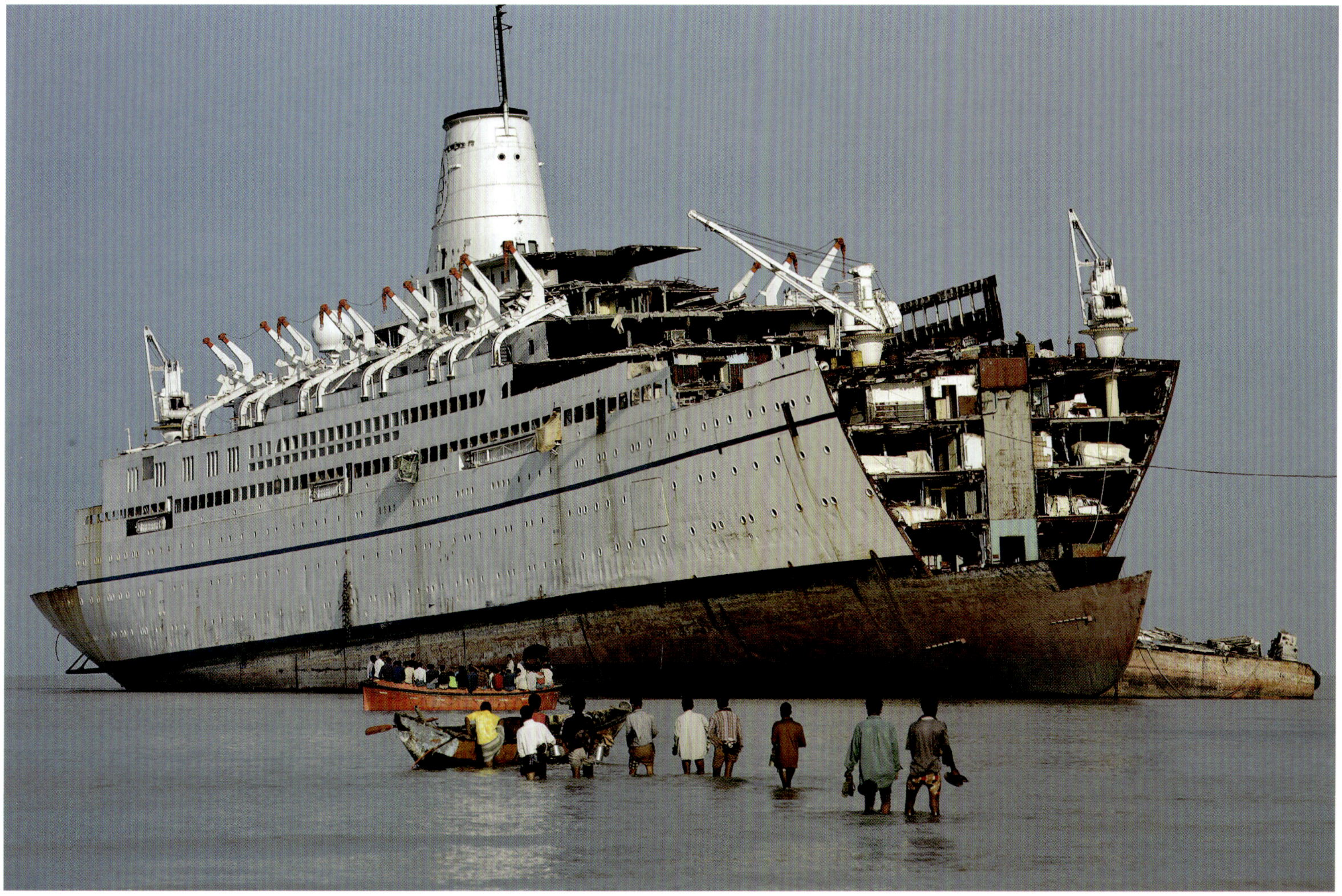

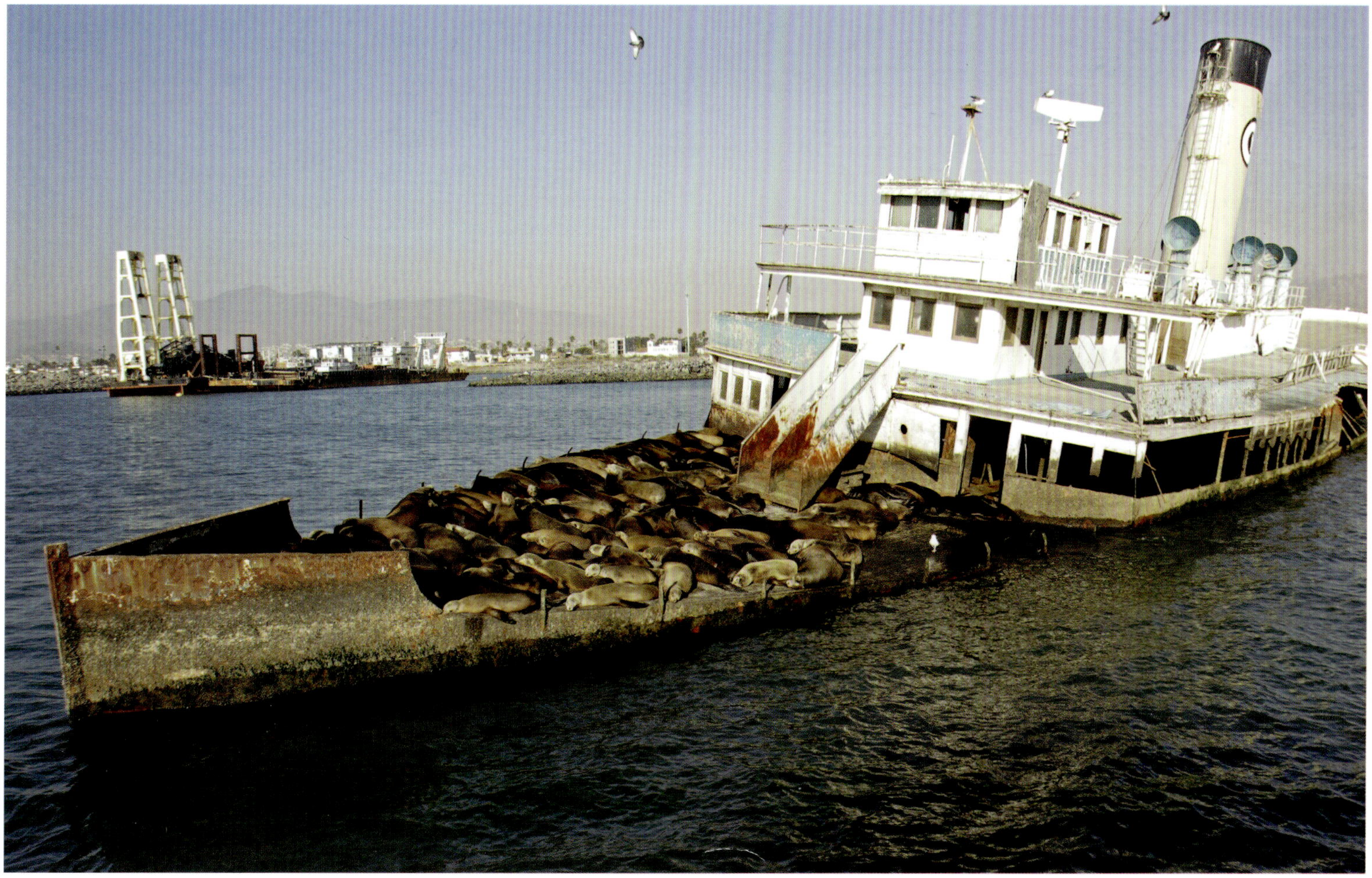

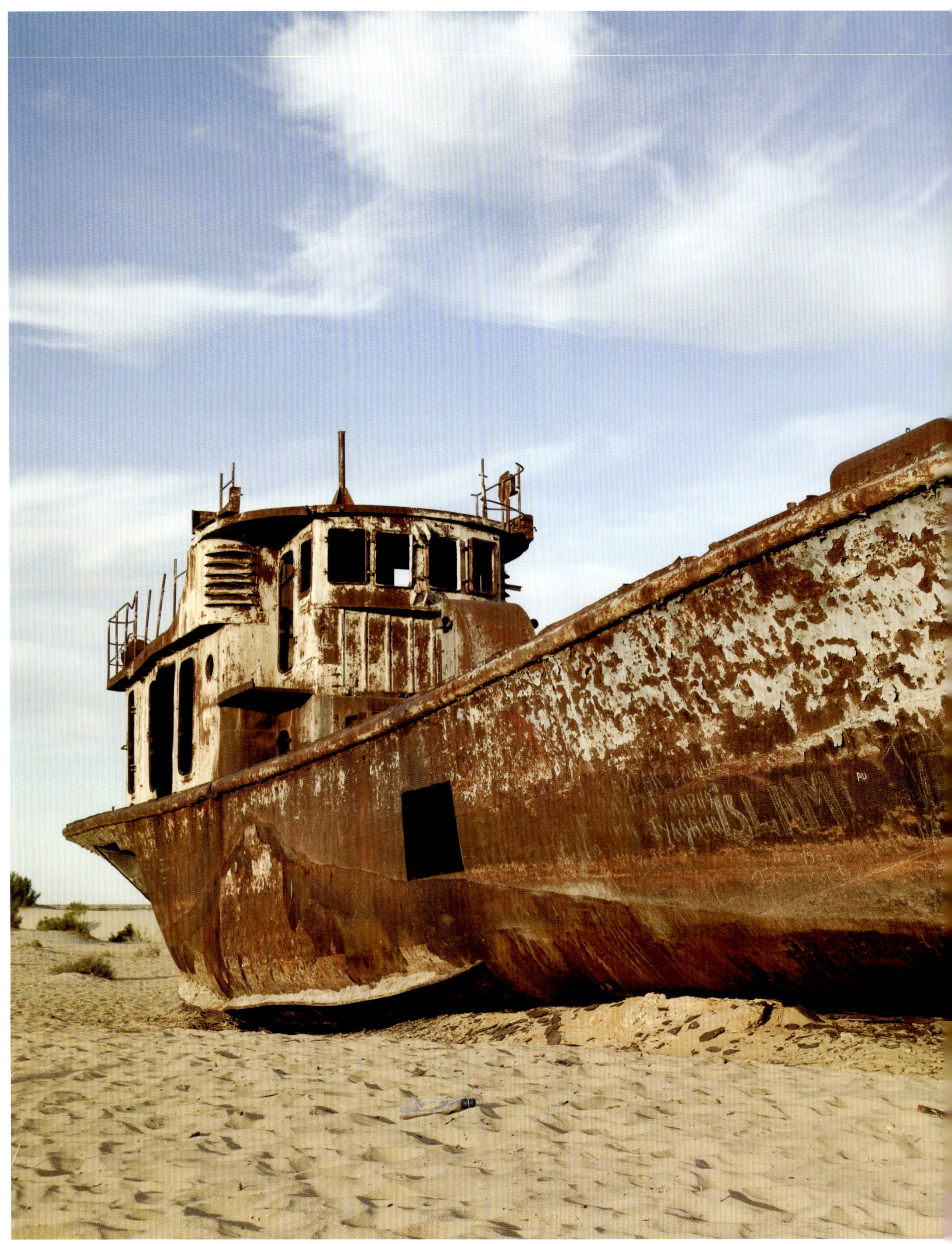

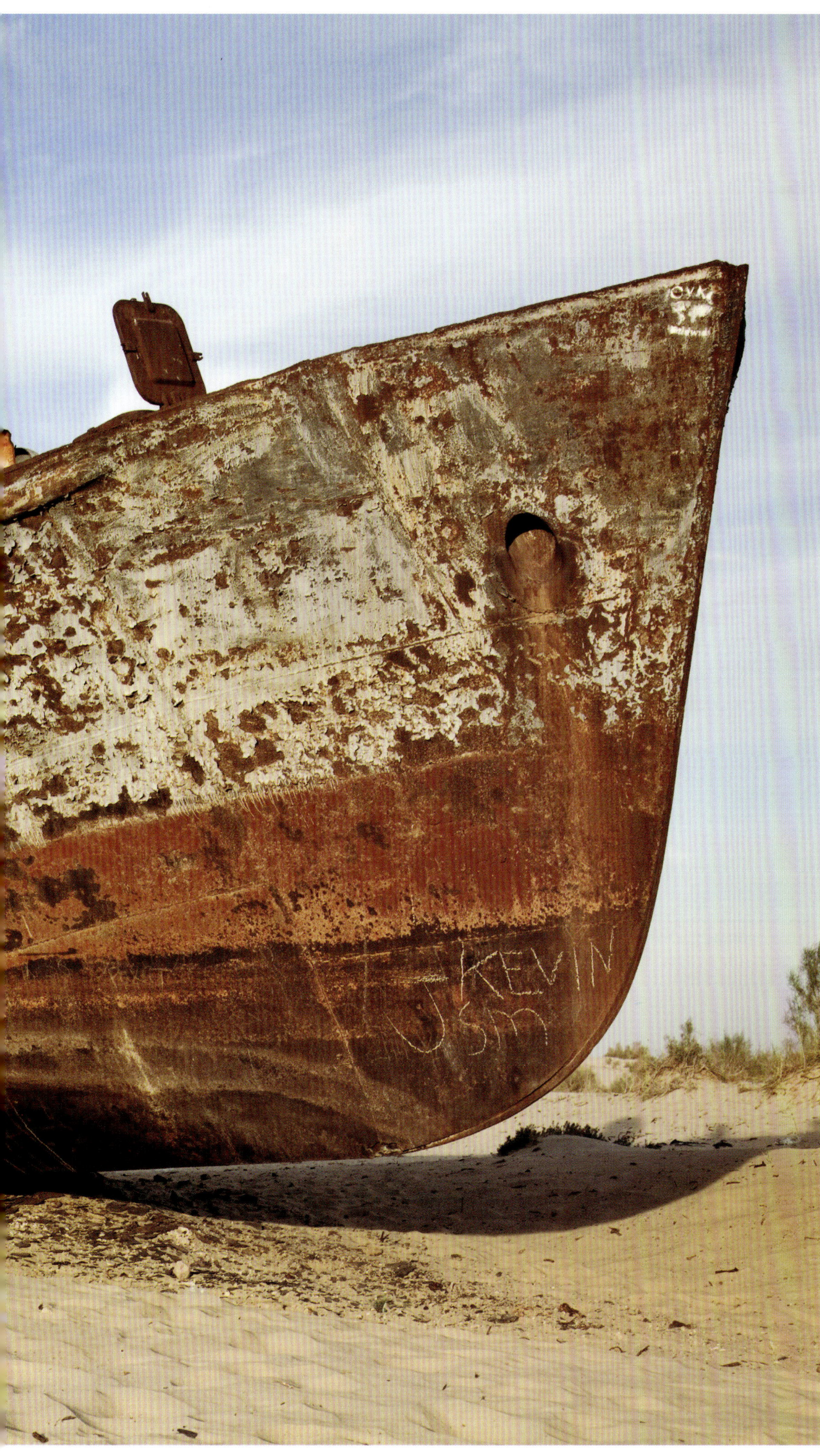

**Mo'ynoq, Aral Sea,
Karakalpakstan, Uzbekistan**
Mo'ynoq was once Uzbekistan's
busiest and most populated port.
The massive retraction of the Aral
Sea, shrinking since the 1960s after
the Soviet diversion of its feed
rivers, has decimated the local Aral
Sea fishing industries. This fishing
boat is one of many wrecks rusting
on the exposed seabed, over which
it once made a livelihood.

Bessie White, Fire Island, Long Island, New York, United States
The keel of the Canadian four-masted coal schooner *Bessie White*, which sank when it ran aground in heavy fog in 1922. All the crew survived the incident, but 950 tons of coal was lost. This wreckage was exposed by the effects of Hurricane Sandy in 2012.

SS *Dicky*, Dicky Beach, Sunshine Coast, Queensland, Australia
The SS *Dicky* was a single-screw coastal trader vessel operating around the coast of Australia in the late 1880s and early 1890s. On 4 February 1893 it was lost when bound for Brisbane, driven ashore in rough weather.

American Star, Fuerteventura, Canary Islands, Spain
The once-proud bows of the *American Star* lean at a crazy angle on the coast of Fuerteventura. The ship was originally the cruise liner SS *America*, built in 1940 for the United States Lines. The ship ran aground after breaking away from tow ships in an Atlantic storm.

Moreton Island, Queensland, Australia
While it is unusual to see wrecks in such concentration, these 15 vessels were actually deliberately sunk to form a breakwall for small boats in the township of Tangalooma.

SS Nornen, near Berrow, Somerset, England
The remains of the SS *Nornen*, a Norwegian sailing vessel that ran aground in freezing, stormy weather on 3 March 1897. The local Burnham lifeboat, crewed by ten courageous men, sailed through the pummelling waves to rescue all the crew, including the ship's dog.

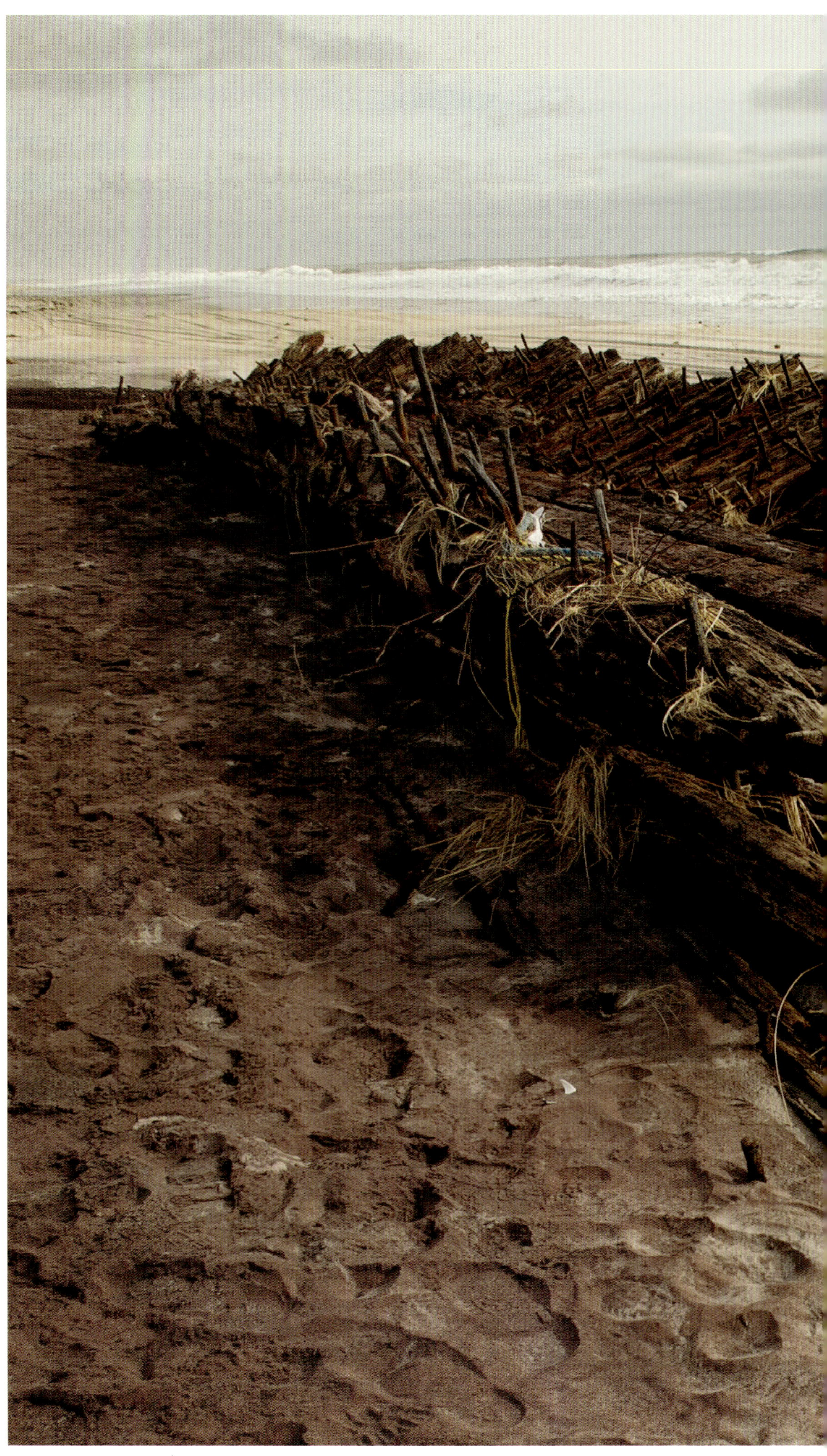

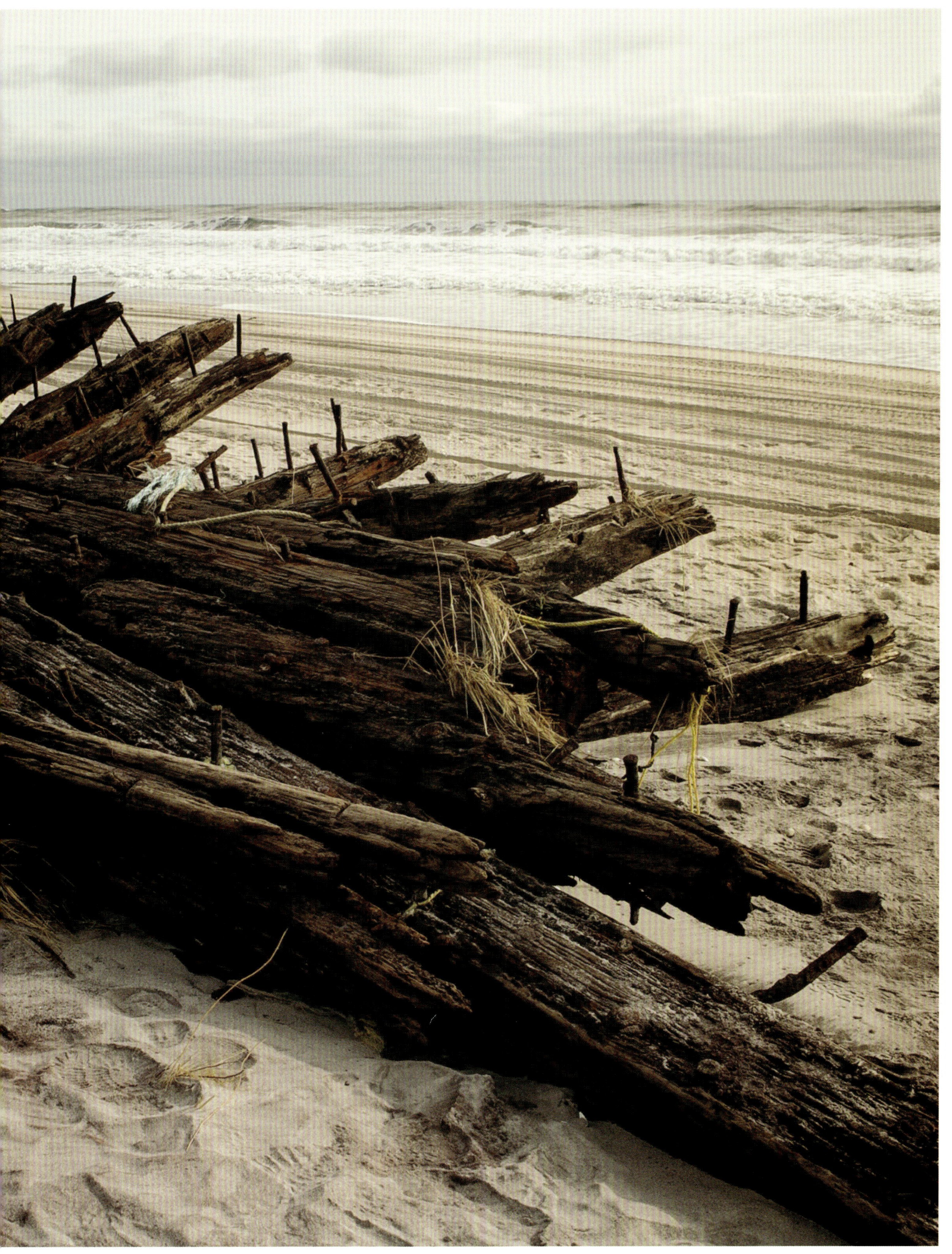

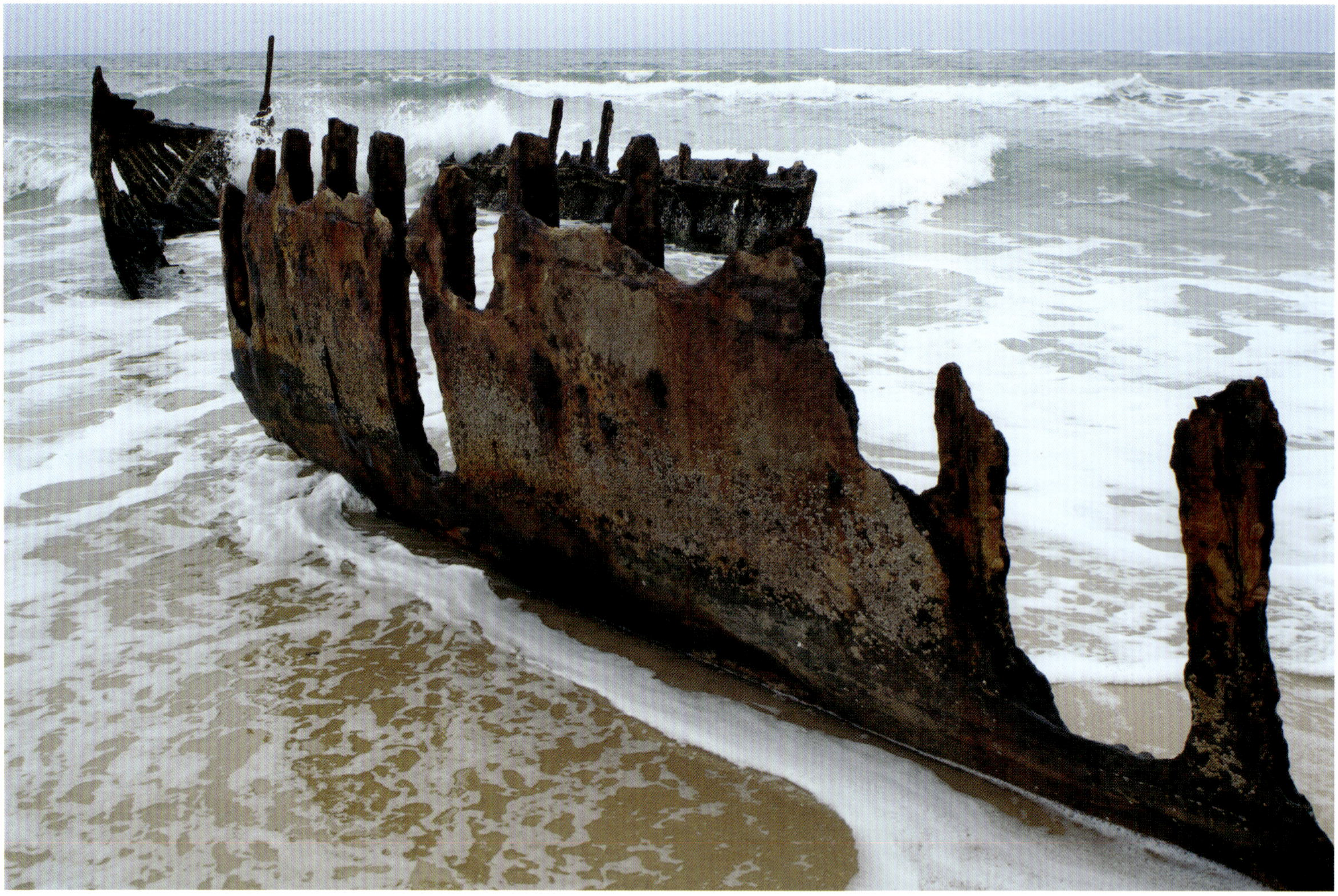

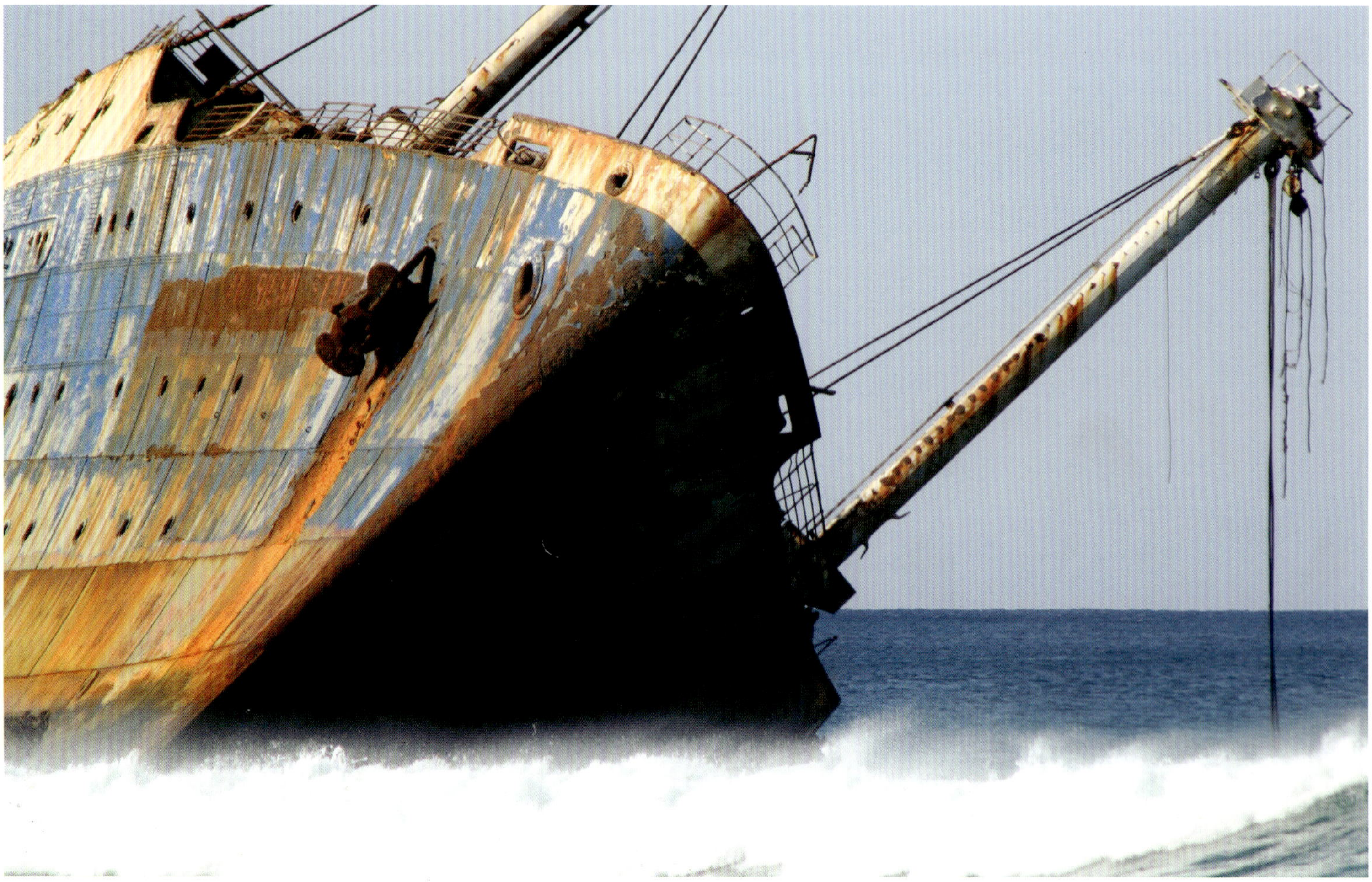

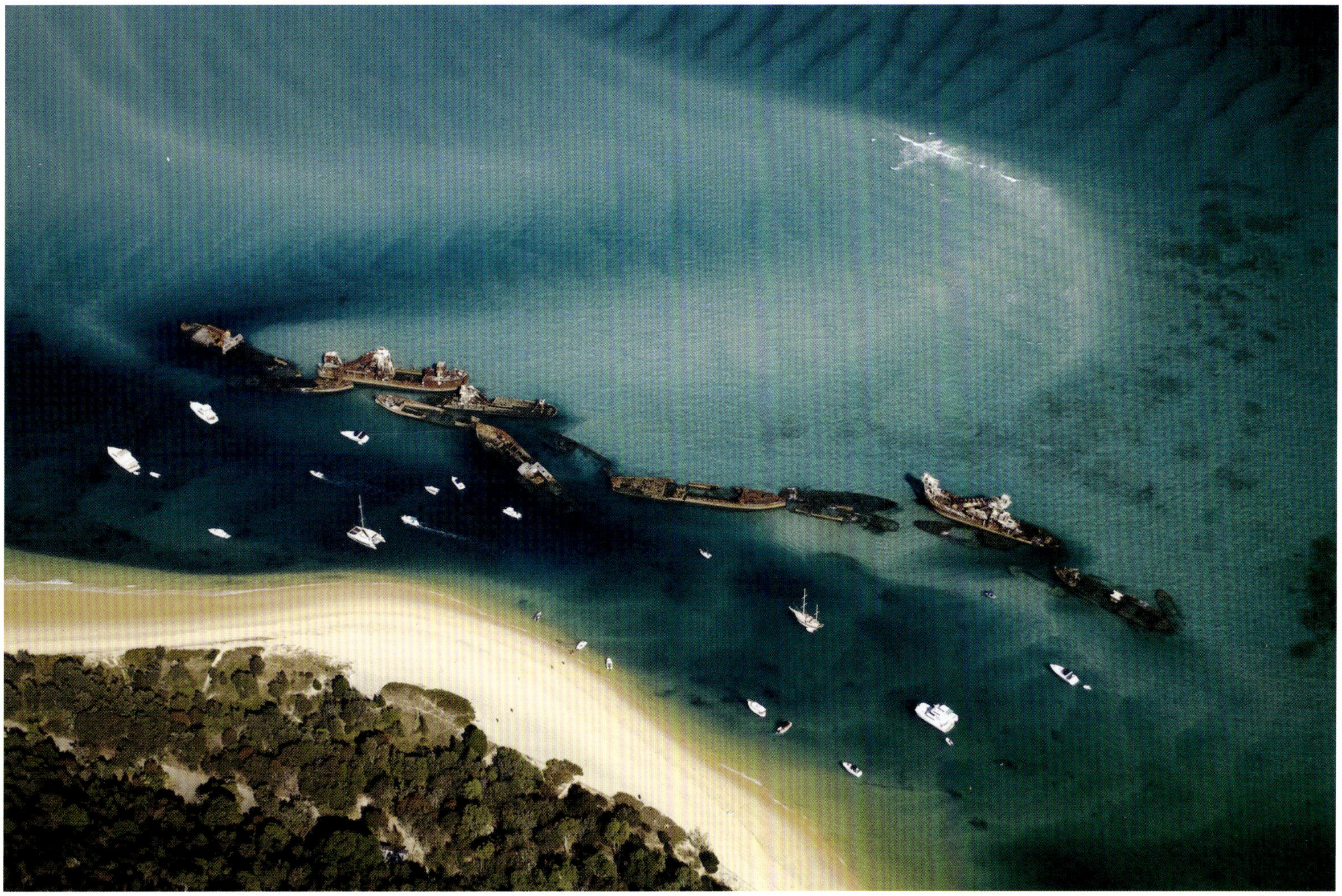

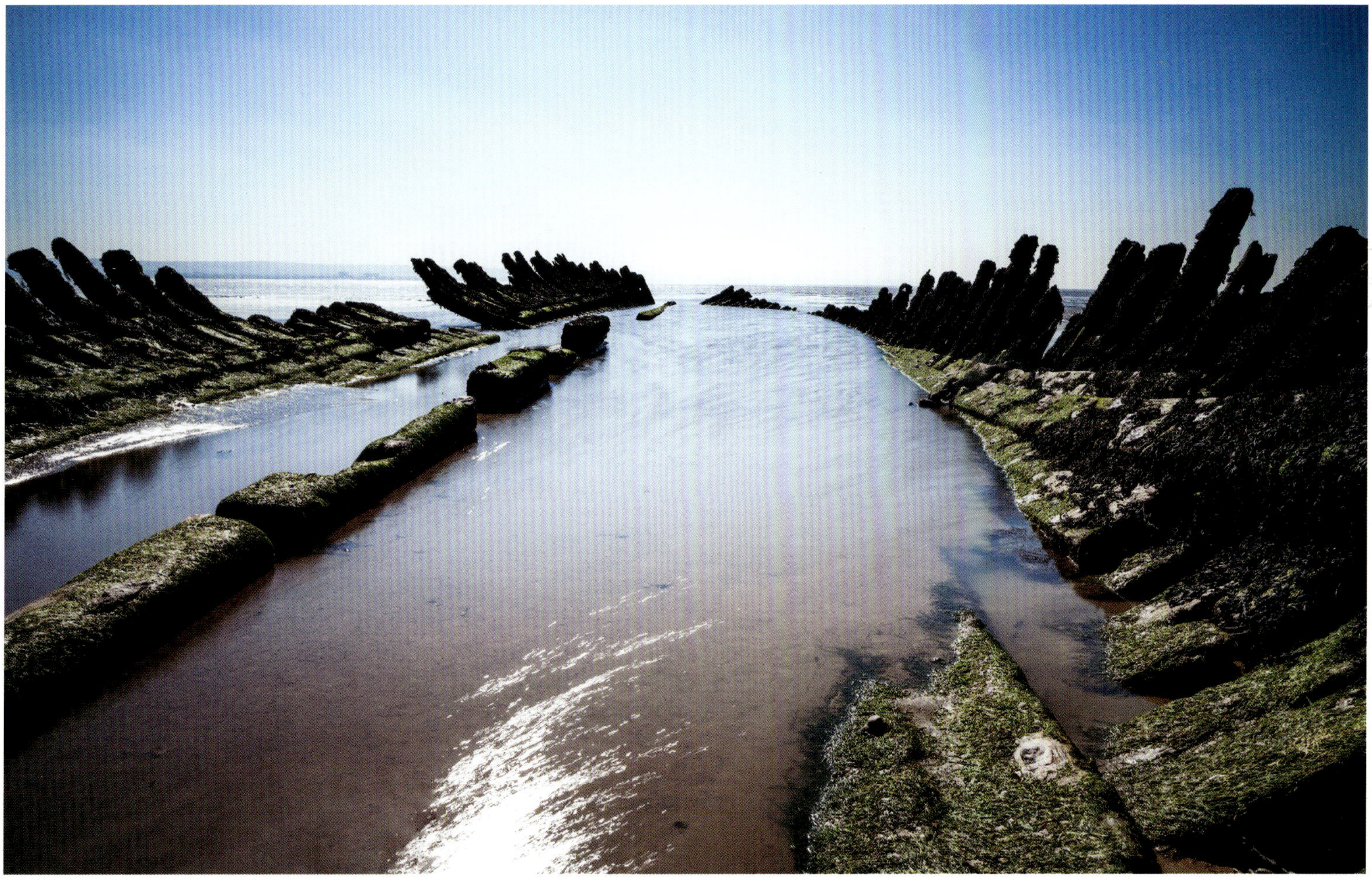

Our Confidence, Bonaire, Leeward Antilles, Caribbean
The historic 18m (60ft) fishing vessel _Our Confidence_ sank on 4 August 2003, settling in 17m (55ft) of water. This little boat had a big history, in its time serving as a World War II refugee boat and a supply ship for hurricane victims.

OVERLEAF:
TOP LEFT:

Hilma Hooker, Bonaire, Leeward Antilles, Caribbean
The wheel of the evocatively titled _Hilma Hooker_ is locked forever in place on the Caribbean seabed. This cargo ship was originally Dutch and called _Midsland_, but went through several name and ownership changes following its launch in 1951. The ship sank through disrepair in 1984 after being impounded for drug smuggling.

BOTTOM LEFT:

SS _Bryansk_, Black Sea, off Odessa, Ukraine
A diver moves past the anchor chain of the SS _Bryansk_, a UK-built Soviet cargo steamer sunk in an air raid near Odessa on 21 August 1941.

TOP RIGHT:

RMS _Titanic_, North Atlantic
Few wrecks have drawn the public's fascination as much as that of the RMS _Titanic_, which sank after hitting an iceberg on 14 April 1912. Here we see an underwater shot of a deck from the documentary _Ghosts of the Abyss_ directed by James Cameron.

BOTTOM RIGHT:

RMS _Titanic_, North Atlantic
One of _Titanic_'s mighty anchors, as seen during the _Ghosts of the Abyss_ documentary. The _Titanic_'s historical narrative is compelling for many reasons, not least that the ship sank on her maiden voyage to New York and that it only had enough lifeboats for about half the people on board.

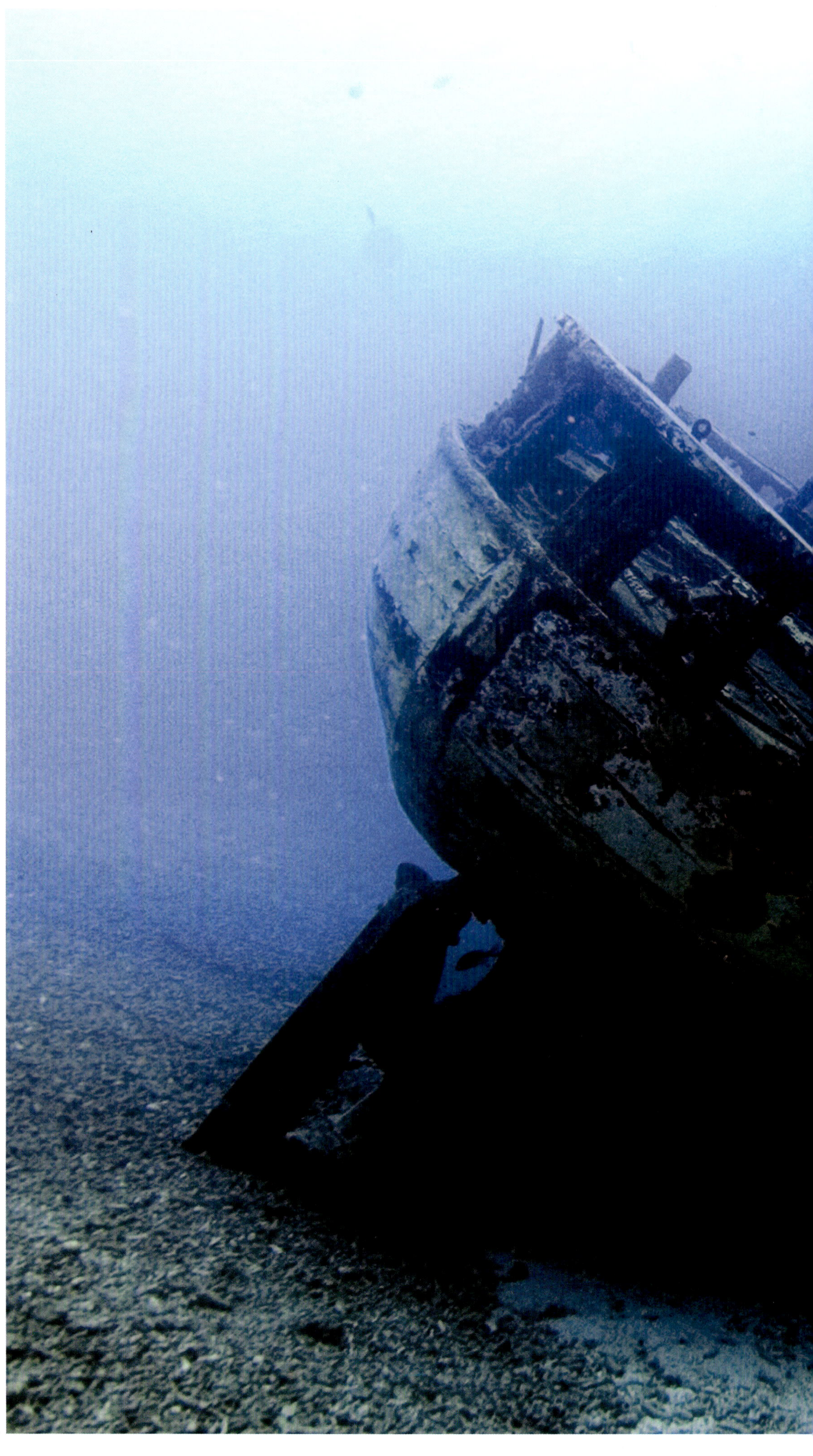

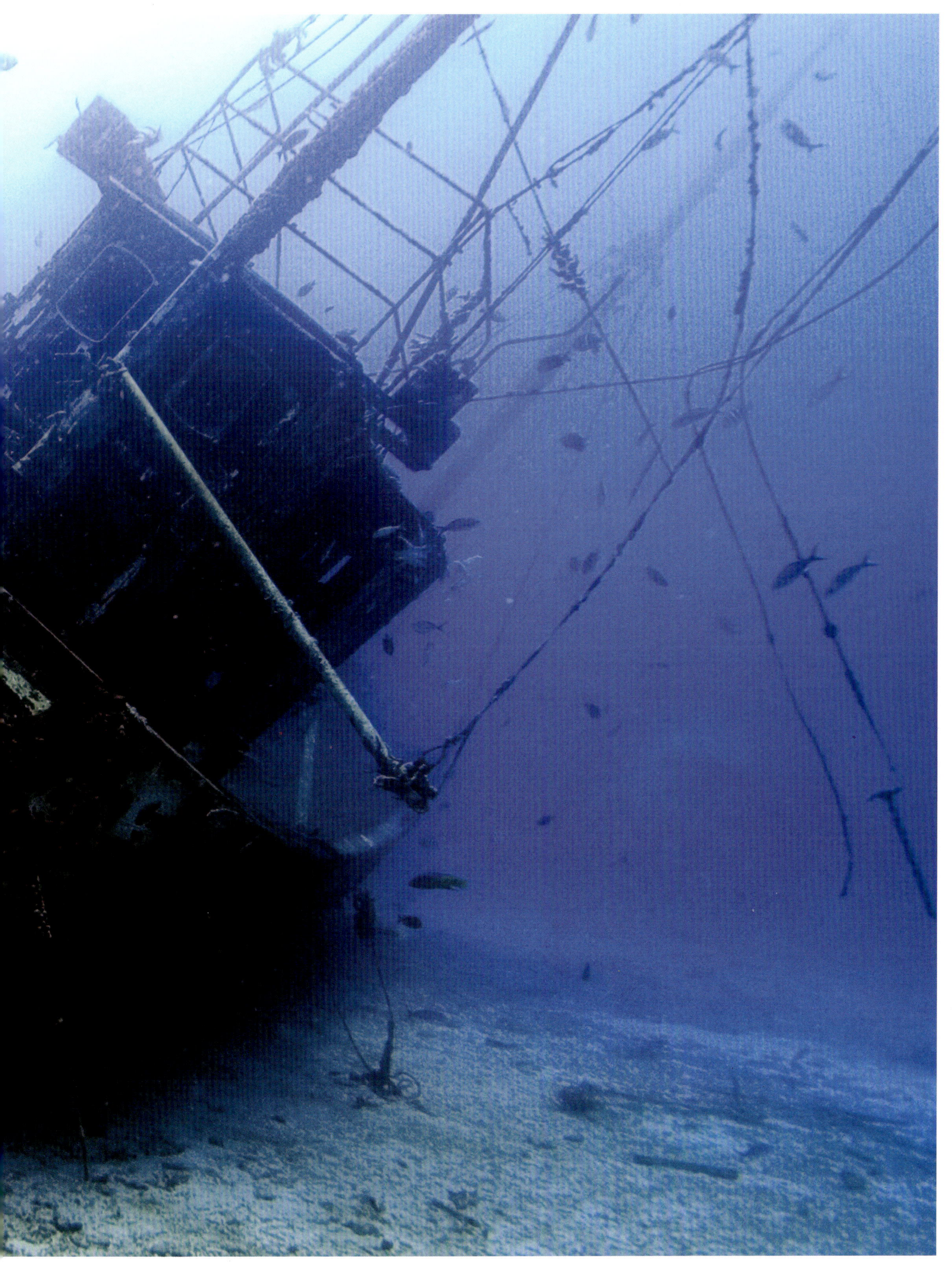

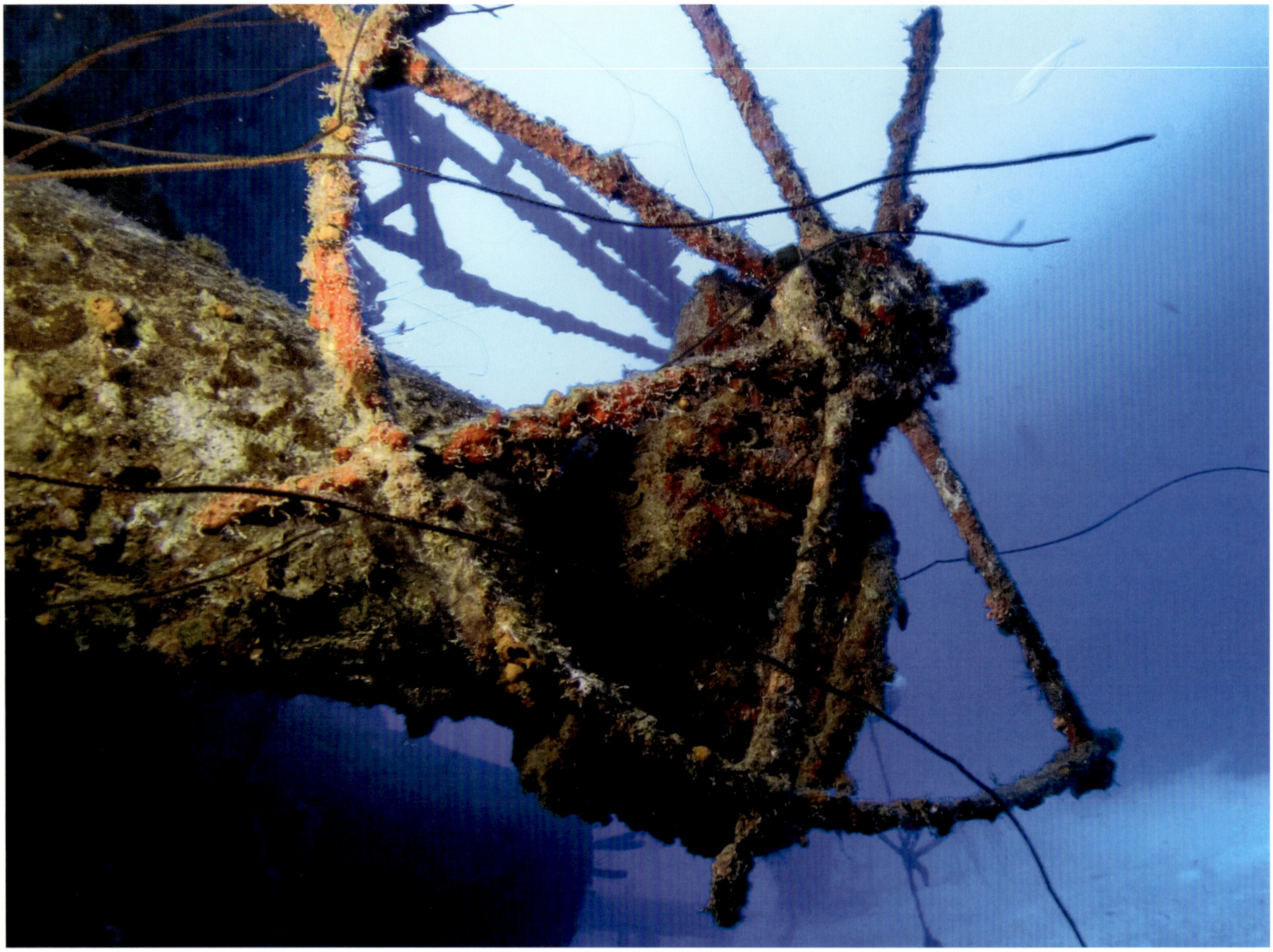

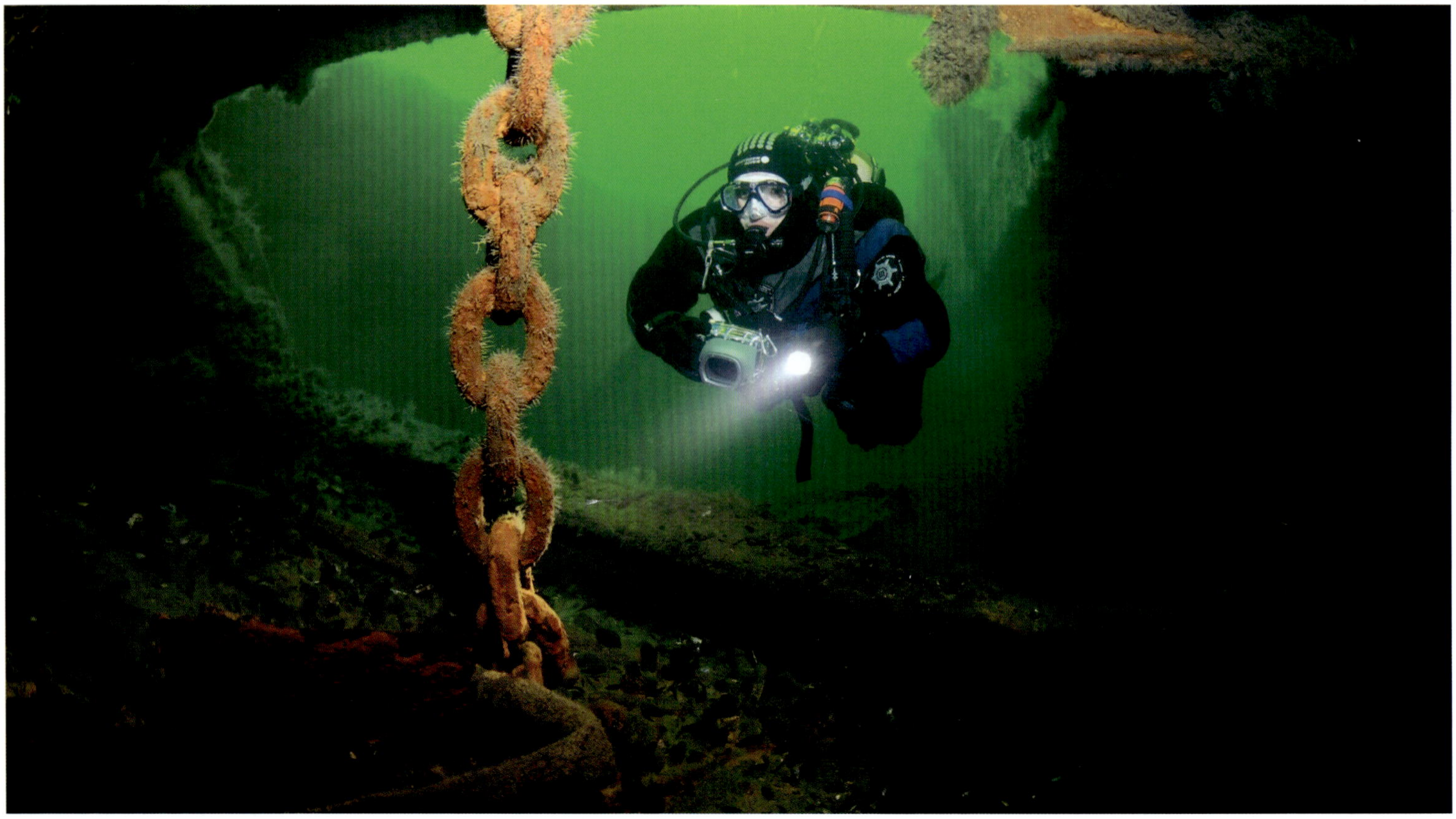

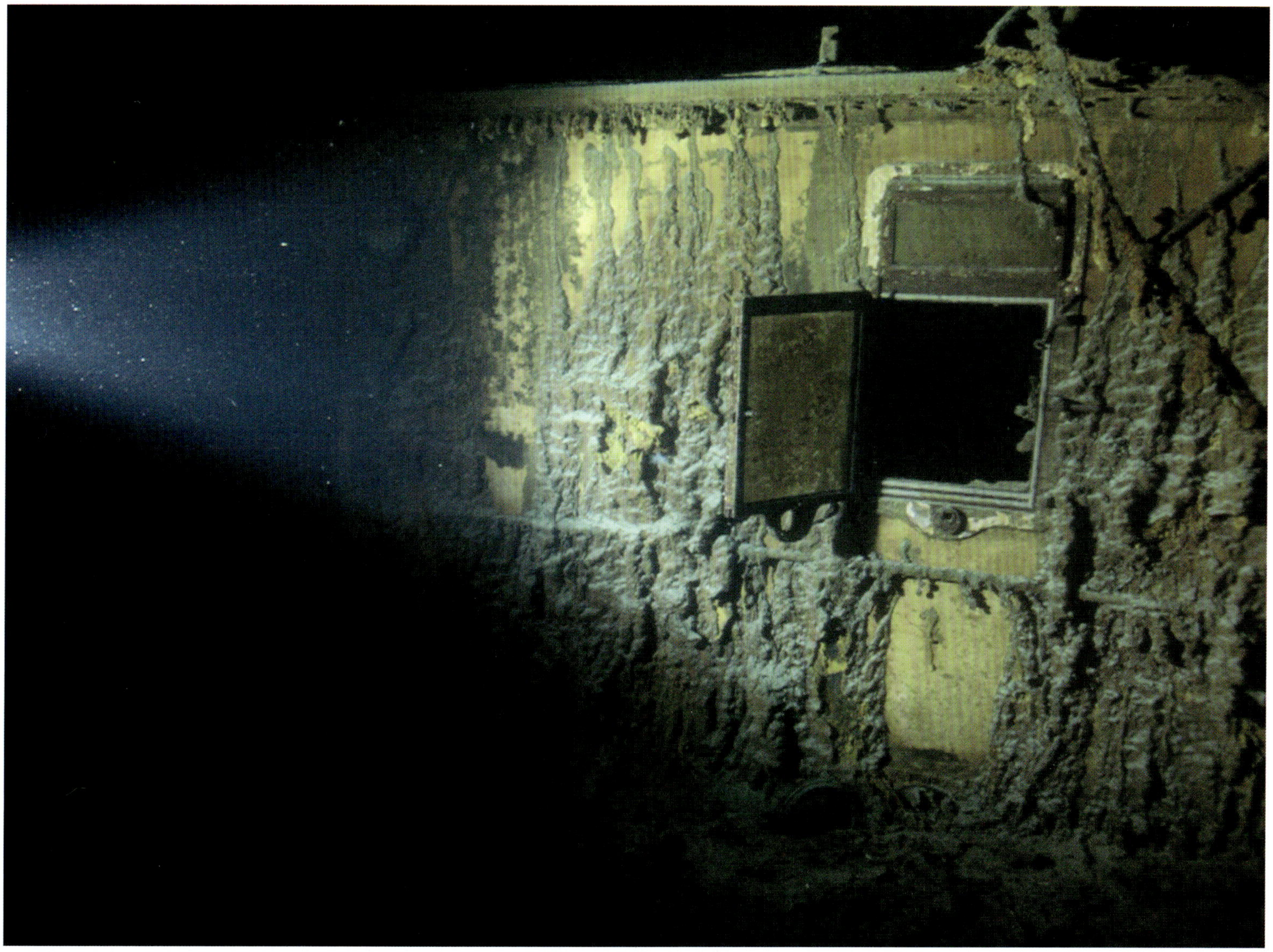

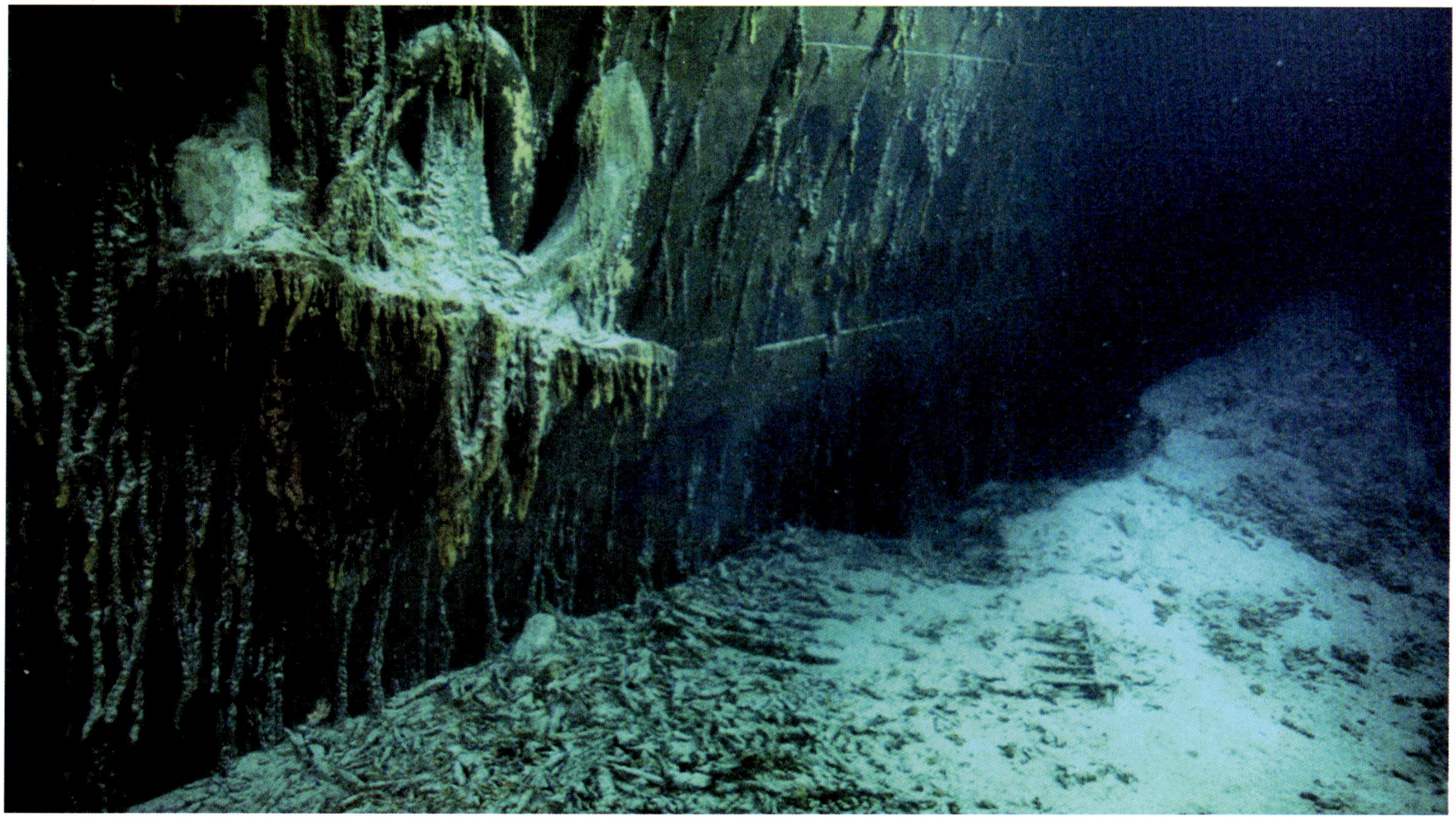

RMS *Titanic,* North Atlantic
Although this photograph of
the bows of the *Titanic* is now
one of the most famous wreck
images, it still has haunting
impact. The wreck – which was
only discovered in 1985 – has been
visited infrequently, as it lies more
than 3,700m (12,000ft) below the
surface in a vast debris field.

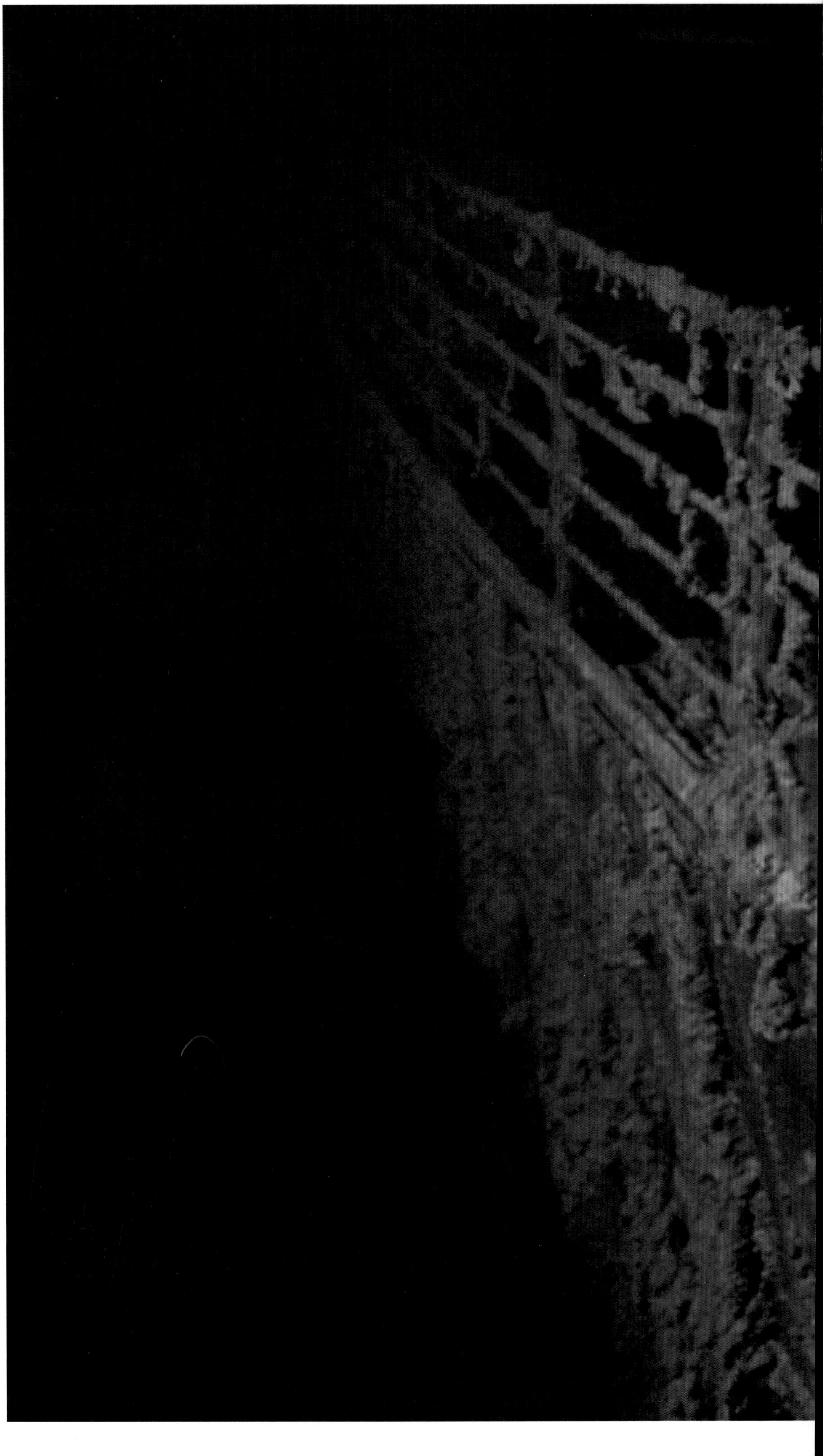

***Desdemona,* Cabo San Pablo,
Patagonia, Argentina**
Apart from its rusted hue, the wreck
of the cargo ship *Desdemona* still
looks remarkably intact. The ship
ran aground on 9 September 1985.
Grounding can be a very destructive
experience for a ship, but sometimes
results in surprisingly little
structural damage.

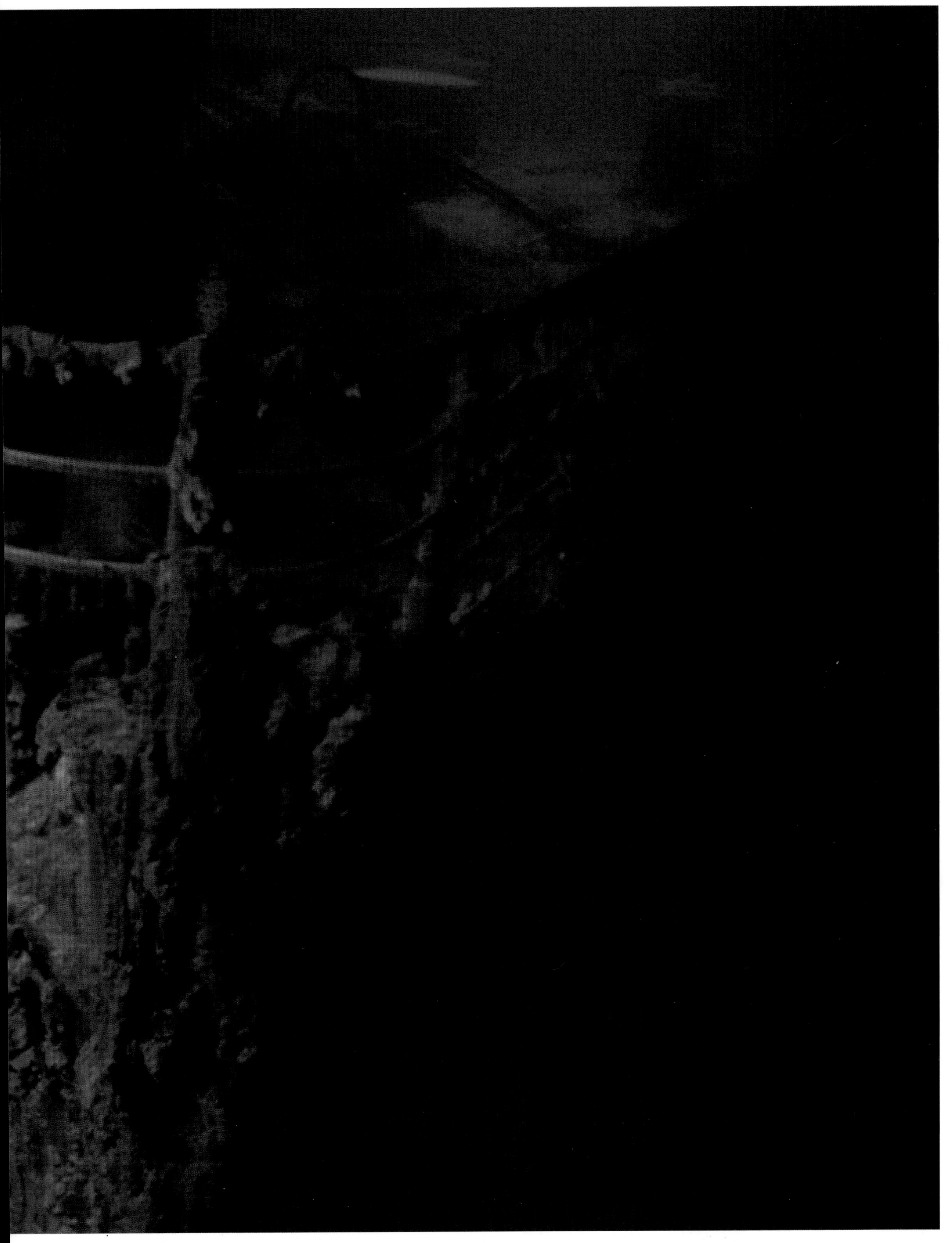

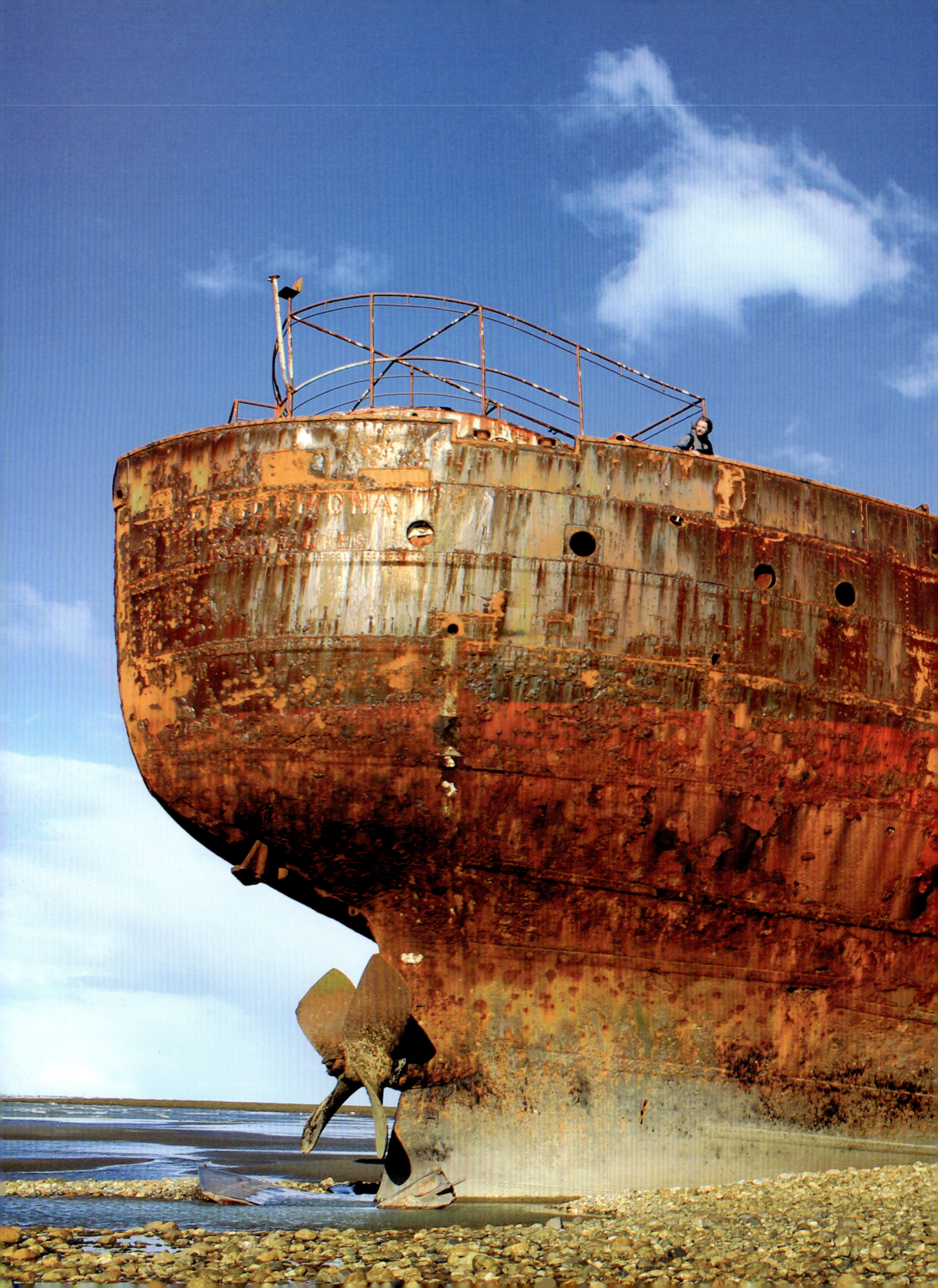

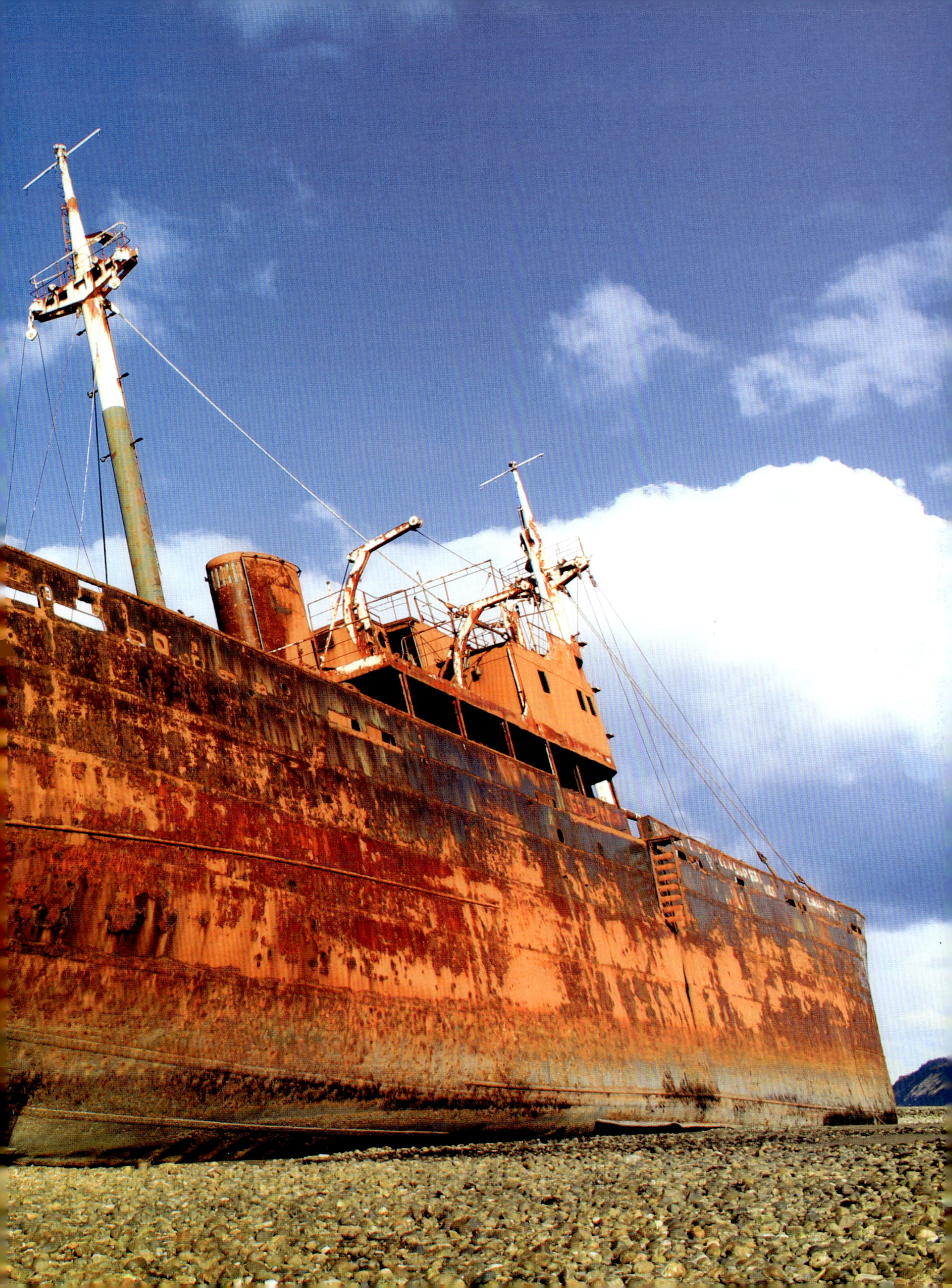

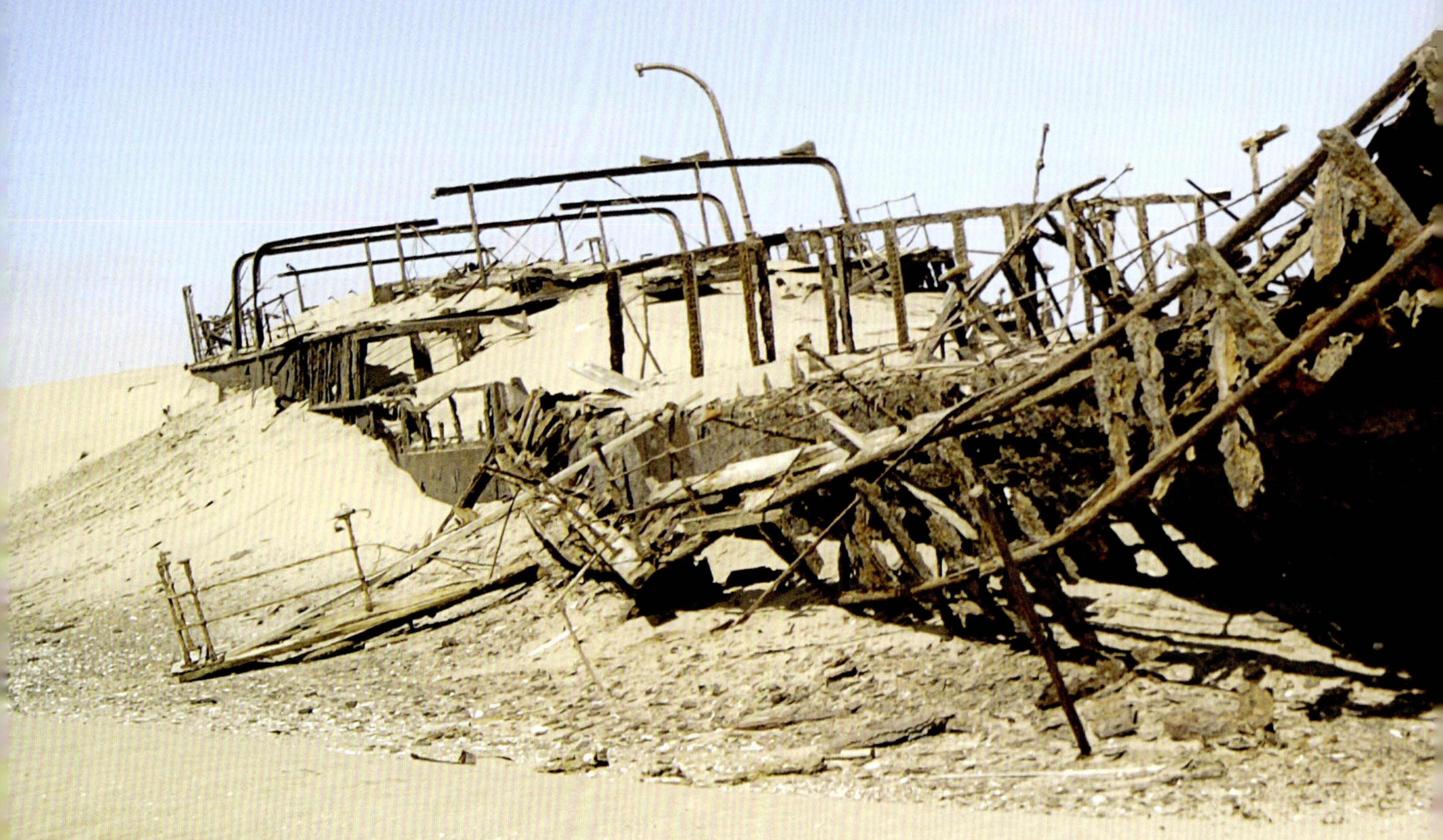

Eduard Bohlen, Skeleton Coast, Namibia
The Skeleton Coast is famously littered with shipwrecks, the product of heavy coastal fogs and large wave systems. This vessel is the cargo ship _Eduard Bohlen_, wrecked in a thick fog on 5 September 1909. Having been destroyed by the sea, the ship is now being claimed by the sand.

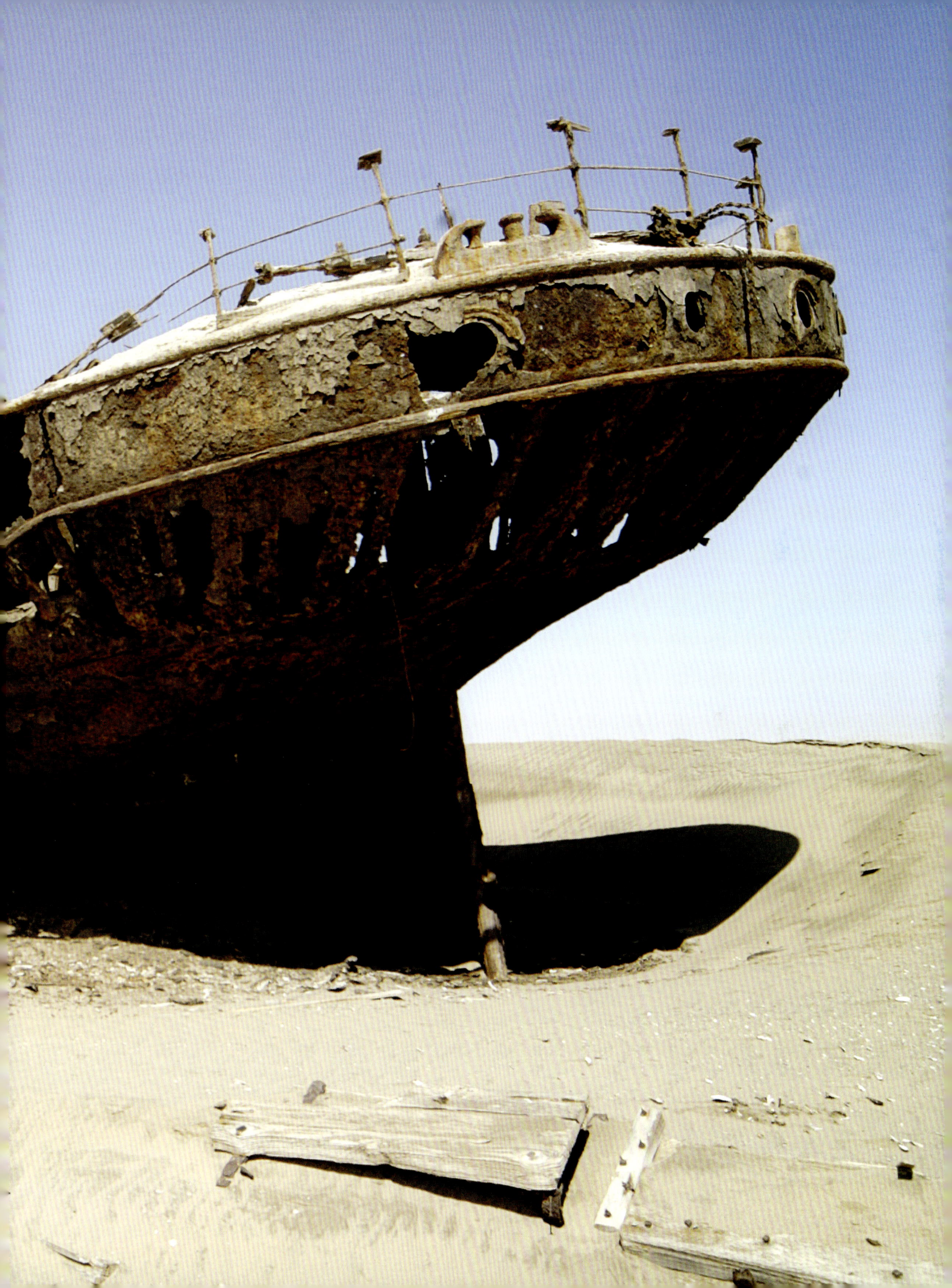

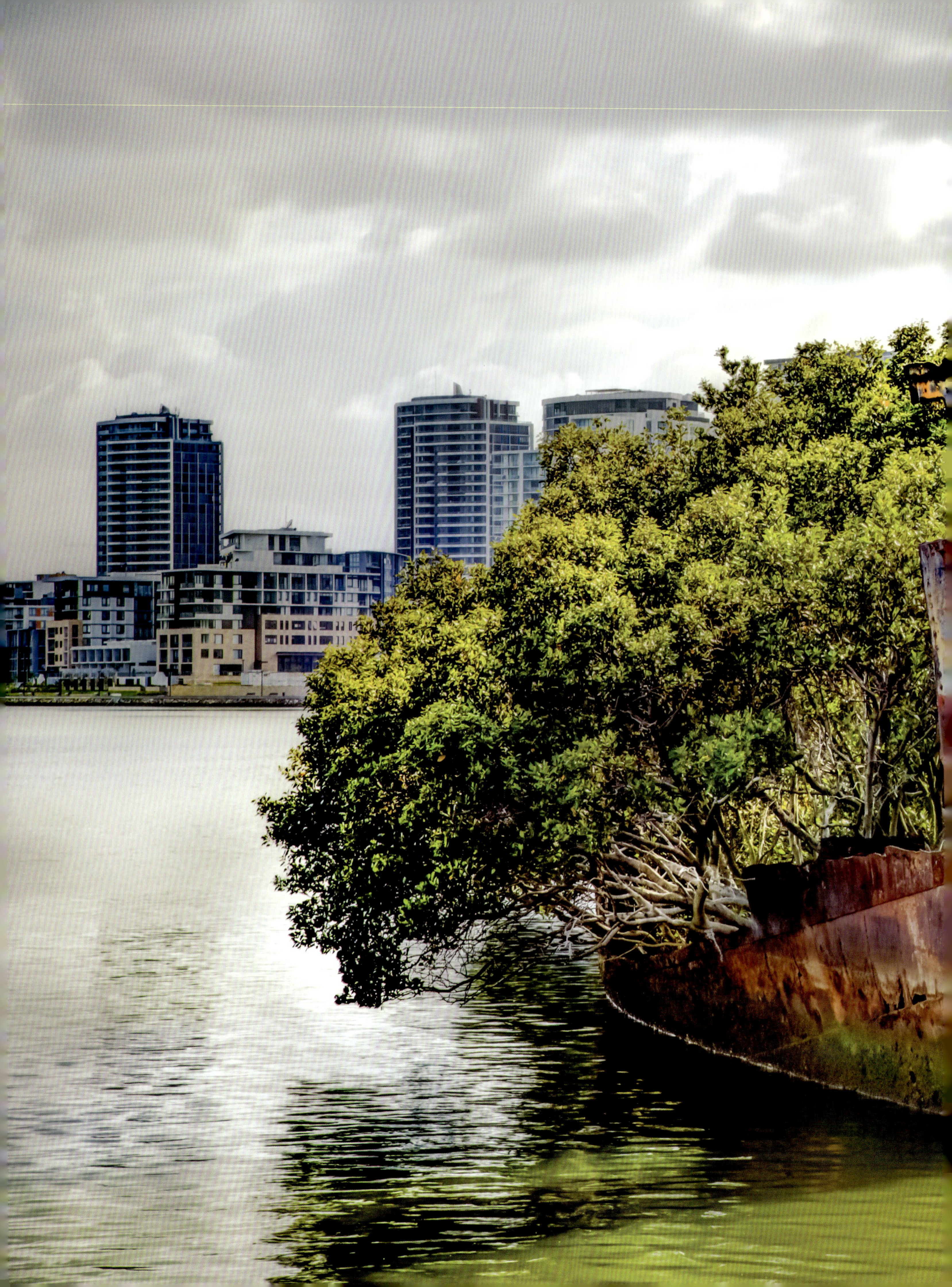

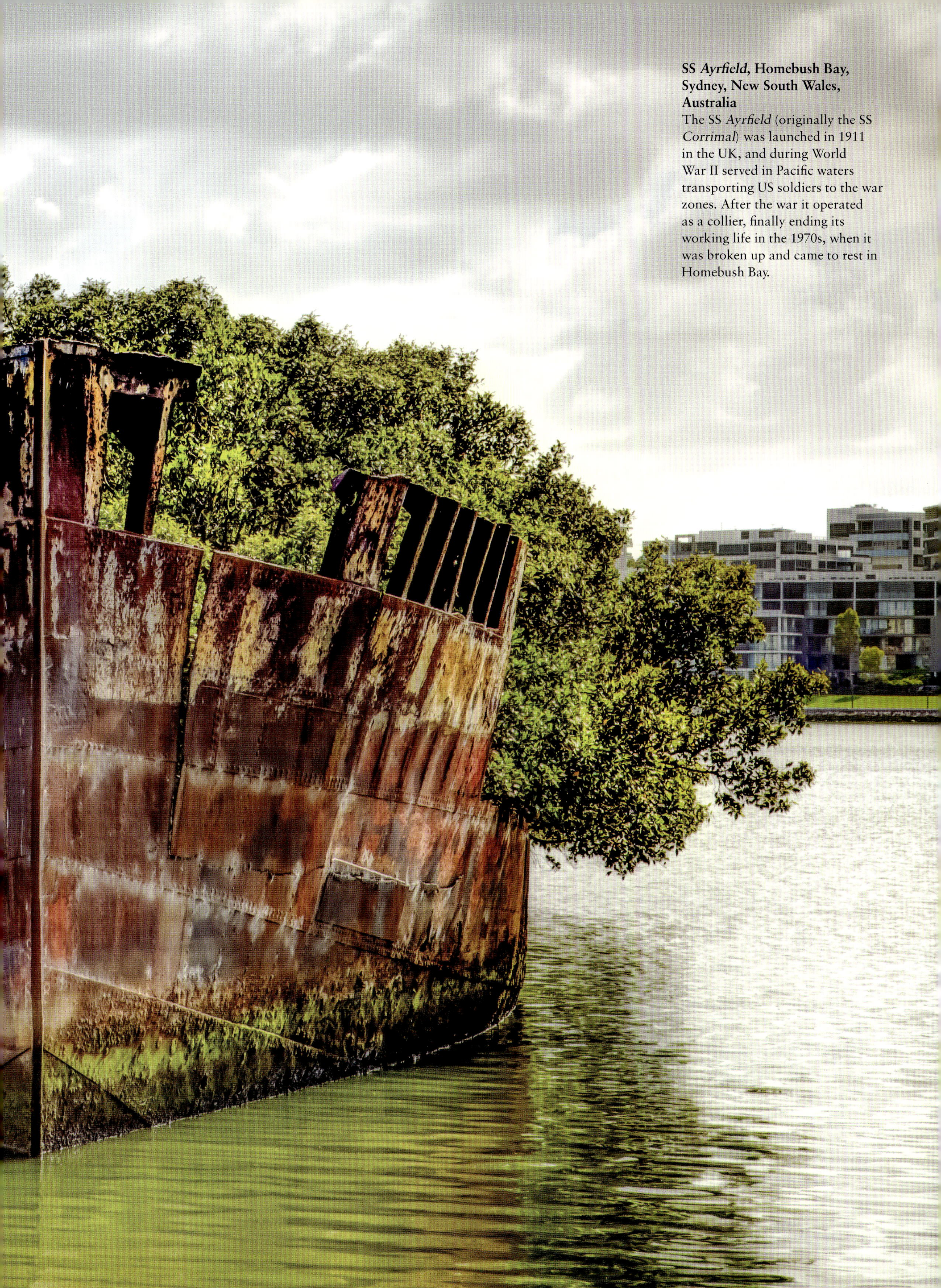

SS *Ayrfield*, Homebush Bay, Sydney, New South Wales, Australia
The SS *Ayrfield* (originally the SS *Corrimal*) was launched in 1911 in the UK, and during World War II served in Pacific waters transporting US soldiers to the war zones. After the war it operated as a collier, finally ending its working life in the 1970s, when it was broken up and came to rest in Homebush Bay.

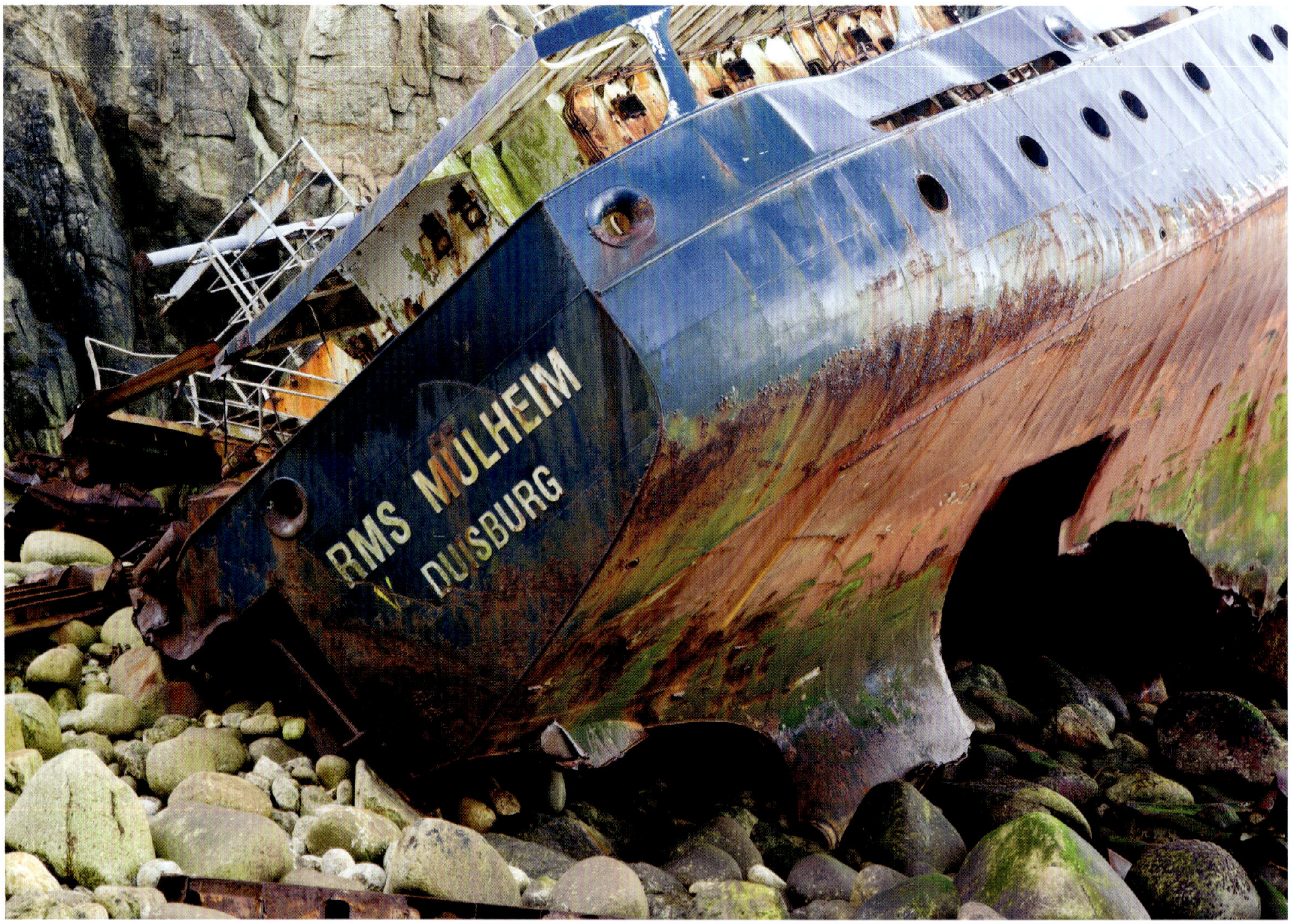
RMS MULHEIM
DUISBURG

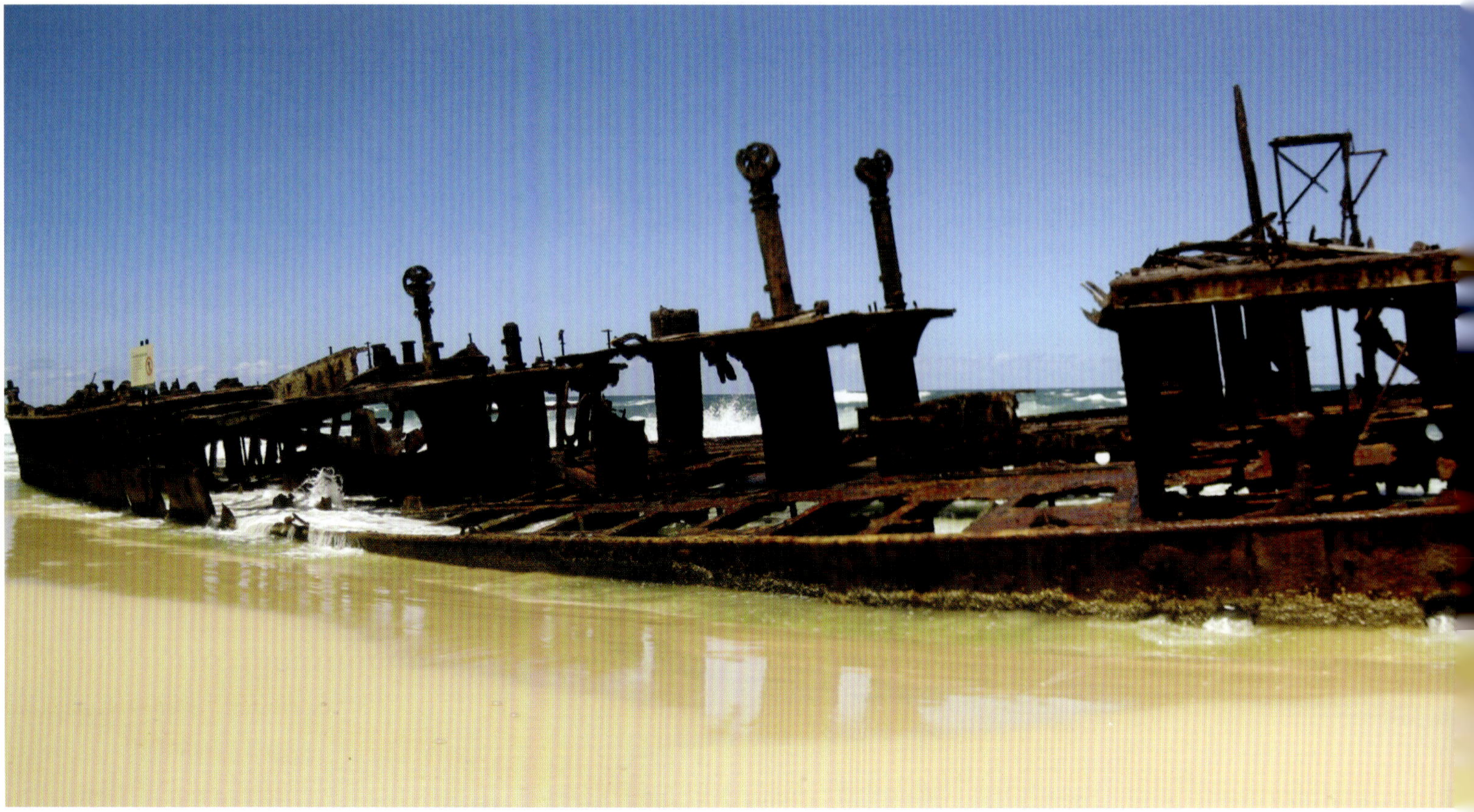

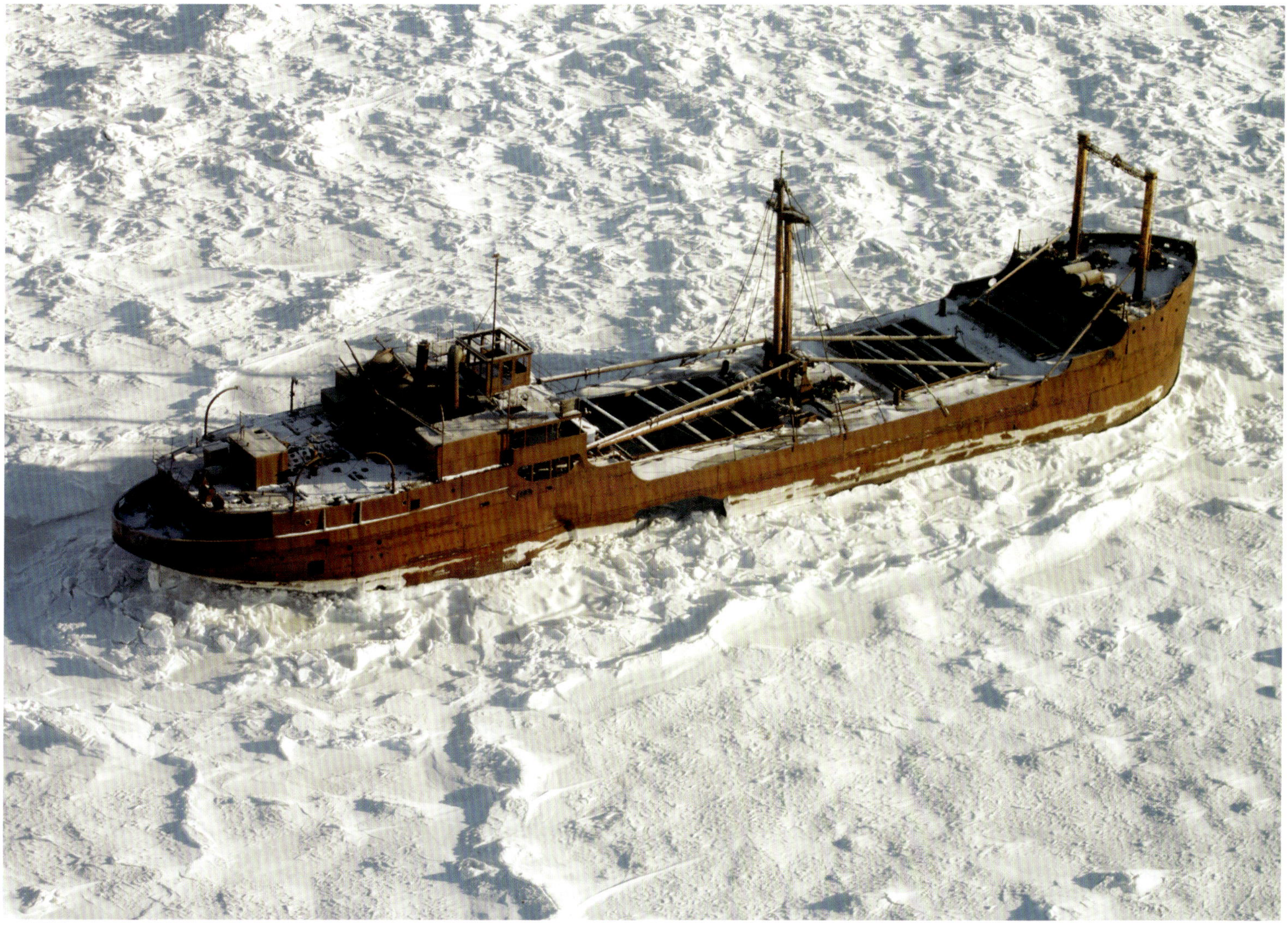

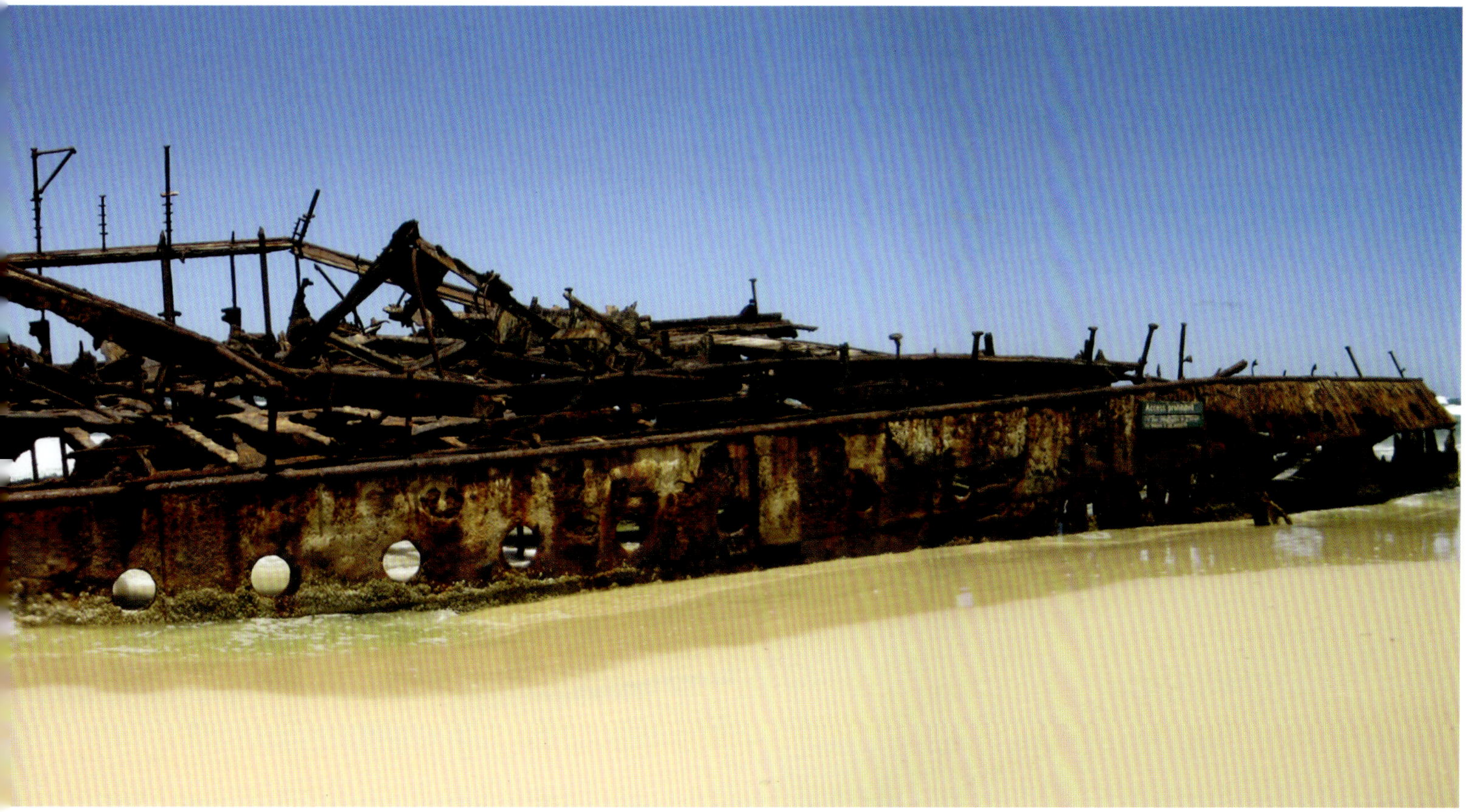

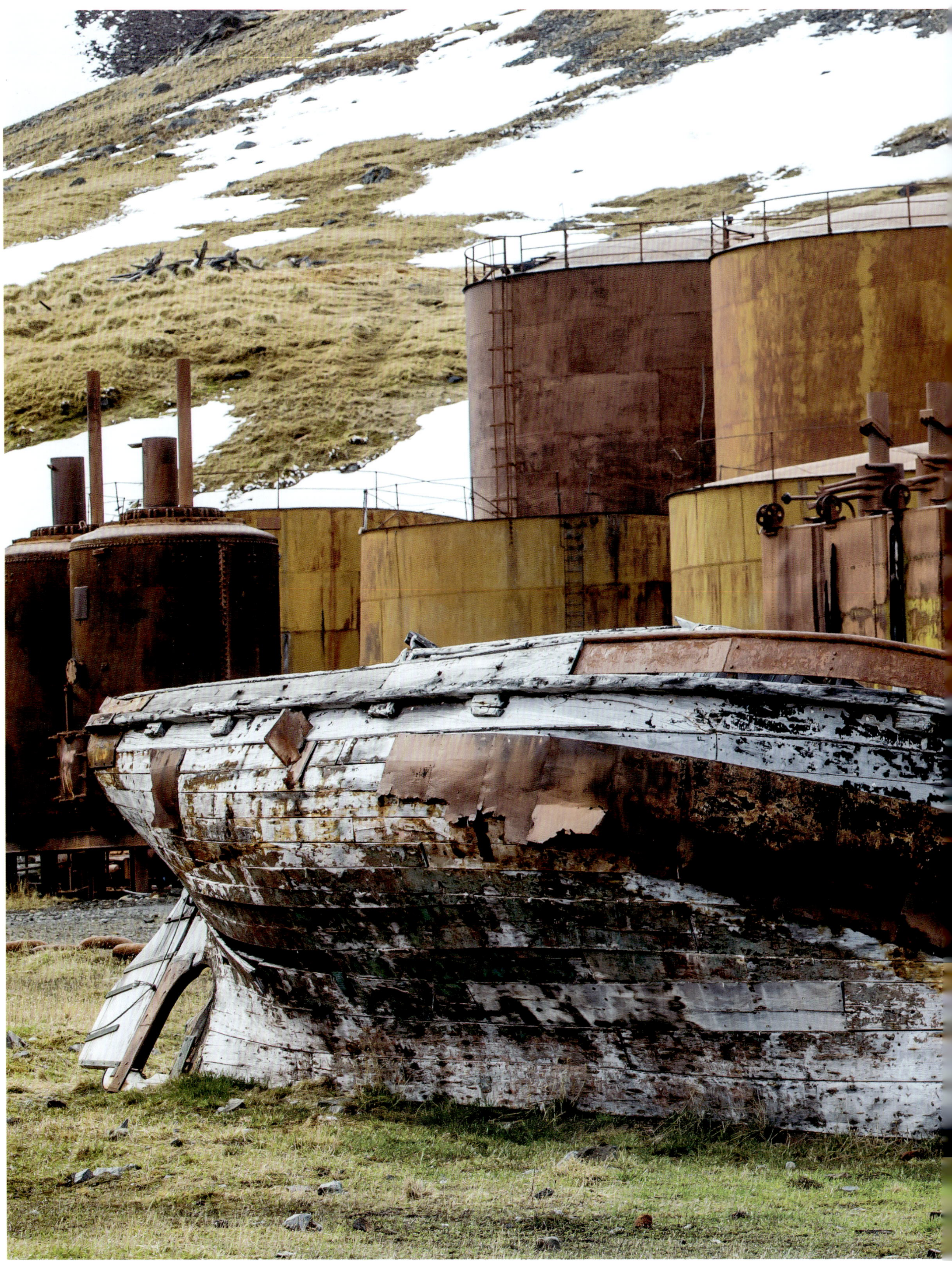

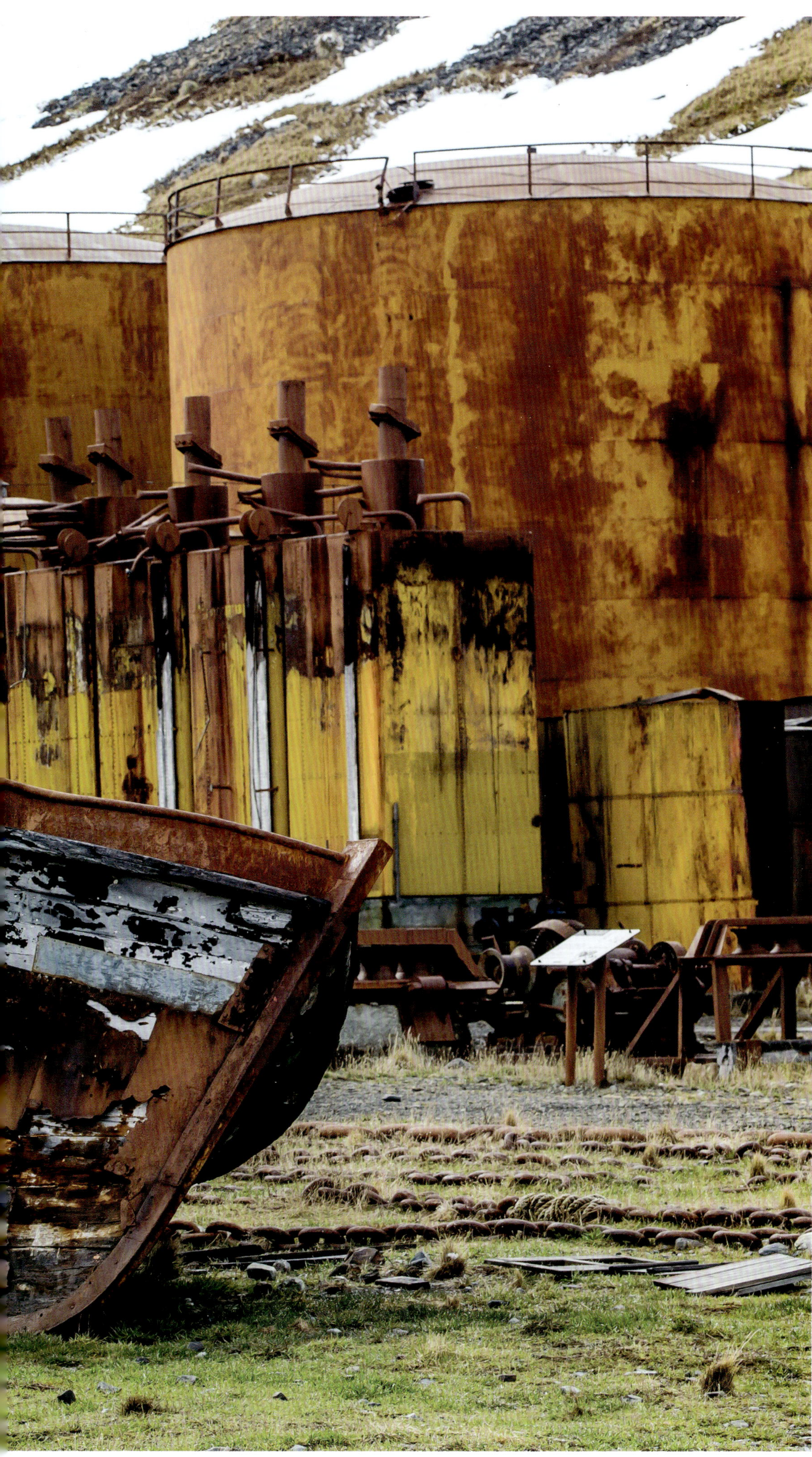

TOP LEFT:

RMS *Mülheim*, Land's End, Cornwall, England

The RMS *Mülheim* was a German cargo ship launched in Romania in 1999. On 22 March 2003, while the ship was sailing for Cork, Ireland, the officer on watch accidentally knocked himself unconscious on the bridge. When he came to the ship was grounding itself on the southwest corner of England.

TOP RIGHT:

SS *Ithaka*, Bird Cove, Hudson Bay, near Churchill, Manitoba, Canada

The SS *Ithaka* was a Canadian freighter launched in 1922. The ship's original name was *Frank A. Augsbury*, and it went through many others before it was renamed *Ithaka* in 1960. The ship was run aground in terrible weather on 14 September 1960, the gravel bank on which she sat ripping out her hull as the waves struck.

BOTTOM:

SS *Maheno*, Fraser Island, Queensland, Australia

The SS *Maheno* was an ocean liner that during World War I served as a hospital ship for ANZAC forces, including during the disastrous Gallipoli campaign of 1915. In July 1935, the ship was under tow when it separated from its tow ship during a cyclone, grounding itself on the coast of Fraser Island.

LEFT:

Leith Harbour, South Georgia, southern Atlantic Ocean

This simple craft, alongside many other relics scattered around Lieth Harbour, is a visible reminder of South Georgia's once-thriving whaling industry. The tanks in the background were used for storing whale oil.

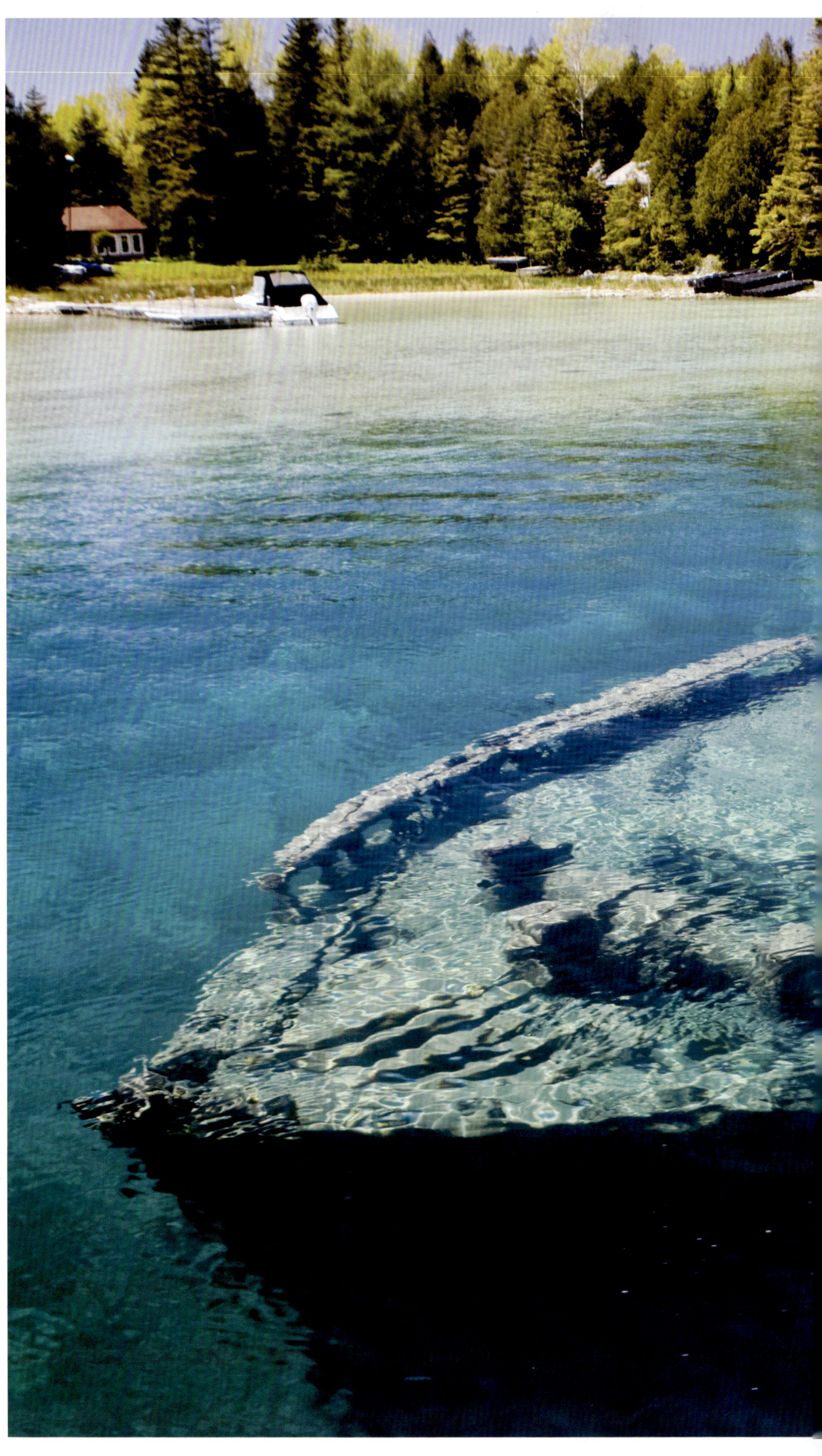

Sweepstakes, **Big Tub Harbour, Fathom Five National Marine Park, Lake Huron, Ontario**
Looking ghostly under the waters of Big Tub Harbour in Lake Huron, *Sweepstakes* was a Canadian schooner built in Burlington, Ontario, in 1867. The ship sank in 1885, but has remained astonishingly well preserved to this day.

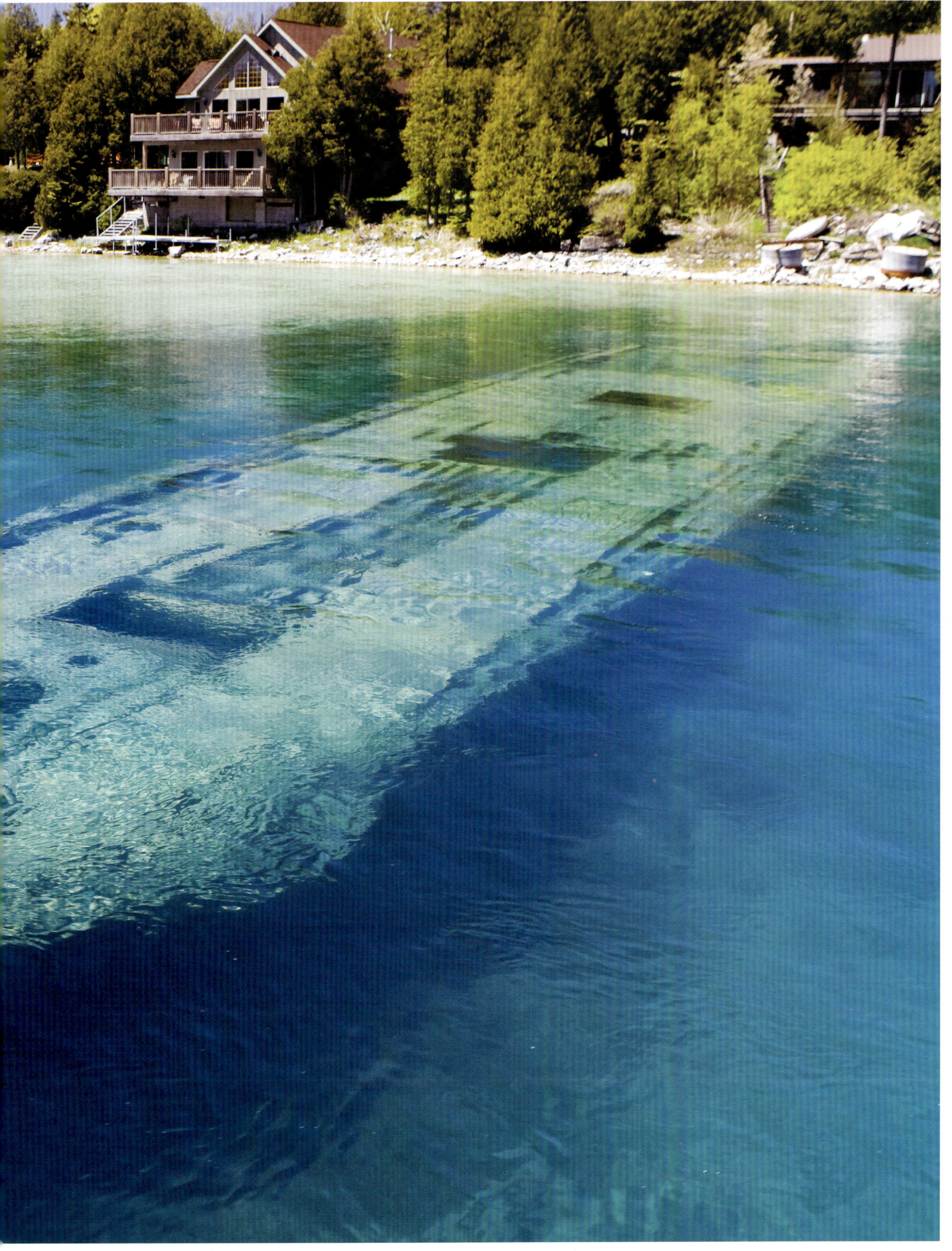

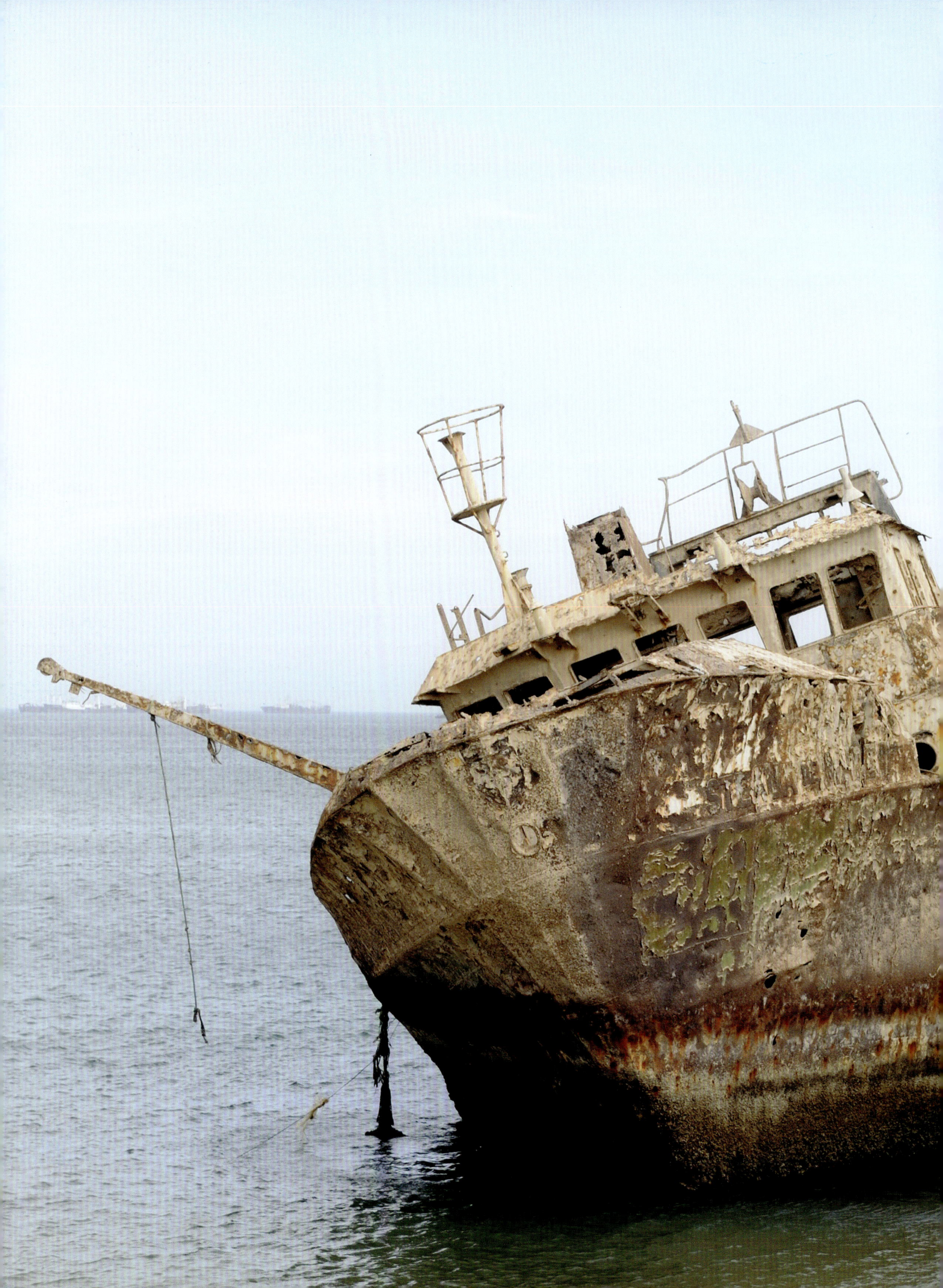

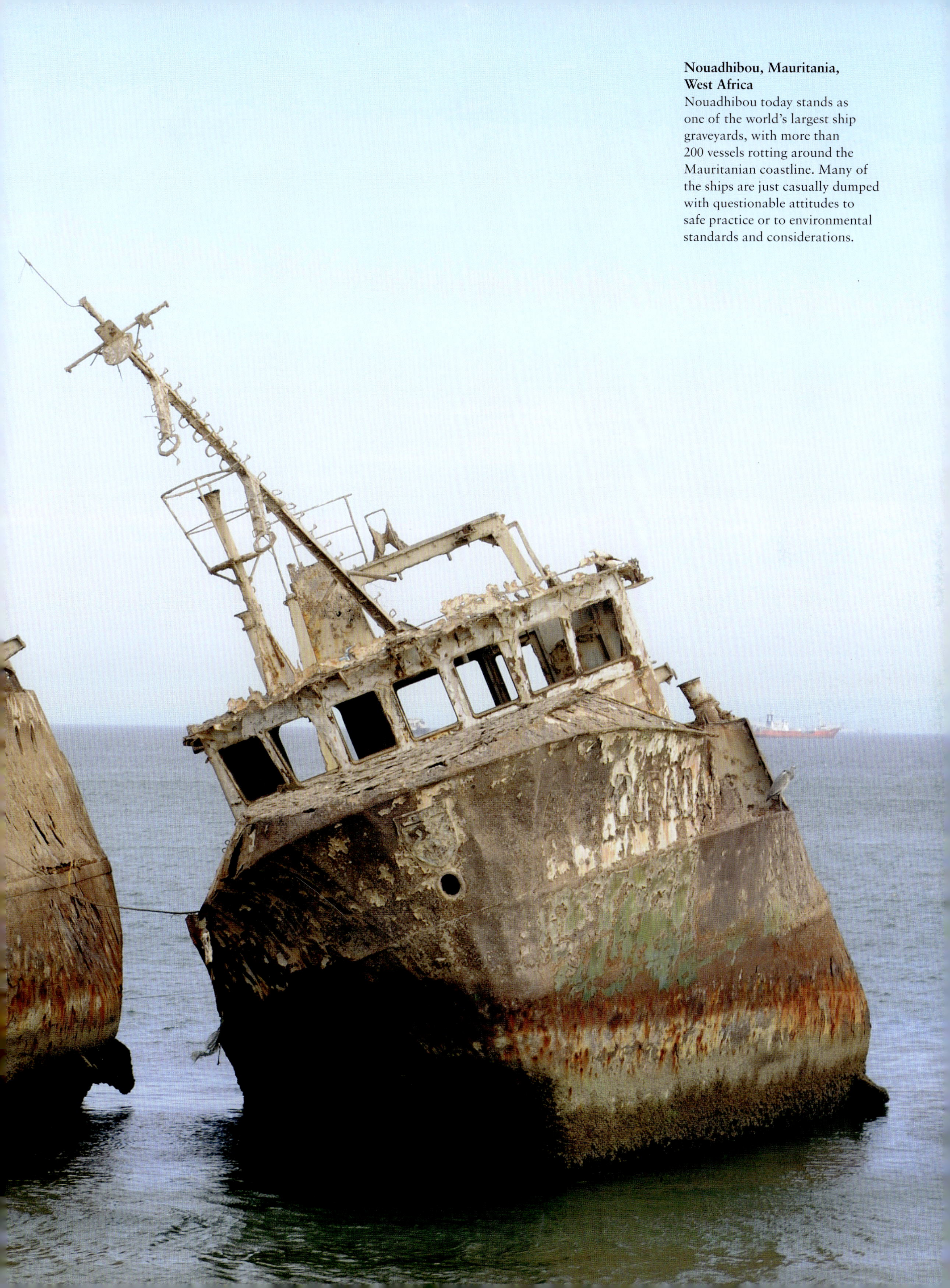

Nouadhibou, Mauritania, West Africa
Nouadhibou today stands as one of the world's largest ship graveyards, with more than 200 vessels rotting around the Mauritanian coastline. Many of the ships are just casually dumped with questionable attitudes to safe practice or to environmental standards and considerations.

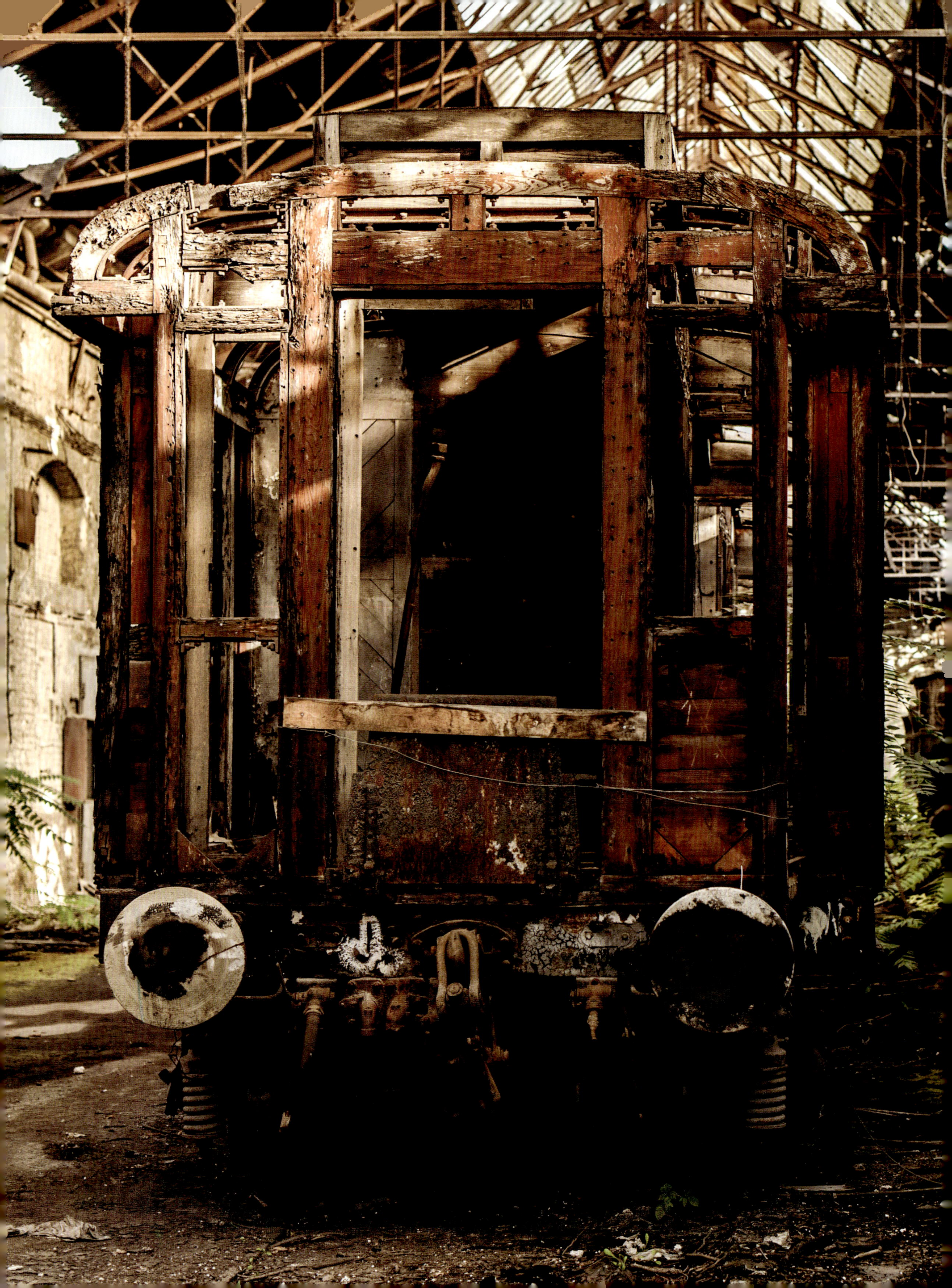

Trains

In our age of air travel and personal vehicles, it is all too easy to forget the global transformation achieved by the development of rail transportation. From the creation of the first full-size steam locomotive in 1804, courtesy of British inventor Richard Trevithick, the volume of rolling stock and the sheer number and distance of lines proliferated at an extraordinary rate. By the end of the 19th century, almost every continent was criss-crossed by rail lines, linking every major habitation, transporting millions of people and hundreds of millions of tons of freight. The advent of rail, therefore, in essence laid the foundation of the modern world. The emergent rail network made possible the tourism industry, long-distance transportation of goods, increased mining and agricultural outputs (in turn supporting population growth) and, less positively, the ability to deploy armies quickly – without trains, it is unlikely that the Franco–Prussian War and World War I could have been fought so readily. Today, a large percentage of the world's population still relies upon rail travel. At the same time, rail locomotives, carriages and wagons of yesteryear litter many of our urban zones and wilderness spaces. They remind us that technology only remains modern for so long, before time, changing fortunes and the environment make it obsolete.

LEFT:
Istvantelek Rail Workshop, Budapest, Hungary
This derelict wood-framed train carriage sits in an abandoned rail shed in Hungary. Wood-framed coaches were standard until the 1950s, when steel-framing took over. Some of the carriages at Istvantelek are believed to have transported Hungarian Jews to the death camps in 1944.

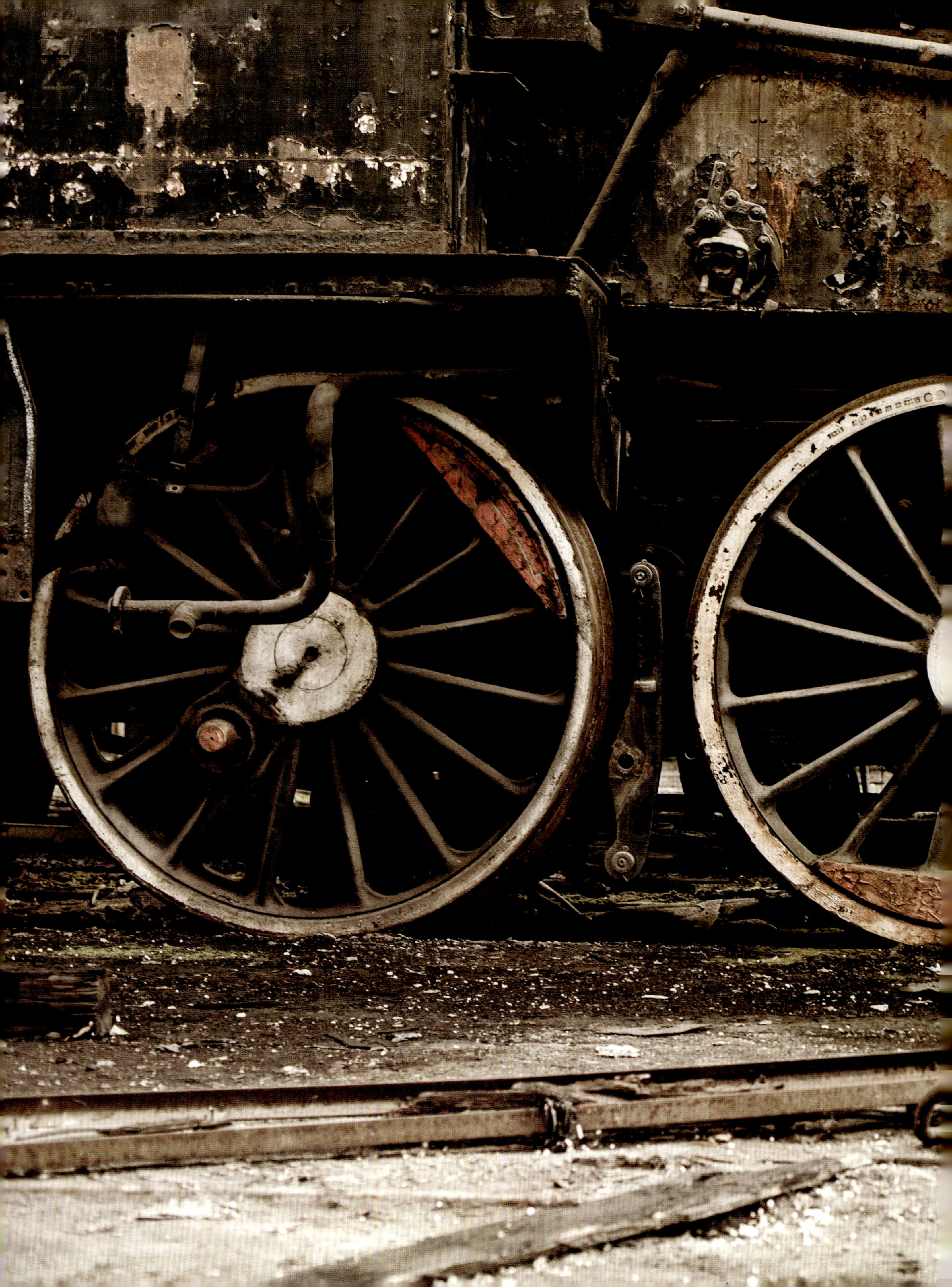

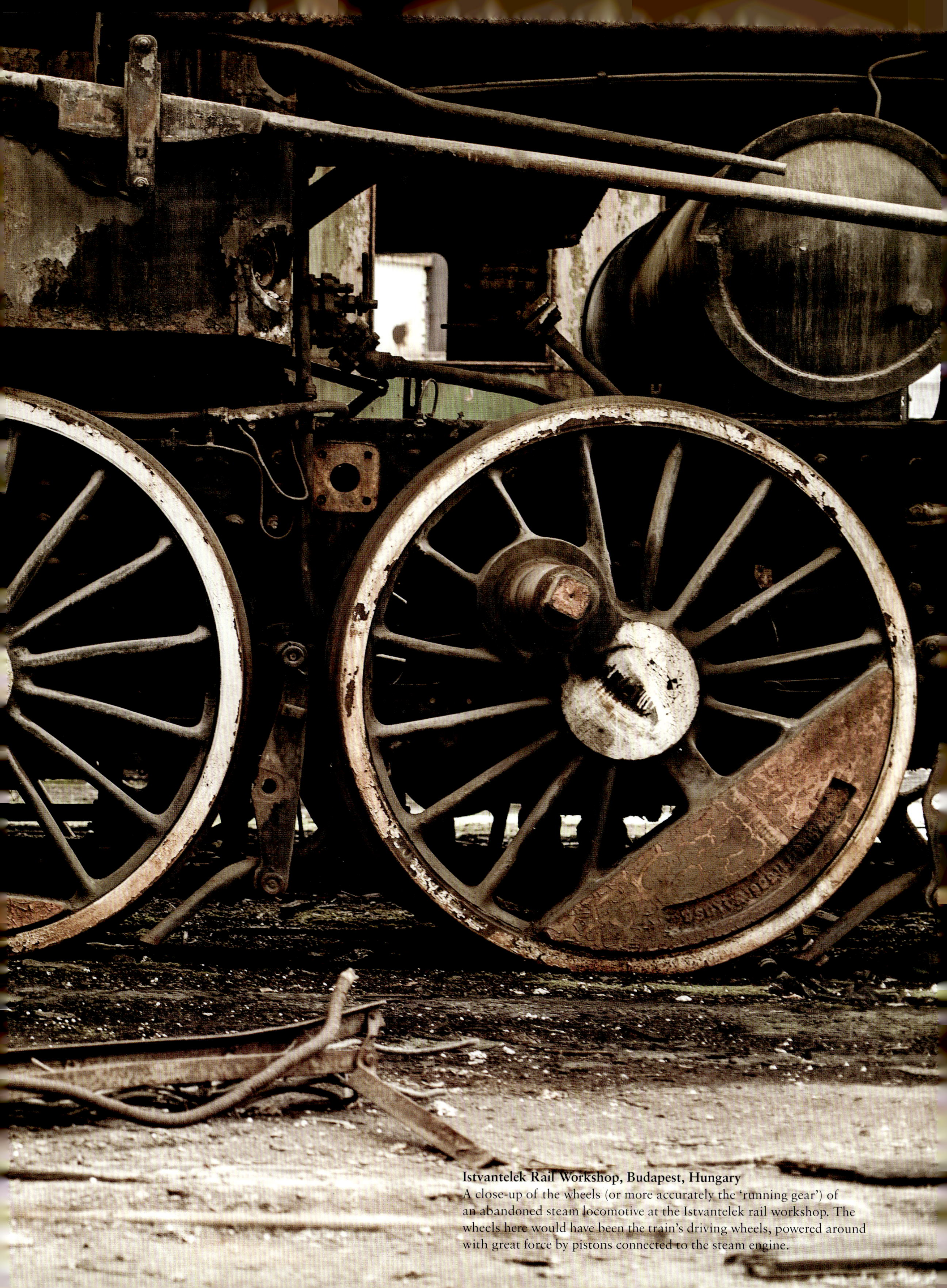

Istvantelek Rail Workshop, Budapest, Hungary
A close-up of the wheels (or more accurately the 'running gear') of
an abandoned steam locomotive at the Istvantelek rail workshop. The
wheels here would have been the train's driving wheels, powered around
with great force by pistons connected to the steam engine.

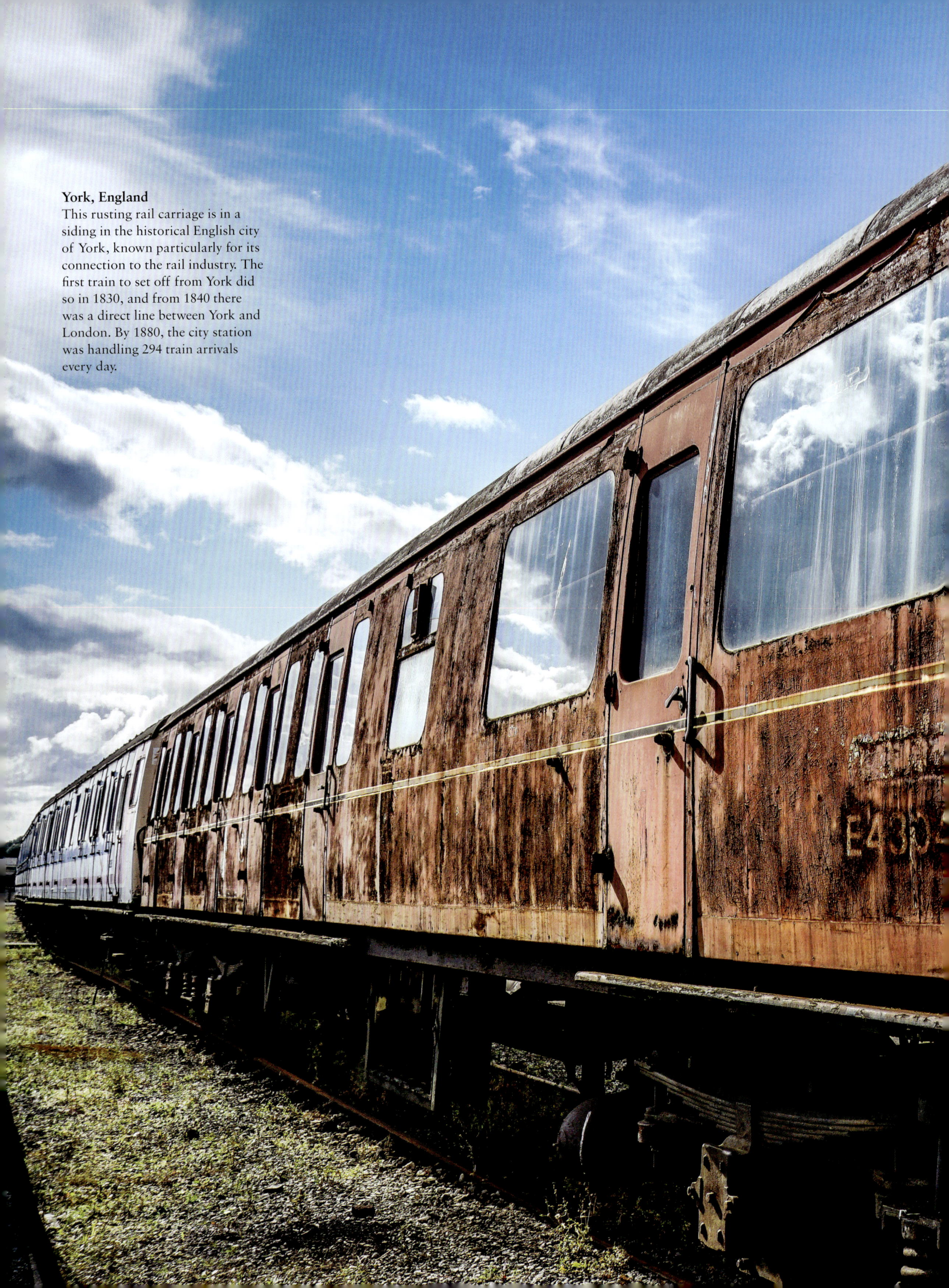

York, England
This rusting rail carriage is in a siding in the historical English city of York, known particularly for its connection to the rail industry. The first train to set off from York did so in 1830, and from 1840 there was a direct line between York and London. By 1880, the city station was handling 294 train arrivals every day.

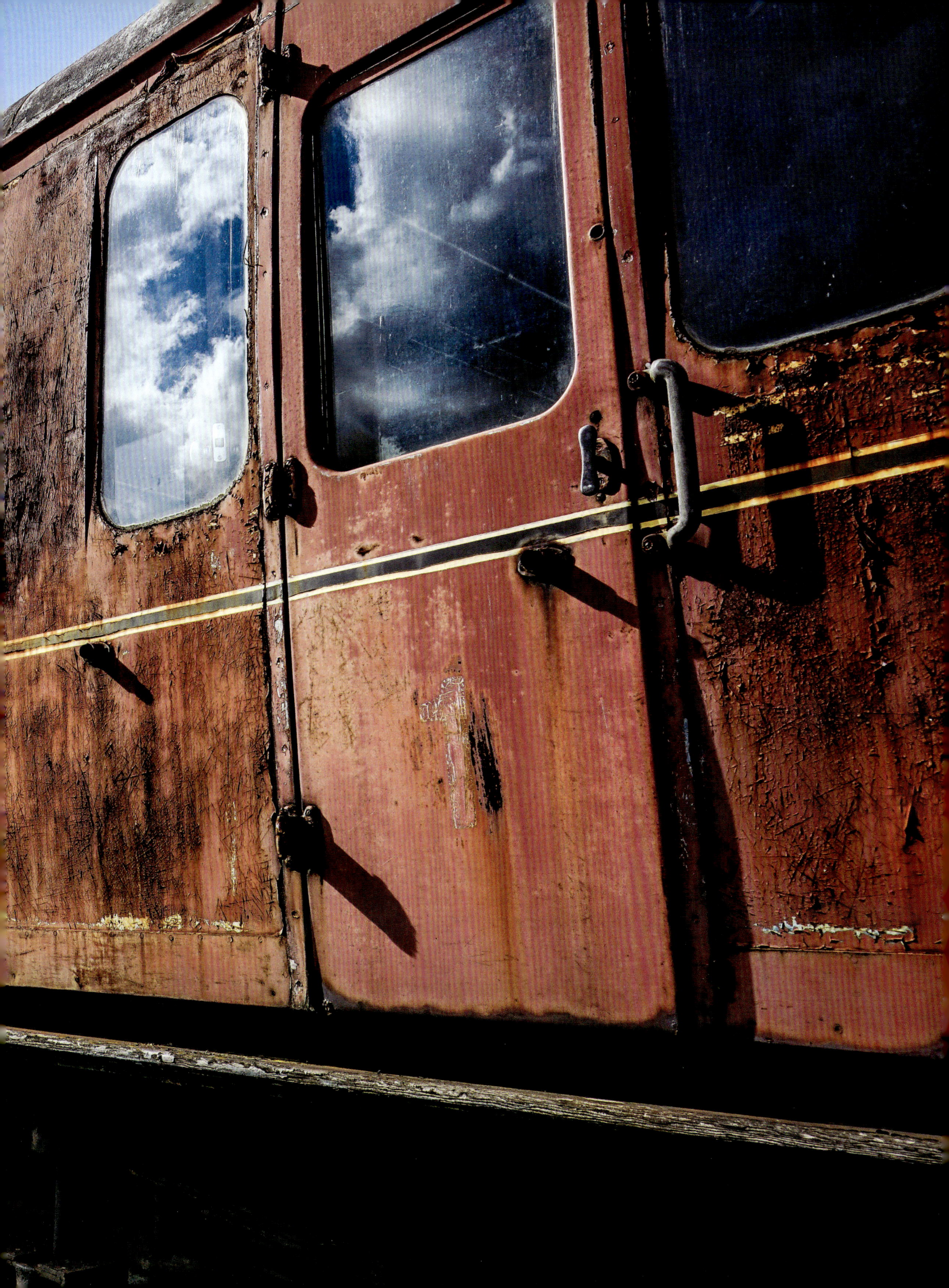

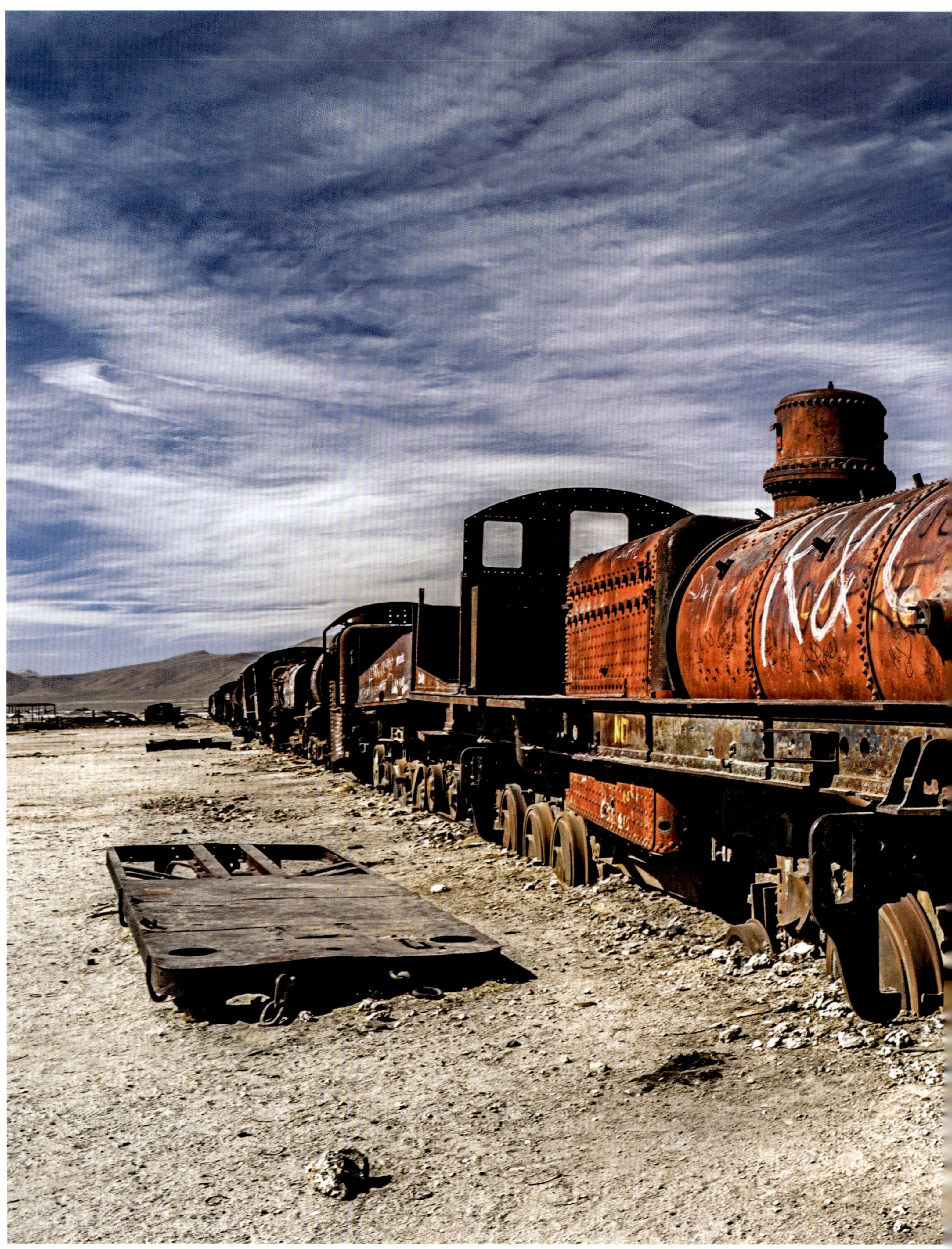

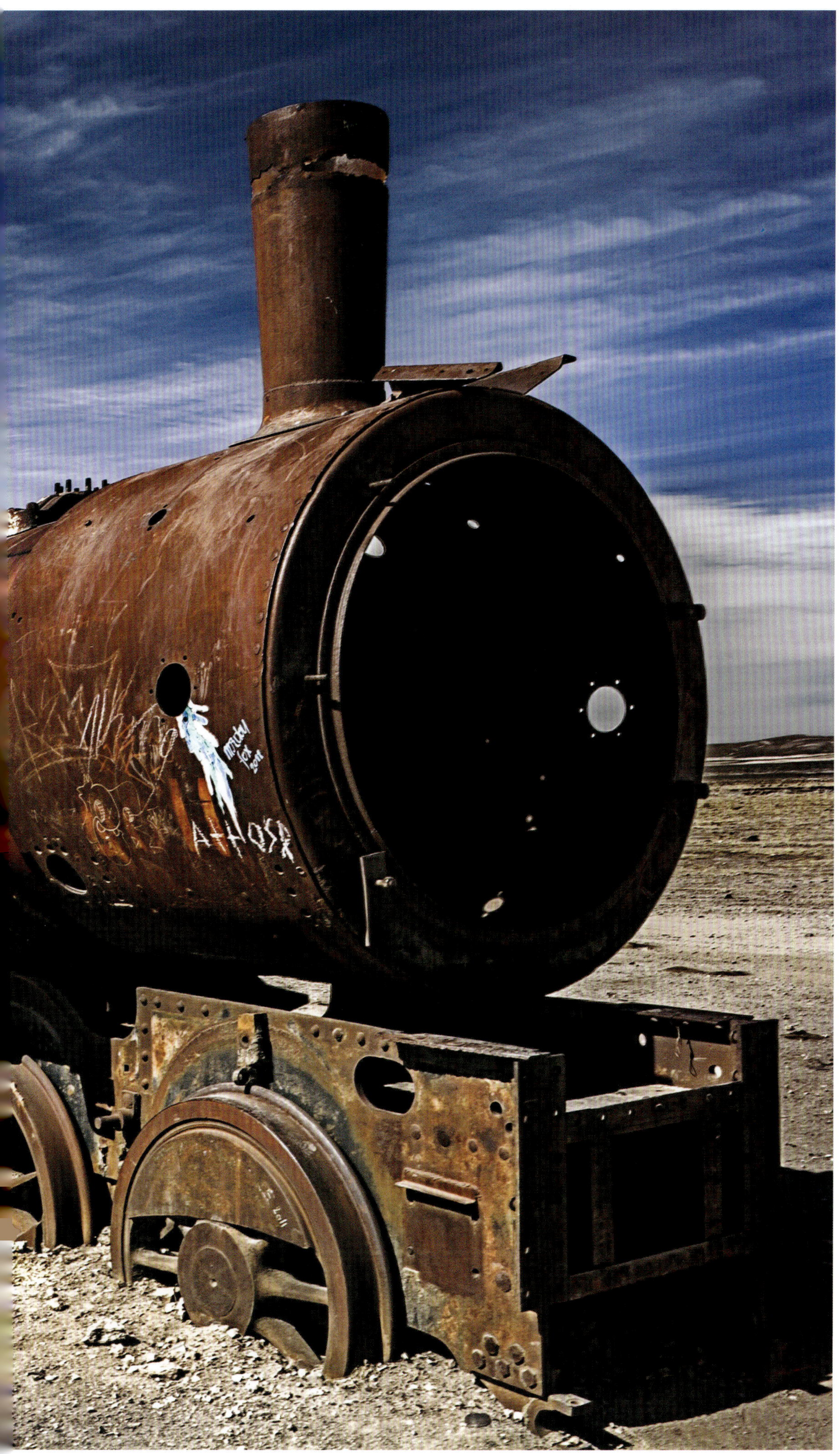

LEFT:

Salar de Uyuni, Bolivia
Located in a high-altitude Andean plain, Uyuni is the desolate Bolivian graveyard for dozens of decrepit trains and carriages, many of them relics of the steam age. A large percentage of the trains found there were originally built in the United Kingdom and exported to South America in the 1800s and first half of the 20th century.

OVERLEAF:

TOP LEFT:

Salar de Uyuni, Bolivia
This powerful locomotive is another of the specimens found at the Salar de Uyuni train graveyard, Bolivia. Salar de Uyuni was once a major transport hub in the region, but was eventually abandoned in the 1940s due to changing commercial realities.

BOTTOM LEFT:

Salar de Uyuni, Bolivia
The empty boiler of this locomotive at Salar de Uyuni still manages to evoke a sense of strength. The atmosphere from the surrounding salt flat is highly corrosive, the salts blown continually against the locomotives by the mountain winds.

RIGHT:

Salar de Uyuni, Bolivia
Many of the locomotives at the Uyuni site were originally used for transporting minerals mined from the Andes Mountains to the Pacific Ocean ports. The decline of Salar de Uyuni was brought about by the collapse in the Bolivian minerals industry during the 1940s.

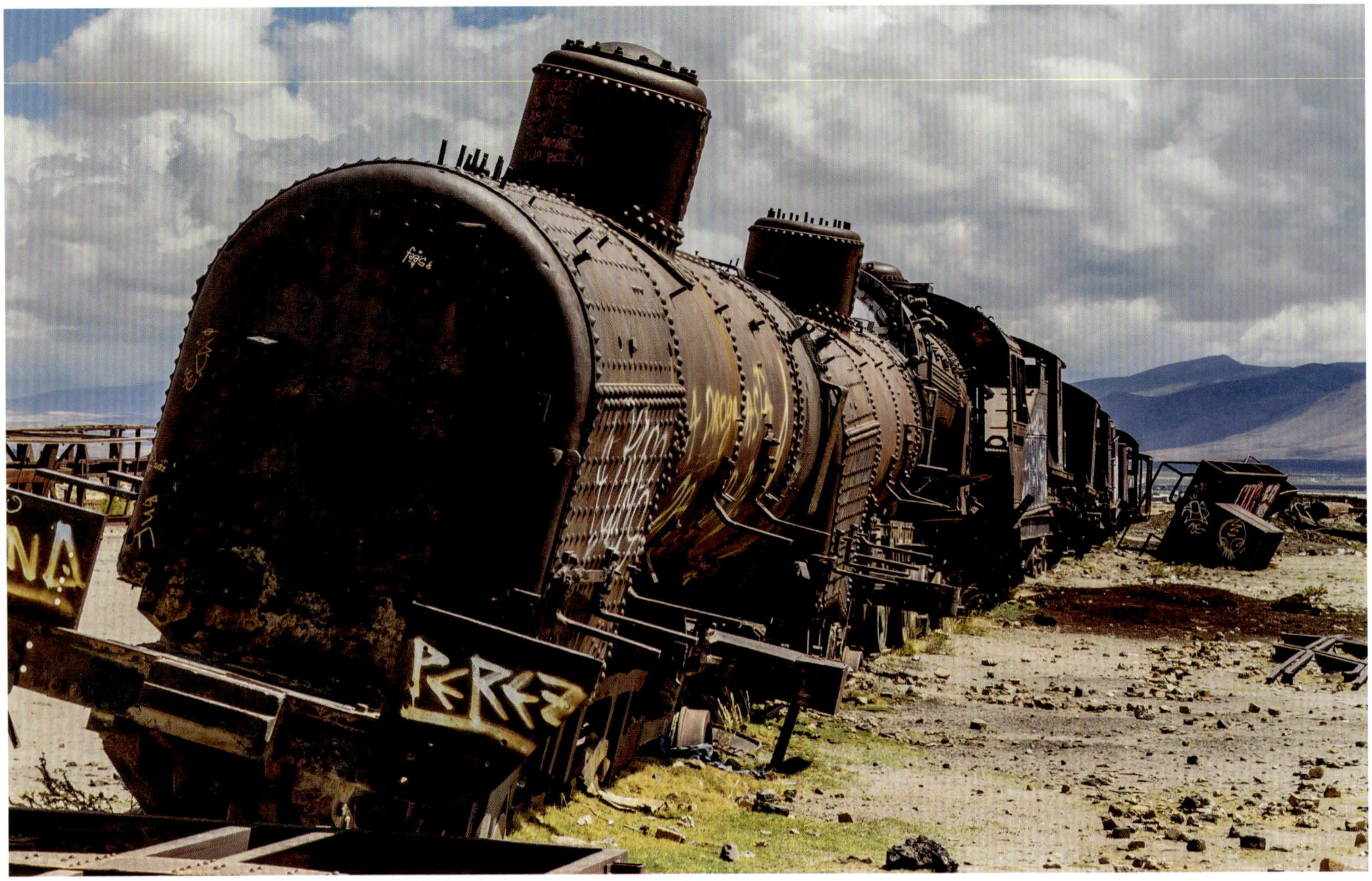

NA
PEREE

"ASI ES LA VIDA"
se necesita
un mecánico
con experiencia
¡URGENTE!

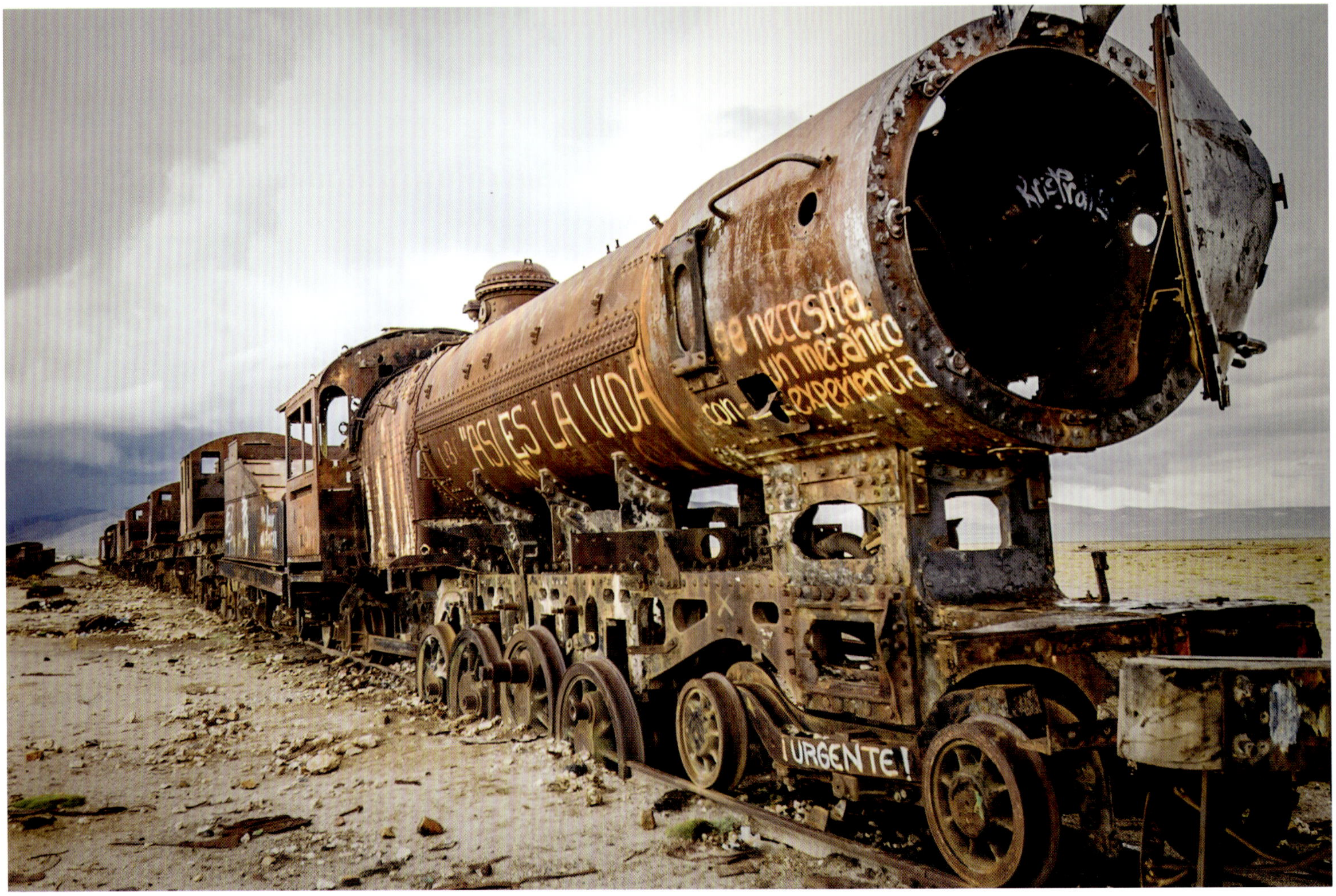

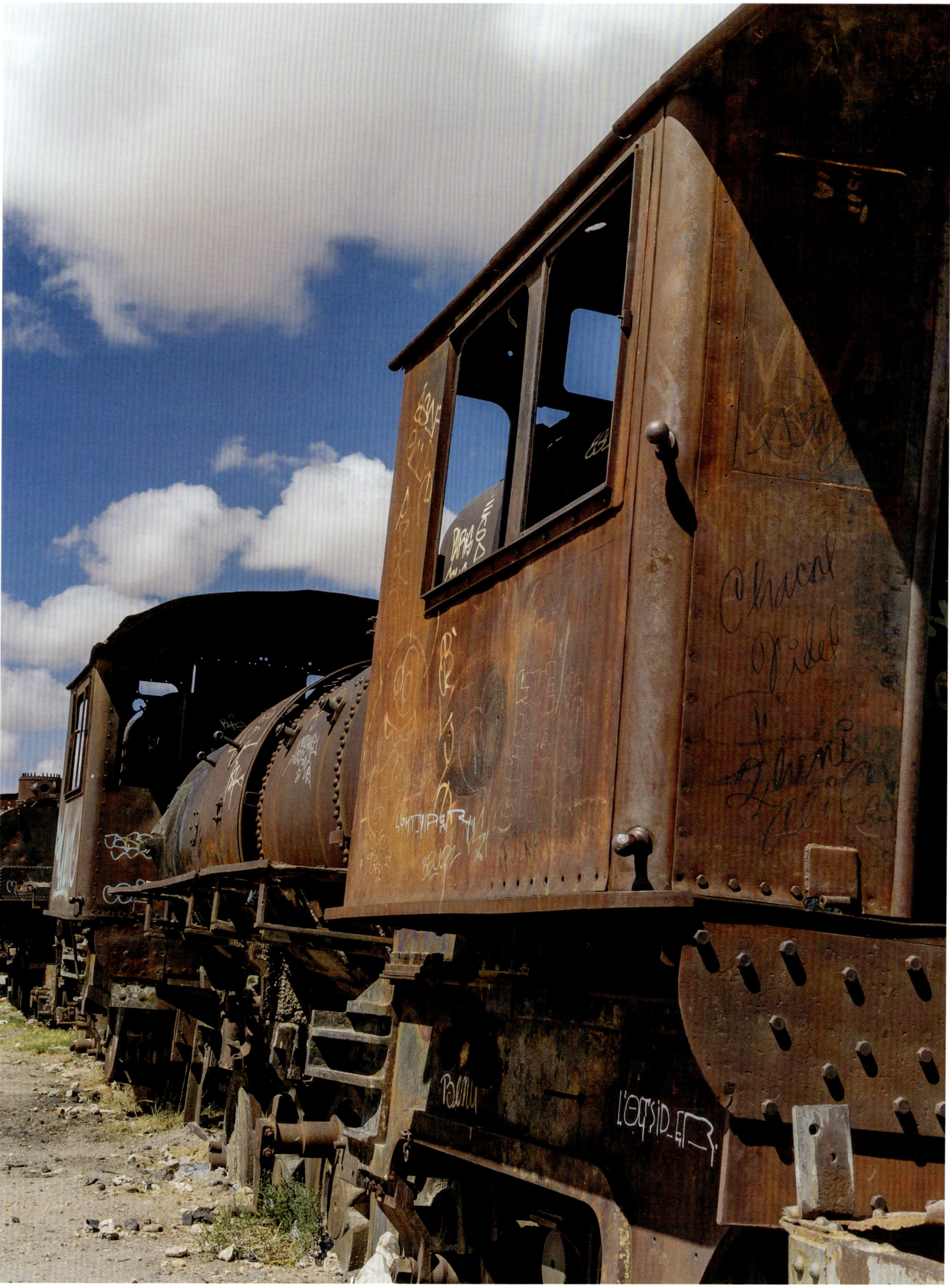

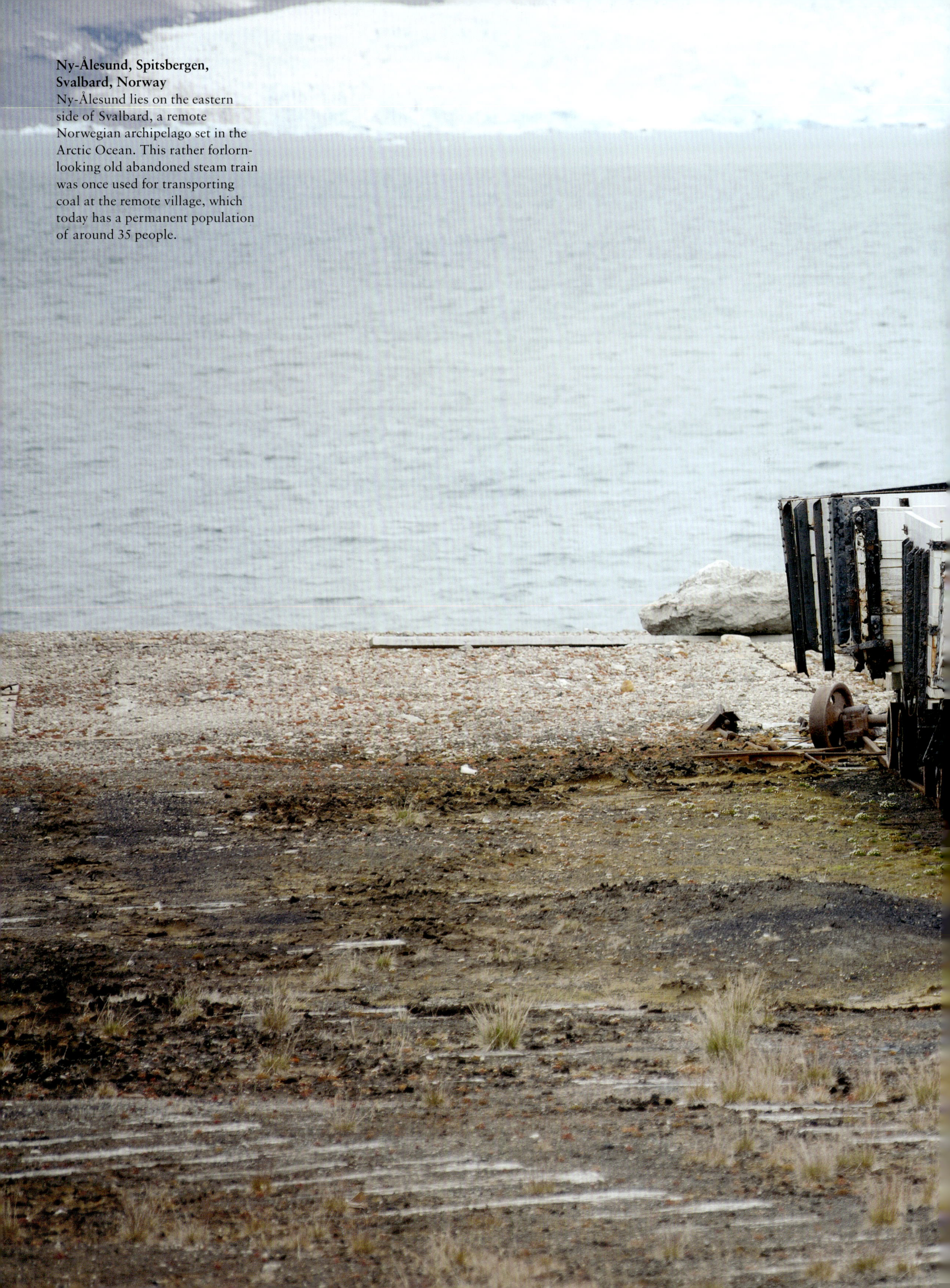

Ny-Ålesund, Spitsbergen, Svalbard, Norway
Ny-Ålesund lies on the eastern side of Svalbard, a remote Norwegian archipelago set in the Arctic Ocean. This rather forlorn-looking old abandoned steam train was once used for transporting coal at the remote village, which today has a permanent population of around 35 people.

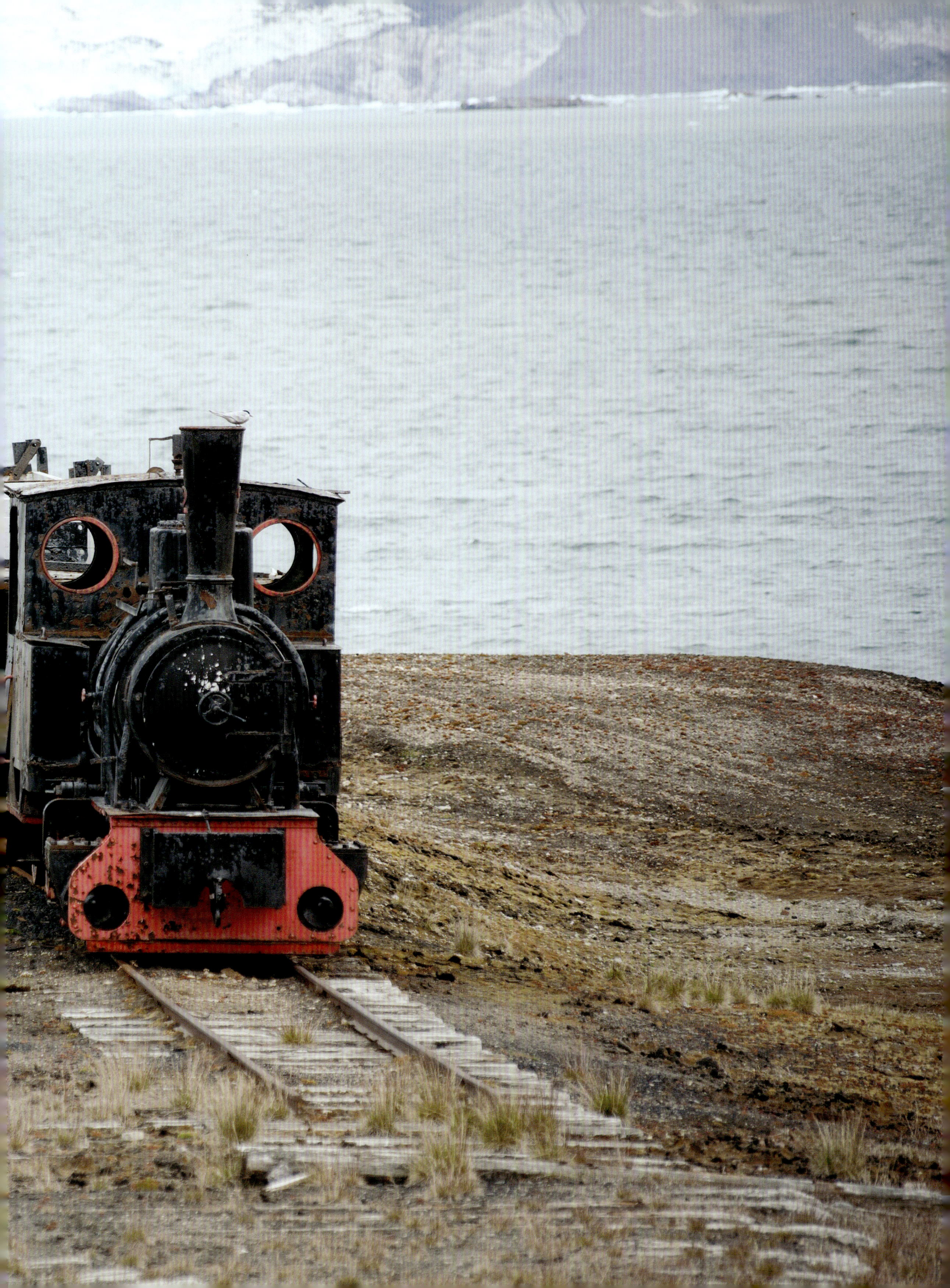

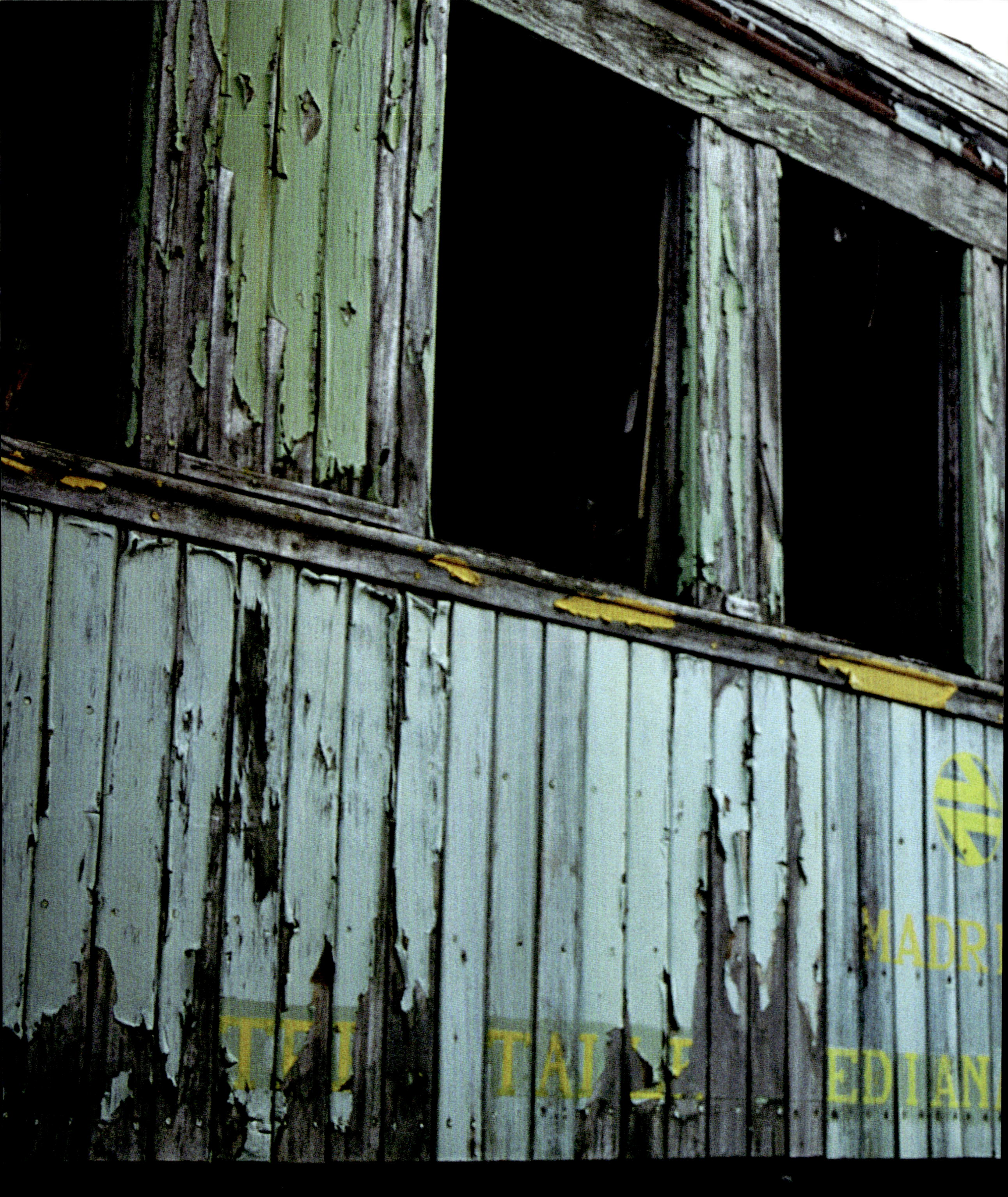
MADRI
EDIAN
TAL
20-M

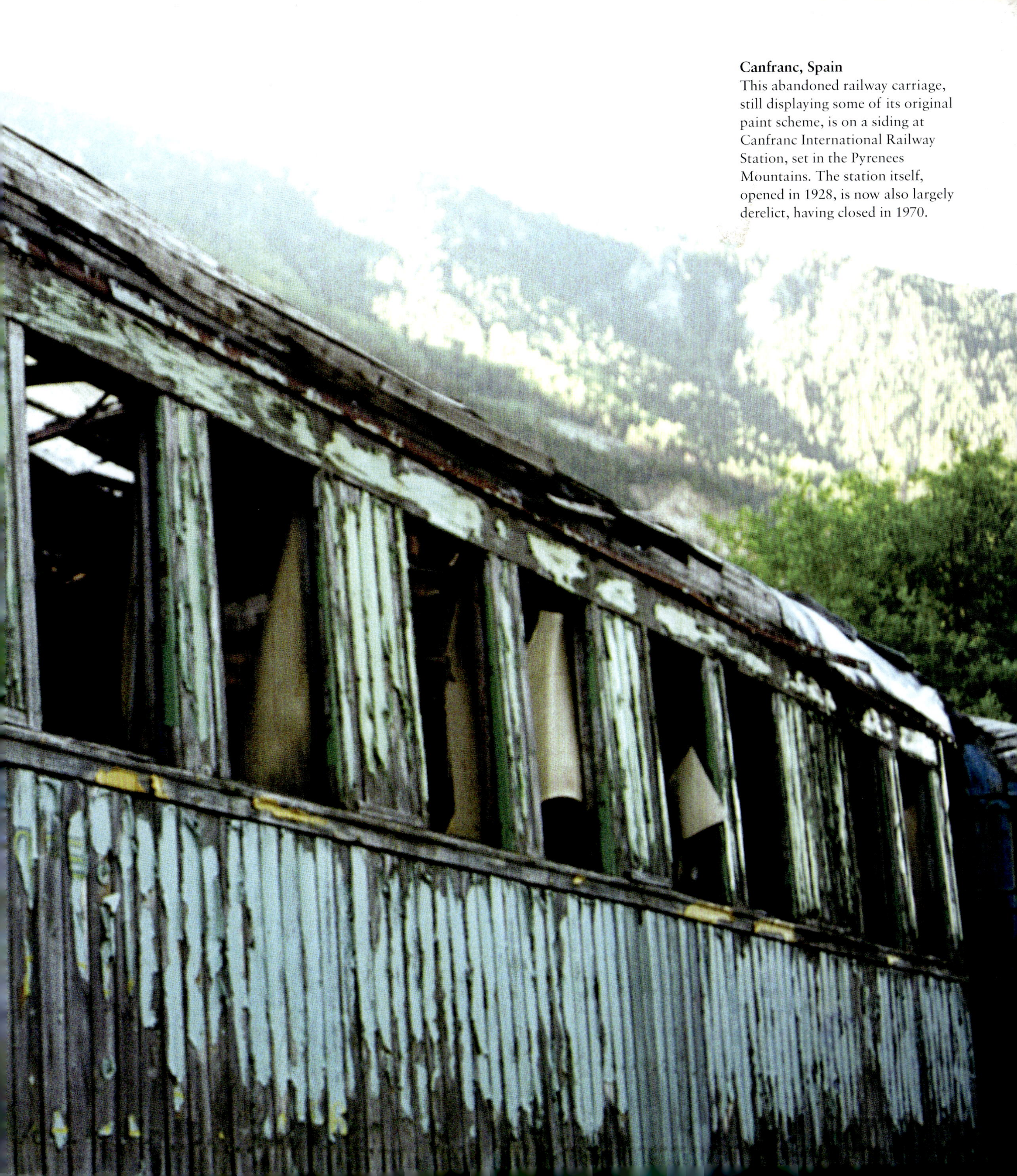

Canfranc, Spain
This abandoned railway carriage, still displaying some of its original paint scheme, is on a siding at Canfranc International Railway Station, set in the Pyrenees Mountains. The station itself, opened in 1928, is now also largely derelict, having closed in 1970.

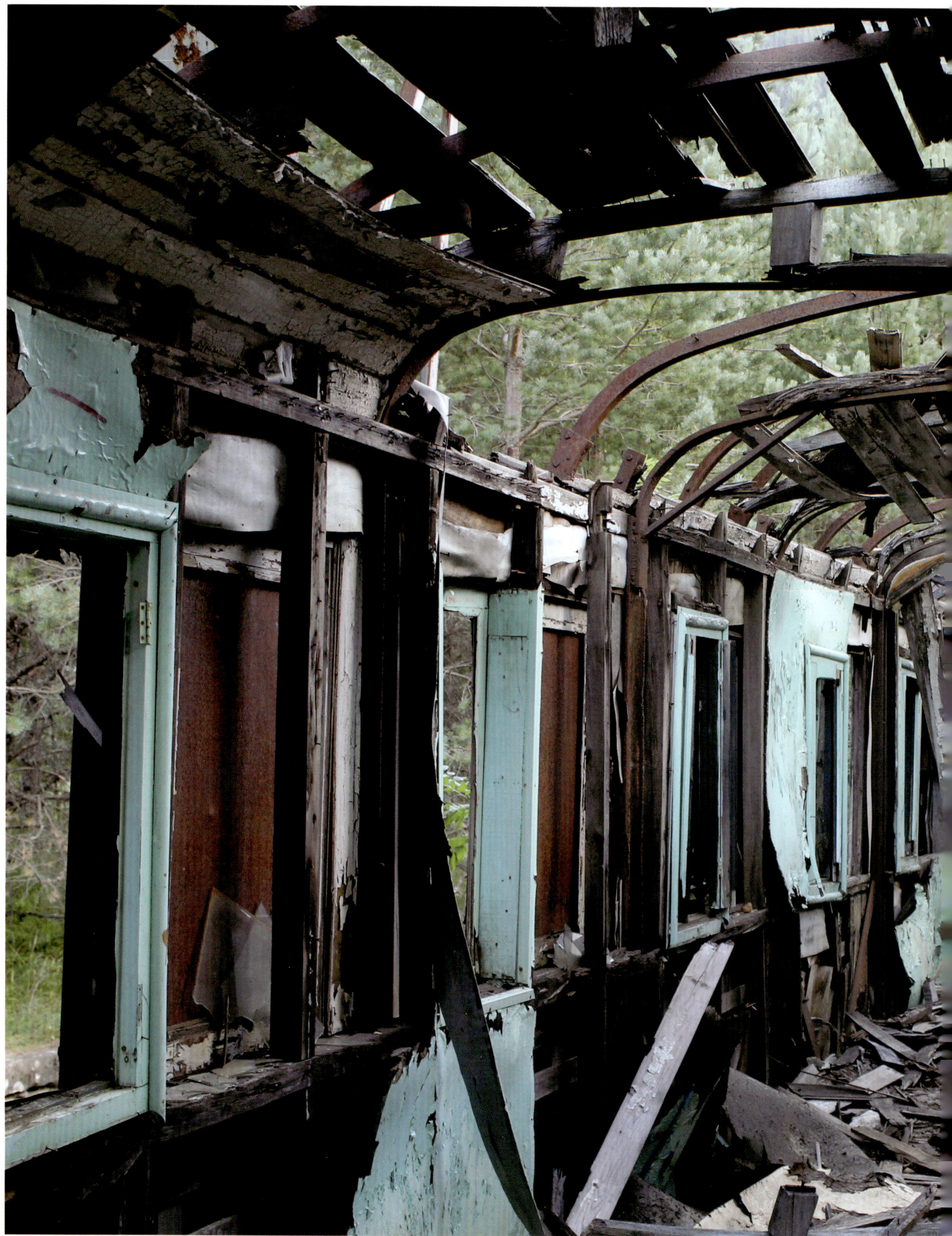

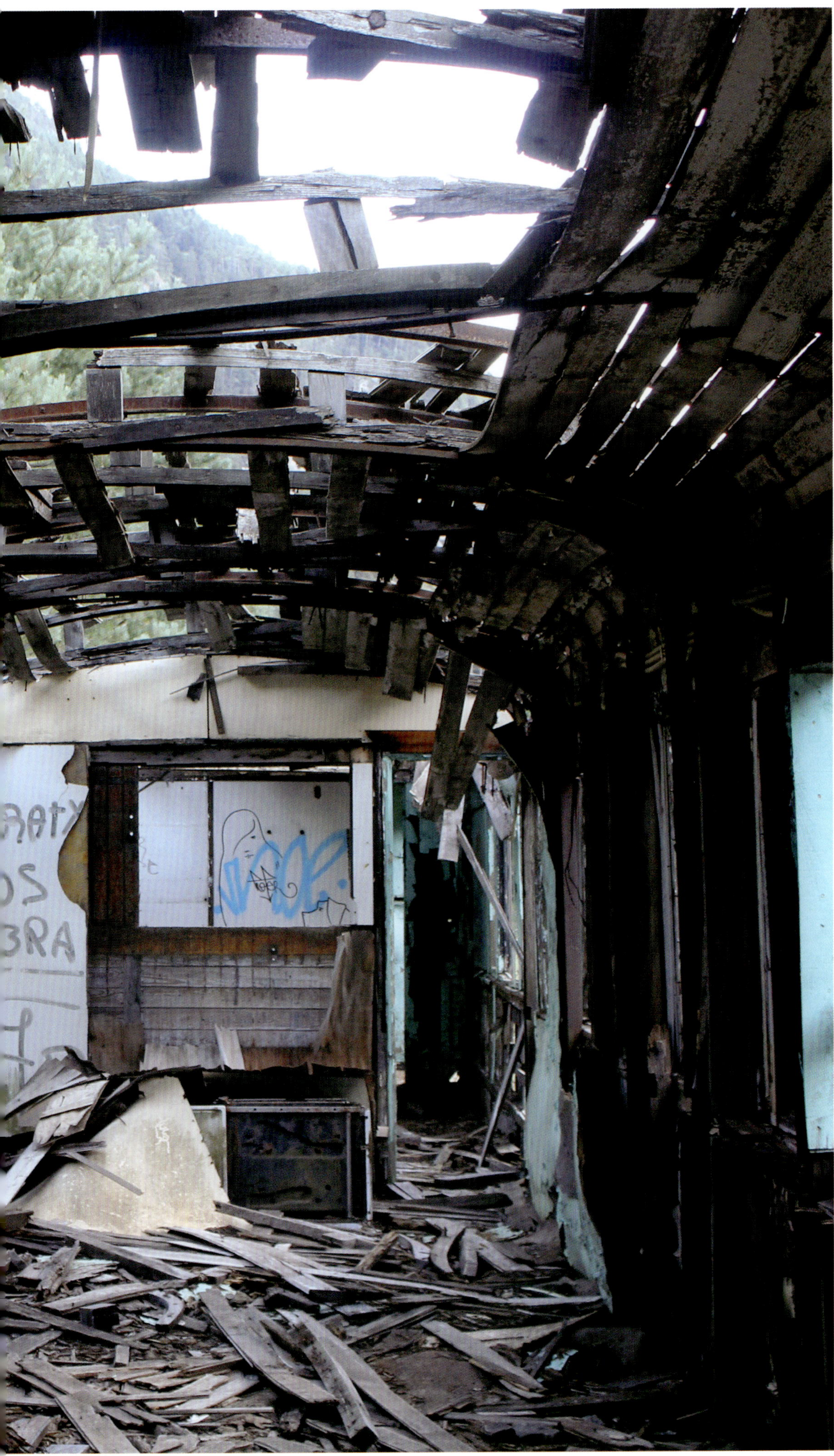

Canfranc, Spain
The roof of this carriage at
Canfranc has finally given up
against the elements, and collapsed
inwards. Much of the rail traffic
from Canfranc was across the
Franco–Spanish border, but the
collapse of a key bridge across
the mountains in 1970 led to the
failure of the station's business.

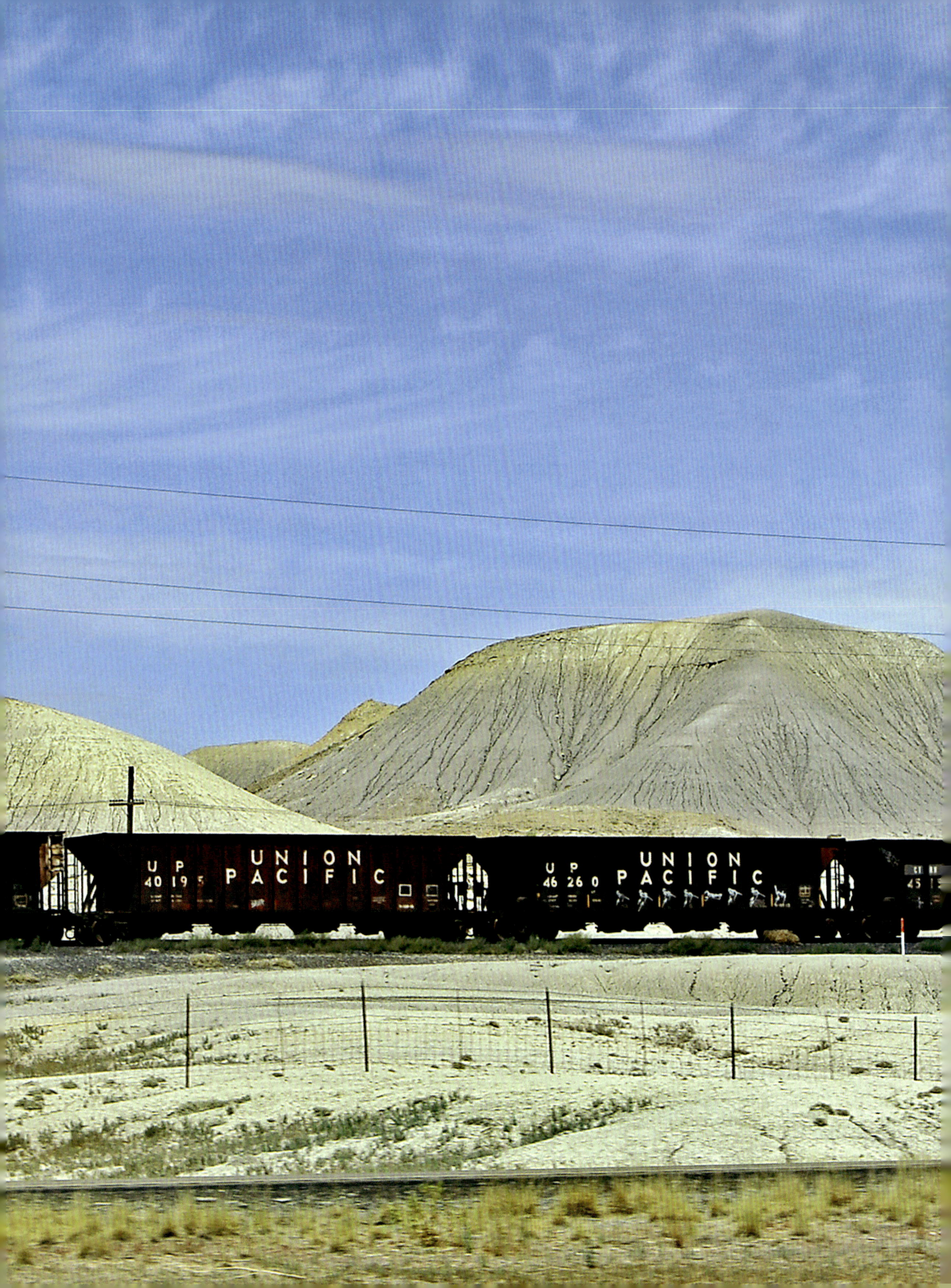
U P 40195 UNION PACIFIC
U P 46260 UNION PACIFIC

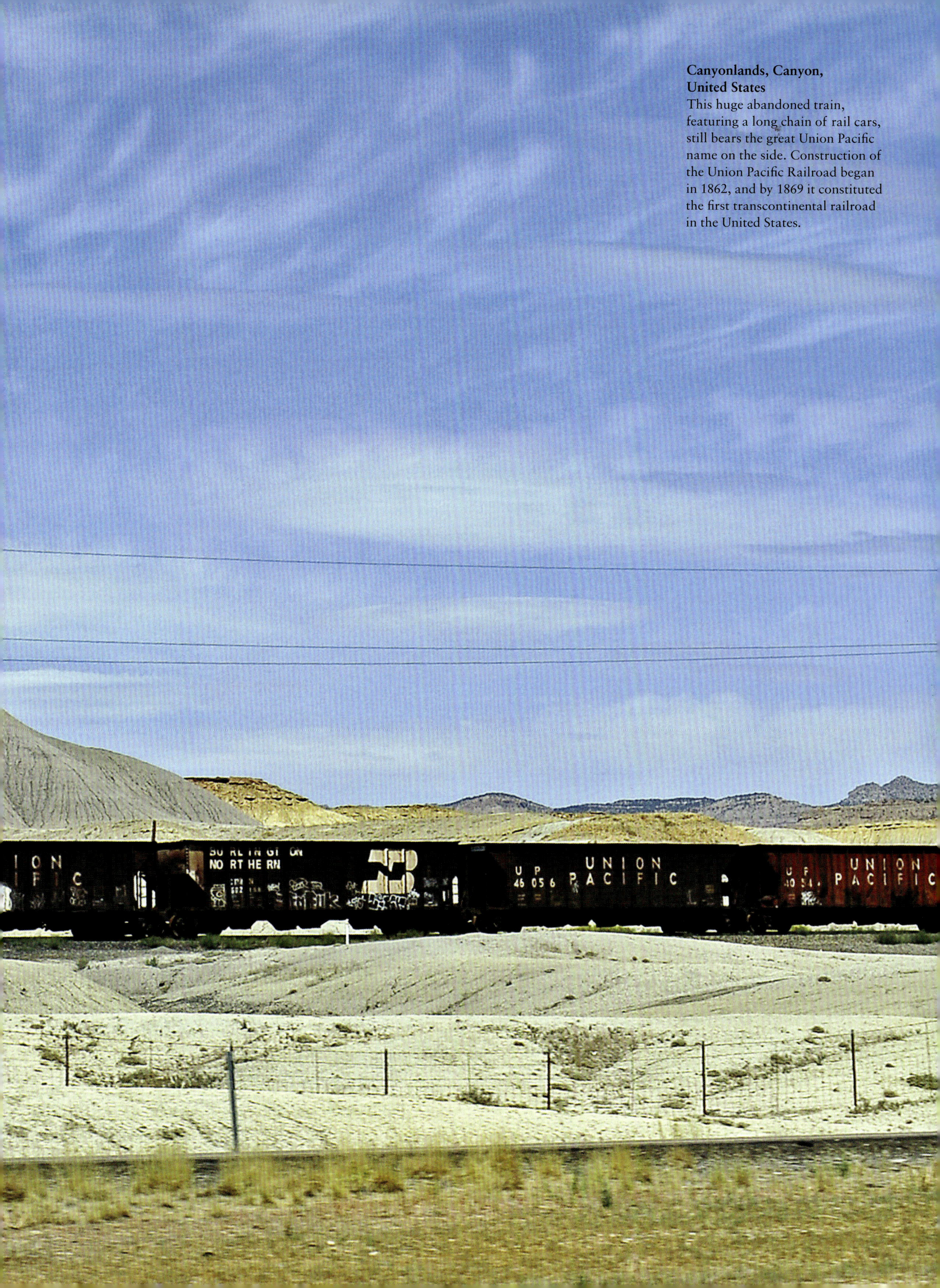

Canyonlands, Canyon, United States
This huge abandoned train, featuring a long chain of rail cars, still bears the great Union Pacific name on the side. Construction of the Union Pacific Railroad began in 1862, and by 1869 it constituted the first transcontinental railroad in the United States.

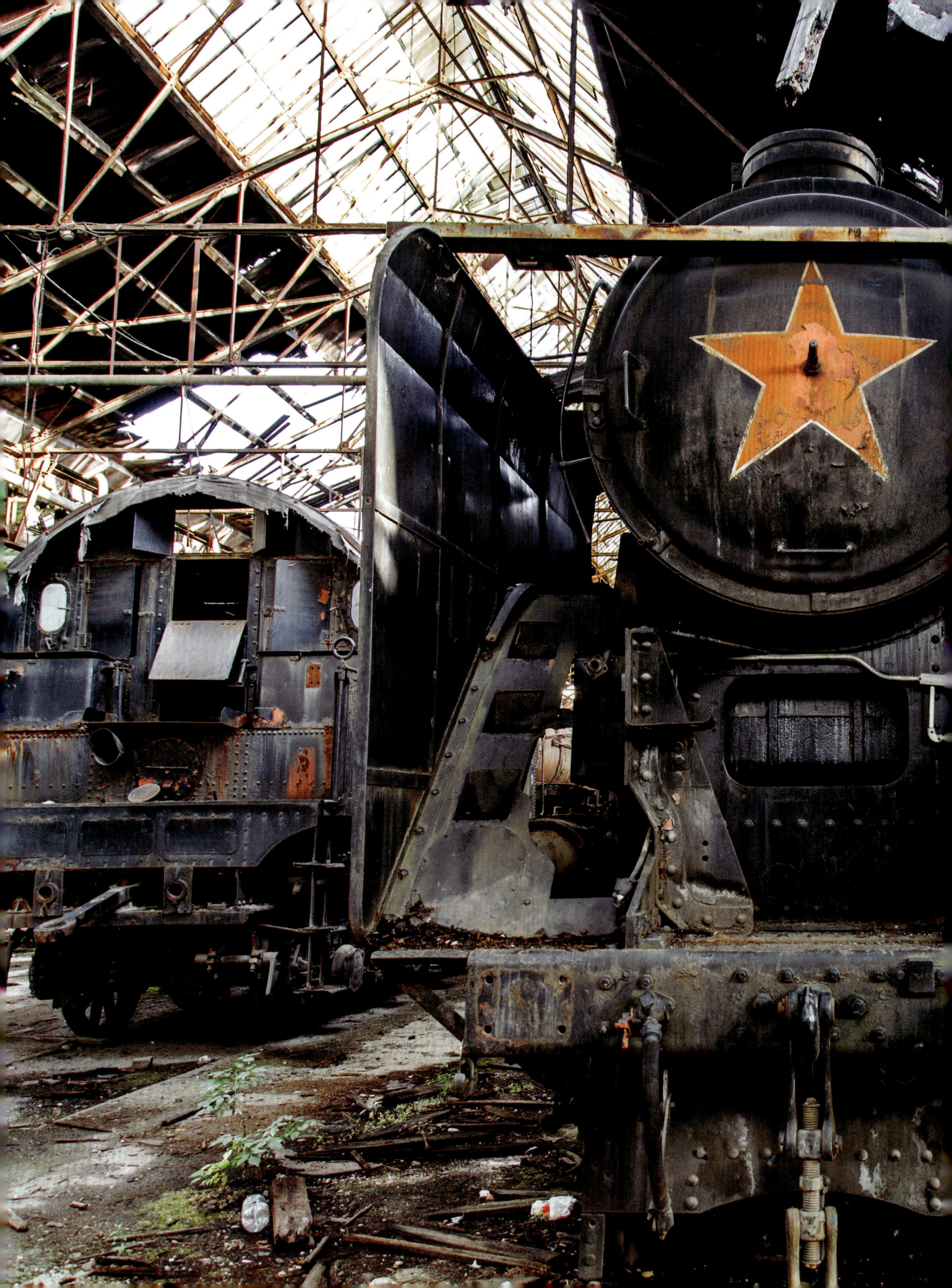

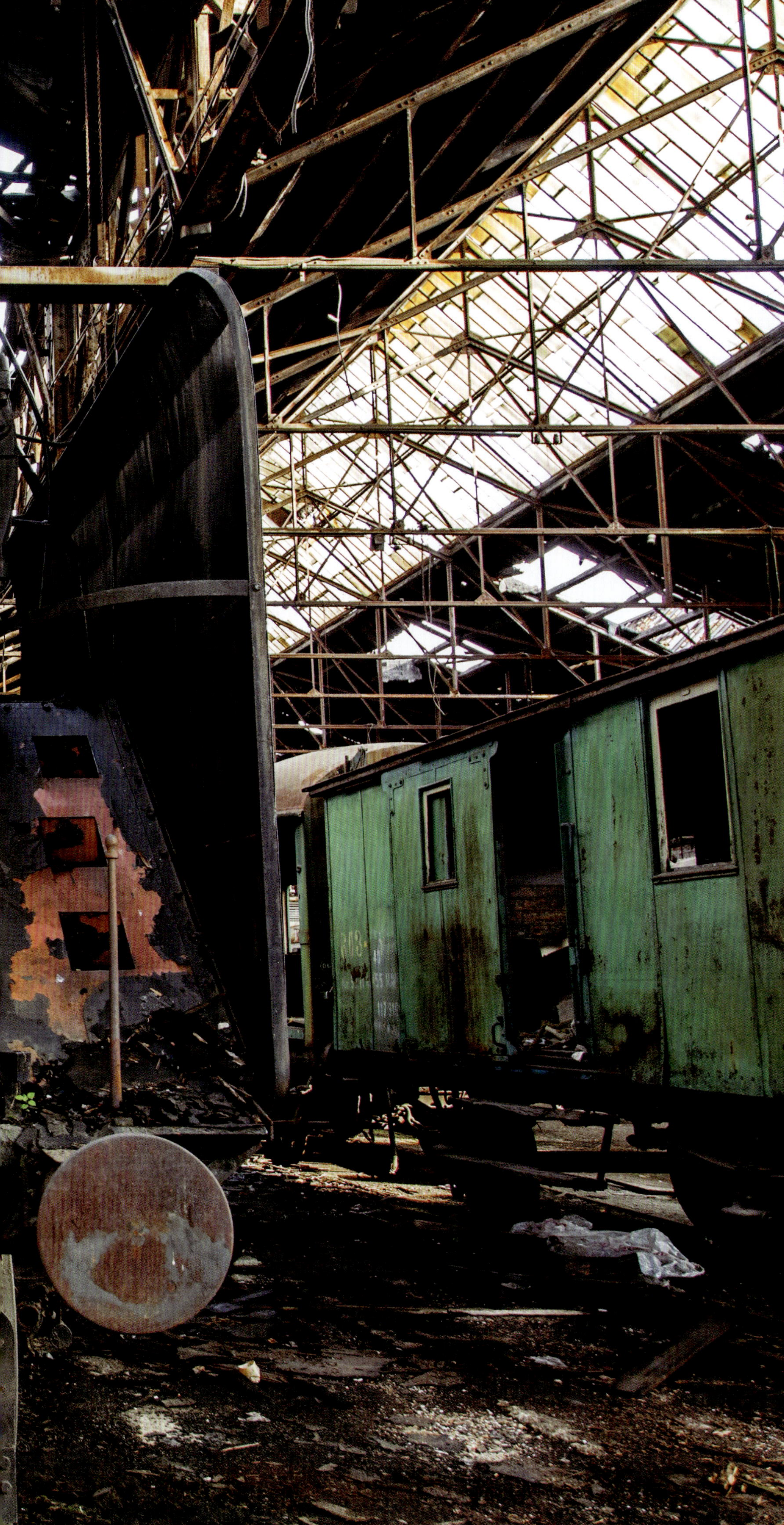

Istvantelek Rail Workshop, Budapest, Hungary
This MAV Class 424 locomotive in the derelict Istvantelek rail workshop, probably in use by the Soviet military, still bears the defiant red star of the communist era. Carriages in the vicinity of the locomotive often contain discarded passenger tickets from the 1960s.

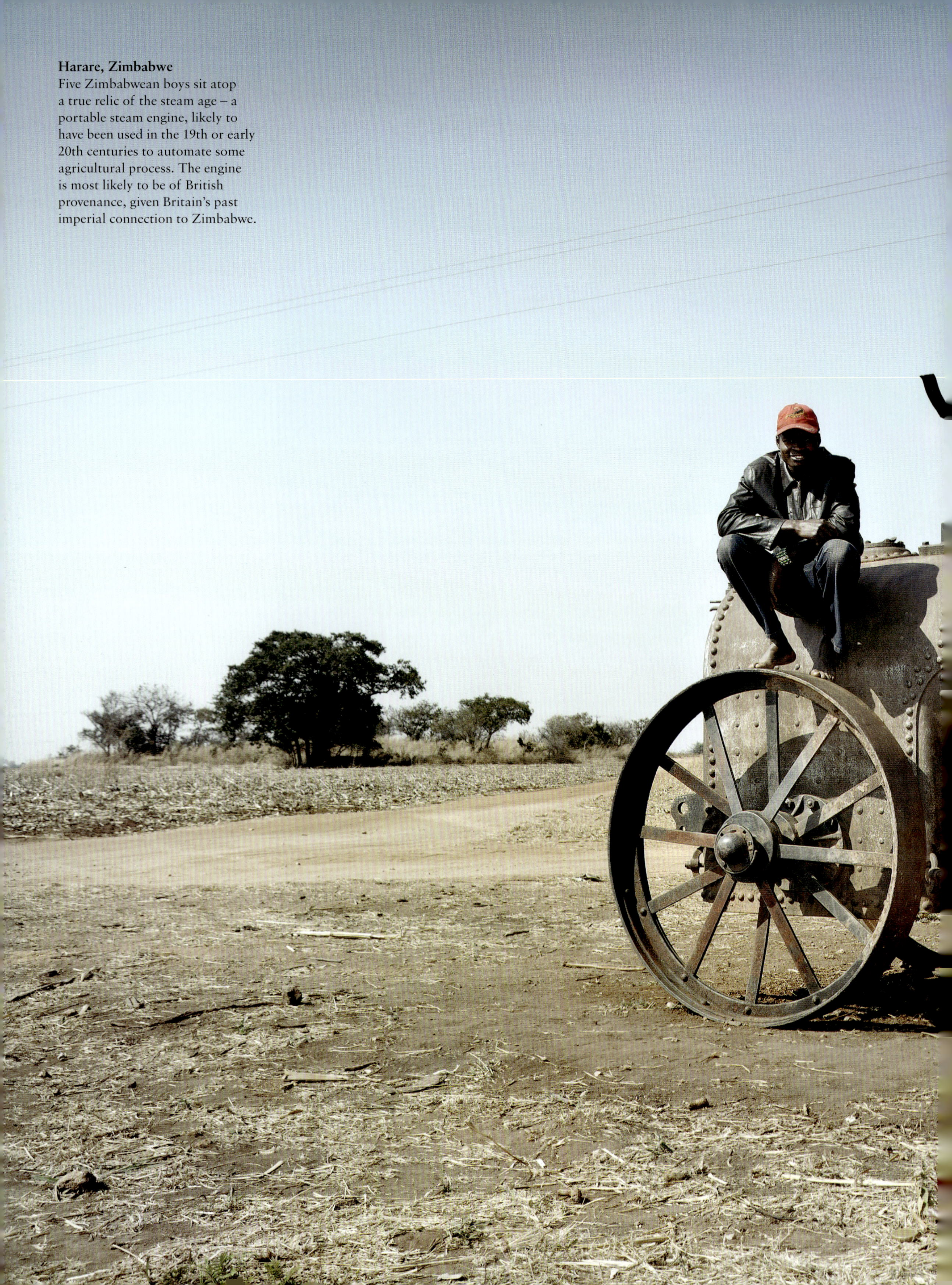

Harare, Zimbabwe
Five Zimbabwean boys sit atop
a true relic of the steam age – a
portable steam engine, likely to
have been used in the 19th or early
20th centuries to automate some
agricultural process. The engine
is most likely to be of British
provenance, given Britain's past
imperial connection to Zimbabwe.

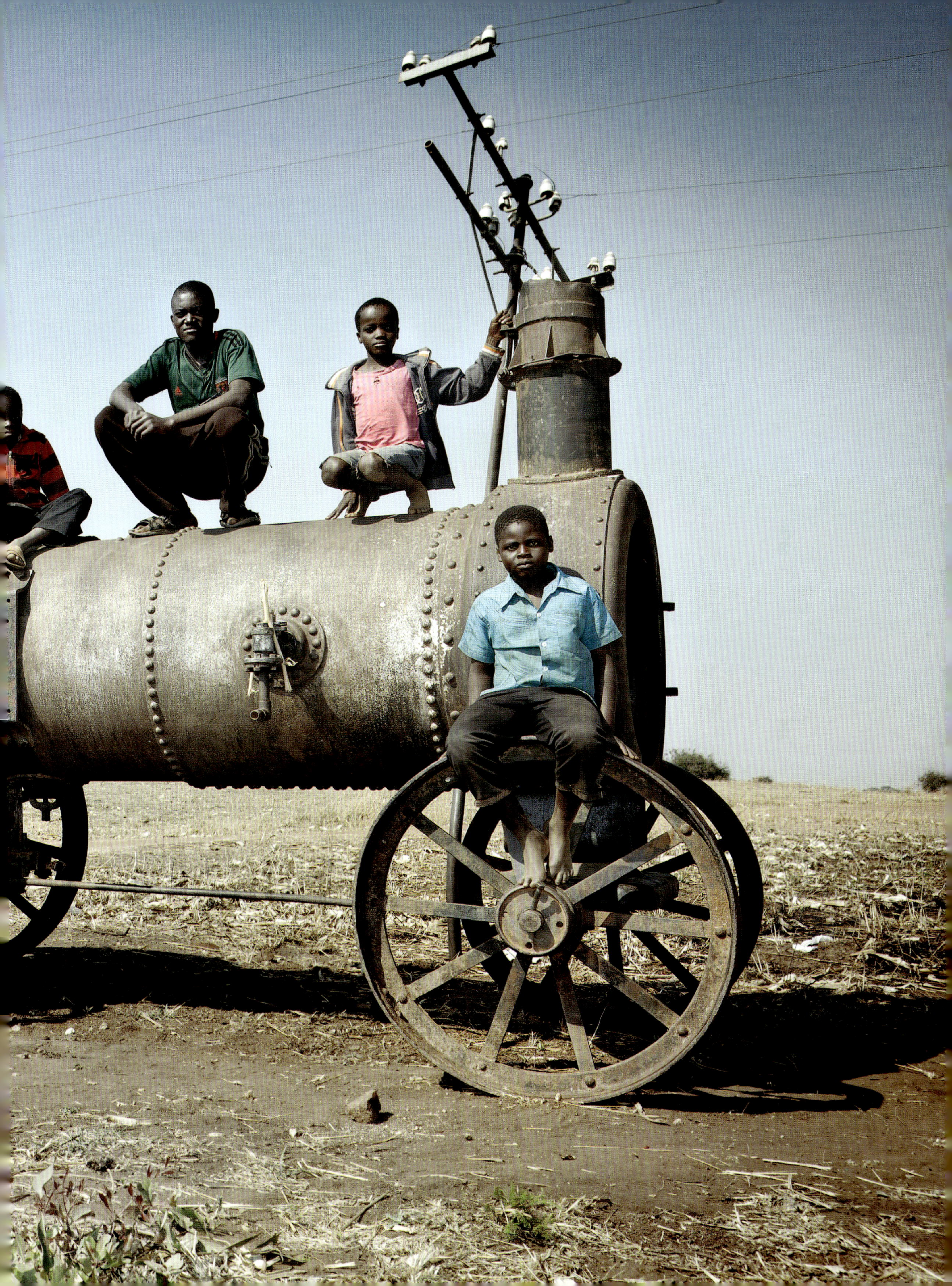

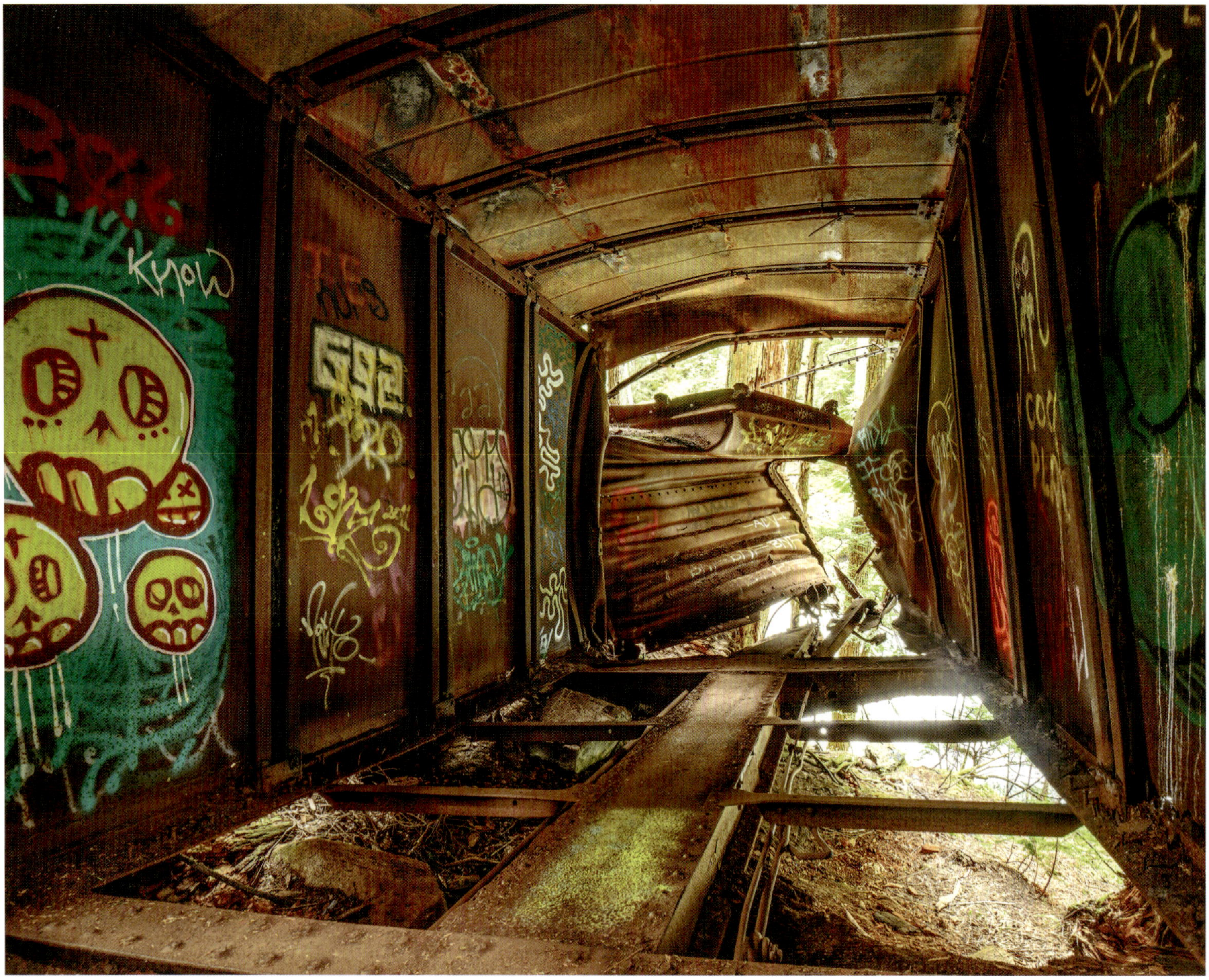

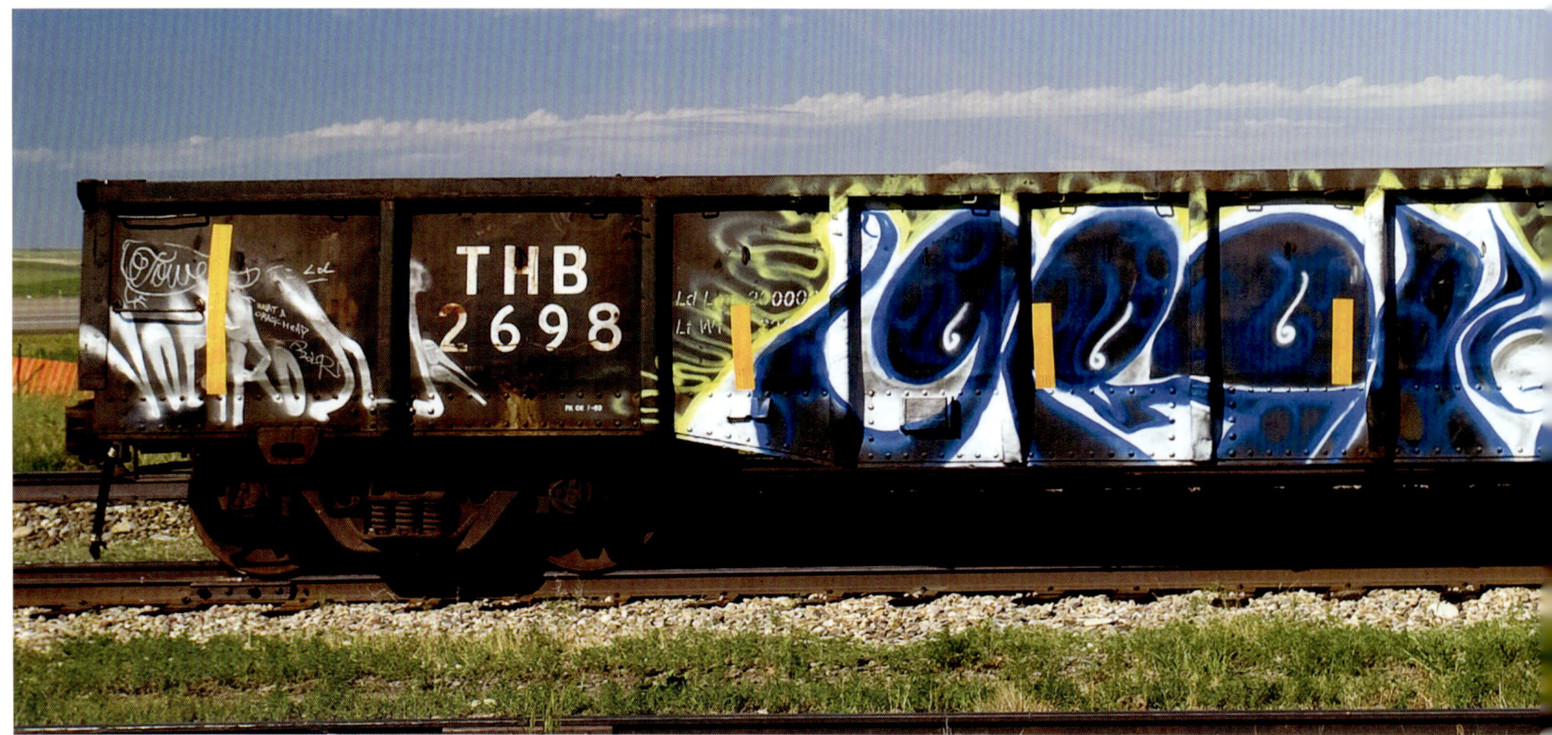

THB
2698

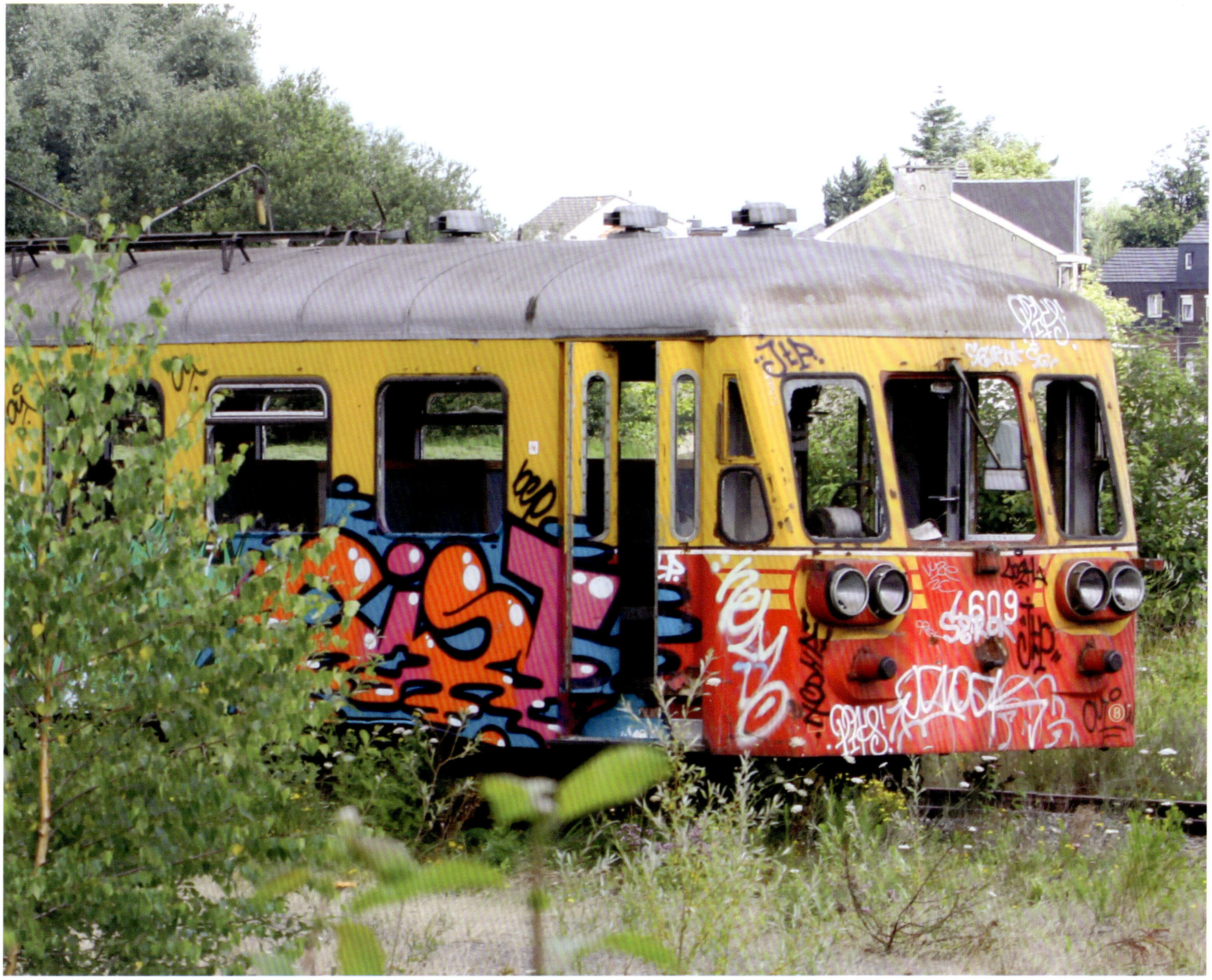

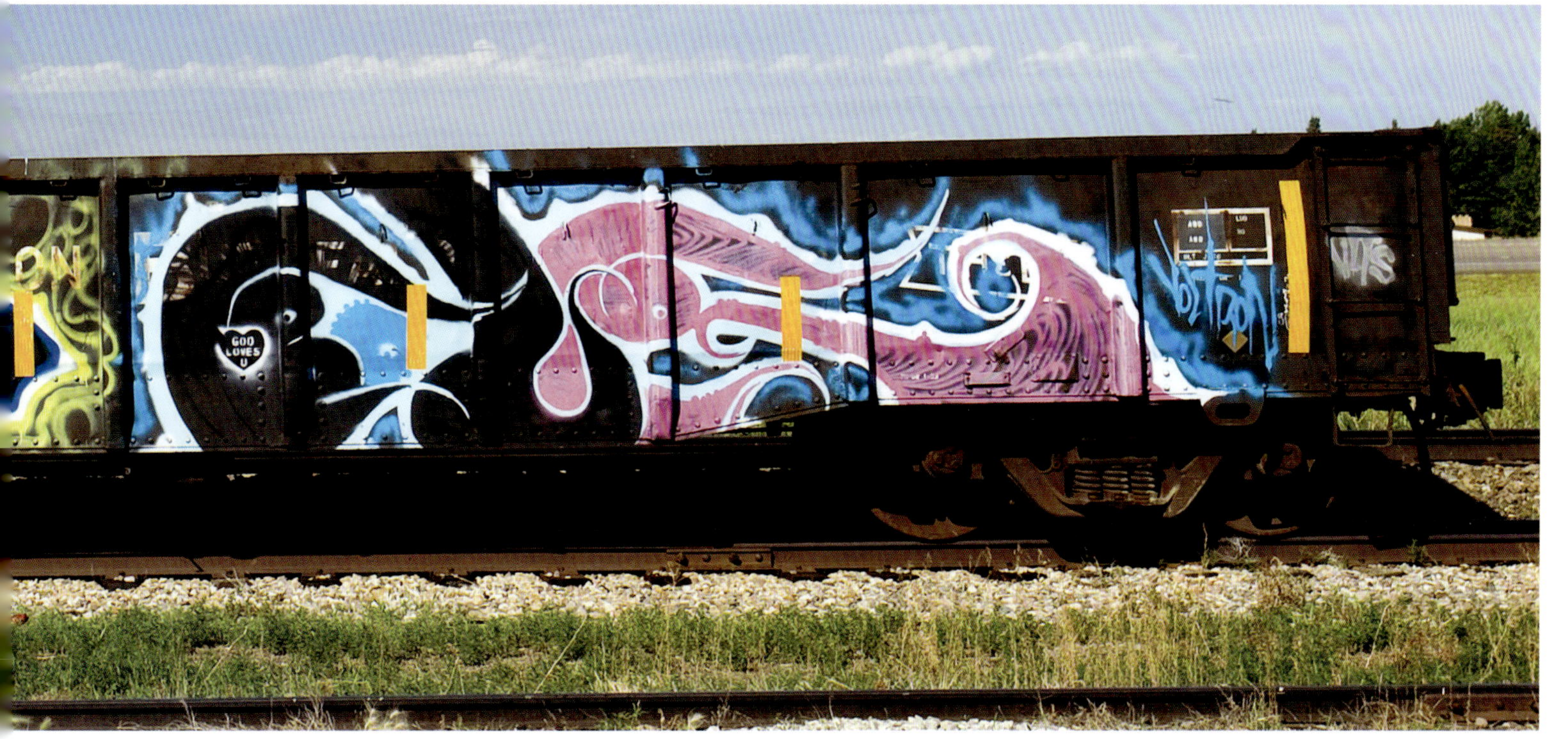

TOP LEFT:

Whistler, British Columbia
This smashed carriage is part
of the wreckage of a crash that
occurred in 1956 near Whistler,
British Columbia. The train had
been thoroughly overloaded with
lumber, and, when going double its
speed limit, came off the tracks in
a rock cutting.

TOP RIGHT:

Hennegau, Mons, Belgium
This vintage rail car has been
well decorated by local artists in
Hennegau, Belgium. Using pre-
prepared stencils, some graffiti
artists have decorated operating
trains with elaborate artworks in
as little as three minutes.

BOTTOM:

Alberta, Canada
The side of this abandoned rail
truck makes the perfect surface for
an extended piece of graffiti. Cars
such as these were generally used
to carry bulk raw materials, such
as coal or iron ore.

RIGHT:

**Las Grutas, Provincia de Chubut,
Patagonia, Argentina**
The interior of an Argentinian
cattle truck, one of many
vehicles in a railway graveyard
in Las Grutas, Argentina. Beef
production is one of Argentina's
largest industries, and the country
is today the third-largest beef
exporter in the world.

OVERLEAF:

Paranapiacaba, São Paulo, Brazil
This passenger train has clearly
reached the end of its line in
Paranapiacaba, São Paulo. The
district of Paranapiacaba was
built to house the workers of the
British-run São Paulo Railway,
established in the second half of
the 19th century.

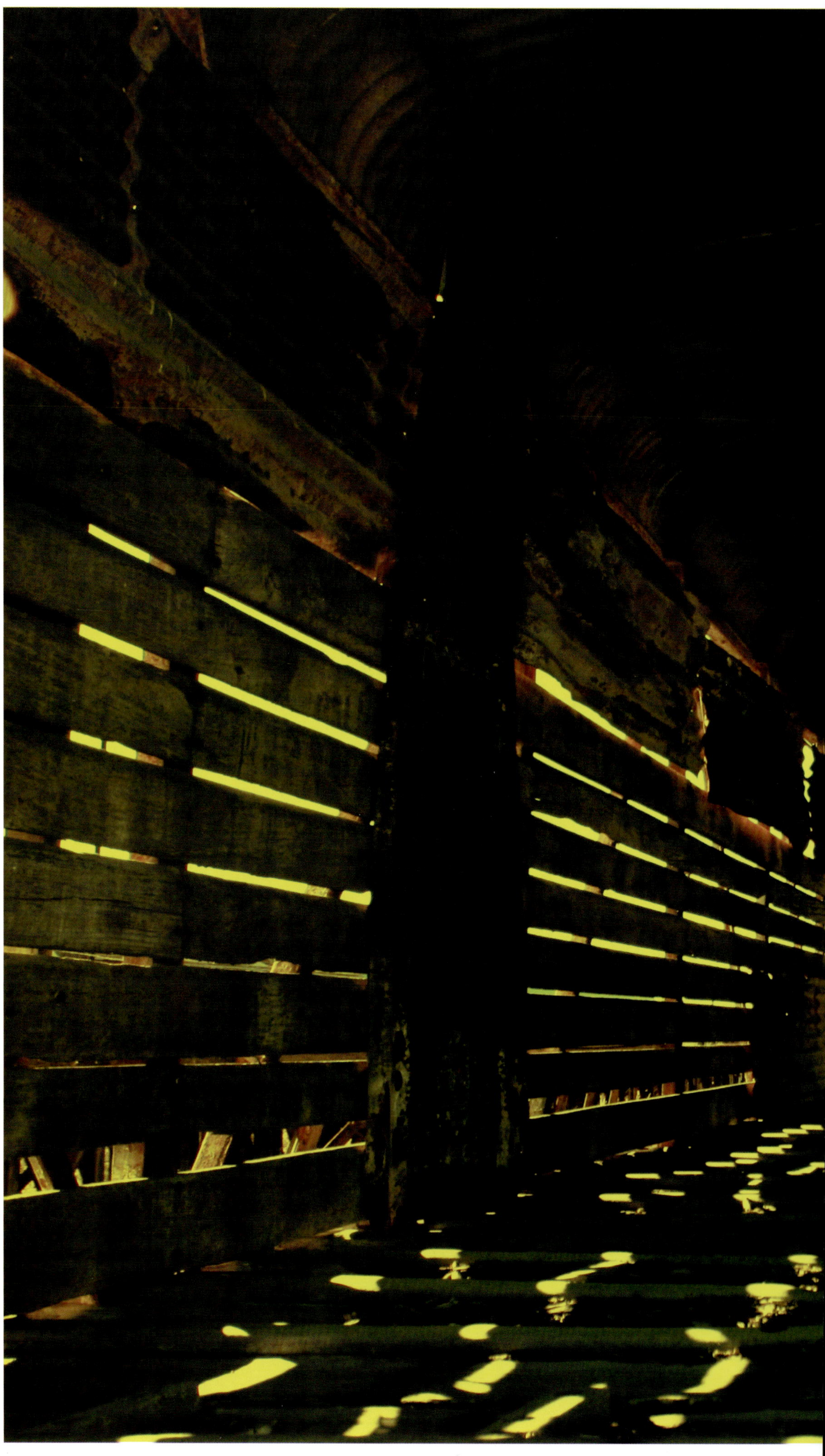

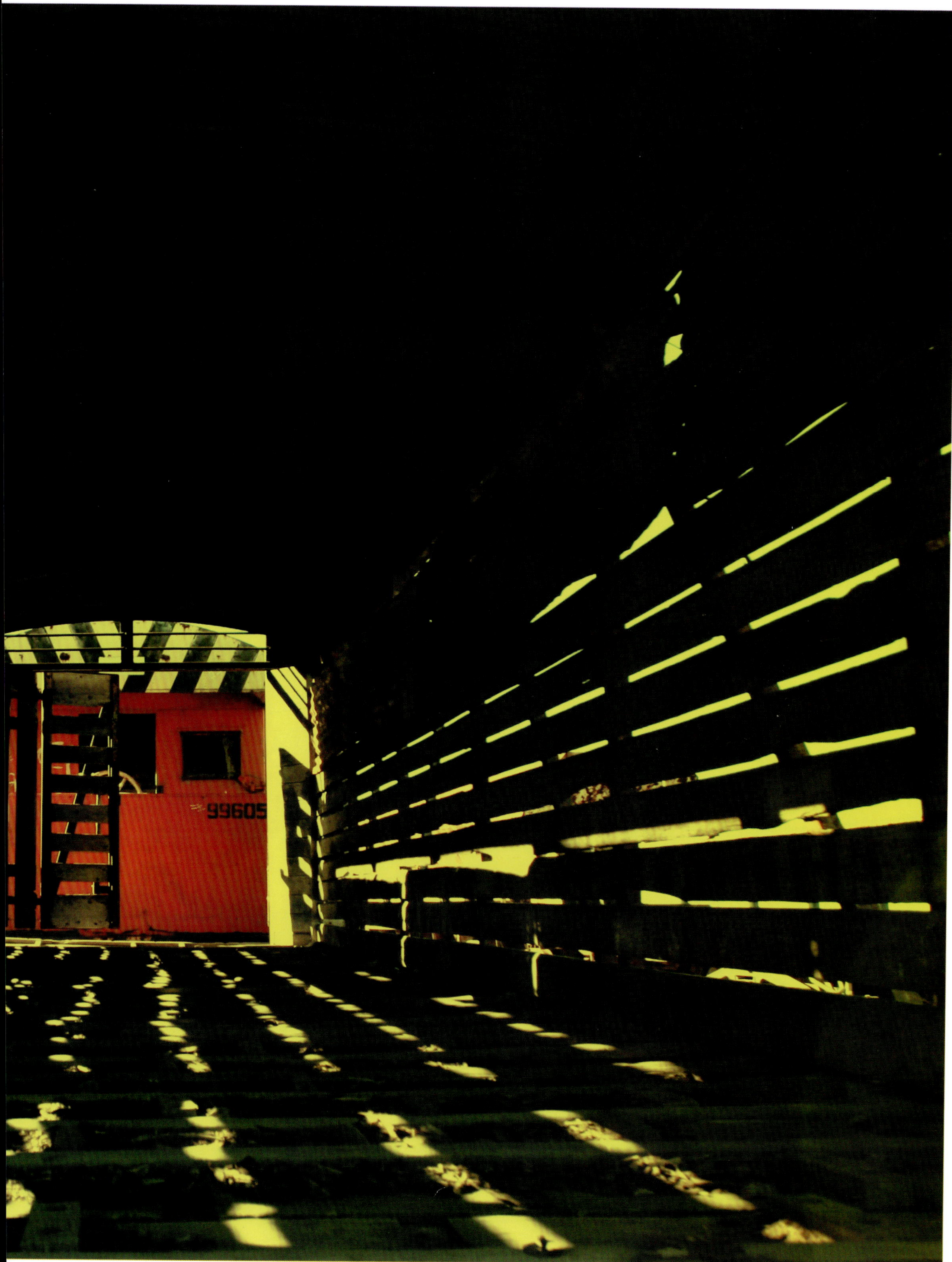

99605

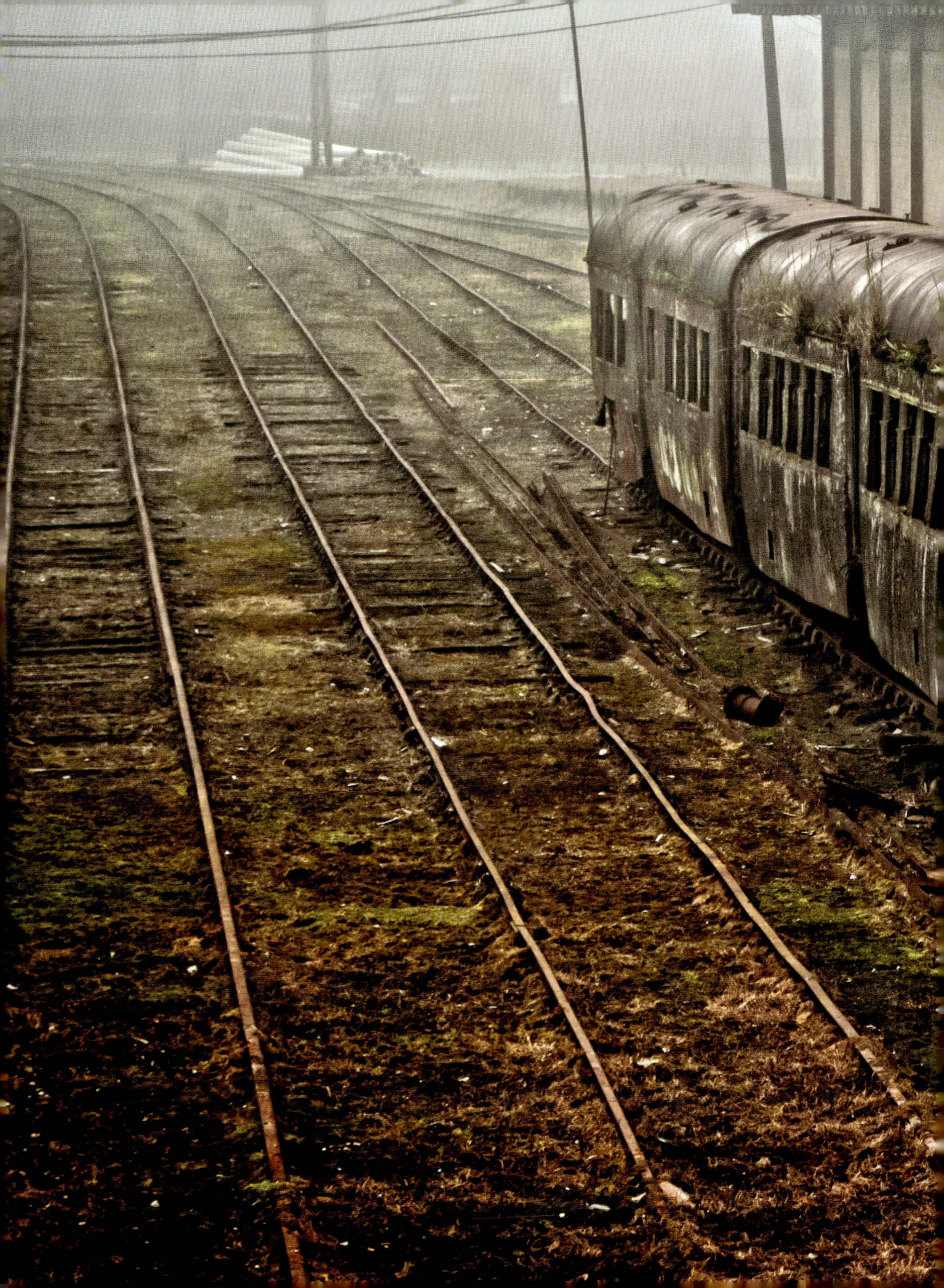

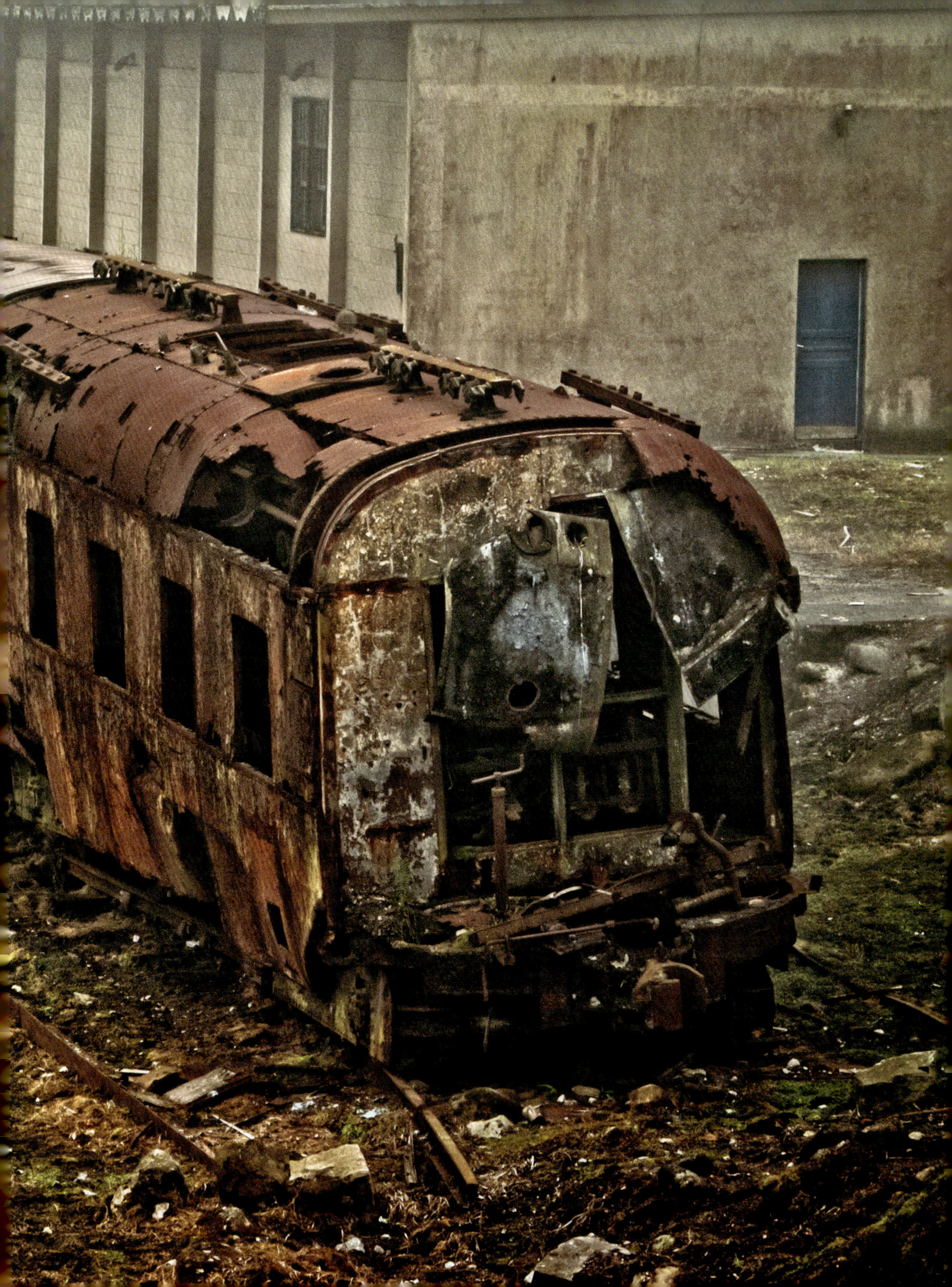

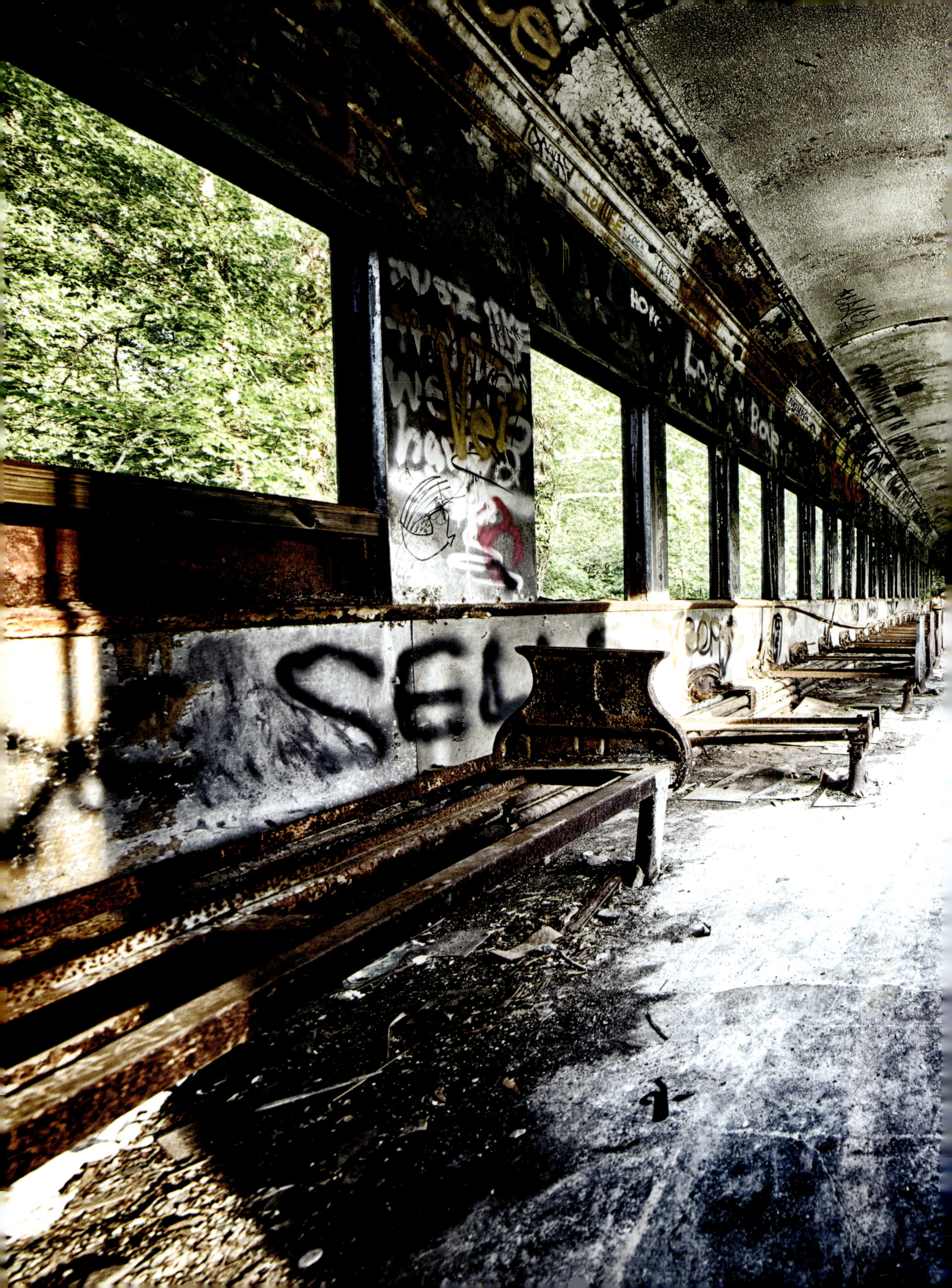

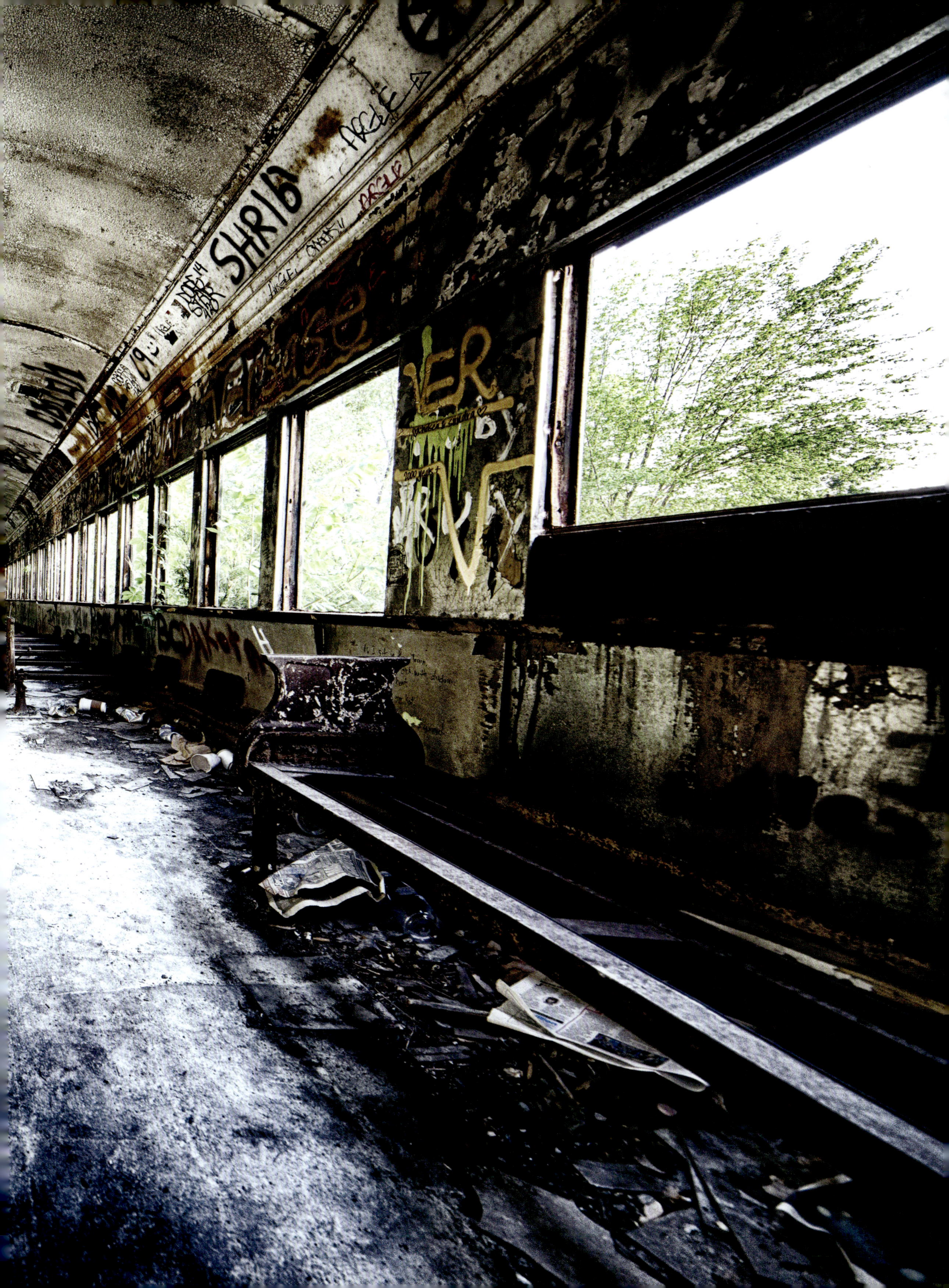

Lambertville, Hunterdon County, New Jersey, United States
This derelict rail car, once packed with New Jersey commuters, now lies silent and gaunt. Although many old rail cars certainly look inviting and quaint, they often had severe issues relating to safety, particularly in terms of crash resilience and passenger comfort.

Akhalkalaki, Georgia
Showing a resourceful repurposing, Georgian engineers have converted this old train carriage into a functional river bridge, each end of the carriage set on concrete plinths. Such arrangements are not uncommon – carriage bridges are also seen in India and other parts of the world.

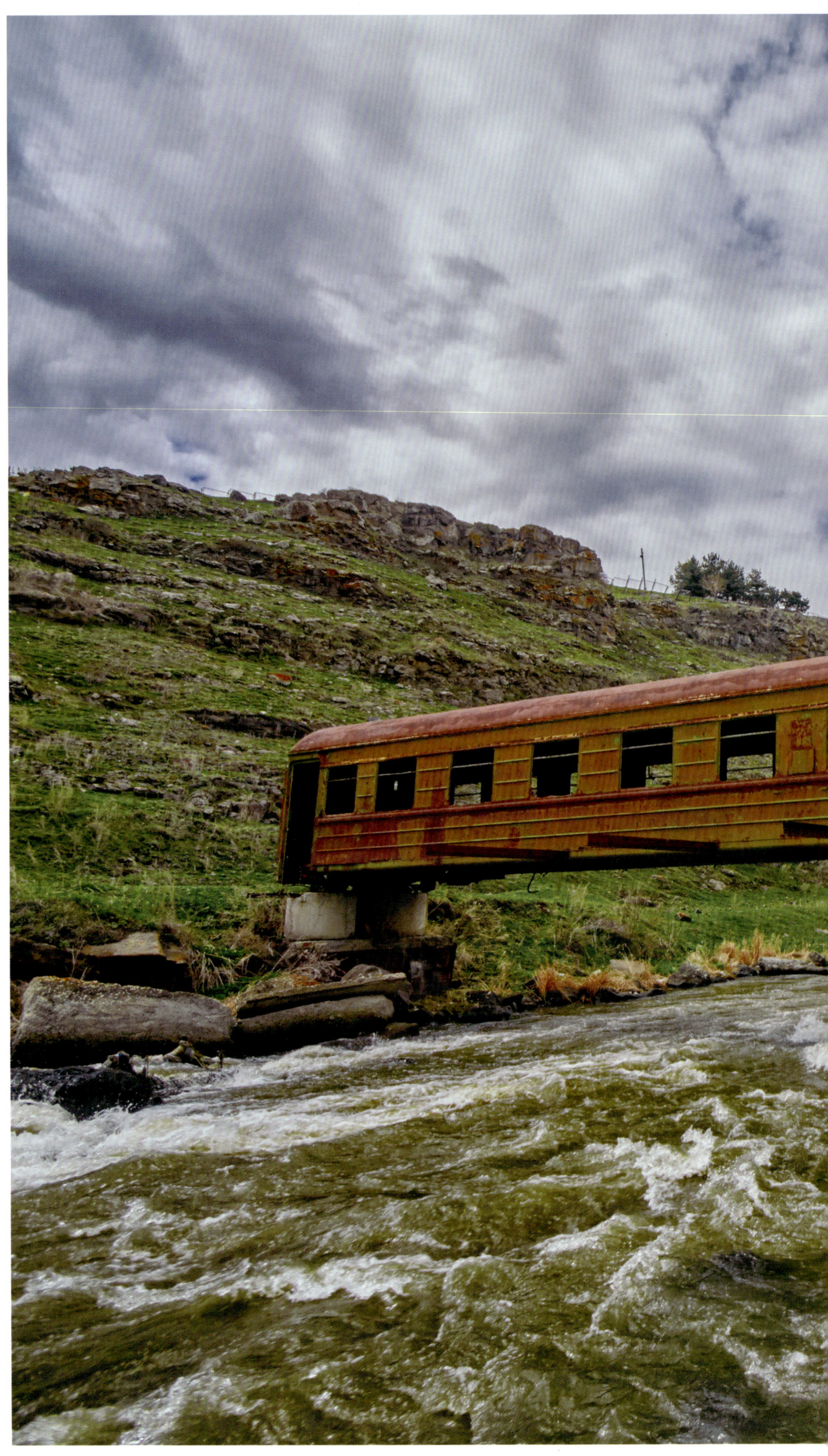

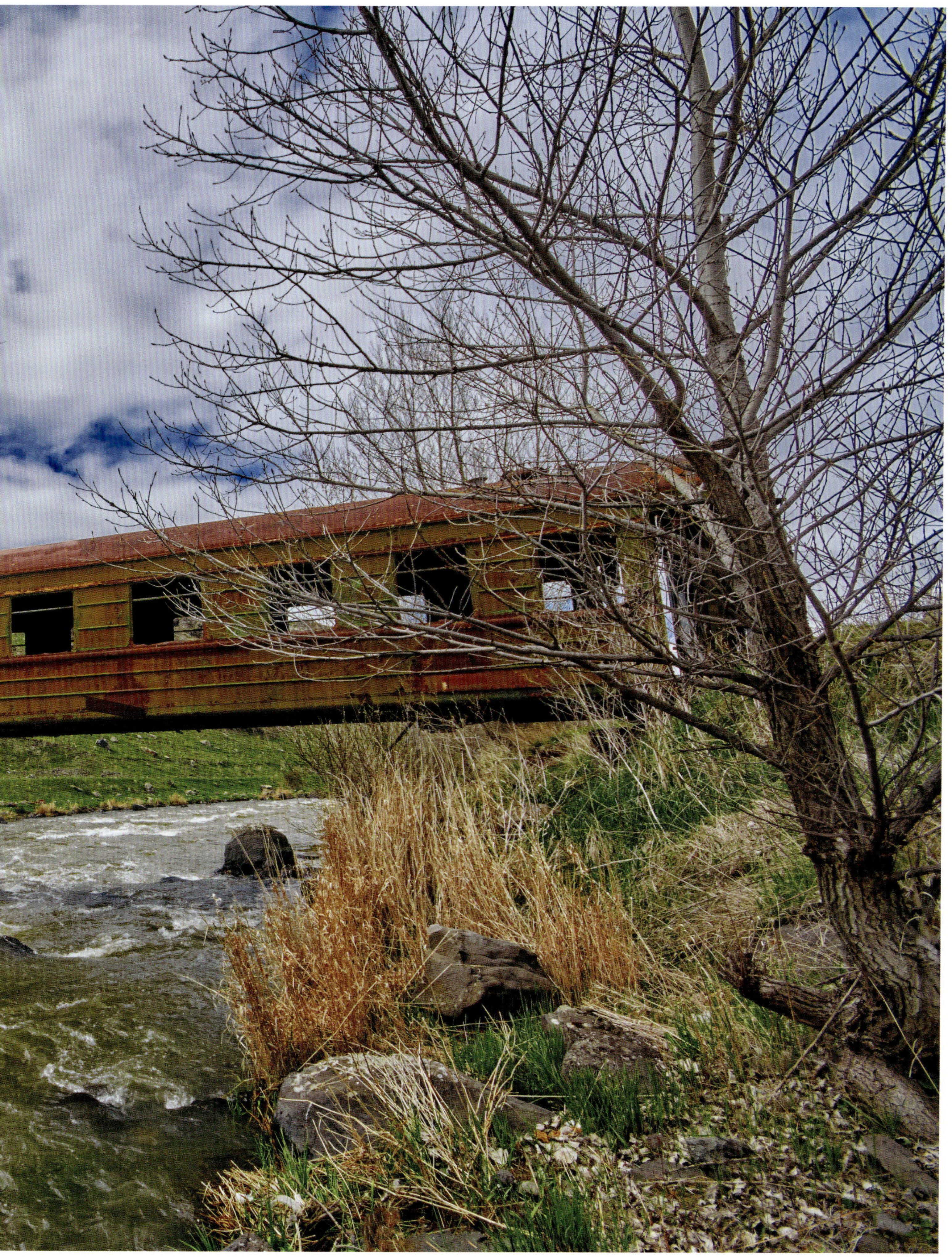

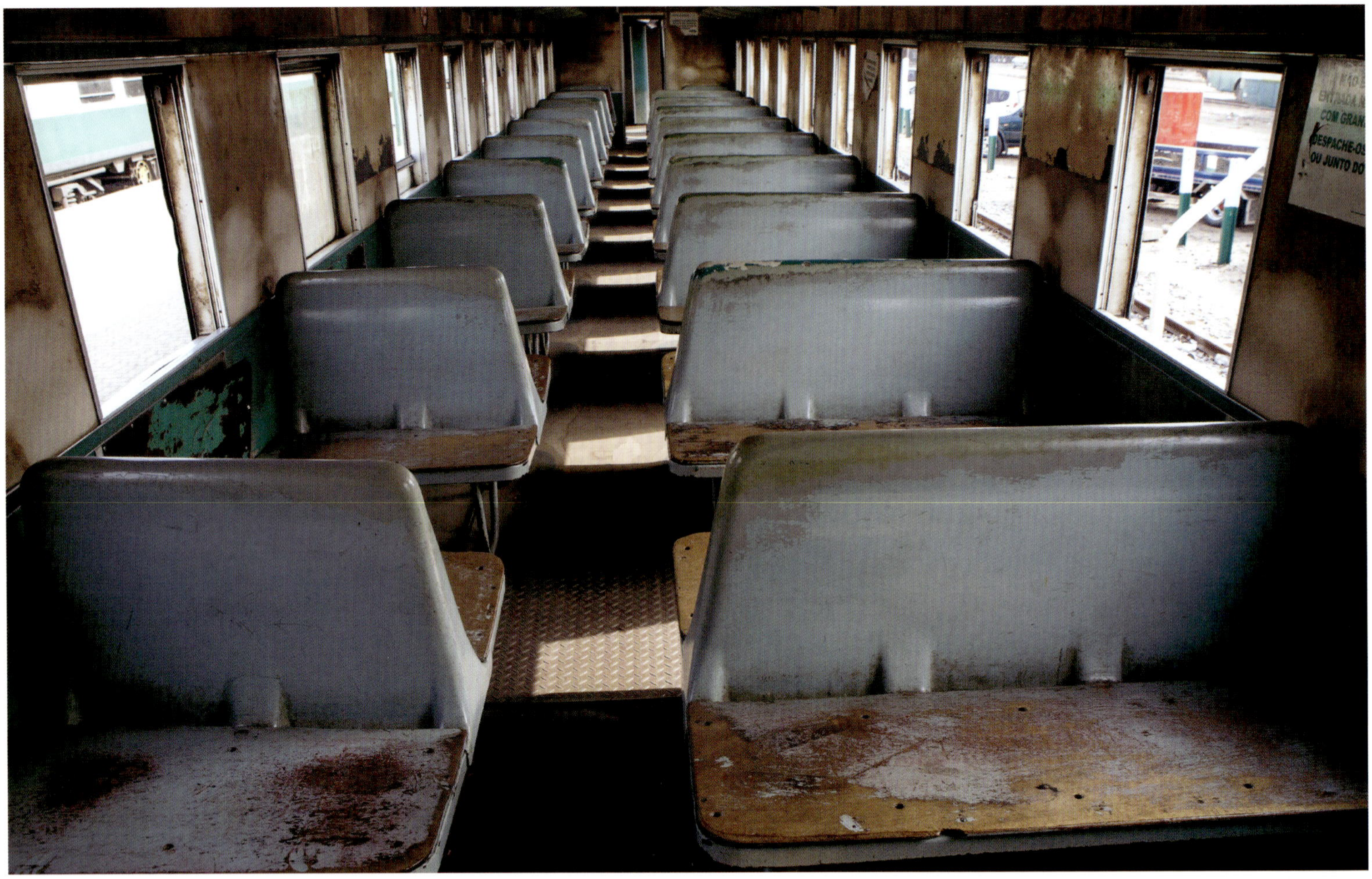

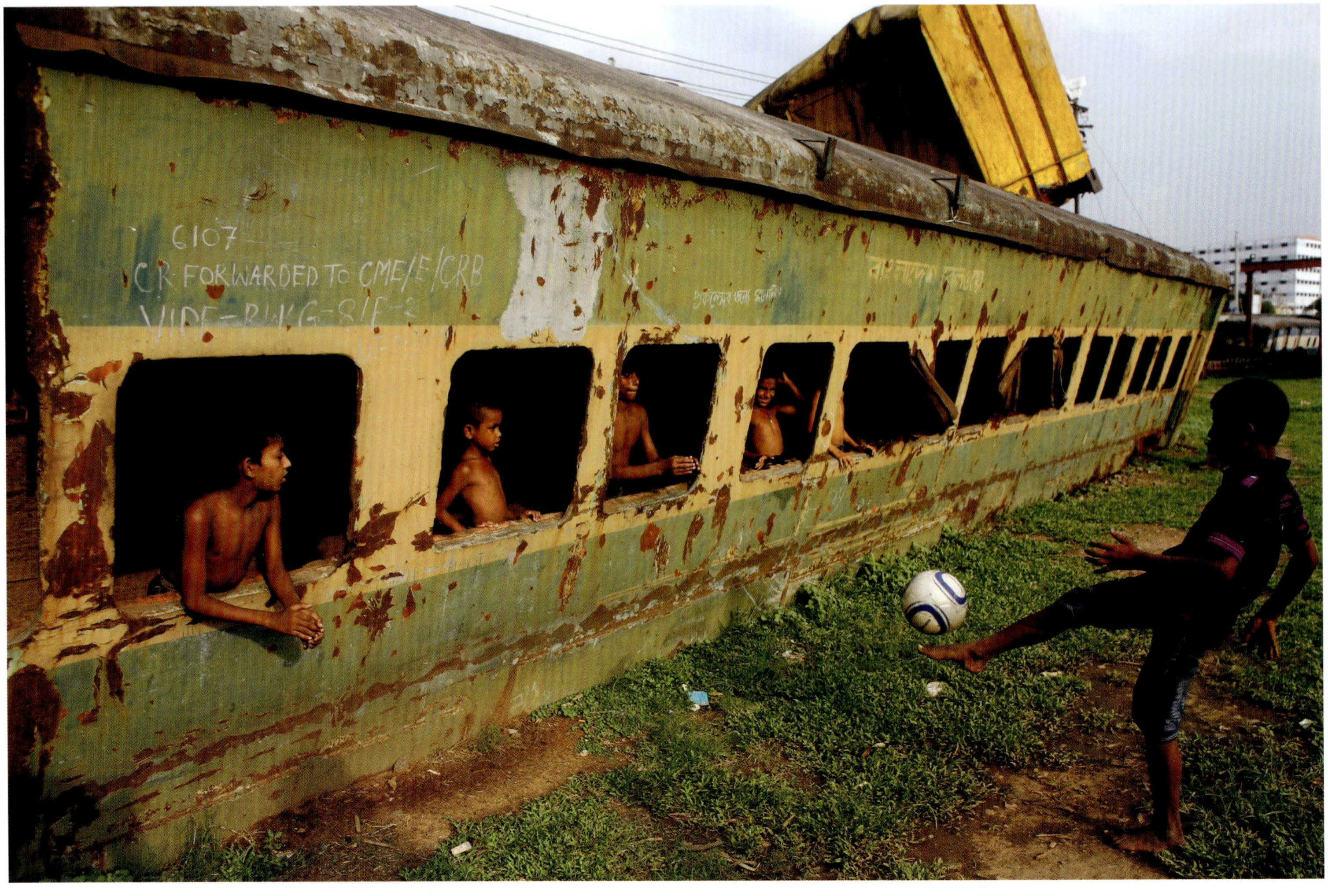
6107
C.R FORWARDED TO CME/E/CRB

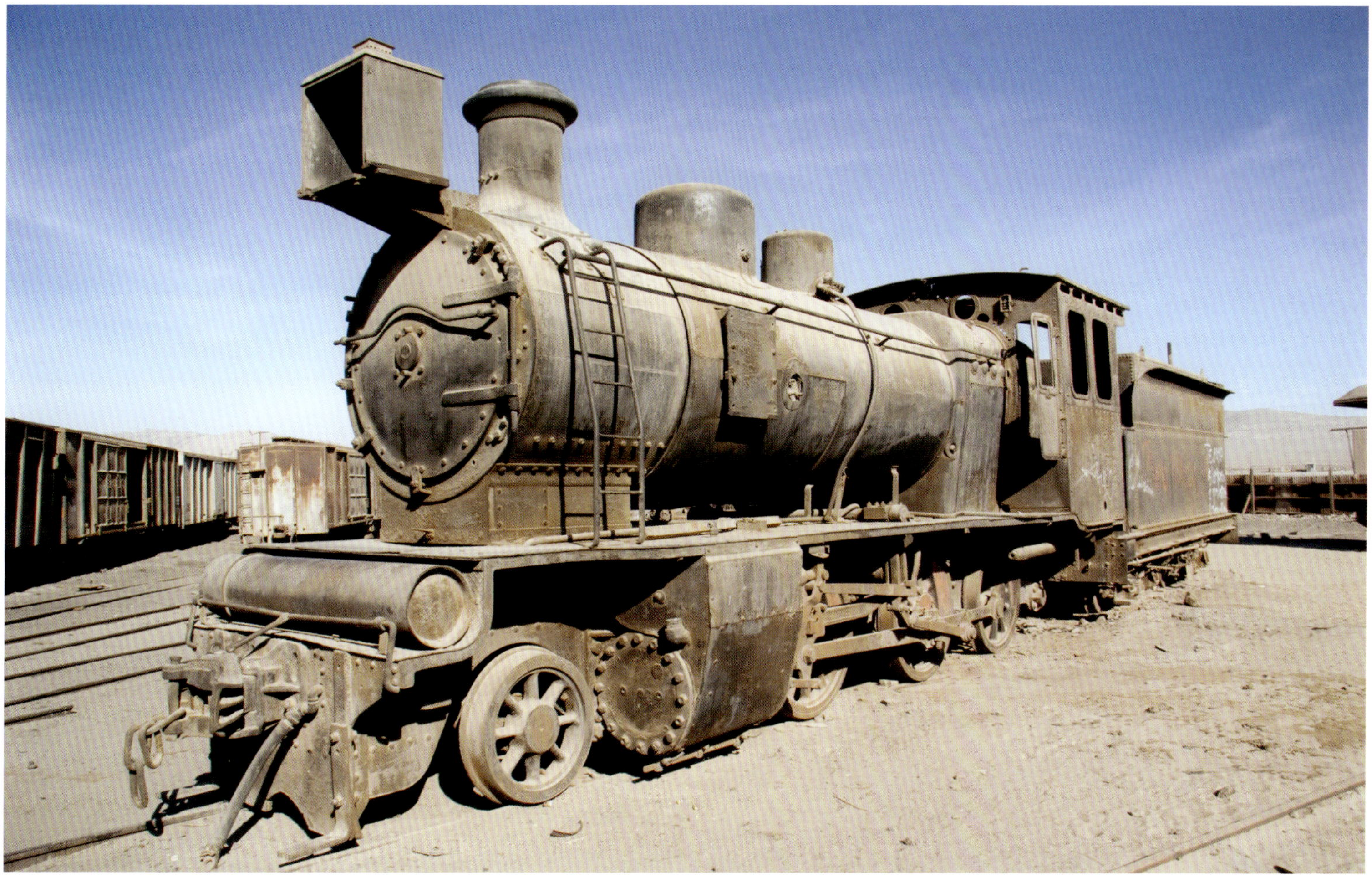

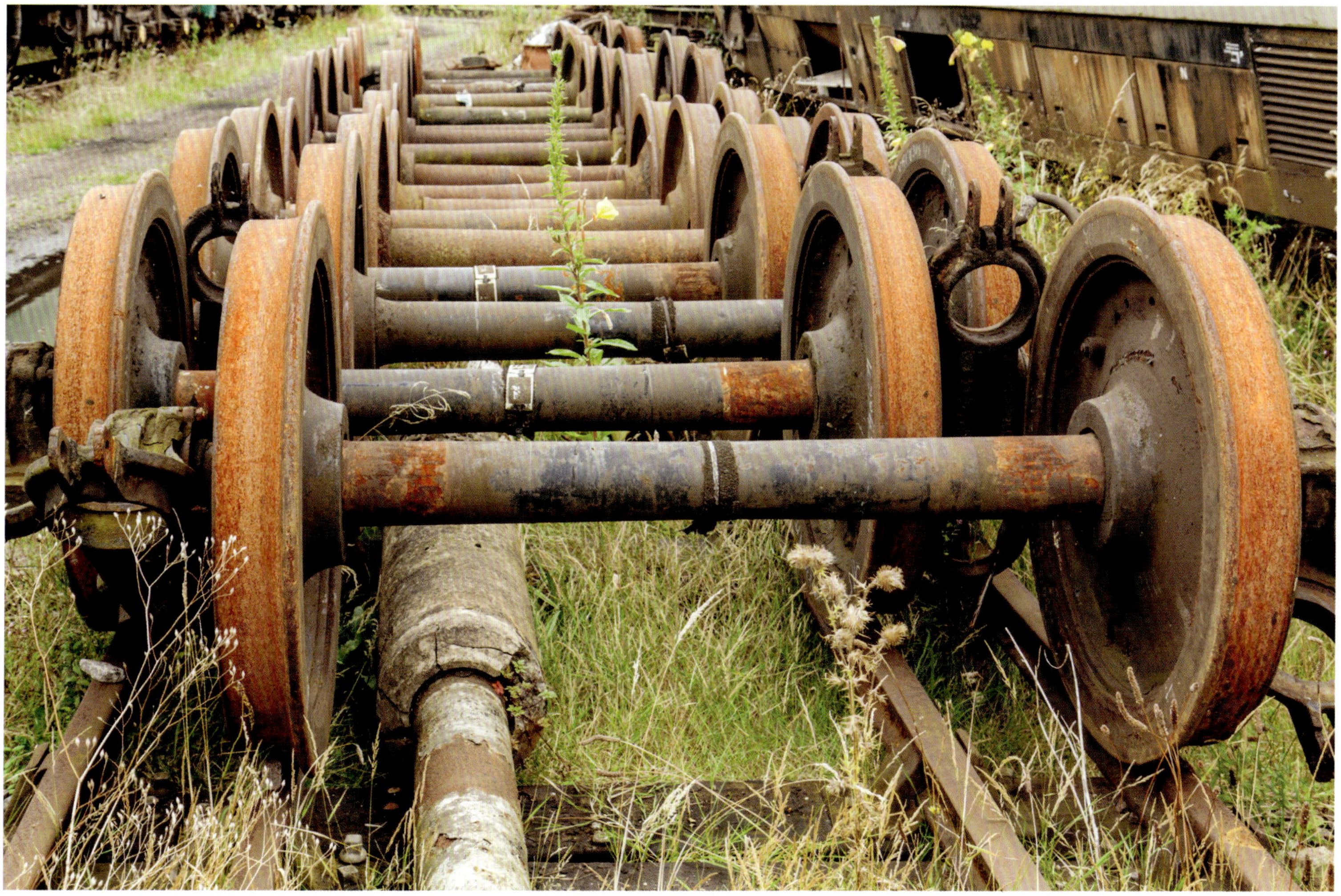

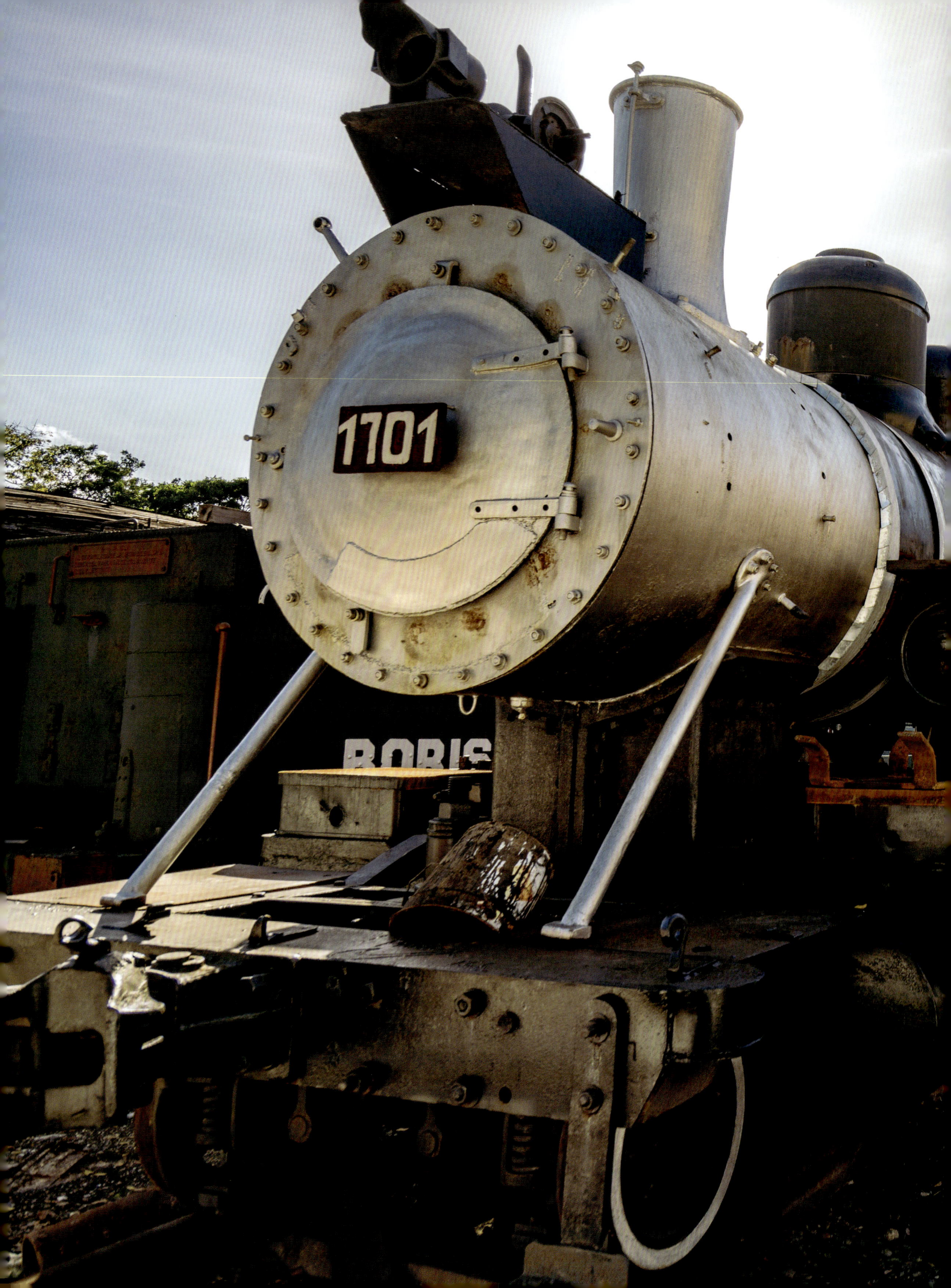

1701
BORIS

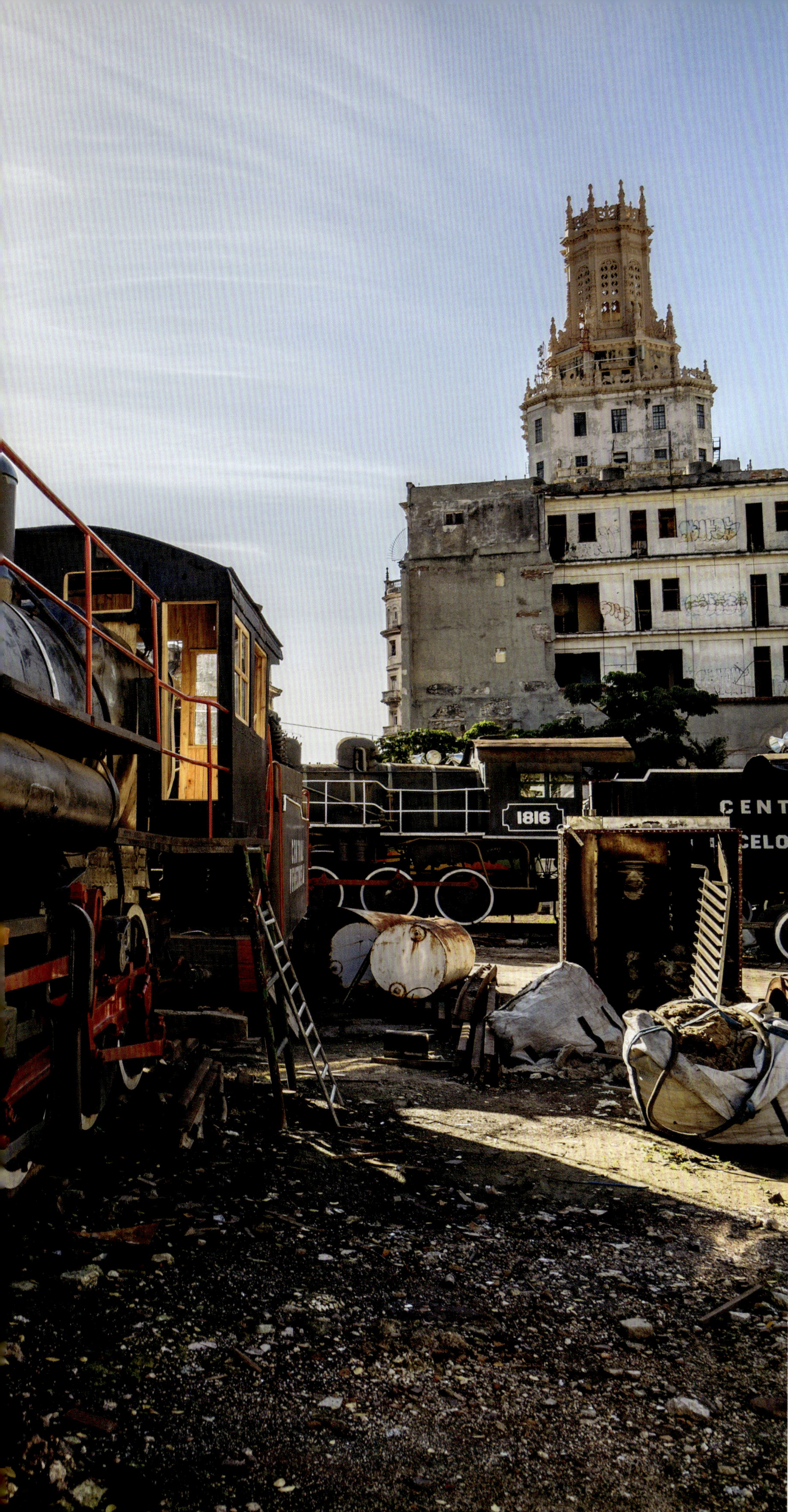

PREVIOUS PAGE:
TOP LEFT:

Maputo, Mozambique

An abandoned rail carriage in Maputo Station, Mozambique. Old locomotives and carriages contain many recyclable materials, such as electric cabling, steel panels and window glass – note how all the windows have gone here.

BOTTOM LEFT:

Dhaka, Bangladesh

This old railway carriage has become an intrinsic part of a football game in Dhaka, Bangladesh. Today, the state-owned Bangladesh Railway carries more than 65 million passengers every year.

TOP RIGHT:

Antofagasta Region, Chile

A sturdy old steam locomotive abandoned in Chile. The large box-like structure over the chimney would have held a headlight, designed to throw a broad beam of light onto the tracks during night journeys across remote parts of the country.

BOTTOM RIGHT:

Ruddington, Nottinghamshire, England

These rusted train wheel bogies for a locomotive or railway carriage are to be found at the Nottingham Transport Heritage Centre, Ruddington, Nottinghamshire. Nottingham's main railway station was built in 1848 by the Midland Railway Company, and by the end of the century the city had two other major stations.

LEFT:

Havana, Cuba

A vintage rail locomotive sits in a yard in Havana. Cuba actually has one of the oldest rail networks in the world; the National Railway Company of Cuba, *Ferrocarriles de Cuba*, first opened in 1837. Only in the first half of the twentieth century did diesel and electric trains steadily begin to replace steam propulsion.

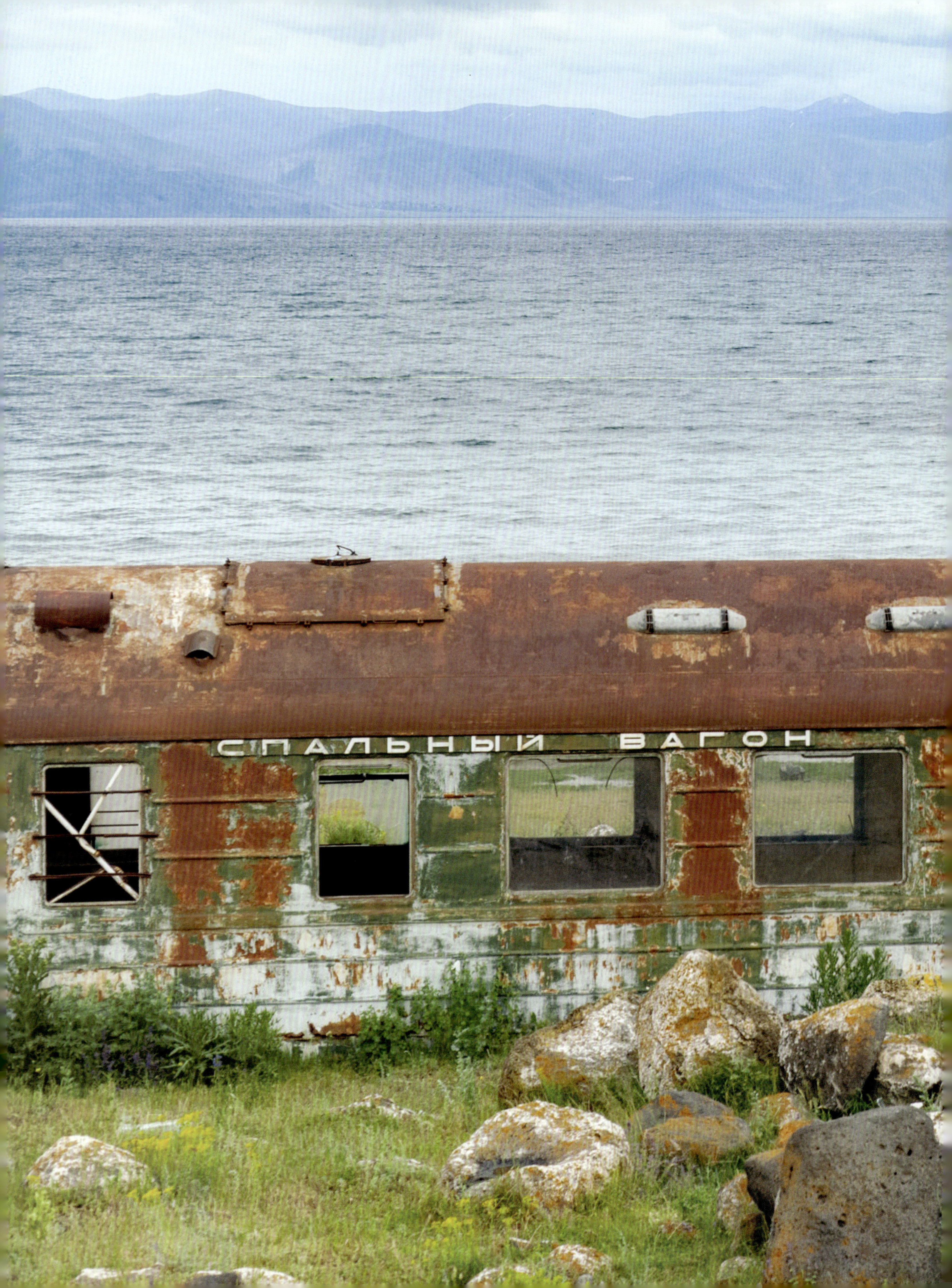
СПАЛЬНЫЙ ВАГОН

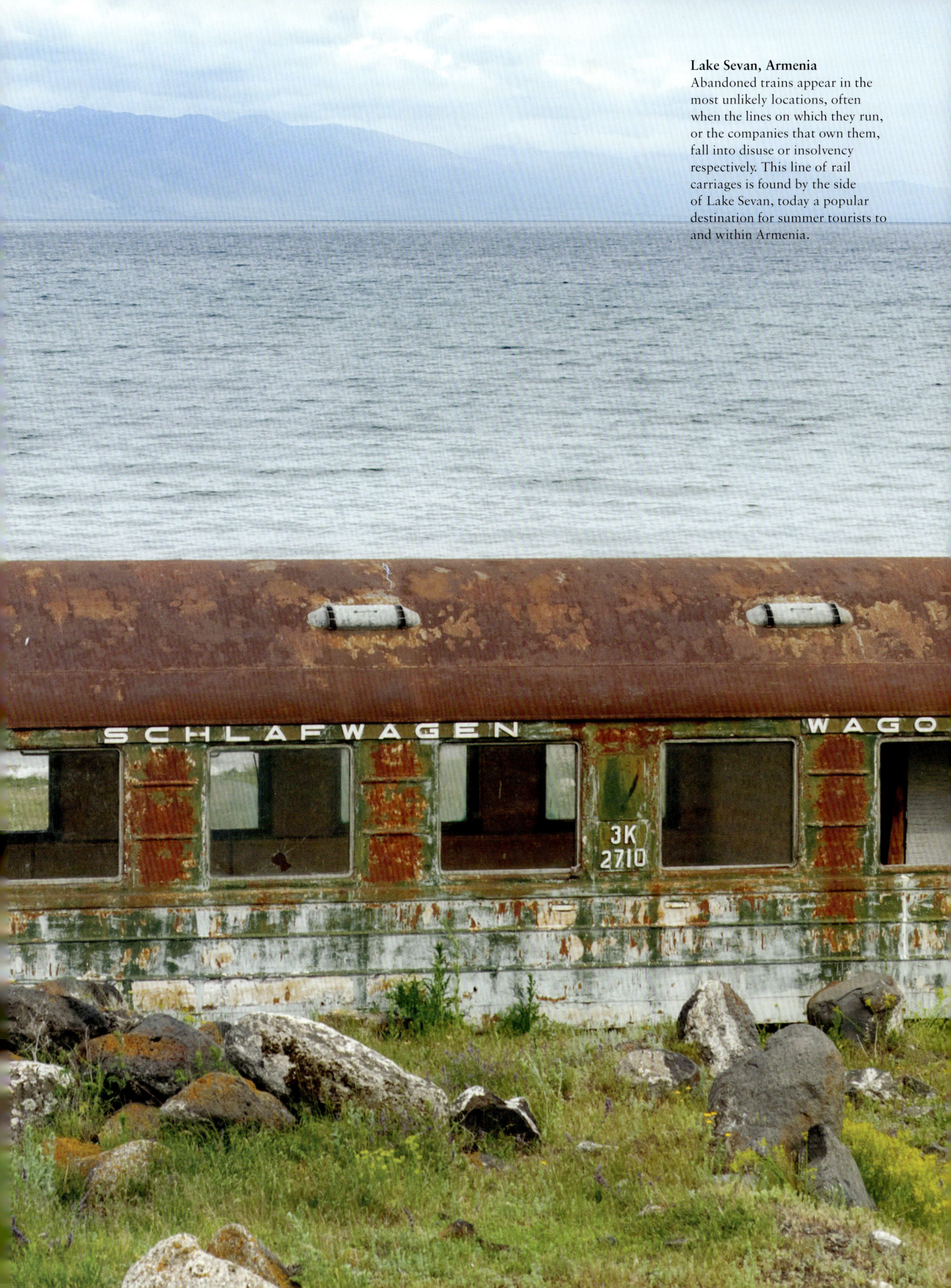

Lake Sevan, Armenia
Abandoned trains appear in the most unlikely locations, often when the lines on which they run, or the companies that own them, fall into disuse or insolvency respectively. This line of rail carriages is found by the side of Lake Sevan, today a popular destination for summer tourists to and within Armenia.

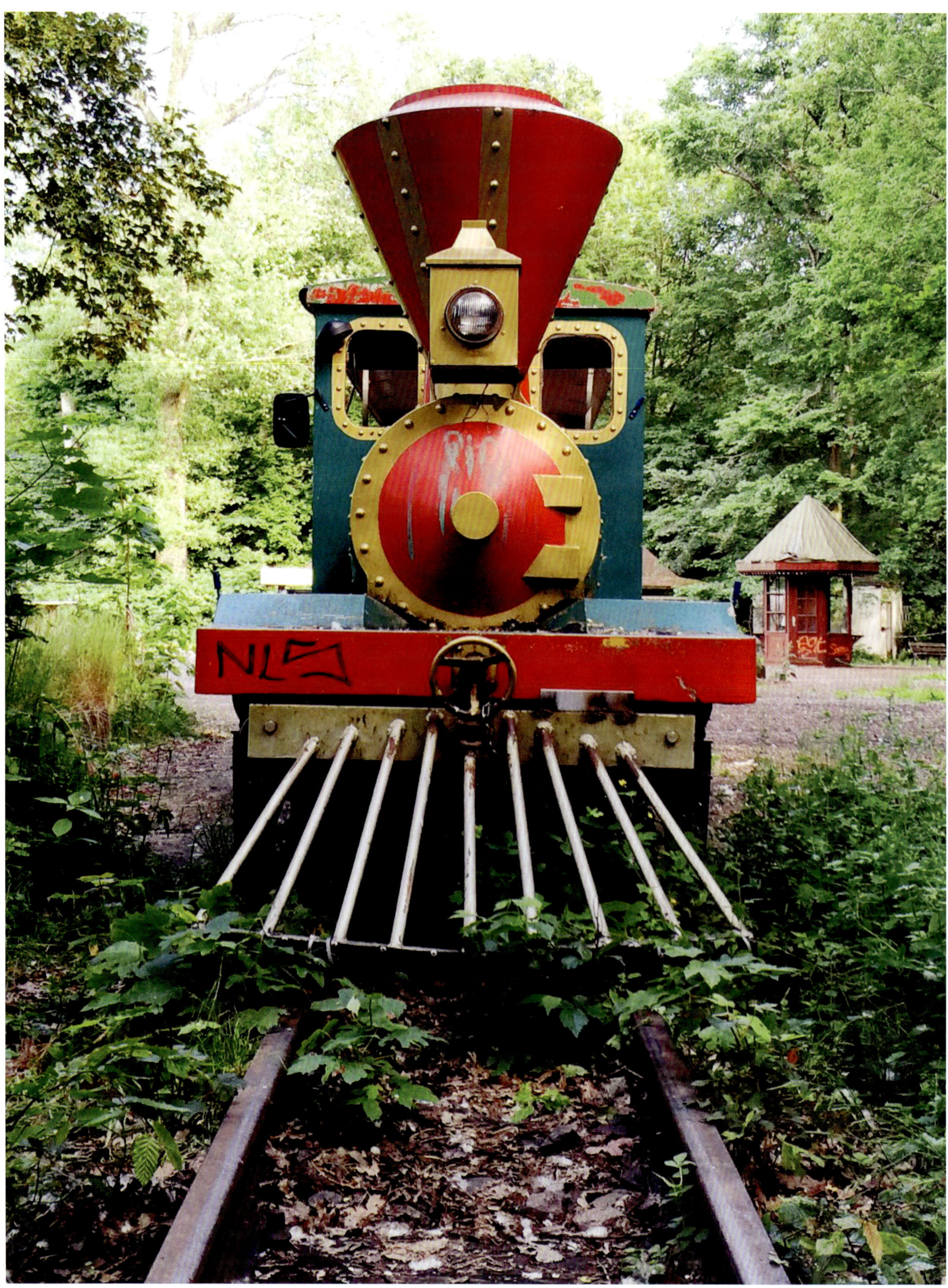

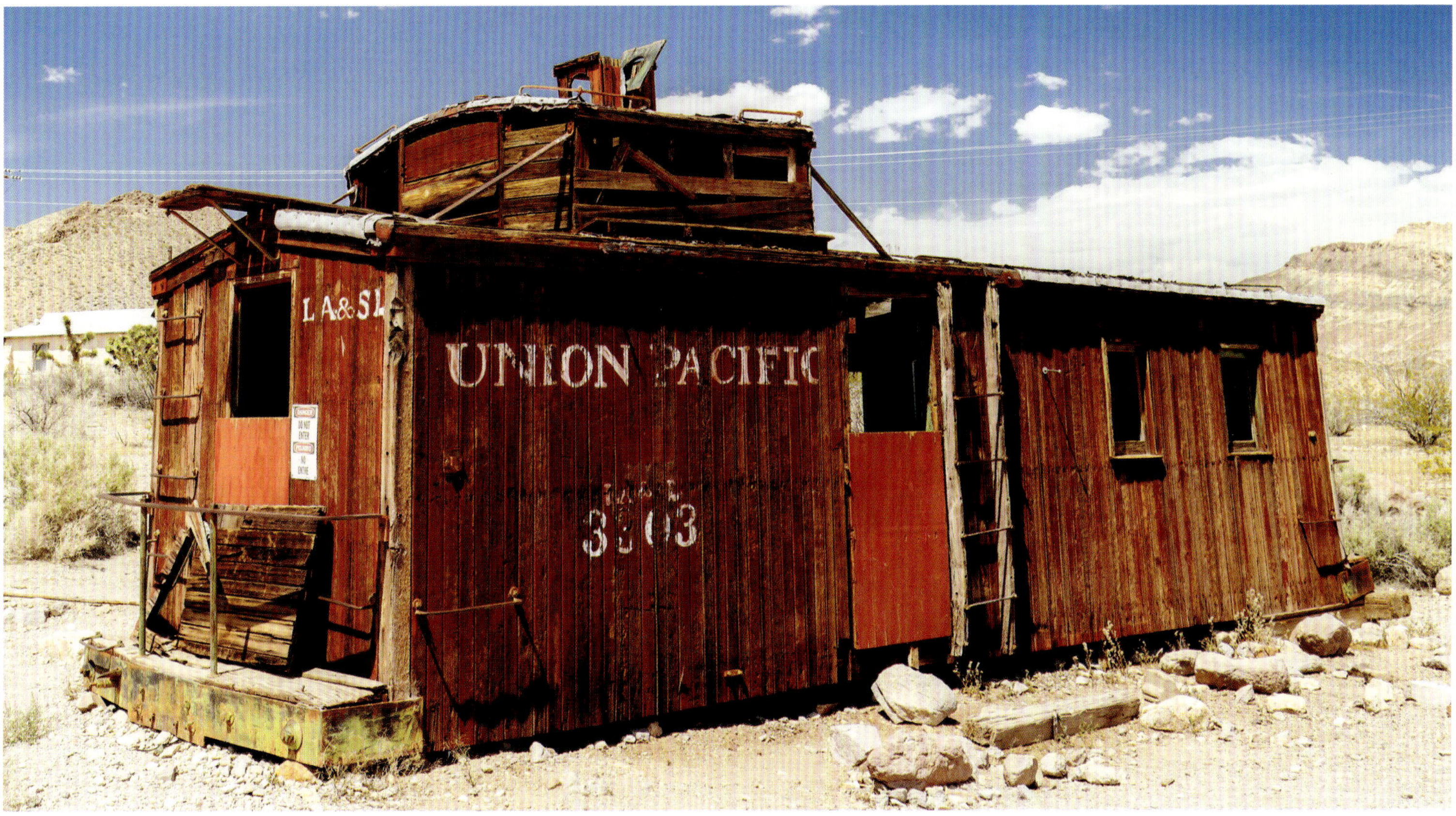

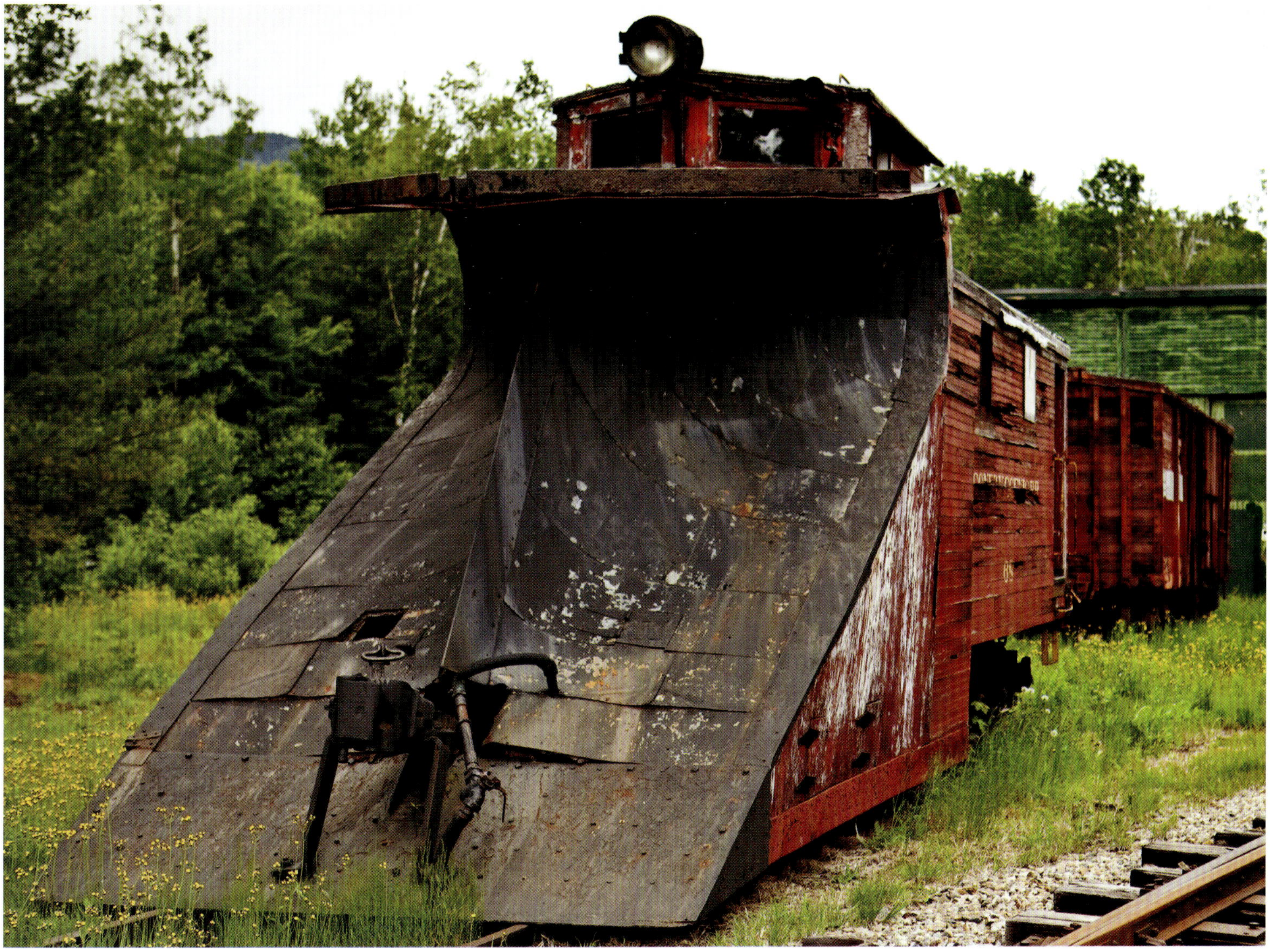

Spreepark, Berlin, Germany

The jaunty colours of this train are explained by the context of its surroundings. Spreepark is an abandoned theme park in Berlin that opened in 1969 but that went insolvent in 2001. Today, the park remains the home to ageing rides and exhibits, such as this train.

Rhyolite, Nye County, Nevada, United States

This old Union Pacific Railroad car is in the ghost town of Rhyolite in Nevada. The town itself developed as a gold-mining settlement from 1905, but its fortunes peaked too quickly and by 1920 it was deserted.

Bartlett, New Hampshire, United States

Here displayed at the Bartlett Roundhouse, an historic railroad service facility in Bartlett, New Hampshire, we see Russell Snow Plow #68. The giant blades at the front of the locomotive would have been capable of pushing aside even the heaviest of snowfalls.

Ayrshire, Scotland

Ayrshire, where we find these abandoned pieces of rail history, was once a major hub for rail services along the east coast of Scotland. The rail lines facilitated the development of the coal industry in the region, plus connections with urban areas such as Glasgow and Paisley.

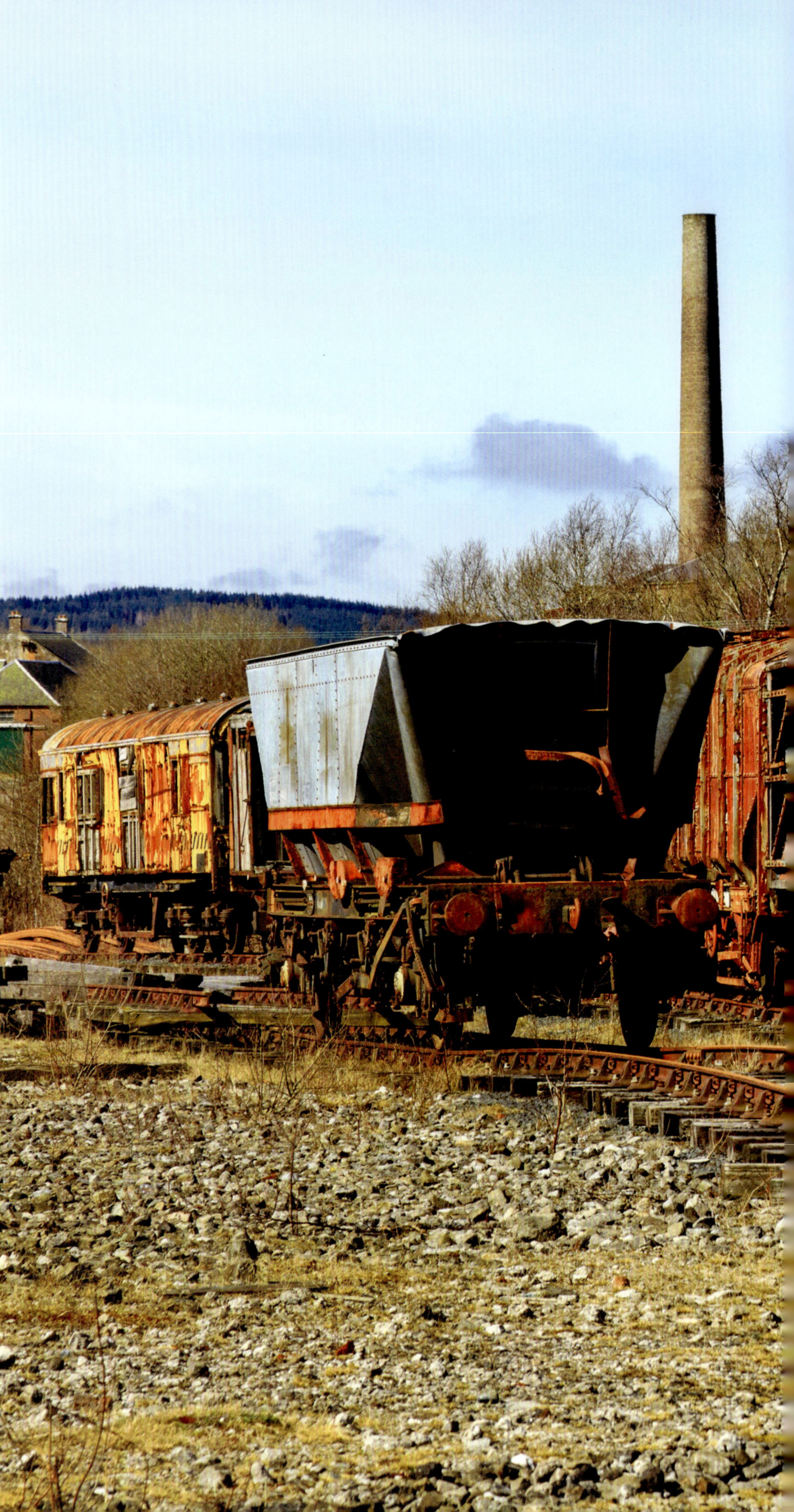

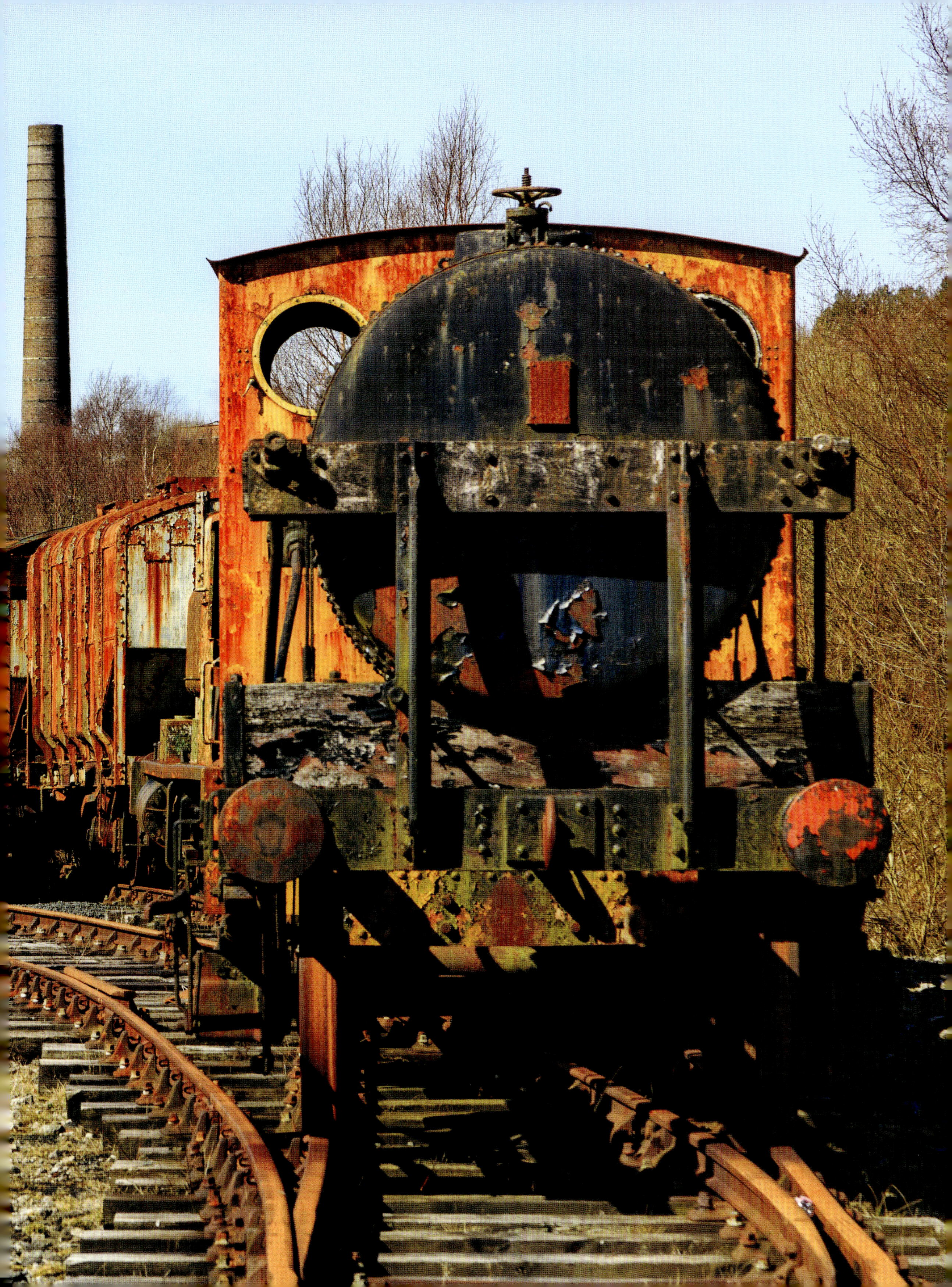

Ayrshire, Scotland
Another of the rusted and stripped
specimens found in Ayrshire, this
one sat rather optimistically on
rails. This diesel-powered vehicle
is actually a train shunter, used to
push trains, wagons and carriages
manually between platforms.
Operating shunting engines can
be dangerous work, especially for
personnel assisting the shunting
manoeuvre from ground level.

**Minas de Riotinto, Huelva
Province, Spain**
Steam locomotives were central
to the industrialization of mining
during the 19th century. Here this
locomotive is in a section of the
RioTinto mining area in Spain.
Typical materials mined in this
area were gold, silver and copper.

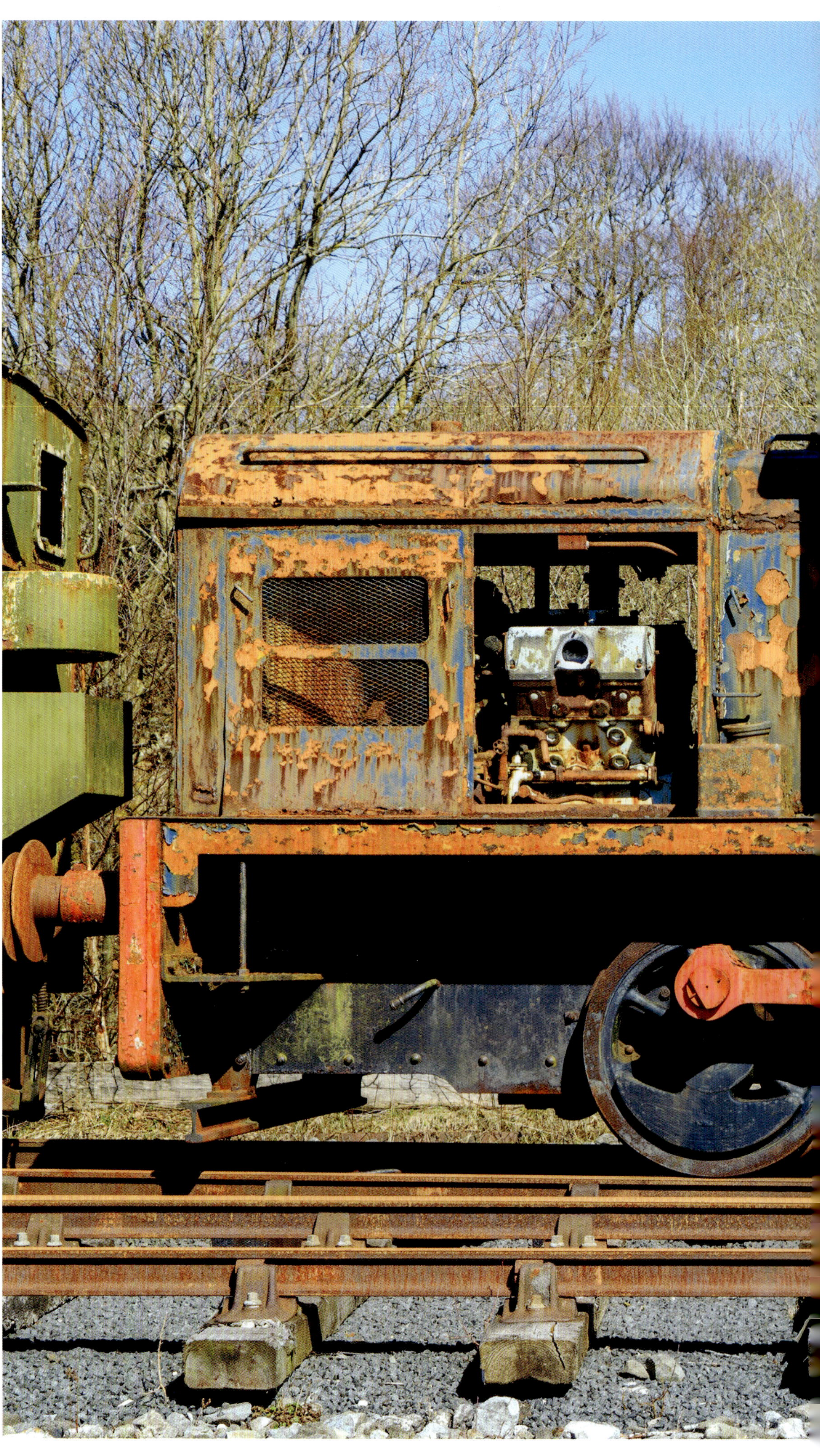

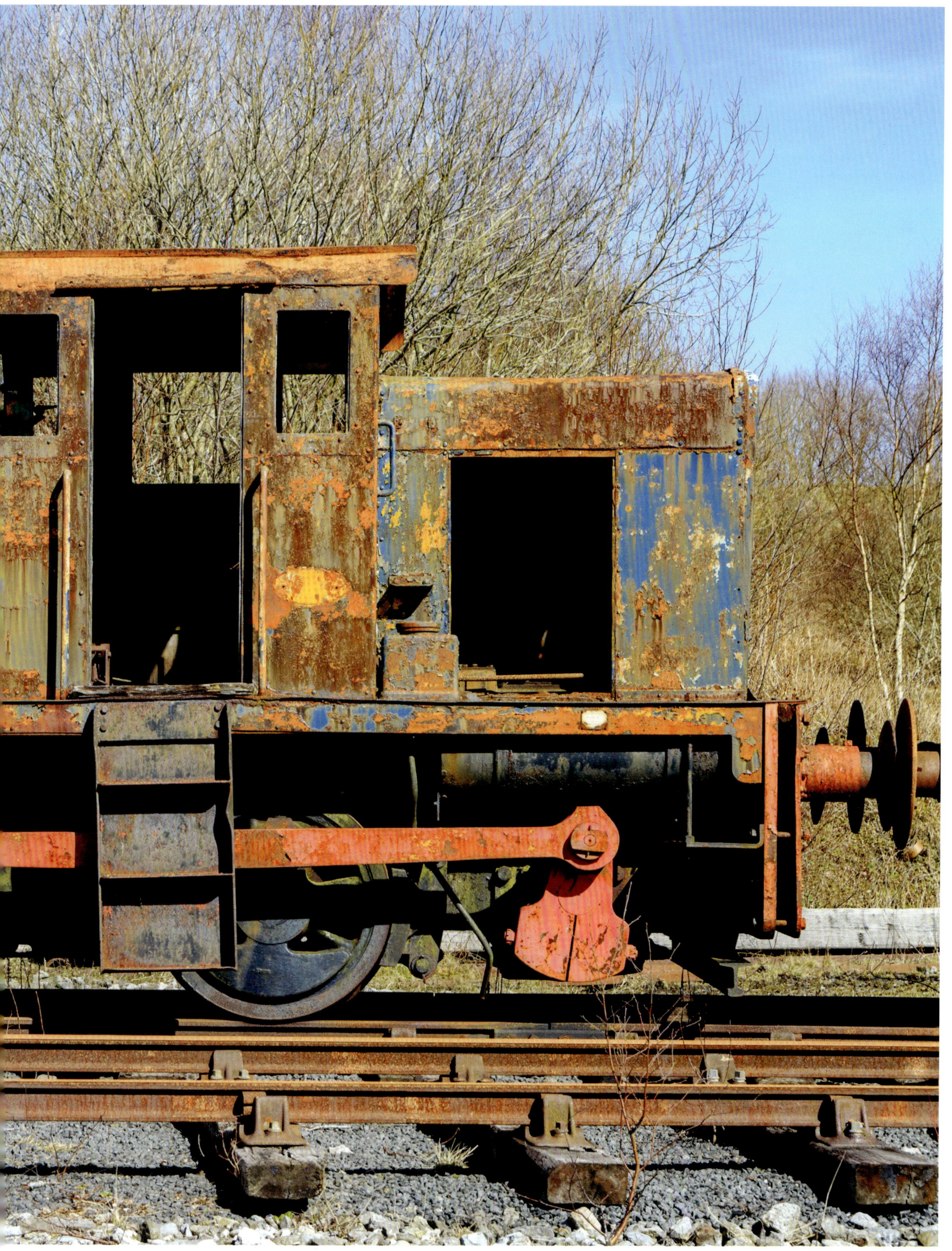

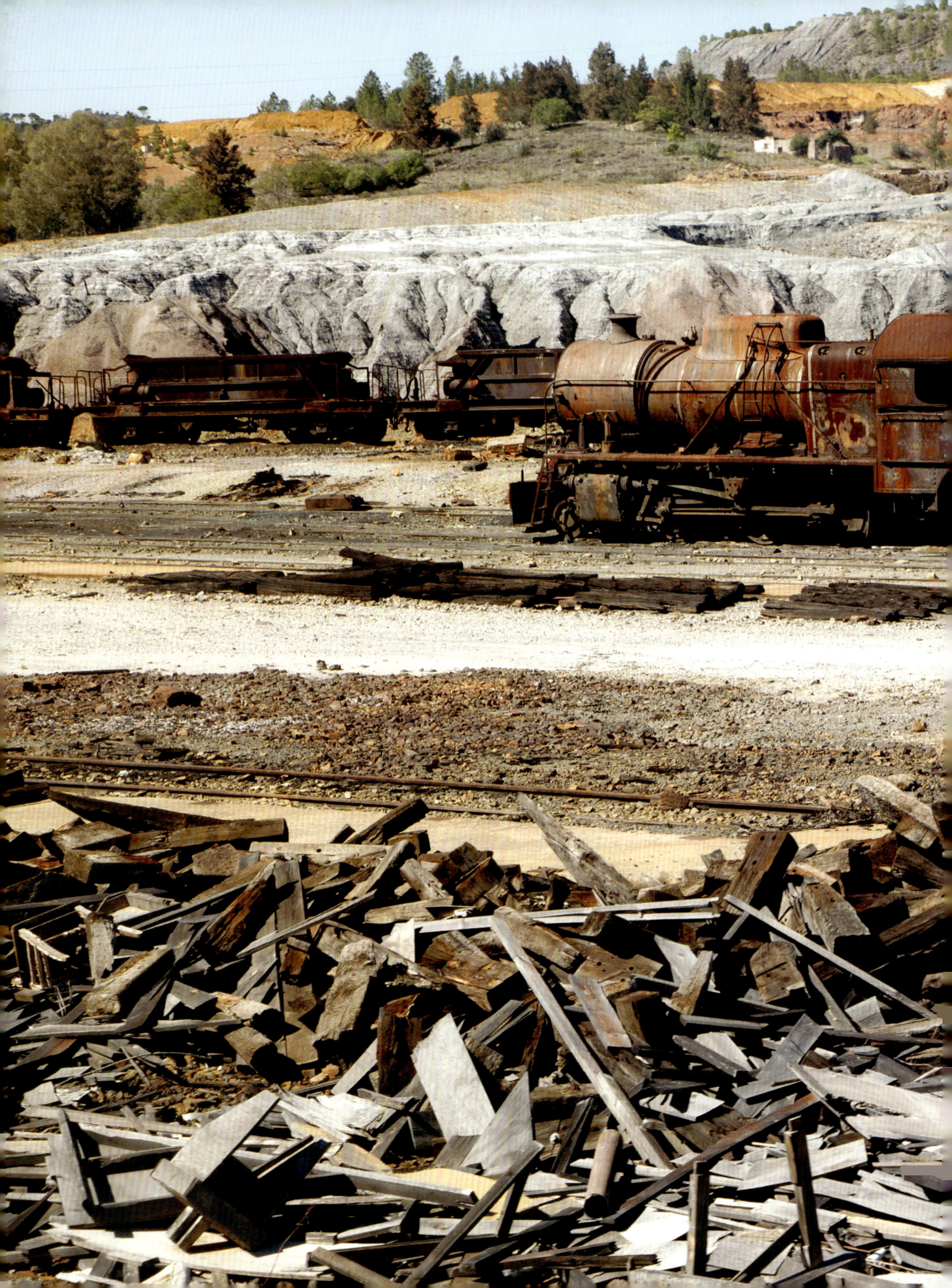

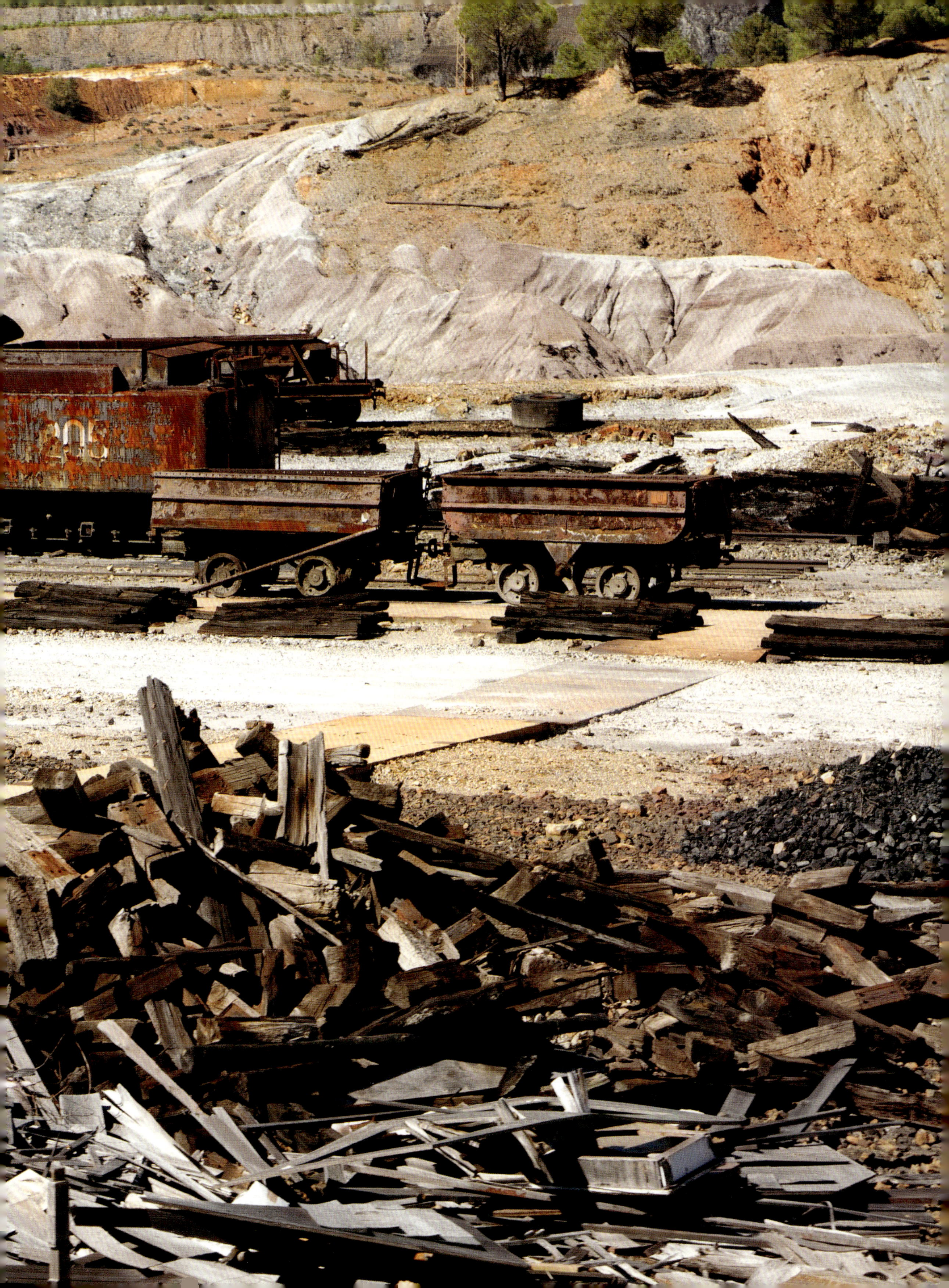

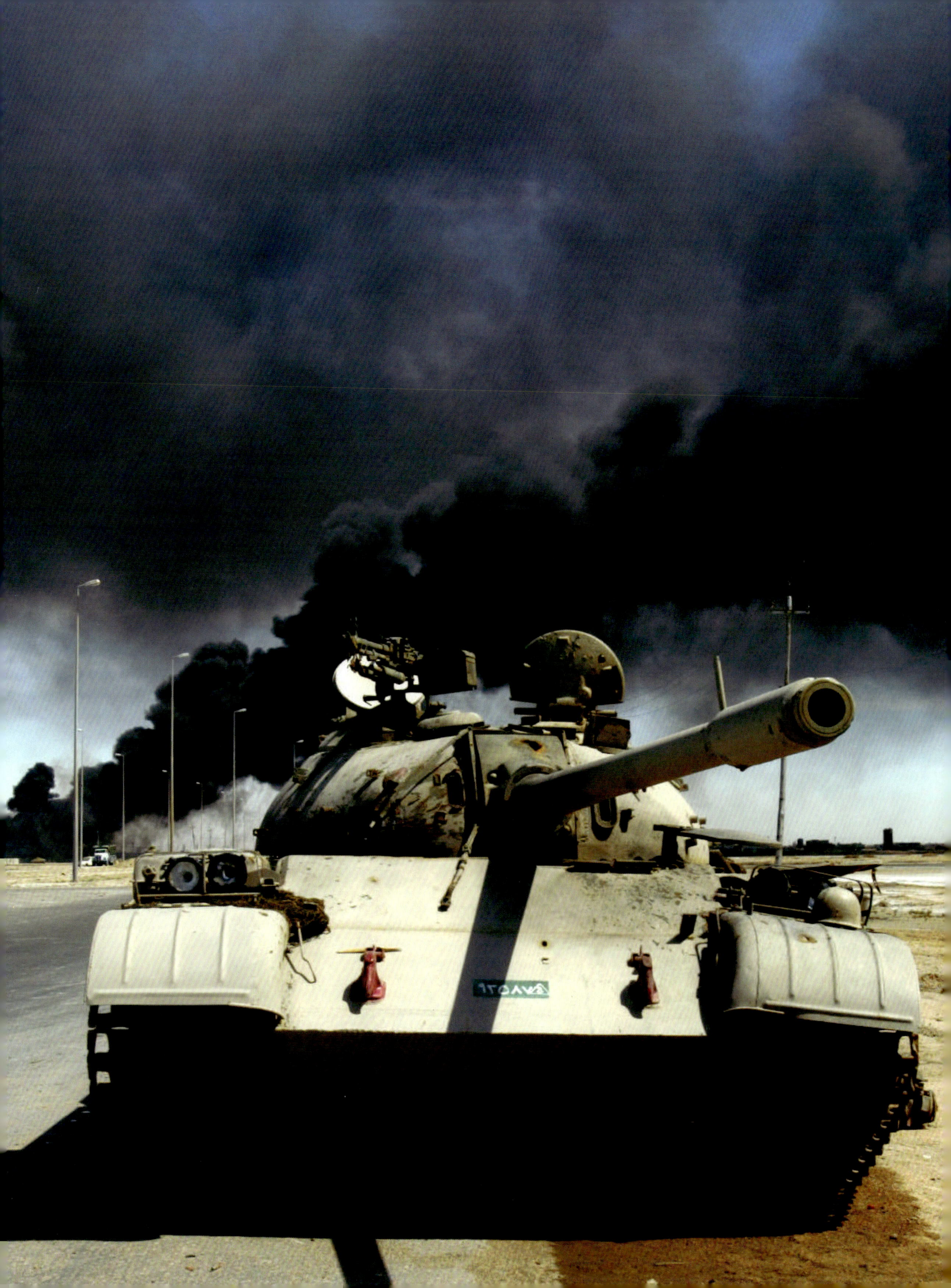

Military Vehicles

The world is littered with the remnants of military vehicles. Produced, and destroyed, in their hundreds of thousands, they can be found in every corner of the globe: a US amphibious vehicle rotting in the surf line of a Pacific atoll; a German Panzer standing silent in a clearing in Russian woodland; a Soviet tank with its turret blown off in an Afghan valley; and countless other scenarios. In many instances, the wrecked military vehicle speaks of an obliterative end, turned from a rumbling, powerful vehicle into an inert dead weight through the impact of a missile, the detonation of a mine, or the consuming flames of an incendiary device. Looking at the outside destruction of such vehicles, it is always chilling to consider the experience of those on the inside. (It is little wonder that some British tank crews in North Africa followed the practice of carrying a pistol on their laps, as an alternative route to death should their tank be hit and catch fire.) Yet as a balance to the sense of vulnerability given in the photographs that follow, there also remains an aura of the sheer durability of military vehicles – a main battle tank is a huge block of high-grade steel and iron, and disposing of such a mechanical entity is no easy task, even for professional scrappers. Because of this resilience, tanks and military vehicles may prove to be our most enduring wrecks.

LEFT:

T-55 Main Battle Tank, near Basra, Iraq
An Iraqi T-55 main battle tank lies static on a road on the outskirts of Basra, 3 April 2003. At the time the picture was taken, the tank had only just been abandoned, in response to Coalition advances following the invasion of Iraq on 20 March. Leaving the vehicle was a good choice – those Iraqi tank crews who chose to fight were almost invariably destroyed.

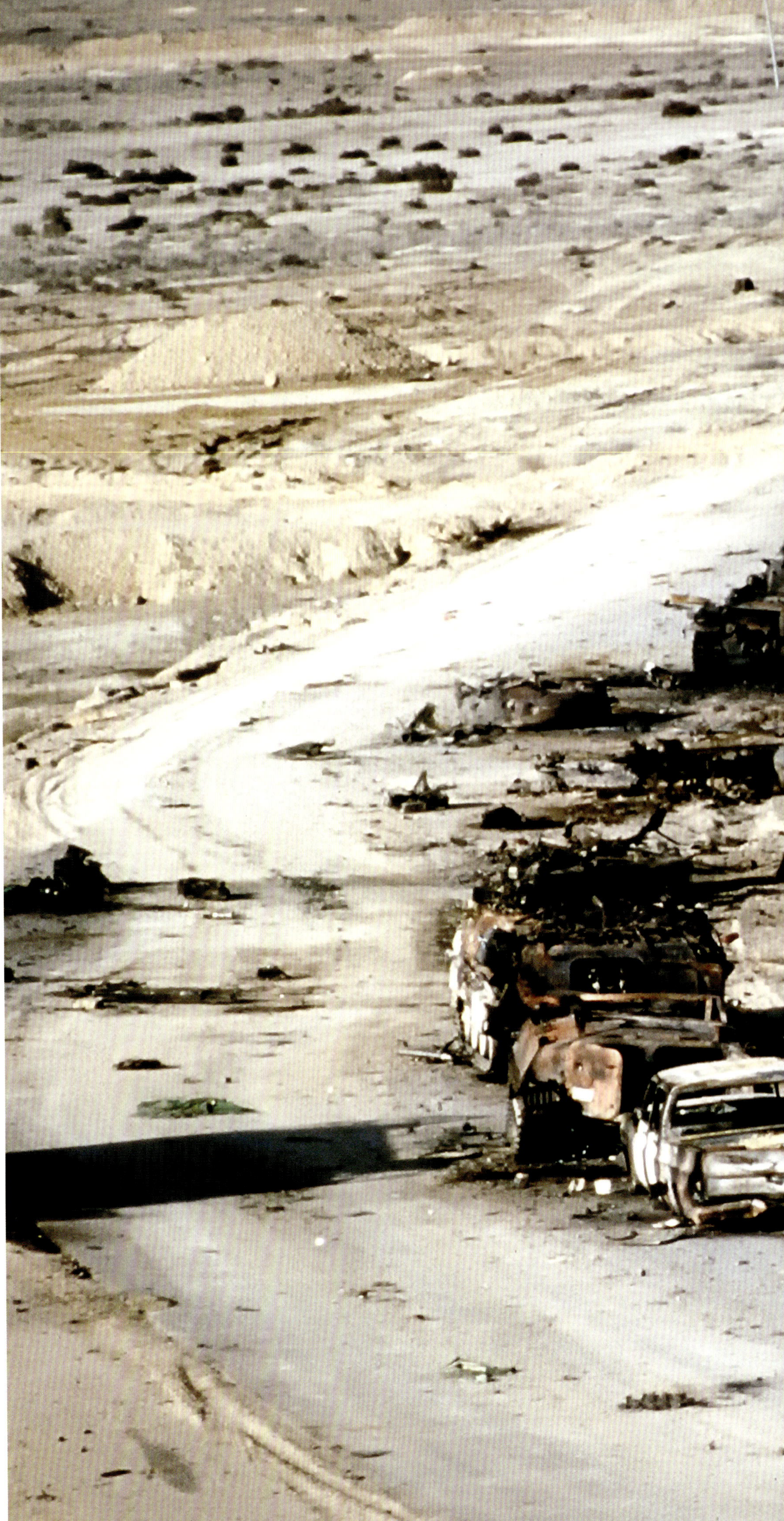

Highway 8, Mutla Ridge, Kuwait
Iraqi military vehicles, smashed
and burnt out, are strewn across
Highway 8 in Kuwait in April
1991. They and countless others
had been destroyed the previous
February in a merciless air attack
by the US Air Force, Marine Corps
and Navy, as the Iraqis attempted
to flee Kuwait following the launch
of the Coalition's successful
Operation *Desert Storm*.

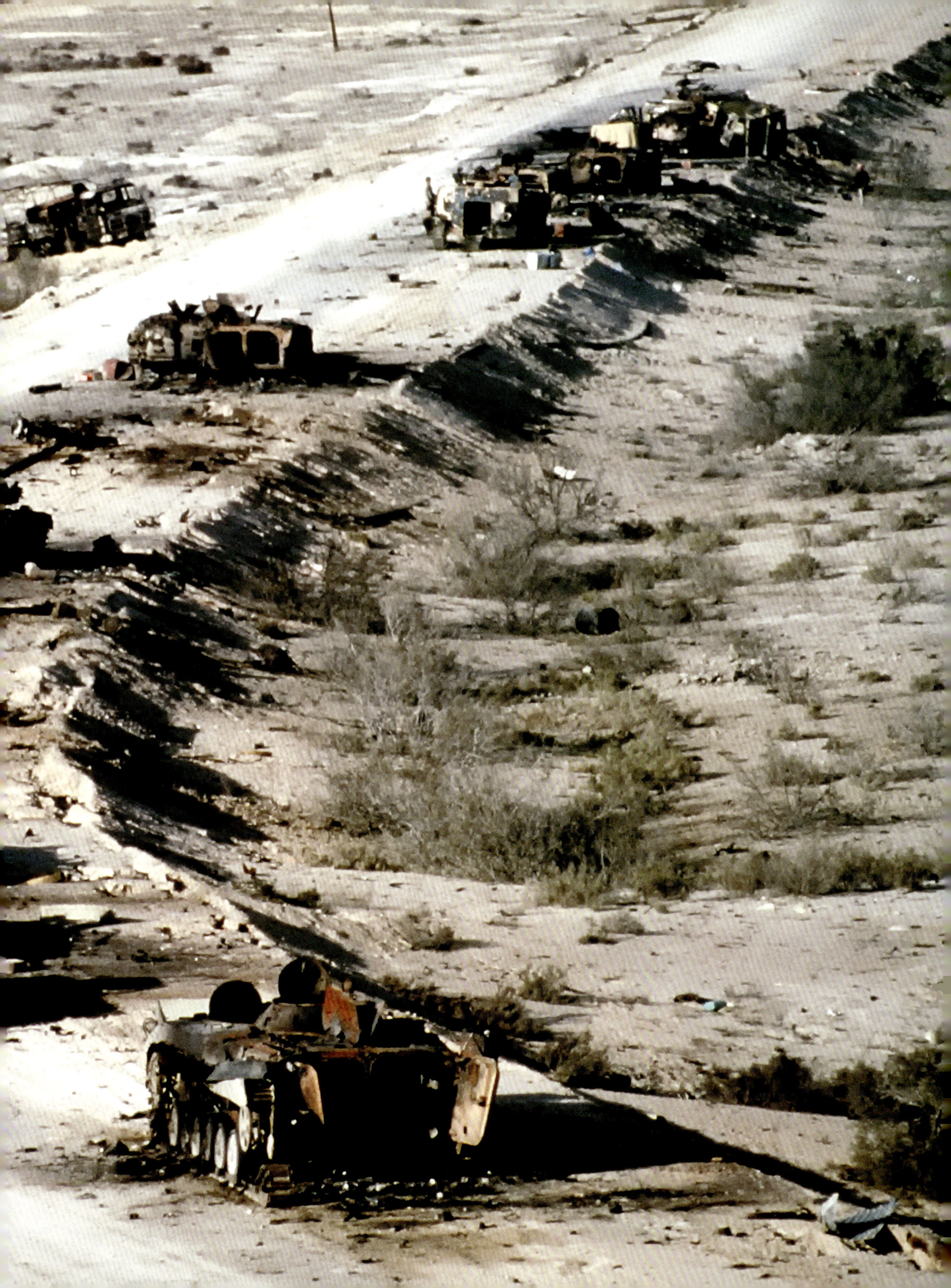

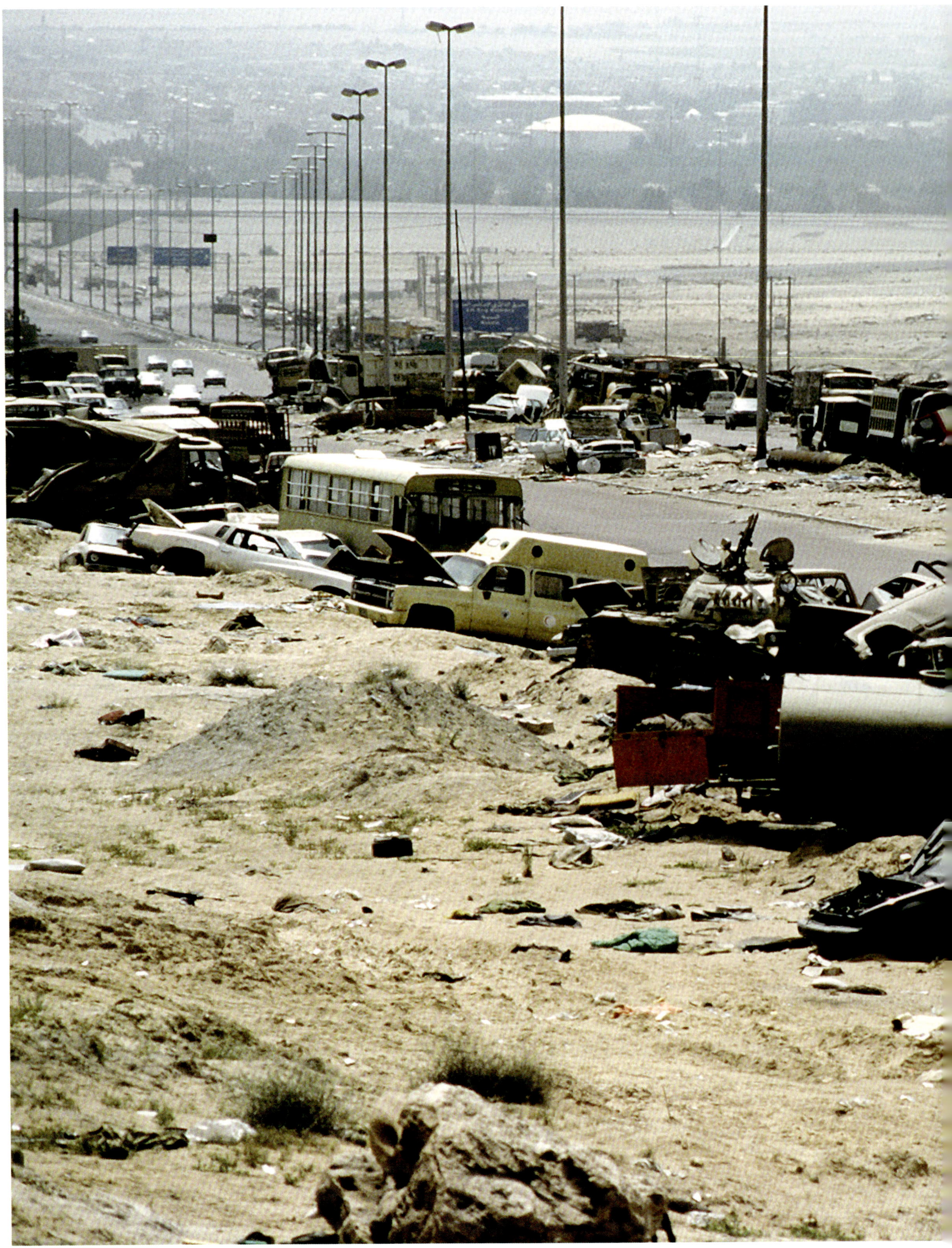

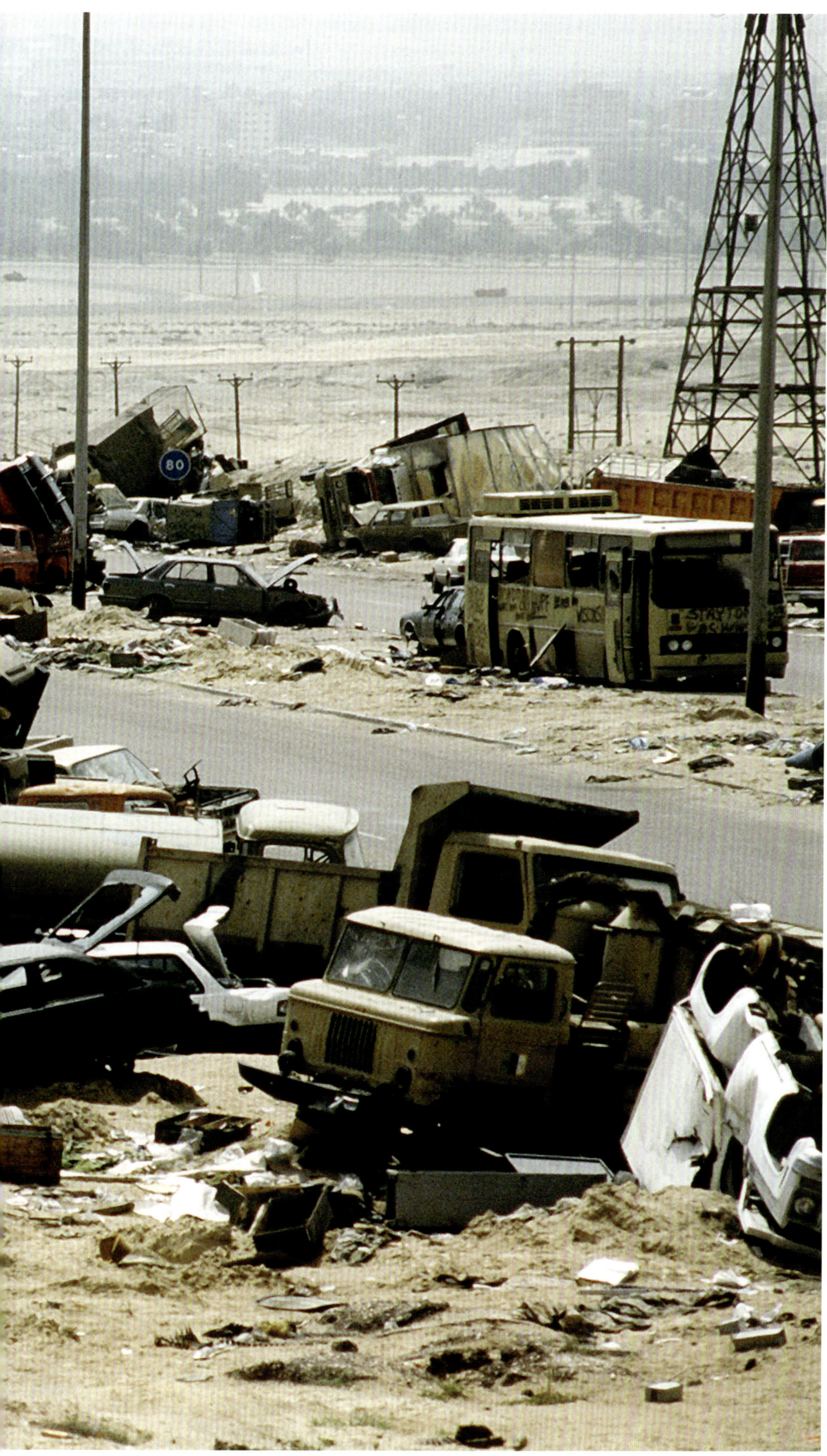

LEFT:

Highway 80, Kuwait

A view of the 'Highway of Death', Highway 80 (a road east of Highway 8), showing the high numbers of civilian vehicles that were also destroyed in the US air attack in February 1991. This picture was taken the following April, the destroyed vehicles shunted to the side of the road like so much refuse.

OVERLEAF:

TOP LEFT:

BMP Infantry Fighting Vehicle, Wakhan Corridor, Badakhshan, Afghanistan

The shell of a Soviet BMP infantry fighting vehicle (IFV) sits alone in the Wakhan Corridor, a strip of territory in northeastern Afghanistan. The vehicle was doubtless destroyed during the Afghan–Soviet War of 1979–89.

BOTTOM:

9K33 OSA 6x6 Self-Propelled Anti-Aircraft System, Benghazi, Libya

The wrecked vehicle here is a Libyan Army 9K33 OSA 6x6 self-propelled anti-aircraft system, the vehicle destroyed in a Coalition air strike in 2011. The vehicle was clearly ready for action, with its blast shield raised at the back, but despite having considerable anti-aircraft resources the Libyan Army was unable to shoot down a single Coalition aircraft.

TOP RIGHT:

Western Desert, Egypt

This initially uninteresting-looking wreck carries some considerable historical weight. It belonged to the Long Range Desert Group (LRDG), an elite British raiding and reconnaissance unit frequently fighting behind German lines in North Africa between 1940 and 1943. The LRDG often operated alongside the fledgling Special Air Service (SAS).

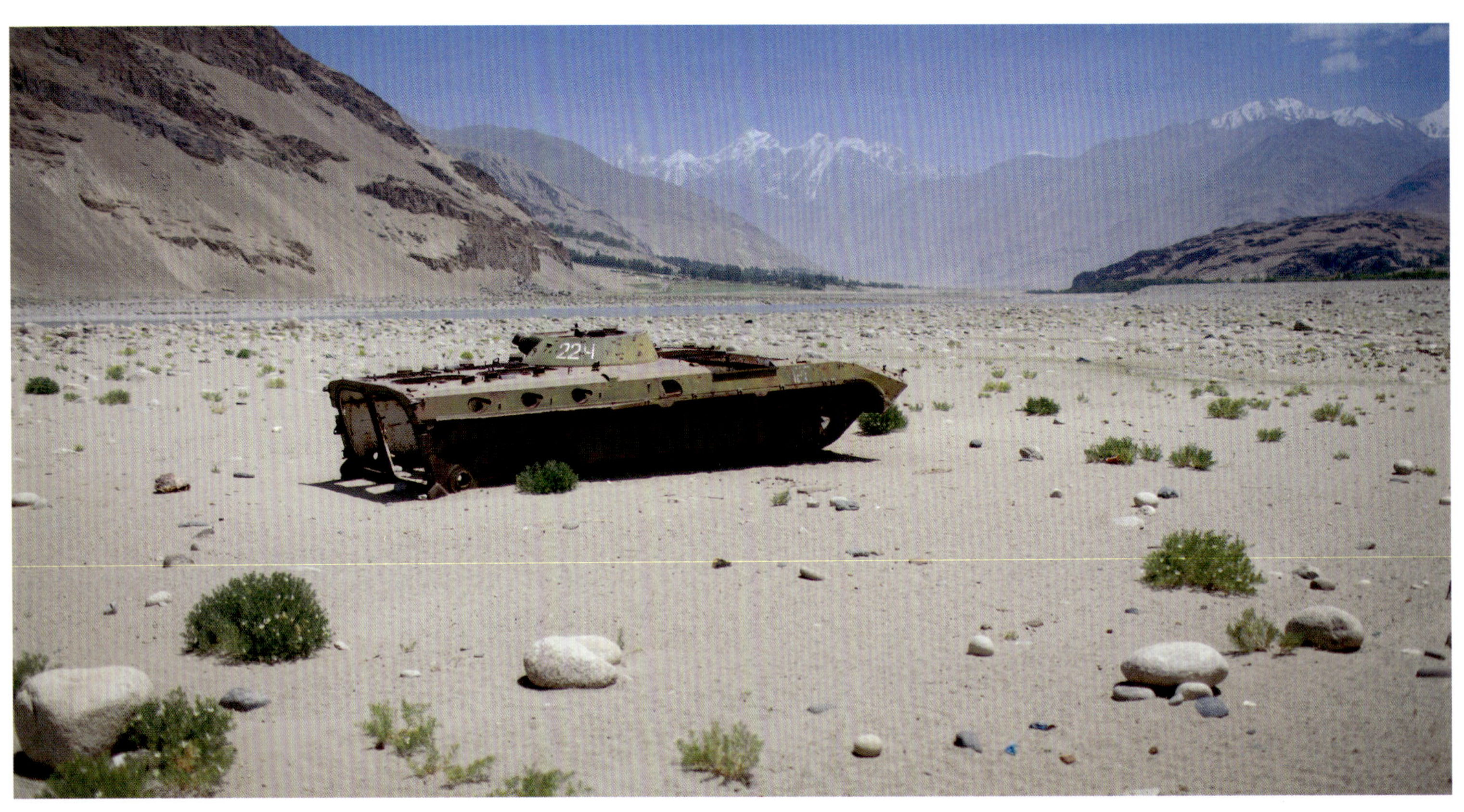

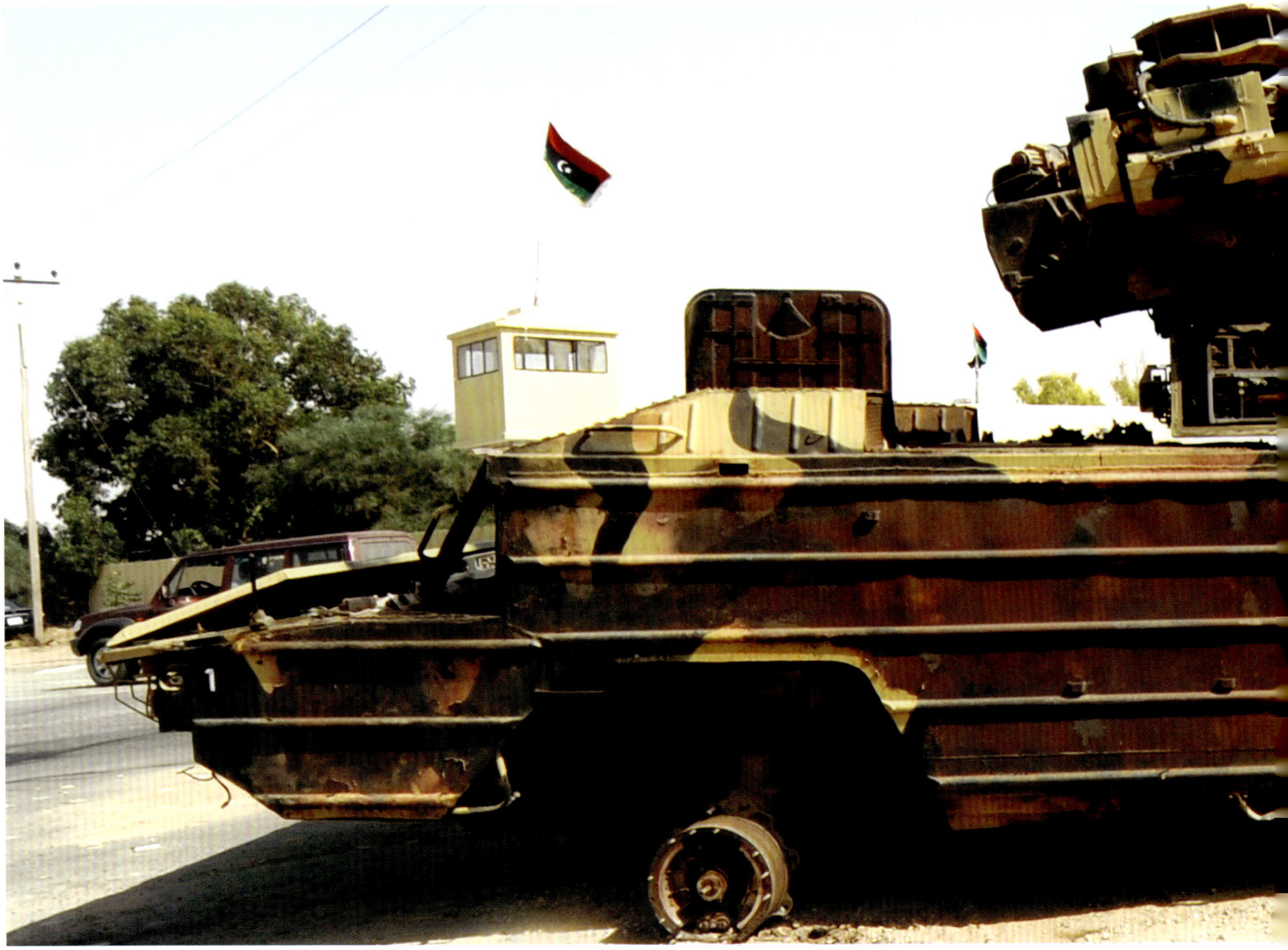

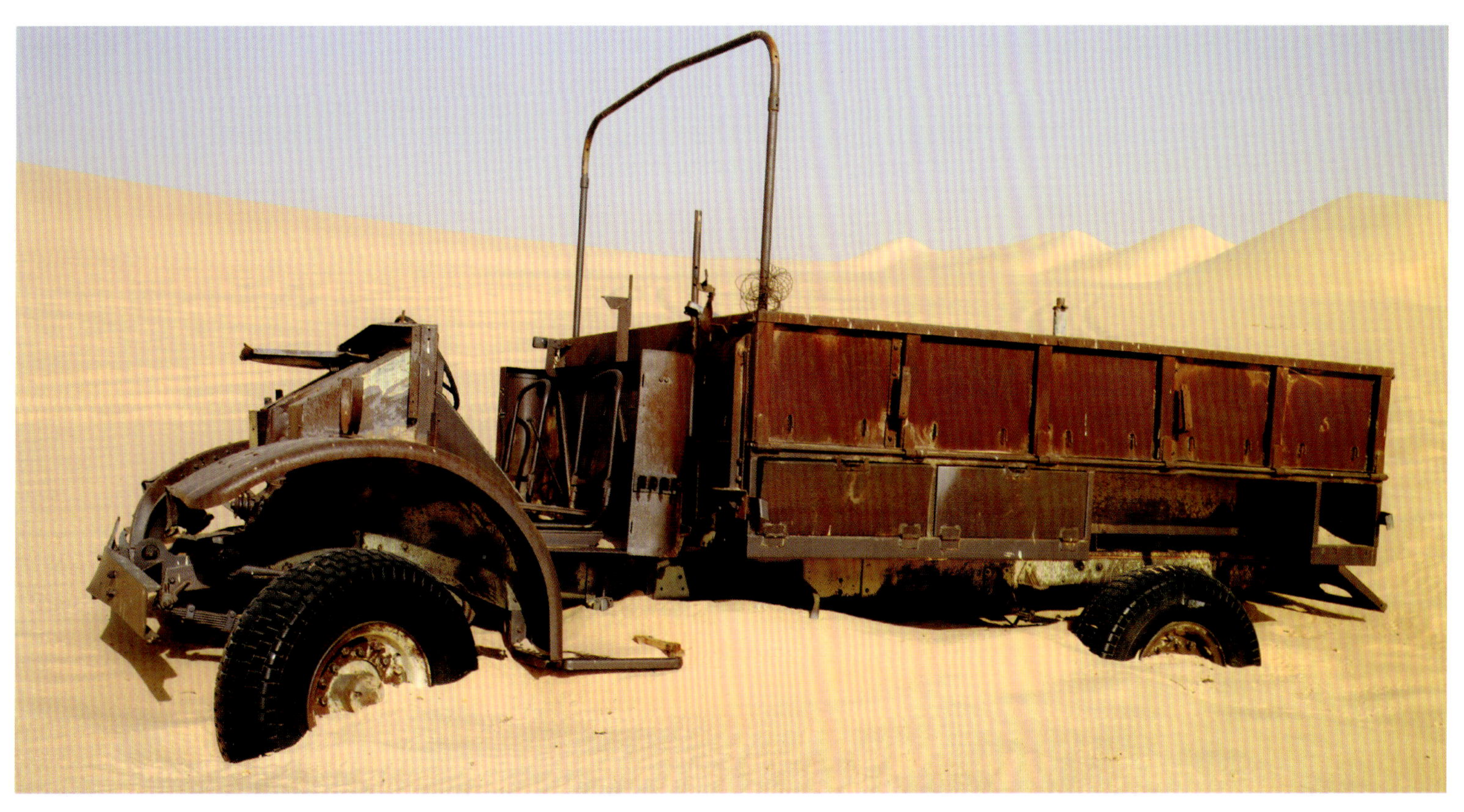

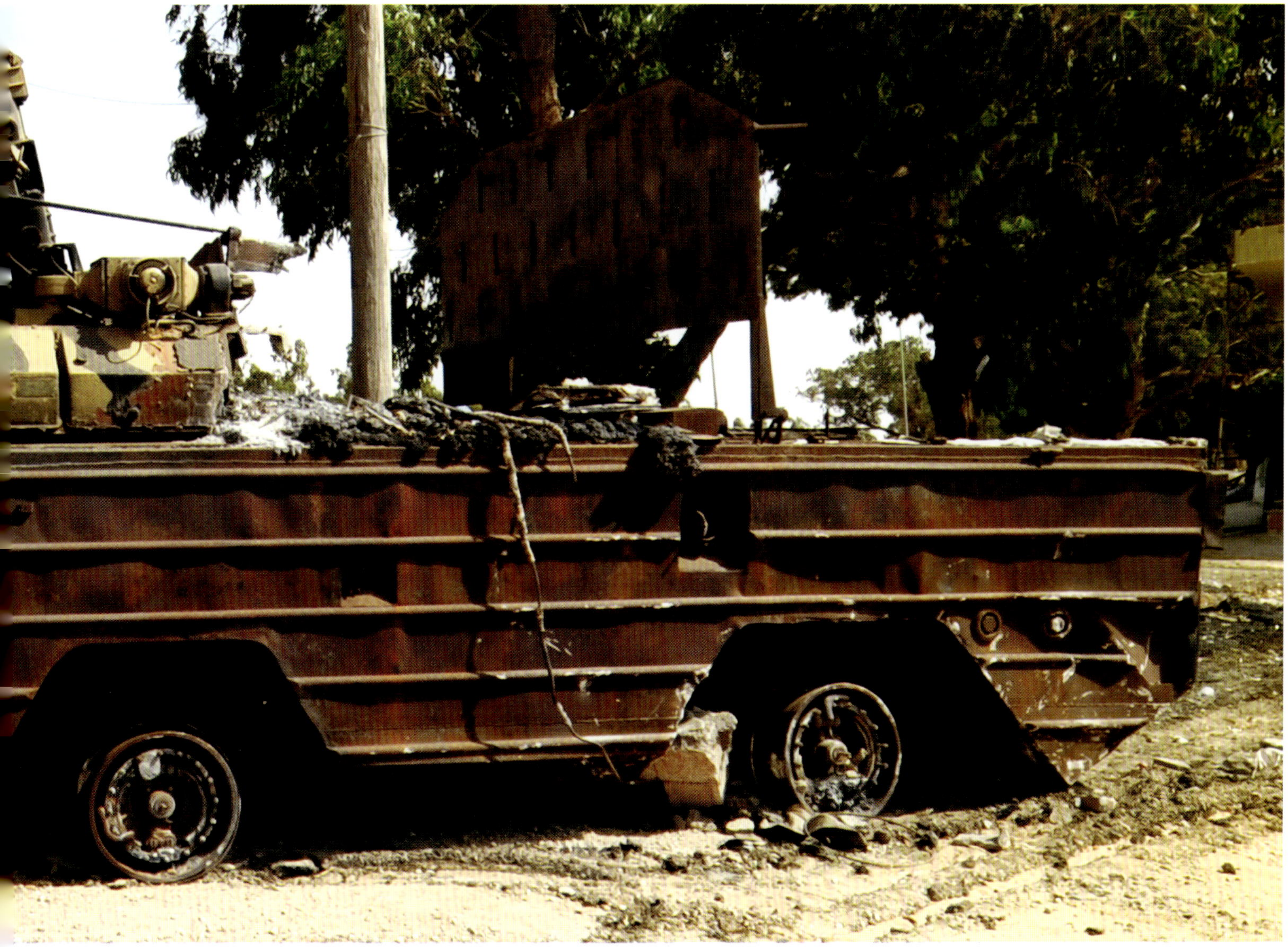

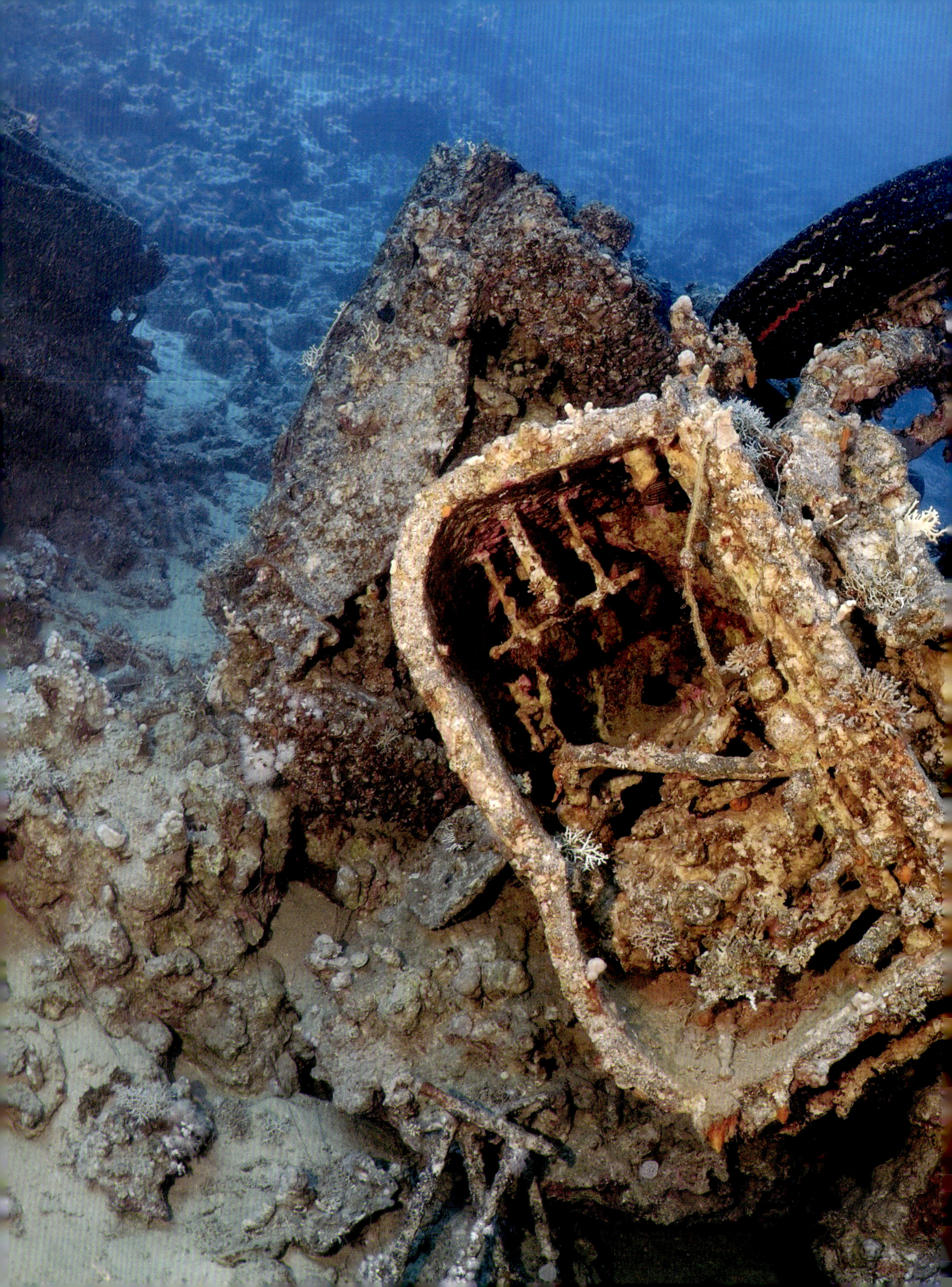

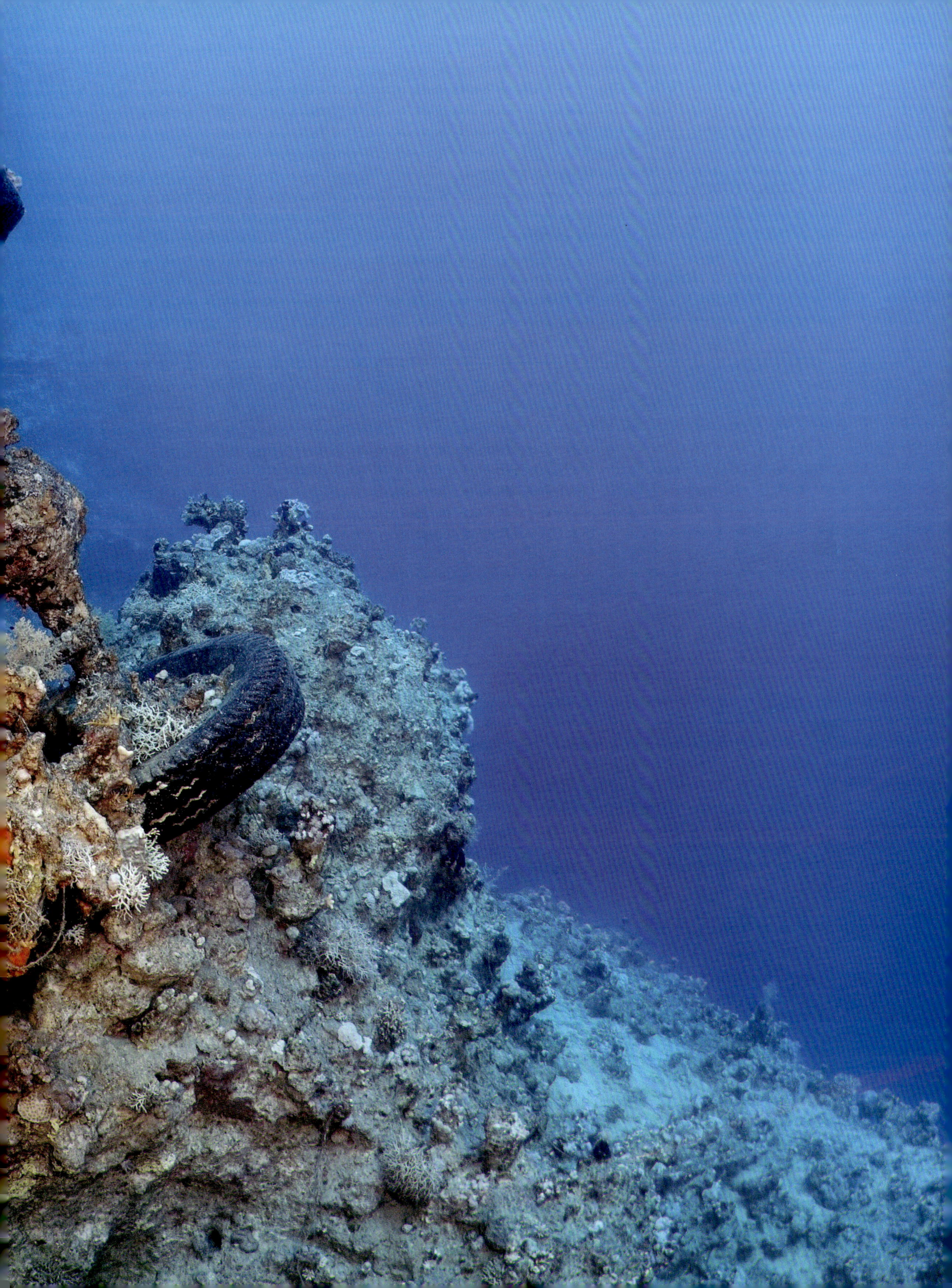

Bedford Truck, Sharm el-Sheikh, Red Sea, off Sinai Peninsula

This rusted Bedford truck sits at a crazy angle on the bottom of the Red Sea, having been dumped there by Egyptian forces during the Suez Crisis of 1956. This truck and many other vehicles were originally sold to Egypt by the UK, but were destroyed (pushed off a cliff into the sea) to prevent them falling into the hands of the advancing Israeli forces.

RIGHT:

Sharm el-Sheikh, Red Sea, off Sinai Peninsula

The numerous vehicles destroyed by Egypt during the Suez Crisis today form a graveyard off the Red Sea coast at Sharm el-Sheikh. Here, amid the Bedford trucks, we can also see British-manufactured Bren Gun Carriers (the tracked vehicles).

OVERLEAF:

TOP LEFT:

Type 95 Light Tank, Betio, Tarawa, Gilbert Islands

The wreck here is that of a Japanese Type 95 light tank, destroyed in the failed attempt to stop US amphibious forces landing on Tarawa on 20 November 1943. These beaches were the location for fighting of quite horrifying intensity – in a thin island only 3.2km (2 miles) long, more than 6,000 soldiers were killed.

BOTTOM LEFT:

M42 Duster Anti-Aircraft Vehicle, Gulf of Aqaba, Red Sea, Jordan

This vehicle is an American-made M42 Duster Anti-Aircraft Vehicle, operated by Jordan in the 1950s and 1960s. It was dropped into the Red Sea as an artificial reef on 1 September 1999 by the Jordanian Royal Ecological Diving Society.

RIGHT:

T-55 Main Battle Tank, near Basra, southern Iraq

This Iraqi T-55 was discovered at an abandoned Iraqi base by members of 2 Close Support Regiment, Royal Logistical Corps, while patrolling to the west of Basra, southern Iraq, in April 2003. It is in a large trench, dug to protect the vehicle from observation and gunfire, although not from overhead air strikes, which destroyed much of the Iraqi defences in 2003.

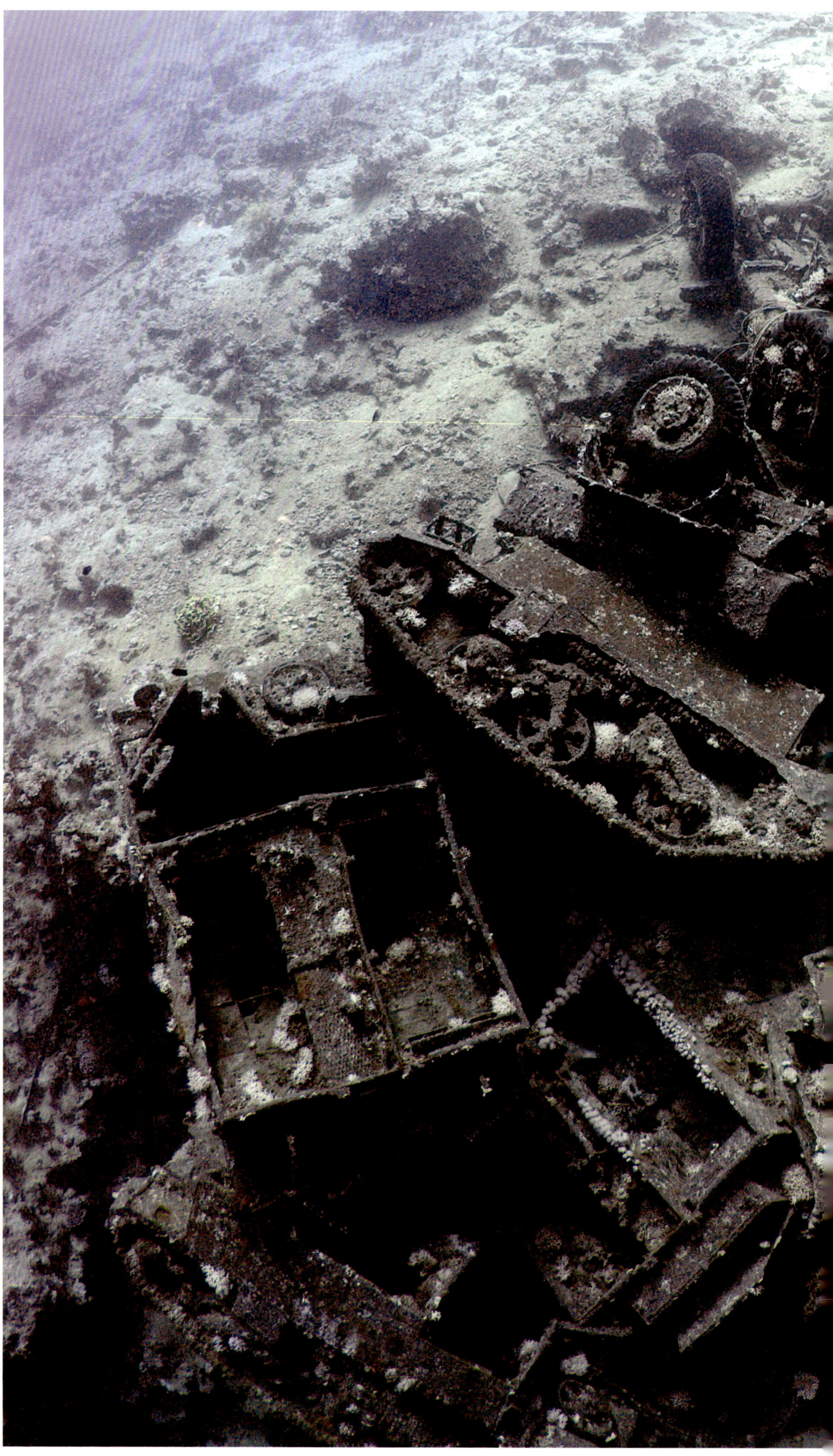

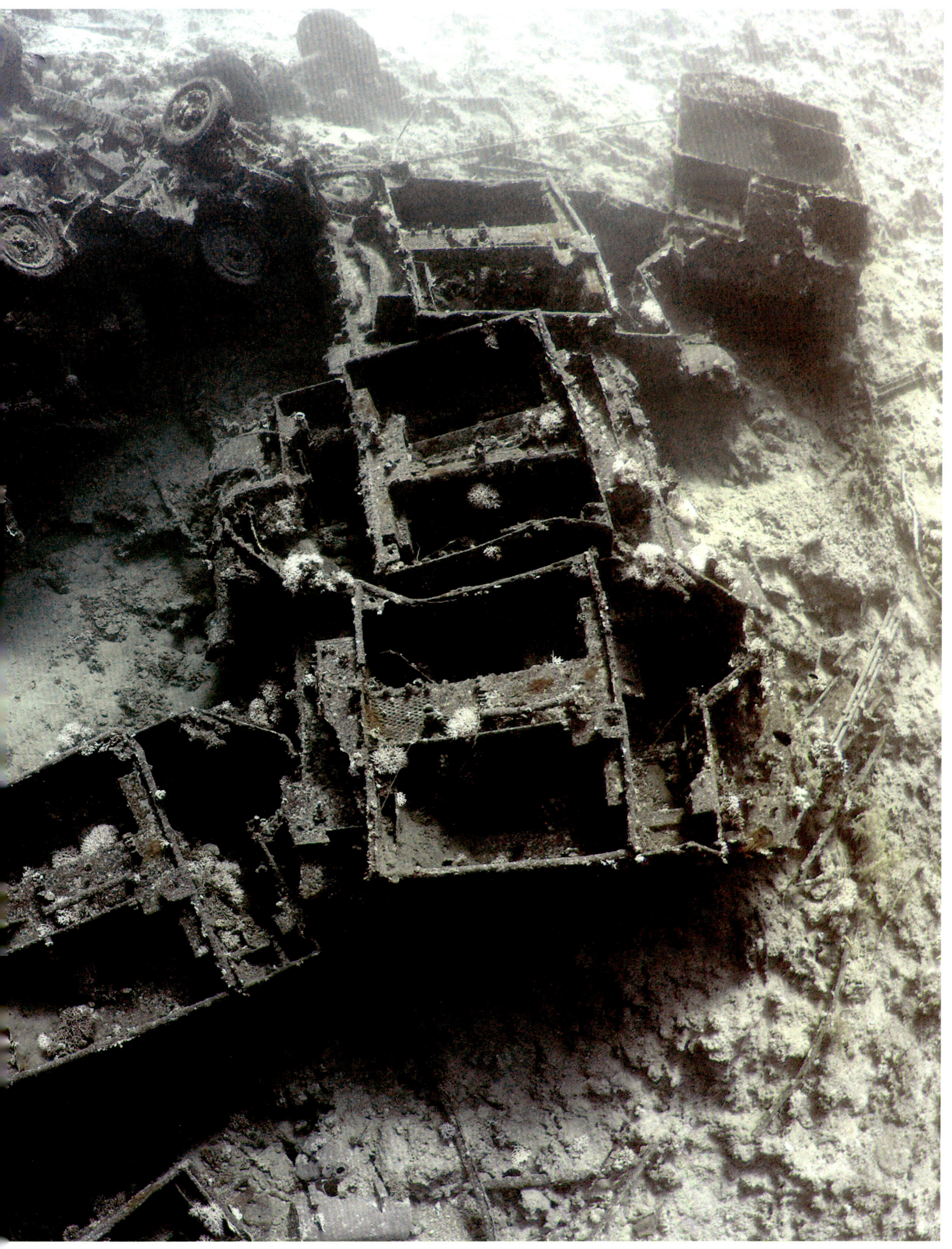

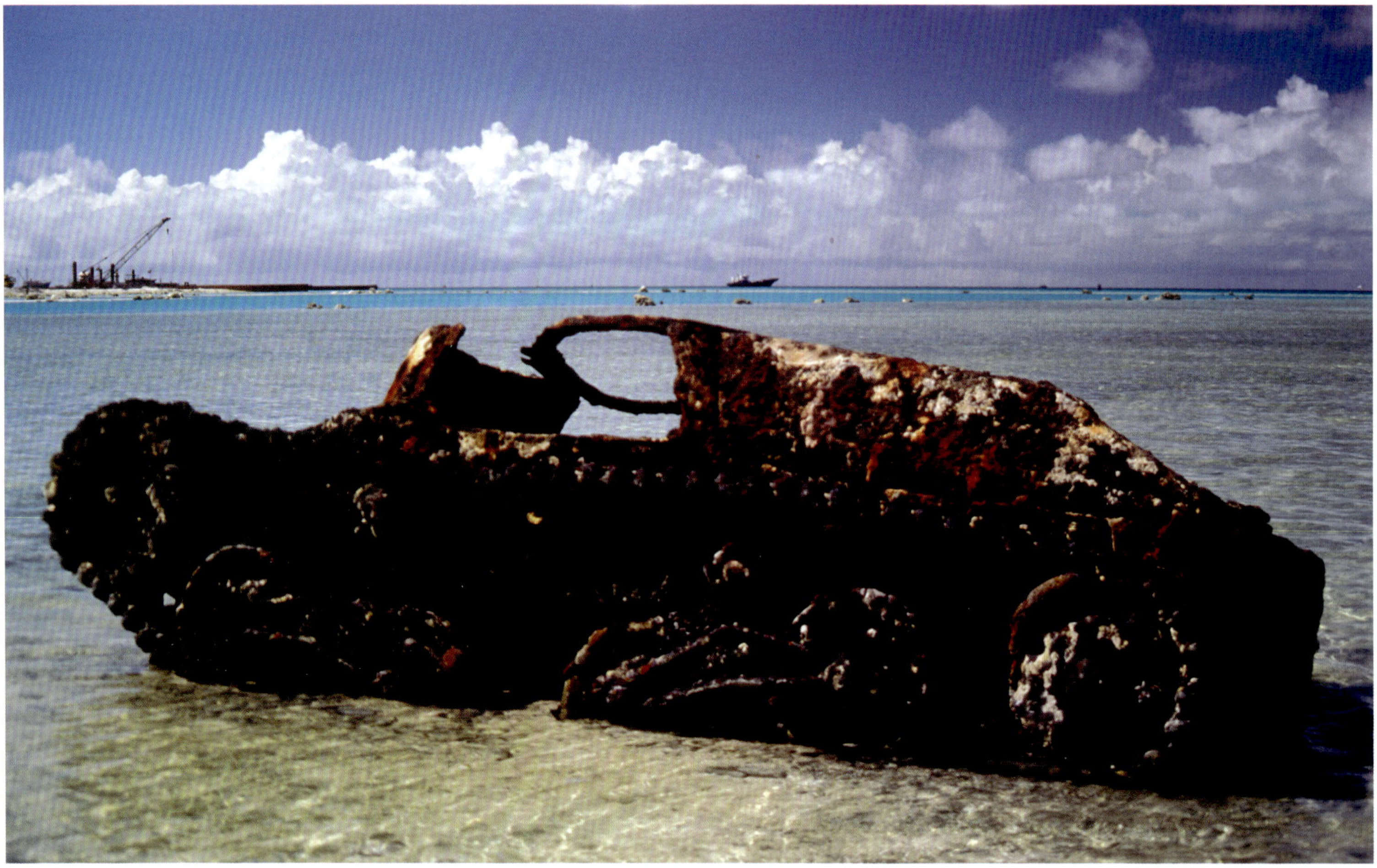

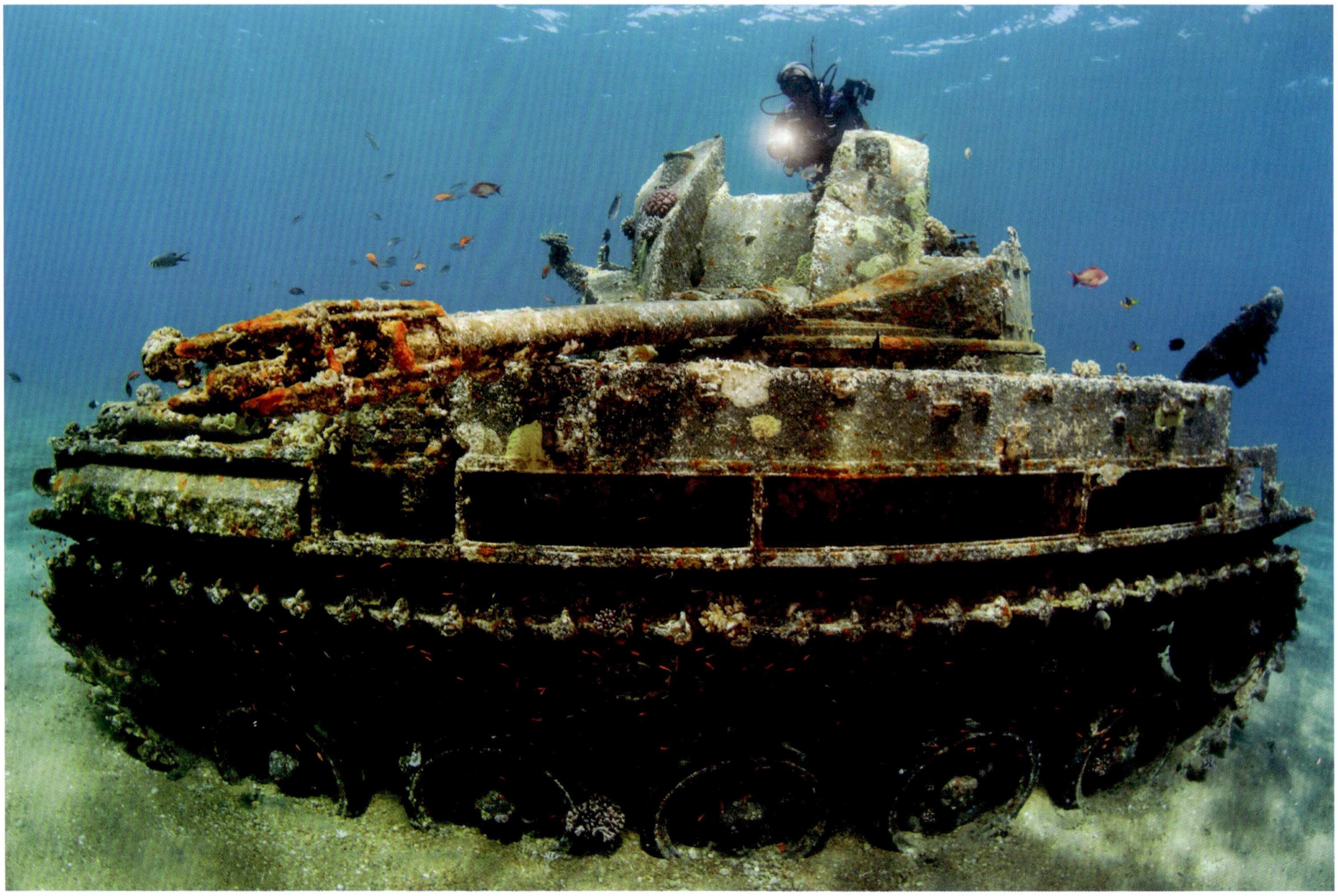

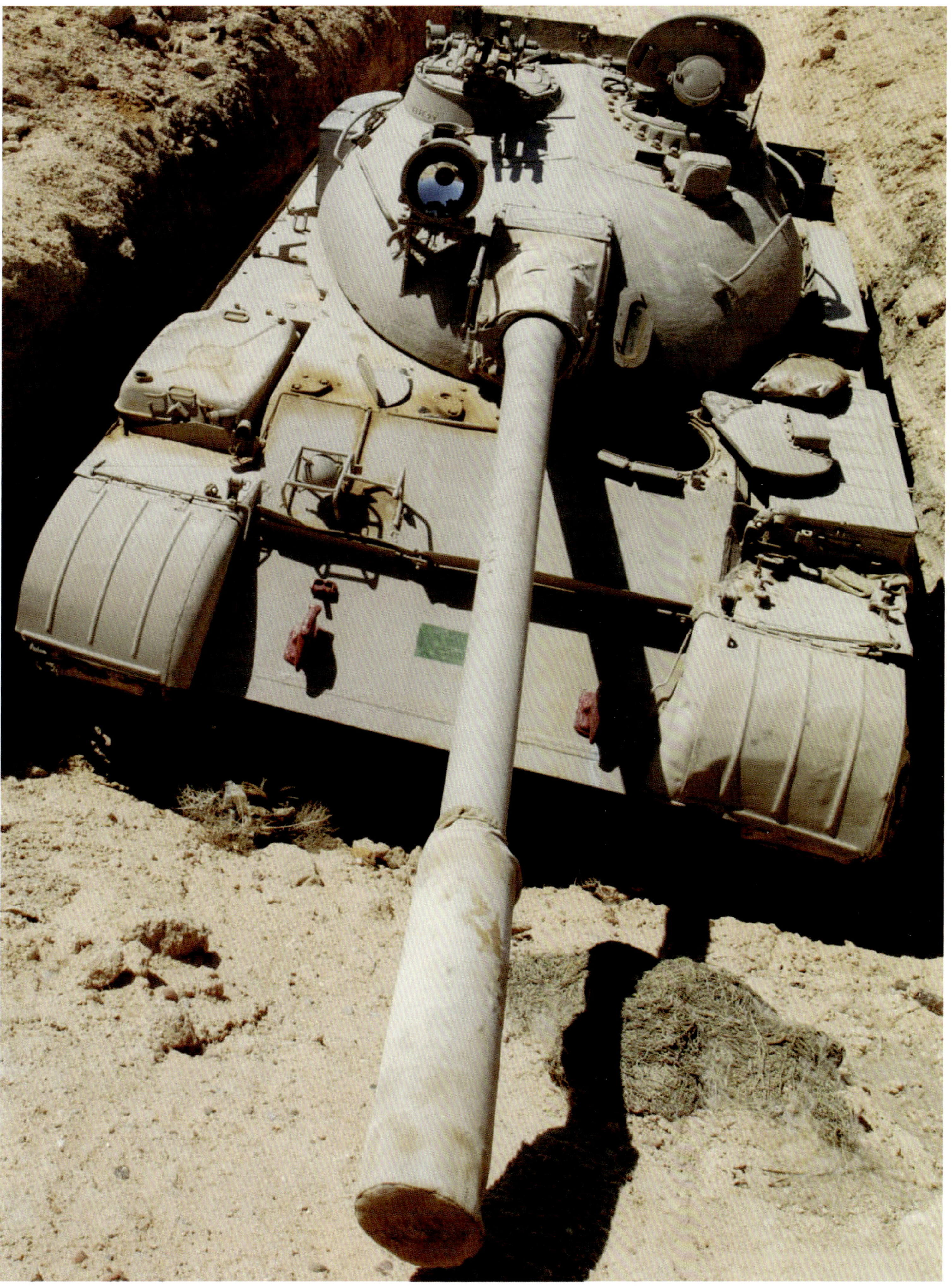

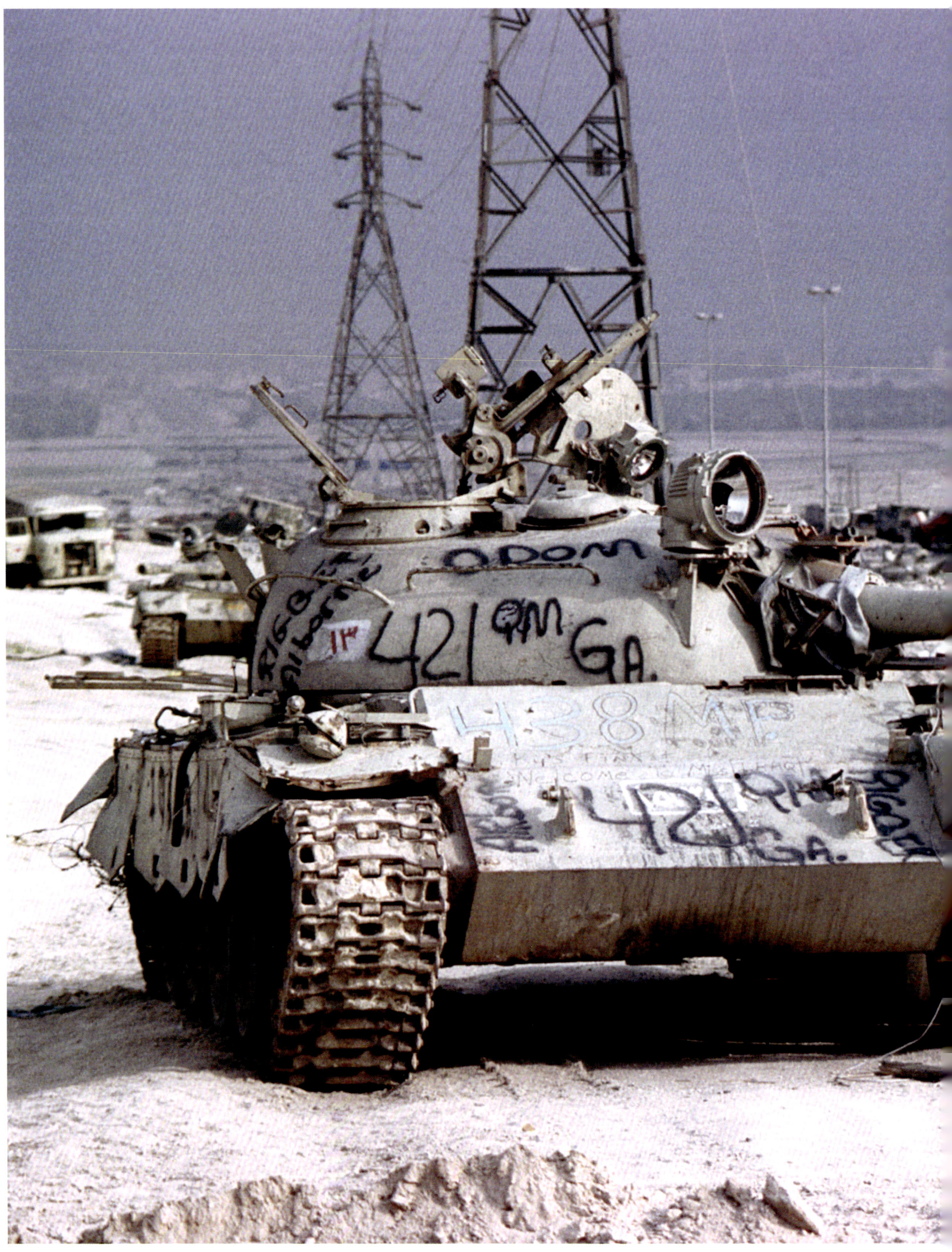
ODOM
421 OM GA.
438 MP
421 OM GA.

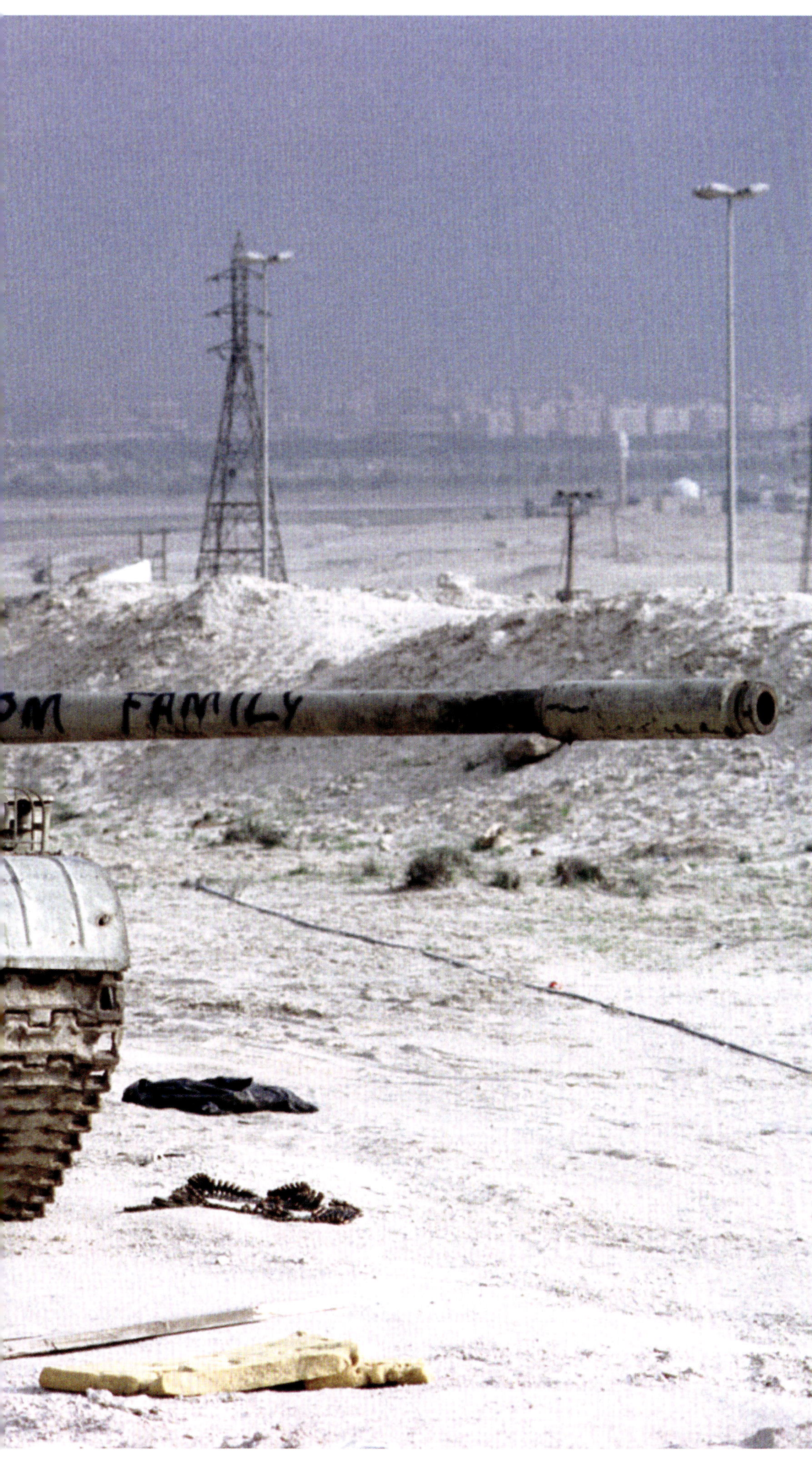

T-55 Main Battle Tank, Highway 80, Kuwait City, Kuwait
One of the many Iraqi T-55 tanks that were abandoned or destroyed along the 'Highway of Death' in Kuwait in 1991. Iraq's armoured force was severely depleted following the 1990–91 Gulf War. Wrecks frequently attract graffiti in war zone areas, typically daubed in political or racial slogans by the winning side.

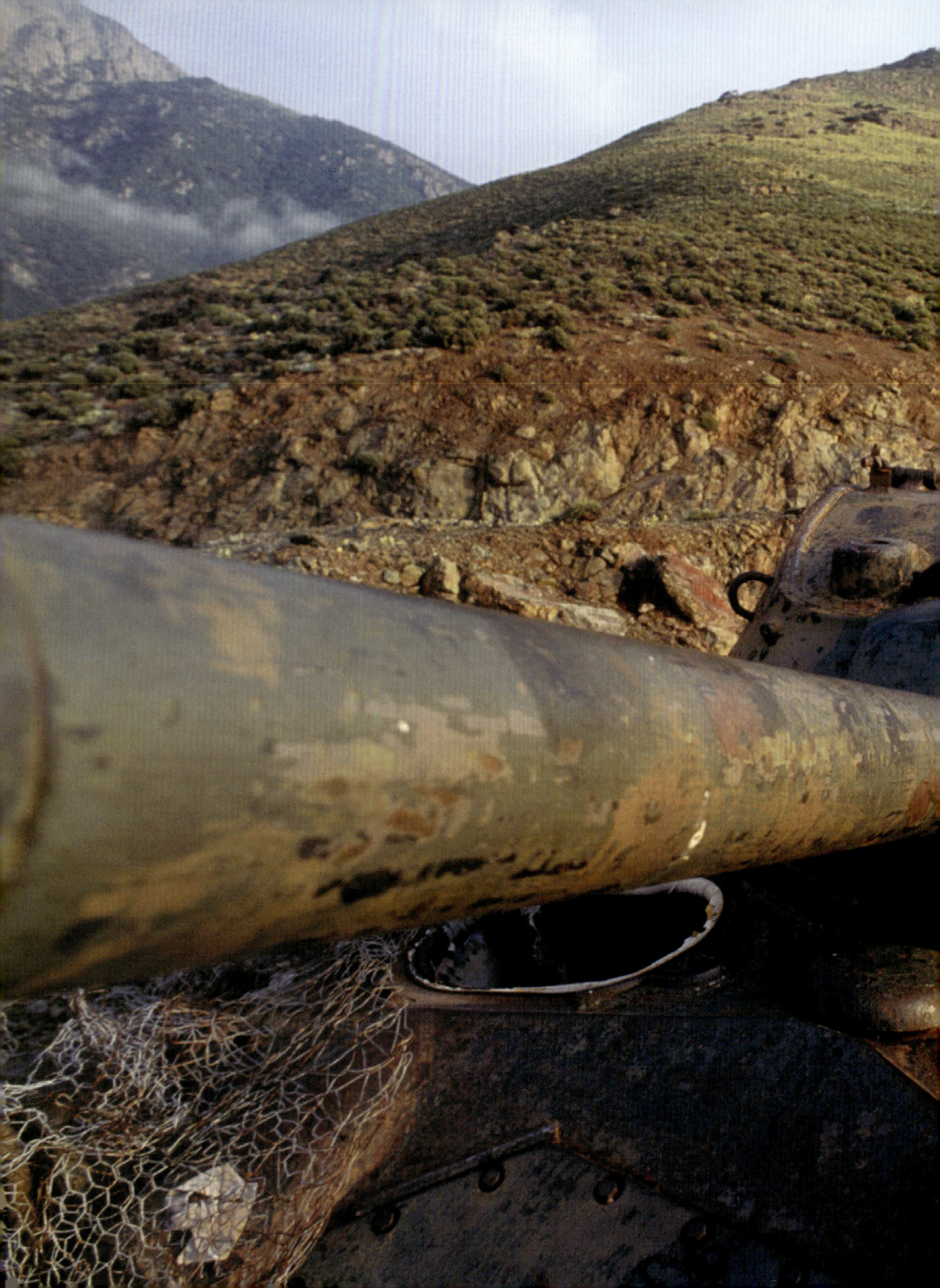

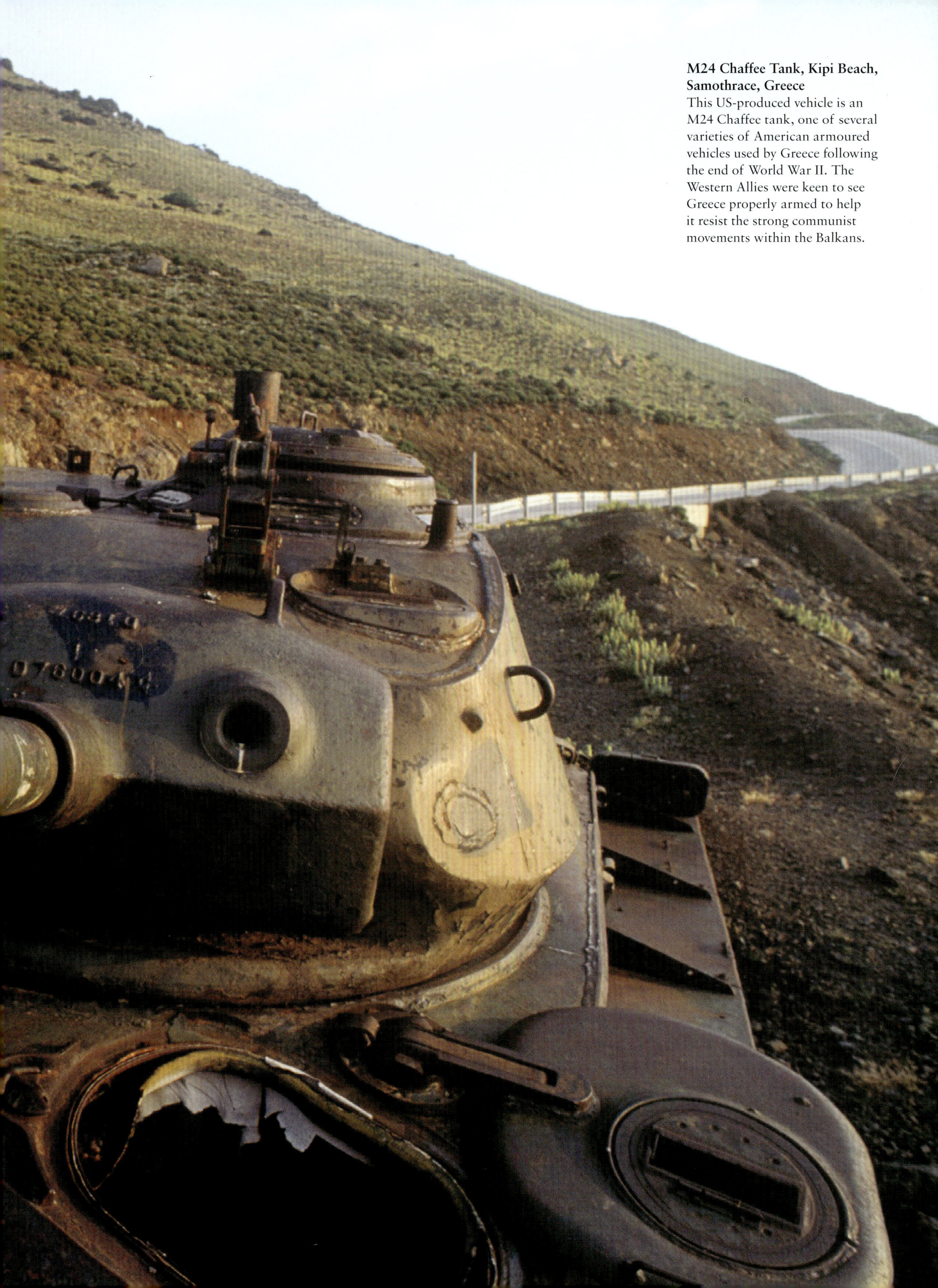

M24 Chaffee Tank, Kipi Beach, Samothrace, Greece
This US-produced vehicle is an M24 Chaffee tank, one of several varieties of American armoured vehicles used by Greece following the end of World War II. The Western Allies were keen to see Greece properly armed to help it resist the strong communist movements within the Balkans.

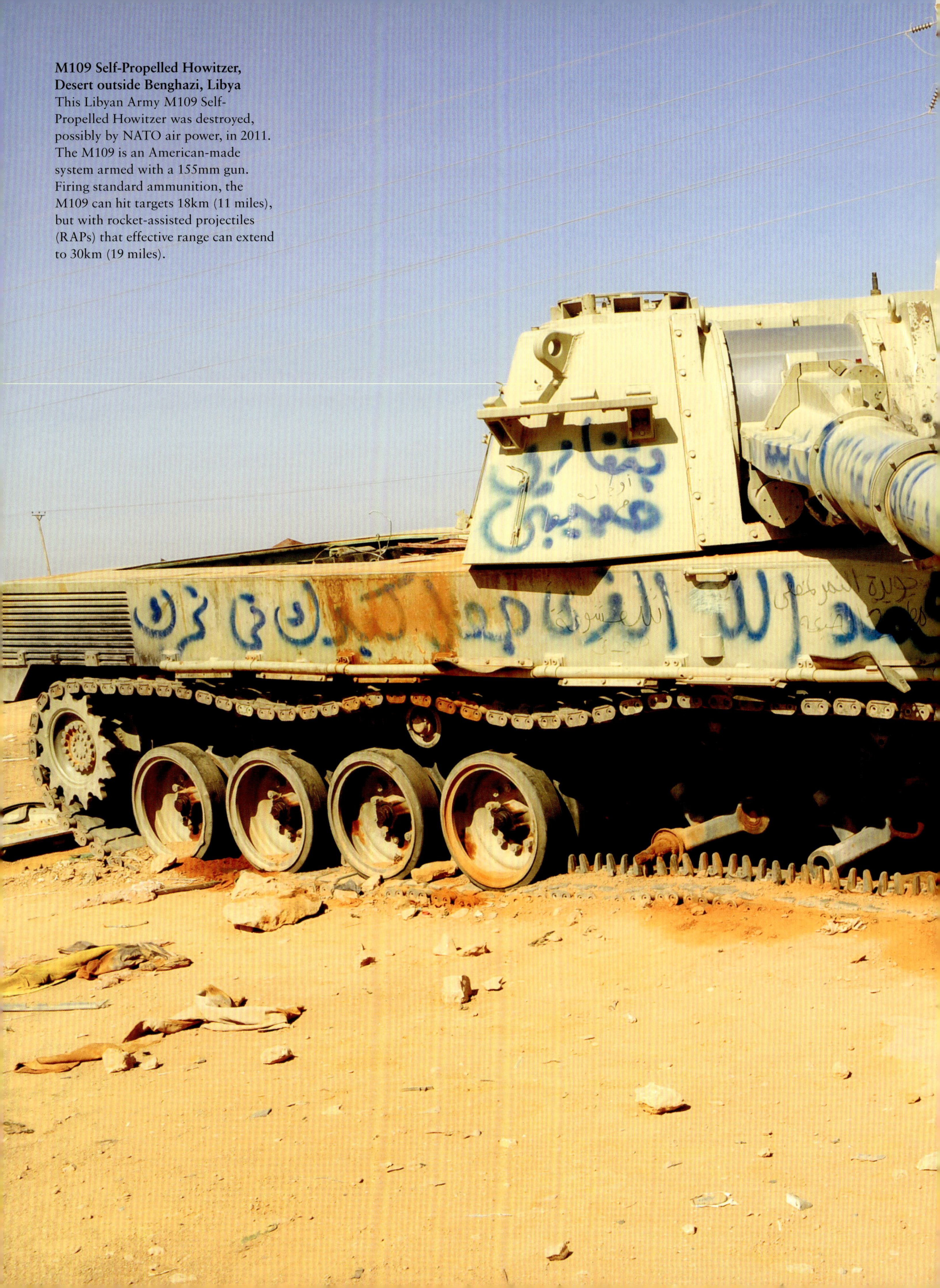

**M109 Self-Propelled Howitzer,
Desert outside Benghazi, Libya**
This Libyan Army M109 Self-
Propelled Howitzer was destroyed,
possibly by NATO air power, in 2011.
The M109 is an American-made
system armed with a 155mm gun.
Firing standard ammunition, the
M109 can hit targets 18km (11 miles),
but with rocket-assisted projectiles
(RAPs) that effective range can extend
to 30km (19 miles).

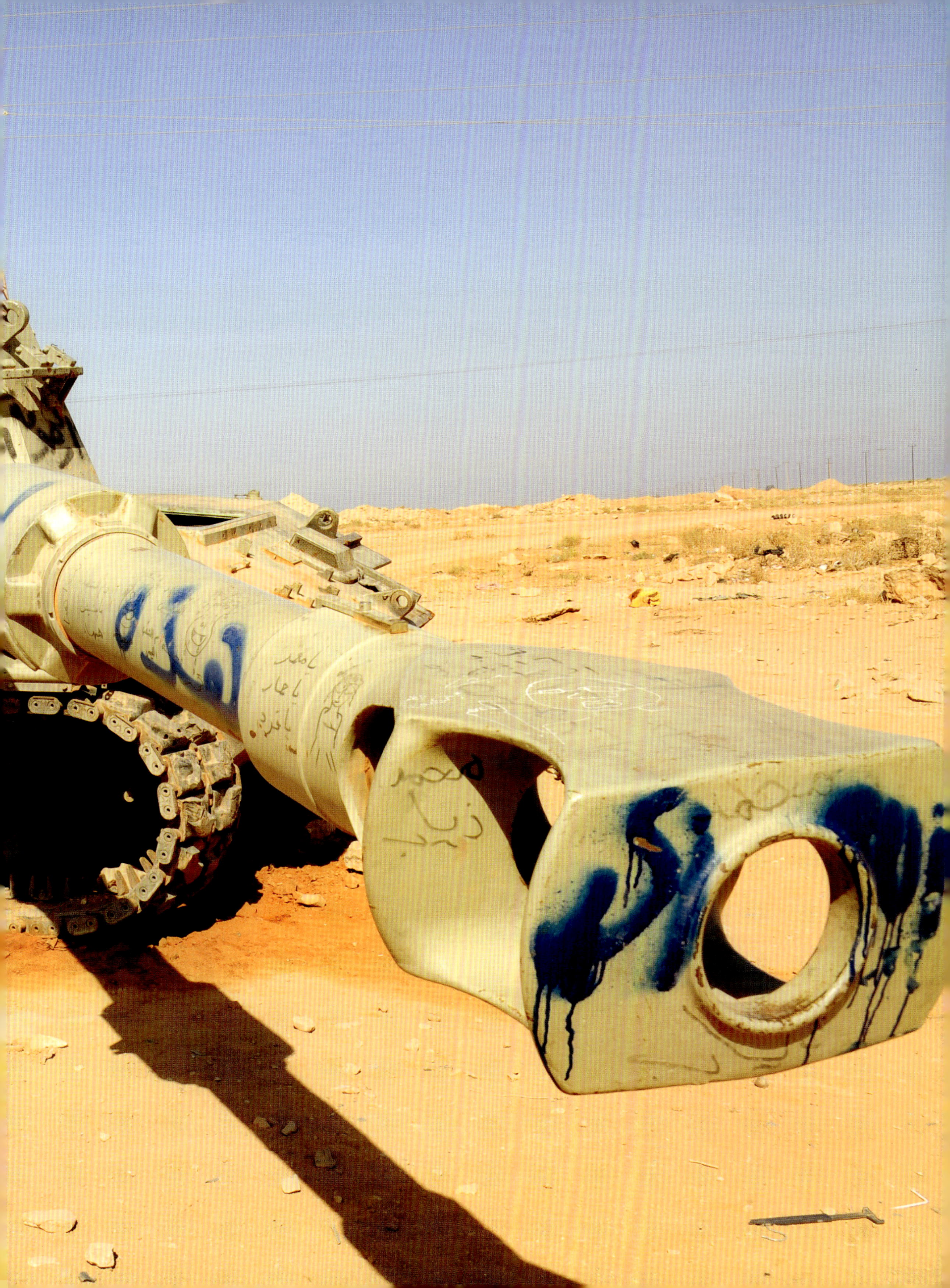

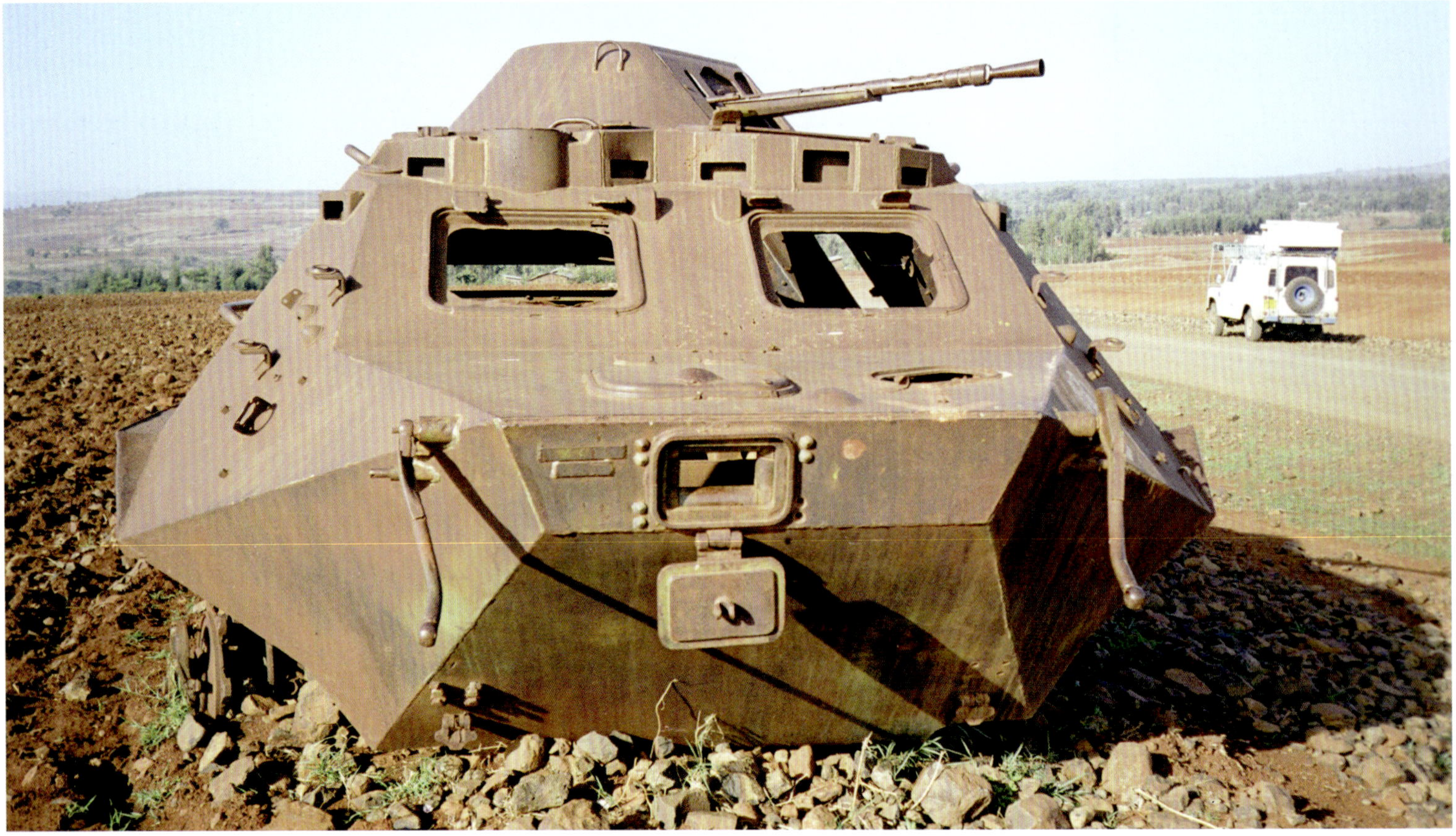

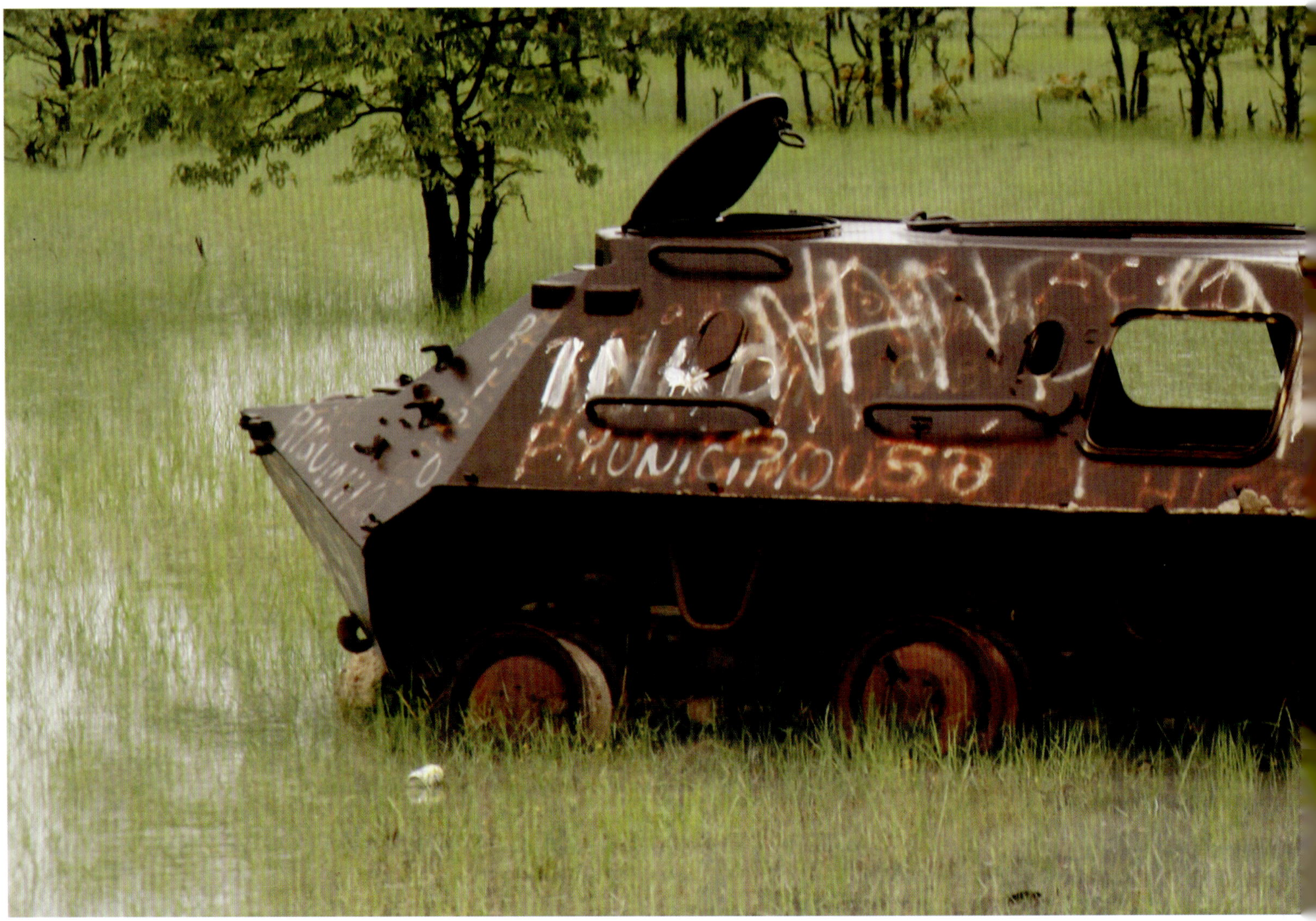

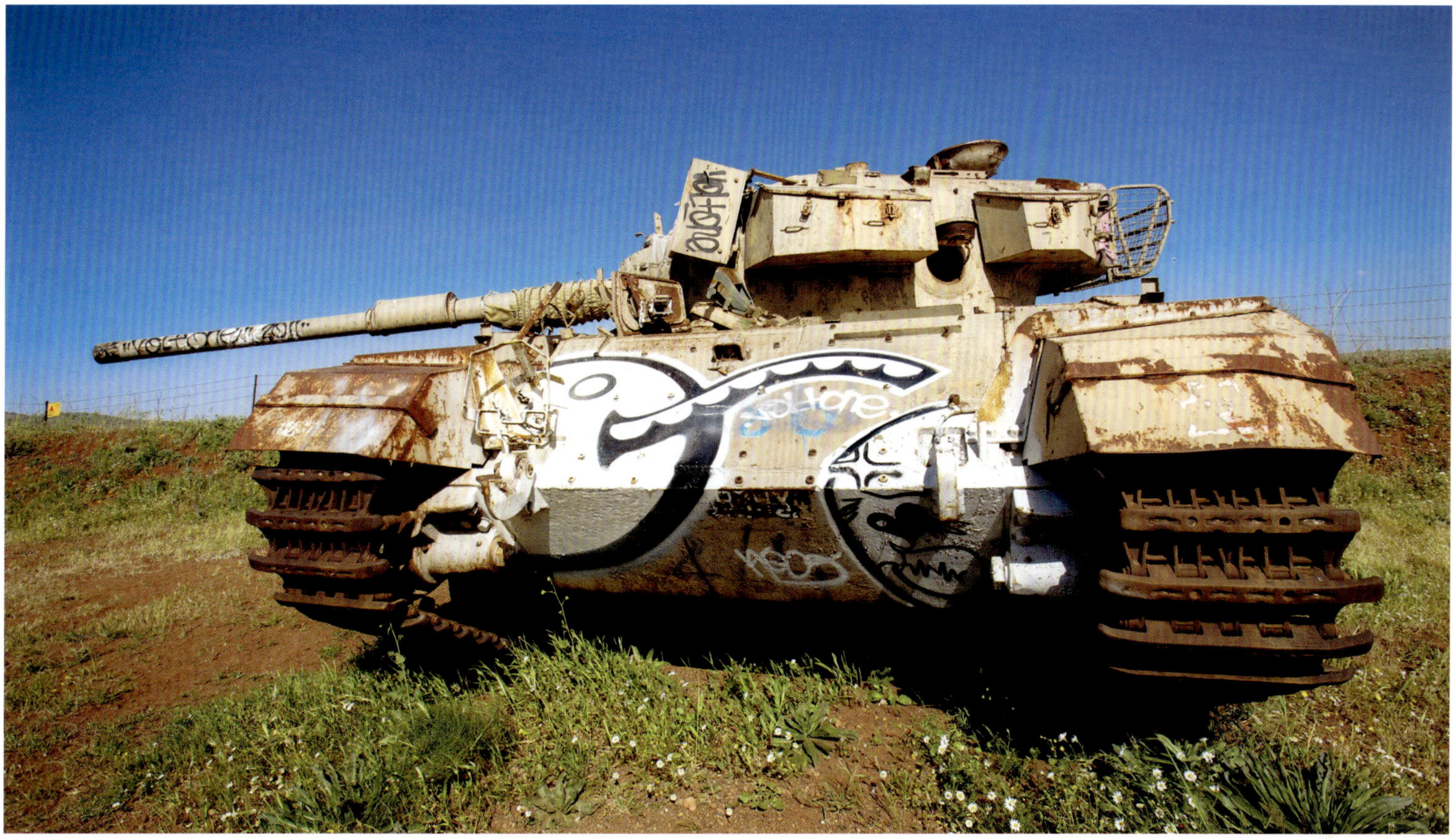

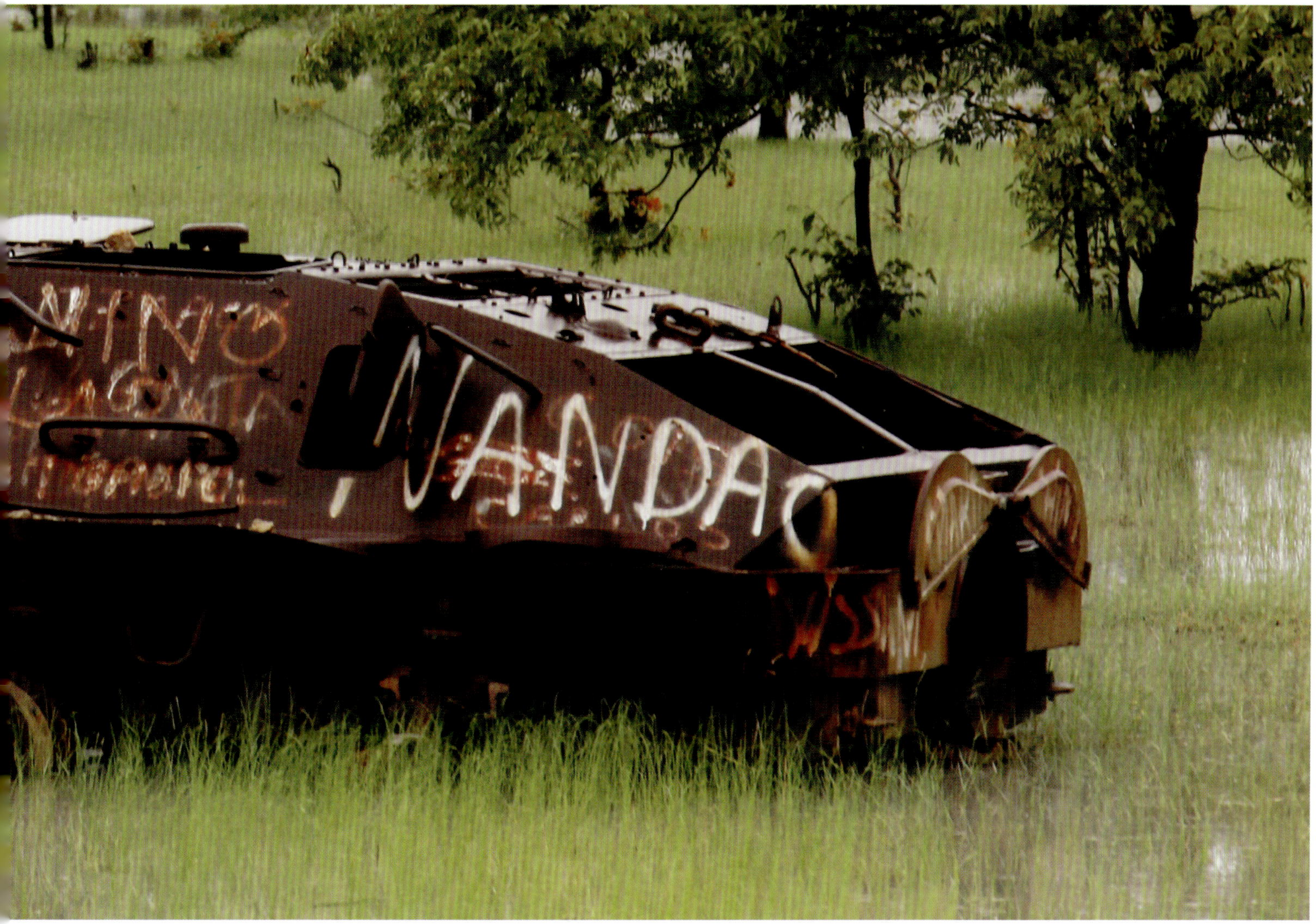

NANDA

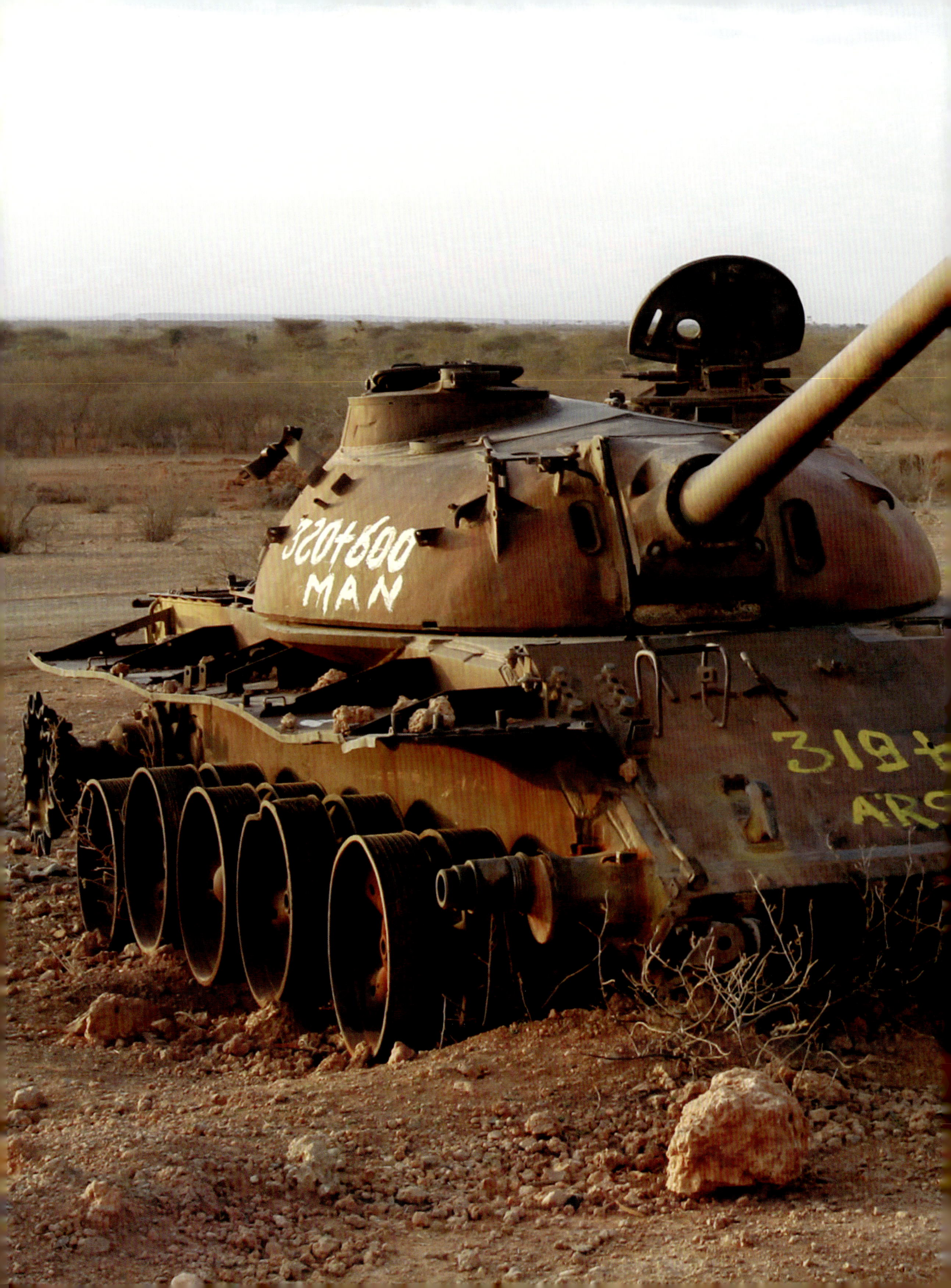
3204600
MAN
319%
AR

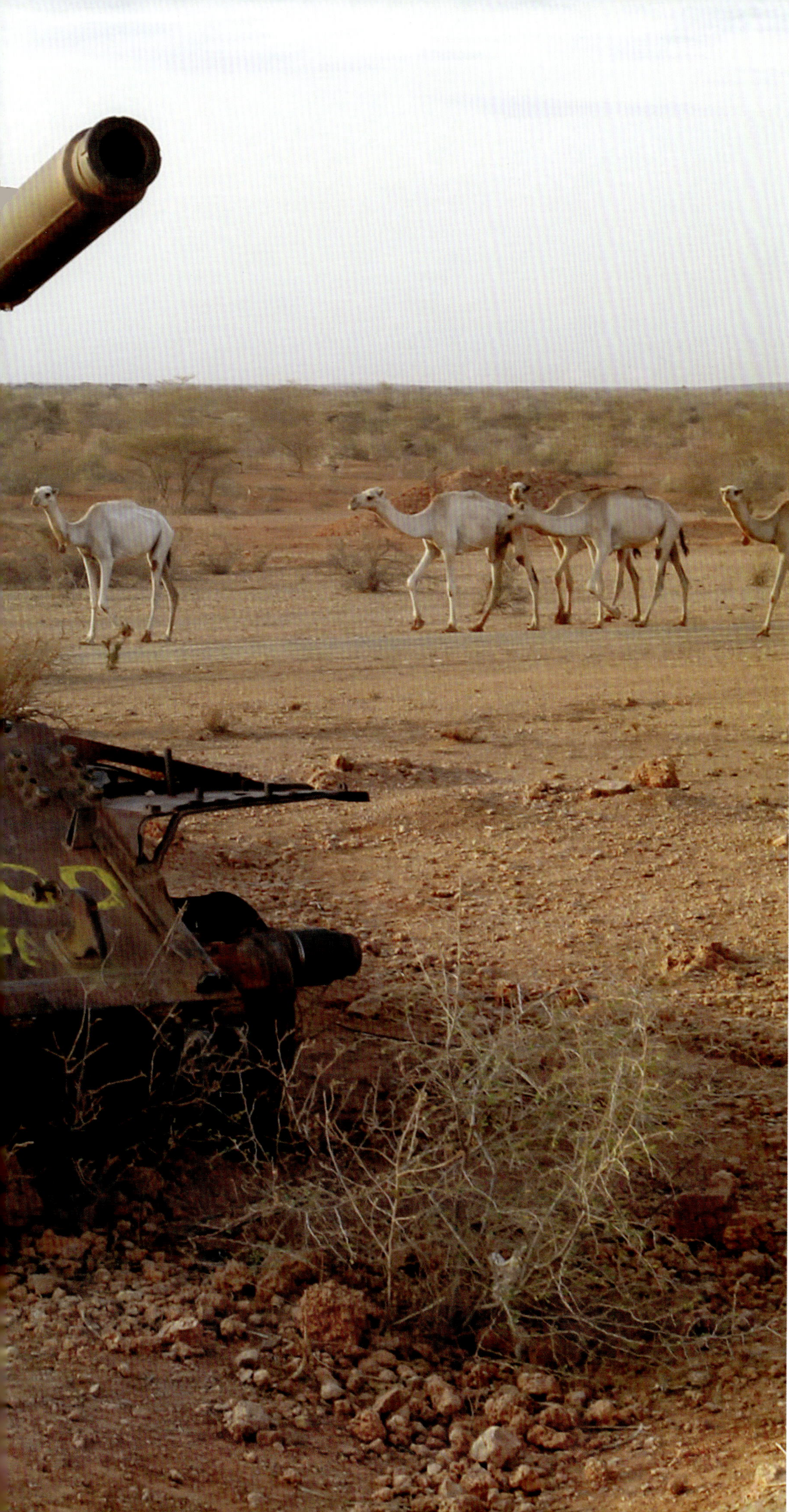

TOP LEFT:

BTR-60 Armoured Personnel Carrier, Federal Democratic Republic of Ethiopia

Since 1945, Ethiopia has historically relied heavily on Soviet/Russian military vehicles for its armed forces, and many of these vehicles have been destroyed in the country's internecine conflicts. The wreck here is that of a BTR-60, an eight-wheeled armoured personnel carrier (APC) fitted with a 14.5mm KPVT heavy machine gun in its turret.

BOTTOM:

BTR-60 Armoured Personnel Carrier, Cunene Province, Angola

The Angolan Civil War lasted from 1975 until 2002, and was one of the bloodiest conflicts on the African continent, costing more than 500,000 lives. Equipment from the war still litters the bush, such as this BTR-60 infantry fighting vehicle (IFV).

TOP RIGHT:

Sho't Tank, Golan Heights, Israel

This Israeli Defense Forces (IDF) Sho't tank stands on the Golan Heights, a reminder of the intense tank battle that took place there during the 1973 Yom Kippur War. The Sho't was essentially a British Centurion tank, upgraded for Israeli service.

LEFT:

T-55 Tank, Dolo Ado, near the Ethiopia–Somalia border

Camels stroll past the wreckage of a T-55 tank in the scrublands of Ethiopia. In total during the Cold War era, Ethiopia purchased more than 1,200 T-55 tanks from the Soviet Bloc, as well as hundreds of other armoured vehicles that helped sustain the country's periodic conflicts.

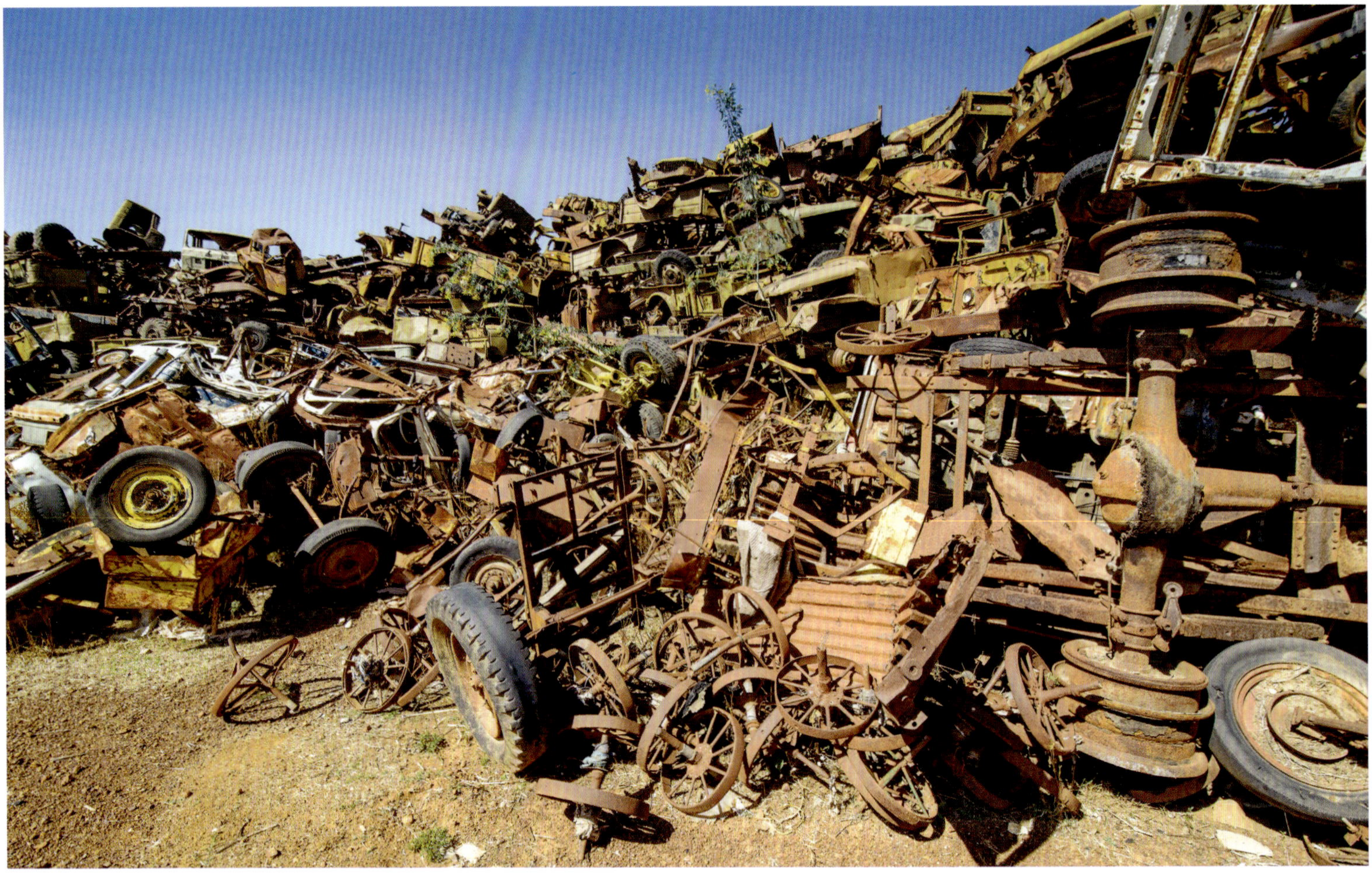

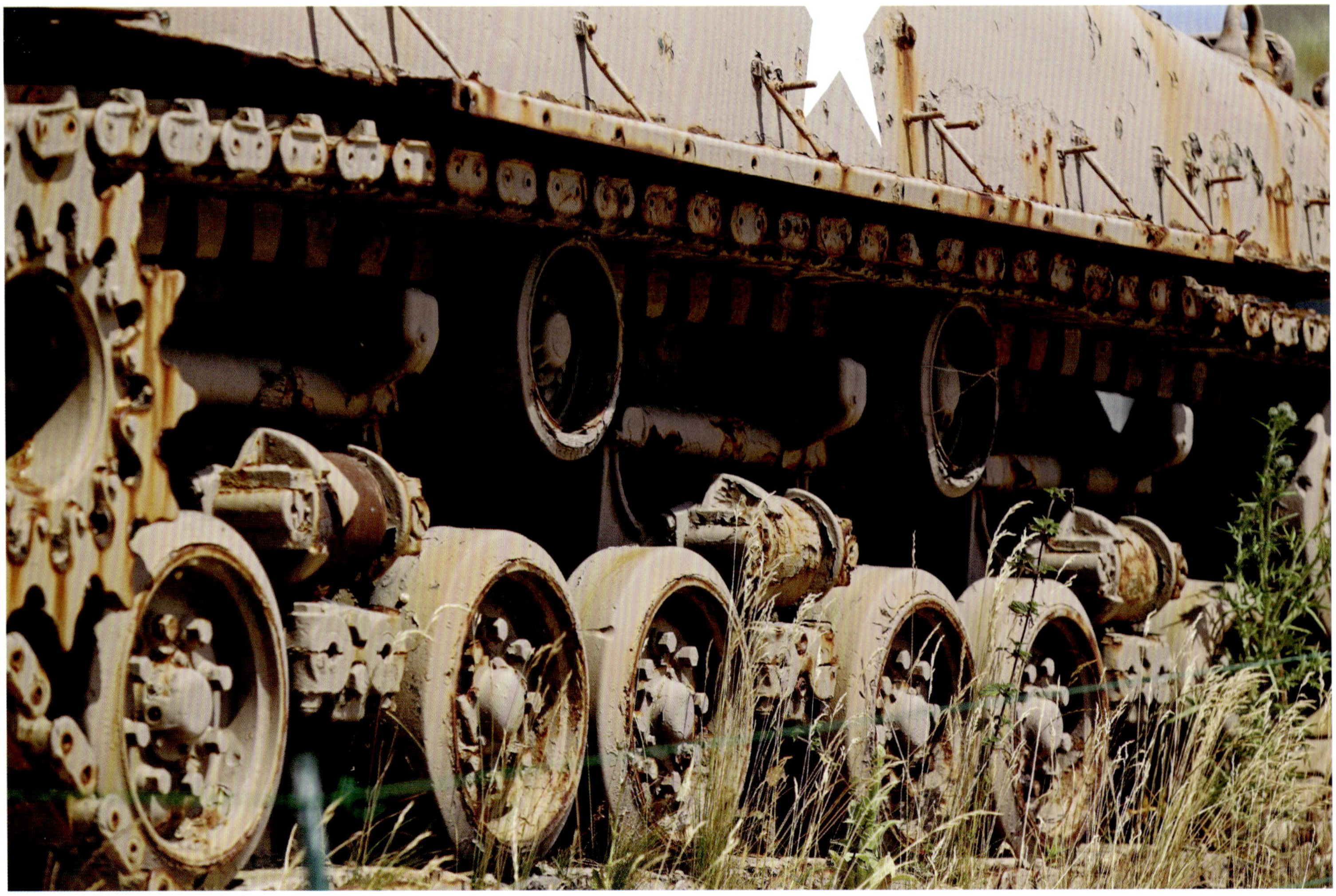

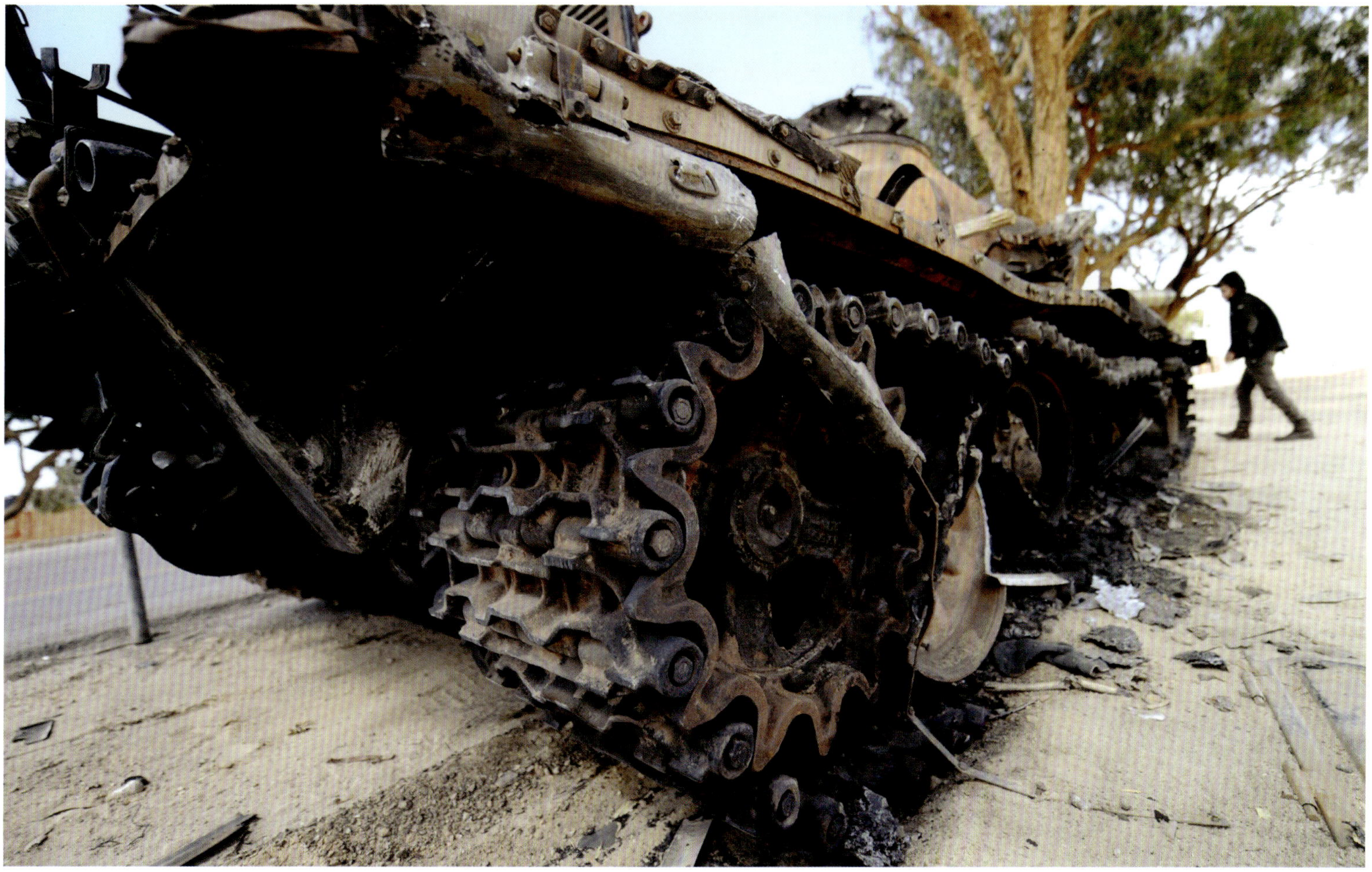

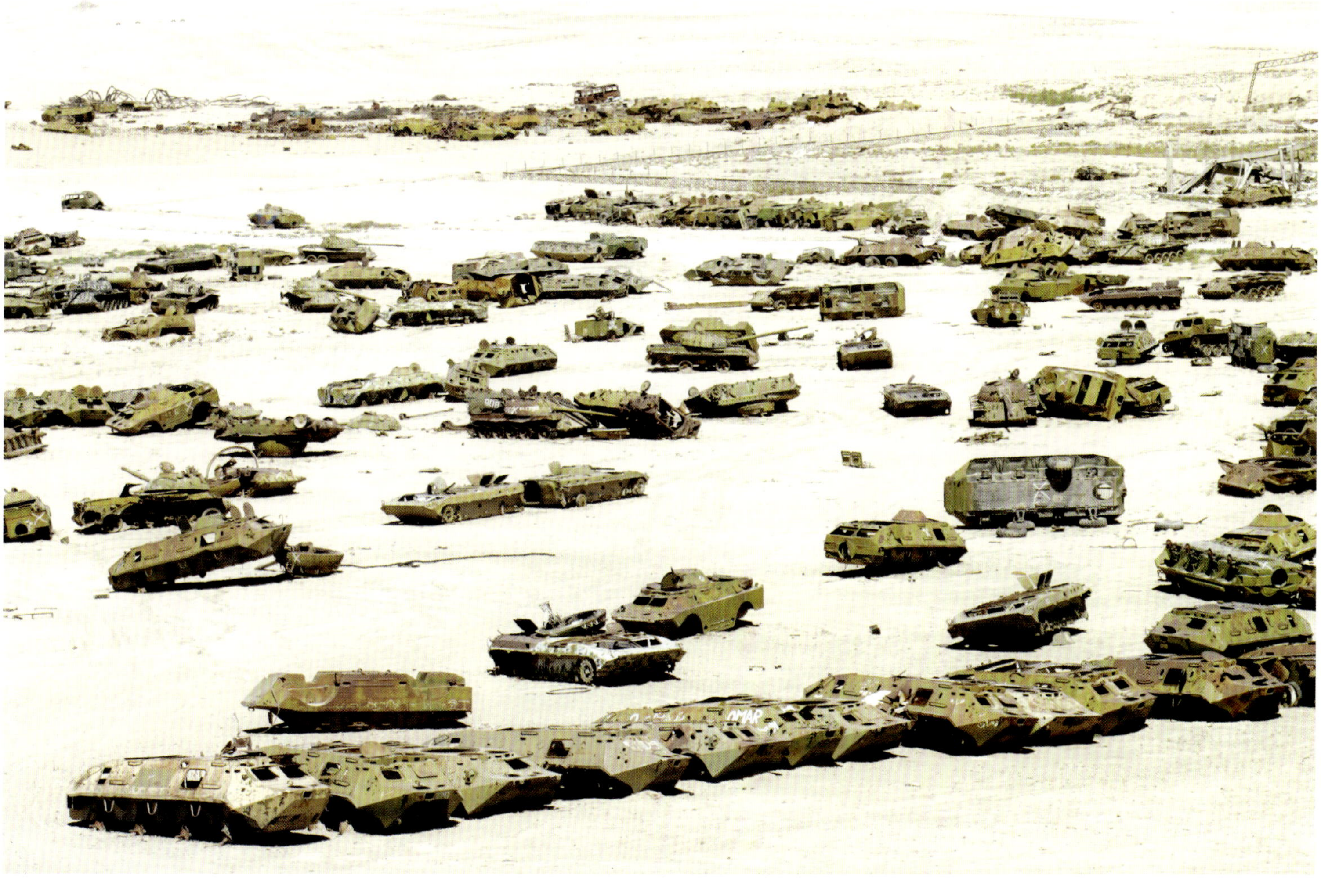

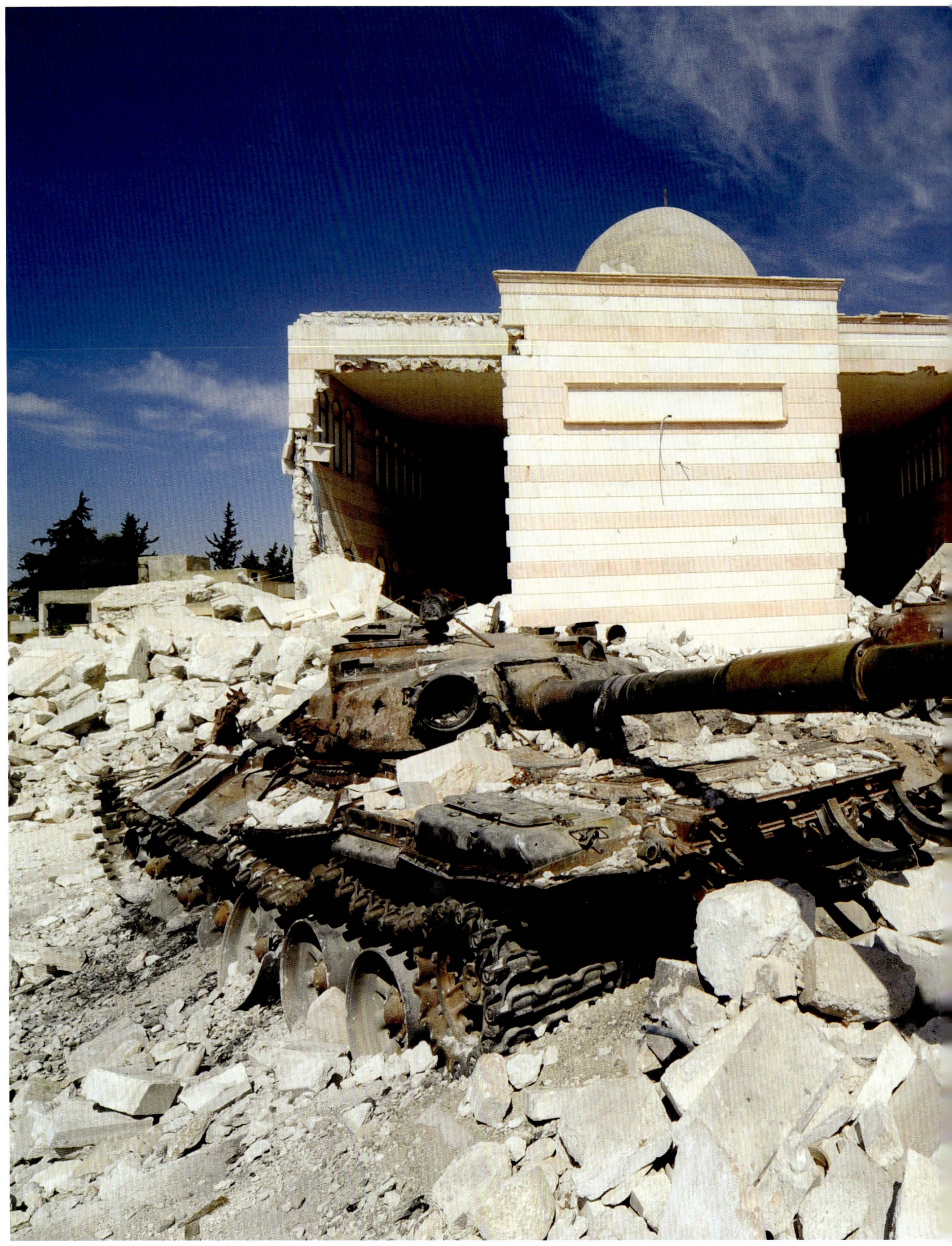

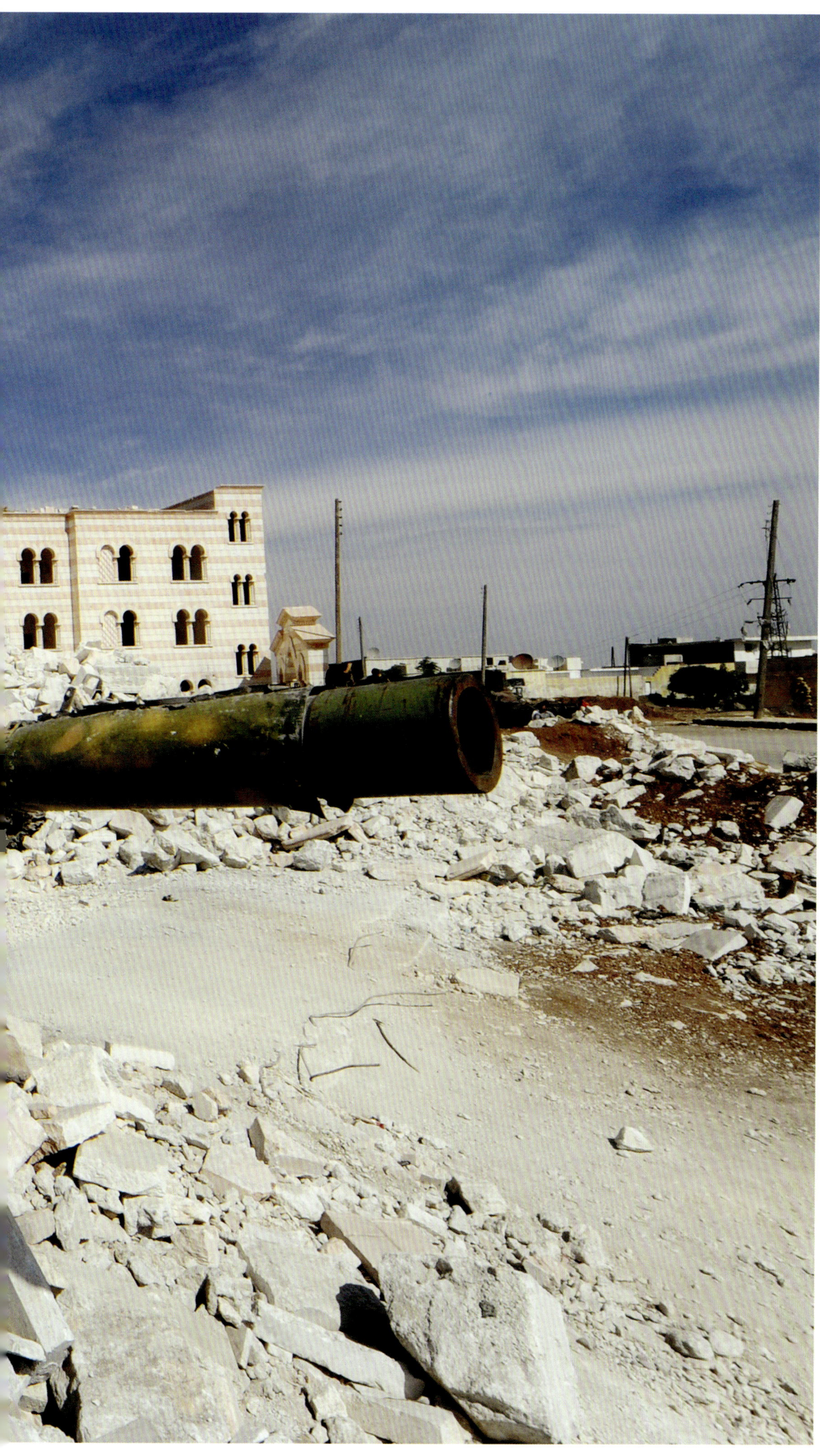

PREVIOUS PAGE:

TOP LEFT:

Asmara, Eritrea
A vehicle cemetery in Eritrea, containing a mixture of military and civilian vehicles. Vehicles are, by their nature, relatively expensive machines to maintain and run, so countries such as Eritrea have often had to dump large numbers of military vehicles during periods of economic hardship.

BOTTOM LEFT:

M4 Sherman Tank, Utah Beach, Normandy, France
Here we see a close-up of the track system of a US M4 Sherman tank, which today stands as a memorial to those Allied personnel who lost their lives during the Normandy landings of 6 June 1944.

TOP RIGHT:

Benghazi, Libya
Local people inspect a tank destroyed in the Libyan Revolution of 2011. Wrecked tanks offer the prospect of high-grade scrap metal, although their very durability means that heavy-duty equipment is needed to cut up and deconstruct their parts.

BOTTOM RIGHT:

Near Kabul, Afghanistan
An unsettling silence seems implied in this photograph of an armoured vehicle graveyard near Kabul in Afghanistan. Most of the vehicles here are relics of the Cold War, being a mixture of Soviet-built tanks, armoured personnel carriers (APCs) and infantry fighting vehicles (IFVs).

LEFT:

T-72 Main Battle Tank, Azaz, Syria
A Russian-made T-72, destroyed in the Syrian Civil War (2011–), sits amid the rubble of an equally devastated district of Azaz. Although the Syrian government had far more armour than the rebels, insurgent forces had access to modern anti-tank missile weaponry.

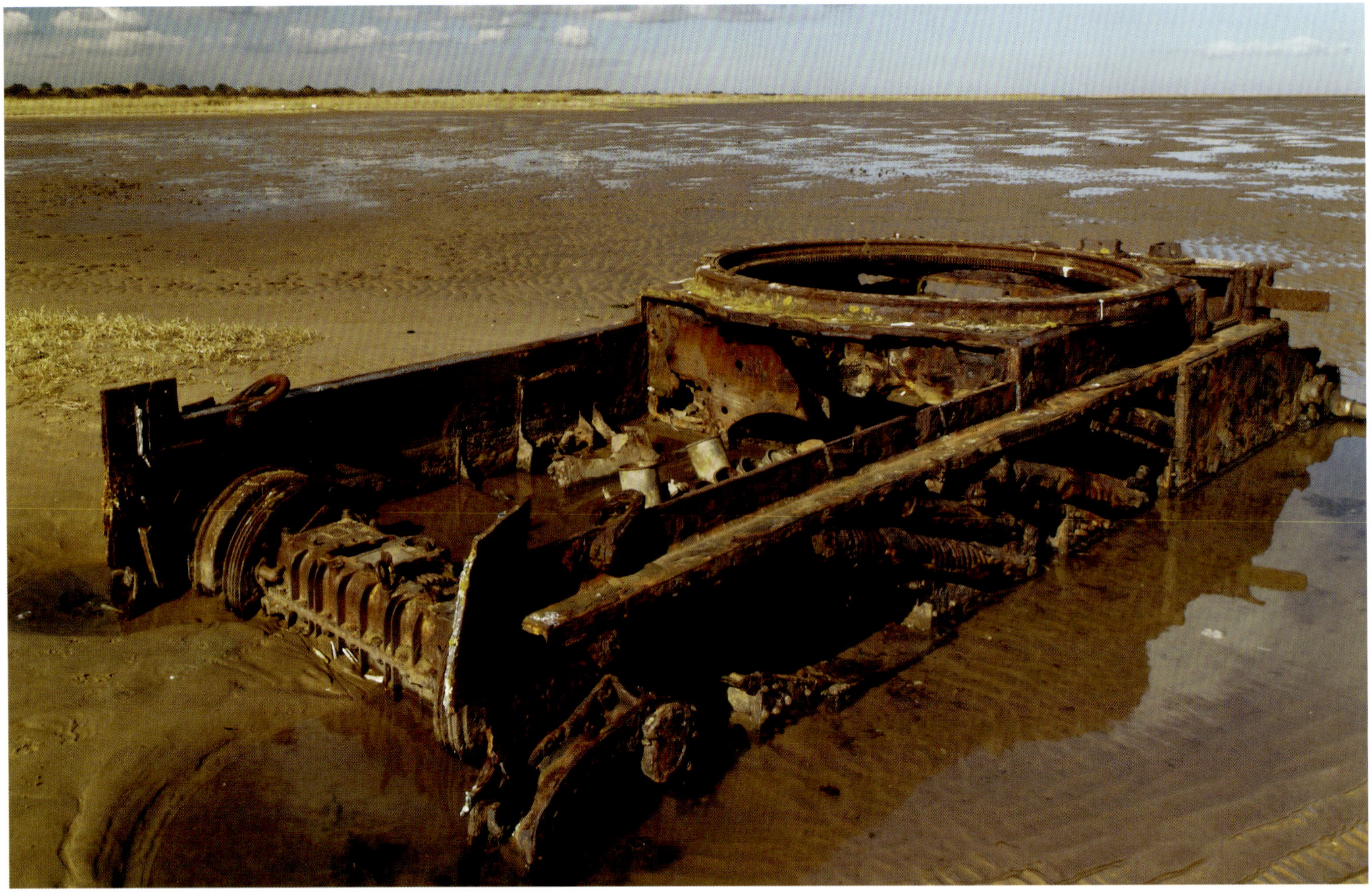

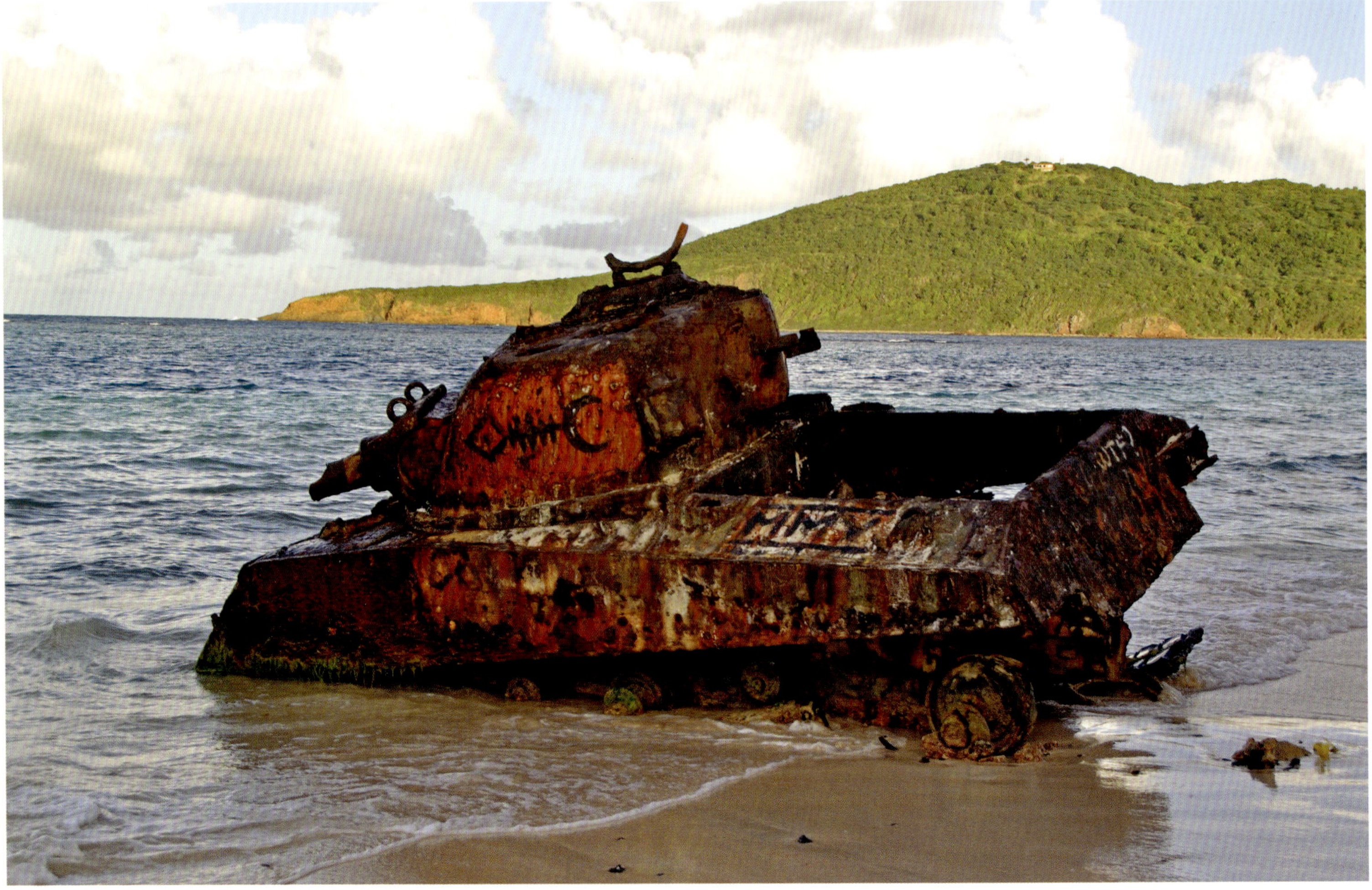

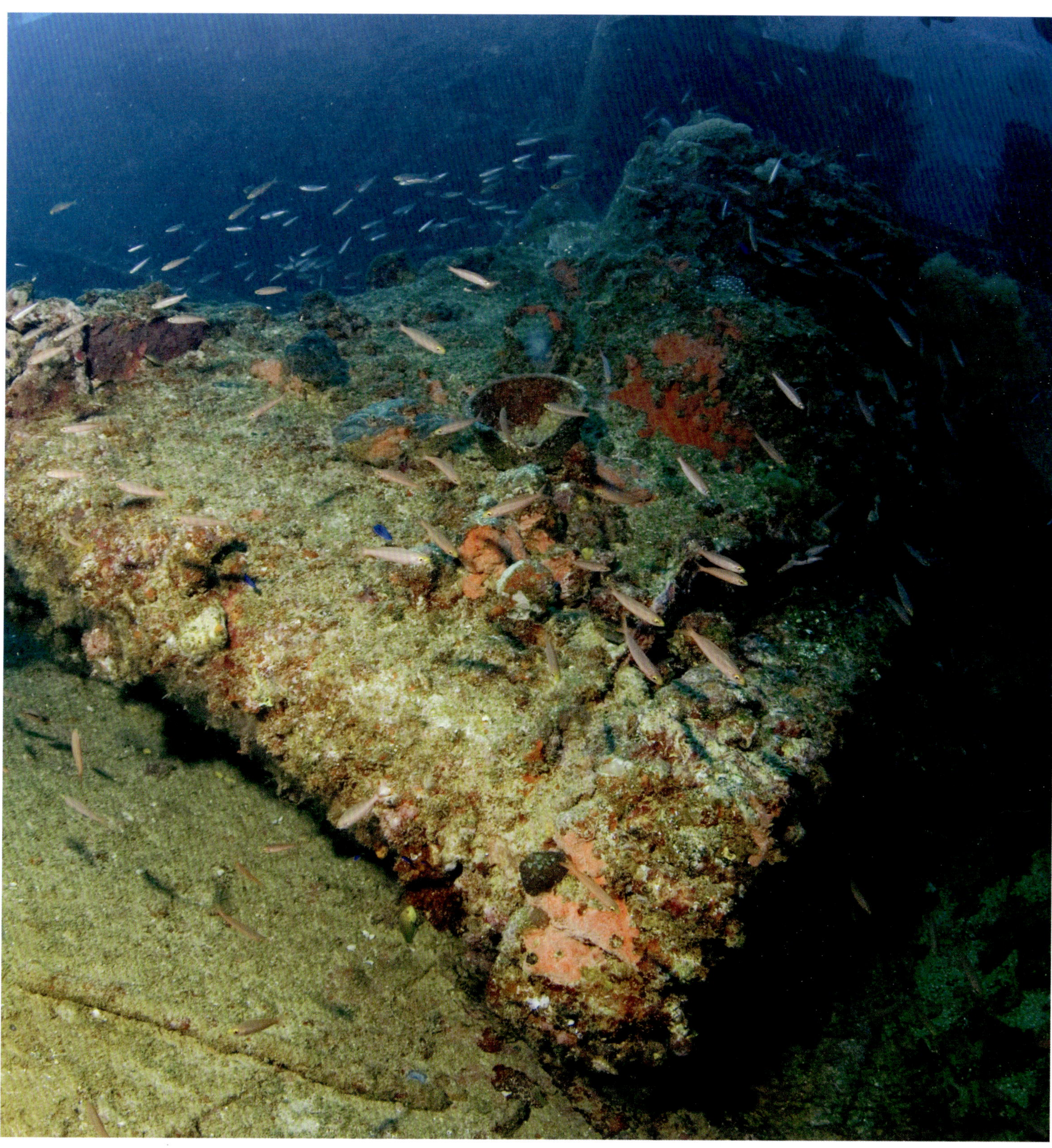

A34 Comet Tank, Saltfleetby-Theddlethorpe Dunes National Nature Reserve, Lincolnshire, England

Embedded in the sand, here are the rotting remains from the hull of an A34 Comet tank. This tank, along with many other military vehicles, was used for target practice, the surrounding beach being designated as a Ministry of Defence (MOD) bombing range between the 1930s and the 1960s.

Isla Culebra, Puerto Rico

The US military conducted firing tests and range practice on several of the beaches around Puerto Rico between the 1930s and the 1970s. This tank is one of the targets that was destroyed in the process. The firing was finally stopped in the 1970s following protests by locals people. The tanks, being far too heavy and awkward to move easily, were left in the edge of the surf to rot.

Type 97 Light Tank, Truk Lagoon, Central Pacific

This submerged Type 97 light tank is actually sitting on the deck of the sunken Japanese cargo ship *Nippo Maru*. On 17 February 1944, the heavily laden ship was attacked and sunk by torpedo-bombers from the carrier USS *Essex*, the ship taking its large consignment of tanks, artillery pieces and ammunition to the bottom of the Pacific.

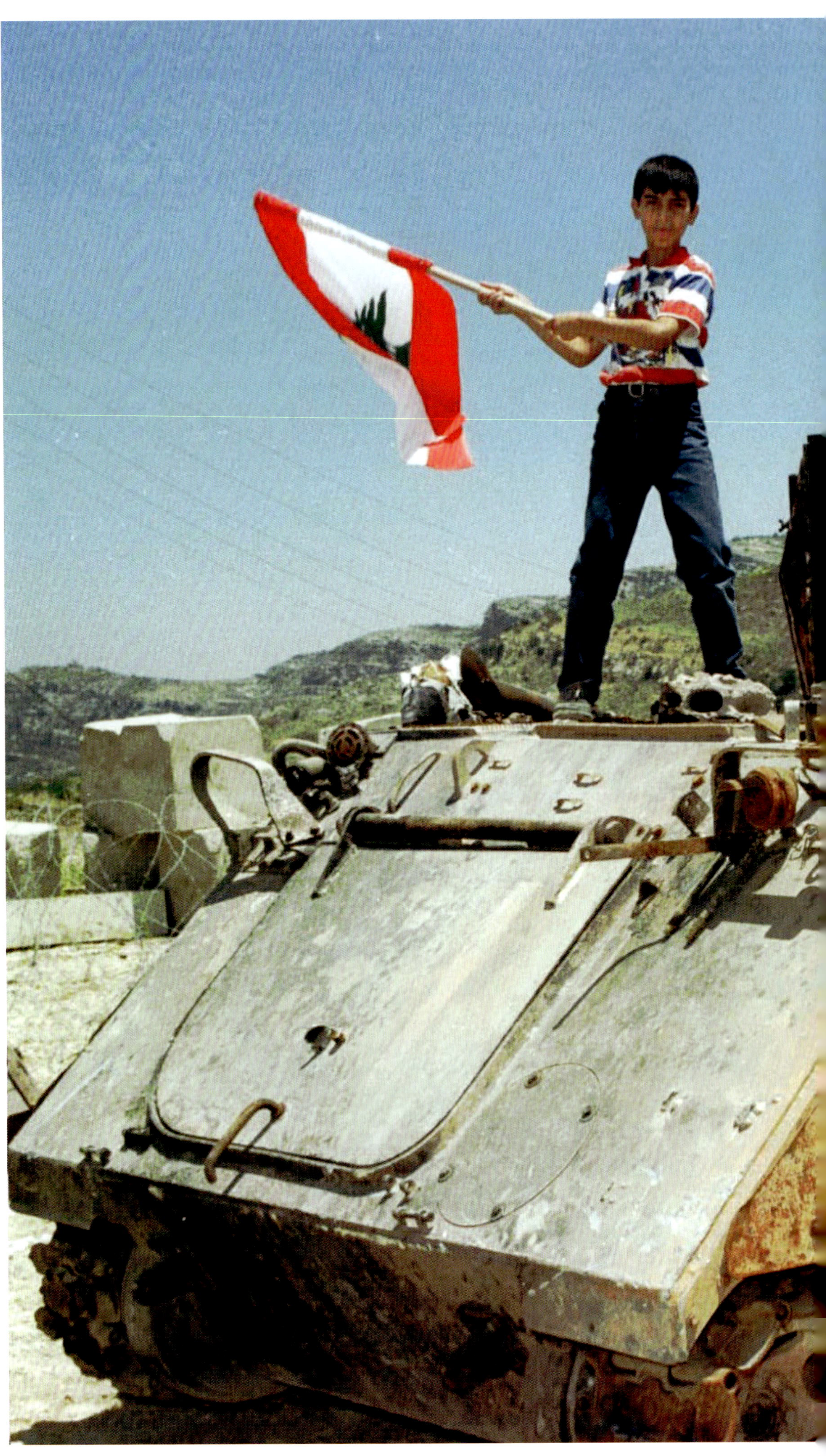

M113 Armoured Personnel Carrier, Jezzine, South Lebanon
Following the withdrawal of the Israeli-backed South Lebanon Army (SLA) from Jezzine in June 1999, local children celebrate by climbing on an abandoned SLA M113 armoured personnel carrier (APC). The child at the bottom is holding a poster of the Lebanese president, Émile Jamil Lahoud.

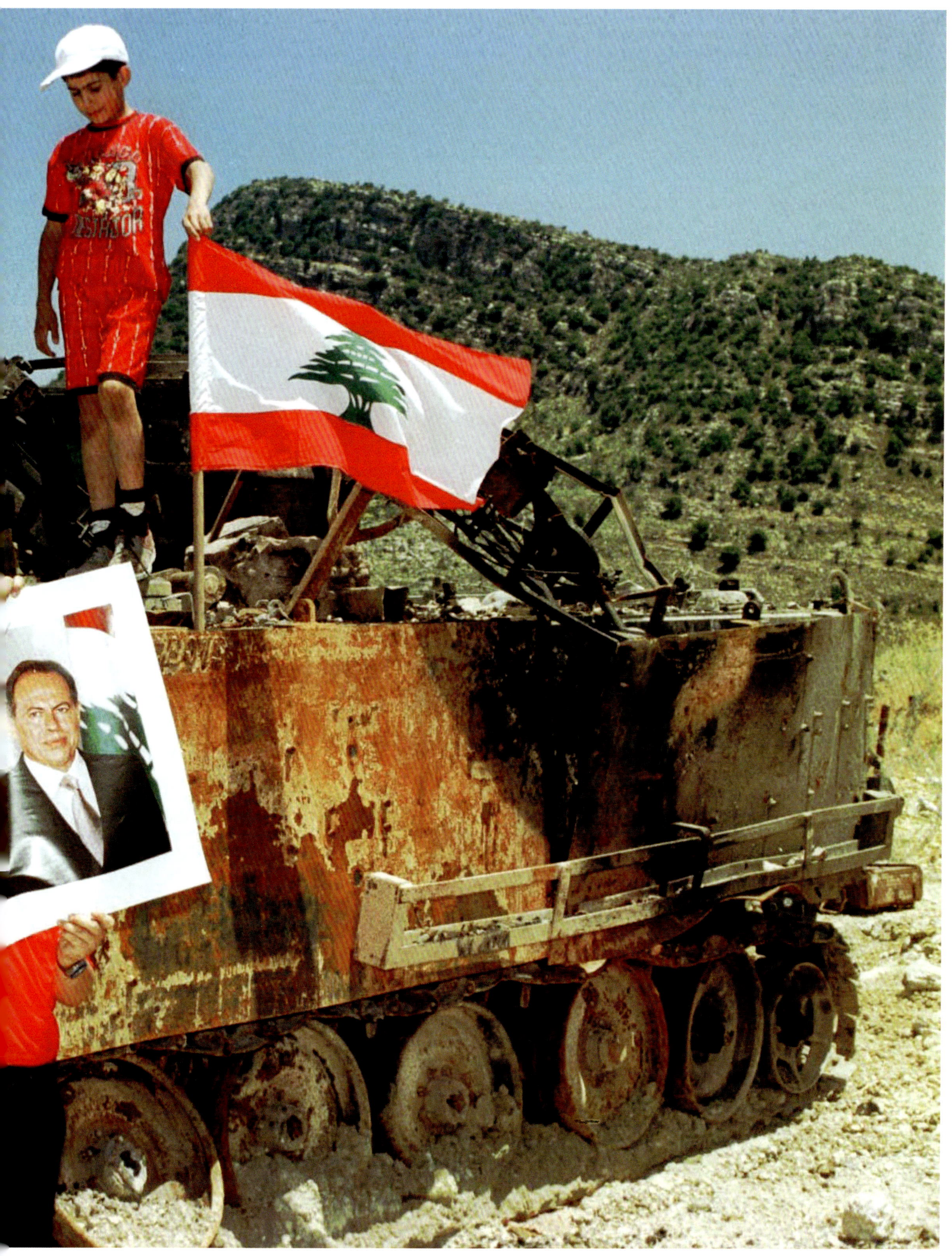

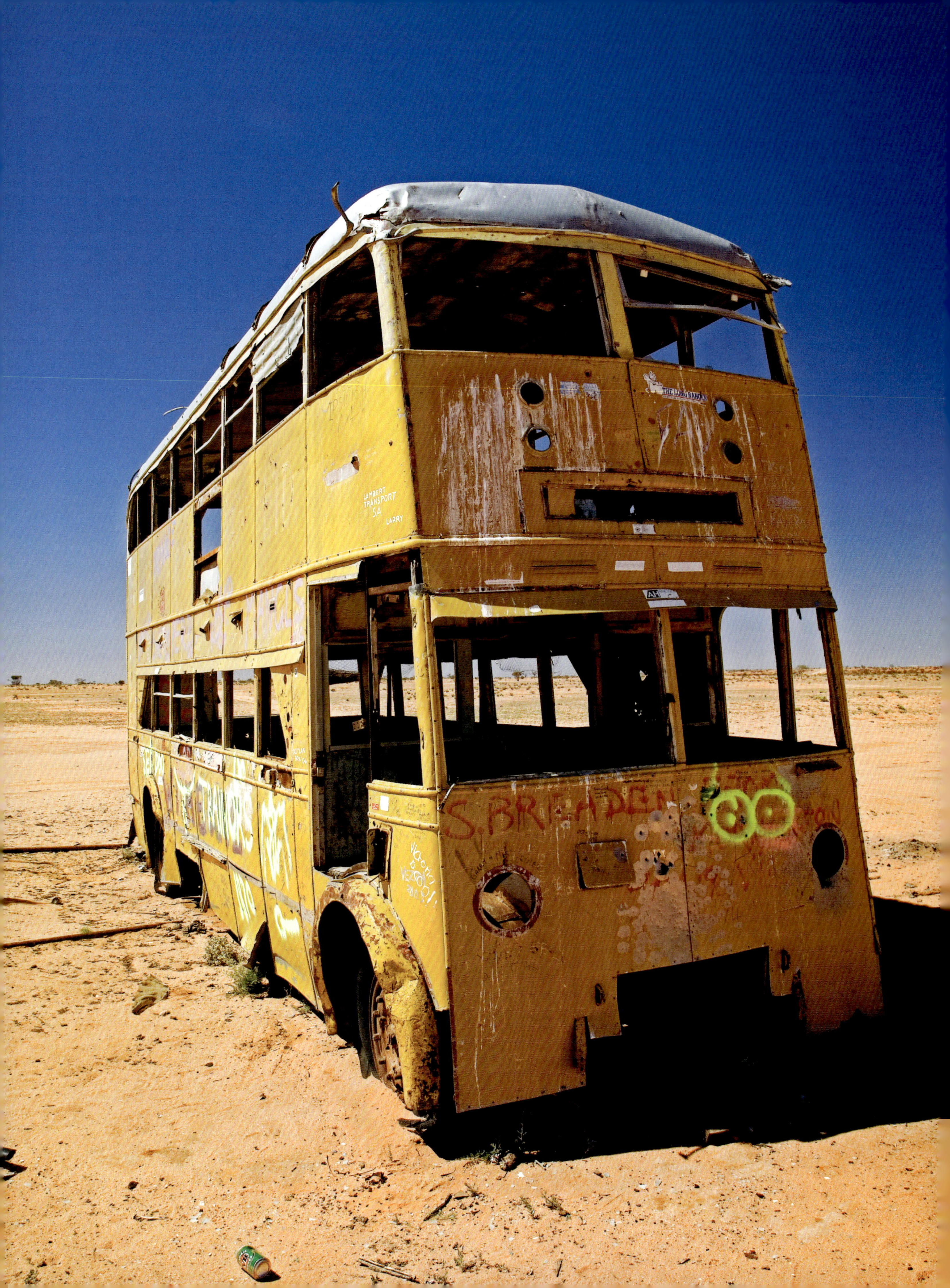

LAMBERT
TRANSPORT
SA
LARRY
S. BREADEN
TRAITORS

Road Vehicles

It is often surprising the degree of emotional attachment human beings can forge between themselves and the vehicles in which they travel, particularly cars. Yet it is understandable. The cars that we own and drive play their part within a specific time period in our lives, and hence become infused with the memories and emotions of that period. While abandoned military vehicles suggest violence, drama and human extremes, civilian wrecks speak of the thrum of daily life – running kids to school, collecting the shopping, picking up a date, leaving home, going on holiday. It is the very normality of the activities that seems to make the abandoned car speak so eloquently.

The wrecks featured in this chapter cross many different types and purpose of vehicle. They include school buses, trucks, motorbikes, bicycles, cars (classic and otherwise), tractors and caravans. What is striking about them all is how, through the rust and degradation of age, they still appear so firmly of another historical age. Motor vehicles, being commercial consumer products, are always crafted with the fashions and preferences of the market in mind. Hence, what was once futuristic in design becomes decidedly retro 50 years after it was launched. The vehicles in this chapter therefore refer as much to the passing of cultural time as that of physical time.

Camerons Corner, Strzelecki Track Road, South Australia
This derelict double-decker bus still manages to look strangely cheerful as it sits under the burning sun of the Australian outback. The vehicle is actually a 1952-vintage British Leyland bus, and was formerly used commercially in the Australian city of Sydney.

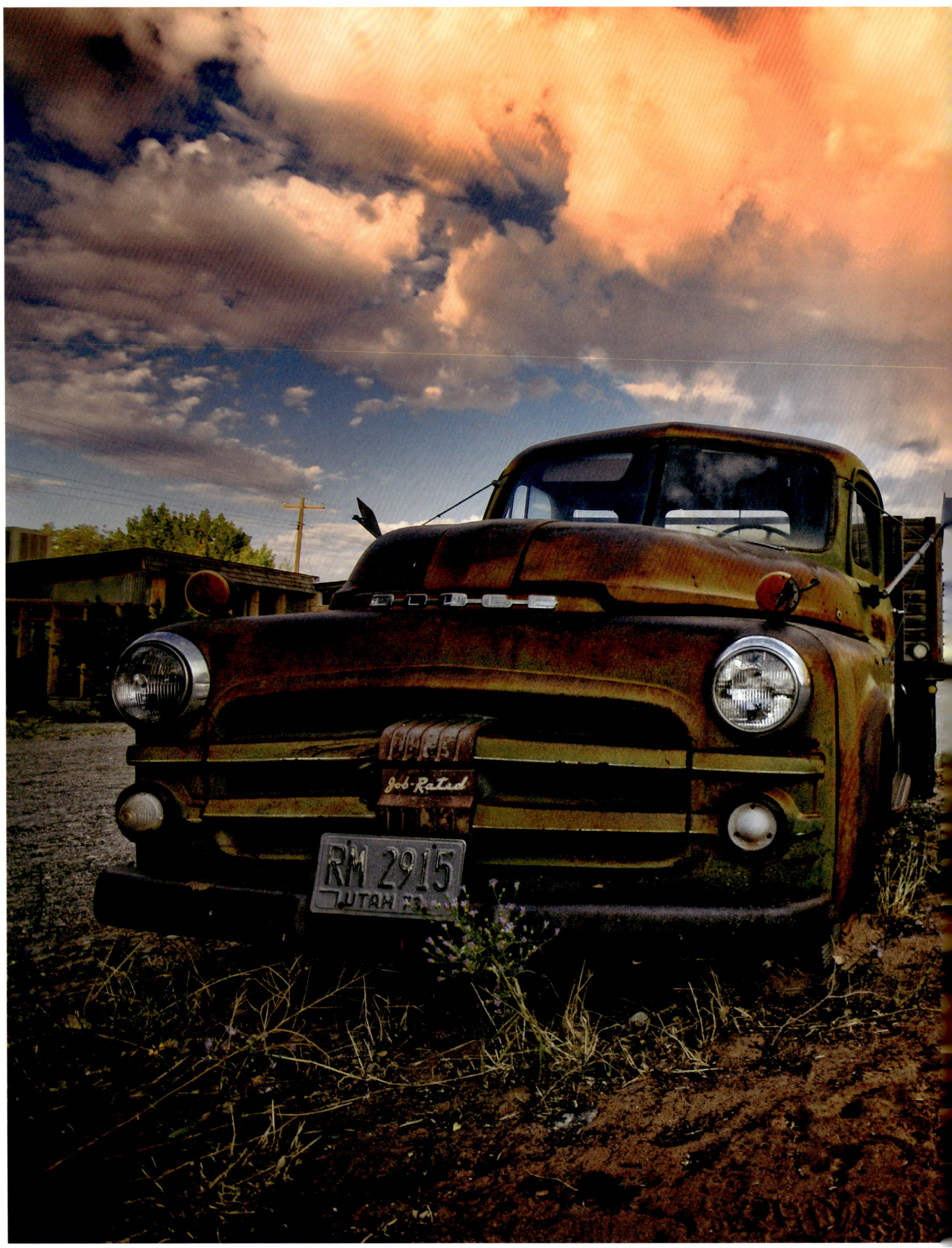

Job-Rated
RM 2915
UTAH 73

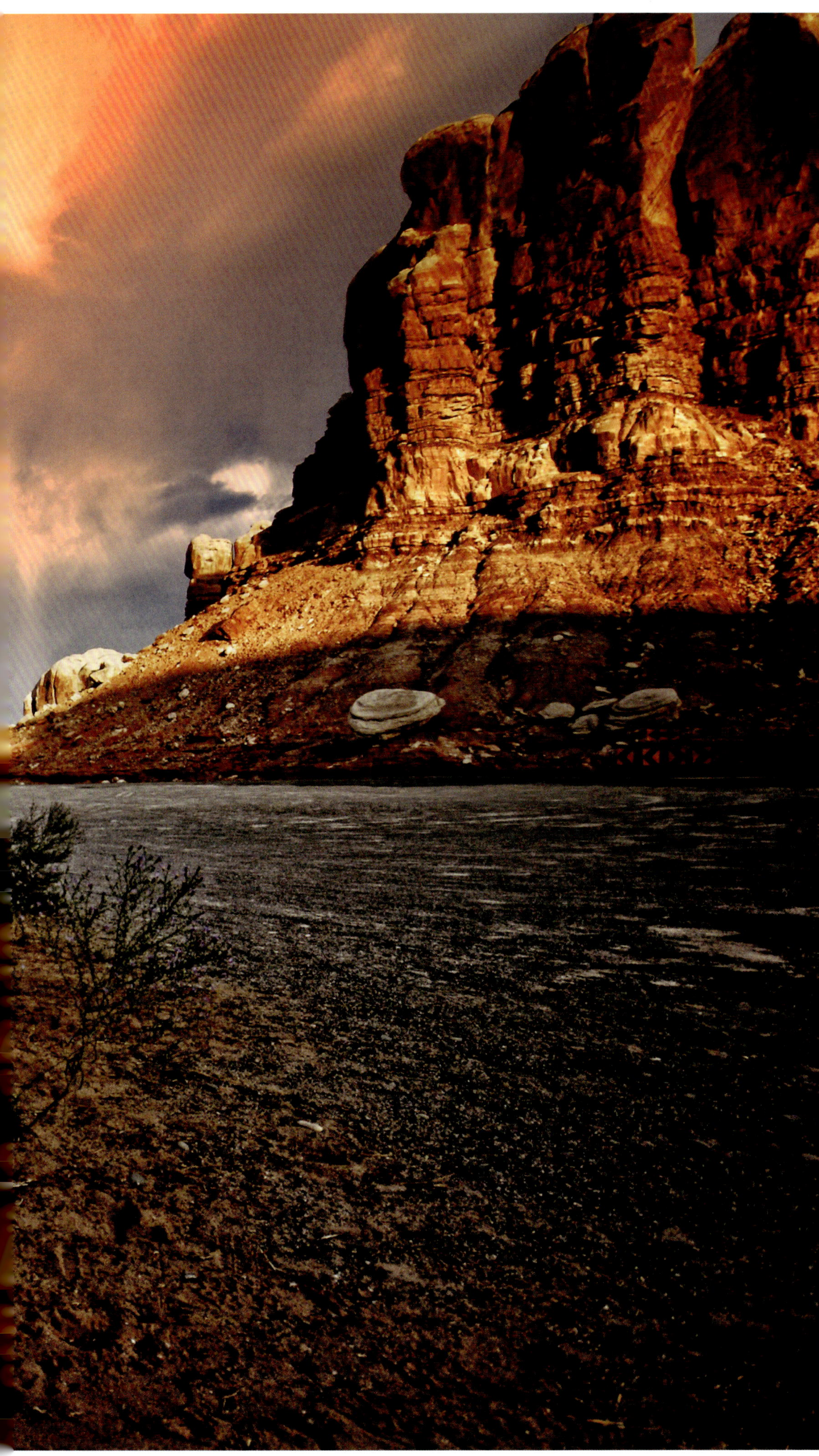

Dodge B pick-up truck, Bluff, Utah, United States
Sitting in one of Utah's many rocky canyons, here we see a 1951 Dodge B pick-up truck, slowly giving way to rust. The B-series pick-up vehicles were produced between 1948 and 1953. They provided the buyer with hard-wearing and robust utility vehicles, ideal for farmyard and light commercial applications.

OVERLEAF:

TOP LEFT:

Oulu, Finland
A bicycle emerges from the water of a Finnish river. Unwanted bicycles litter the world's scrapyards, waterways and derelict ground. In London alone, around 27,000 bicycles are abandoned every year.

BOTTOM LEFT:

Amsterdam, Holland
Amsterdam is a city of bicycles – an estimated 800,000 people in the city use a bicycle on a daily basis. Thousands are abandoned, like this one against this tree. In one case in Vashon Island, Washington, USA, a bicycle was left propped against a tree so long the tree has now grown around it.

RIGHT:

Fish River Canyon, Canon Roadhouse, Namibia
A 'quiver tree' – a local species of aloe plant – grows up through the engine compartment of an old truck. The engine itself was probably long gone, stripped of its parts and used in other vehicles. Given the size of the tree, this probably occurred about half a century ago.

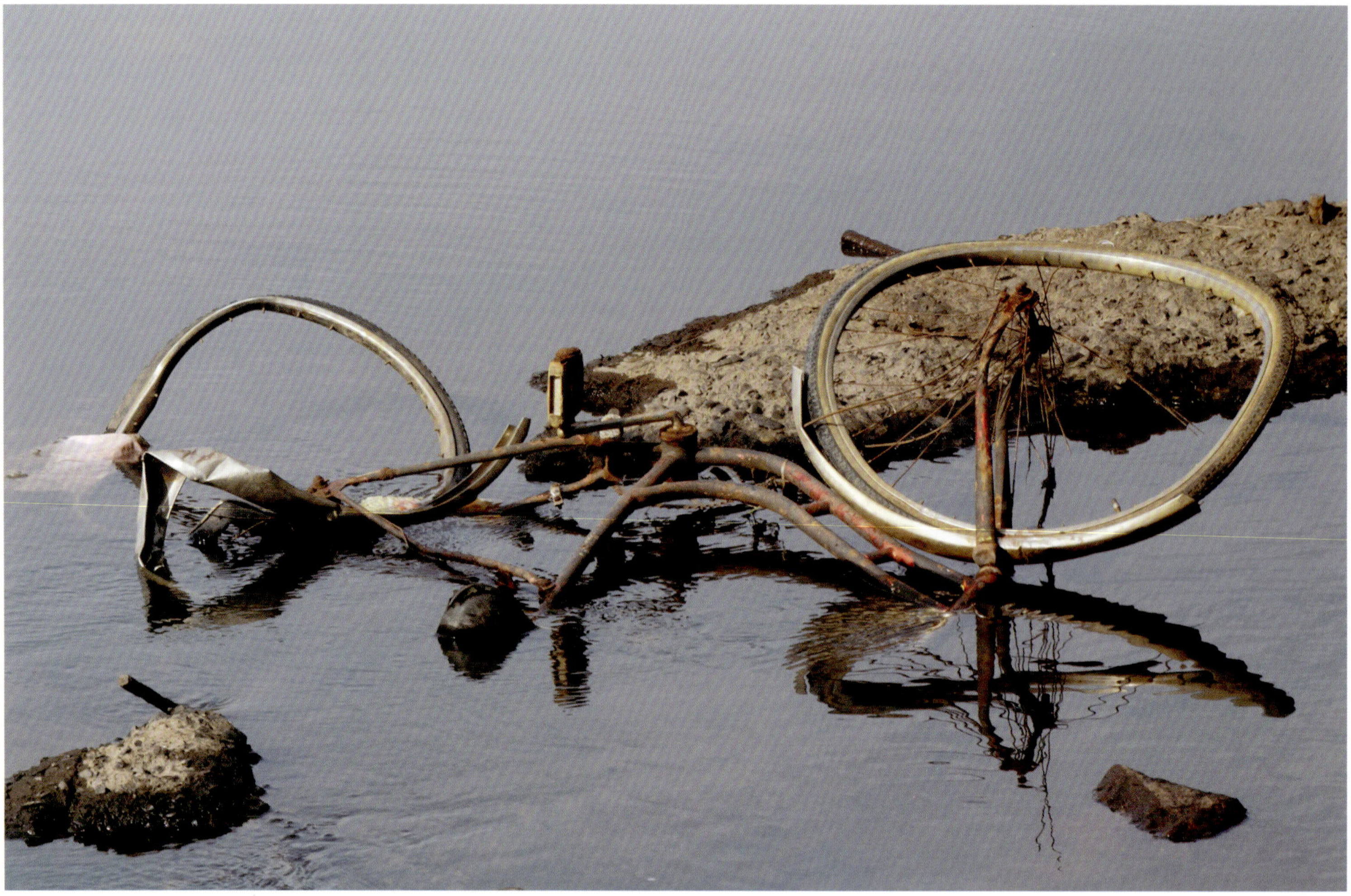

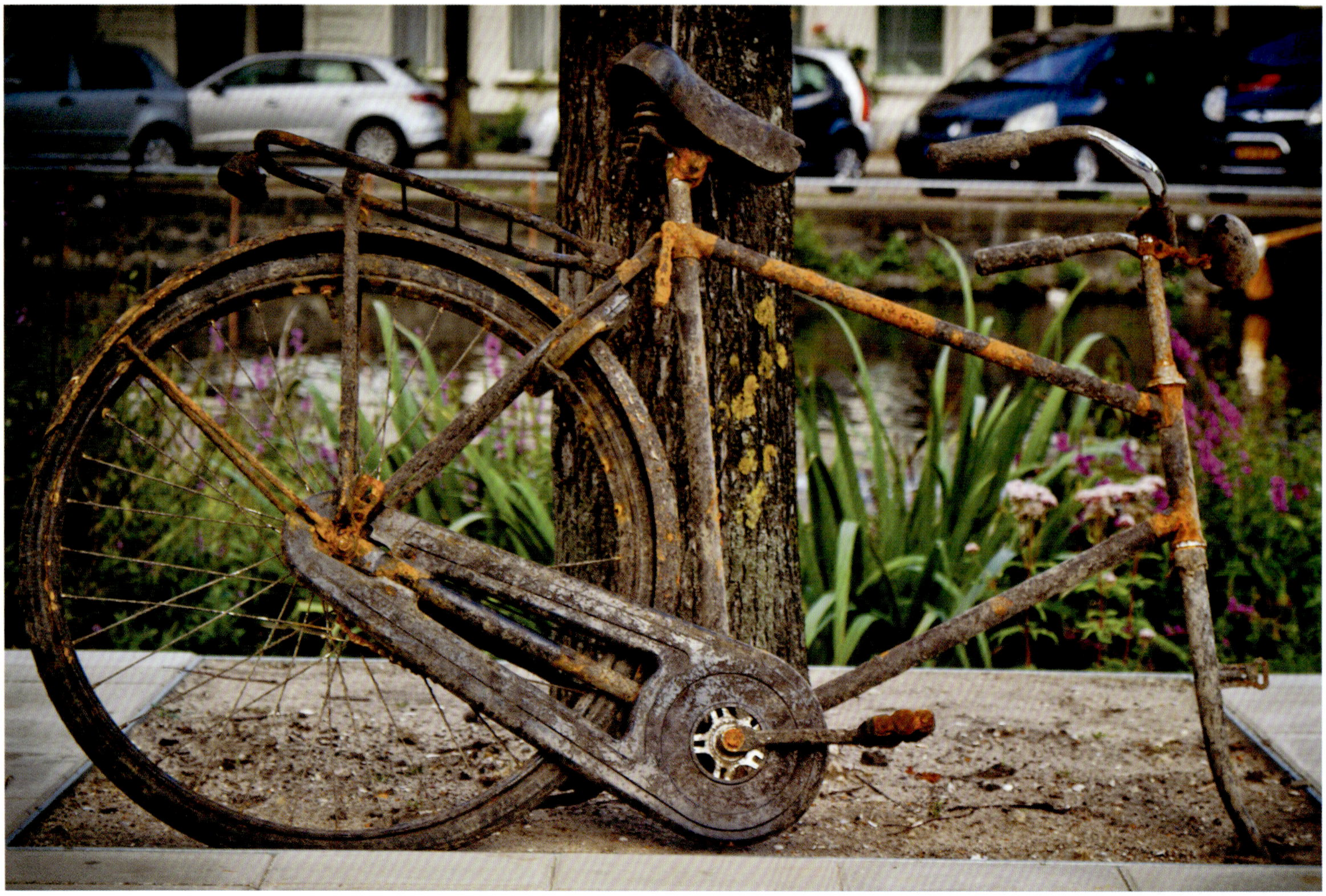

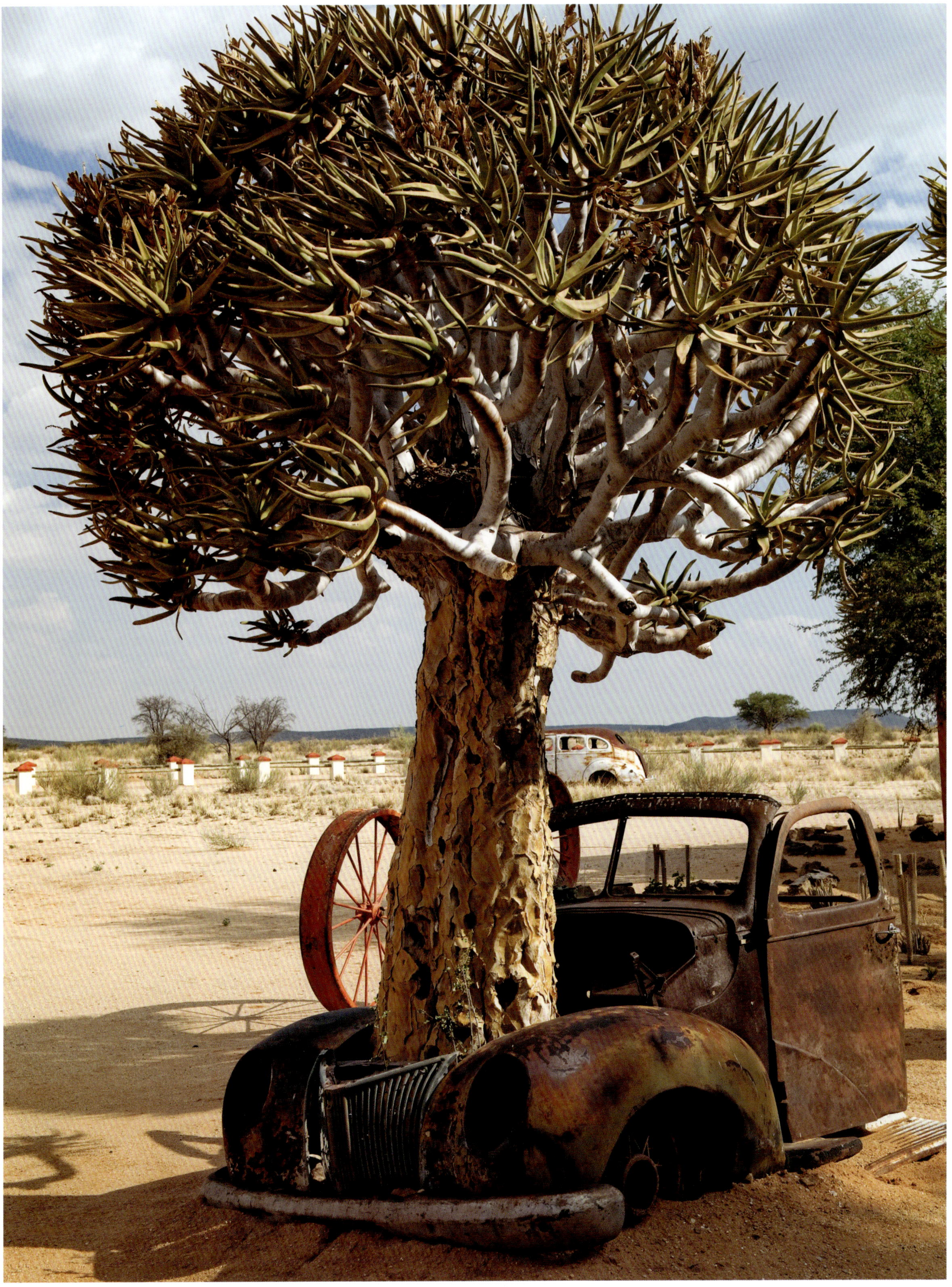

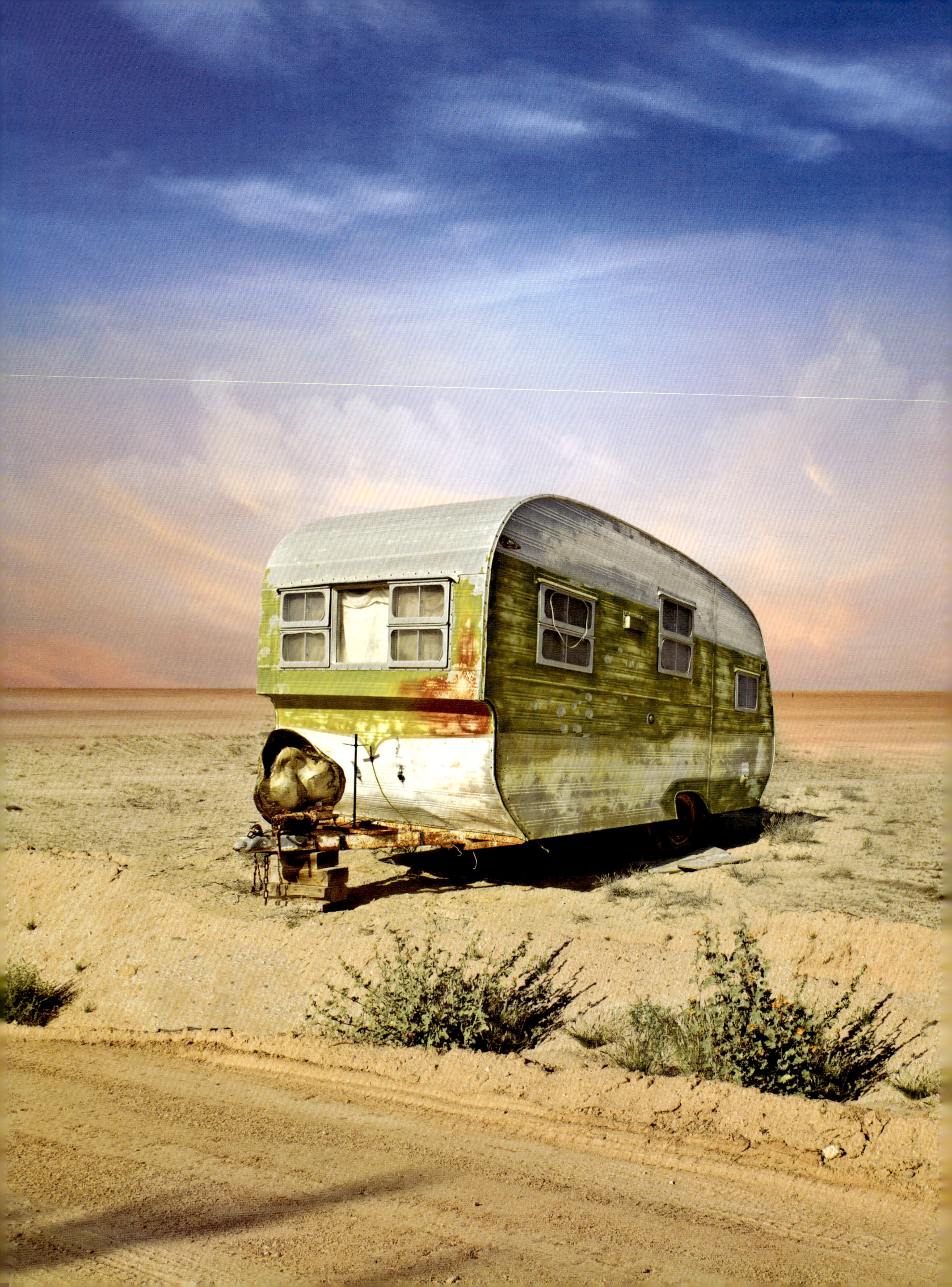

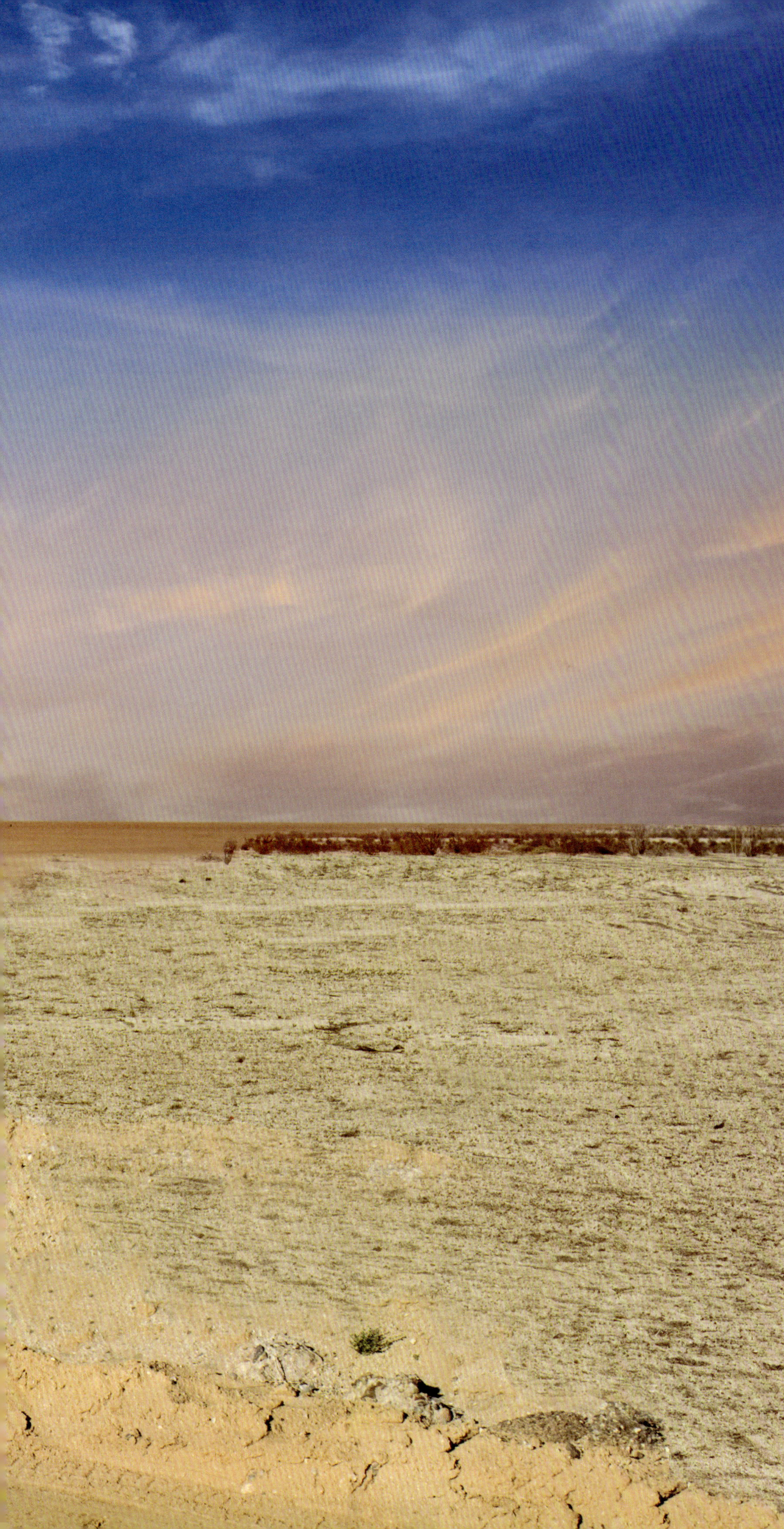

Sonora Desert, United States
The caravan trailer began a
revolution in travel during
the second half of the 20th
century, providing portable
accommodation for millions.
Abandoned caravans are found
in the most desolate and unlikely
locations – this caravan was found
in the Sonora Desert, left at the
side of a dirt road.

OVERLEAF:
TOP:
**Indian, Anchorage, Alaska,
United States**
In the United States, the school bus
is one of the great cultural motifs,
remembered with fondness, dread
or boredom by millions of former
schoolchildren. The passage of
time makes it difficult to identify
the make and model of this bus,
but popular marques from the
1950s and 1960s were GMC,
Chevrolet and Studebaker.

BOTTOM LEFT:
**Brooklyn, New York,
United States**
Abandoned streetcars line up at
the front of Fairway supermarket
in the Red Hook section in
Brooklyn on 17 August 2013.
The vehicles were once operated
by the Brooklyn City Street Car
Company, and today there are
plans to reintroduce streetcars to
between Queens and Brooklyn.

BOTTOM RIGHT:
Asmara, Eritrea
Four buses give each other silent
company in Asmara, Eritrea. The
typical lifespan of a commercial
bus is reckoned at about 25 years
or 402,300km (250,000 miles),
after which it becomes too
expensive to maintain on the road.

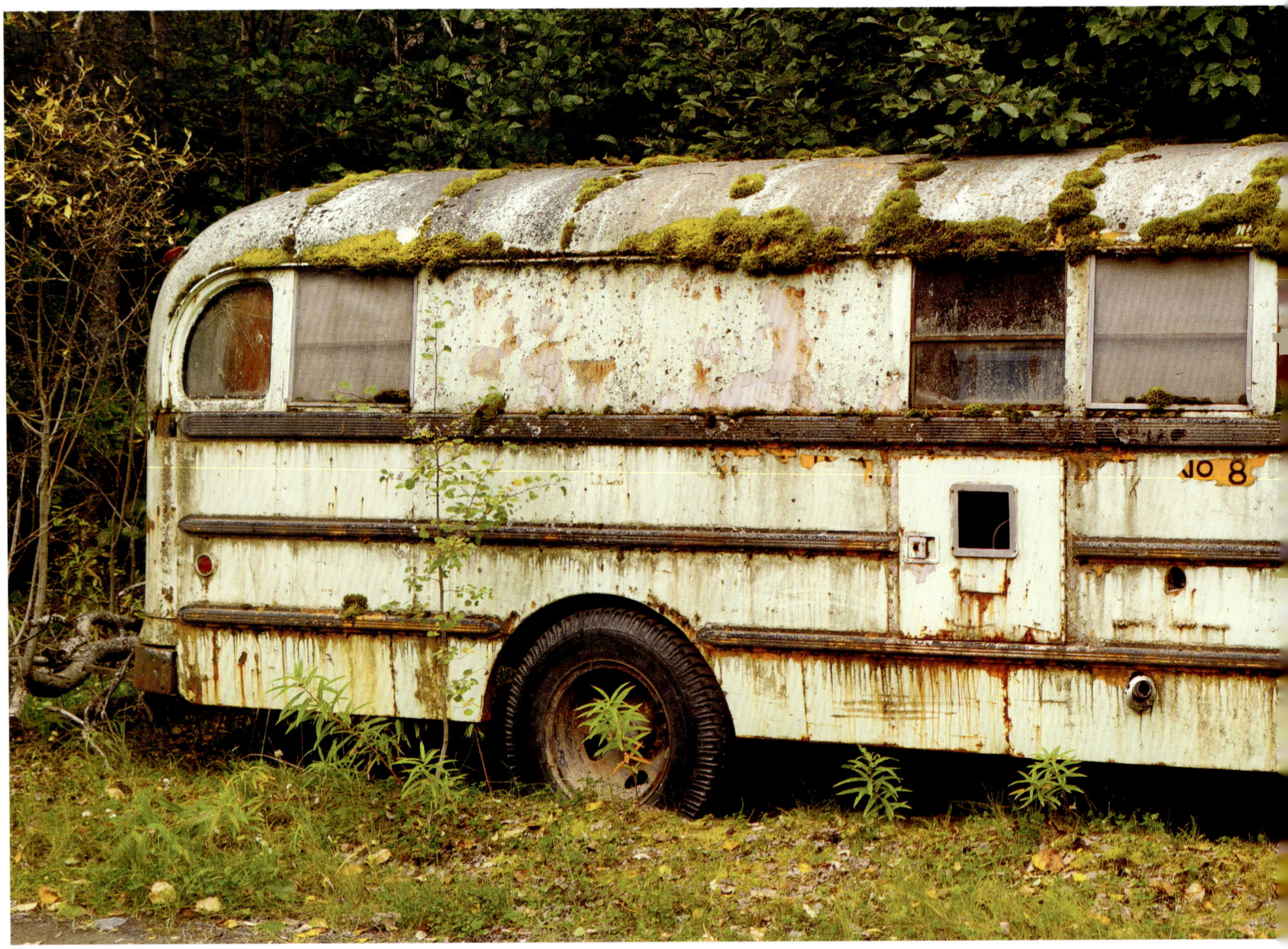

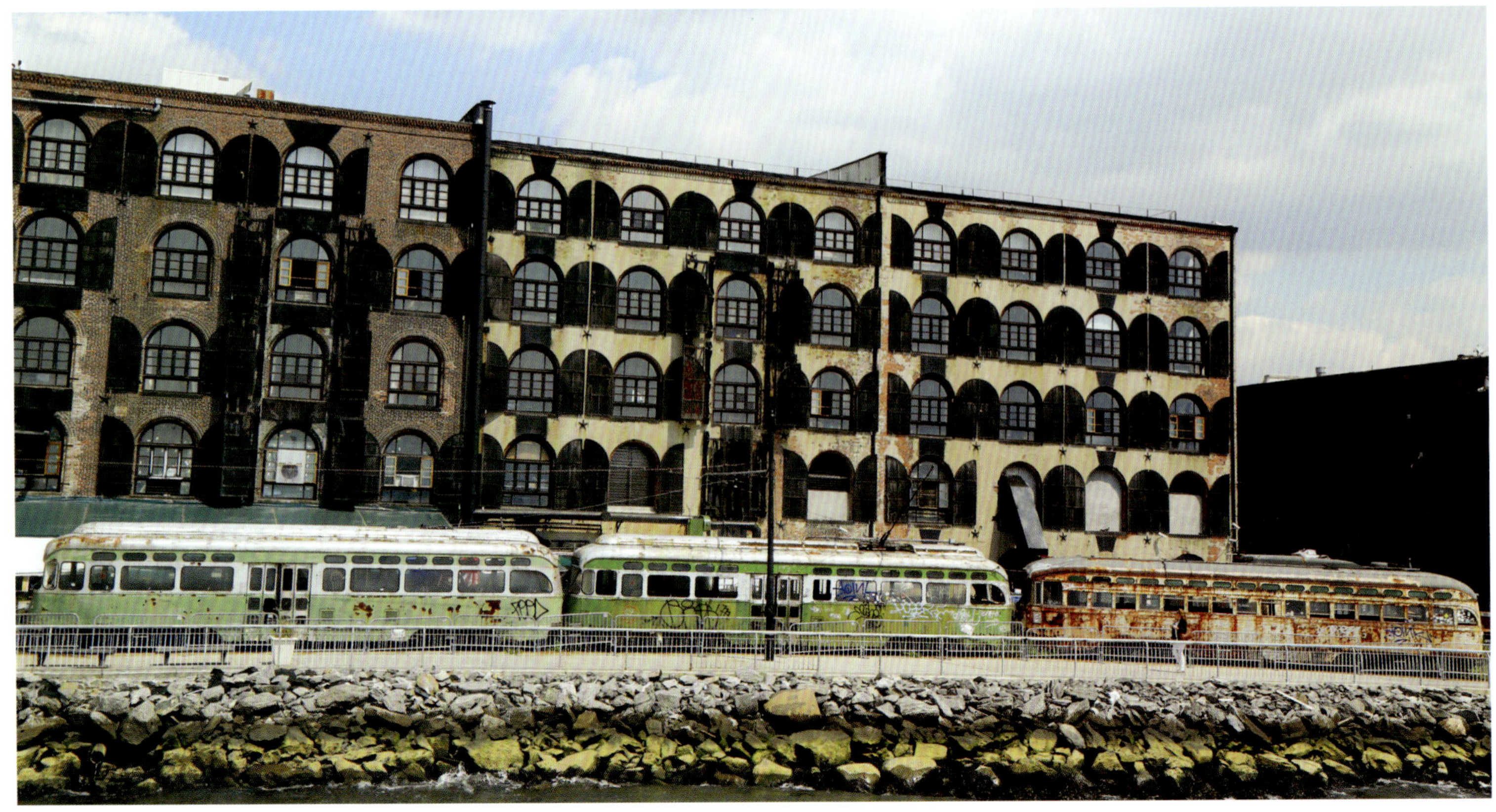

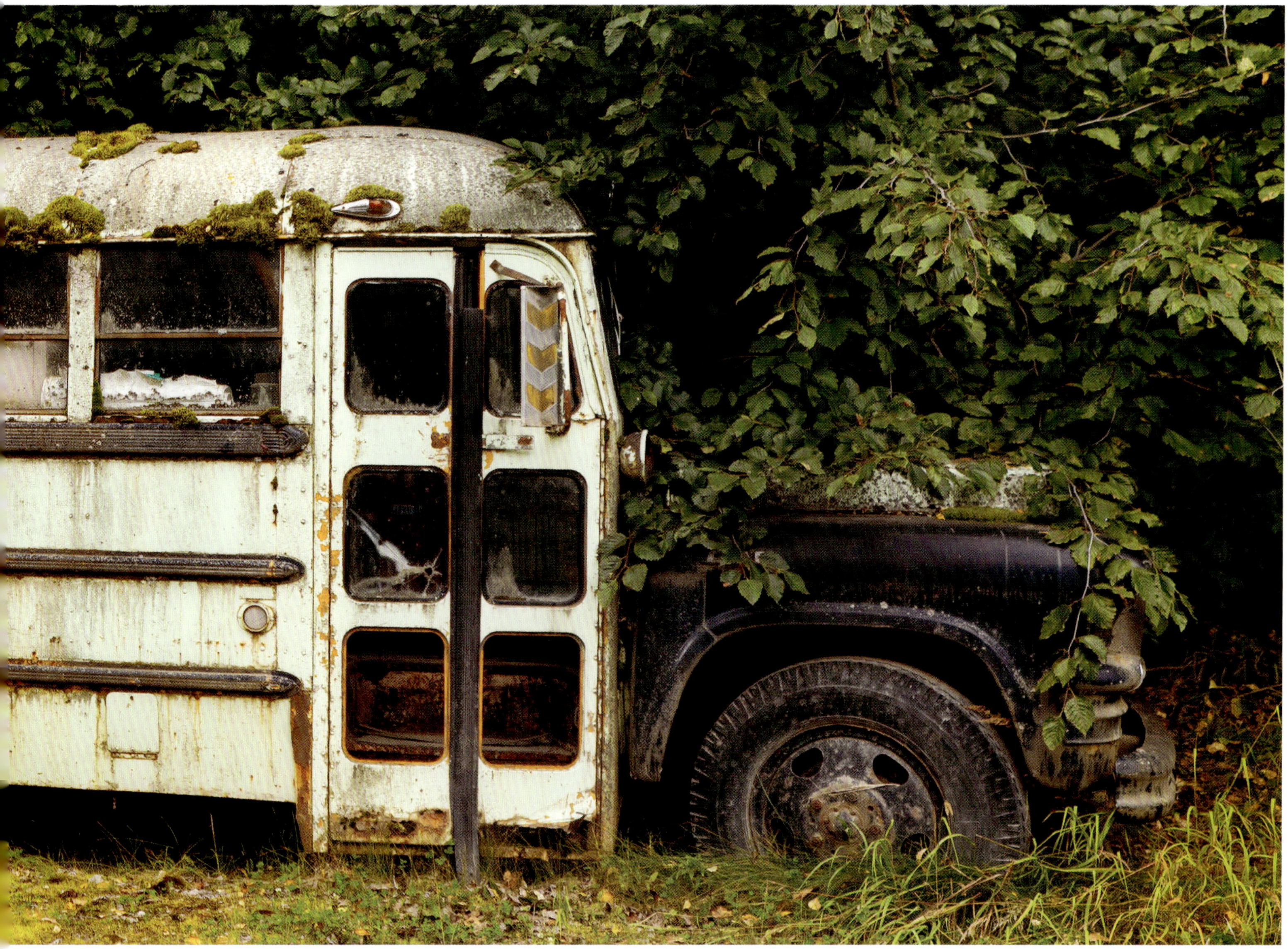

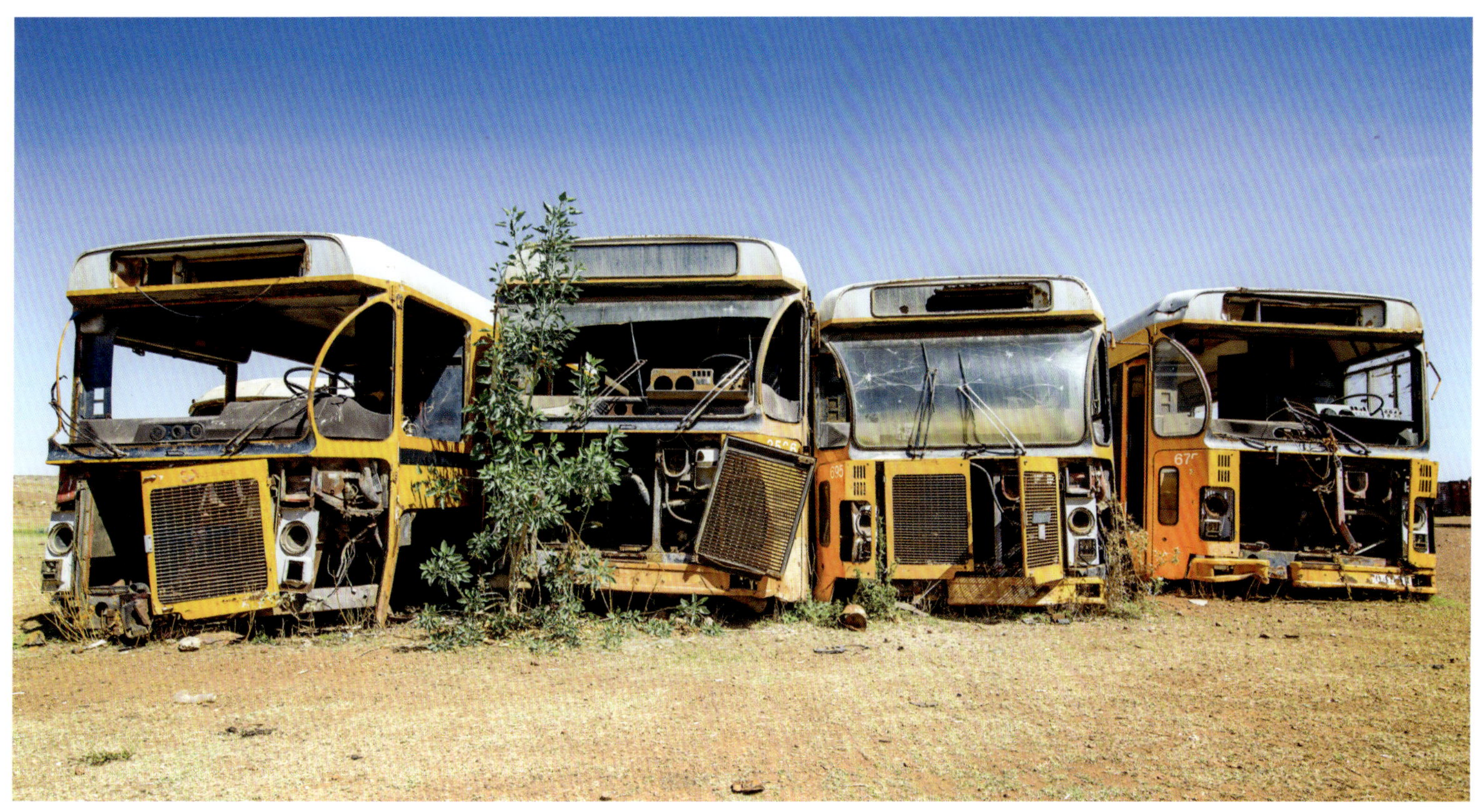

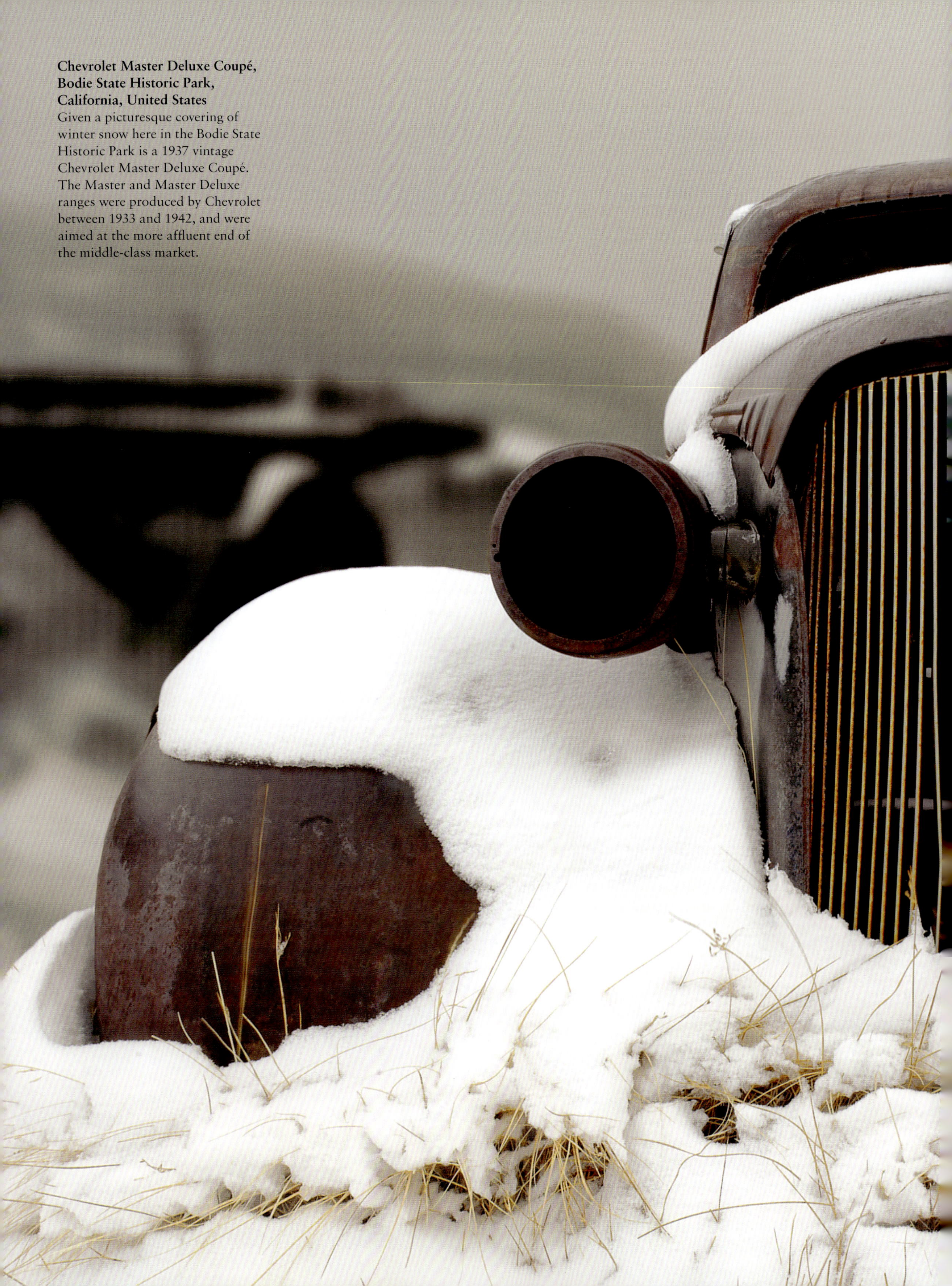

Chevrolet Master Deluxe Coupé,
Bodie State Historic Park,
California, United States
Given a picturesque covering of
winter snow here in the Bodie State
Historic Park is a 1937 vintage
Chevrolet Master Deluxe Coupé.
The Master and Master Deluxe
ranges were produced by Chevrolet
between 1933 and 1942, and were
aimed at the more affluent end of
the middle-class market.

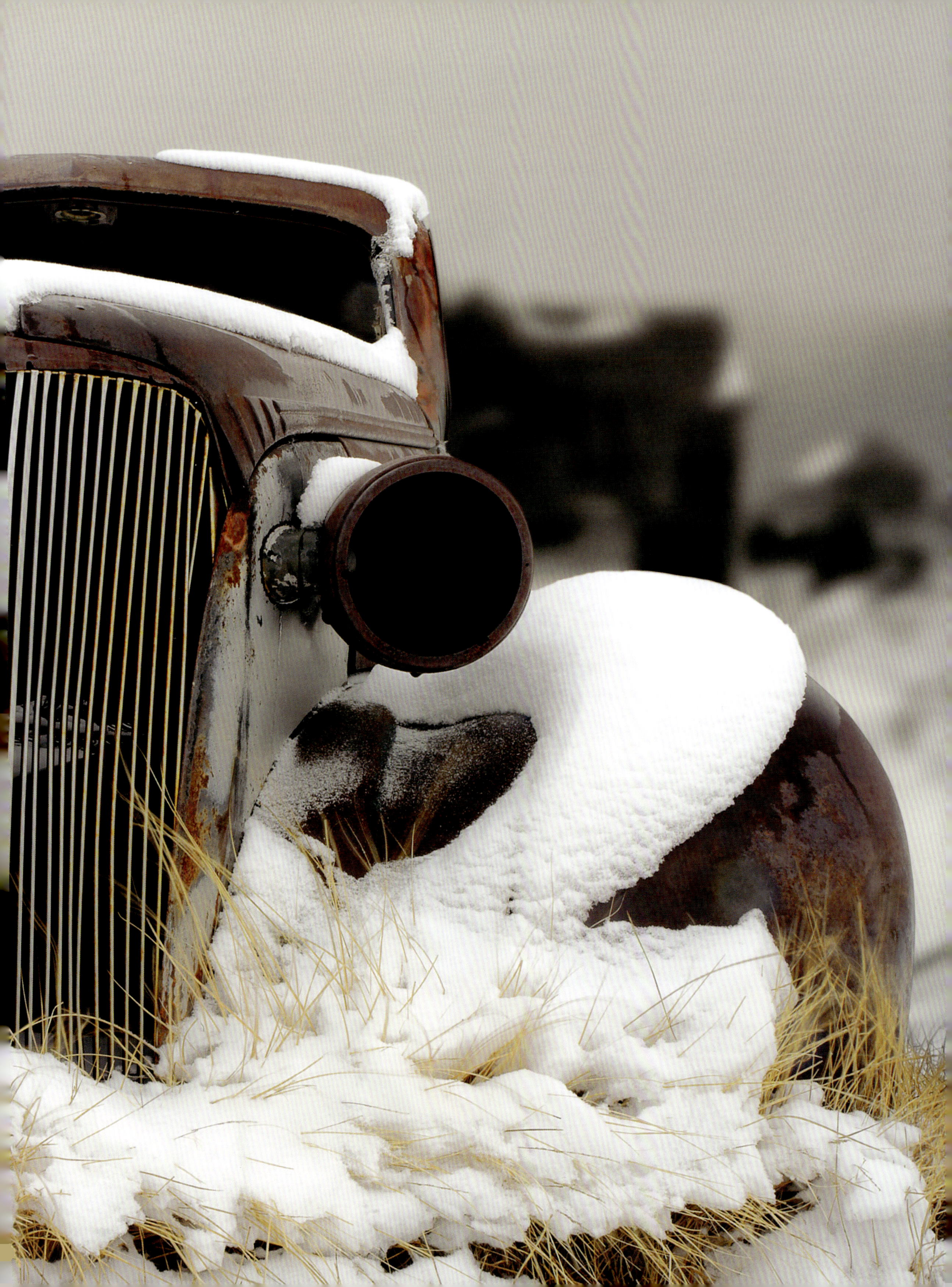

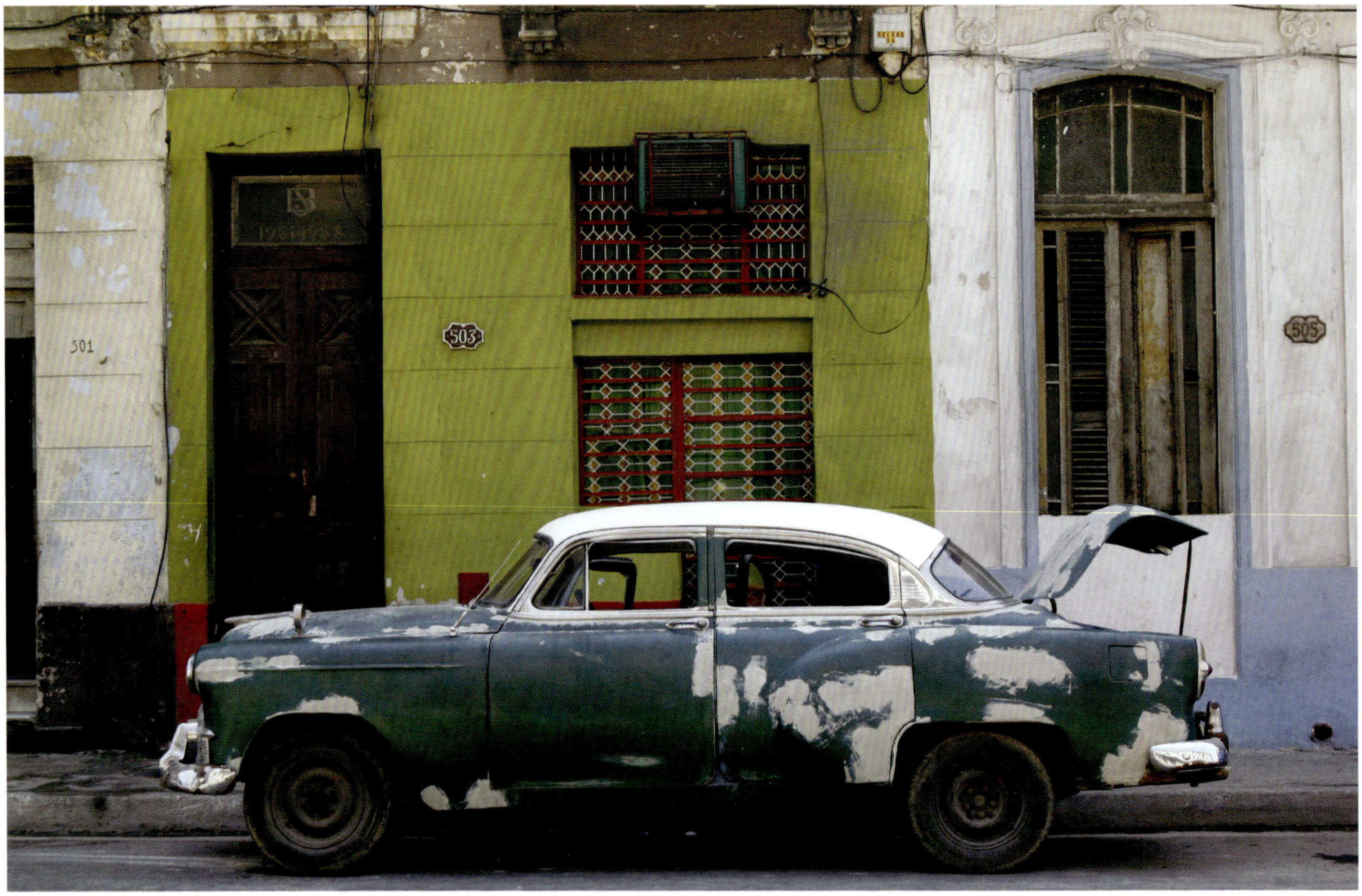

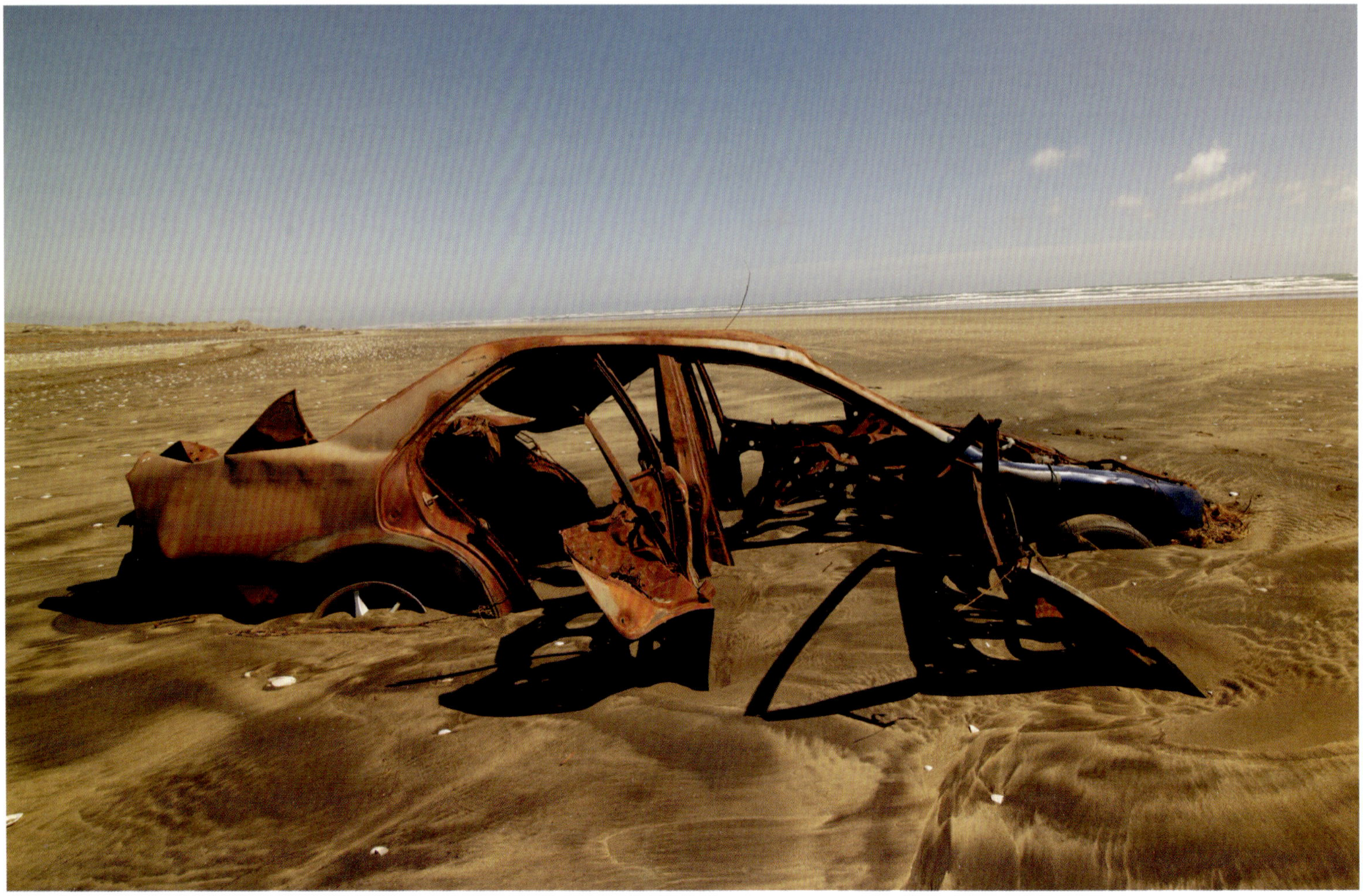

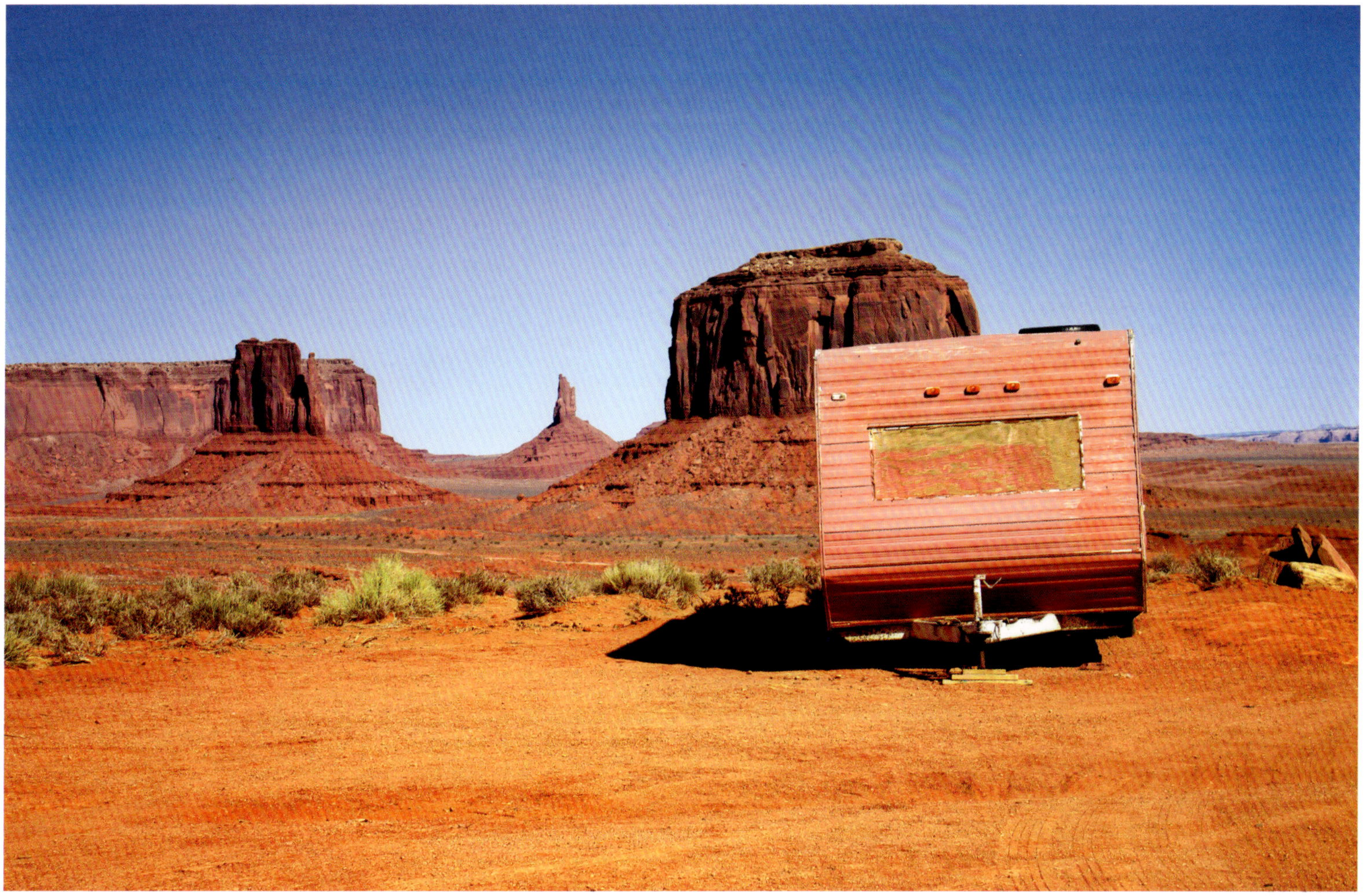

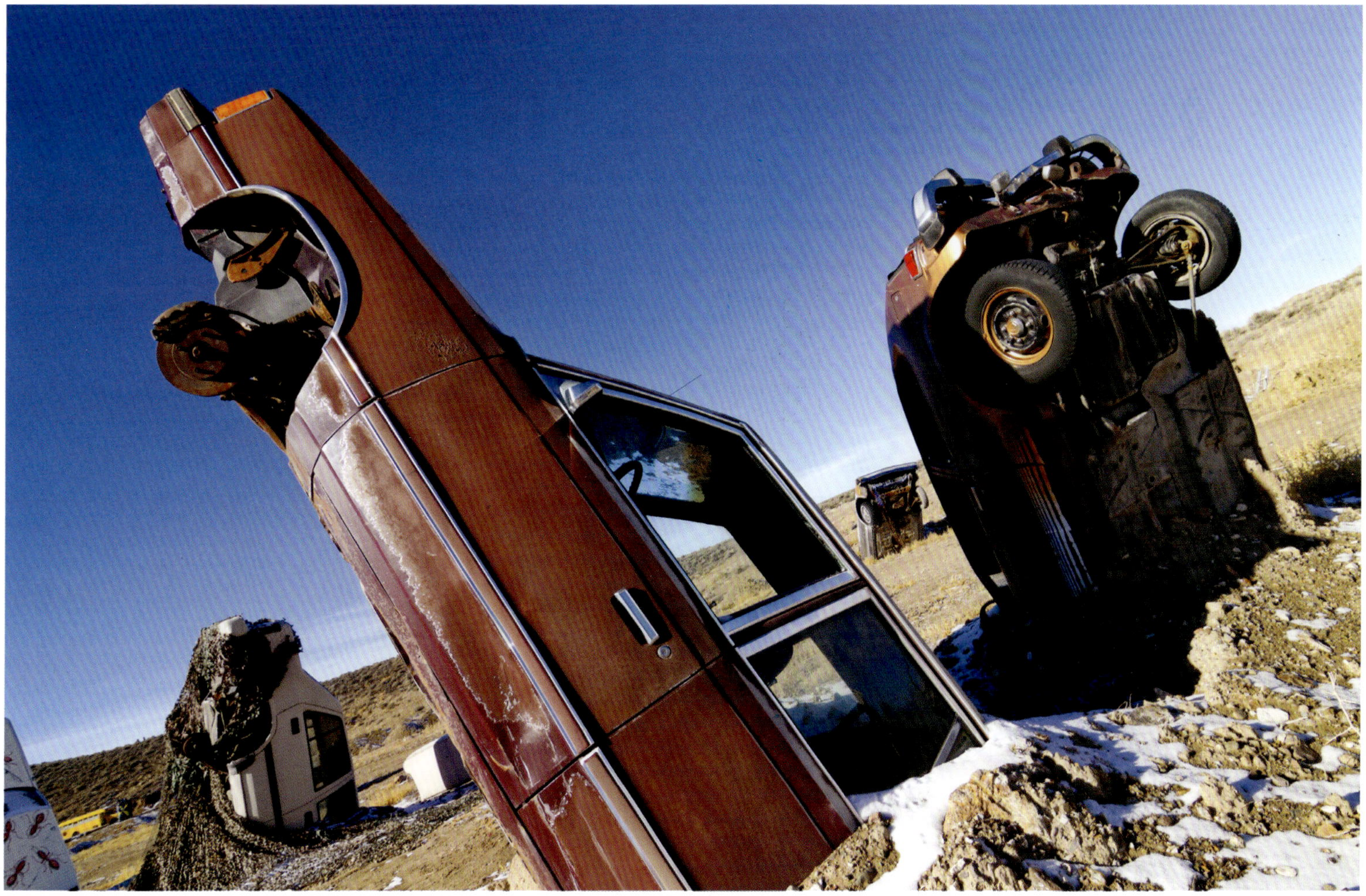

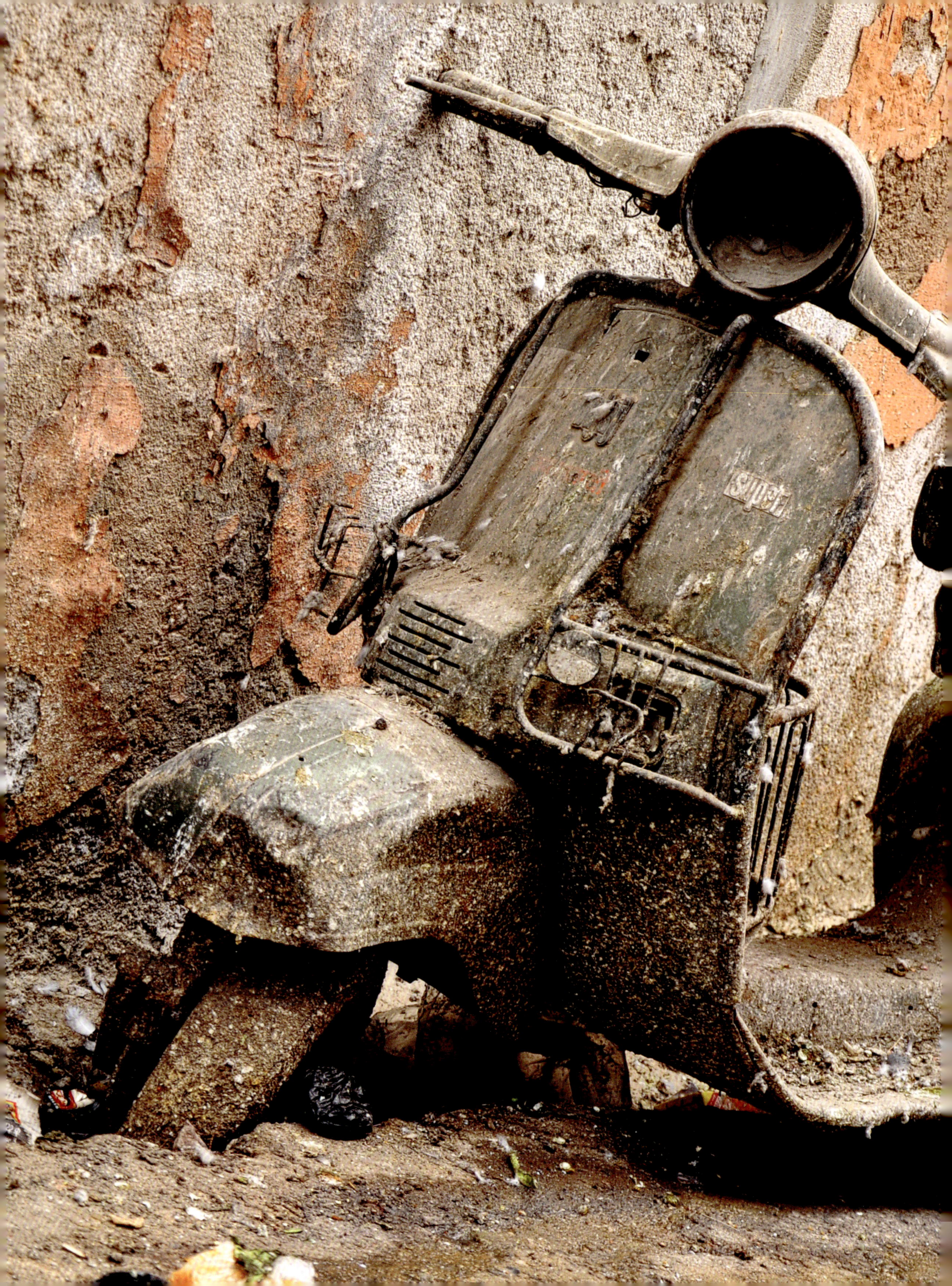

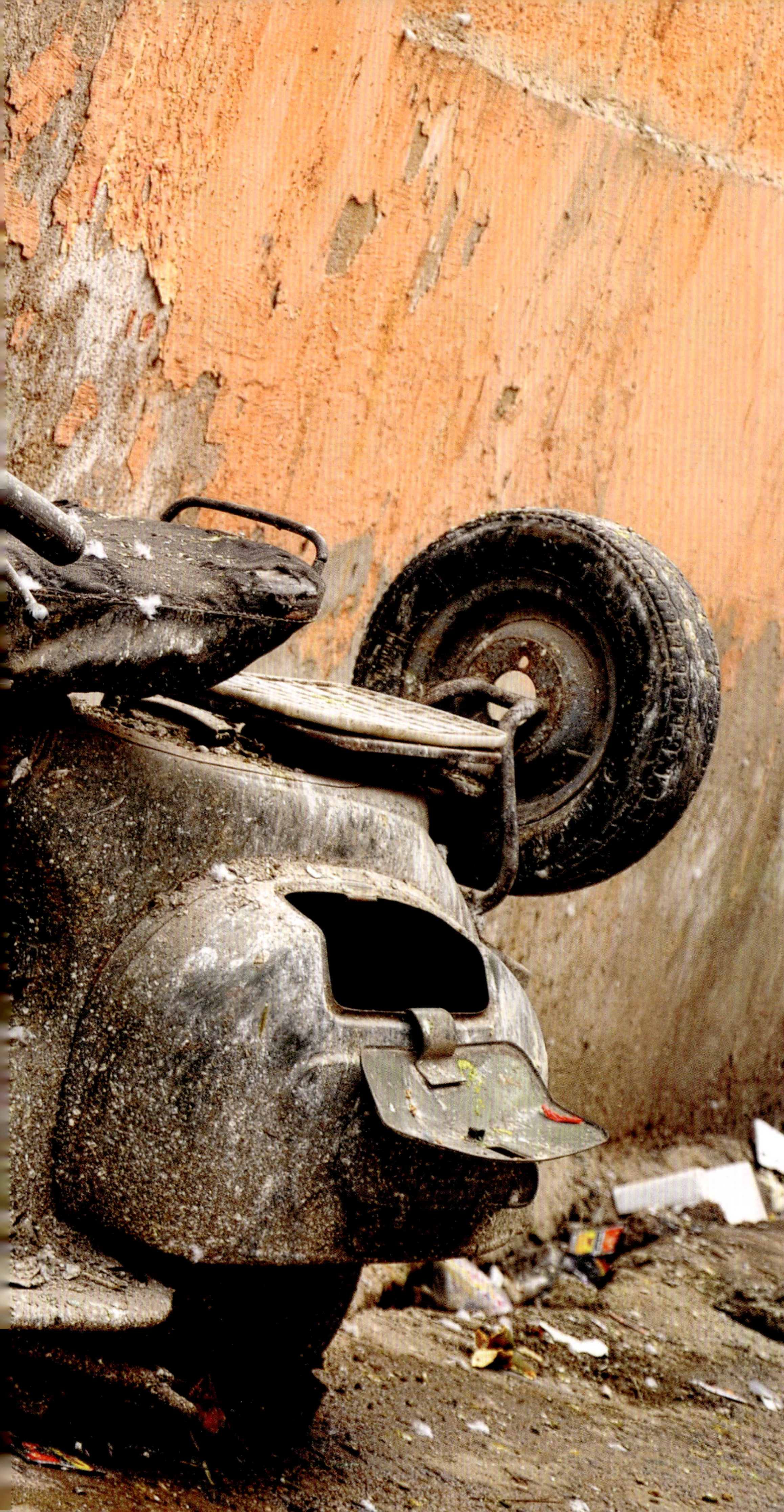

TOP LEFT:

Havana, Cuba

Cuba has long been famous for its vintage American cars, courtesy of the US trade embargo against the island, locked in place in 1960. Chevrolets, Buicks and Studebakers are common, but the old cars need constant work to keep them running – this one is receiving a rudimentary paint retouch.

BOTTOM LEFT:

New Zealand coast

The sand and the sea of the New Zealand coastline are steadily destroying this relatively modern family saloon car. Many vehicles worldwide are claimed by the sea each year, when their owners park them on a clear beach only to come back later and find them submerged in the tidal waters.

TOP RIGHT:

Monument Valley, Arizona–Utah border, United States

The colour of this caravan sits in sympathy with the pink tones in the rocks in Monument Valley. The hot and dry air of the valley will likely ensure that the caravan remains relatively rust-free for many years.

BOTTOM RIGHT:

Goldfield, Nevada, United States

Derelict cars here find a new life in artistic purpose. These are just a handful of more than 40 vehicles displayed creatively in the International Car Forest of the Last Church, a vivid work of installation art and the brainchild of artists Chad Sorg and Mark Rippie.

LEFT:

Jodhpur, India

In the developing world particularly, the humble scooter is the primary form of motorized transportation for millions of people, the bikes ridden to destruction on the city streets. The bike here has been abandoned in the gutter in Jodhpur, India, a country with around 37 million motorcycles or mopeds.

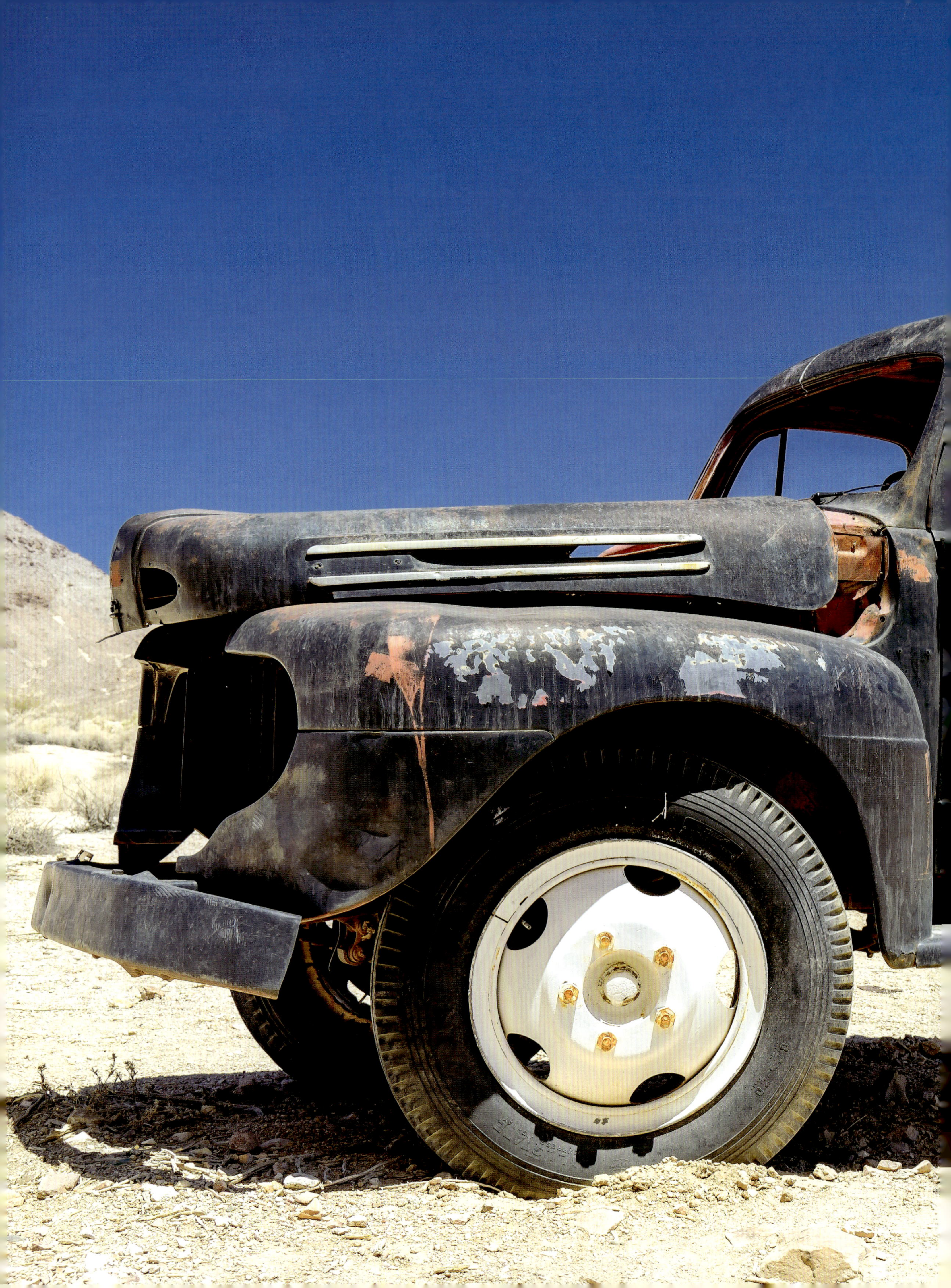

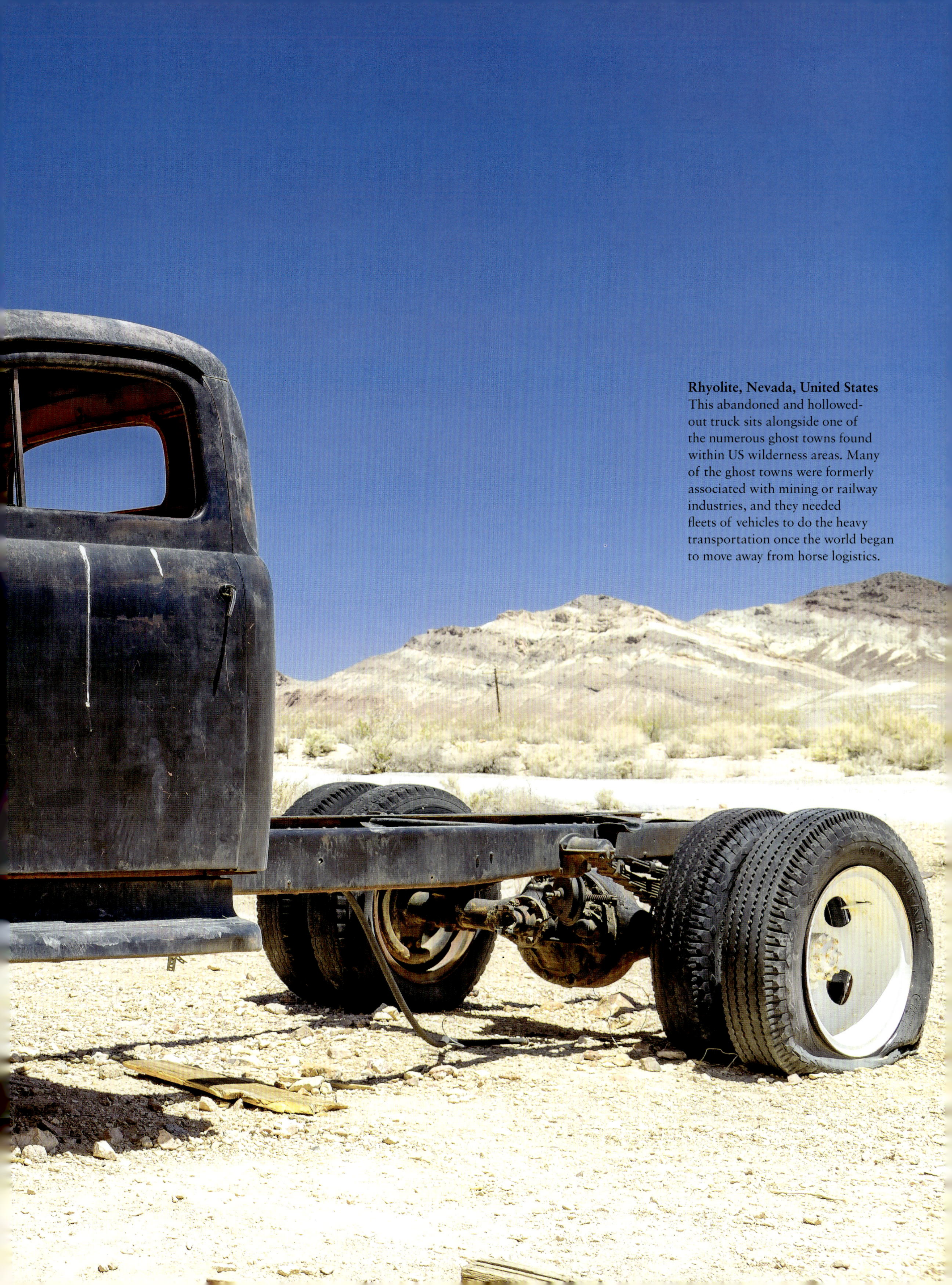

Rhyolite, Nevada, United States
This abandoned and hollowed-out truck sits alongside one of the numerous ghost towns found within US wilderness areas. Many of the ghost towns were formerly associated with mining or railway industries, and they needed fleets of vehicles to do the heavy transportation once the world began to move away from horse logistics.

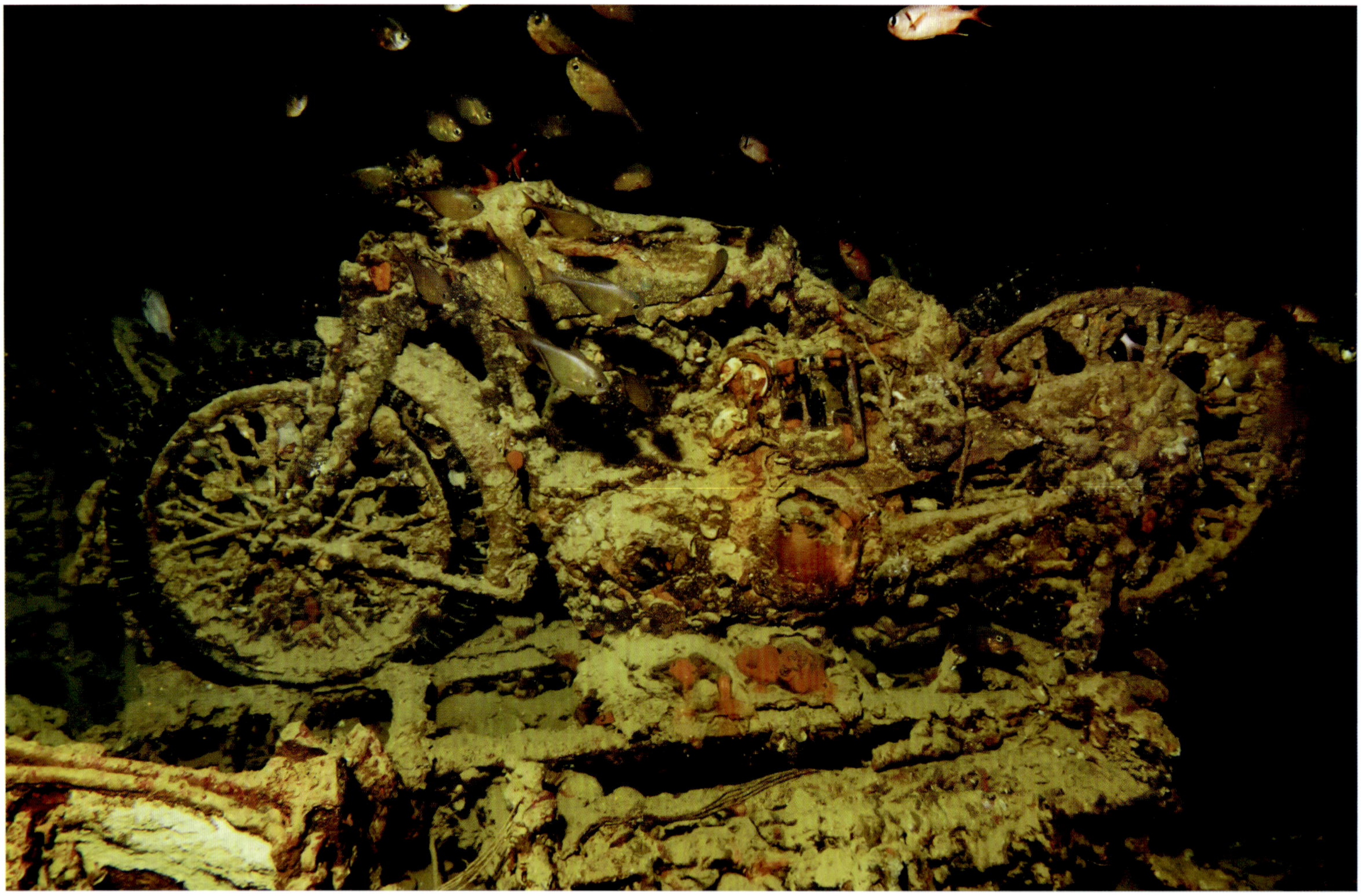

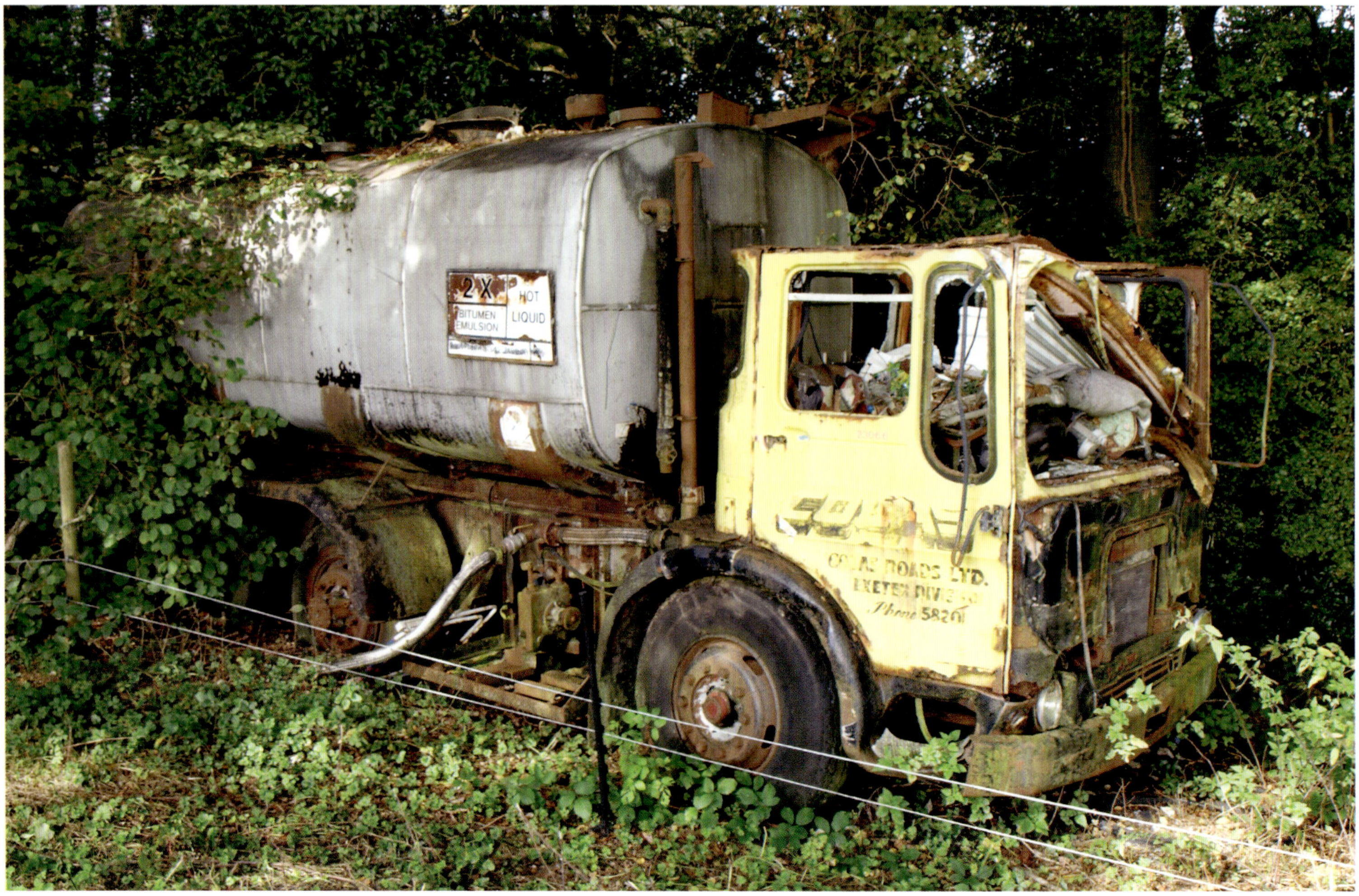

2X
BITUMEN
EMULSION
HOT
LIQUID
COLAS ROADS LTD.
EXETER DIVISION
Phone 58201

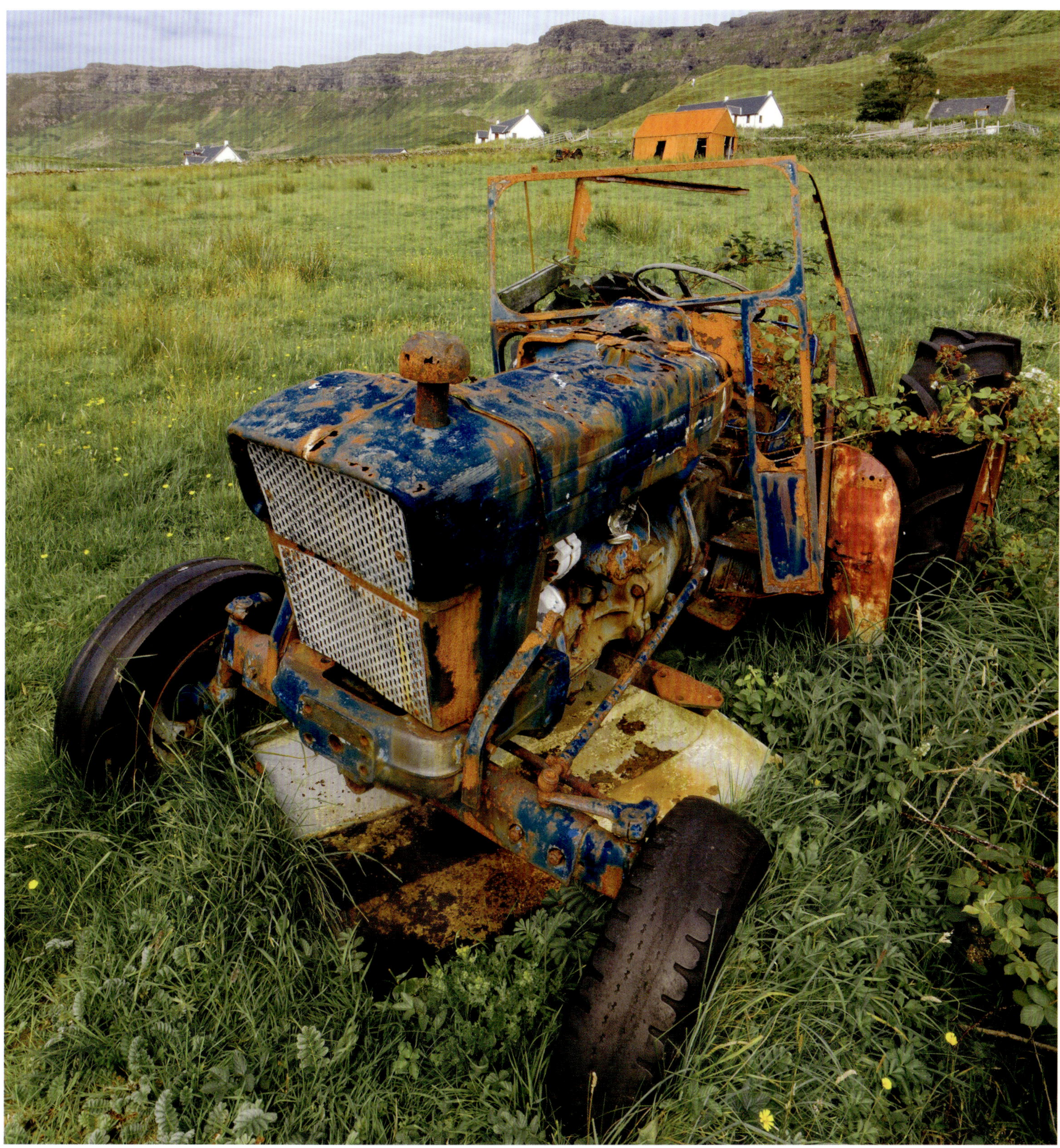

Sharm el-Sheikh, Egypt
On 6 October 1941, the British merchant vessel SS *Thistlegorm* was sunk at anchor by German air attack, two bombs sending the ship to the bottom. *Thistlegorm* was very heavily laden with motorcycles, trucks, aircraft, armoured vehicles and even two steam locomotives. Today, the ship is listed as one of the best international wreck dive sites.

Devon, England
A tanker vehicle rots in woodland in rural Devon. The truck appears to be an Associated Equipment Company (AEC) Mammoth Major, probably built in the 1950s or 1960s. The AEC company was founded in 1912, and provided both civilian and military vehicles until the marque disappeared in the 1970s, the company taken over by British Leyland.

Isle of Eigg, Scottish Inner Hebrides
This vintage tractor, likely to be of the 1940s or 1950s, decays on the farm that it once served. The first petrol-powered tractor was manufactured in 1892, and in the 20th century such vehicles revolutionized farming, freeing farm workers and horses from back-breaking labour and speeding up crop ploughing and harvesting.

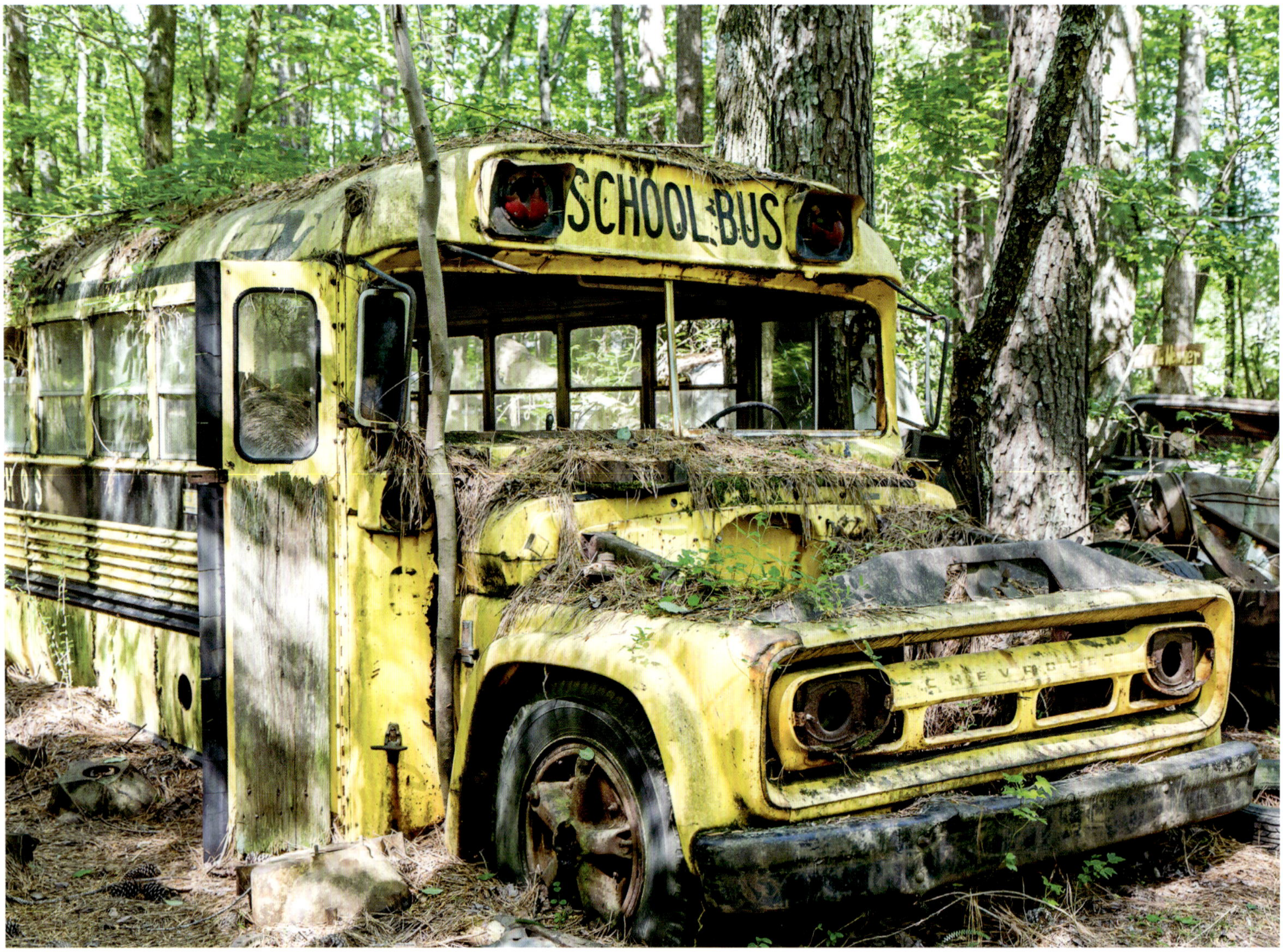

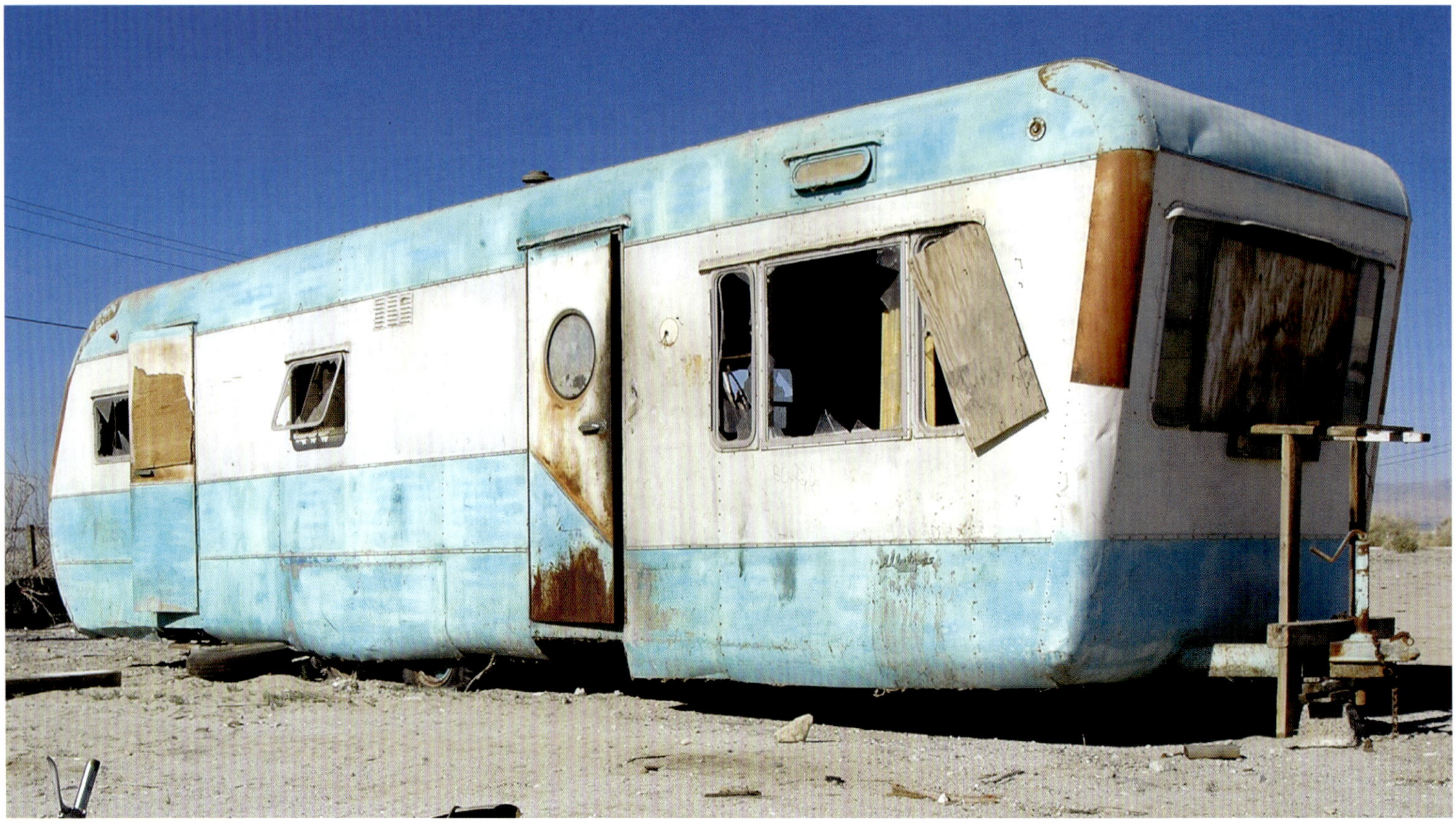

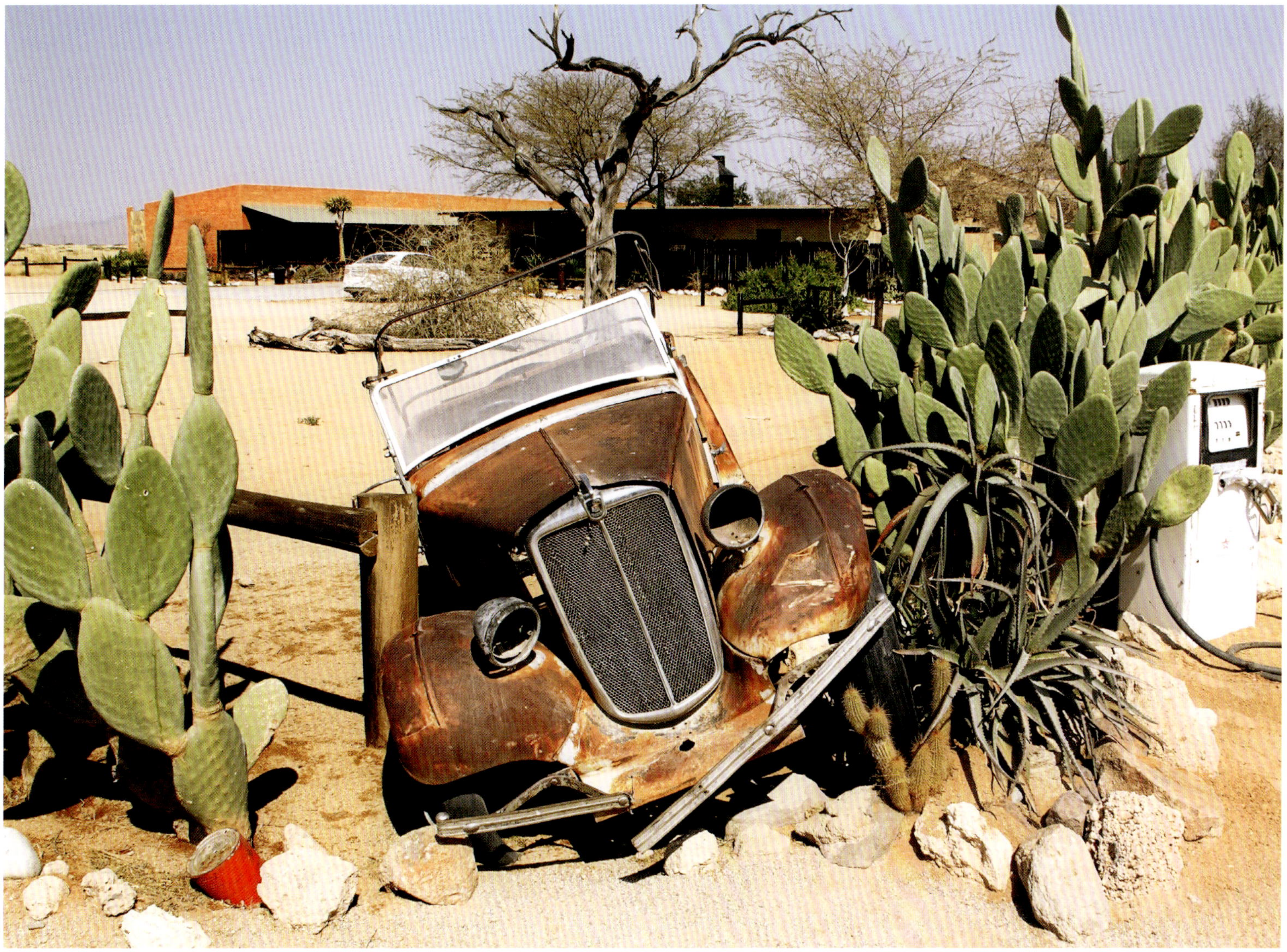

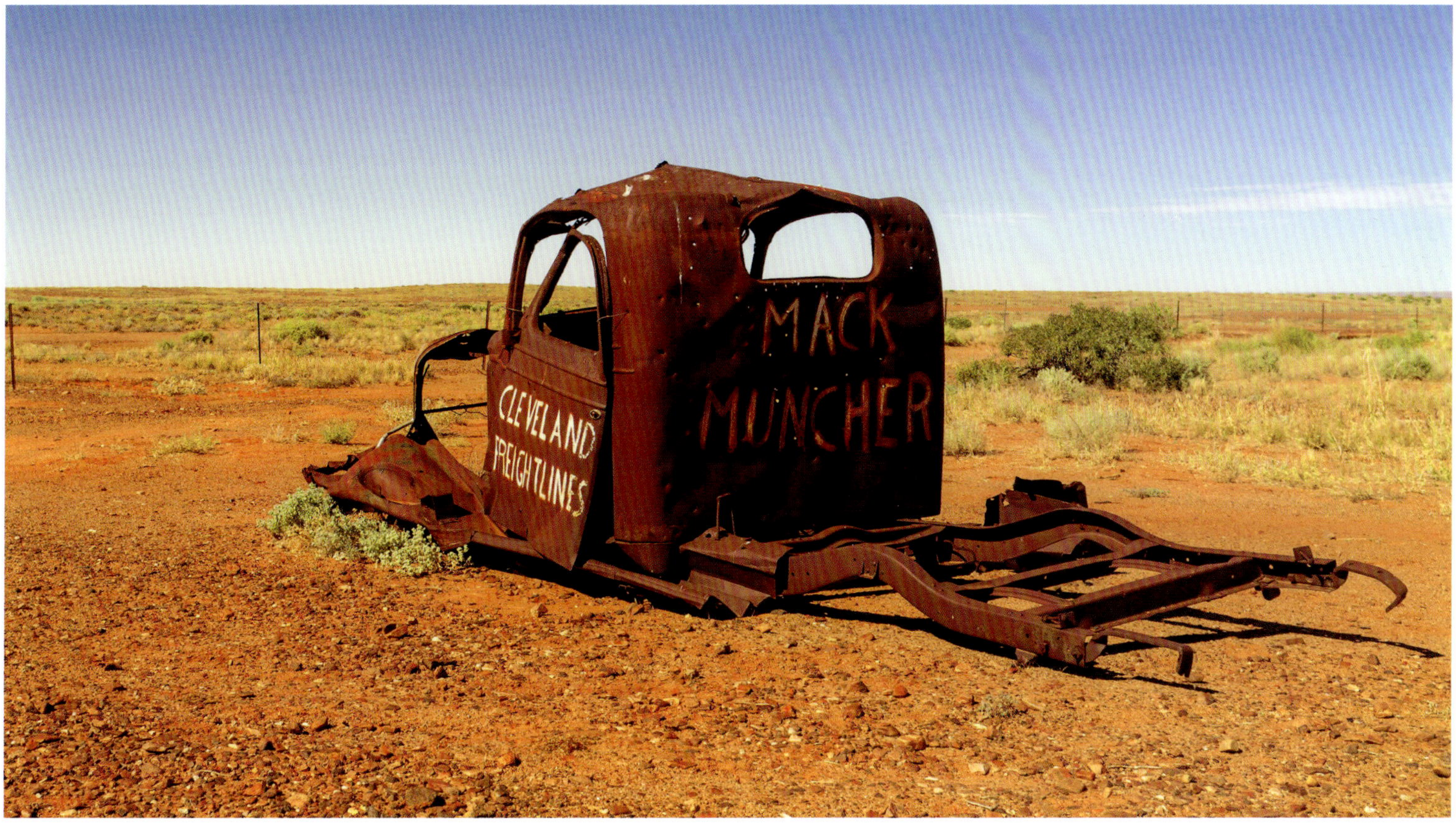

MACK
MUNCHER
CLEVELAND
FREIGHTLINES

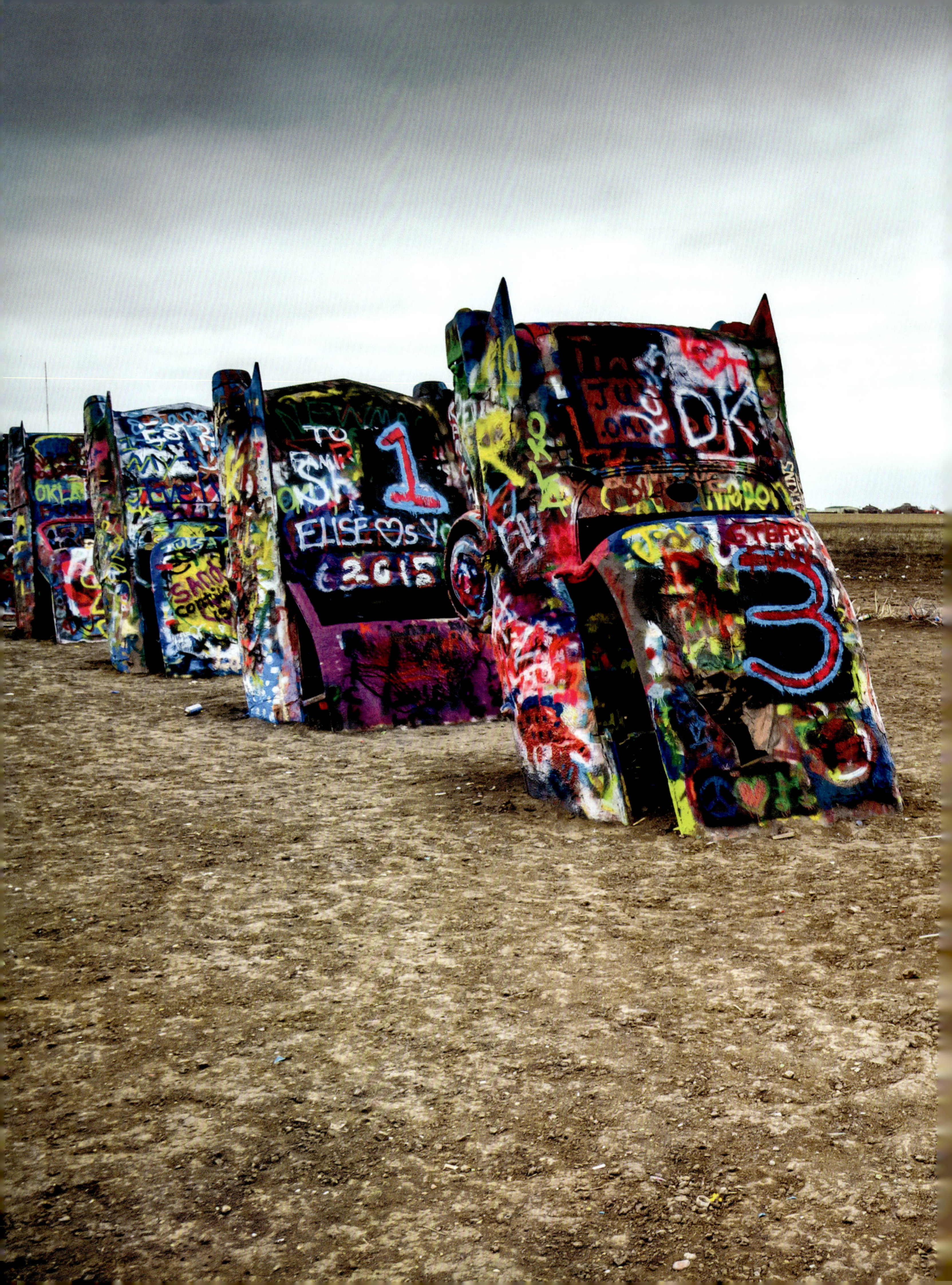

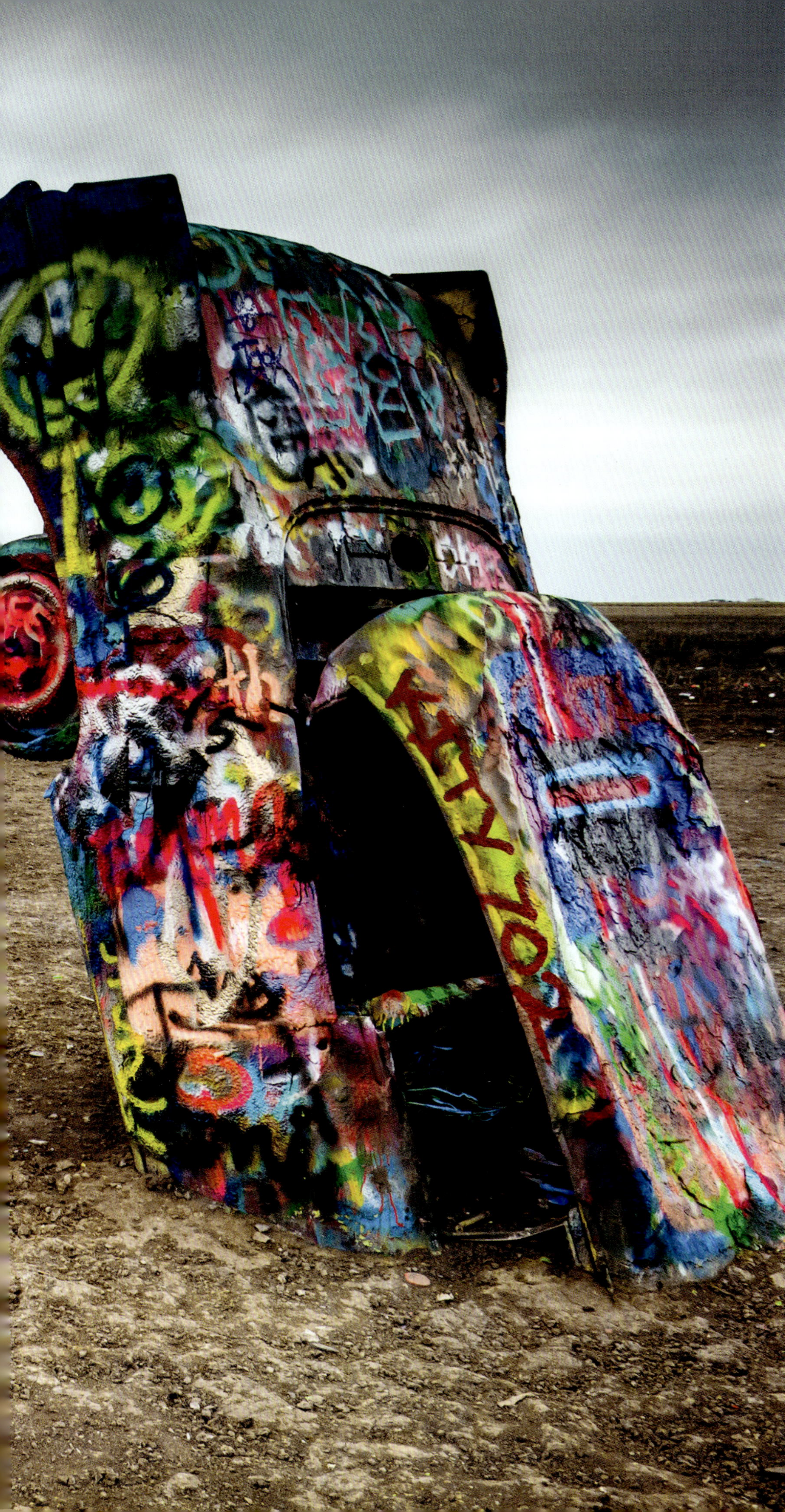

PREVIOUS PAGE:

TOP LEFT:

Detroit, Michigan
United States
Somewhere in Detroit, this yellow Chevrolet school bus lies inert and unused. The Chevrolet company is still one of the leading manufacturers of school buses in North America.

BOTTOM LEFT:

Salton Sea, Salton City, California, United States
An abandoned mobile home on the shores of the Salton Sea. The Salton Sea is a shallow lake in the Colorado Desert. Its highly salty waters and exposed location make it rather hostile to vehicles, and the area has many wrecks dotted around its arid landscape.

TOP RIGHT:

Solitaire, Namibia
Cactus plants frame this rusted old car in Solitaire, a small and isolated settlement in the Khomas Region of central Namibia near the Namib-Naukluft National Park. The vehicle probably belonged to the first inhabitants of the settlement, who put down roots there in the late 1940s.

BOTTOM RIGHT:

Edwards Creek, Oodnadatta Track, South Australian outback
The Australian outback, one of the most arid and inhospitable zones in the world, is as hard on vehicles as it is on people. This truck has been weathered by the elements until little remains apart from the shell of the cab and the chassis framework.

LEFT:

Route 66 in Amarillo, Texas, United States
These wrecks form part of the Cadillac Ranch, a public art installation created in 1974 by Chip Lord, Hudson Marquez and Doug Michels. The half-buried vehicles represent the evolution of Cadillac vehicles from 1949 to 1963. Although the paint schemes have changed over time, the vehicles always attract graffiti.

153

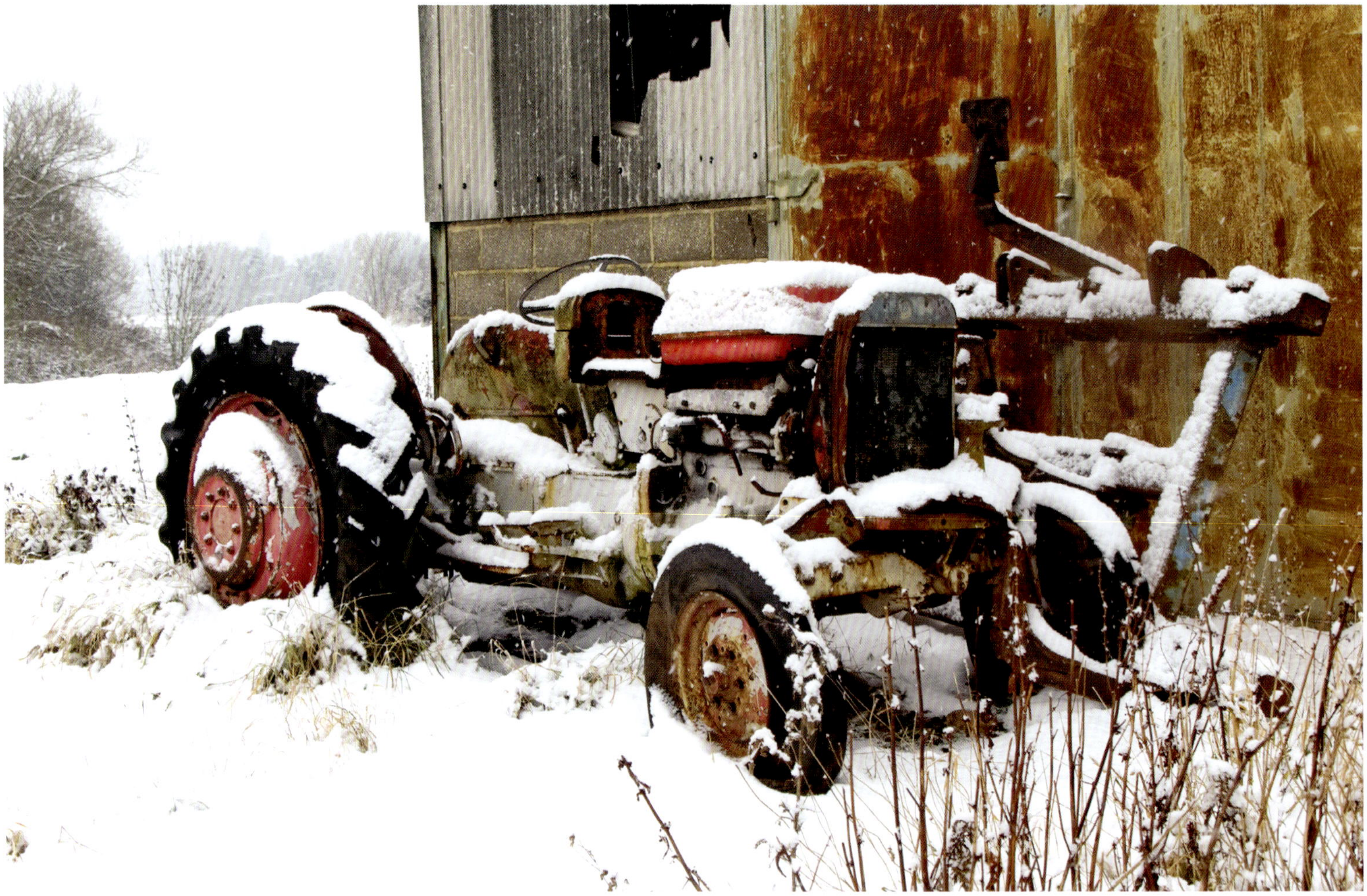

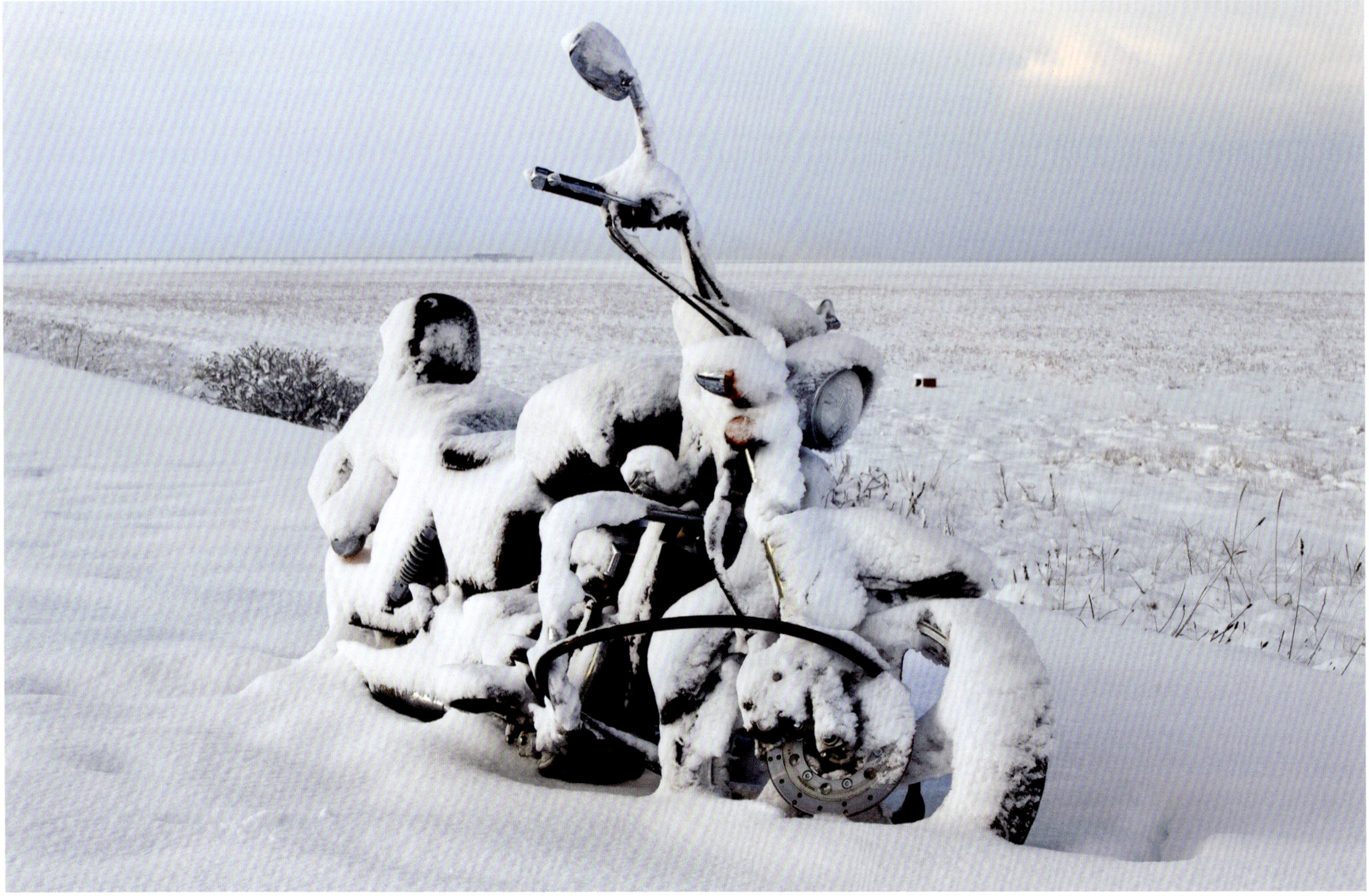

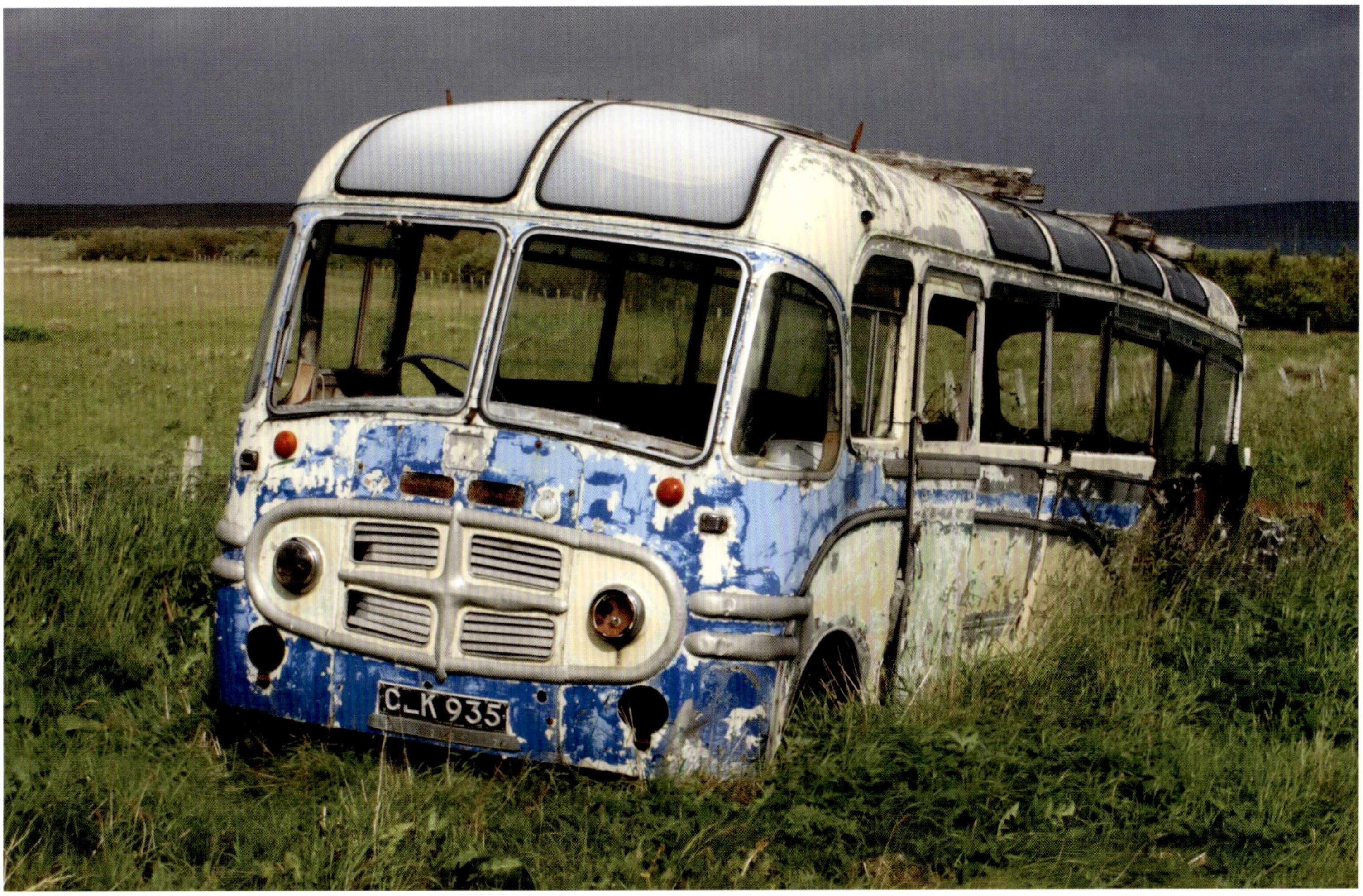

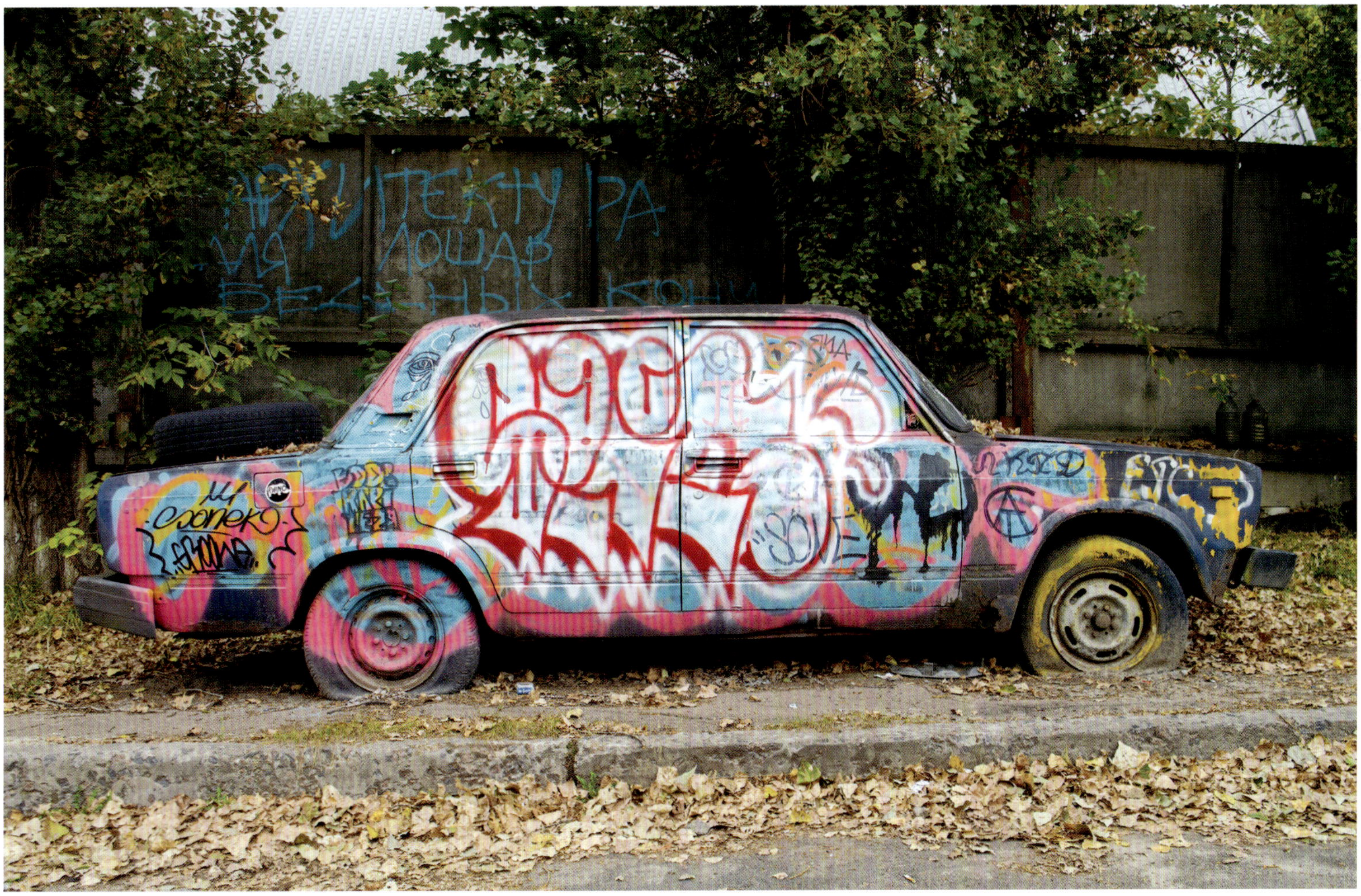

TOP LEFT:

Bunny, Nottinghamshire, England

An abandoned tractor gets a picturesque blanket of snow at this farm in Nottinghamshire. The United Kingdom was once home to a significant number of tractor manufacturers, and some survive to this day, such as JCB.

BOTTOM LEFT:

Southport, Merseyside, England

Sometimes extreme weather compels the sudden abandonment of a vehicle. This motorcycle has been parked up and left by the side of a road following very heavy and unexpected snowfall in the north-east of England.

TOP RIGHT:

Hoy, Orkney, Scotland

This 50-year-old bus, abandoned in a field in the Orkney Isles, was produced by the British Bedford company, which was founded in 1930 and became a world-leading manufacturer of trucks, supplying them to commercial and military customers. The company disappeared in the 1980s under a familiar pattern of buy-outs and declining sales.

BOTTOM RIGHT:

Kiev, Ukraine

What could become an eyesore – an abandoned car on a road in the Ukrainian city of Kiev – is transformed by extremely colourful street art and graffiti.

RIGHT:

Båstnäs, Värmland, Sweden

As if finding some peace among the forest trees, these abandoned and moss-covered cars are becoming part of the scenery. The stack of vehicles includes a Volkswagen Beetle, a car originally created as a vehicle to boost civilian car ownership in Nazi Germany. Although Hitler authorized a nationwide saving scheme for the vehicles, few citizens actually received the car during the 1930s and war years.

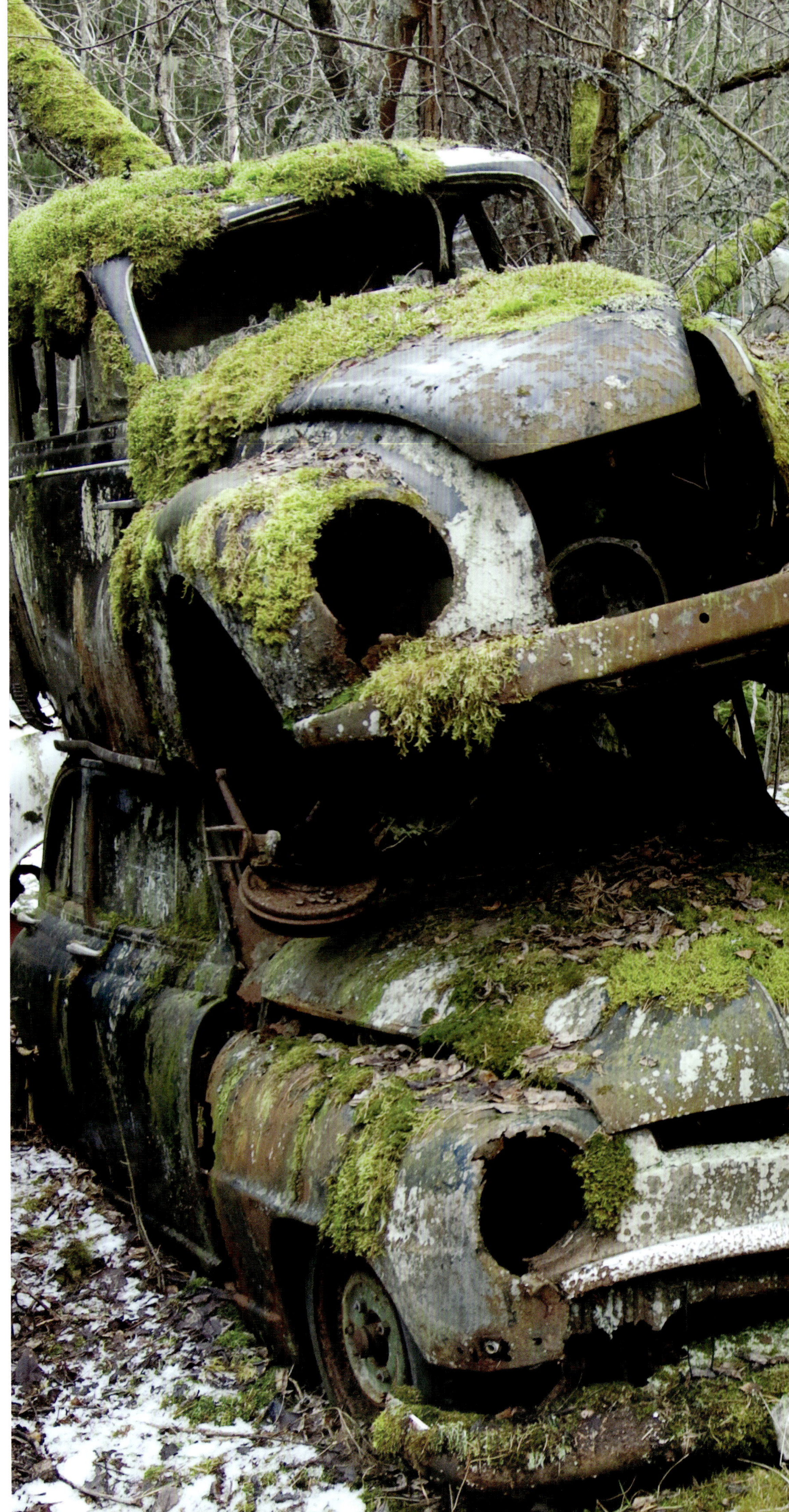

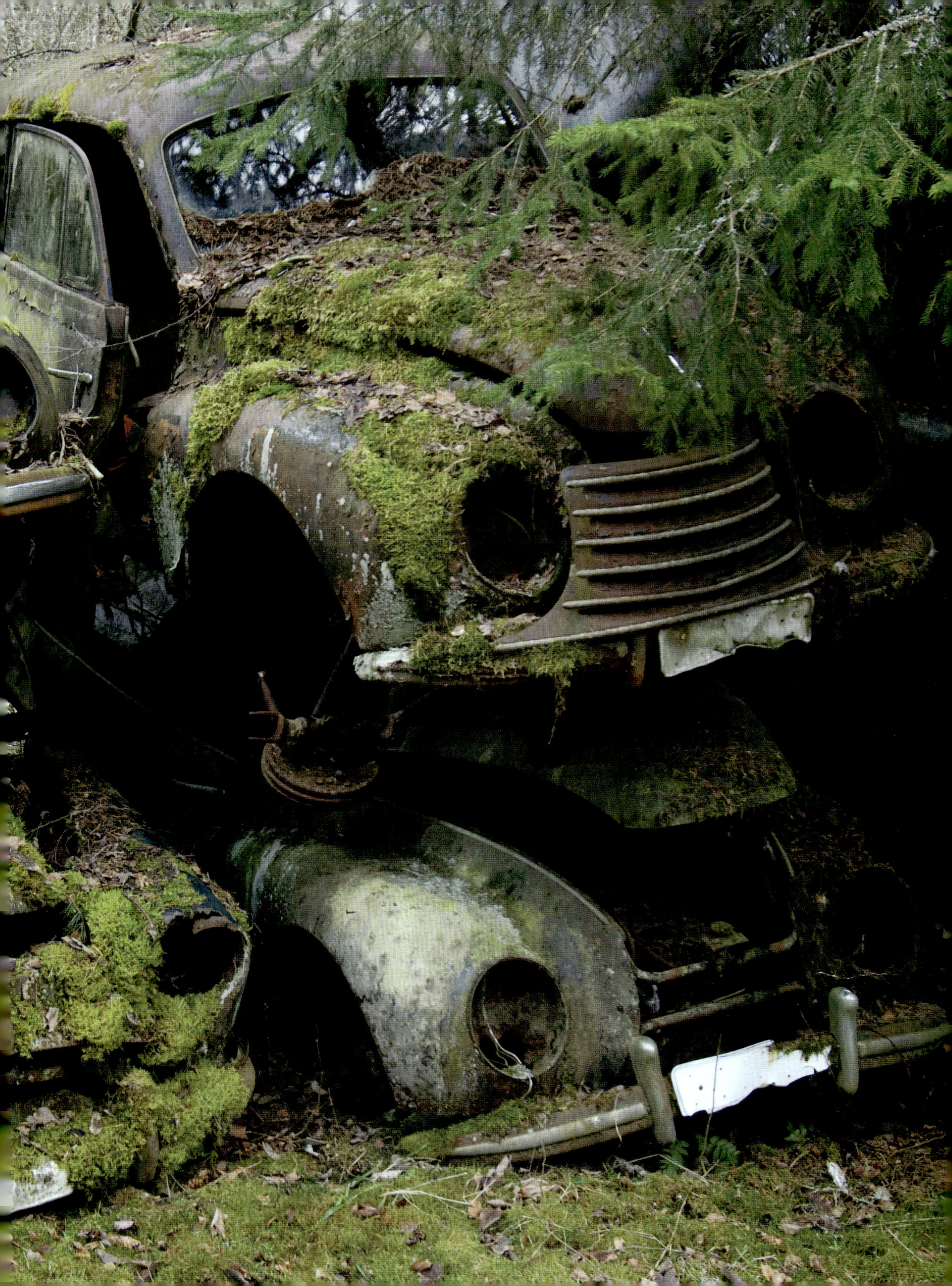

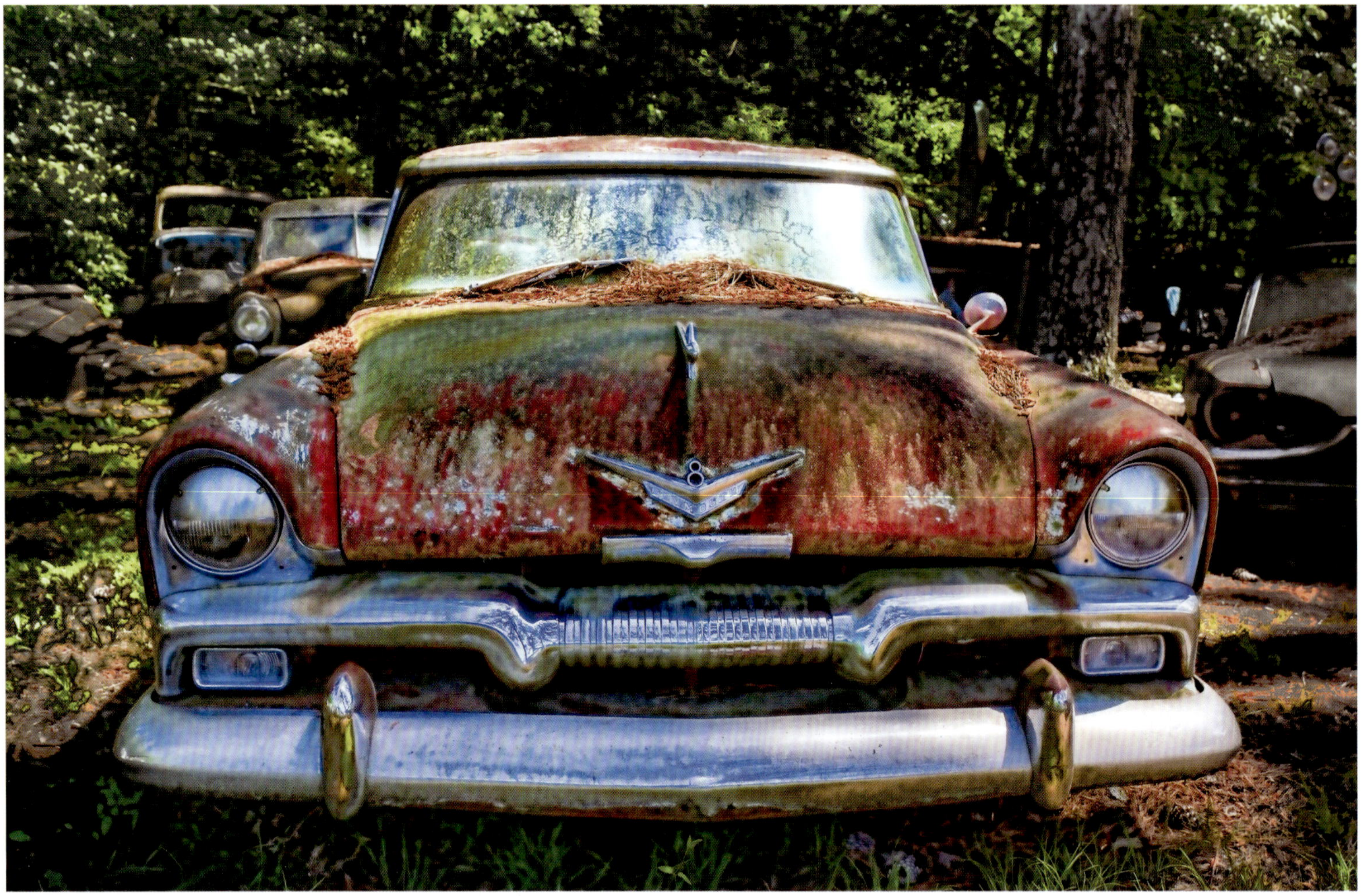

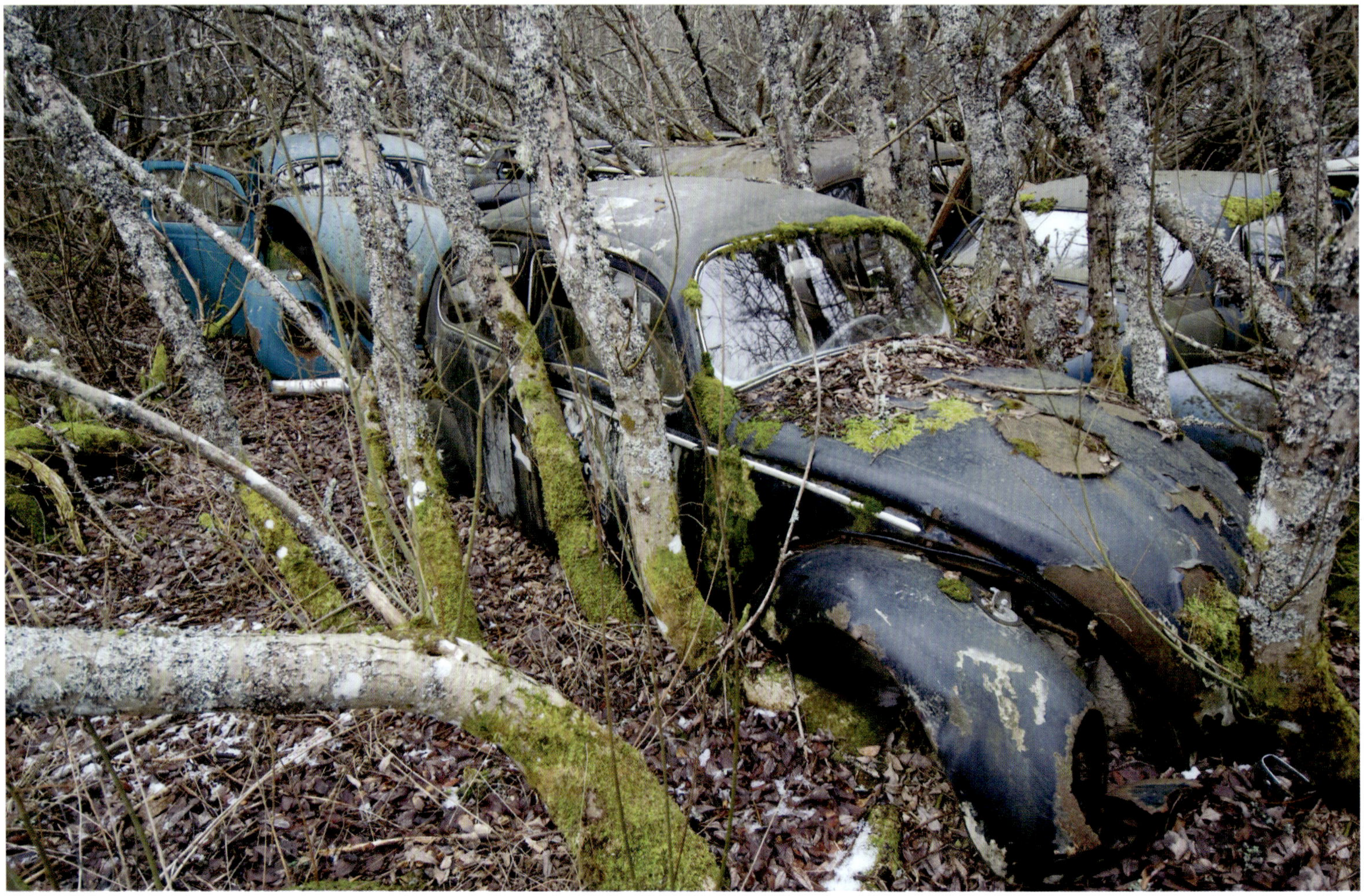

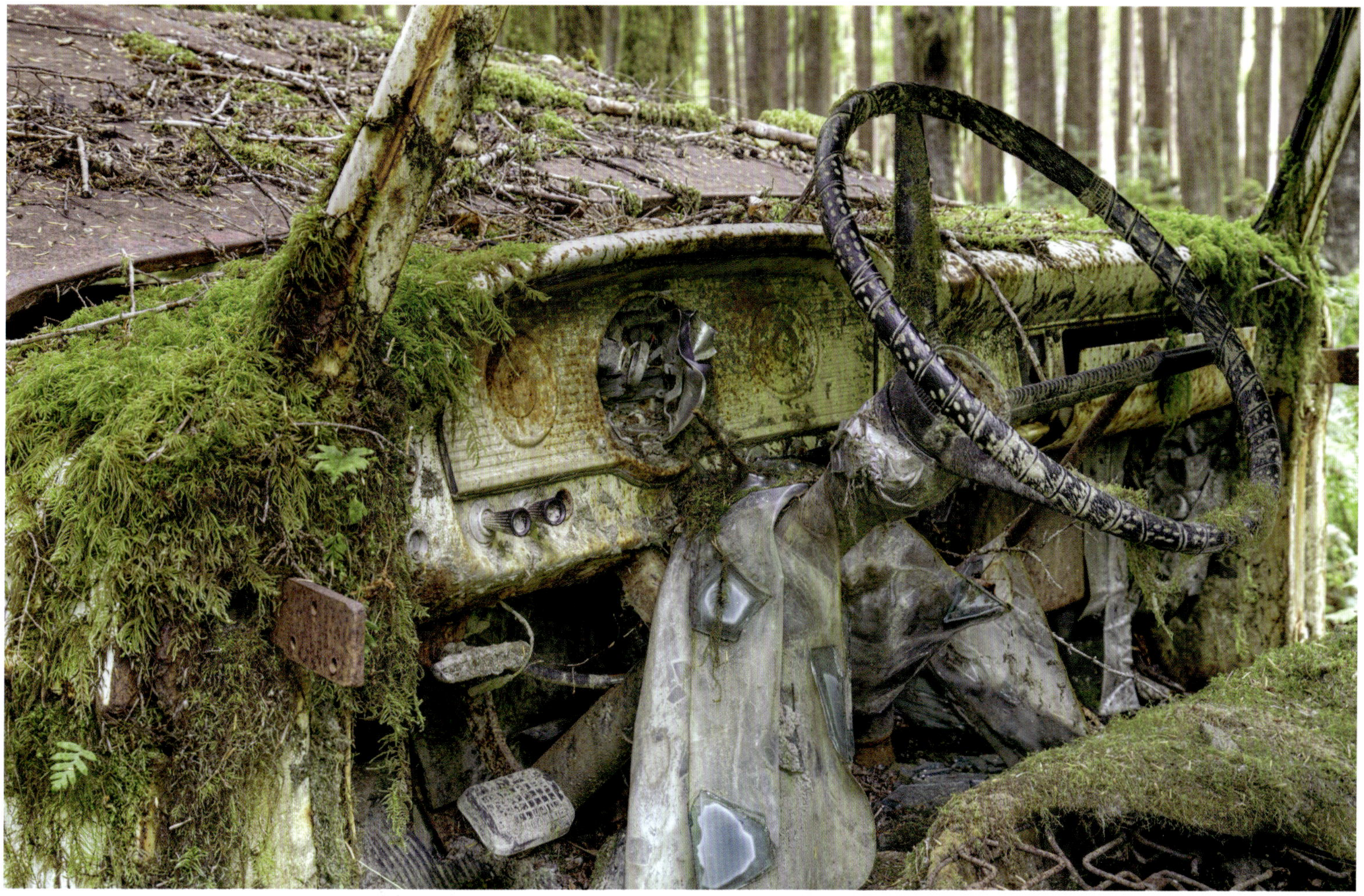

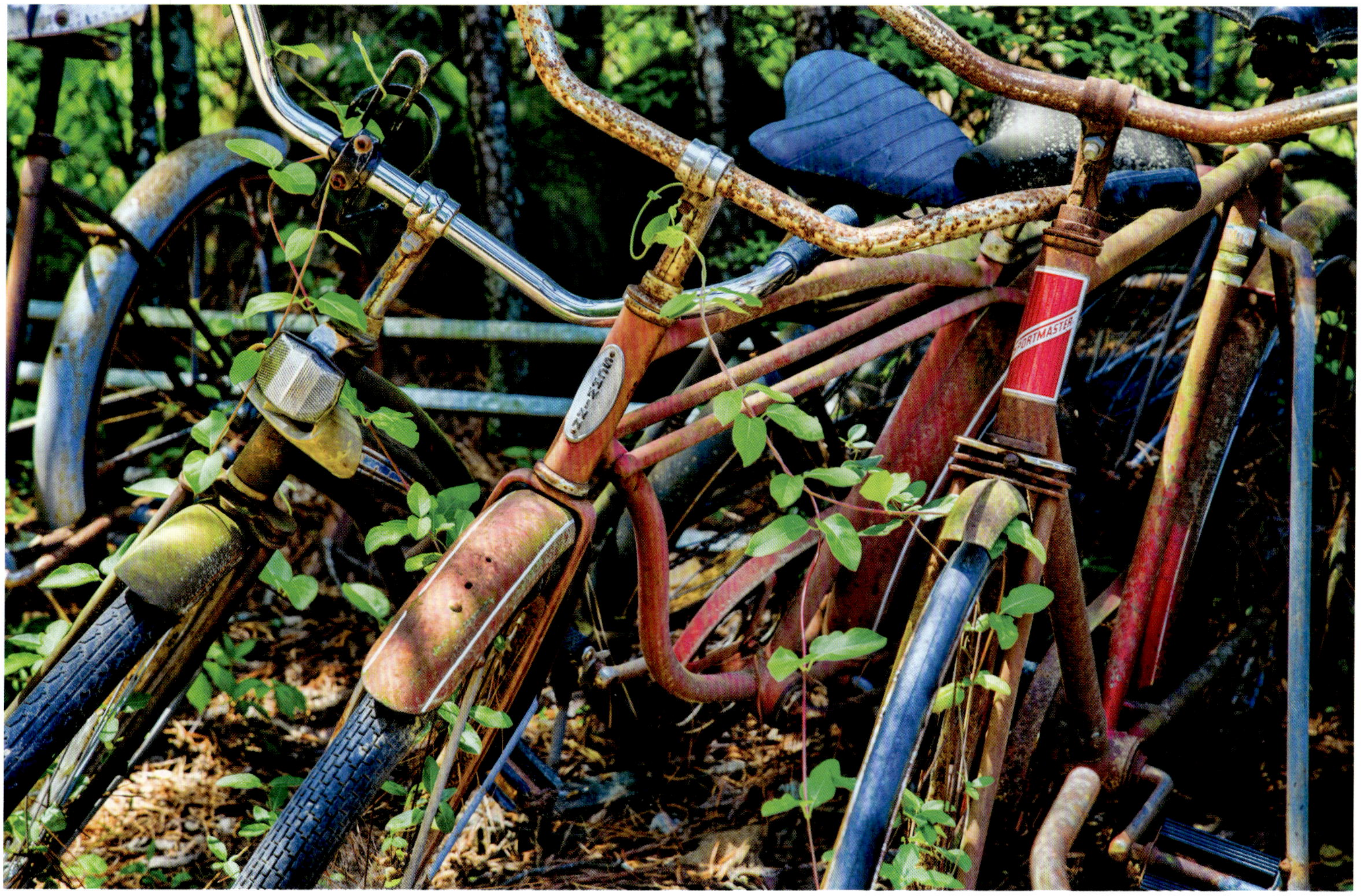

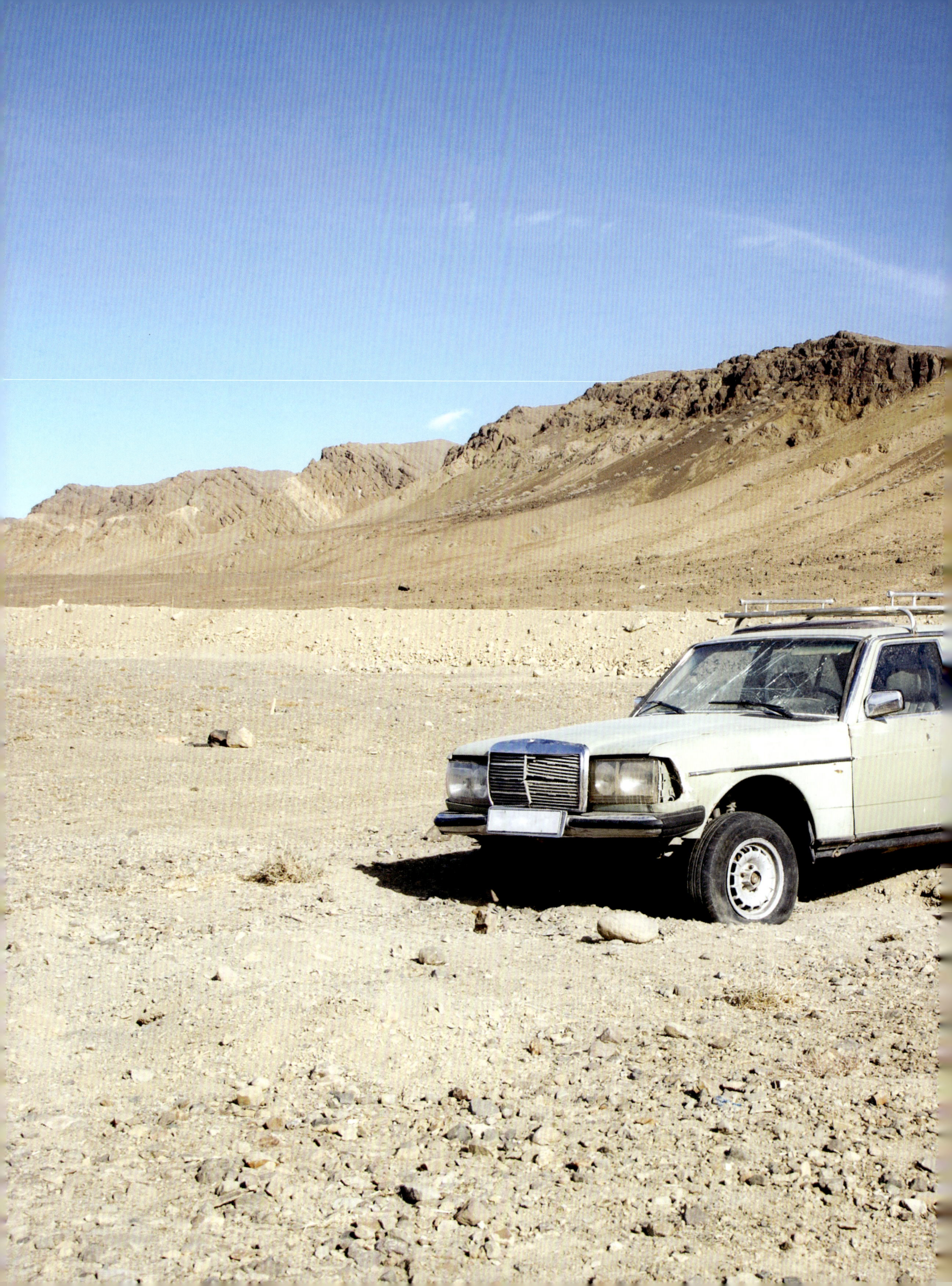

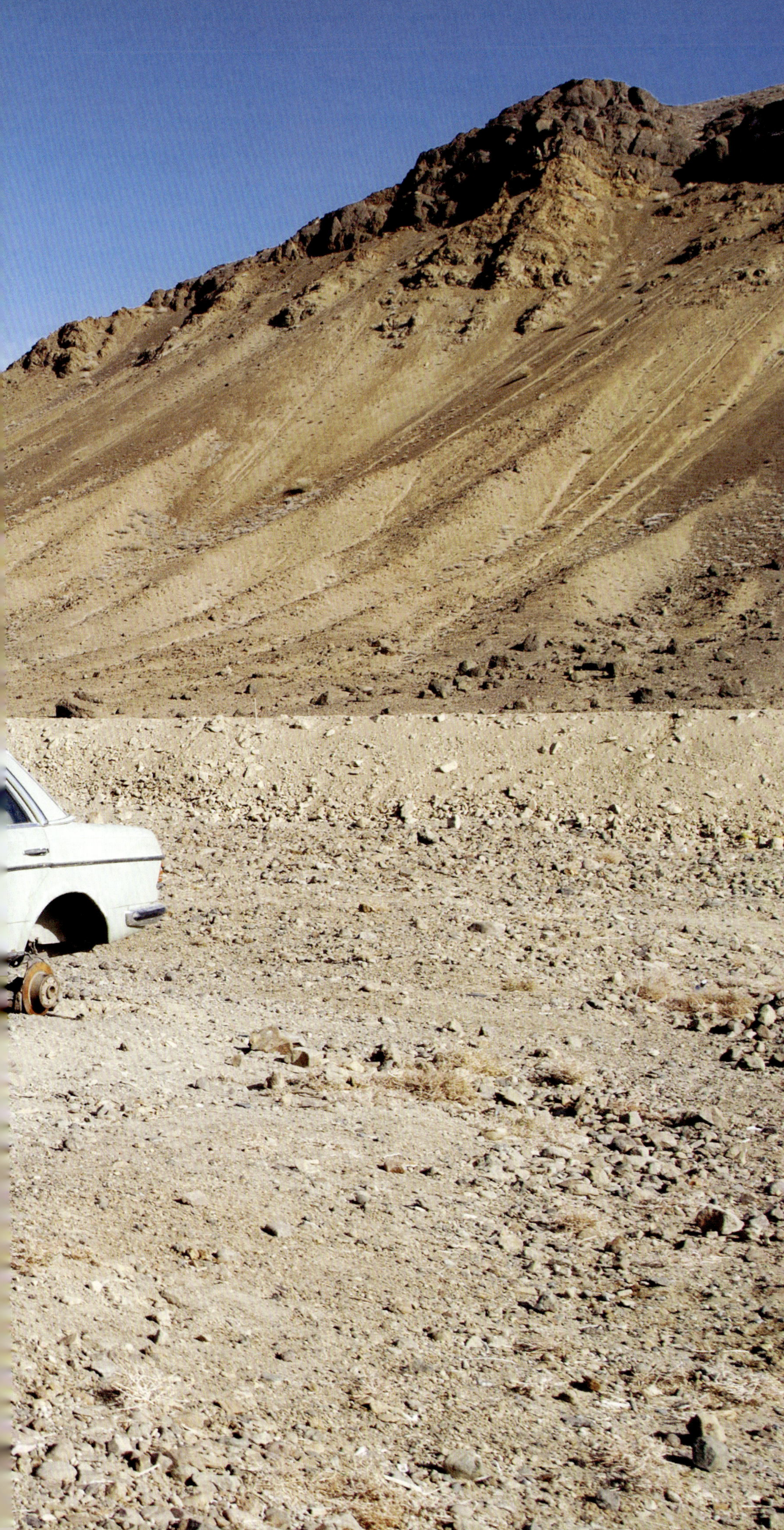

White, Georgia, United States
A resident of Old Car City in White, Georgia, the world's largest known classic car junkyard. Thousands of abandoned cars, including many great American classics of the 1950s and 1960s, sit among the woodland, creating a memory-laden living museum.

BOTTOM LEFT:

Båstnäs, Värmland, Sweden
Another view of the Swedish car graveyard in Båstnäs, Värmland, which contains more than 1,000 vehicles. The graveyard site was originally a giant scrapyard established in the 1950s, but which went out of business in the 1980s.

TOP RIGHT:

Olympic National Park, Washington, United States
Moss is claiming the dashboard of this abandoned Ford pick-up truck, dating from 1963, decaying in the middle of the green rainforest in Olympic National Park, Washington.

BOTTOM RIGHT:

White, Georgia, United States
Vintage cars are not the only vehicles to litter the 13-hectare (32-acre) site of Old Car City – here we also see a collection of bicycles. It is estimated by the owners of the junkyard that 95 per cent of visitors are photographers.

LEFT:

Gobi Desert
This old Mercedes chose one of the most remote places to die – in Gobi Desert of Central Asia. Note how the rear wheel has been removed – abandoned cars provide a ready source of salvage for those who still have vehicles to run.

Hudson, New Hampshire
If an abandoned car does not
end up in a crusher, then rust
is the force most likely to claim
it. Rust-prevention treatments
were only partly successful in
the motor vehicle industry until
very recently, and even operable
vehicles would often need regular
bodywork maintenance to stop
rust spreading.

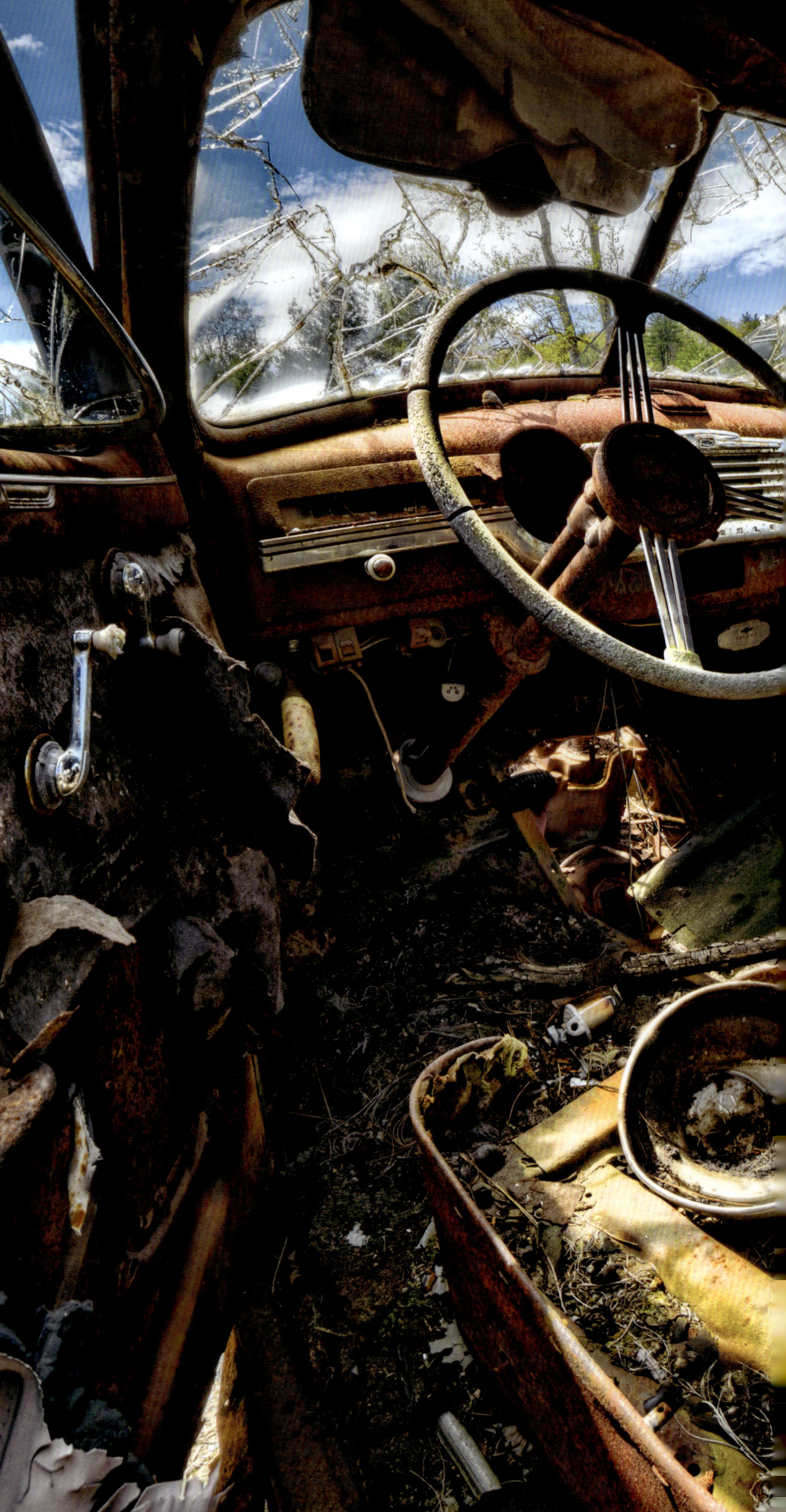

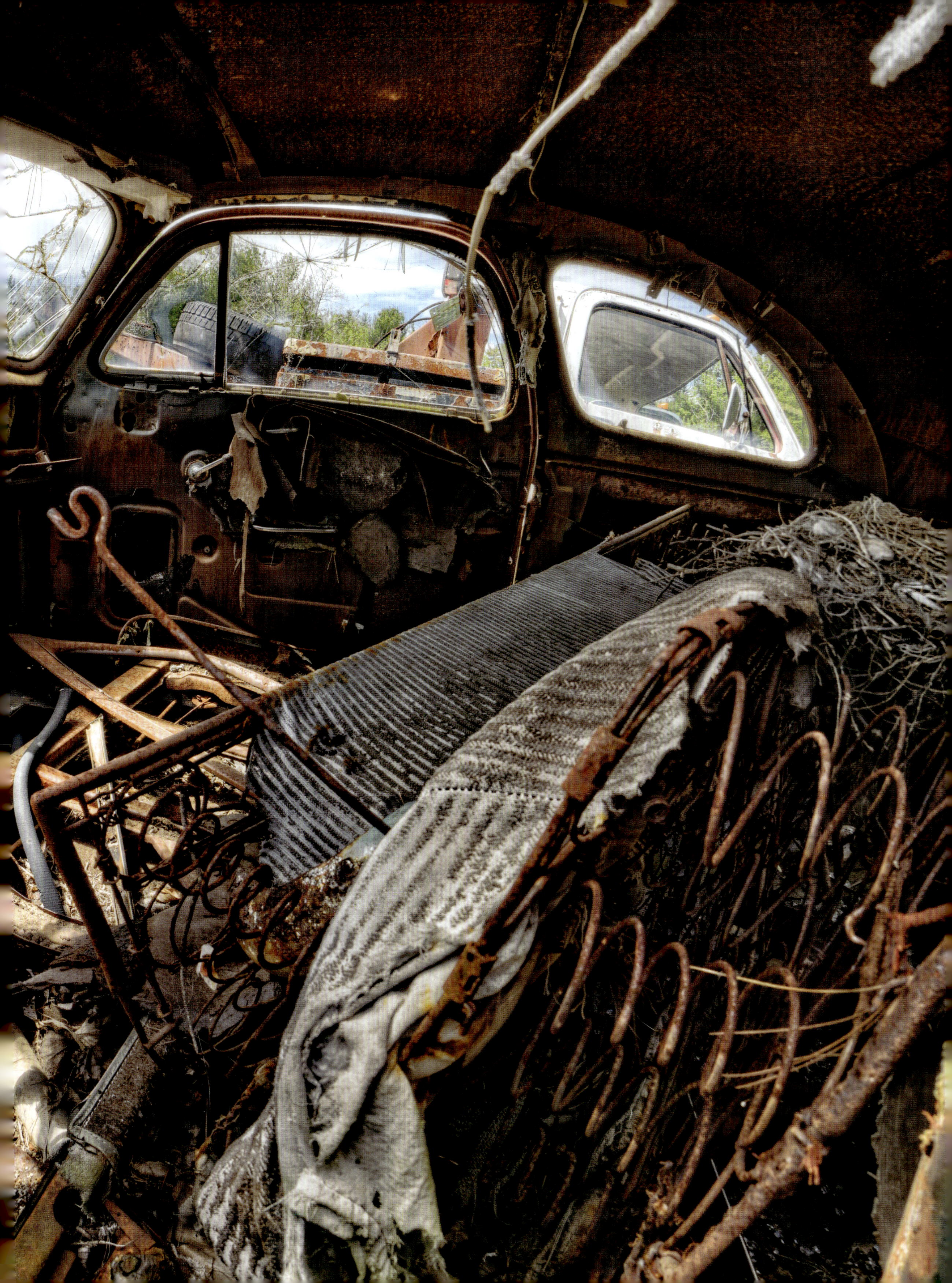

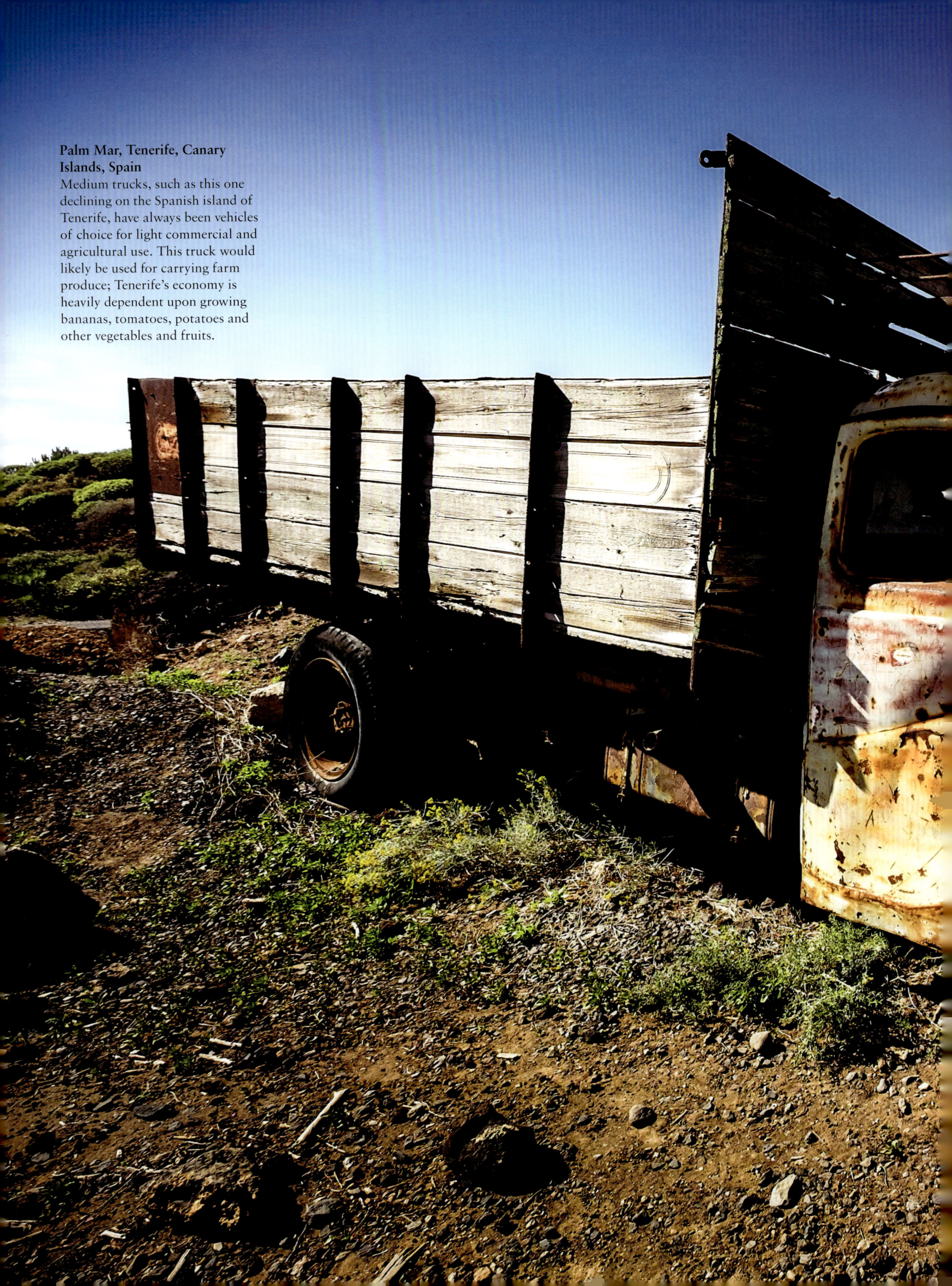

Palm Mar, Tenerife, Canary
Islands, Spain
Medium trucks, such as this one
declining on the Spanish island of
Tenerife, have always been vehicles
of choice for light commercial and
agricultural use. This truck would
likely be used for carrying farm
produce; Tenerife's economy is
heavily dependent upon growing
bananas, tomatoes, potatoes and
other vegetables and fruits.

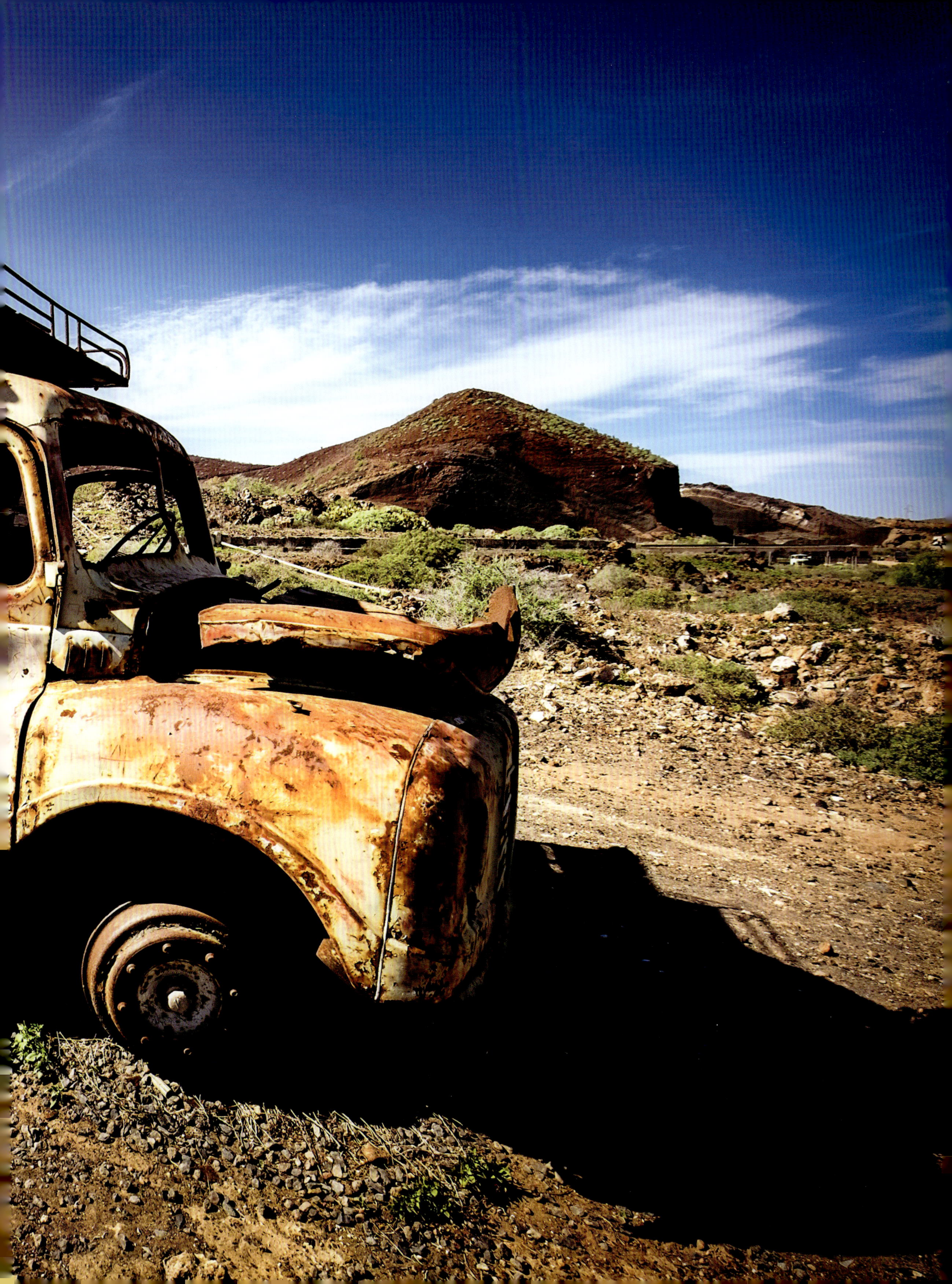

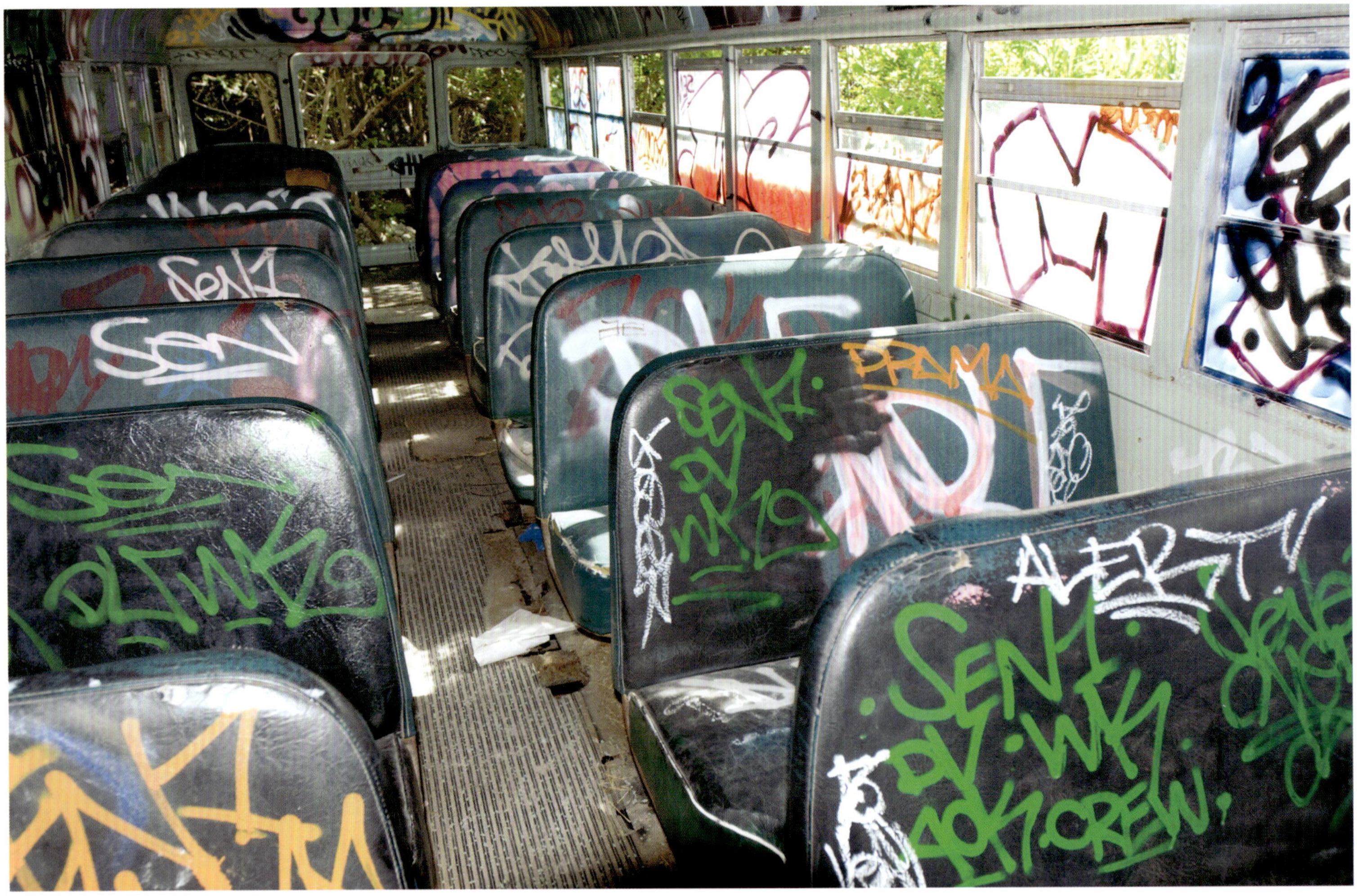

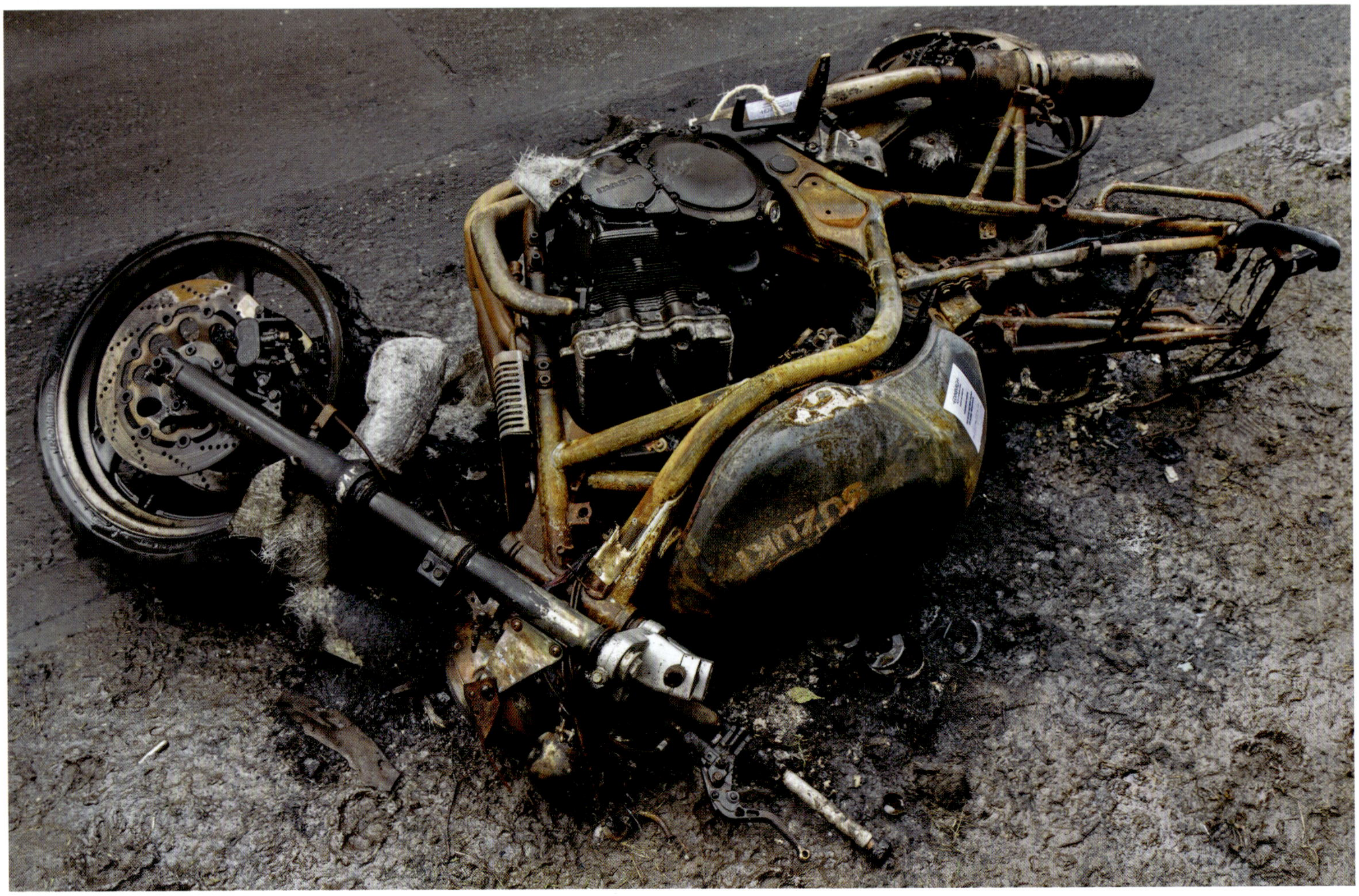

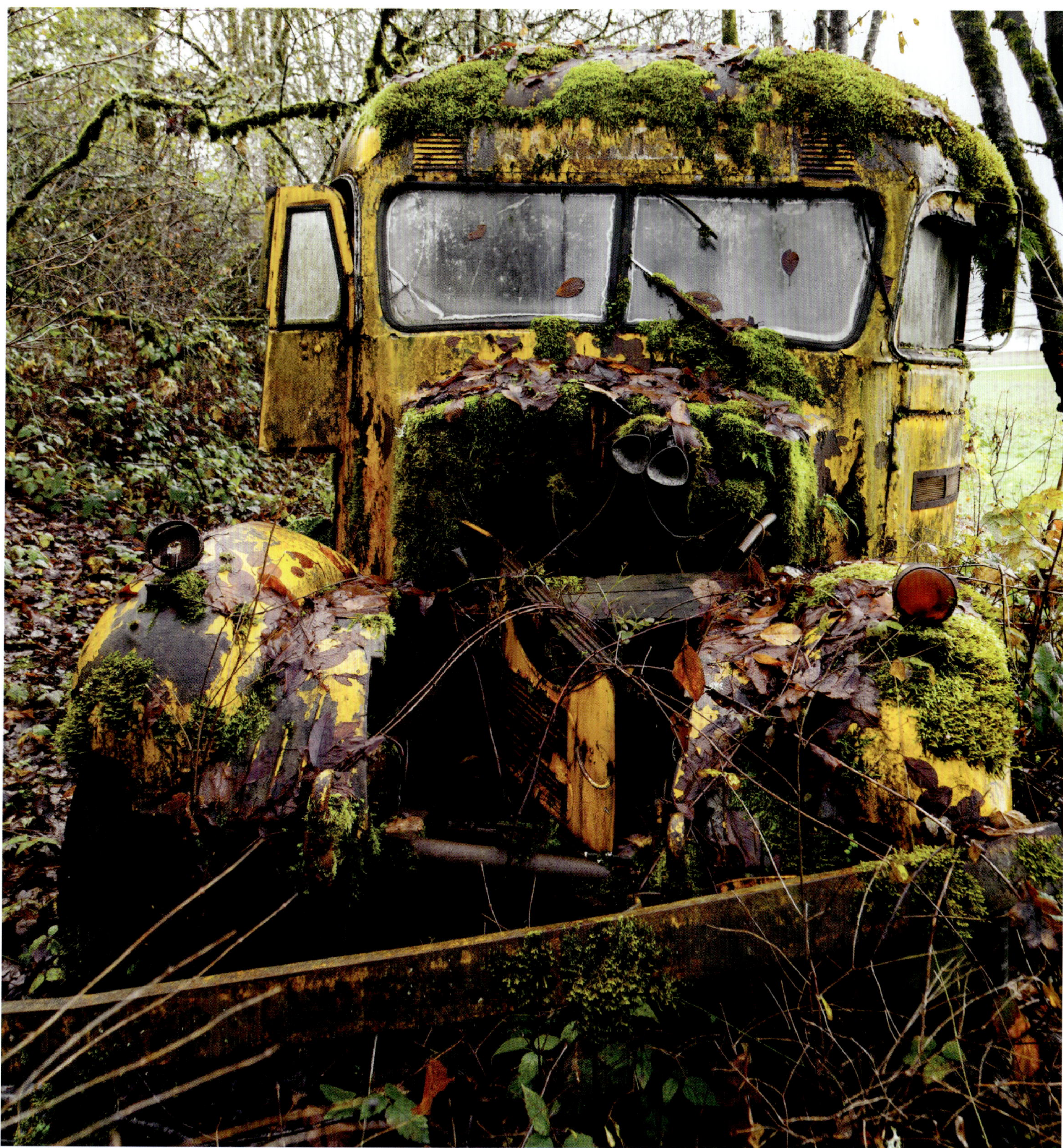

Miami, Florida, United States
In a clear expression of youth getting back at the 'establishment', this abandoned school bus in Florida has been heavily daubed in graffiti, each seat receiving an individual or 'crew' label. School buses have a special place in American cultural iconography, often seen as places of bullying and intimidation, particularly towards the back of the bus.

Leith, Edinburgh, Scotland
Ridden to destruction, this Suzuki motorbike is a charred wreck on this Scottish motorbike track. Modern high-performance road bikes can deliver speeds well in excess of 160km/h (100mph), and acceleration times from 0–96km/h (0–60mph) are measured in just a few seconds. Needless to say, bike riders need skill and experience to handle such power.

Salem, Oregon, United States
Another abandoned school bus sits in woodland in the United States. Although accurate figures are impossible to obtain, it has been estimated that the United States has in the region of 20 million to 50 million abandoned vehicles of one sort or another, lying everywhere from authorized scrapyards through to wilderness settings such this one.

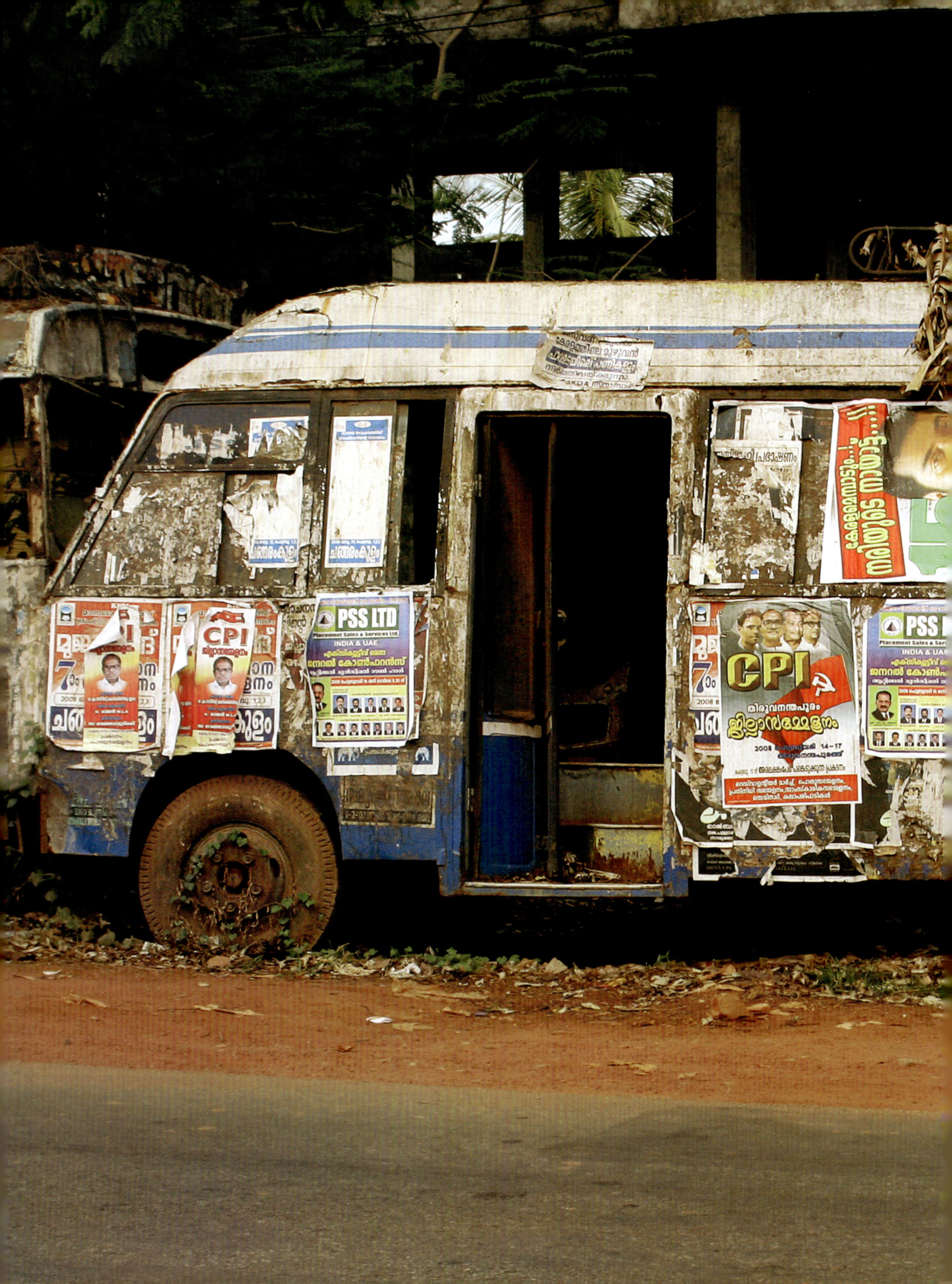

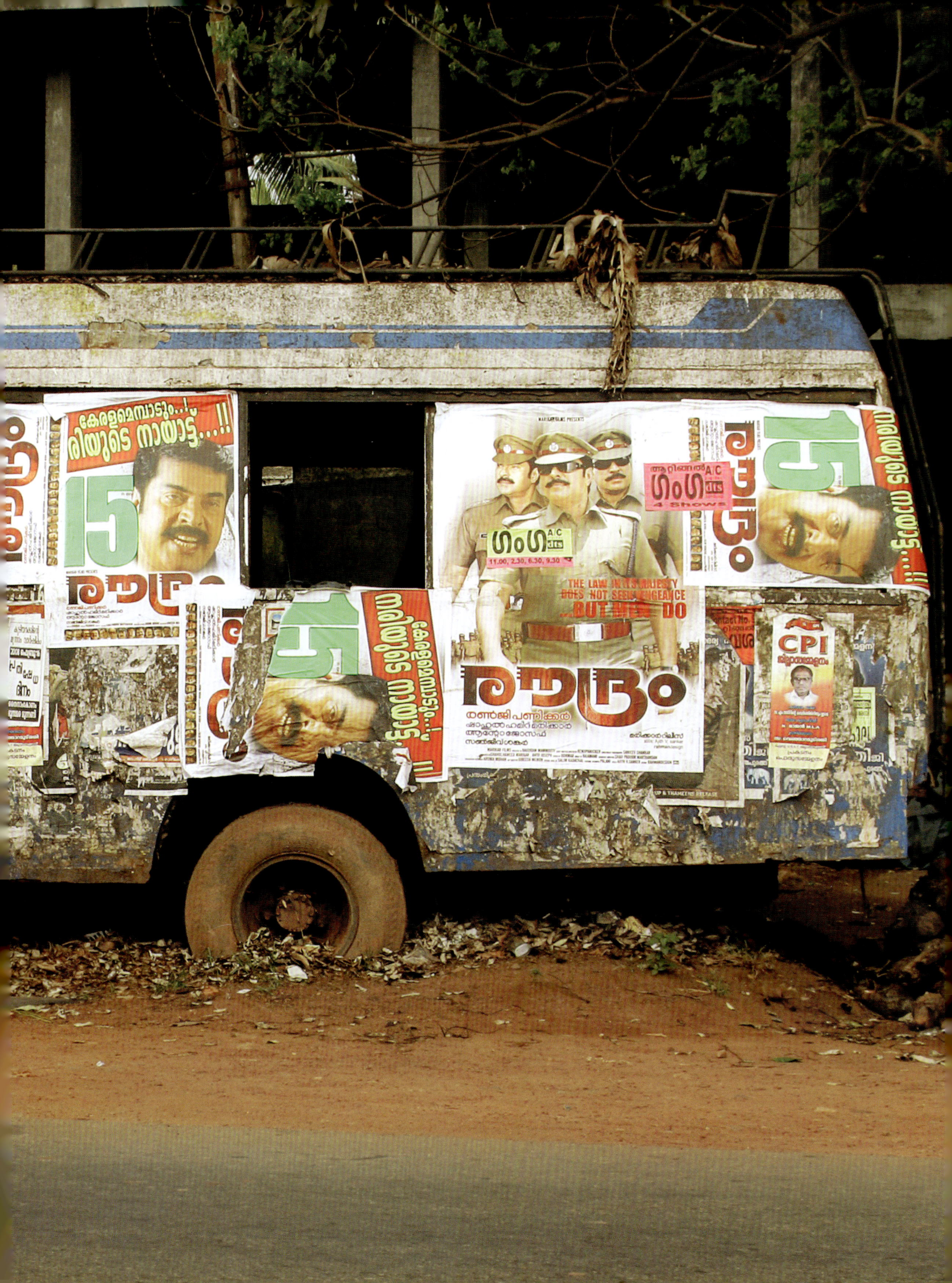
കേരളമെമ്പാടും..!
രിയുടെ നായാട്ട്....!!!
15
രൗദ്രം
WARRIAR FILMS PRESENTS
ഗംഗ A/C
11.00, 2.30, 6.30, 9.30
ആ റീജൻ A/C
ഗംഗ
4 Shows
THE LAW IN ITS MAJESTY
DOES NOT SEEK VENGEANCE
...BUT MEN DO
15
രൗദ്രം
രൗദ്രം
രൗദ്രം
CPI

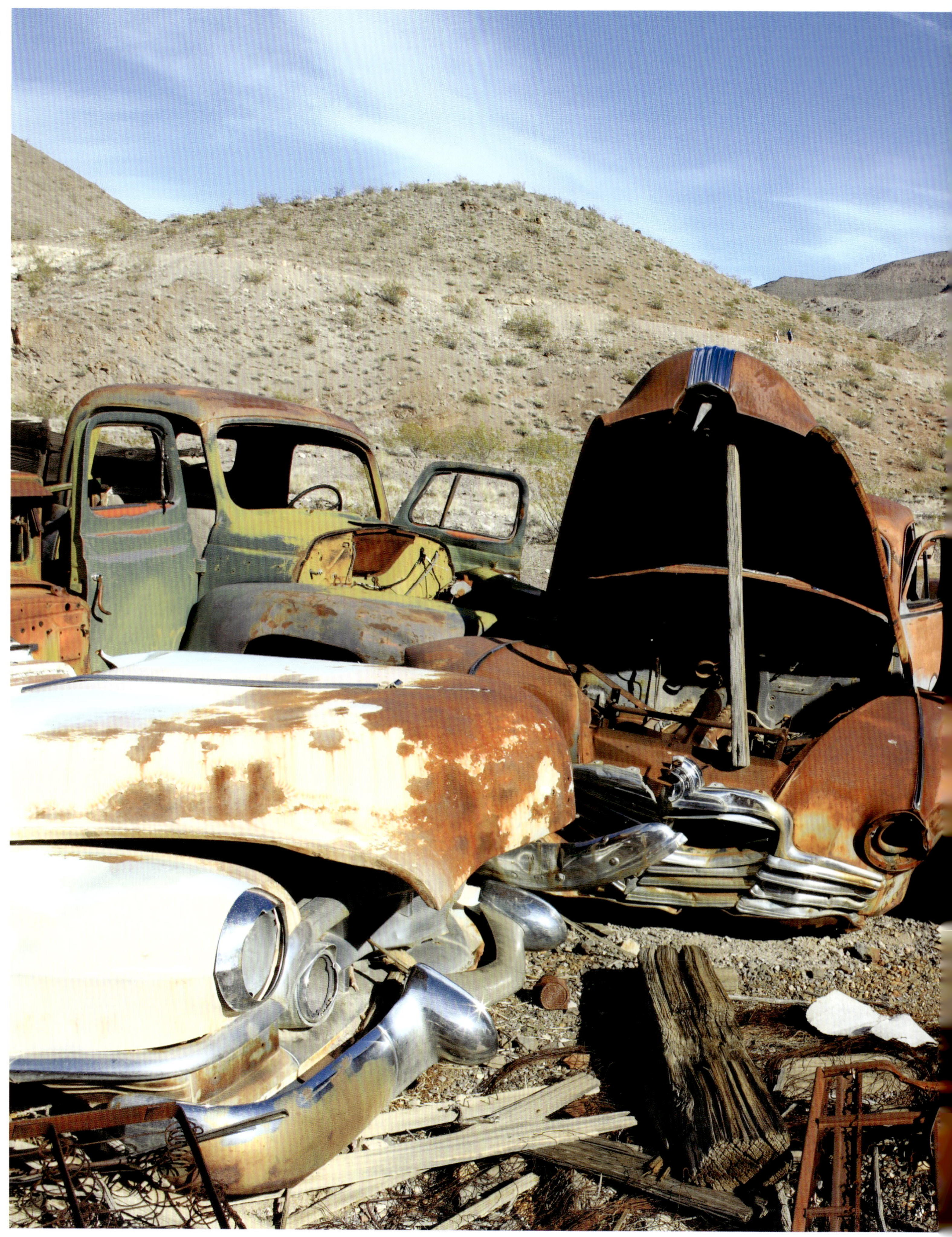

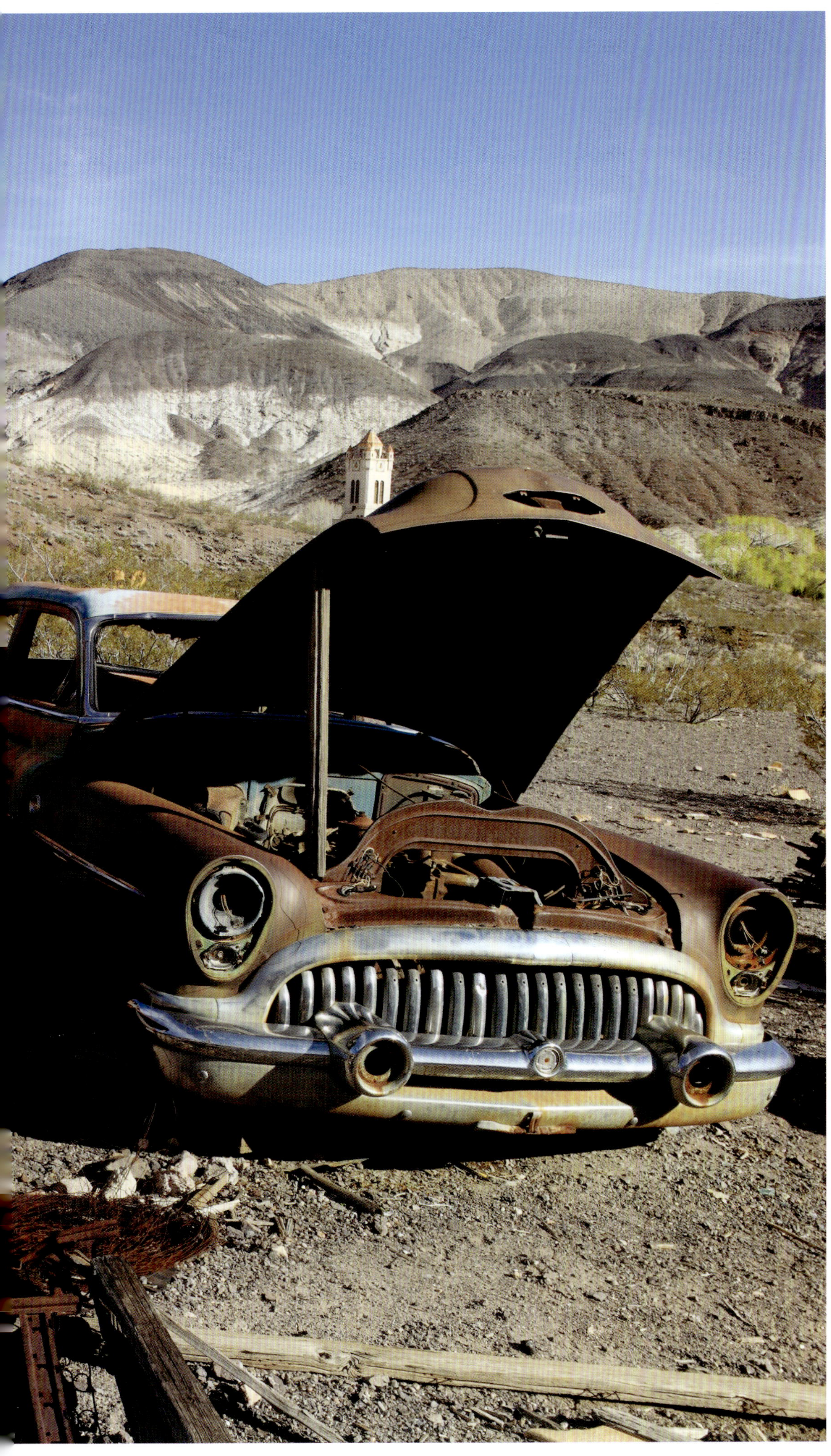

Kerala, India
This defunct bus has found a
new role in life as a display board
for posters advertising movies,
events and political messages.
Despite India's heavy investment
in public transport, the country
still has some of the worst traffic
congestion problems in the world.

LEFT:

**National Park, Death Valley,
United States**
While the main bodywork of
these vintage American cars
has thoroughly rusted, the
chromework still gleams defiantly.
Unless the bodywork has been
physically distorted in some way,
there is always the possibility that
an abandoned vintage car might
be recovered and restored by
enthusiasts.

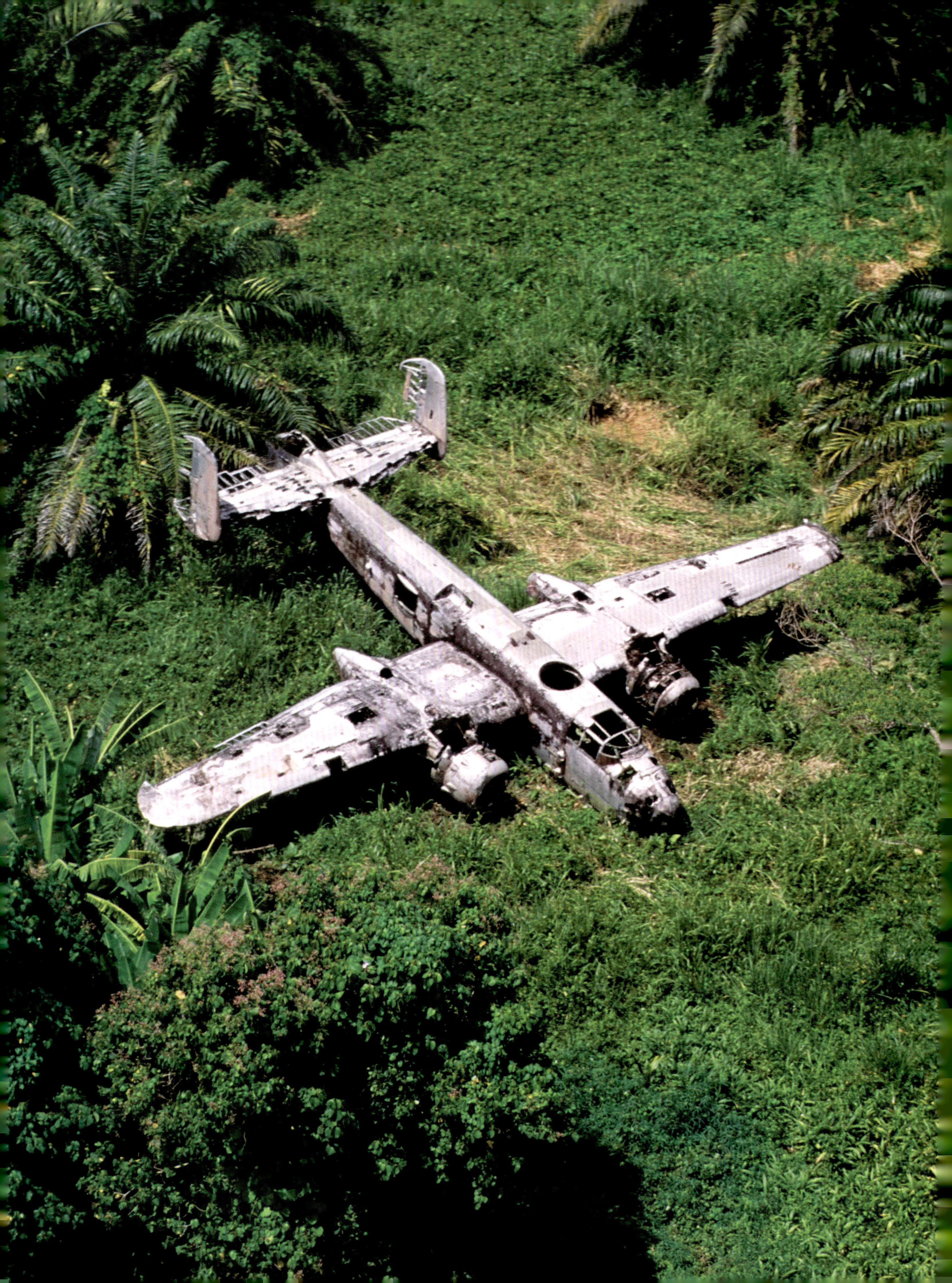

Aircraft

Aircraft seem to have a unique resonance among all the different types of wrecks, although why this is so takes some thought to unpack. Perhaps it is because the aircraft, in its abandoned, rusting and derelict form, stands in such utter historical contrast to the machine when it was in its operational prime. A flying aircraft momentarily escapes the chains of Earth, twisting and turning in the lightness of air. In the case of space vehicles, also touched on in this chapter, the shuttle or rocket even manages to rip free from Earth's gravity, achieving the escape velocity to enter weightless space 100km (62 miles) above the surface of the planet. Yet when the aircraft reaches the end of its flying career, through either obsolescence, accident or conflict, it is as if heavy gravity reclaims the vehicle for good. At the same time, the environment gradually destroys all the technology that enabled the aircraft to lift off in the first place – flight surfaces rust, cockpit dial indicators sit fixed and dead, engines lie inert. Yet the ghostliness of a wrecked aircraft is also often about the drama that once existed inside the fuselage. Many of the wrecks featured here were destroyed in war, real men (for historically they were almost invariably men) dying in the cockpits or gun positions. The silence of their wreckage therefore sits in haunting contrast to the drama of their life.

B-25 Mitchell, near Talasea, West New Britain, Papua New Guinea
The wreck of a US B-25 Mitchell sits in a jungle clearing in Papau New Guinea, its overall contours very well preserved. The Mitchell was used heavily in the Pacific as both a medium bomber and, with its nose packed with machine guns, a strafing gunship. The intact airframe indicates a controlled crash landing.

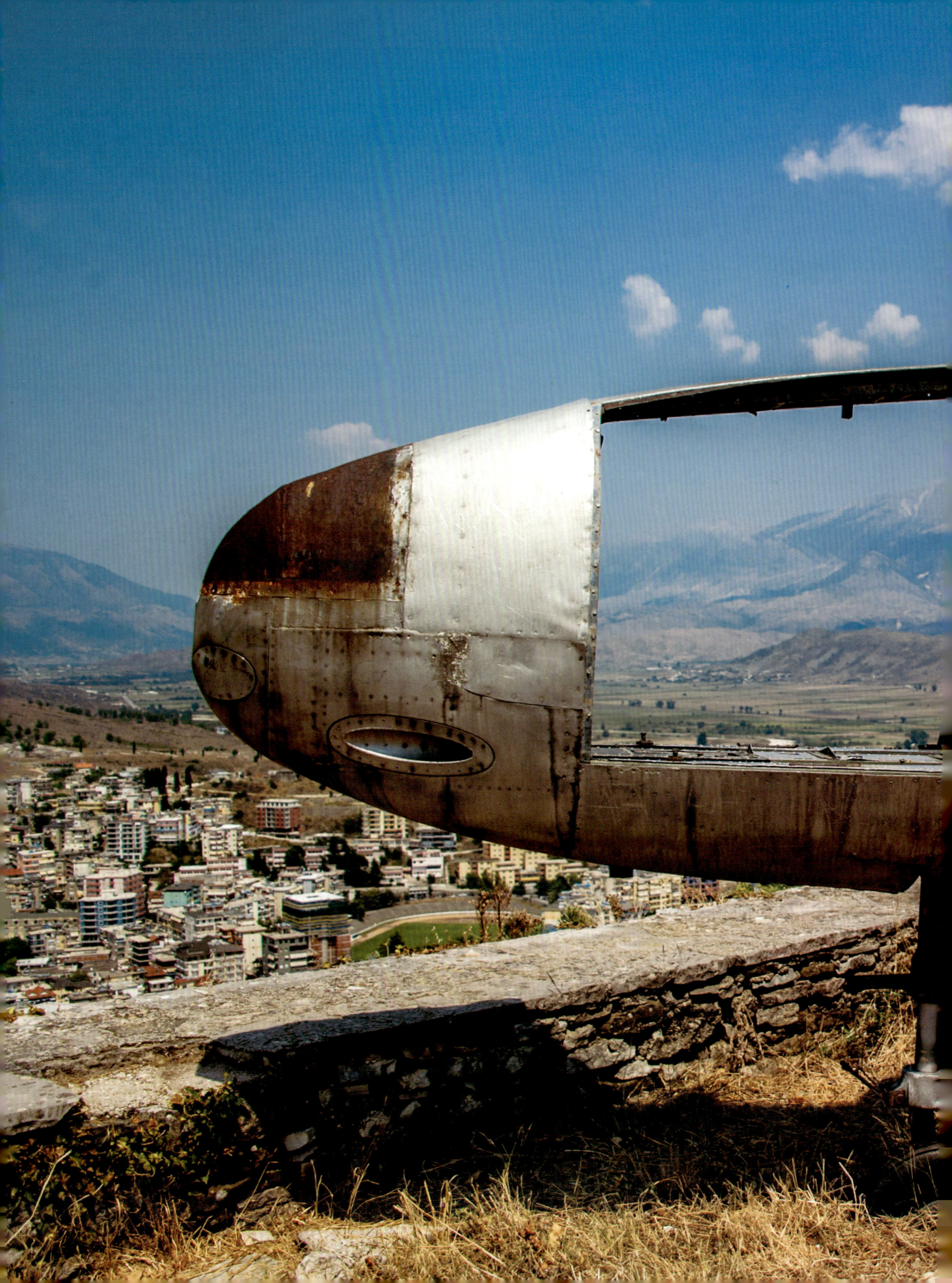

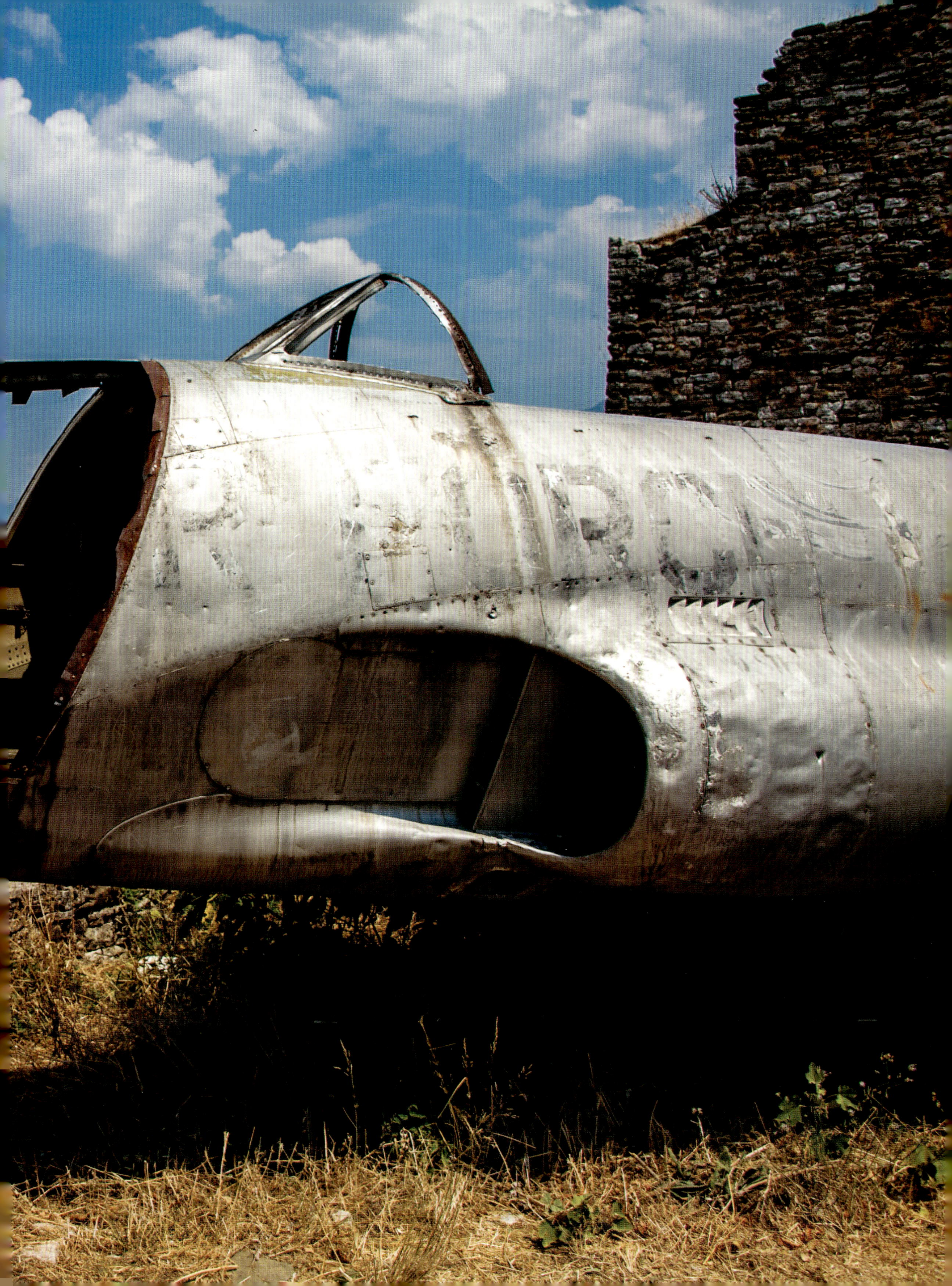

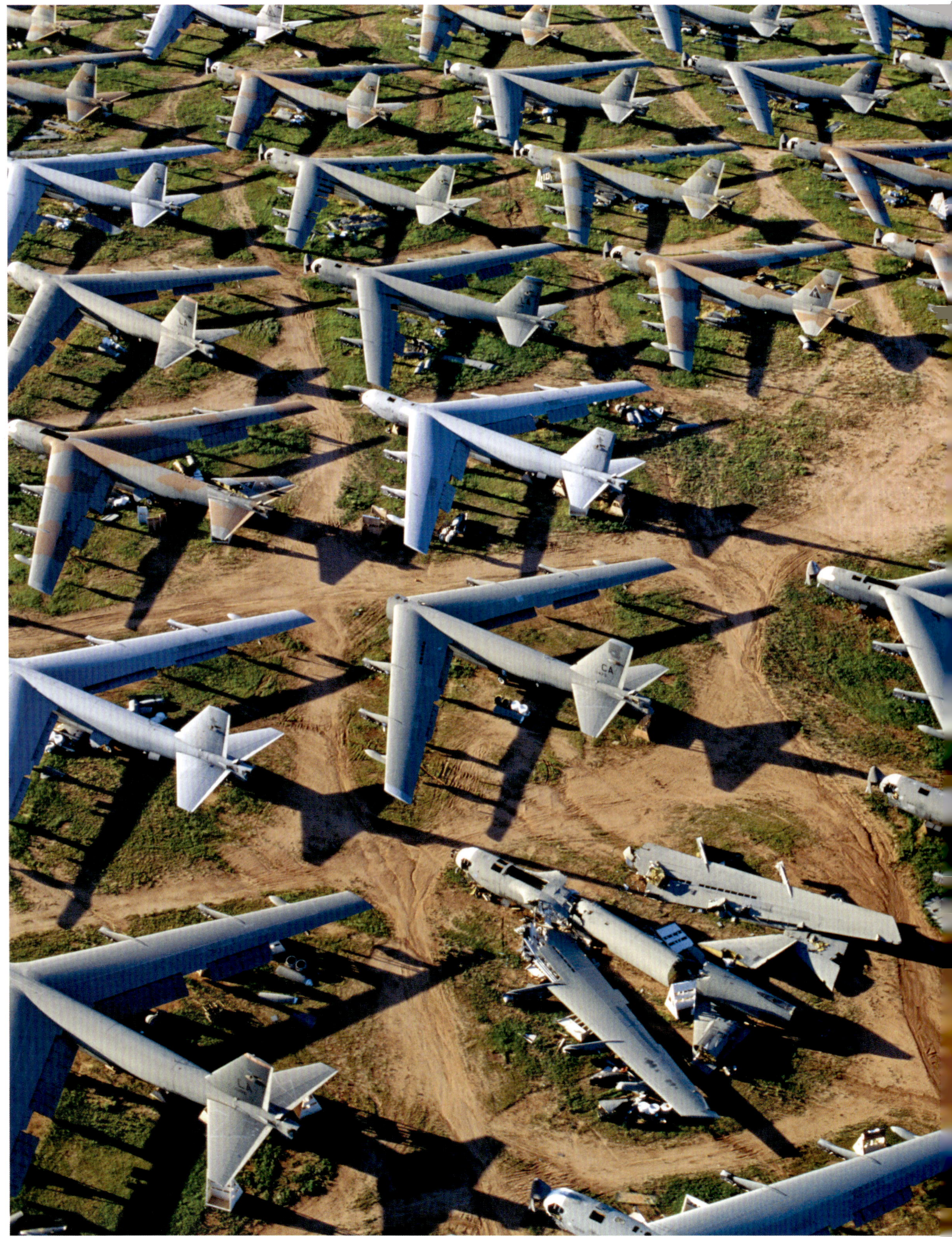

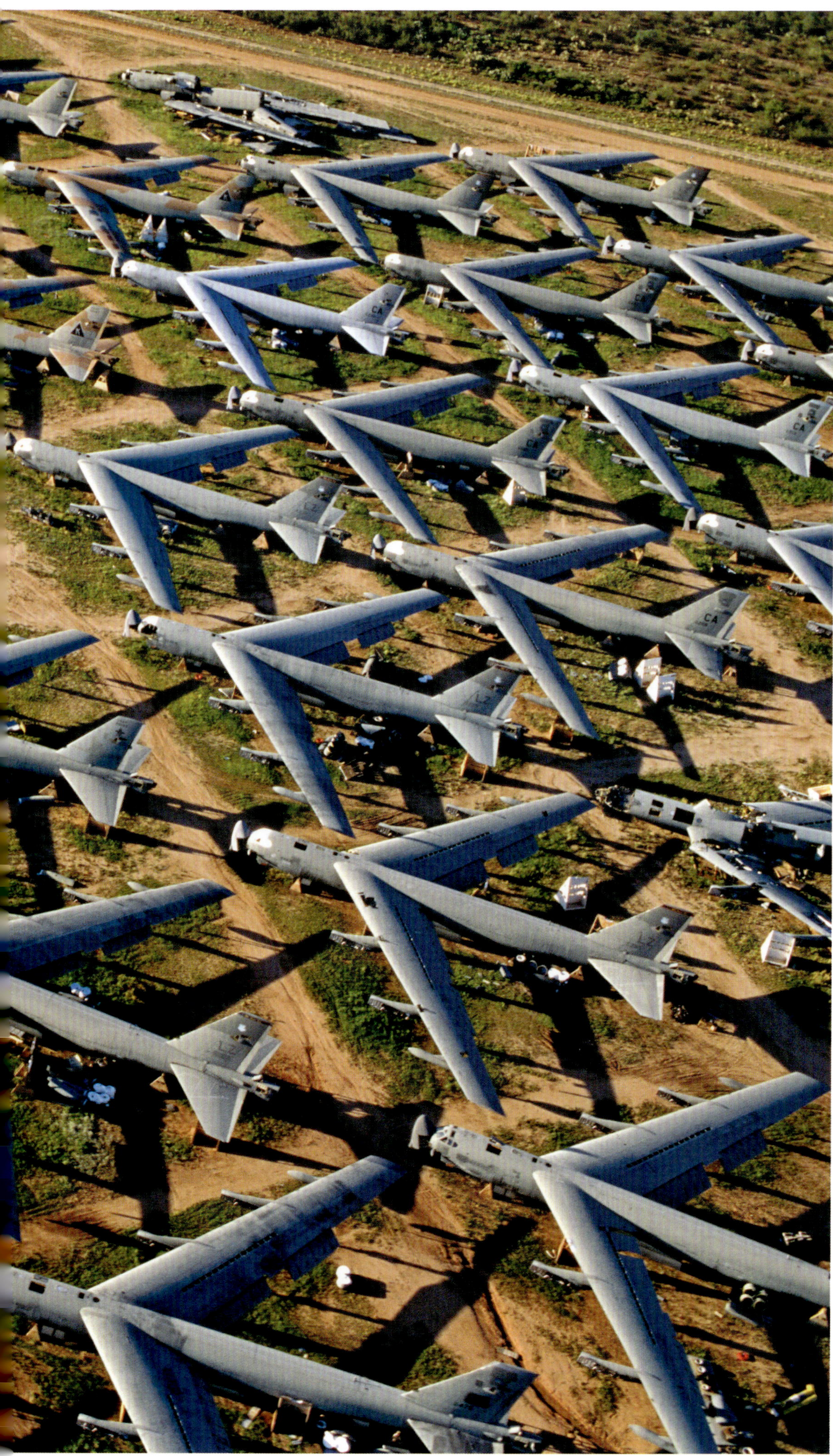

PREVIOUS PAGE:

T-33 Shooting Star, Gjirokastër, southern Albania
A relic of the 1950s jet age watches over the town of Gjirokastër, in southern Albania. This US Air Force T-33 Shooting Star aircraft, on a flight from France to Greece, was forced to land at Tirana Airport in December 1957 due to technical problems. Albania's status as a communist country meant that the aircraft was not returned, and was left in-country to rot.

LEFT:
B-52 Stratofortress, Davis-Monthan Air Force Base, Tucson, Arizona, United States
Sentinels of the Cold War. The B-52 Stratofortress was, and remains, the greatest of the United States' post-World War II bombers. Entering service in 1952, it offered the ability to carry a 32,000kg (70,000lb) payload – including nuclear weapons – over distances of more than 12,900km (8,000 miles). These decommissioned aircraft, abandoned at Davis-Monthan aircraft graveyard awaiting recycling for scrap, still evoke Cold War power with their sense of flying in formation.

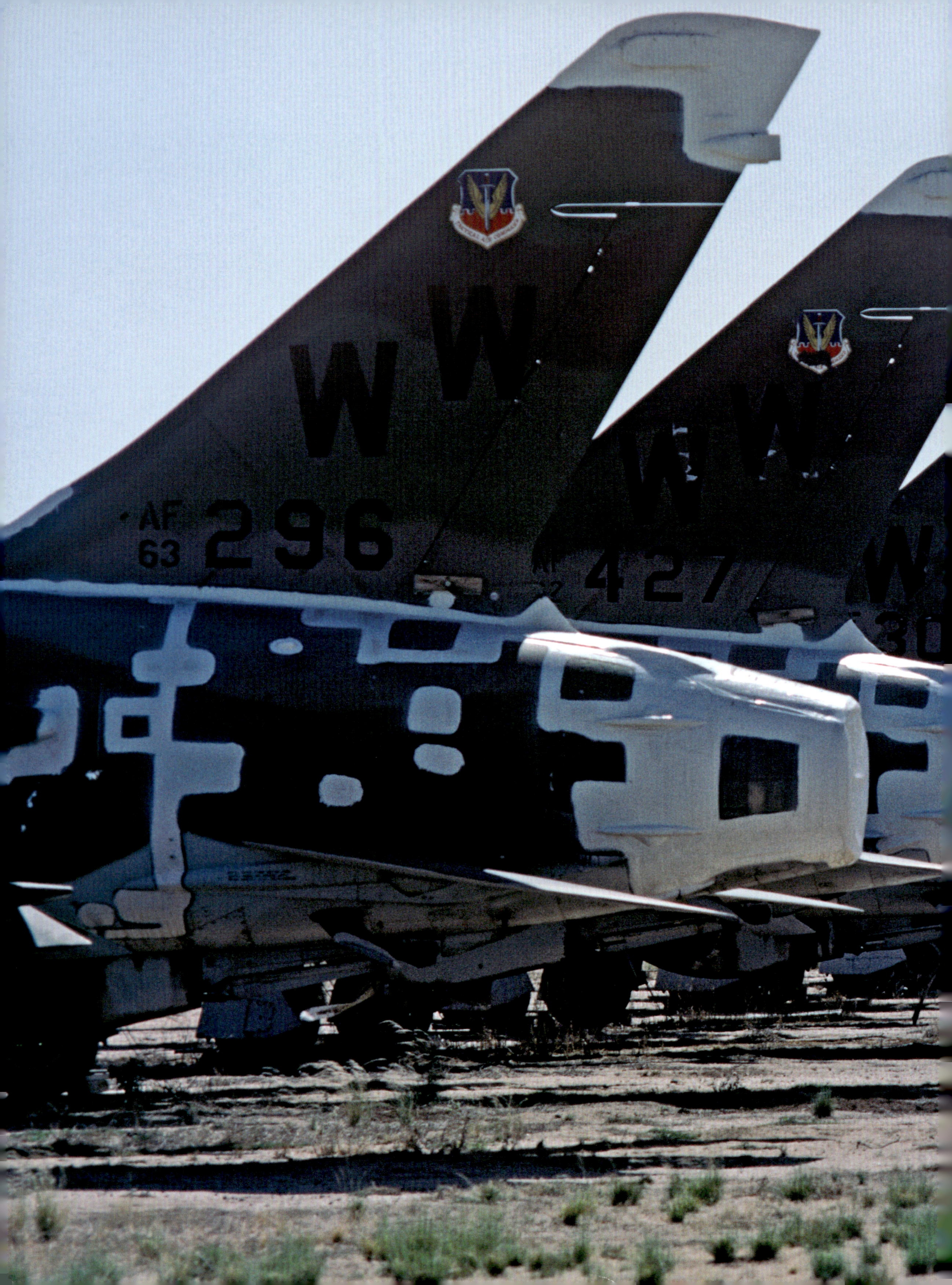

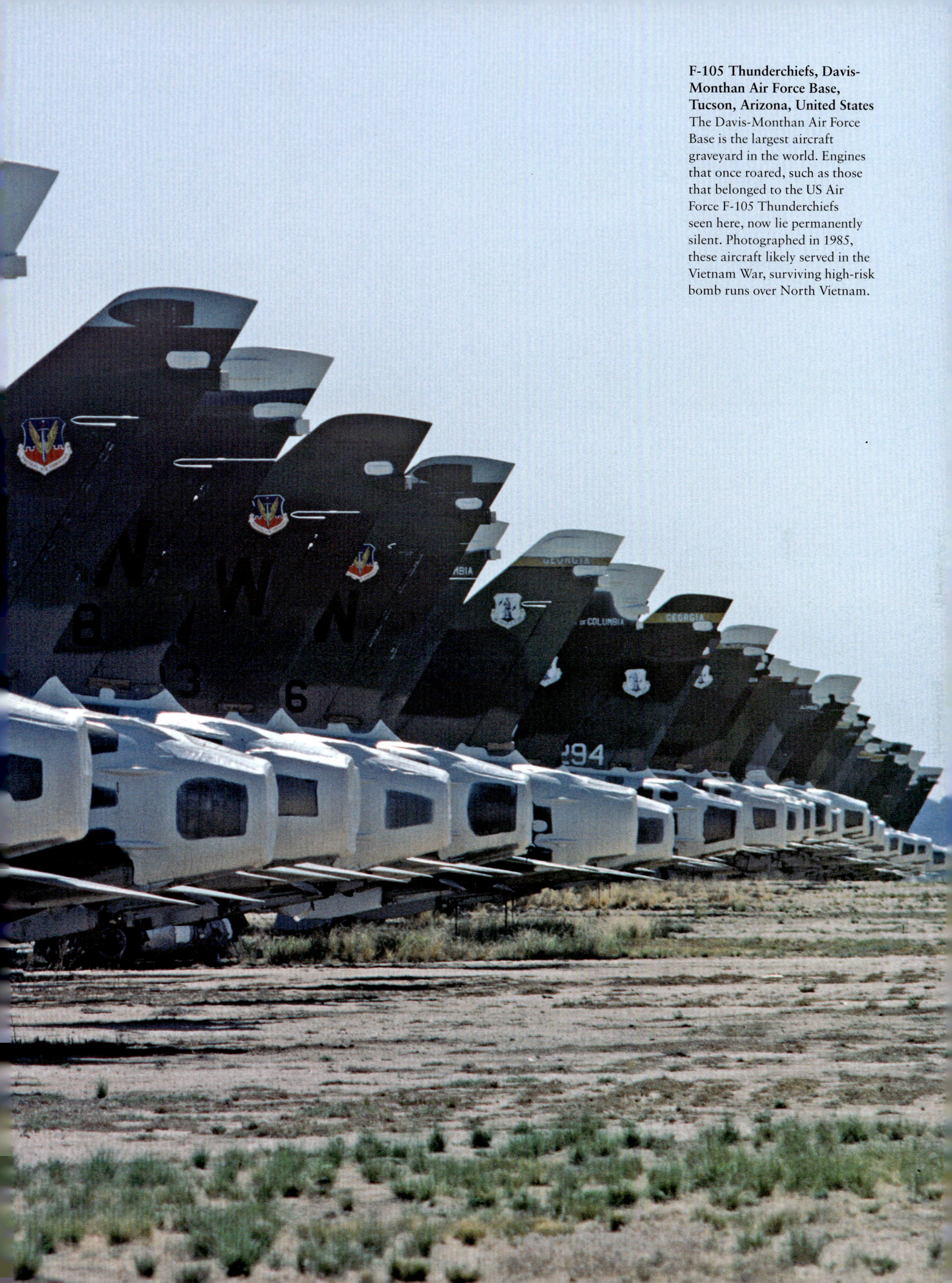

F-105 Thunderchiefs, Davis-Monthan Air Force Base, Tucson, Arizona, United States
The Davis-Monthan Air Force Base is the largest aircraft graveyard in the world. Engines that once roared, such as those that belonged to the US Air Force F-105 Thunderchiefs seen here, now lie permanently silent. Photographed in 1985, these aircraft likely served in the Vietnam War, surviving high-risk bomb runs over North Vietnam.

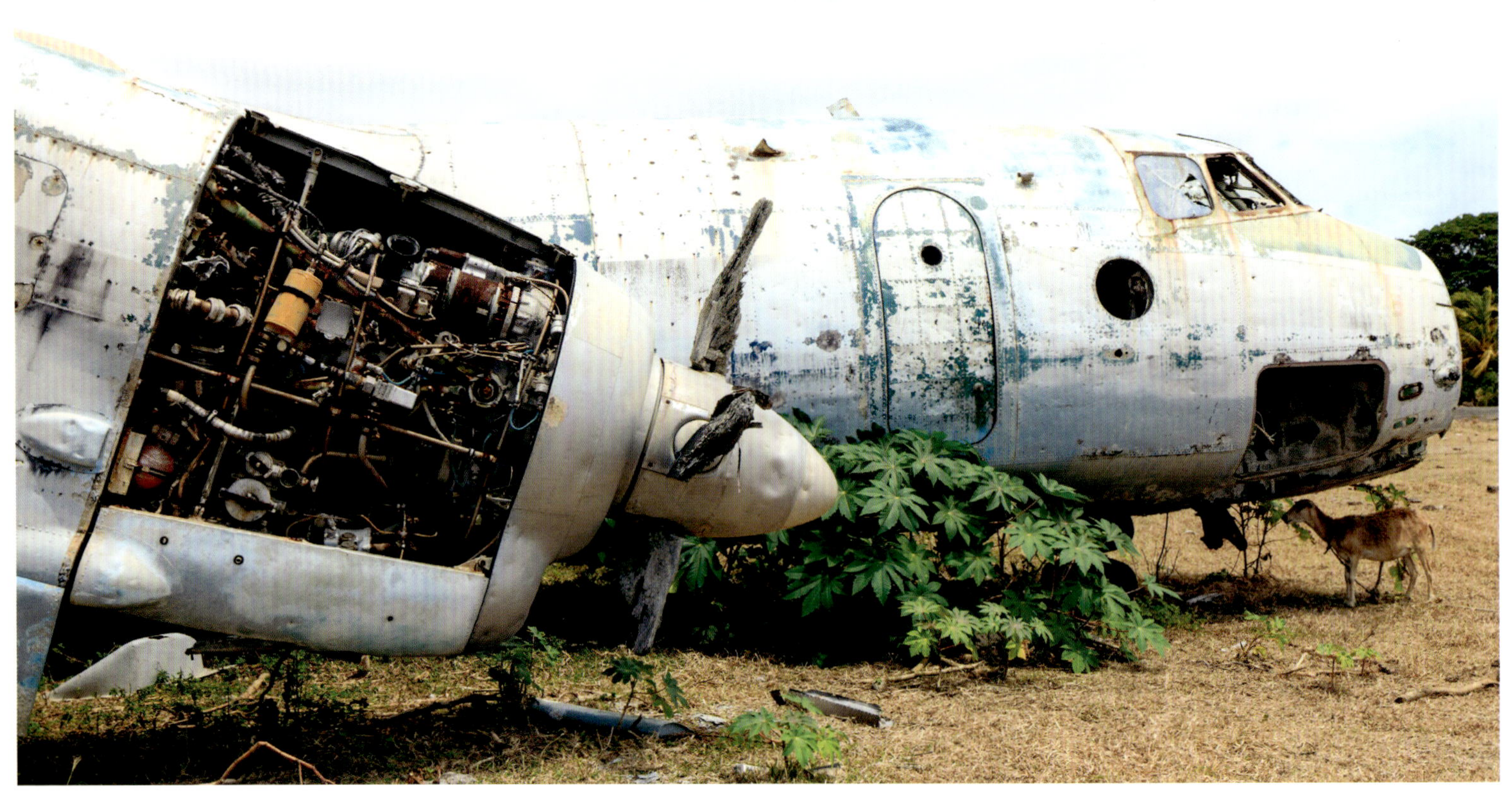

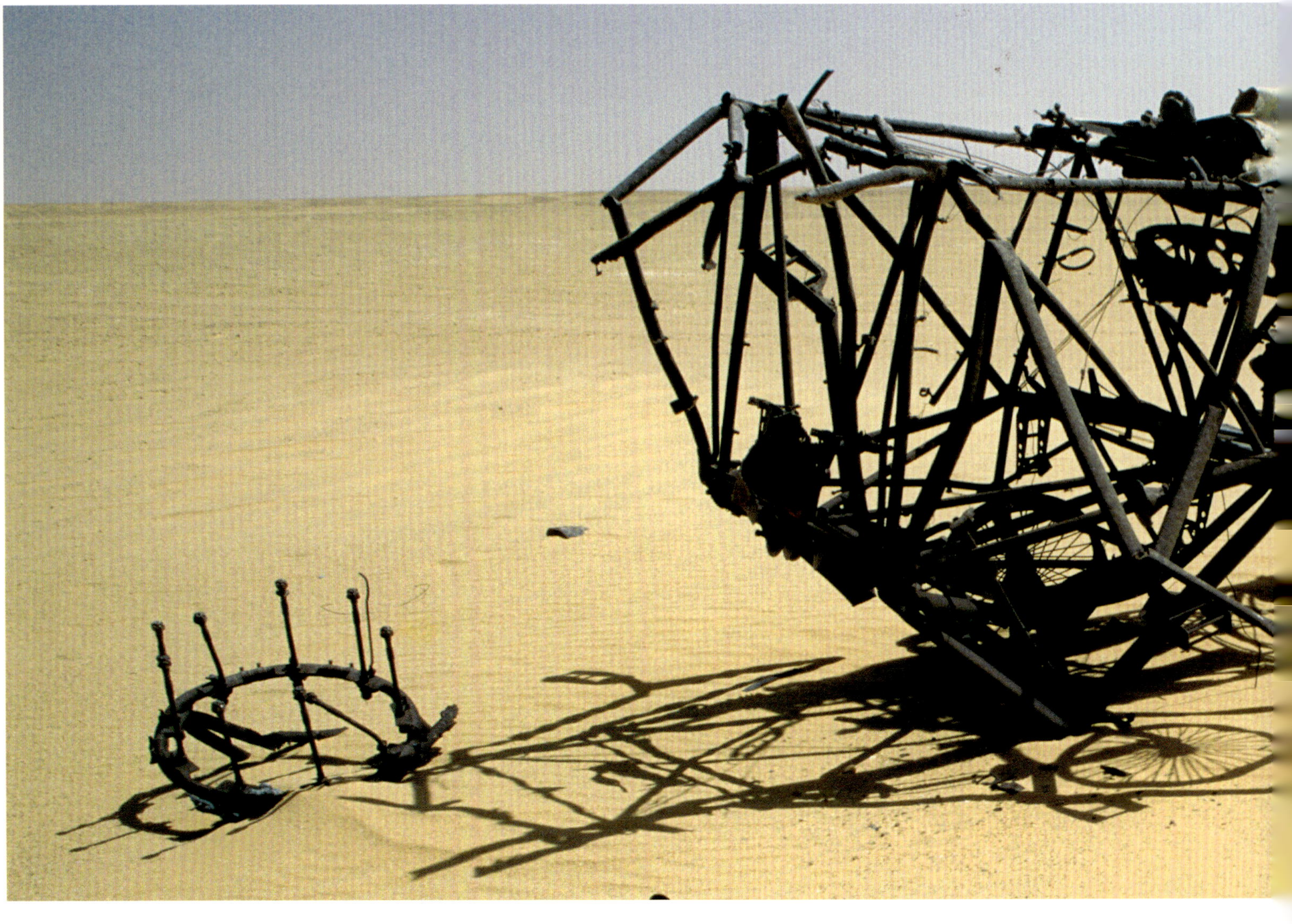

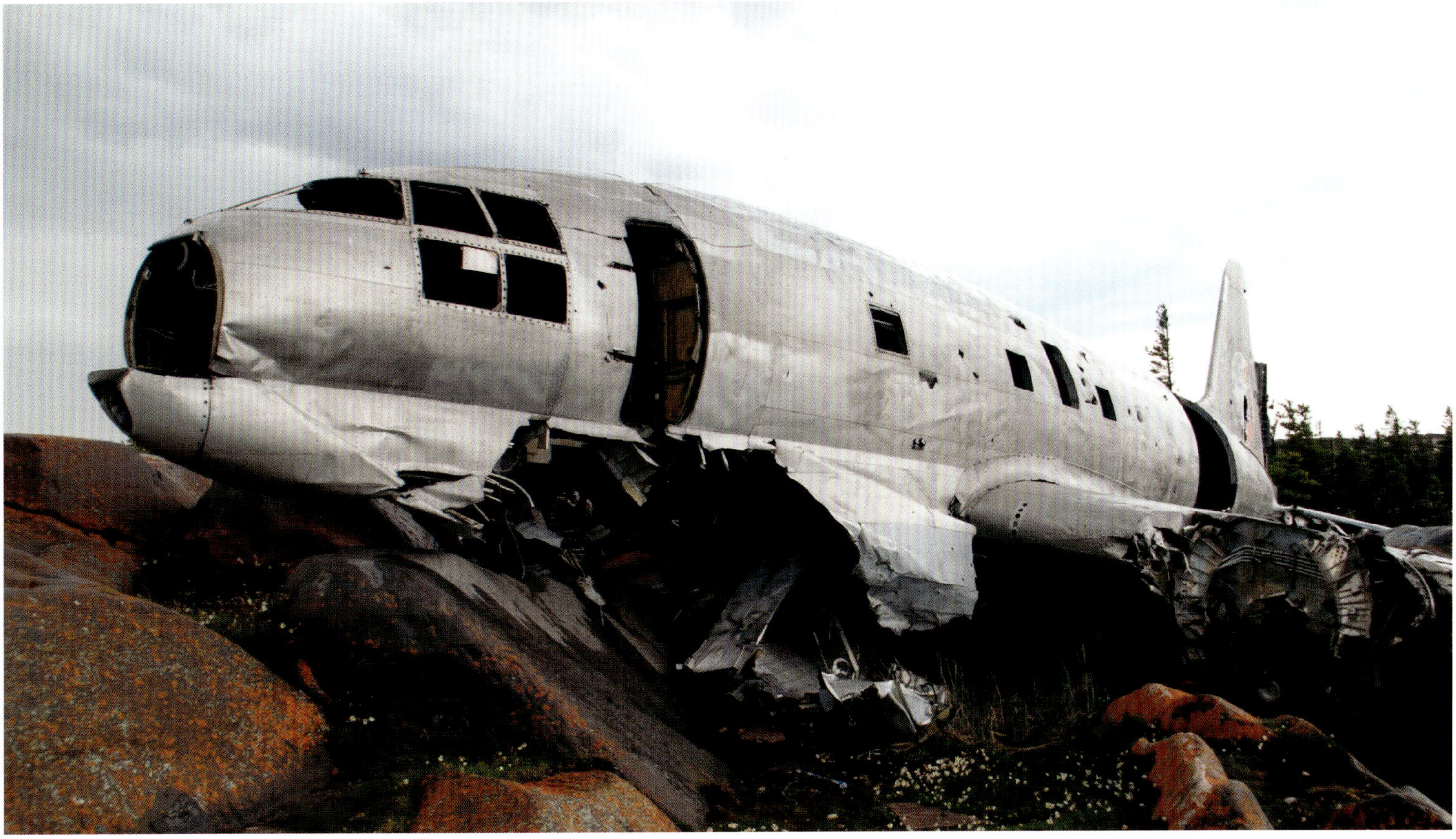

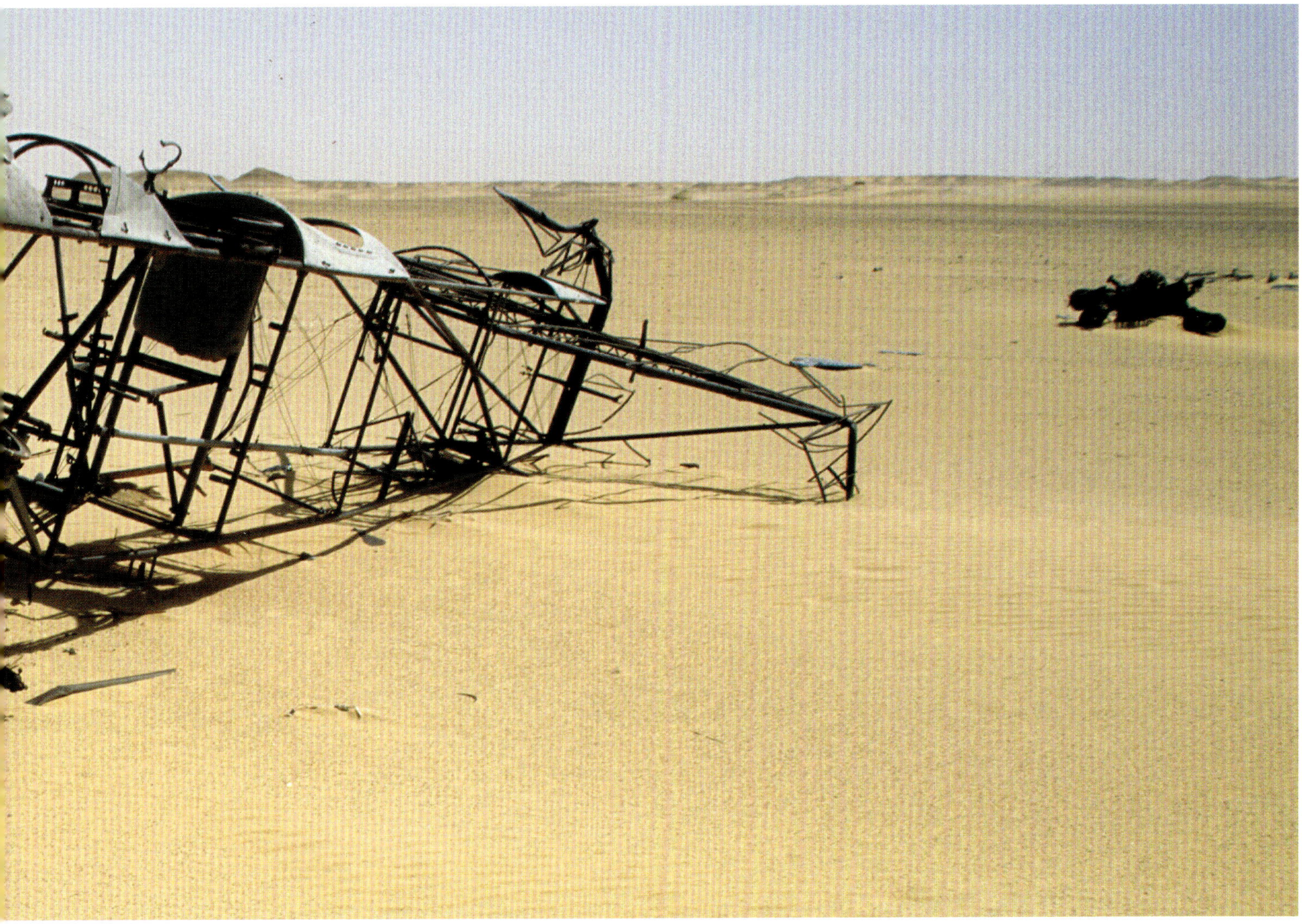

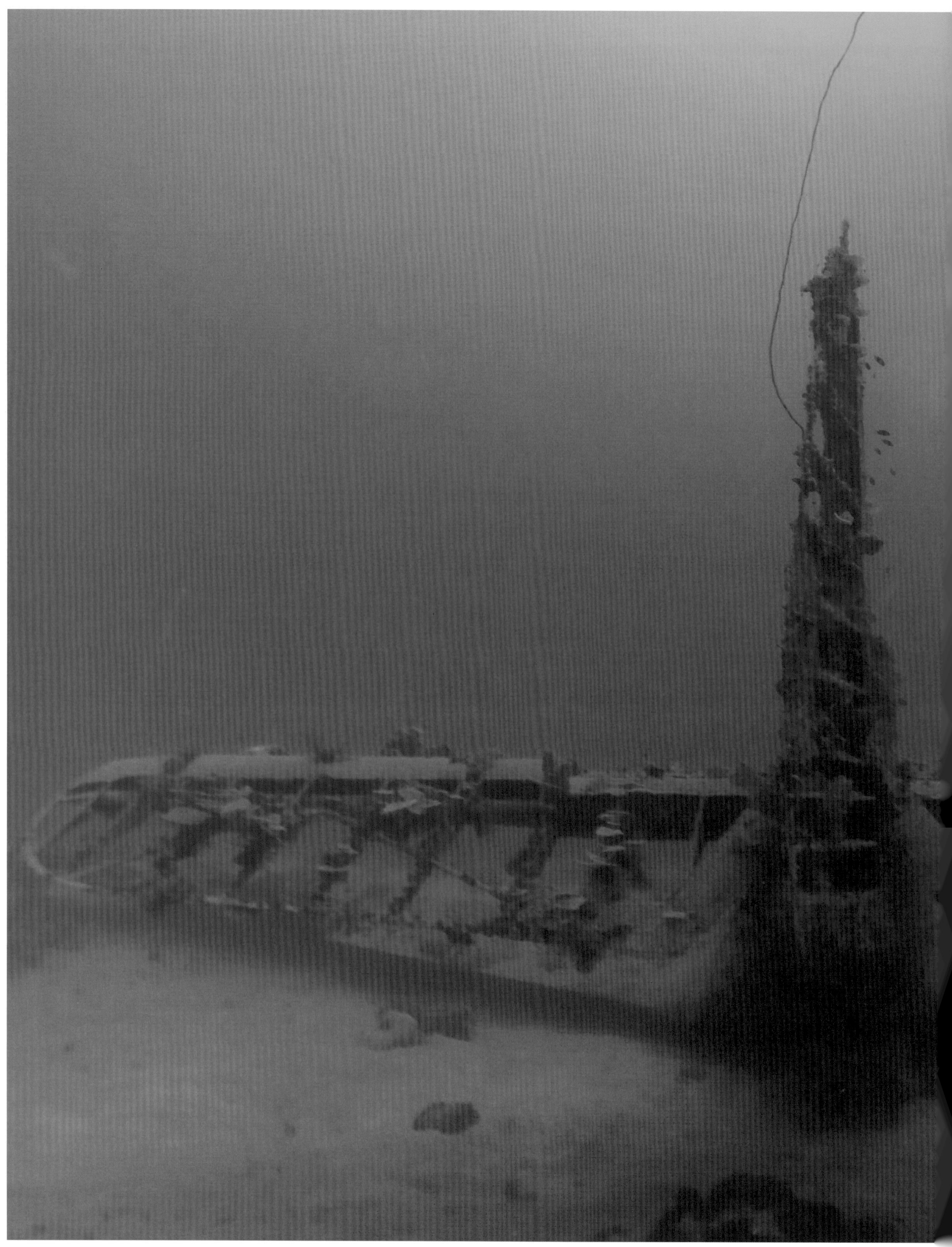

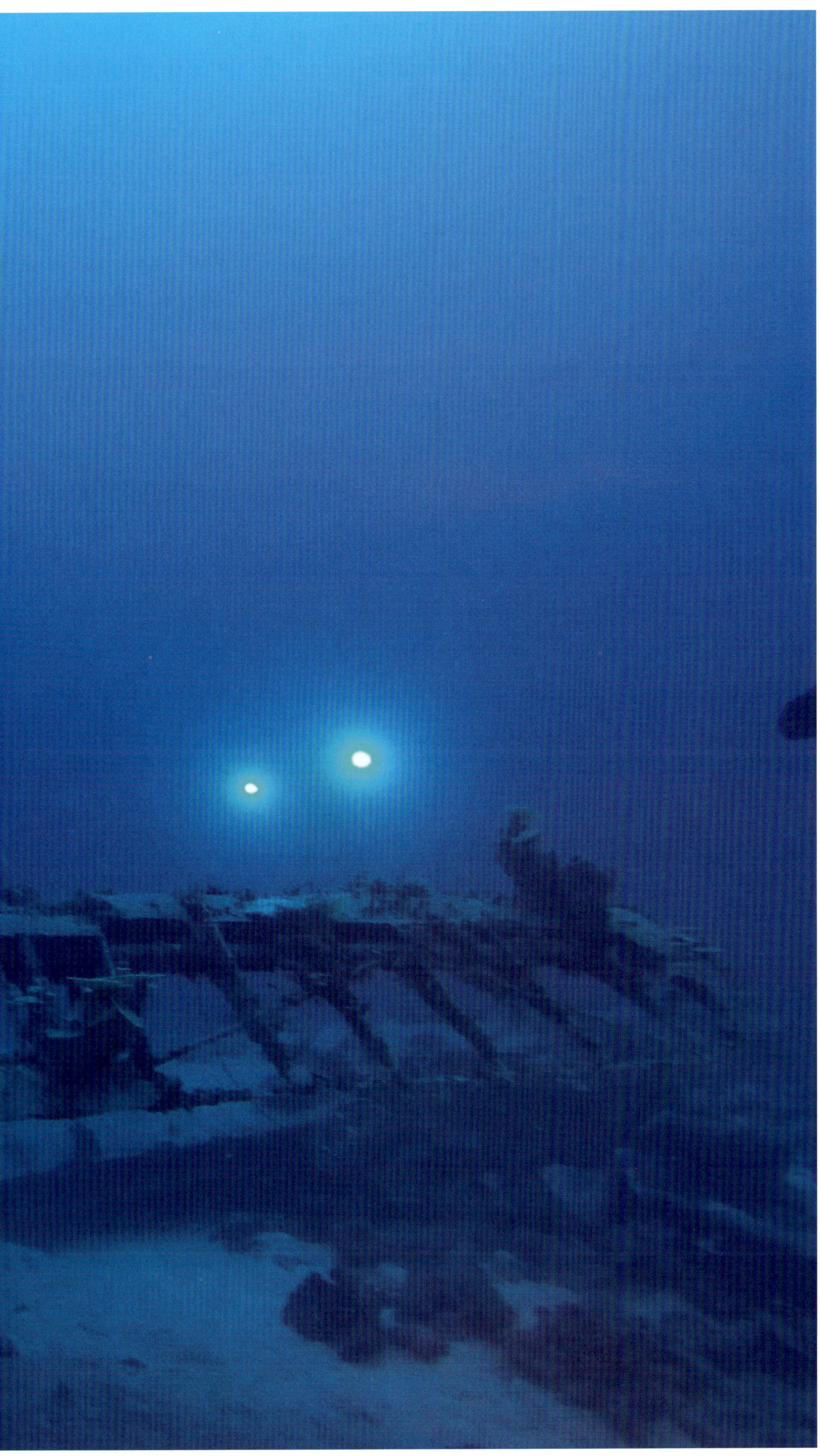

Antonov AN-26, Pearls Airfield, Grenville, Grenada, West Indies

A Russian Antonov AN-26 lies collapsed at Pearls Airfield, Grenada. The aircraft – a particularly successful transport type – was delivered to Grenada by Cuba on 24 October 1983, the day before the US invasion of the island rendered it as junk.

Libya, North Africa

The remains of an Italian fighter aircraft form a skeletal reminder of Italy's involvement in North Africa in World War II. The distribution and location of the wreckage indicate a violent landing. Over the decades since World War II, many wartime relics such as these have been taken for scrap, although some lie preserved in former minefields, still dangerous to this day.

C-46, Churchill, Manitoba, Canada

This C-46 aircraft is known to the locals as 'Miss Piggy', on account of the fact that it once transported pigs. On 13 November 1979, the aircraft crashed following a loss of oil pressure in the left engine. Three of the crew were seriously injured in the impact.

Douglas TBD Devastator, Jaluit Atoll, Marshall Islands, Pacific

The waters around the Marshall Islands are littered with aerial tombstones from World War II. The tailplane of the aircraft here, sitting 28m (92ft) deep off Jaluit Atoll, is from a US Douglas TBD Devastator, one of the primary US Navy carrier-based torpedo-bombers.

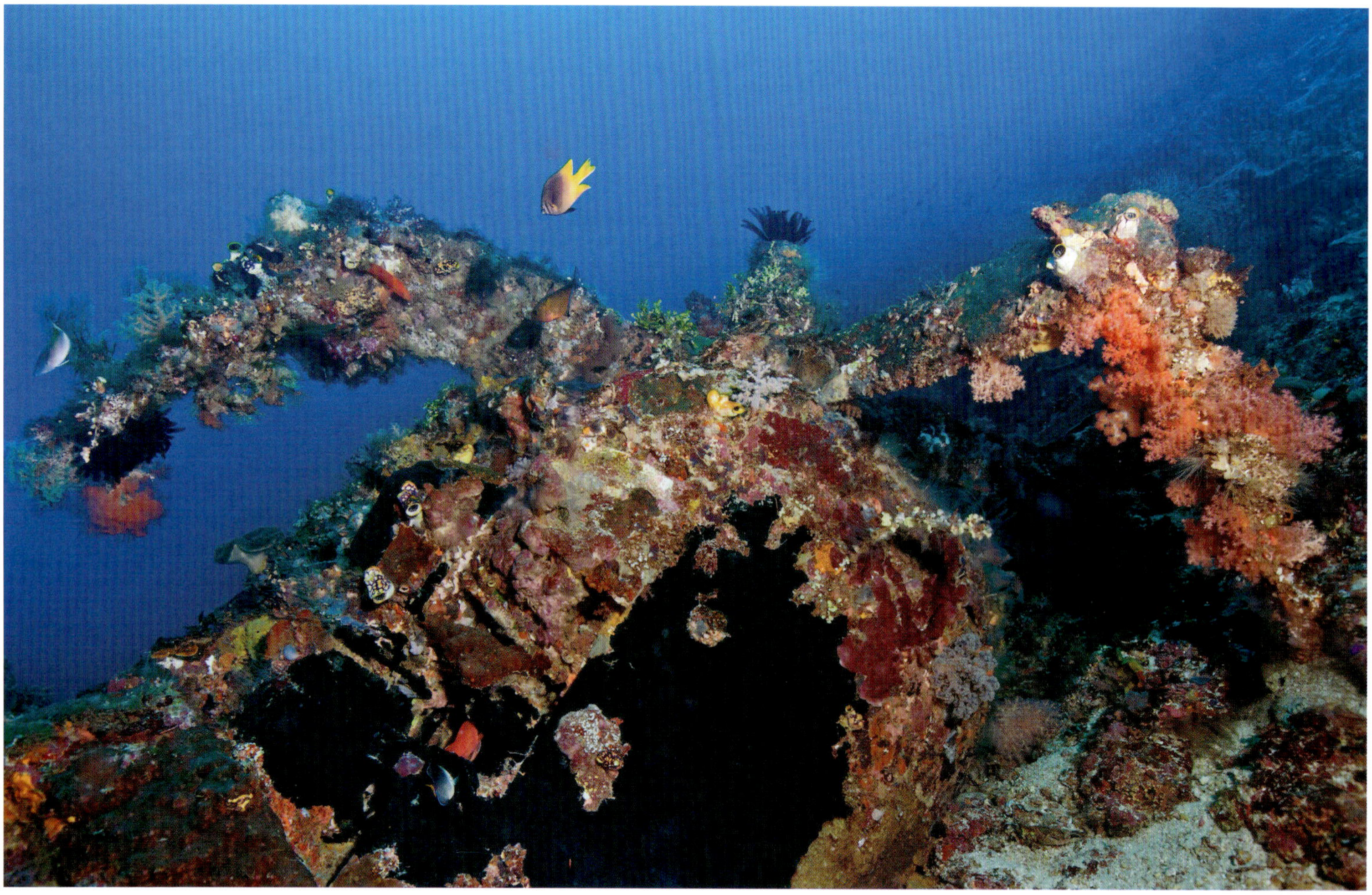

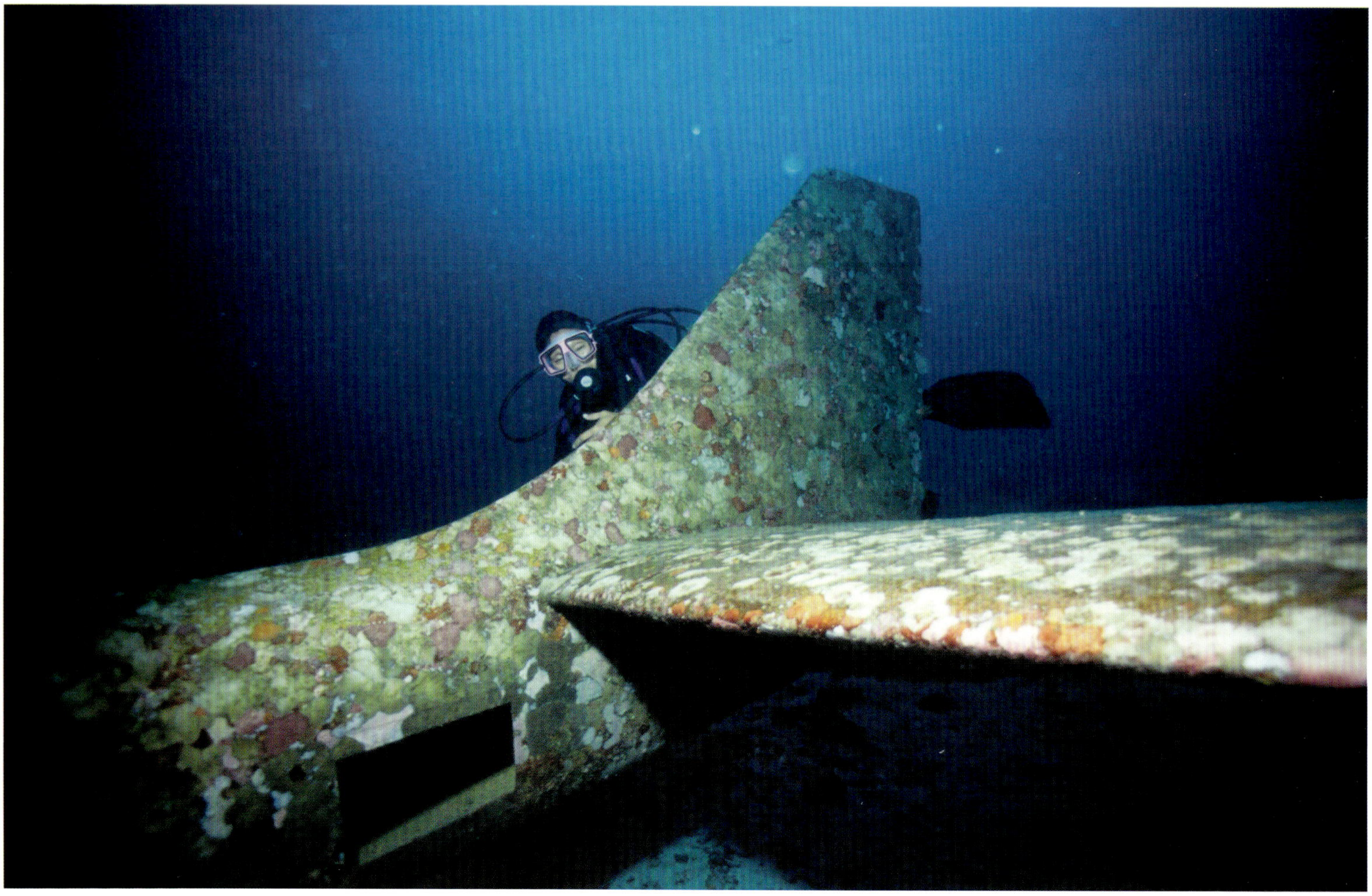

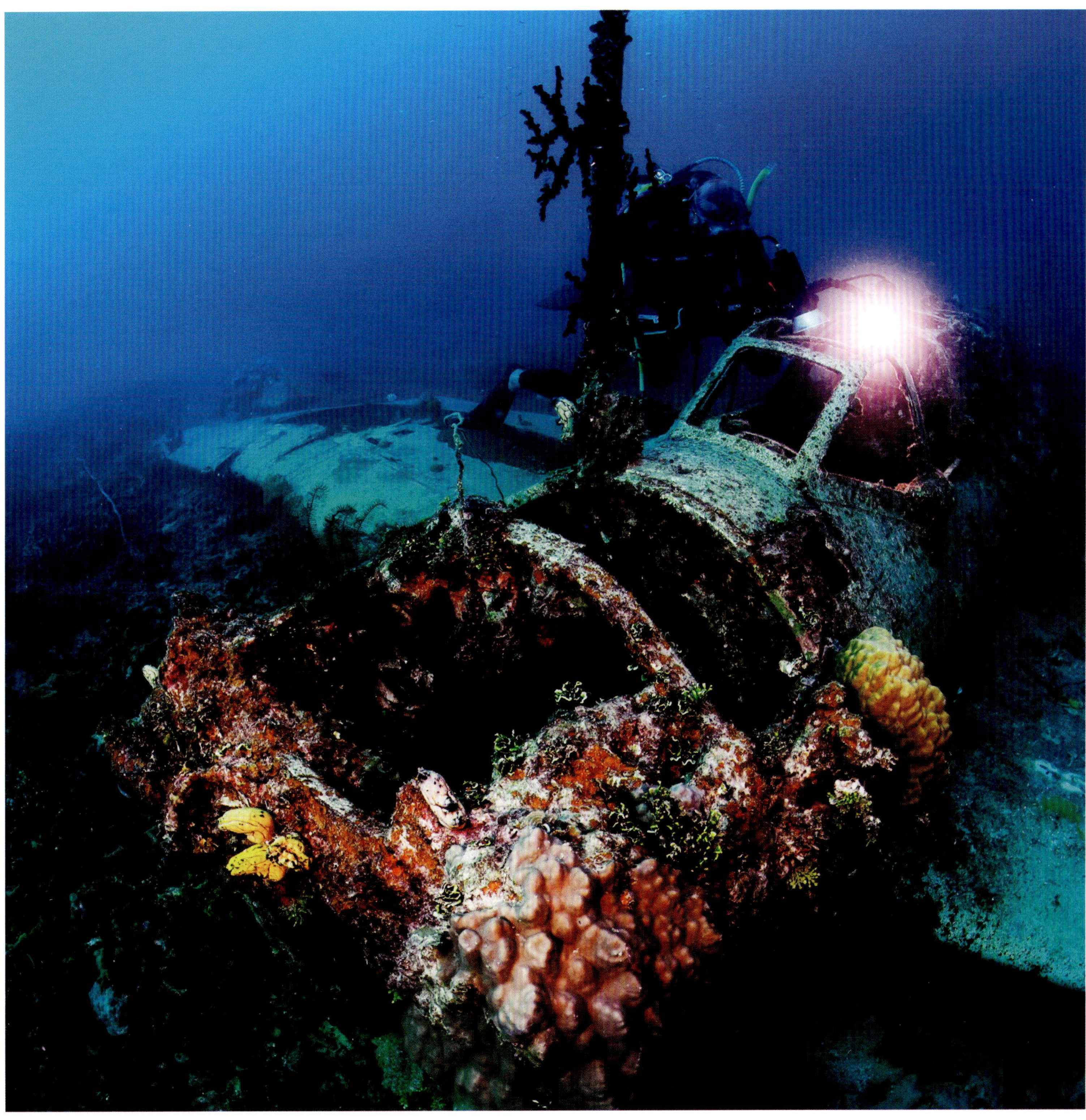

Republic P-47 Thunderbolt, Raja Ampat, Indonesia
The propeller and powerplant of this Republic P-47 Thunderbolt fighter have now become home to multi-coloured aquatic life. The P-47 was known affectionately as the 'Jug', short for the word 'Juggernaut'. It was a powerful aircraft, packing heavy firepower and capable of absorbing immense combat damage and still remaining in the air.

Panagsama Beach, Moalboal, Cebu Island, Visayas, Philippines
While the waters around the Philippines contain numerous wartime relics, this aircraft fuselage actually belongs to a modern commercial Lancair kitplane. The aircraft was donated by the company as the framework for an artificial reef – we can already see coral colonizing the tailplane section of the aircraft.

Mitsubishi A6M Zero Fighter, Sea of Japan
Between 1943 and 1945, Japan's air forces were progressively massacred by the swelling might of the US land- and carrier-based aviation. As many as 50,000 aircraft might have been lost, one of them being this Mitsubishi A6M Zero fighter, shot down over the Sea of Japan. Few of the poorly trained Japanese pilots survived such late-war incidents.

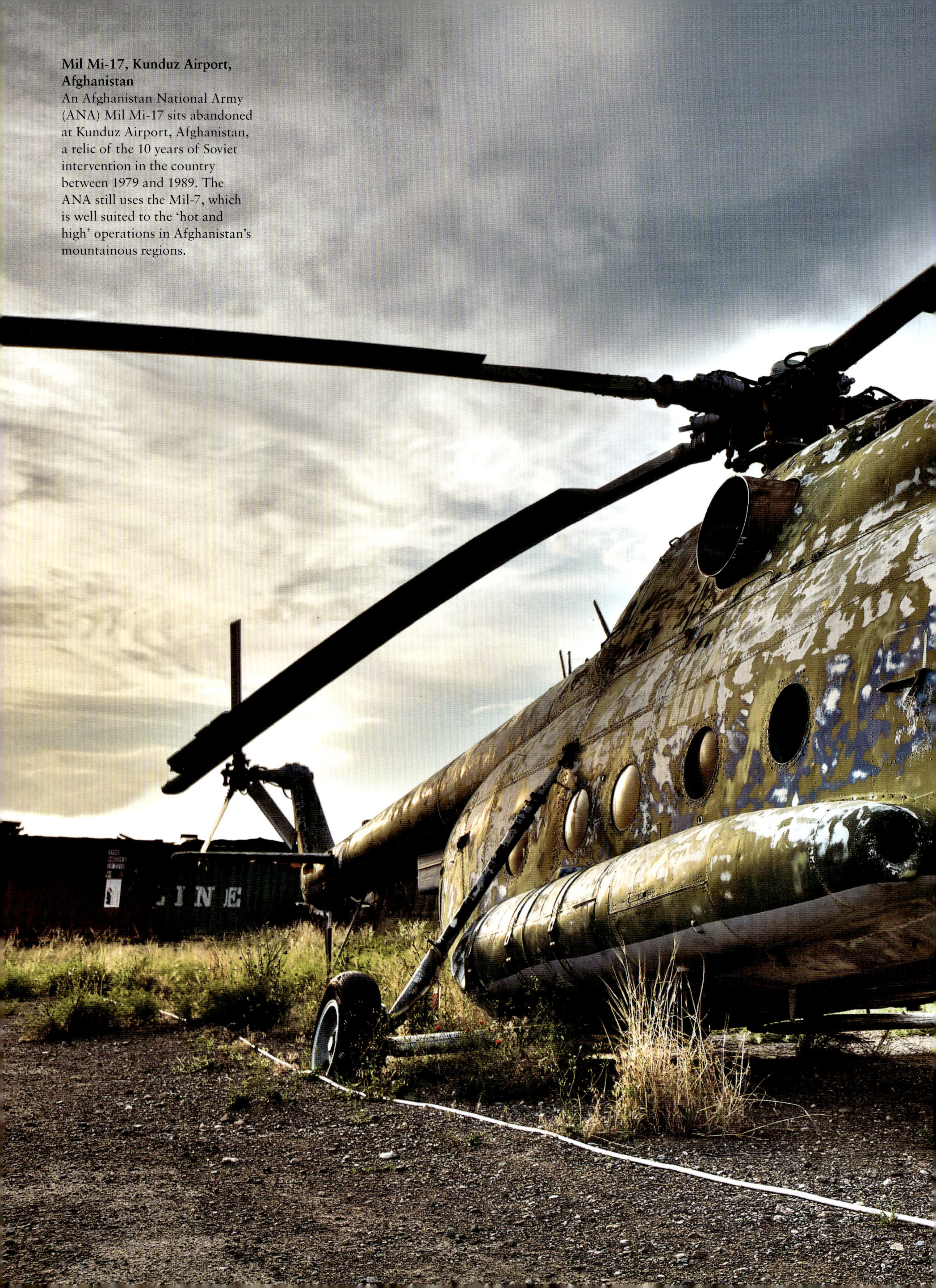

Mil Mi-17, Kunduz Airport, Afghanistan
An Afghanistan National Army (ANA) Mil Mi-17 sits abandoned at Kunduz Airport, Afghanistan, a relic of the 10 years of Soviet intervention in the country between 1979 and 1989. The ANA still uses the Mil-7, which is well suited to the 'hot and high' operations in Afghanistan's mountainous regions.

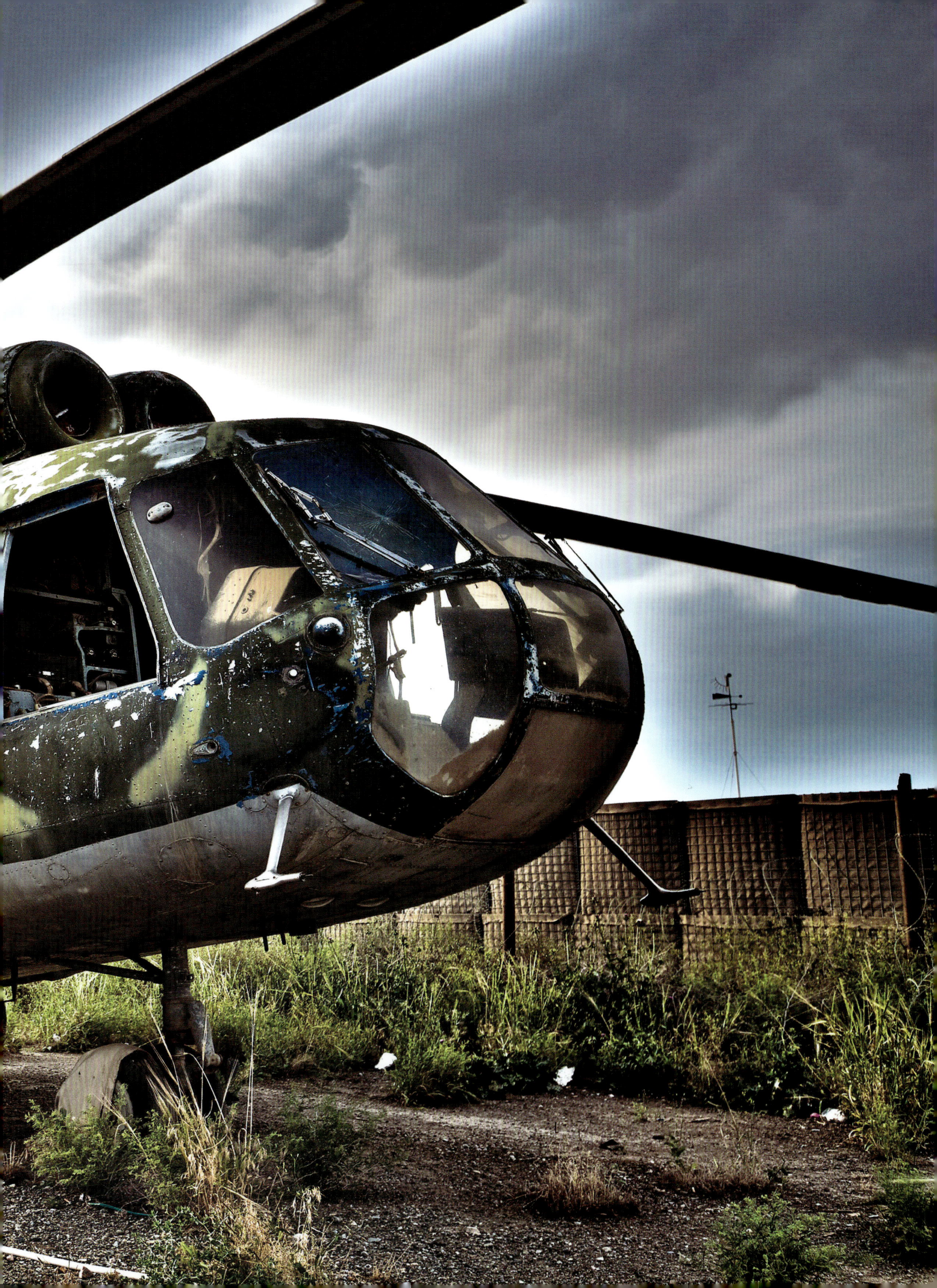

McDonnell Douglas DC-9 Airliner, Parañaque City, Manila, Philippines

Looking utterly incongruous next to a Manila shopping mall sits this tailless McDonnell Douglas DC-9 airliner. It was formerly the property of the airline Cebu Pacific, the Philippines' largest indigenous airline company. In 2014, the Philippines government announced that it would auction off the 12 aircraft abandoned around Manila International Airport.

Douglas DC-3, Otocac, Croatia

The interior of a World War II-era Douglas DC-3 transport aircraft. The DC-3 was the ubiquitous aerial workhorse for the Allies during the war, carrying everything from pack animals and ammunition through to paratroopers and special operations units.

Nevada Desert, United States

The Nevada Desert is littered with aircraft wrecks, such as this one here. The wrecks are the legacy of military and civilian aviation accidents and commercial aircraft abandoned for financial reasons.

North Platte, Nebraska, United States

Wreck repurposing at its best – this defunct US airliner has been converted to a playground attraction in North Platte, Nebraska, taking its place alongside a Vietnam War-era UH-1 Huey helicopter and a fire truck.

Mil-6 Heavy Lift Helicopter, Samara, Russia

The Soviet Union was one of the world's largest producers of helicopters – military and civilian – during the Cold War era. This example, left in a field in the company of other aircraft, is a Mil-6, a heavy-lift helicopter used from 1957 in a wide variety of transport and logistical roles within the Red Army and foreign military forces.

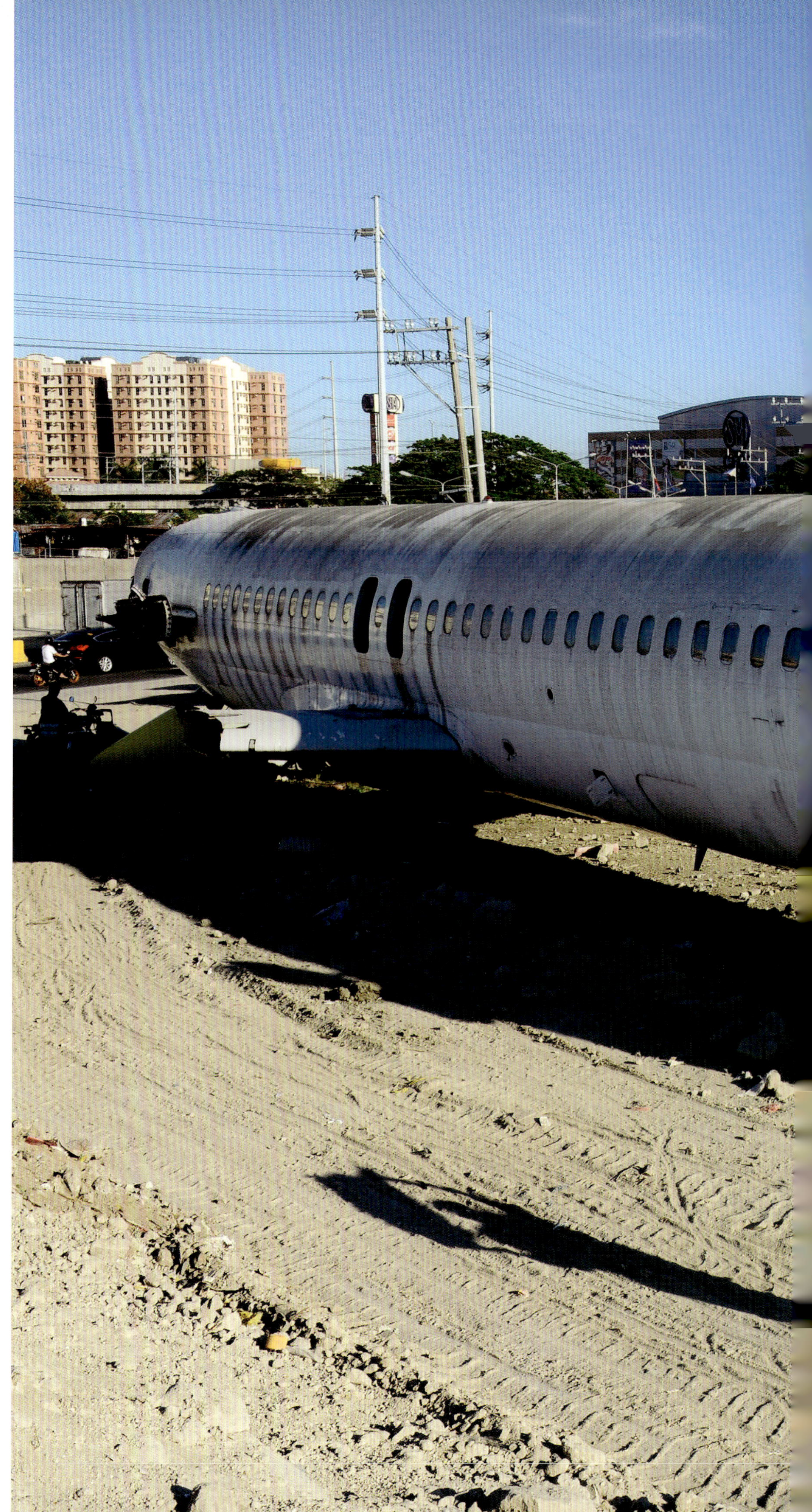

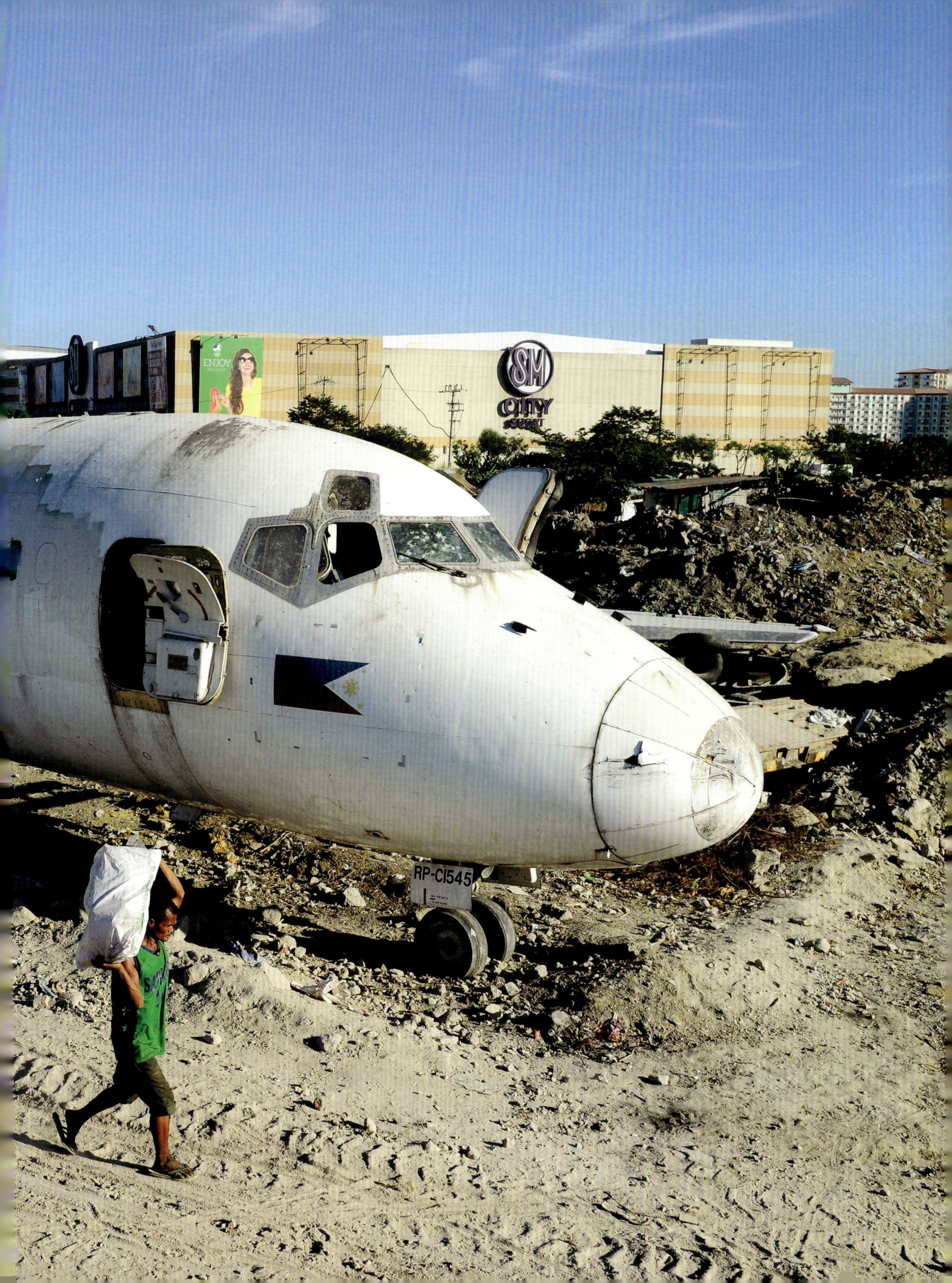
SM
CITY
SUCAT
ENJOY
RP-C1545

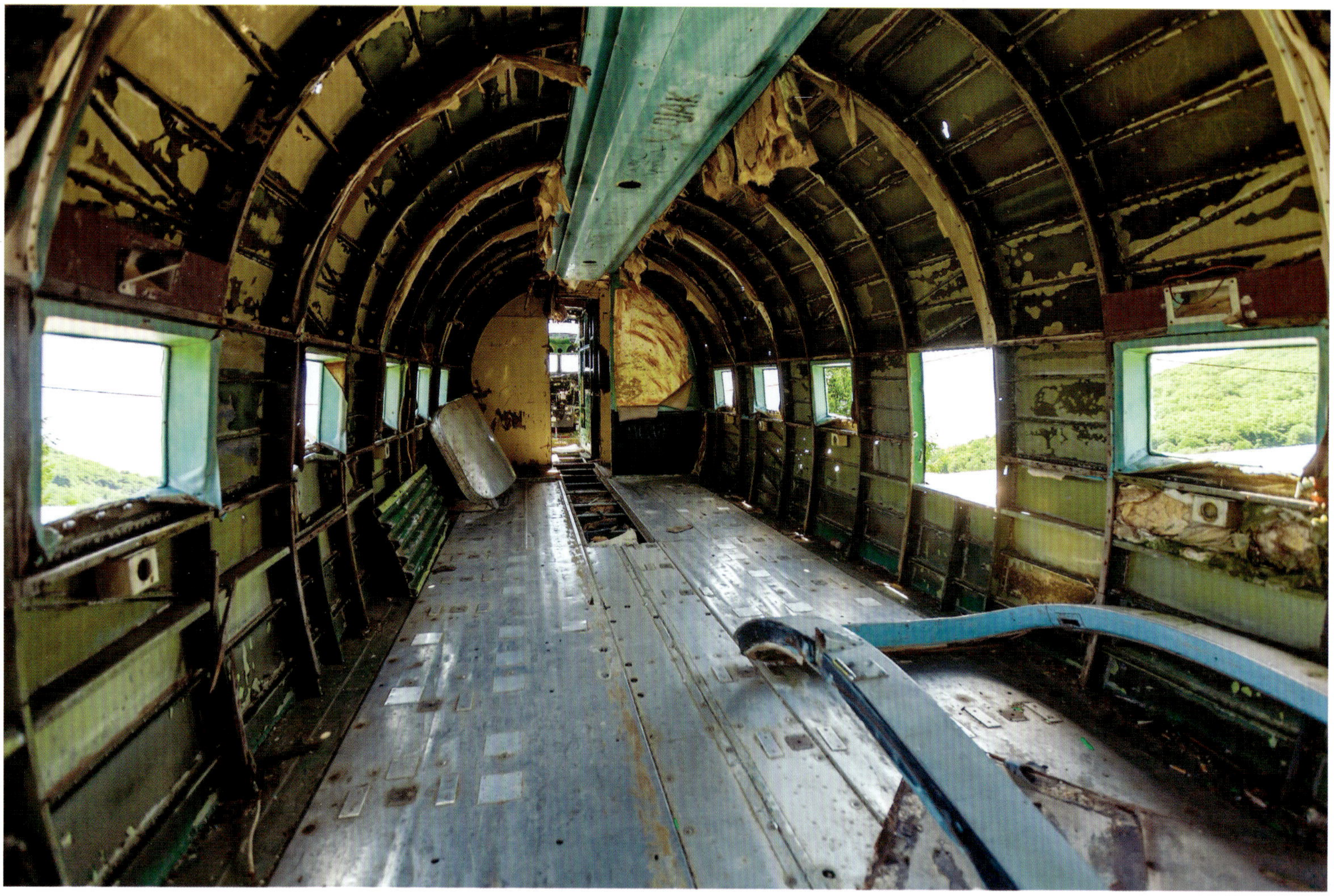

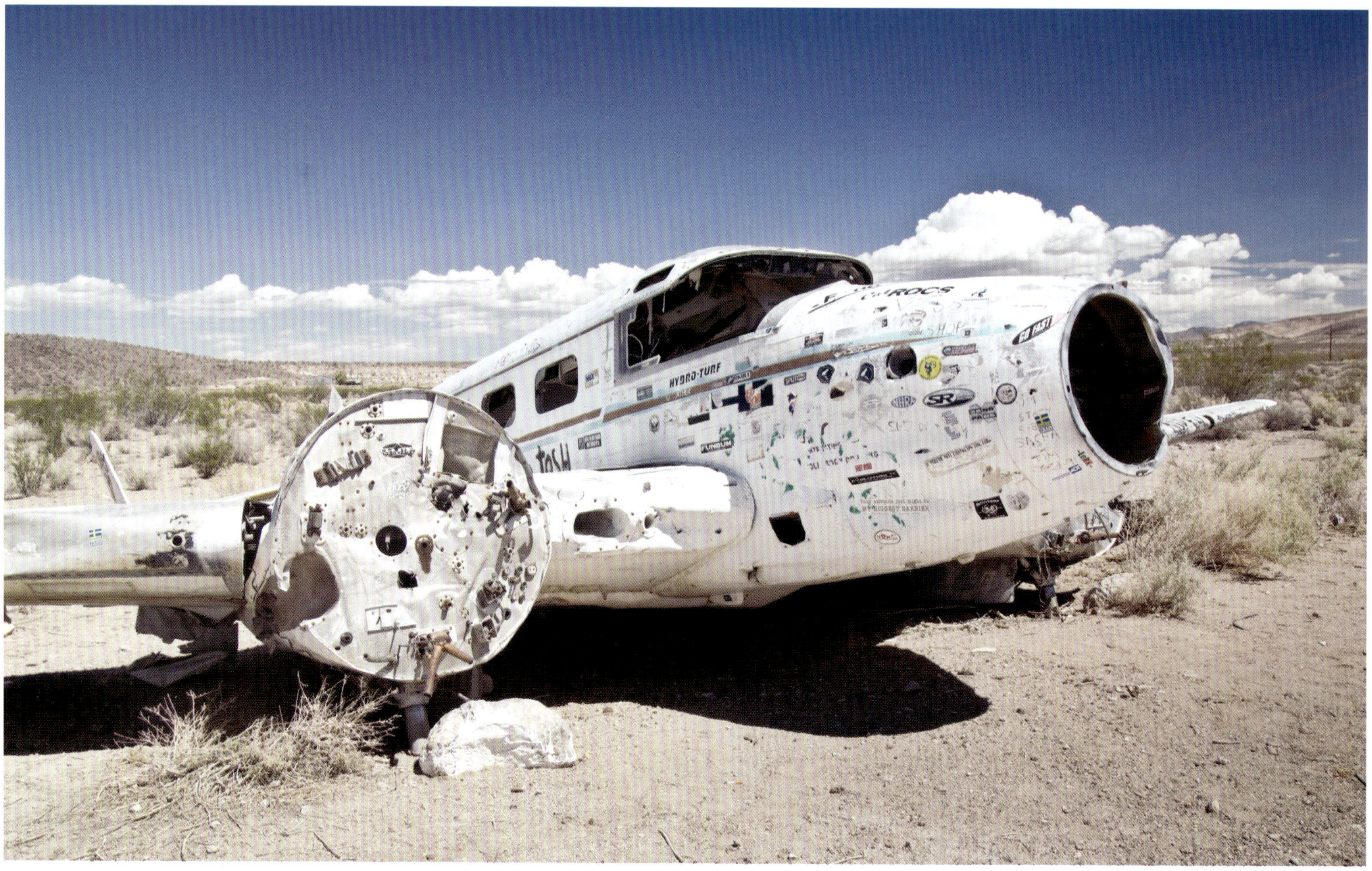

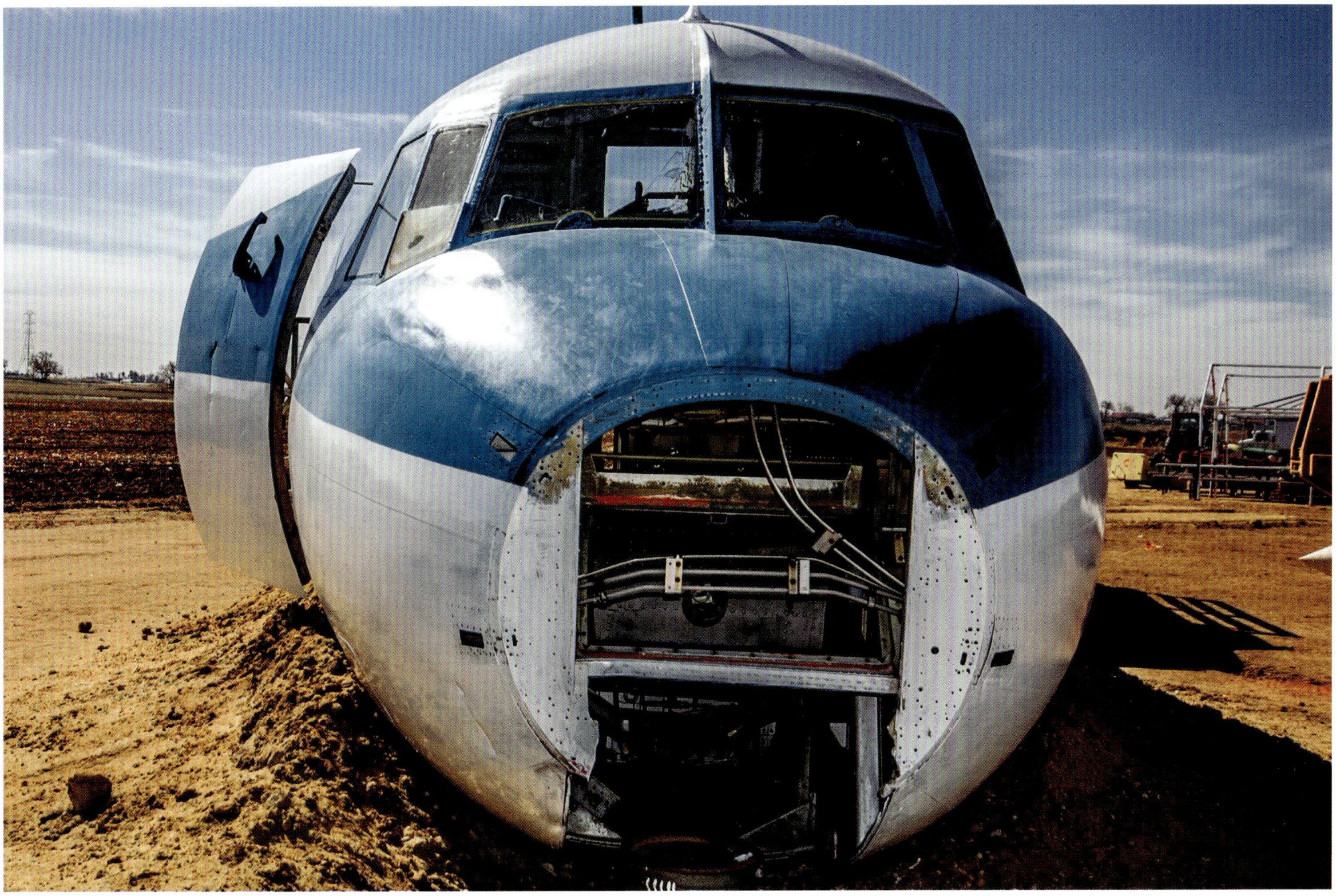

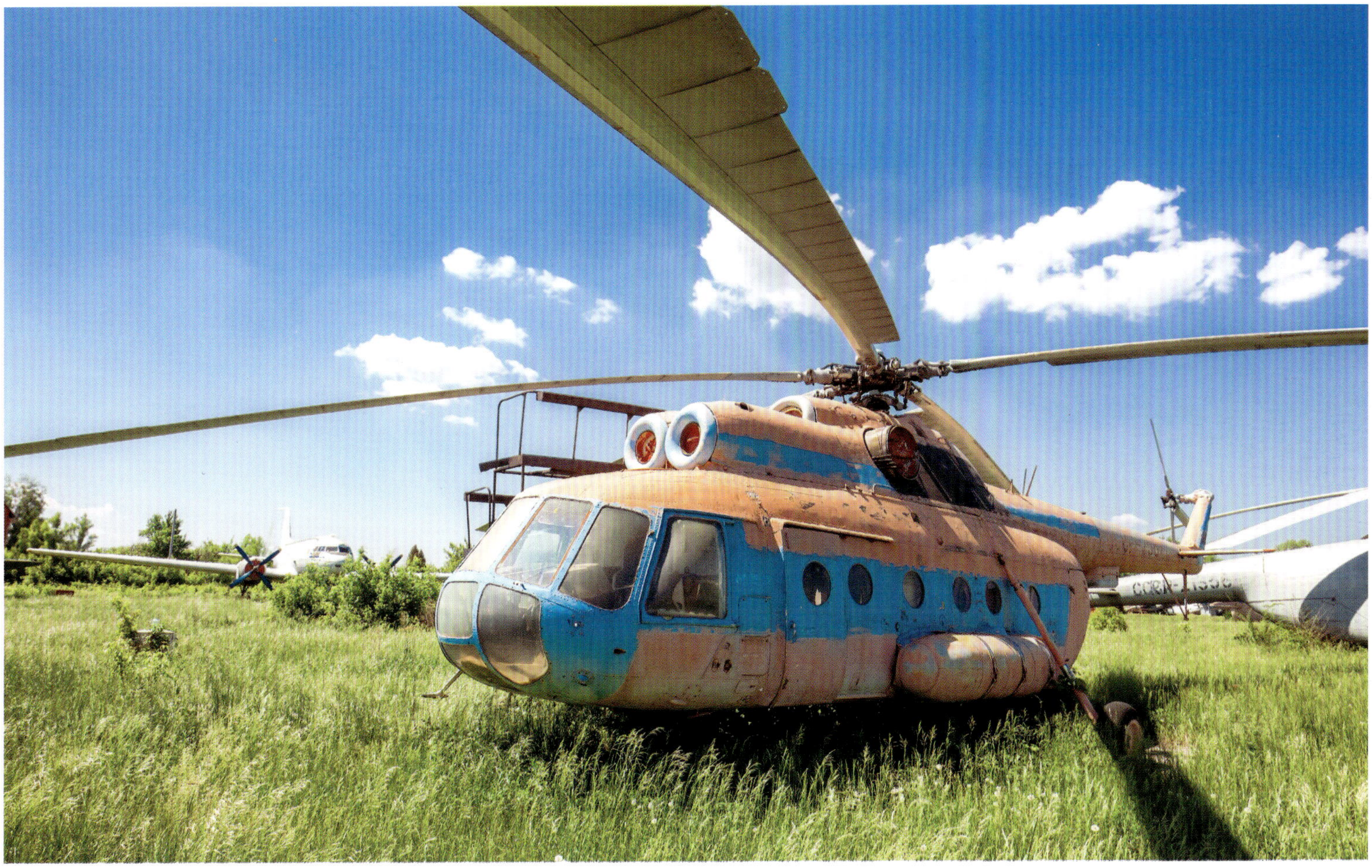

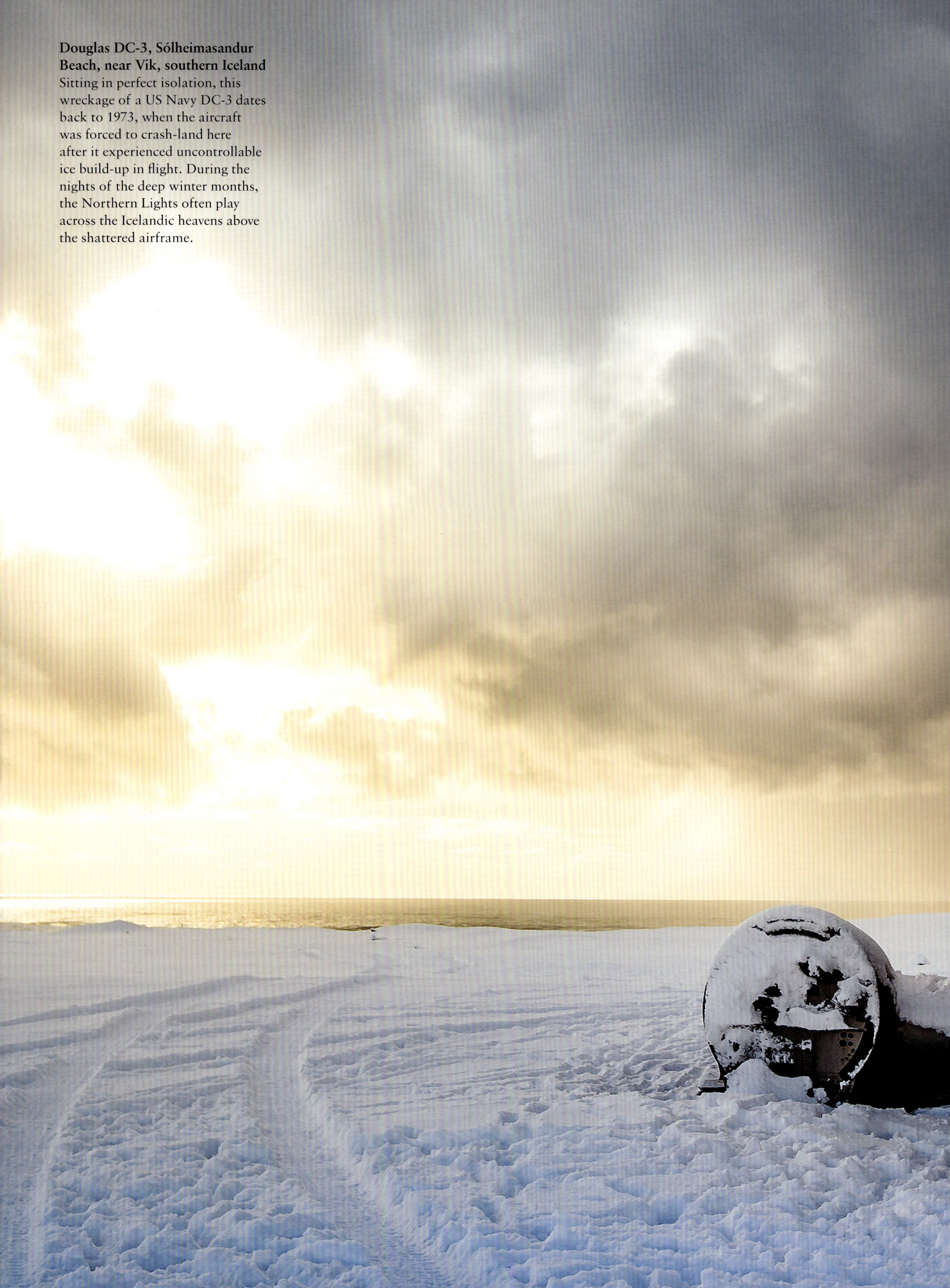

**Douglas DC-3, Sólheimasandur
Beach, near Vik, southern Iceland**
Sitting in perfect isolation, this
wreckage of a US Navy DC-3 dates
back to 1973, when the aircraft
was forced to crash-land here
after it experienced uncontrollable
ice build-up in flight. During the
nights of the deep winter months,
the Northern Lights often play
across the Icelandic heavens above
the shattered airframe.

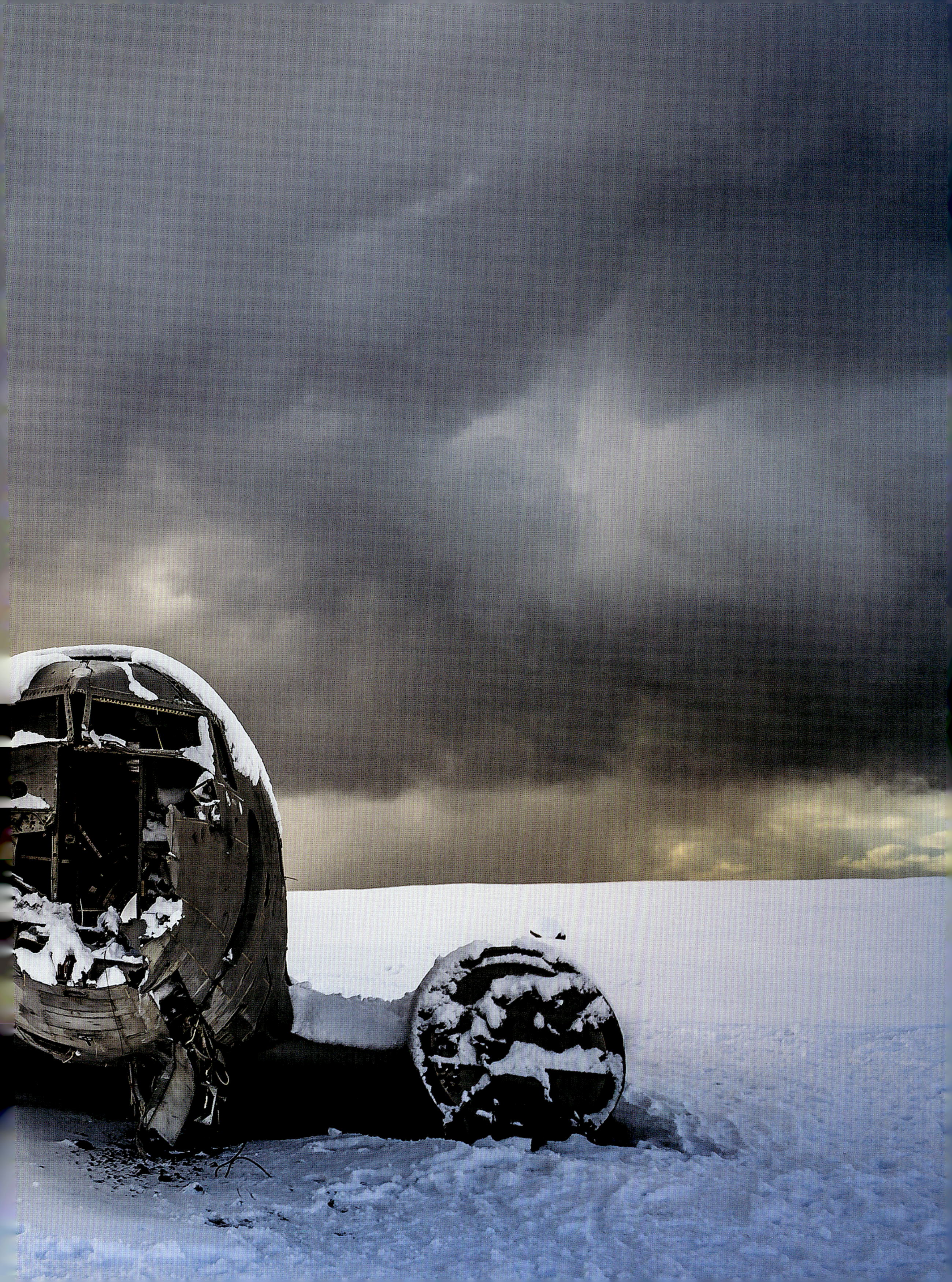

Buran Space Shuttle, Baikonur Cosmodrome, Kazakhstan
In a derelict hangar on the still-active Baikonur Cosmodrome sits the grimy wreck of one of the two Buran space shuttles, the Soviet Union/Russia's only attempt at a space shuttle programme. This shuttle was an operational prototype; the only flying vehicle – OK-1K1 – was destroyed in a hangar collapse in 2002.

Sukhoi Su-15, outskirts of Leningrad, USSR, 1990
The collapse of Soviet communism led to the abandonment of thousands of communist-era vehicles and aircraft. Seen here in 1990, these derelict aircraft appear to be Sukhoi Su-15 fighters, left to rot on a highway.

Mikoyan-Gurevich MiG-15, Karakum Desert, Central Asia
This wreck's silver fuselage in striking contrast to the desert sand, the Mikoyan-Gurevich MiG-15 was a defining jet fighter of the late 1940s and 1950s, known for its exceptional combat manoeuvrability and power.

Hawker Siddeley HS 121 Trident, Nicosia Airport, Cyprus
A reminder of political upheaval and civil war, this Hawker Siddeley HS 121 Trident was damaged beyond repair in the fighting between Turkish and Greek forces following the Turkish invasion of Cyprus on 20 July 1974.

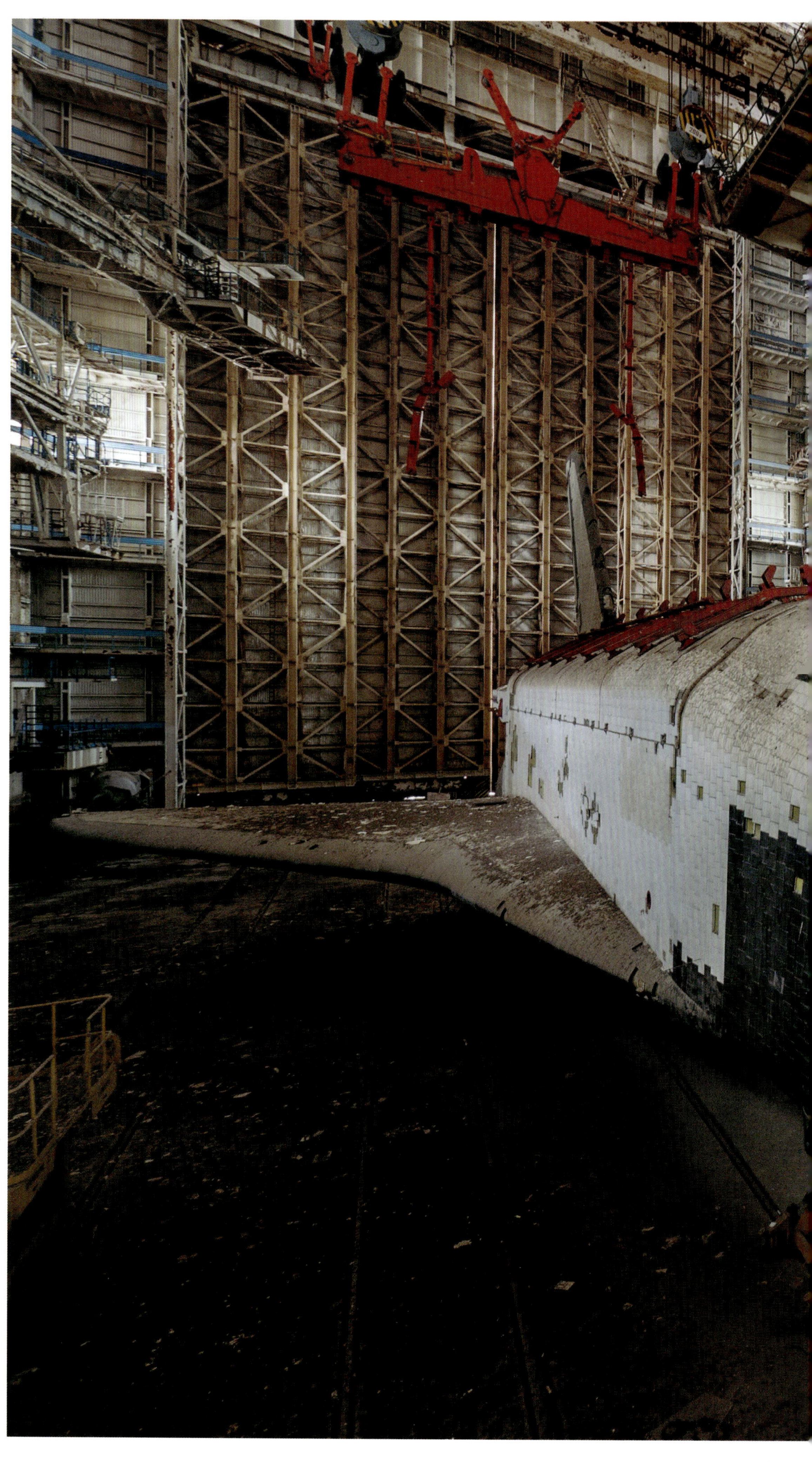

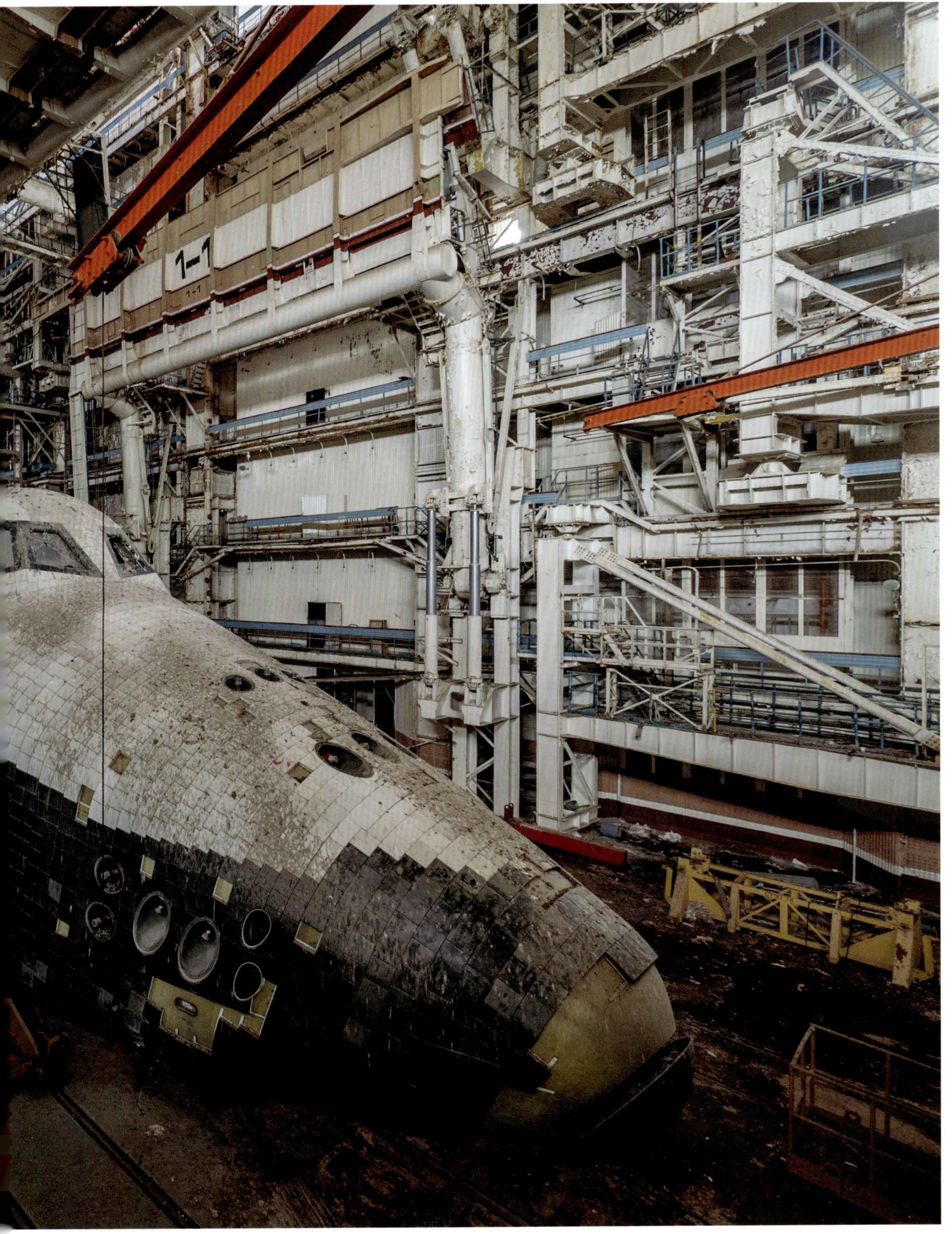

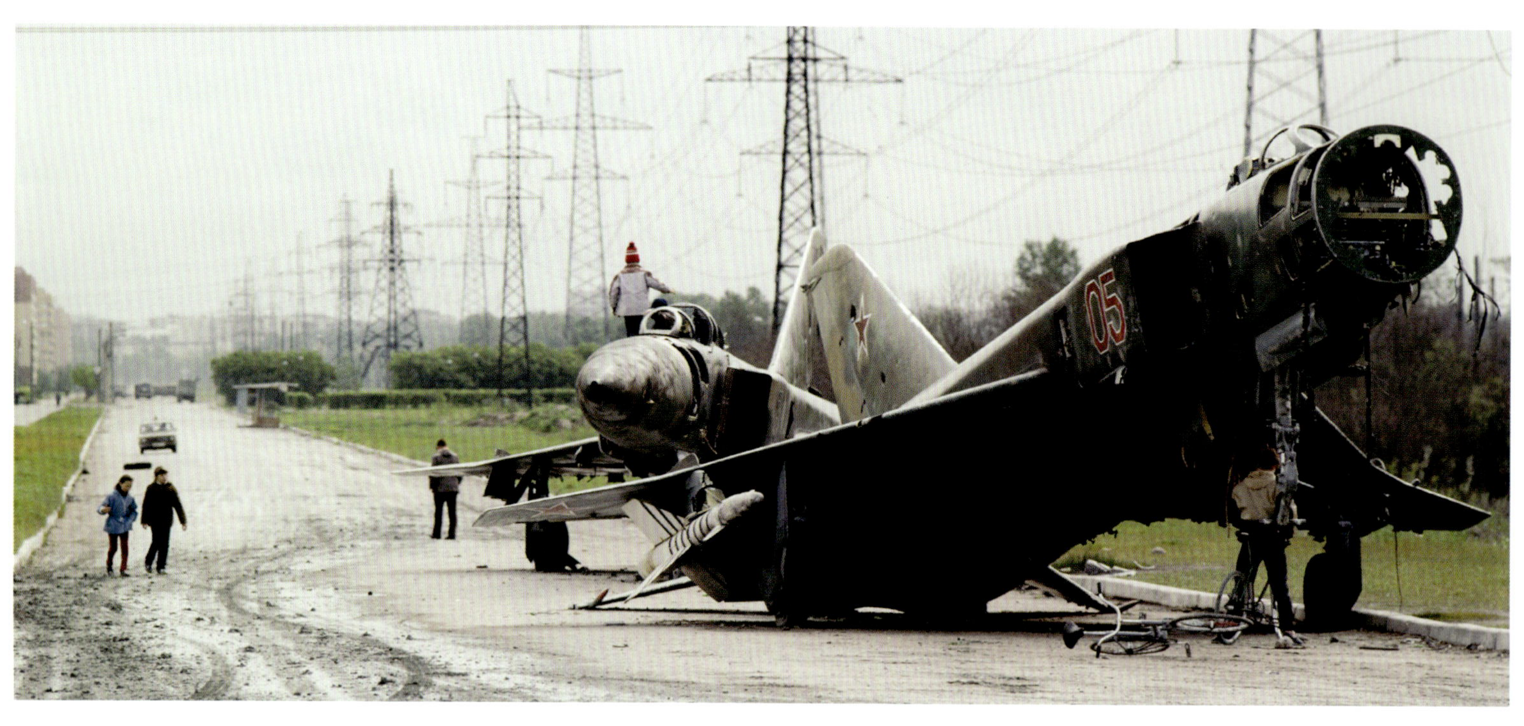

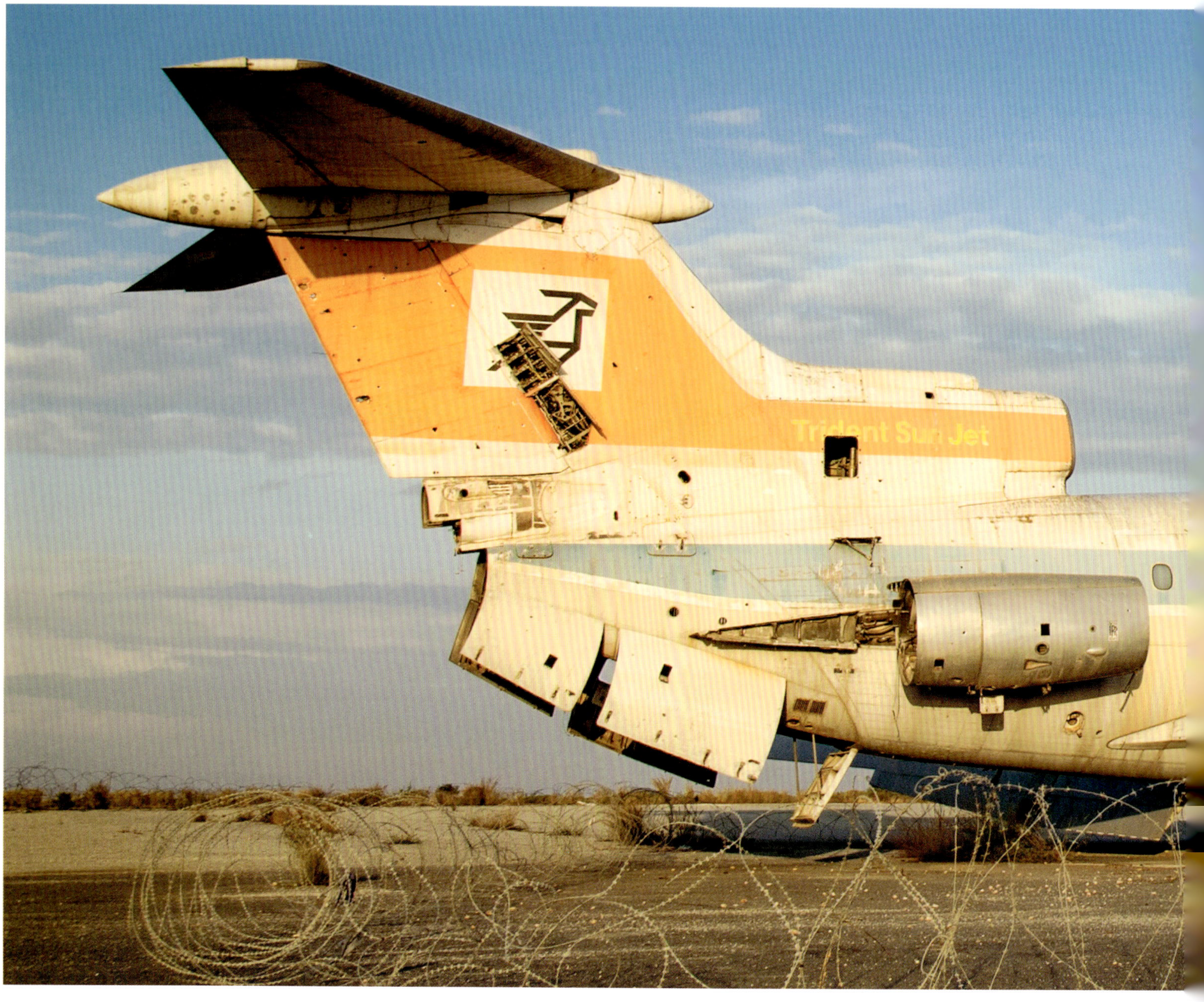

Trident Sun Jet

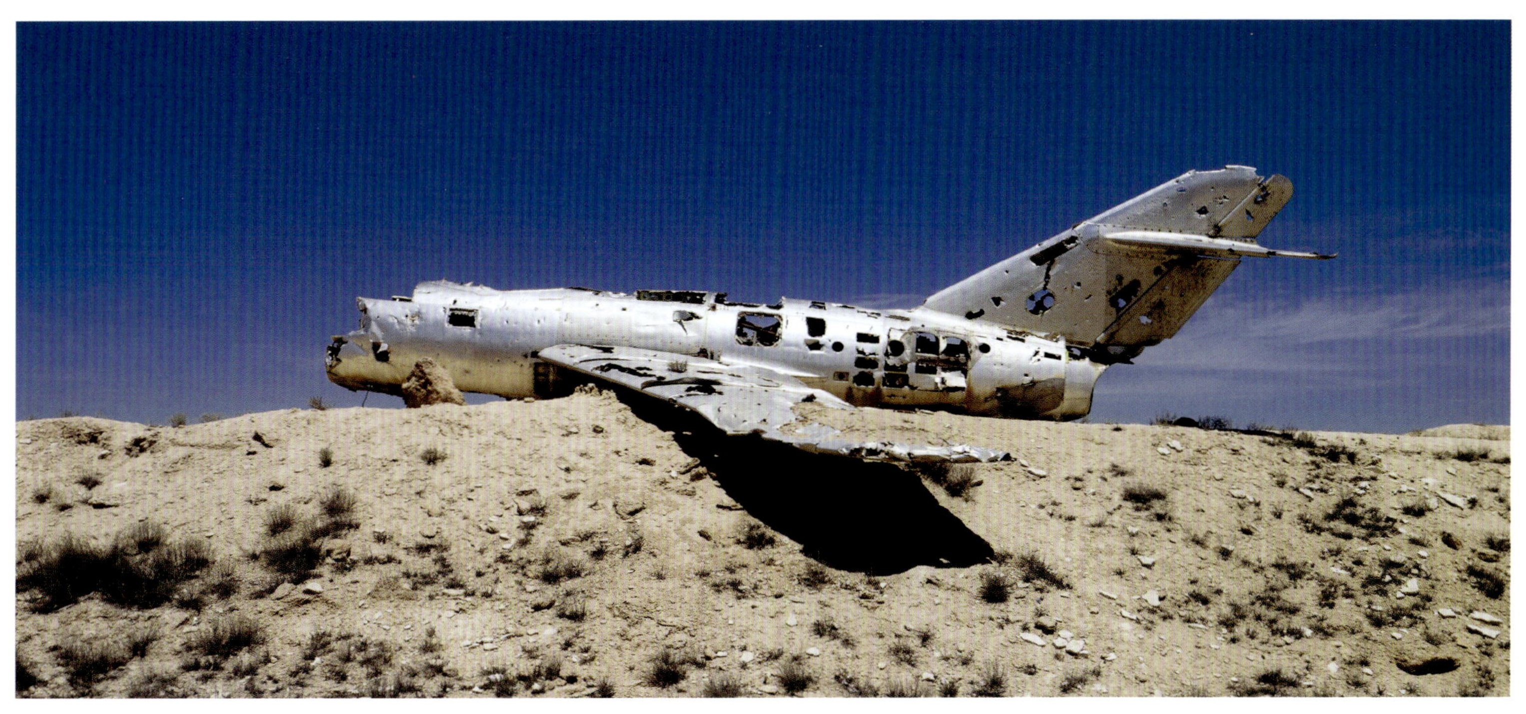

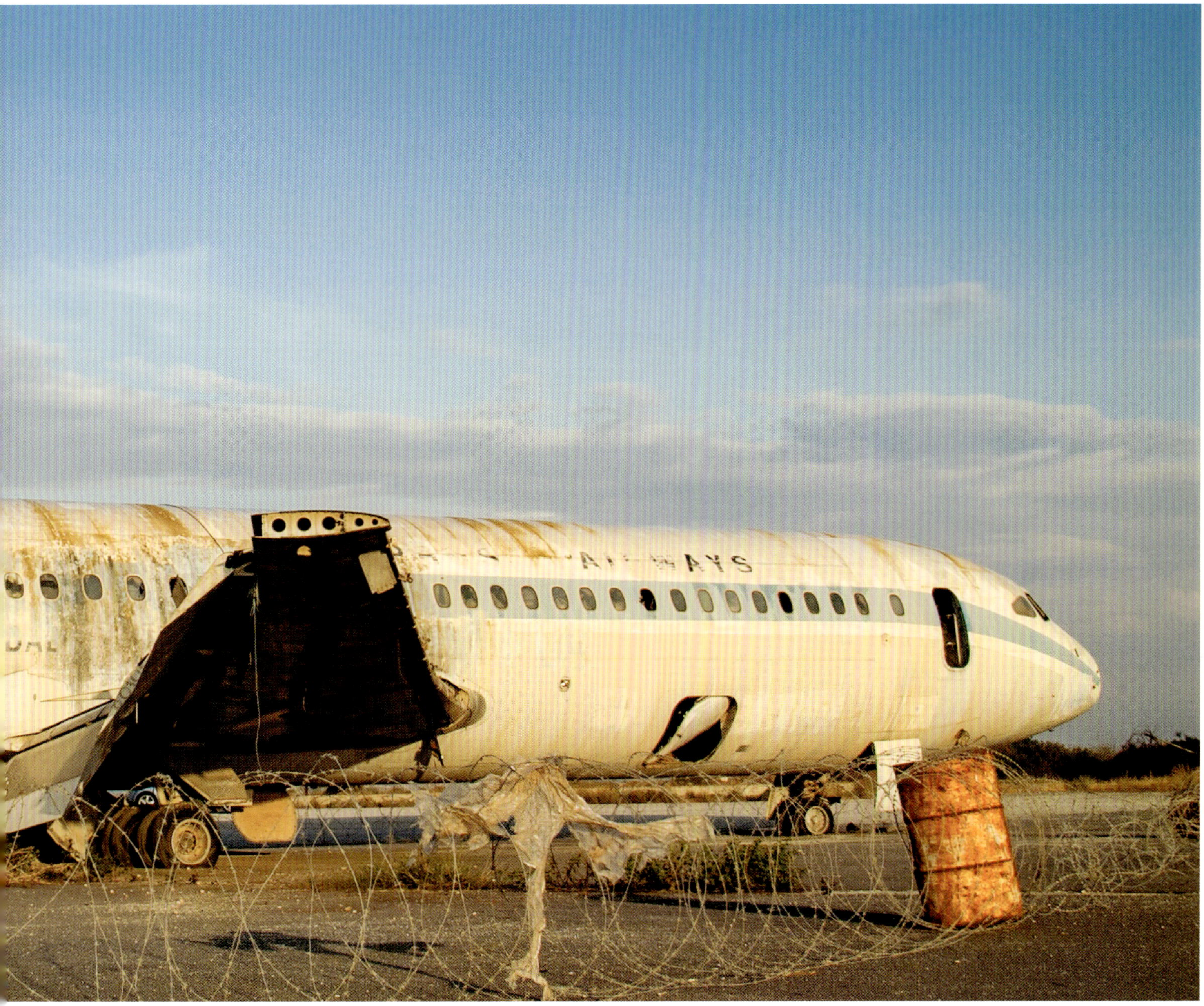

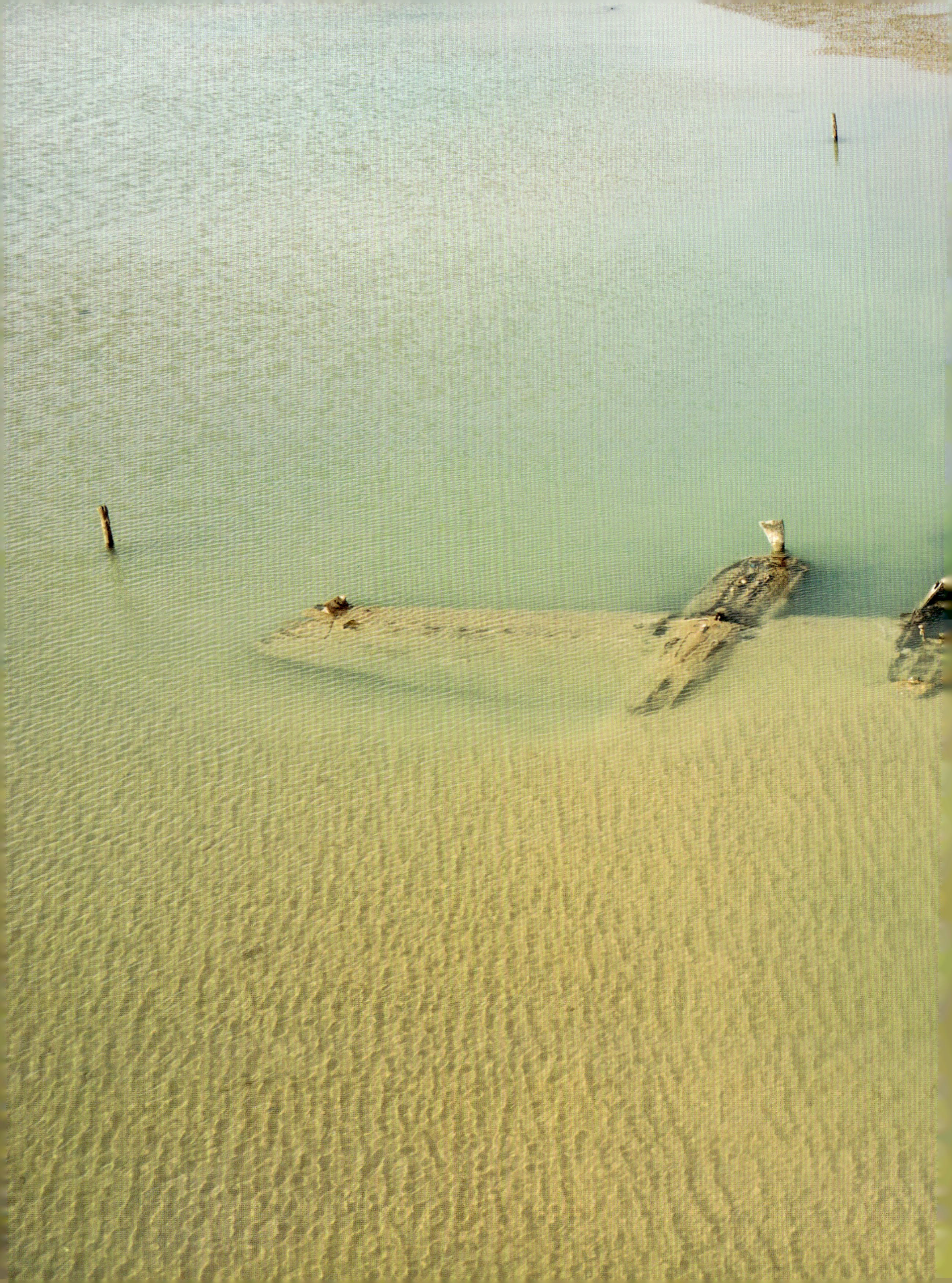

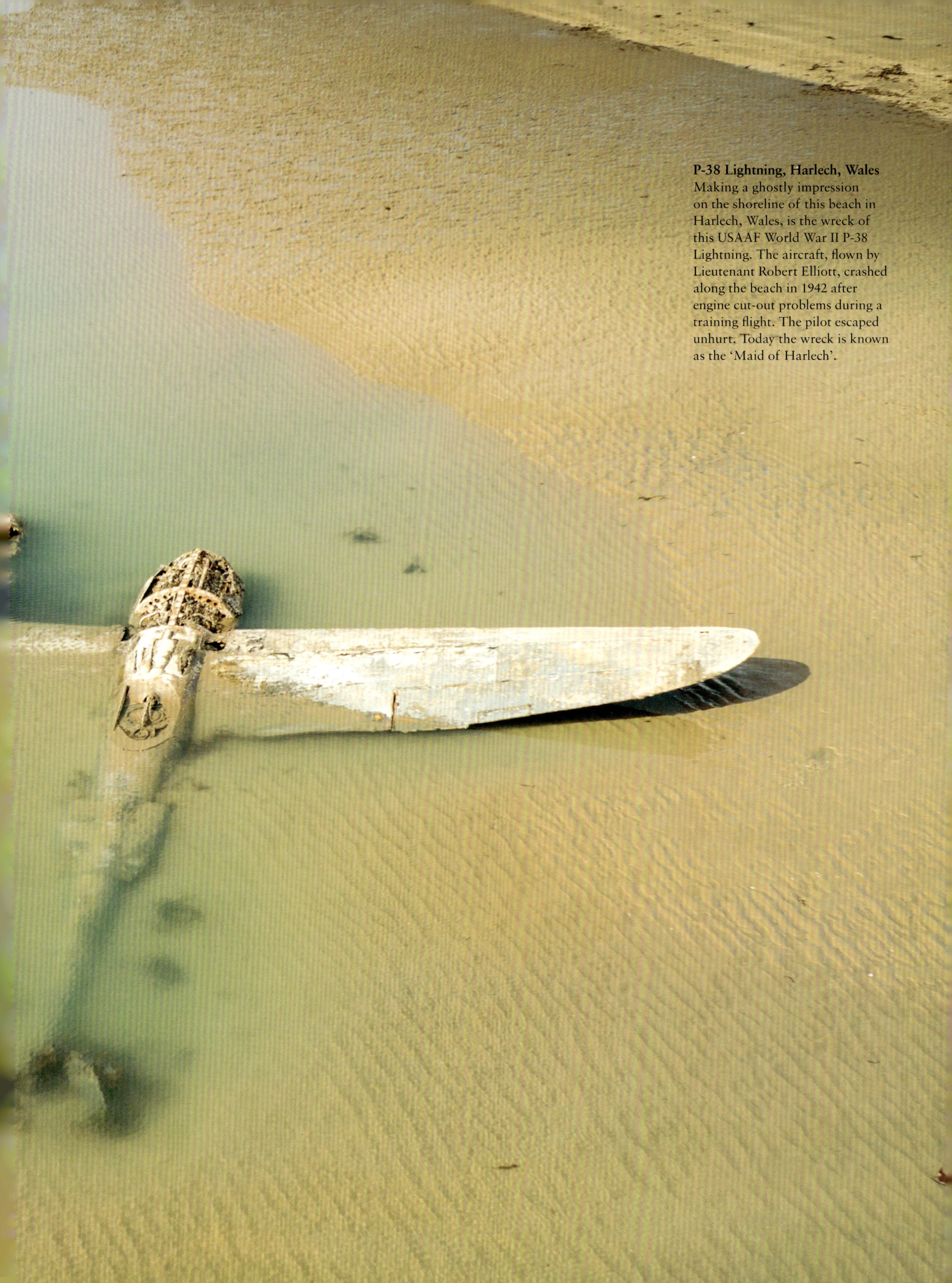

P-38 Lightning, Harlech, Wales
Making a ghostly impression on the shoreline of this beach in Harlech, Wales, is the wreck of this USAAF World War II P-38 Lightning. The aircraft, flown by Lieutenant Robert Elliott, crashed along the beach in 1942 after engine cut-out problems during a training flight. The pilot escaped unhurt. Today the wreck is known as the 'Maid of Harlech'.

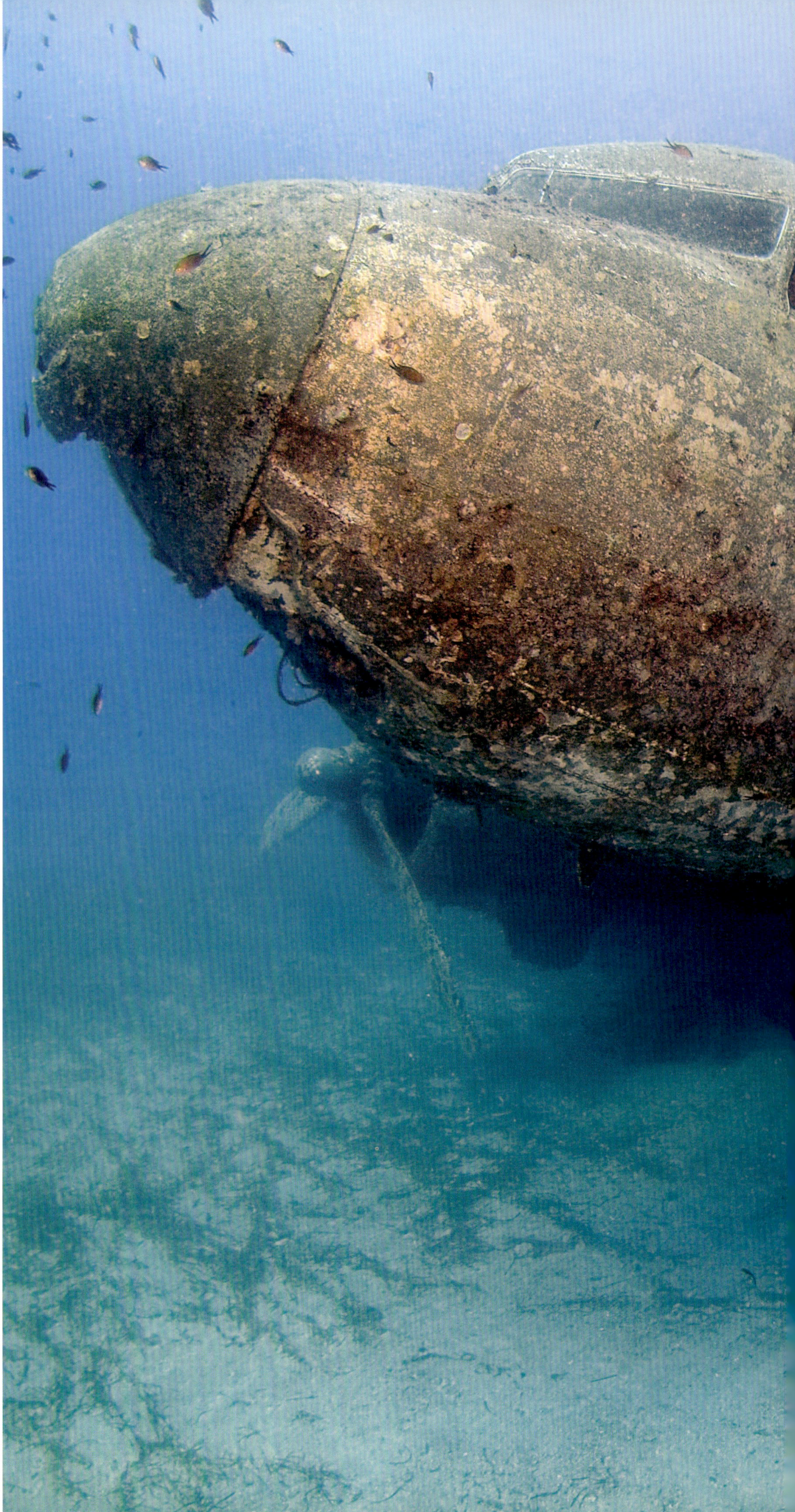

Douglas C-47, Mediterranean Sea, Kas, Turkey
The undersea wrecks of aircraft, if they are at an accessible depth, make some of the most popular destinations for professional and recreational divers. This diver is inspecting the propeller of a Douglas C-47, the aircraft sunk as an artificial reef and dive attraction in July 2009, after a career in the Turkish Air Force.

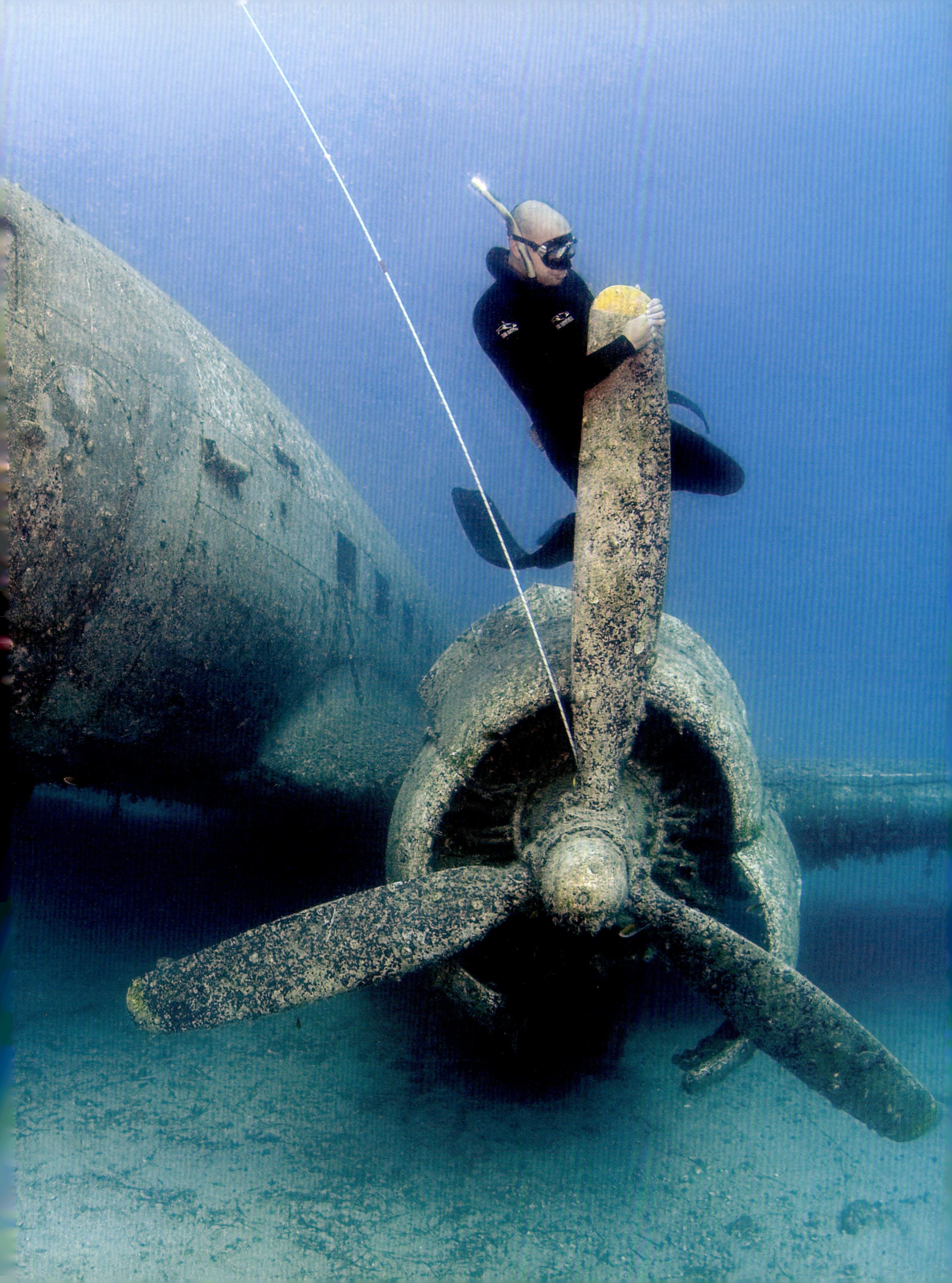

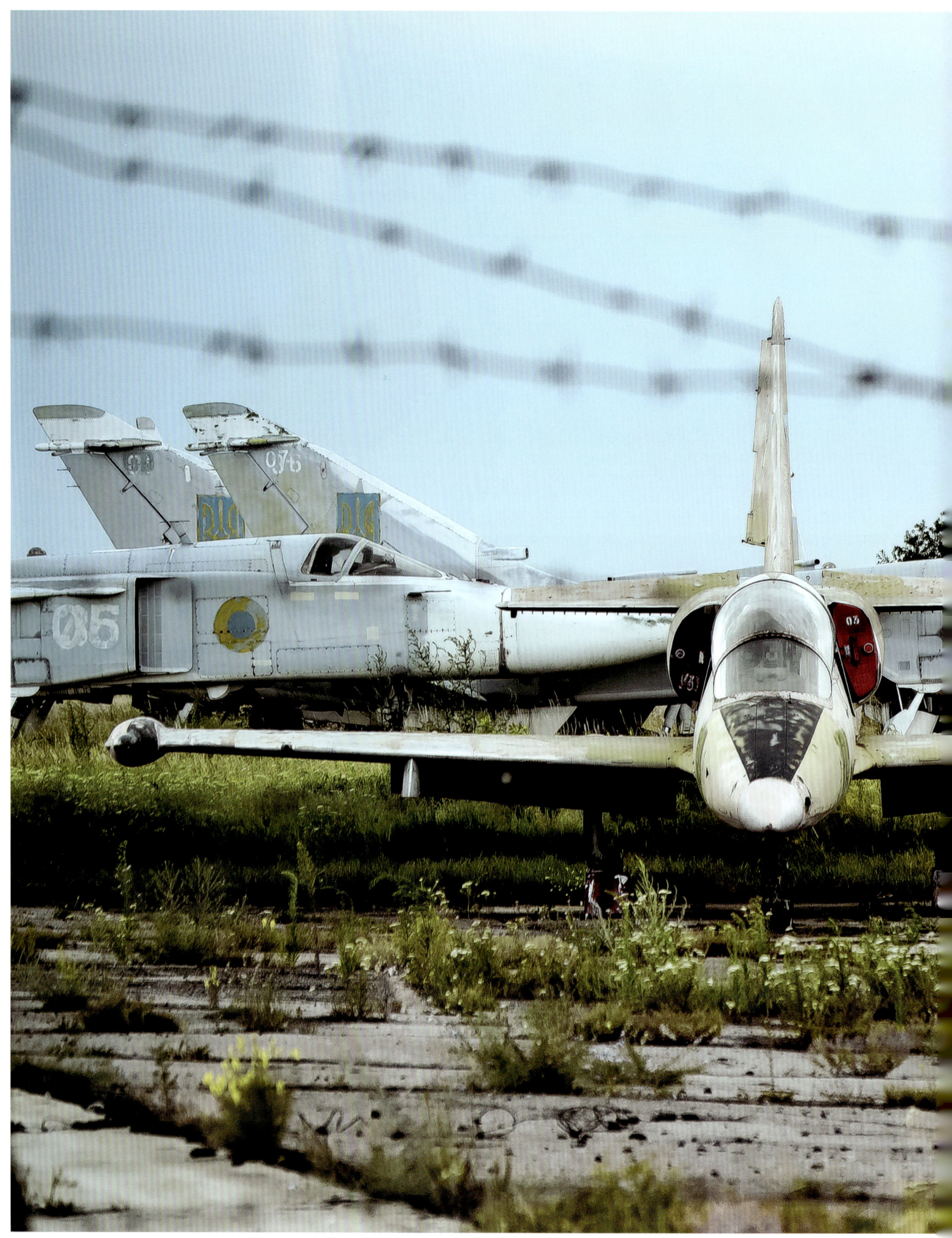

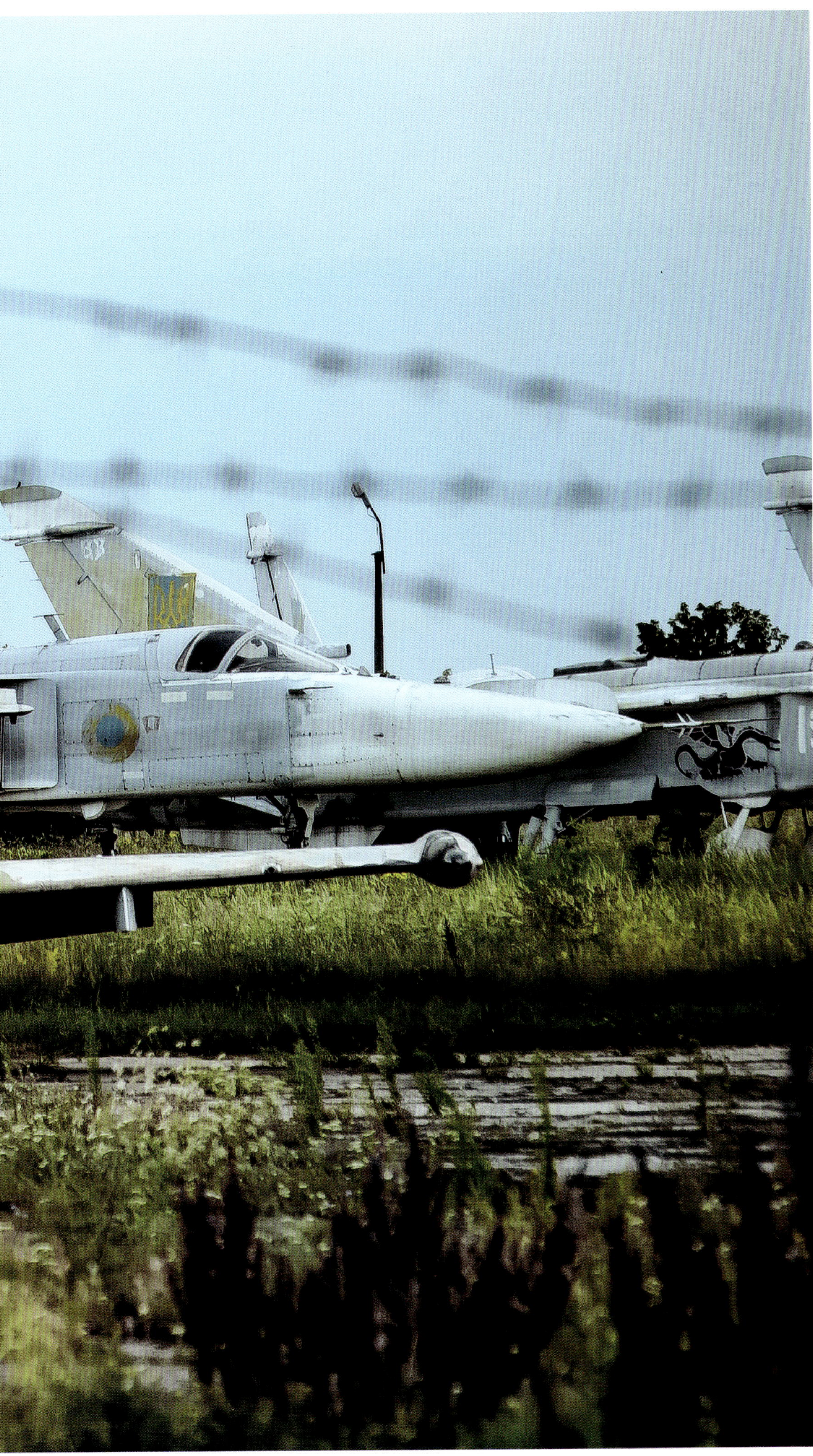

Bila Tserkva, Ukraine
A collection of Soviet-era aircraft huddle together behind barbed wire in this abandoned Ukrainian air base. The aircraft in the background are Sukhoi Su-24M all-weather attack aircraft; when flightworthy, these aircraft had a maximum speed of Mach 1.35. The aircraft in the foreground is an Aero L-39C Albatros jet trainer.

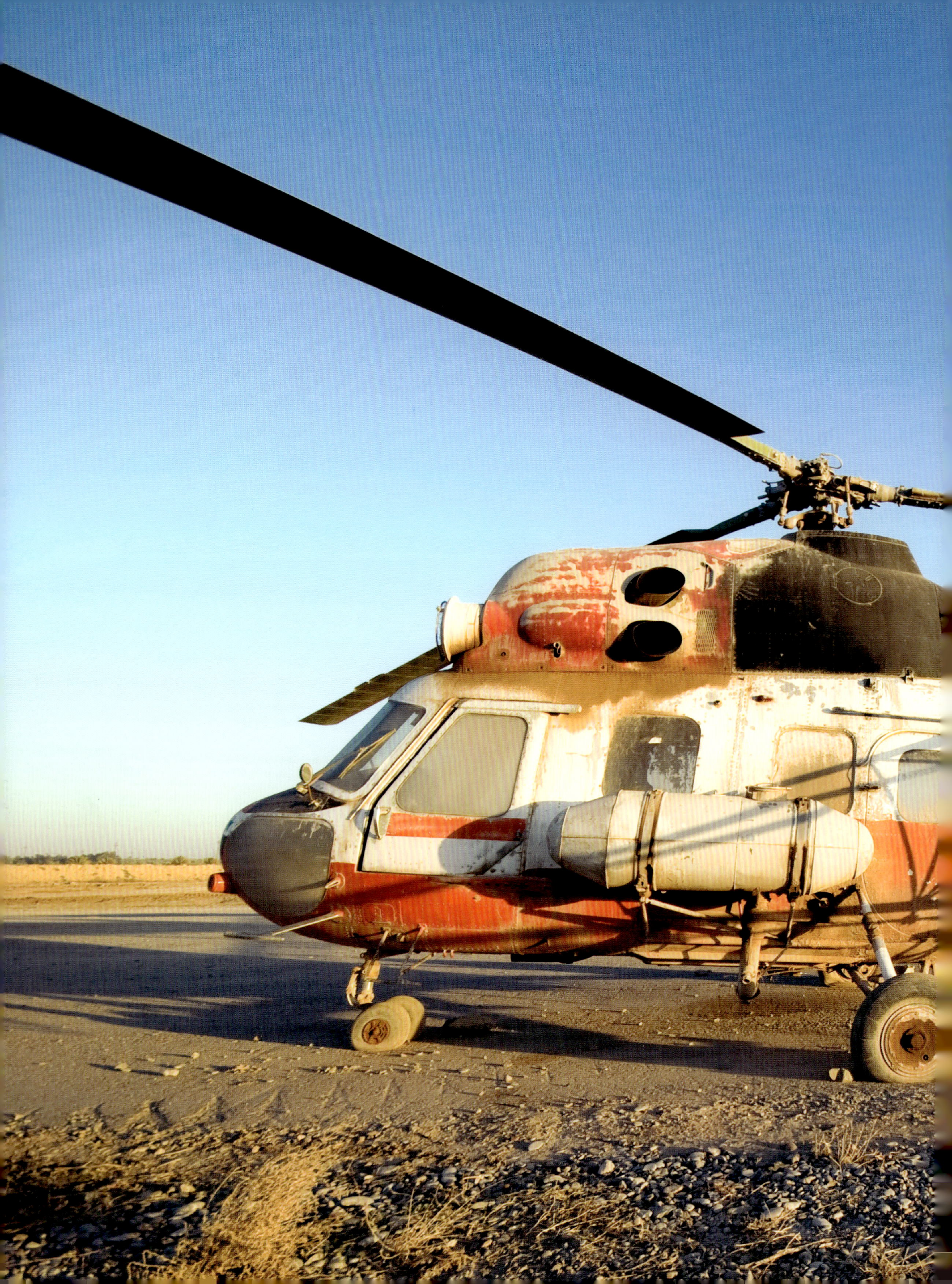

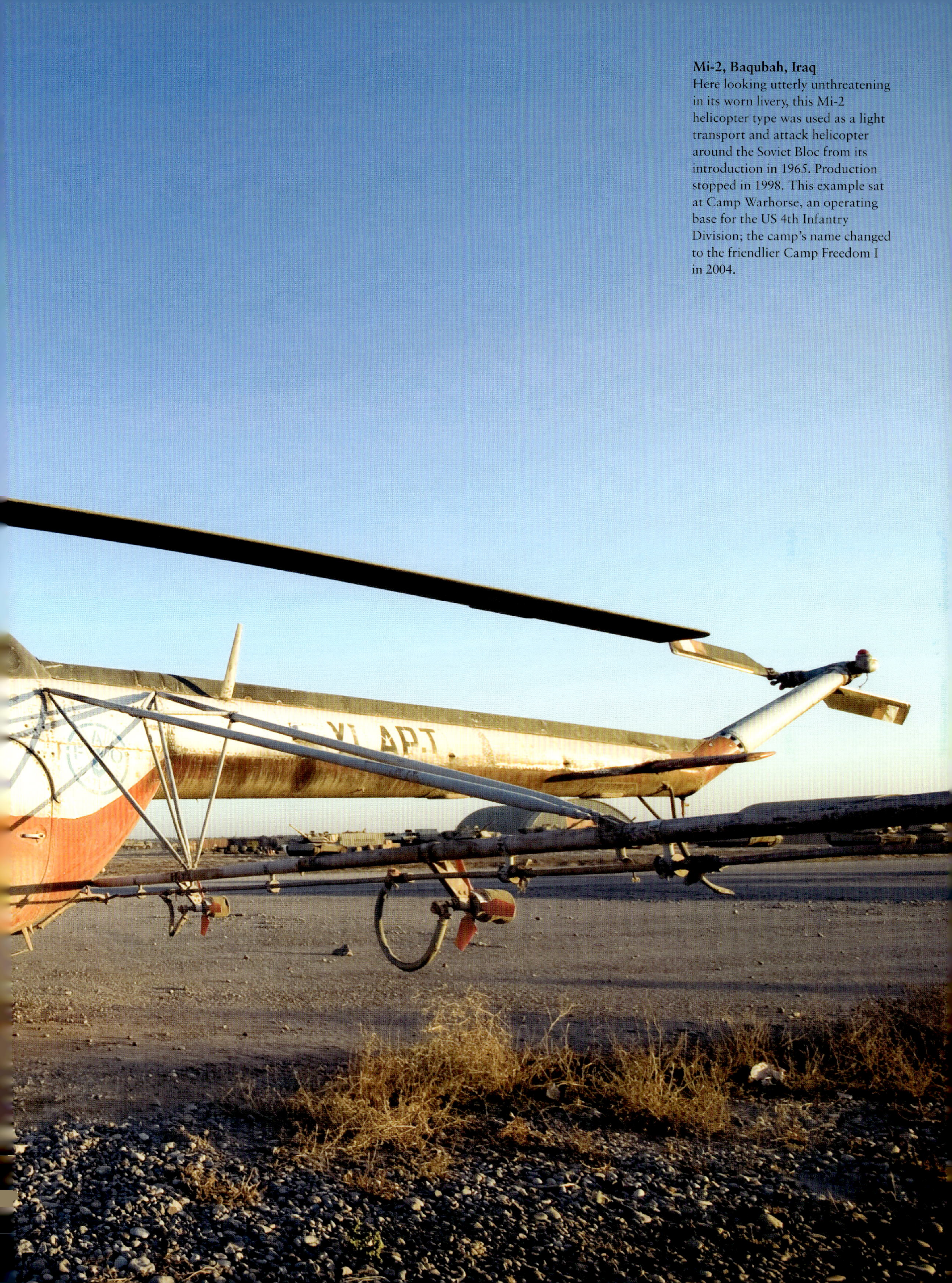

Mi-2, Baqubah, Iraq
Here looking utterly unthreatening in its worn livery, this Mi-2 helicopter type was used as a light transport and attack helicopter around the Soviet Bloc from its introduction in 1965. Production stopped in 1998. This example sat at Camp Warhorse, an operating base for the US 4th Infantry Division; the camp's name changed to the friendlier Camp Freedom I in 2004.

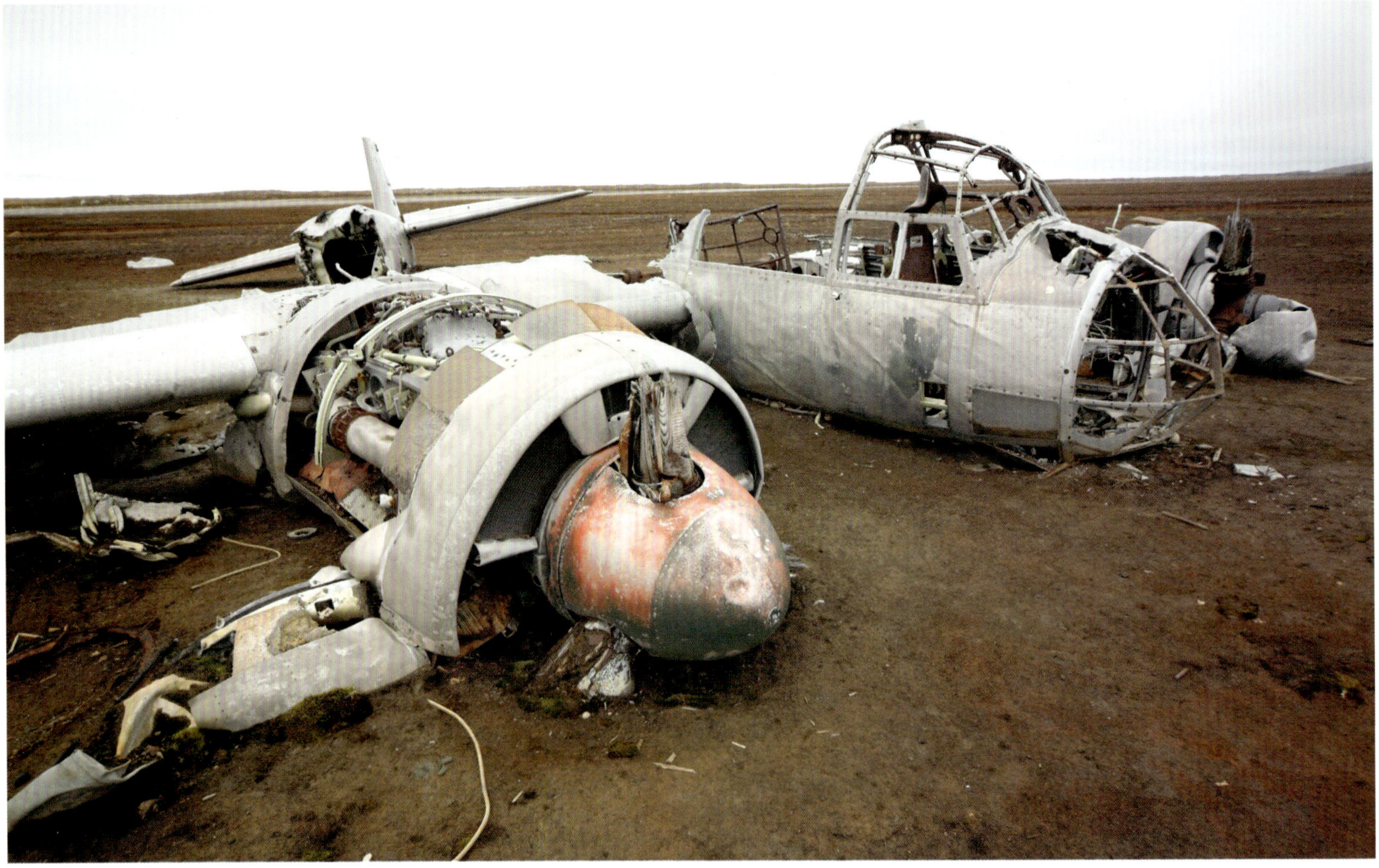

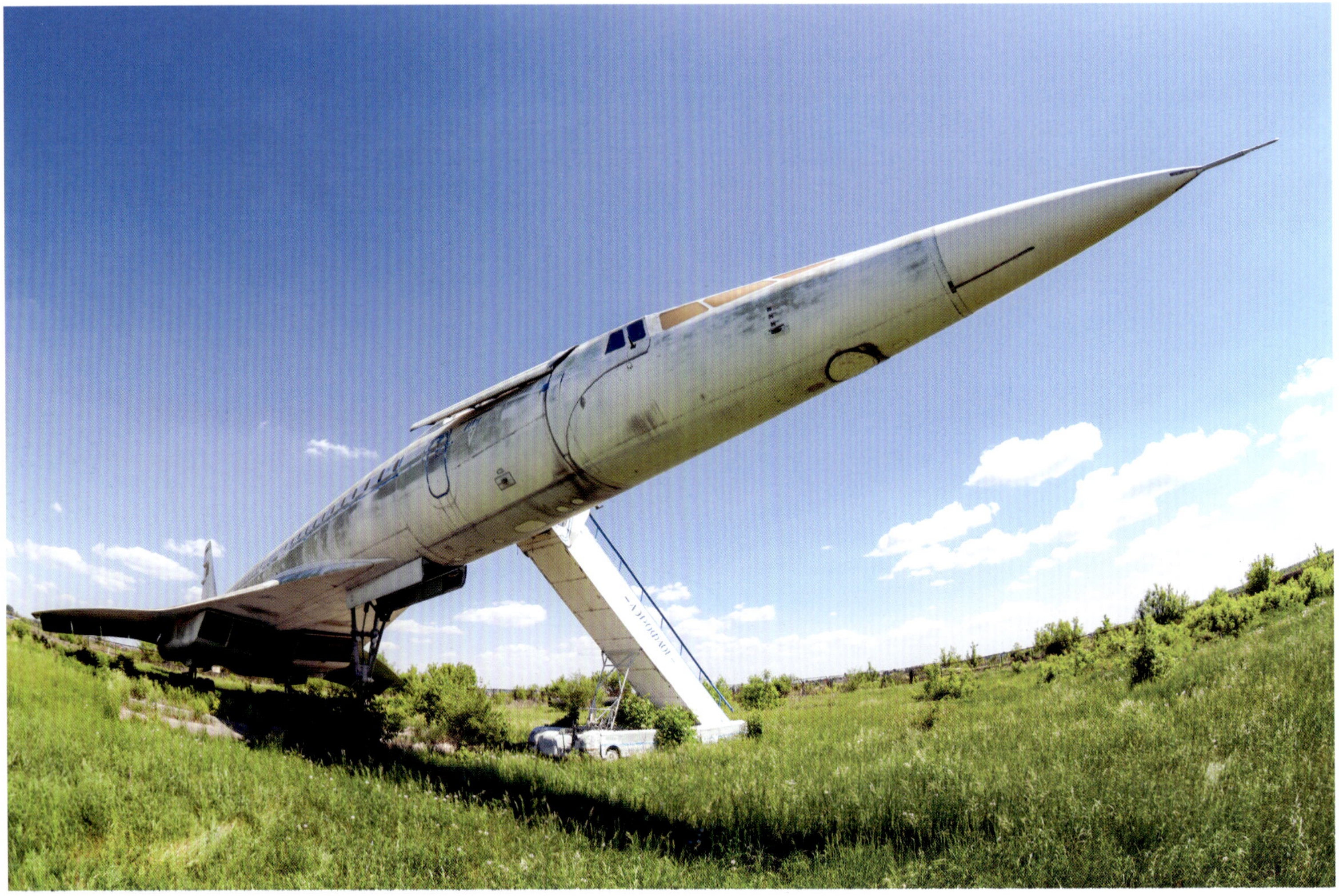

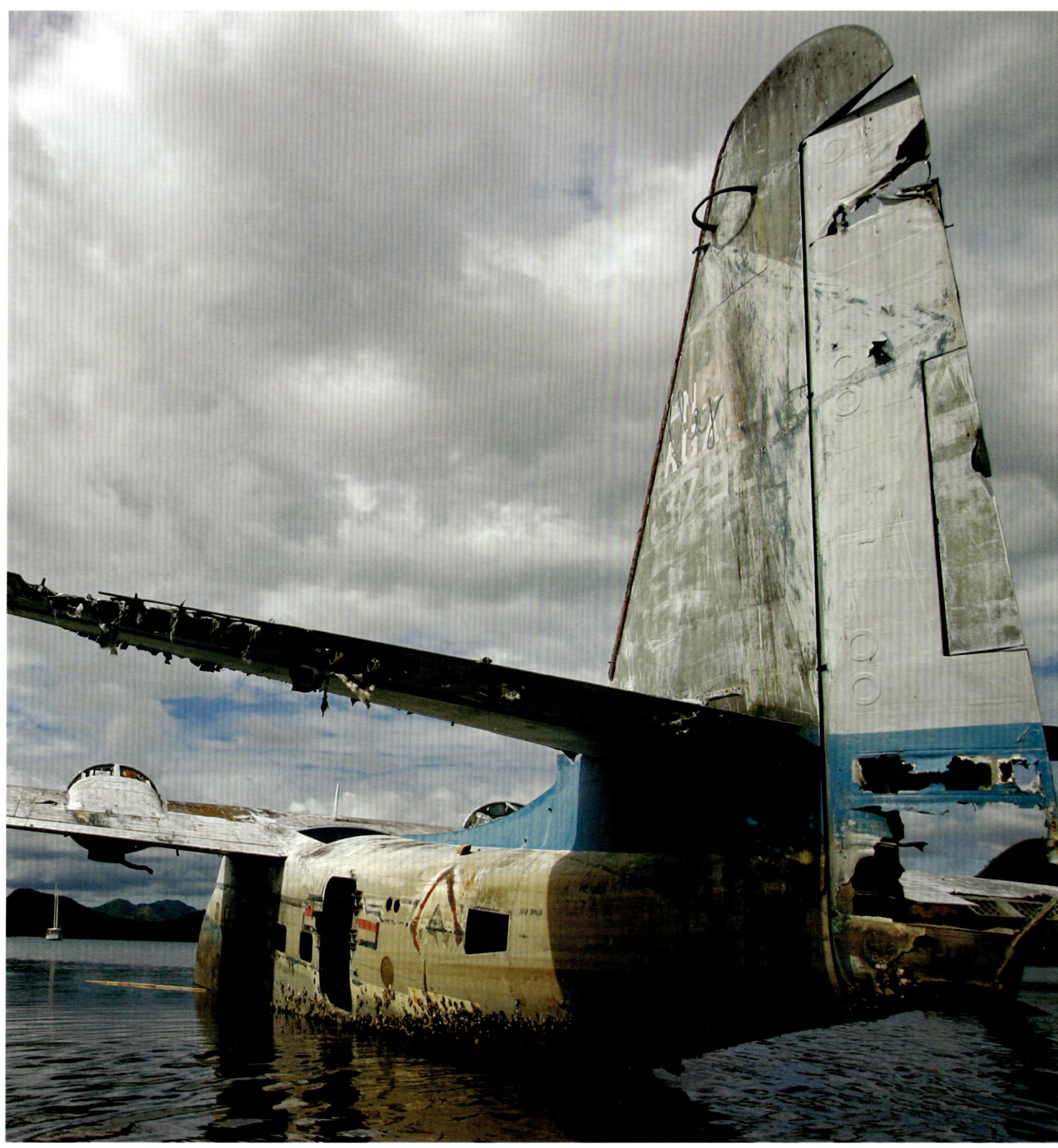

Junkers Ju 88, Kapp Borthen, Norway
This wreckage is that of a German Junkers Ju 88 medium bomber, forced to crash-land here during World War II. The Luftwaffe operated Ju 88s out of Norway mainly in the maritime interdiction role, striking at Allied shipping in the North Sea and ships attempting to transit the Arctic Ocean to Russia.

Tupolev Tu-144, Samara, Russia
Its profile suggesting its sheer speed, the Tupolev Tu-144 was one of only two types of supersonic airliner that went into service, the other being Concorde. It had a maximum cruise speed of 2,120km/h (1,320mph) and a capacity of 140 passengers. The Tu-144 made its first passenger flight in December 1975, and its last in July 1978.

Coron Island, Philippines
This abandoned seaplane off Coron Island in the Philippines still gives a passing impression of seaworthiness. Seaplanes and floatplanes have real utility around the Philippines, with its extremely long coastline and multiple islands. Coron Island is much visited for its superb wreck diving, particularly for its sunken wartime Japanese ships.

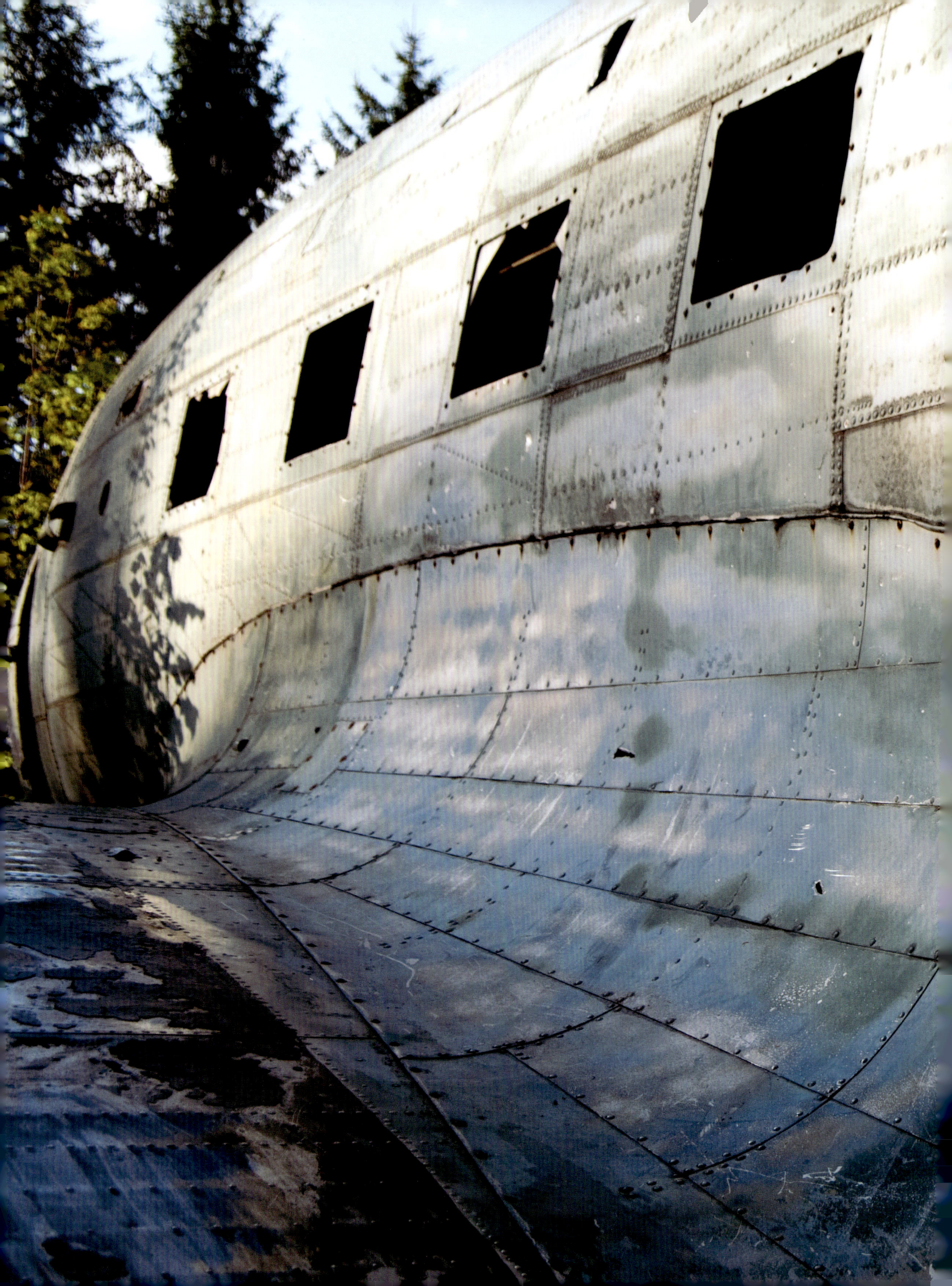

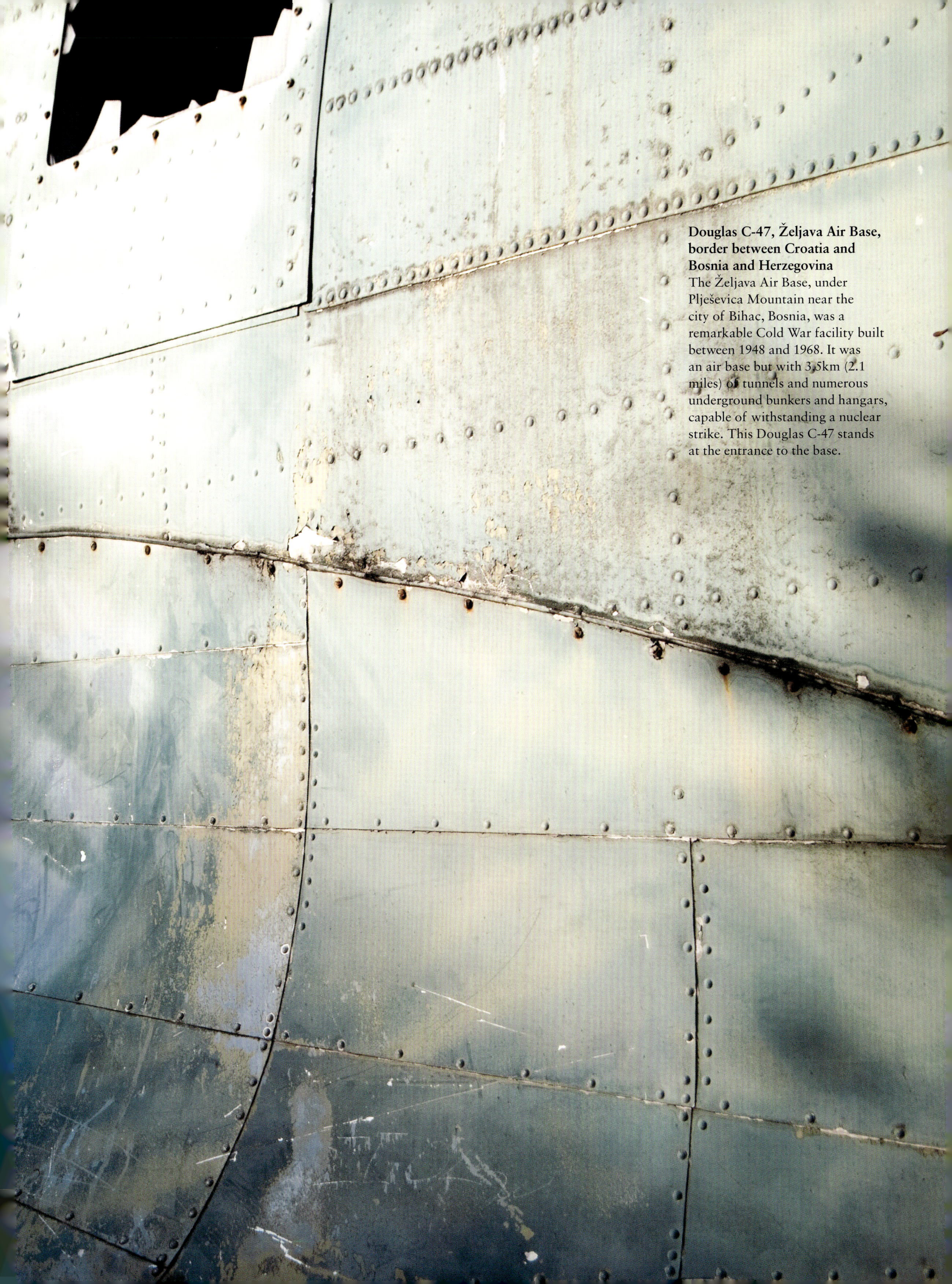

Douglas C-47, Željava Air Base, border between Croatia and Bosnia and Herzegovina
The Željava Air Base, under Plješevica Mountain near the city of Bihac, Bosnia, was a remarkable Cold War facility built between 1948 and 1968. It was an air base but with 3.5km (2.1 miles) of tunnels and numerous underground bunkers and hangars, capable of withstanding a nuclear strike. This Douglas C-47 stands at the entrance to the base.

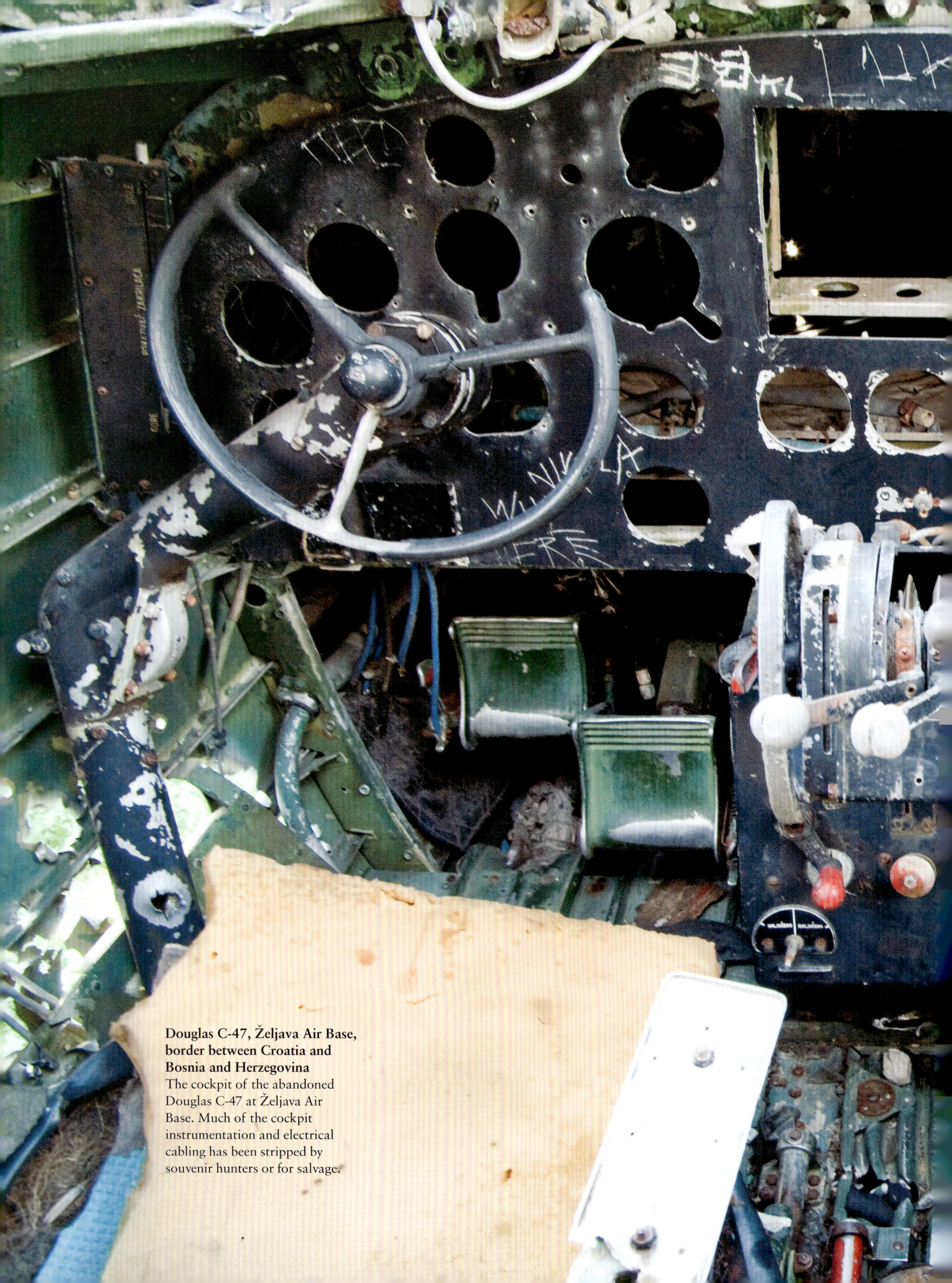

Douglas C-47, Željava Air Base, border between Croatia and Bosnia and Herzegovina
The cockpit of the abandoned Douglas C-47 at Željava Air Base. Much of the cockpit instrumentation and electrical cabling has been stripped by souvenir hunters or for salvage.

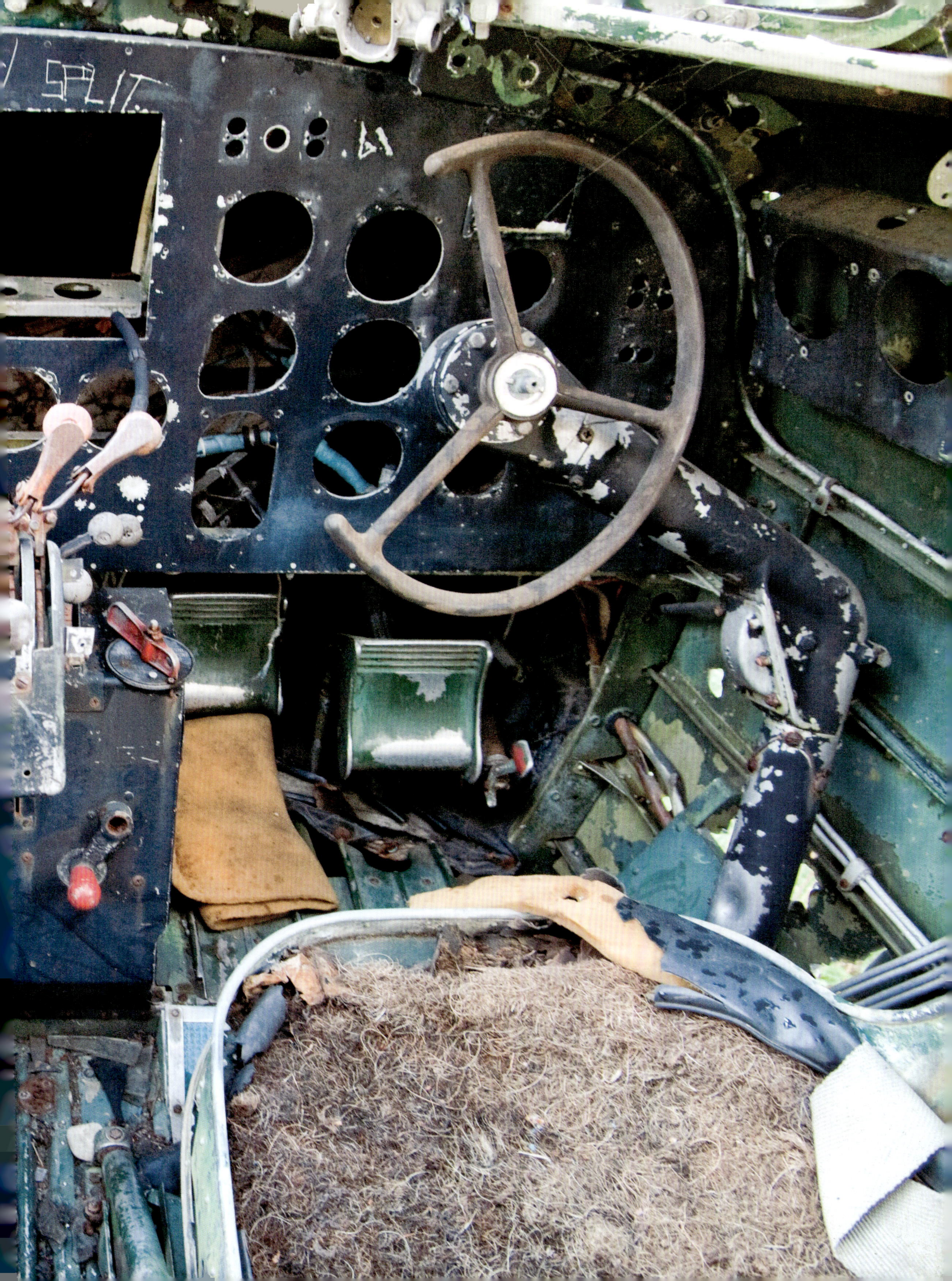

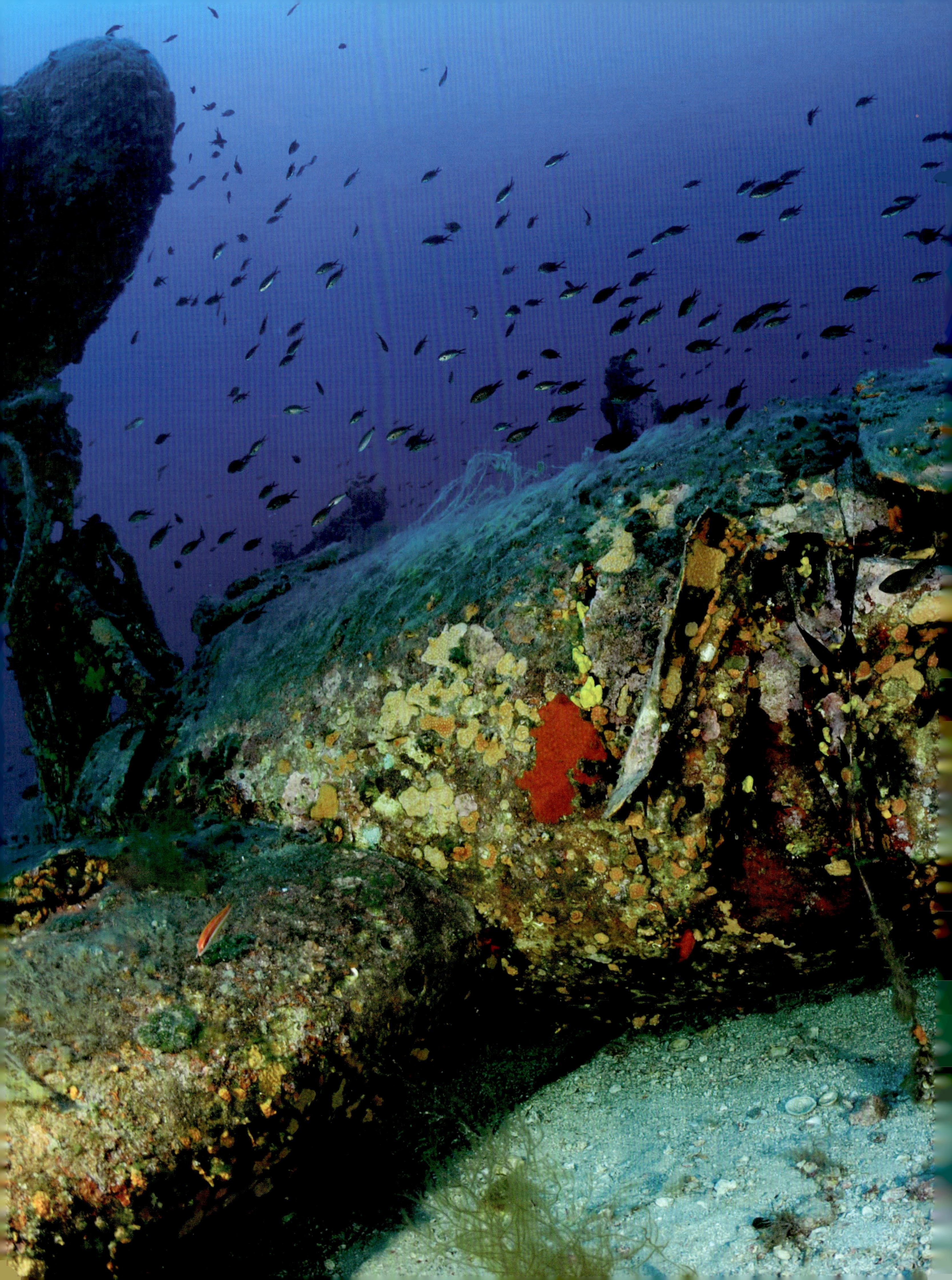

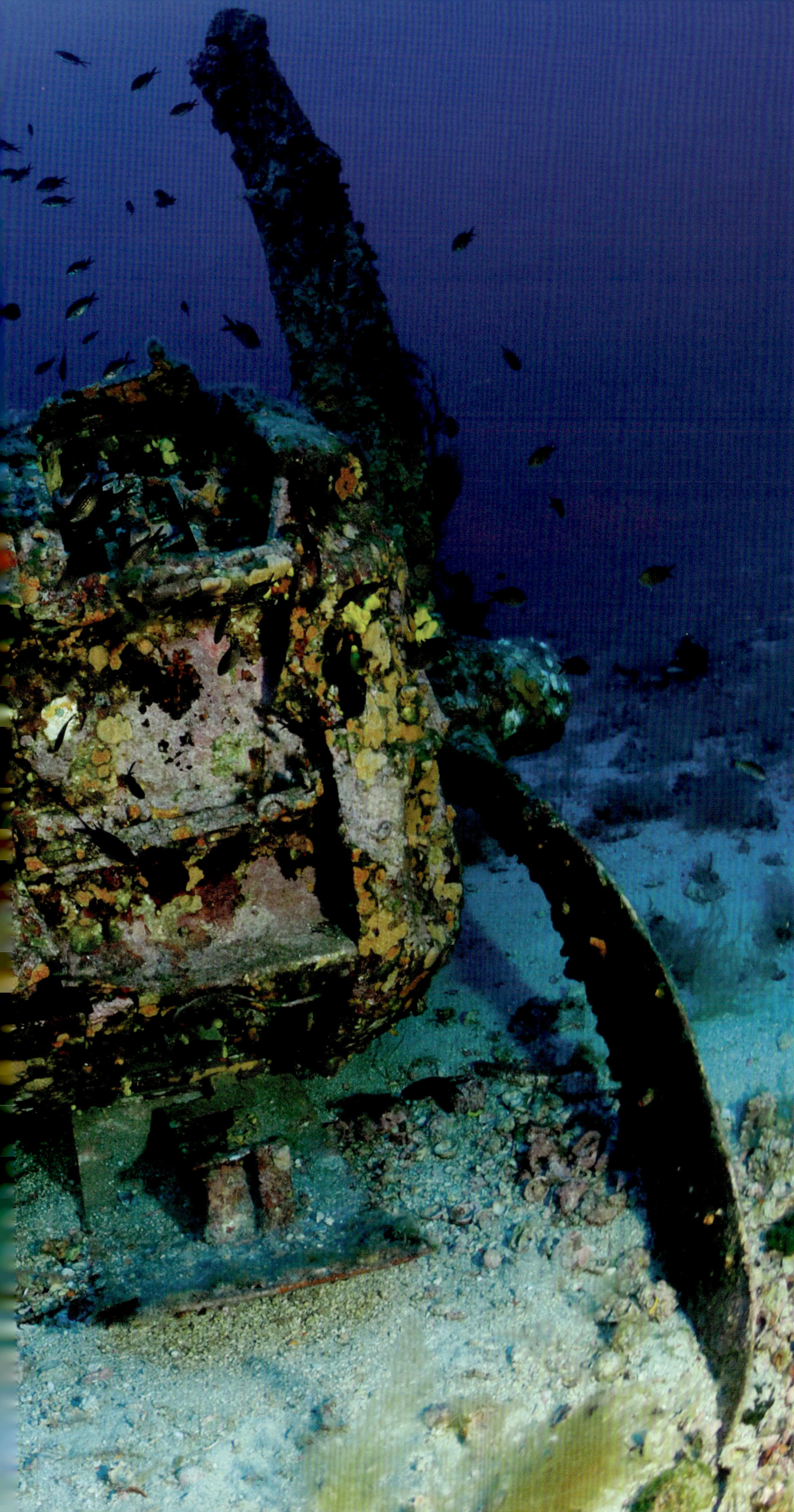

**B-24 Liberator, Vis,
Adriatic Sea, Croatia**
Here we see the submerged
engine of a World War II USAF
B-24 Liberator bomber, one of
15 such aircraft that crashed
around Vis during the conflict.
Three of the crew aboard this
aircraft died when it was shot
down on 17 December 1944. The
engine here is a Pratt & Whitney
turbosupercharged radial type,
generating 1,200hp (900kW).

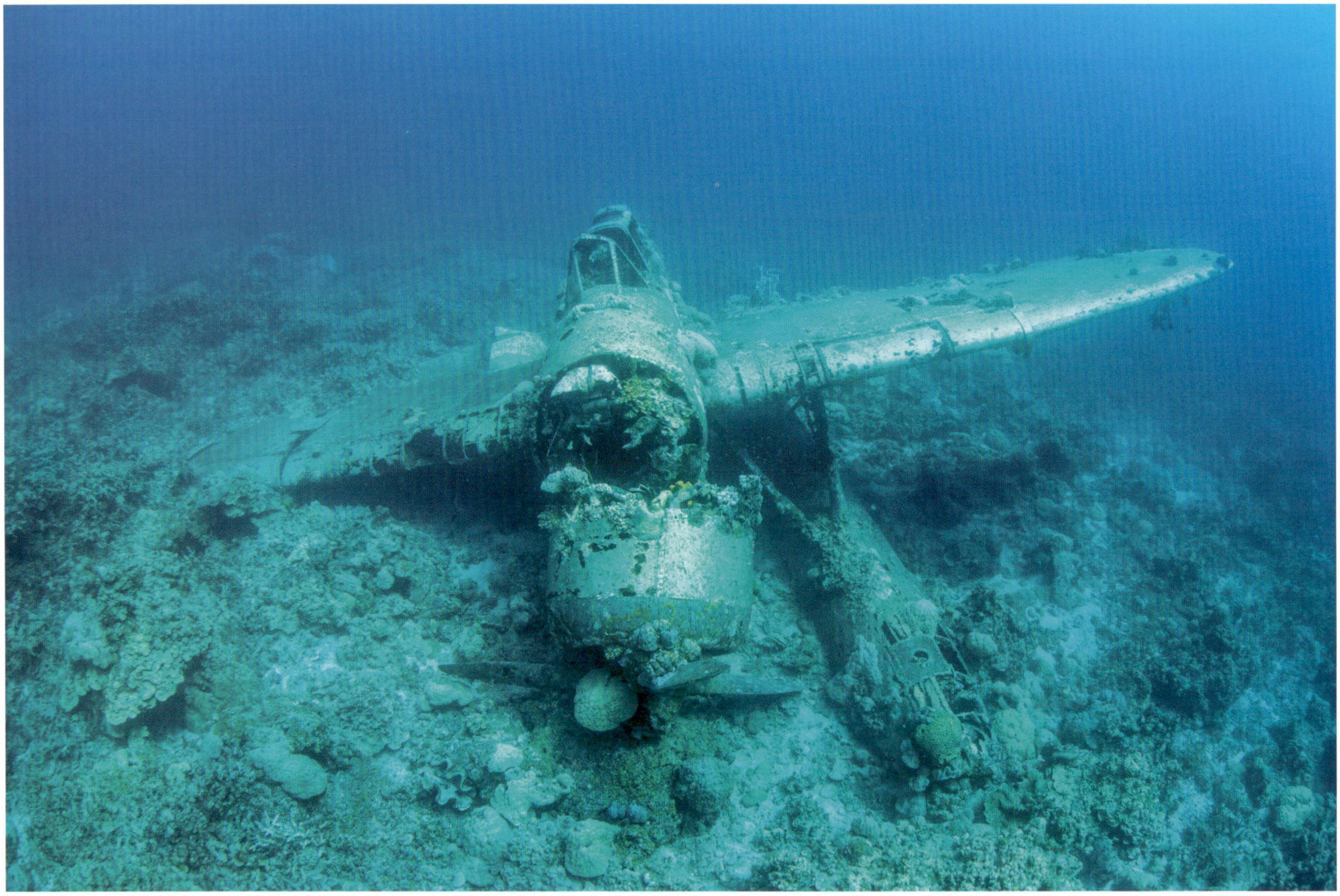

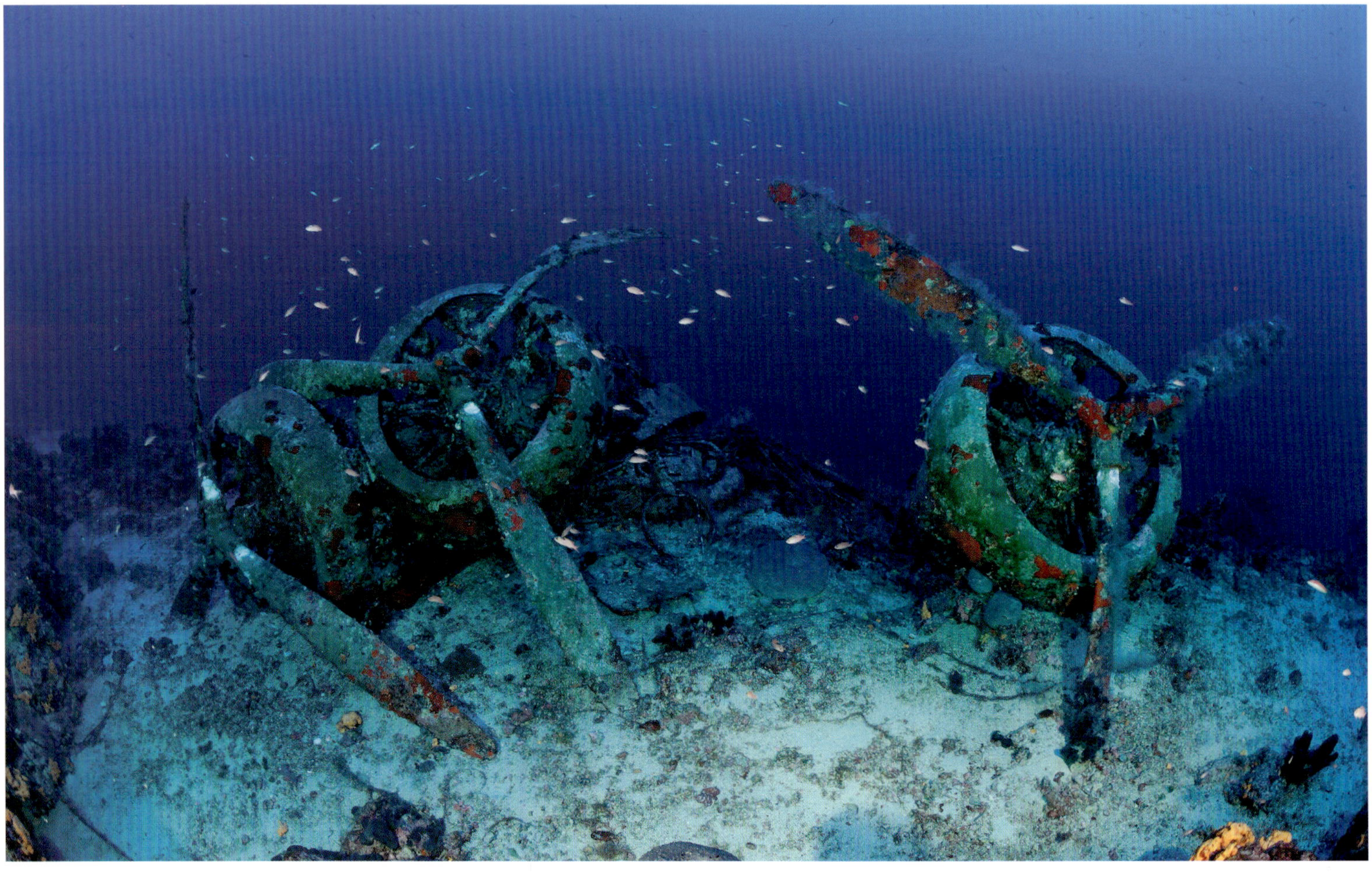

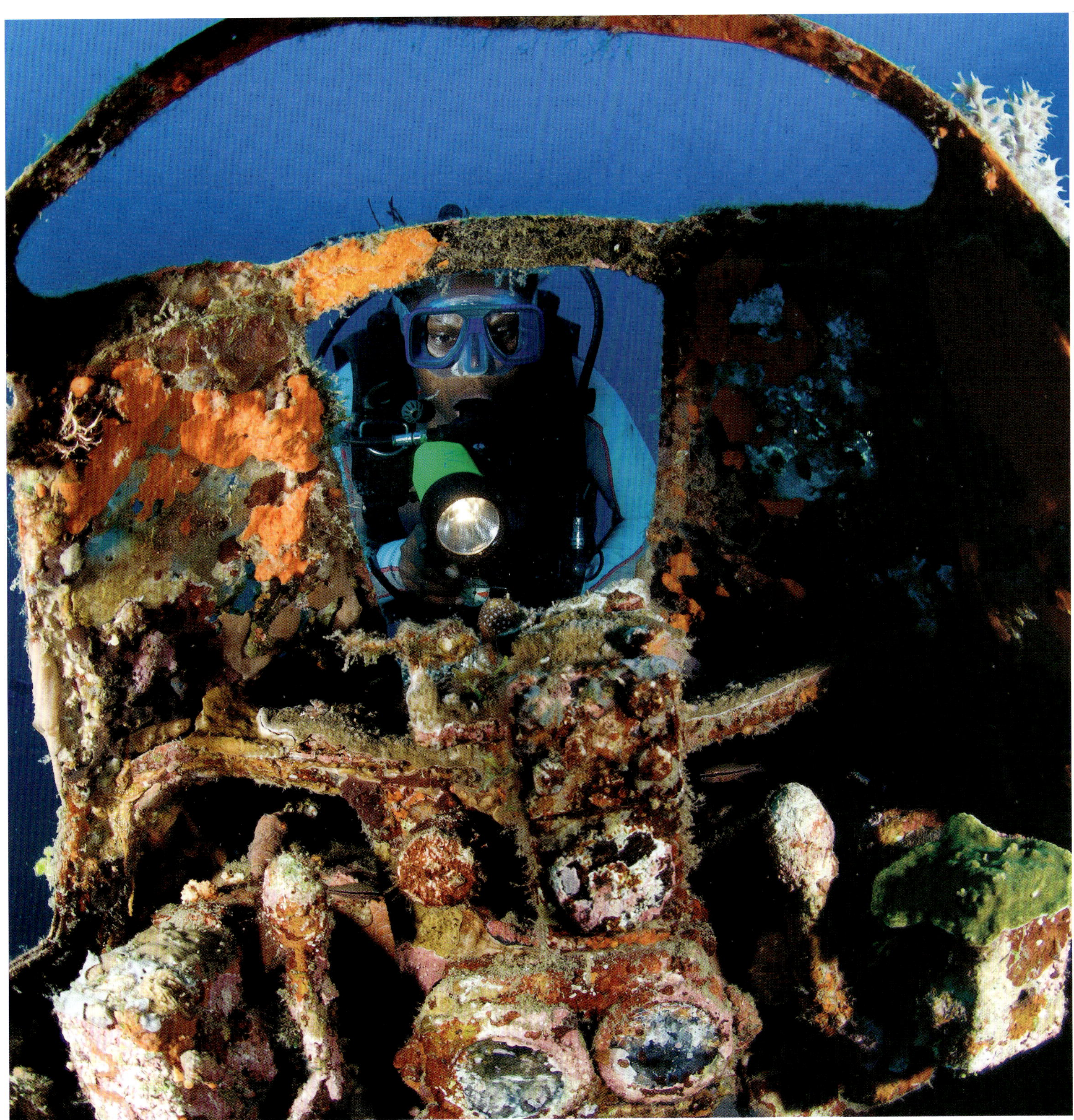

**Aichi E13A, Palau,
Western Pacific**

An Aichi E13A 'Jake' floatplane
lies amid the coral and rocks off
Palau, in 12m (39ft) of water.
The Jake was a Japanese Navy
reconnaissance aircraft, often
deployed from seaplane tenders
and cruisers. Its low speed and
limited defensive armament,
however, made it easy prey for
nimble and powerful American
fighter aircraft.

**Savoia-Marchetti SM.79,
Kas Flying Fish Reef,
Mediterranean, Turkey**

The wreck here is of an Italian
Savoia-Marchetti SM.79 *Sparviero*
(Italian for sparrowhawk) three-
engined bomber. This particular
aircraft was shot down by British
anti-aircraft fire from Meis Island,
and was one of three bombers
destroyed in the action in 1941. All
six of the bomber's crew members
died in the crash.

**Mitsubishi Zero, Kimbe Bay,
Papua New Guinea**

A diver stares into the cockpit of
a Japanese wartime Mitsubishi
Zero, shot down around Papua
New Guinea between 1942 and
1945. Although some of the
cockpit display dials are visible,
most have disappeared now
beneath aquatic life, although
some valuable items have doubtless
been taken by souvenir hunters
over the decades.

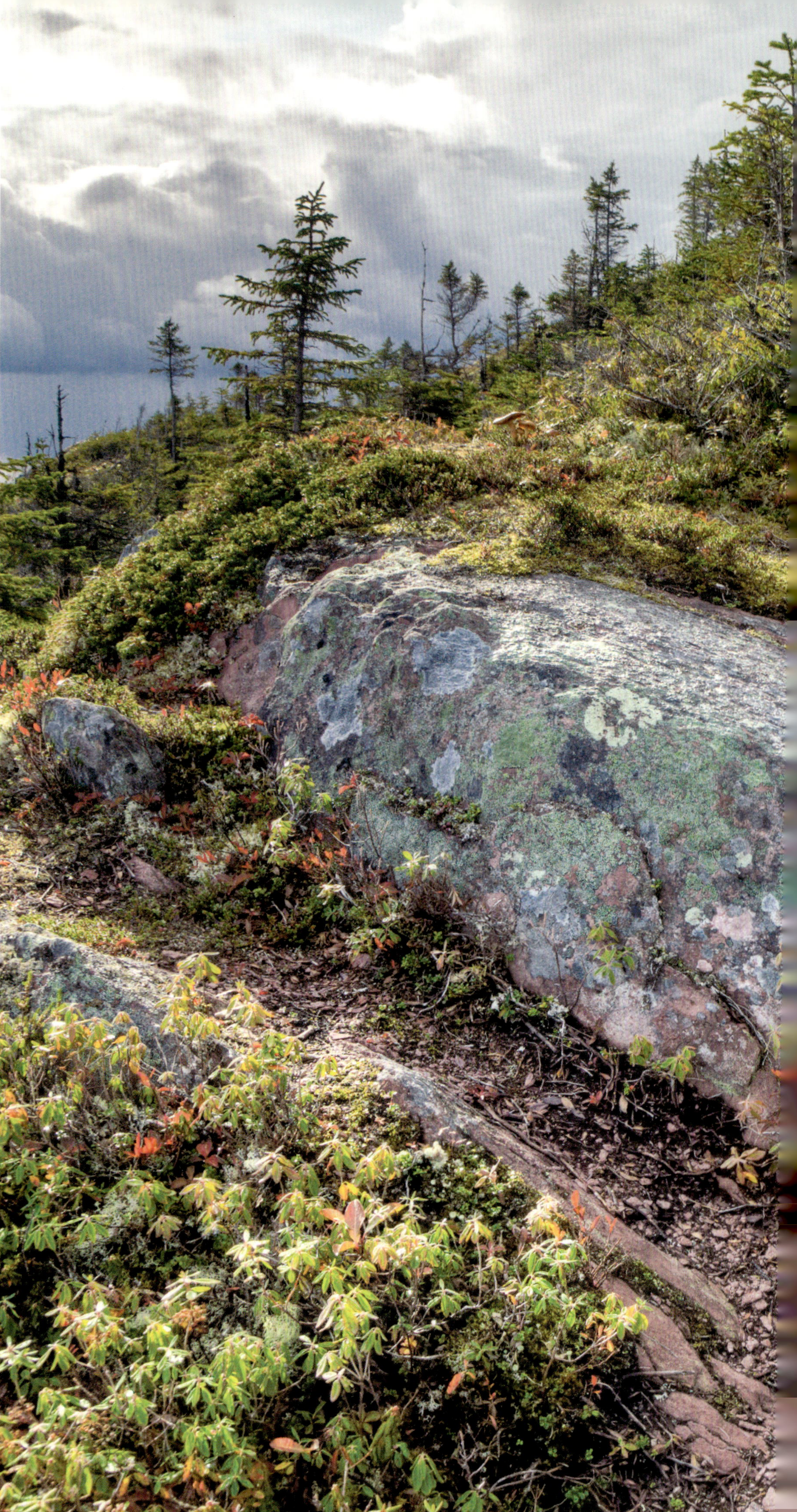

B-26 Peacemaker Bomber, British Columbia, Canada
The engine of a Cold War B-26 Peacemaker bomber lies embedded in a mountainside in British Columbia. The aircraft crashed on 13 February 1950 after three engines caught fire, the crew being forced to jettison their Mk 4 nuclear bomb. Five of the 17-man crew died in the crash or from having bailed out and succumbing to hypothermia in the ocean.

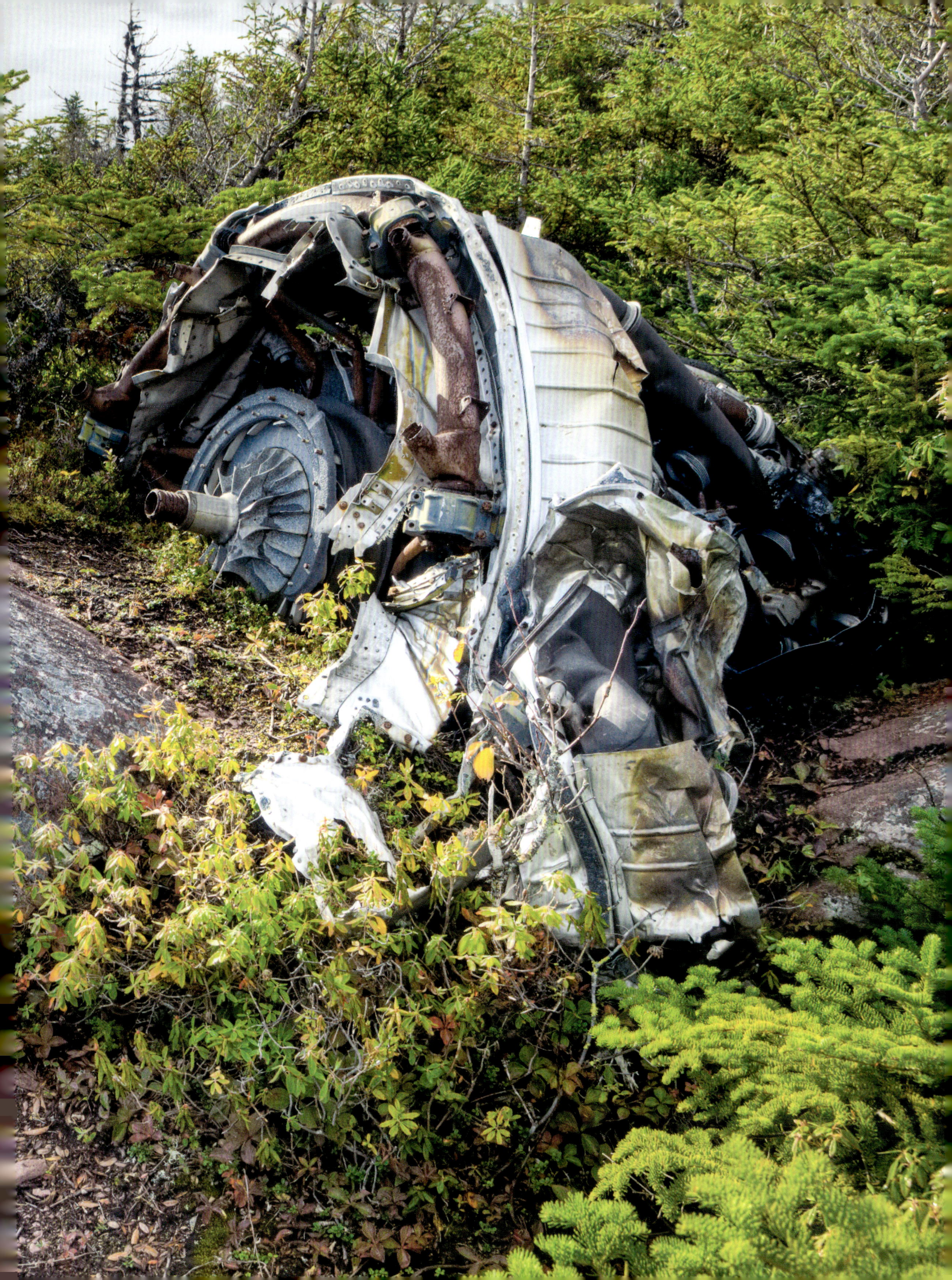

Lockheed Ventura, near Walindi Resort, Papua New Guinea
The jungle steadily reclaims a Lockheed Ventura of the New Zealand Air Force. This aircraft crashed when it suffered from engine failure in September 1944, after completing a bombing mission against Japanese shipping in Rabaul Harbor, New Britain.

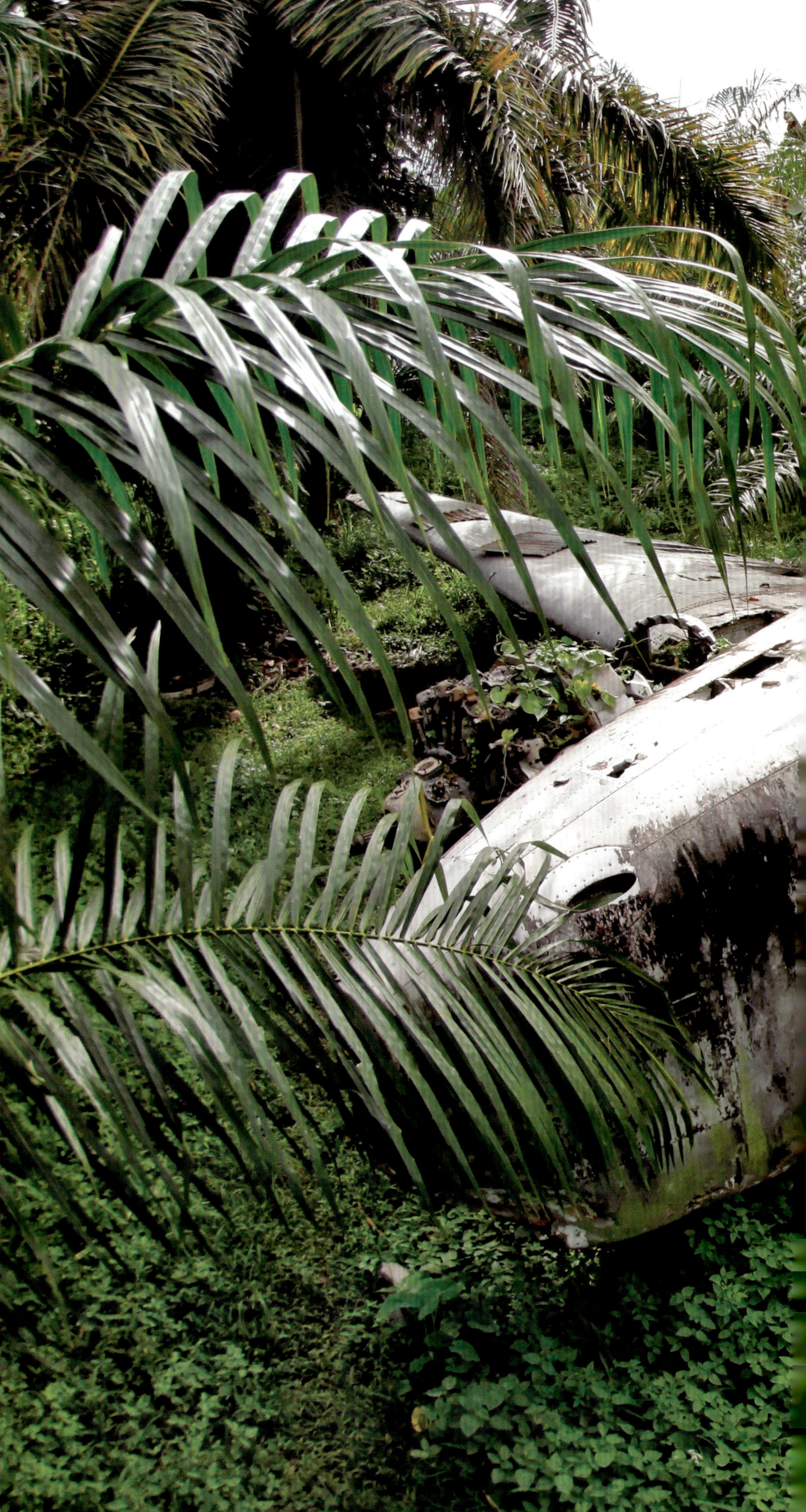

**Antonov AN-2,
Amazon Jungle, Peru**
The well-preserved wreckage of a Soviet Antonov AN-2 aircraft sits in the jungle of Peru, the story behind its crash largely a mystery. The AN-2 was likely sold to Peruvian interests at some point during the Cold War. It was an ideal aircraft for use in remote rural areas, as it could operate from unpaved airstrips.

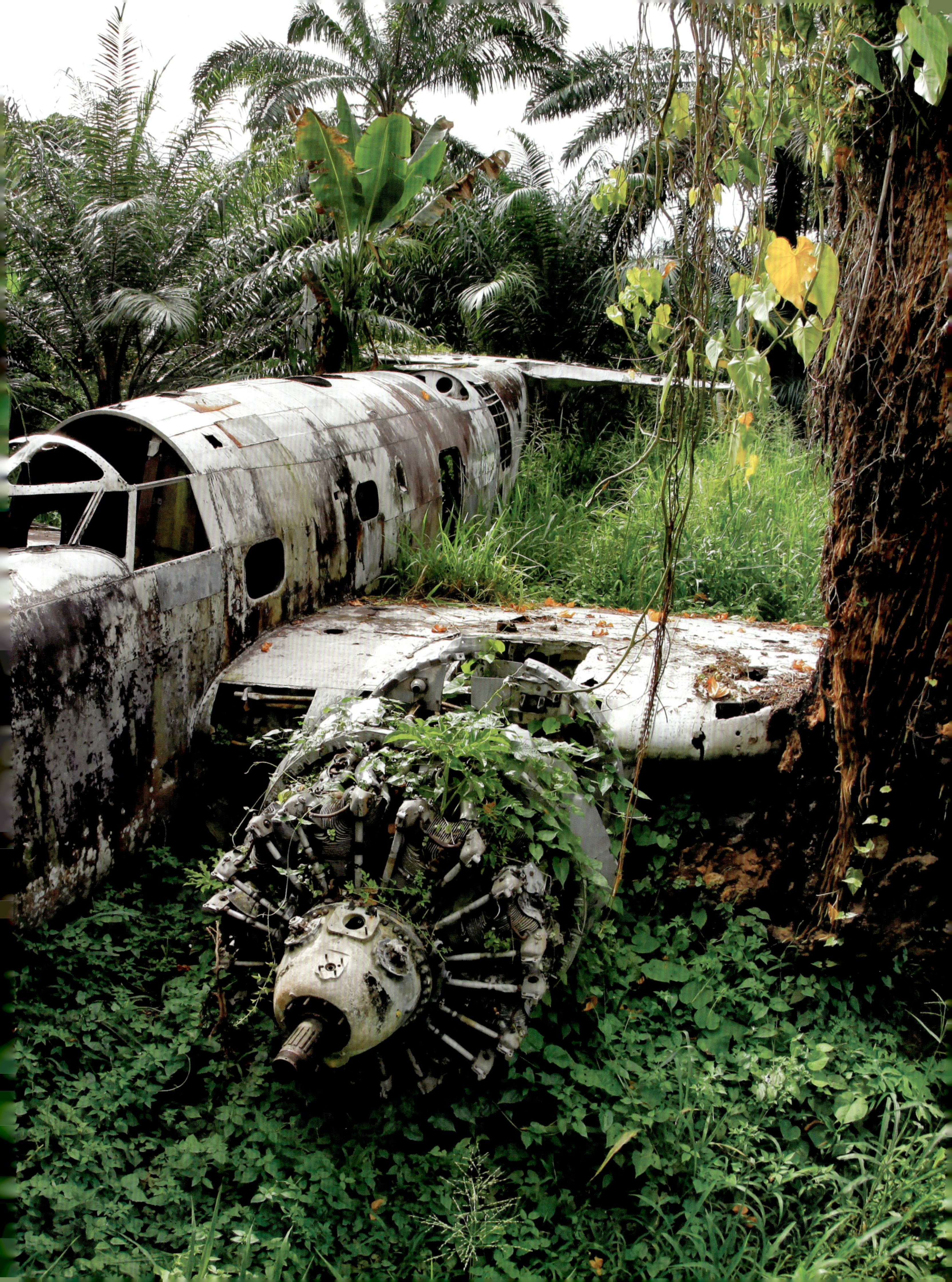

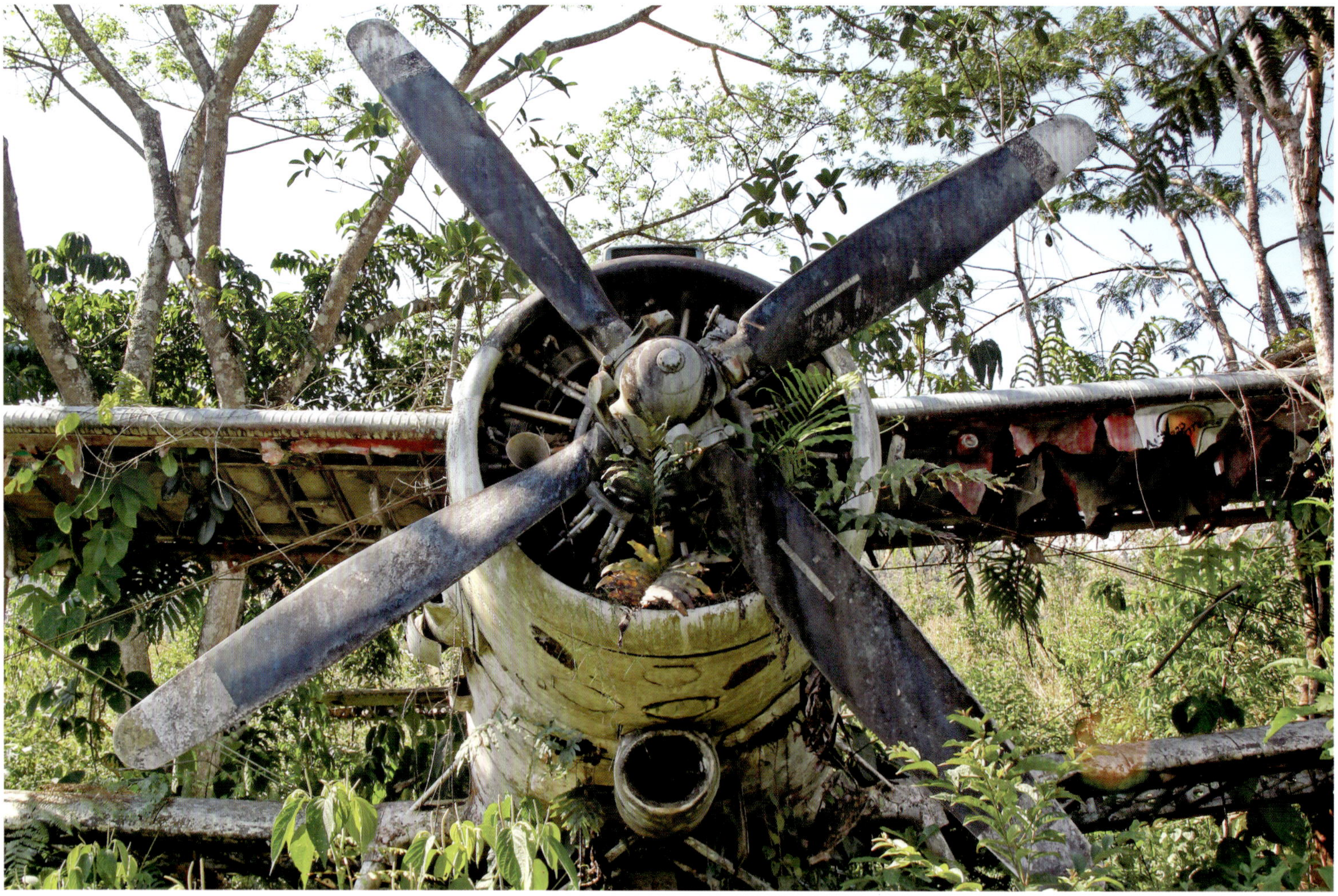

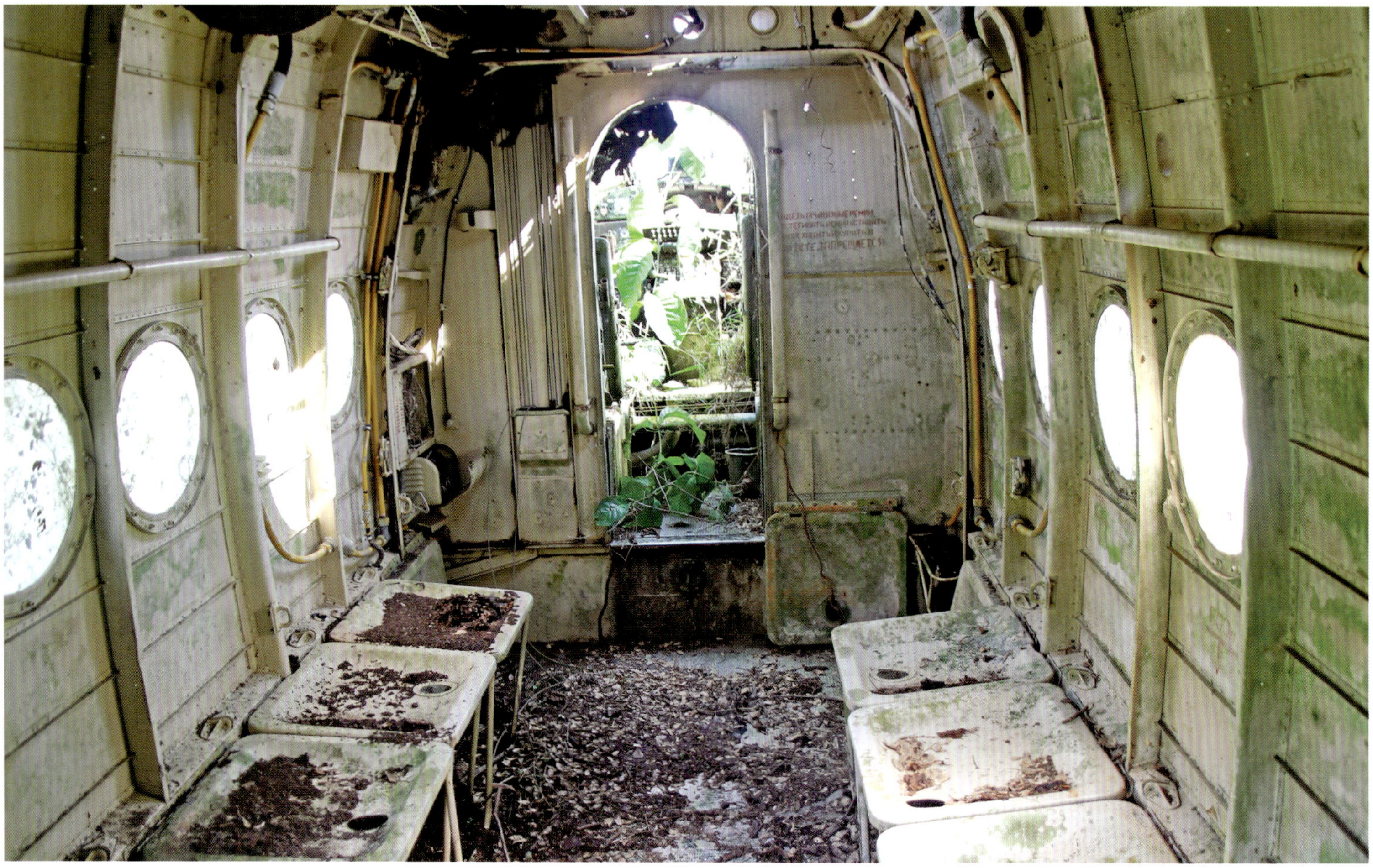

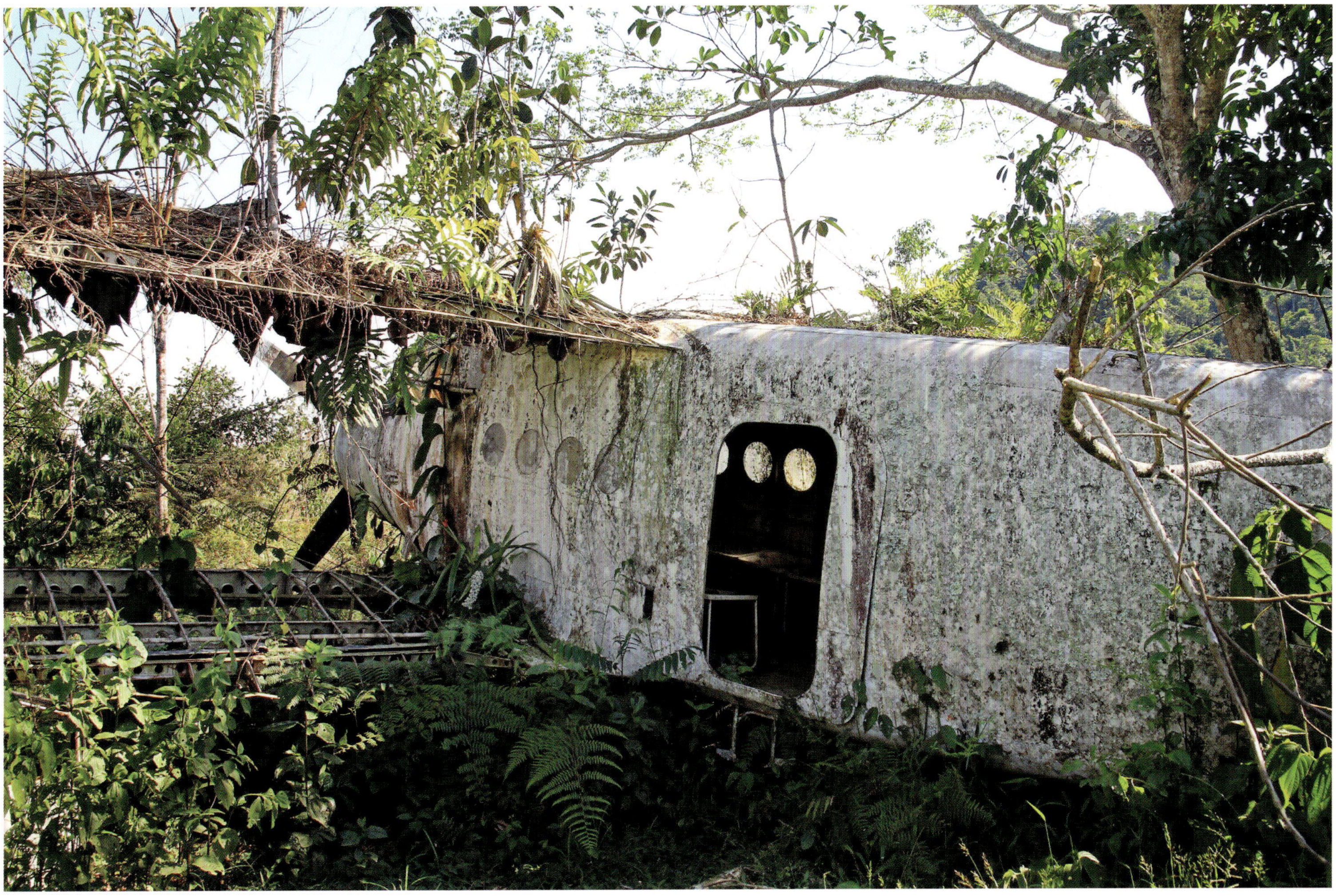

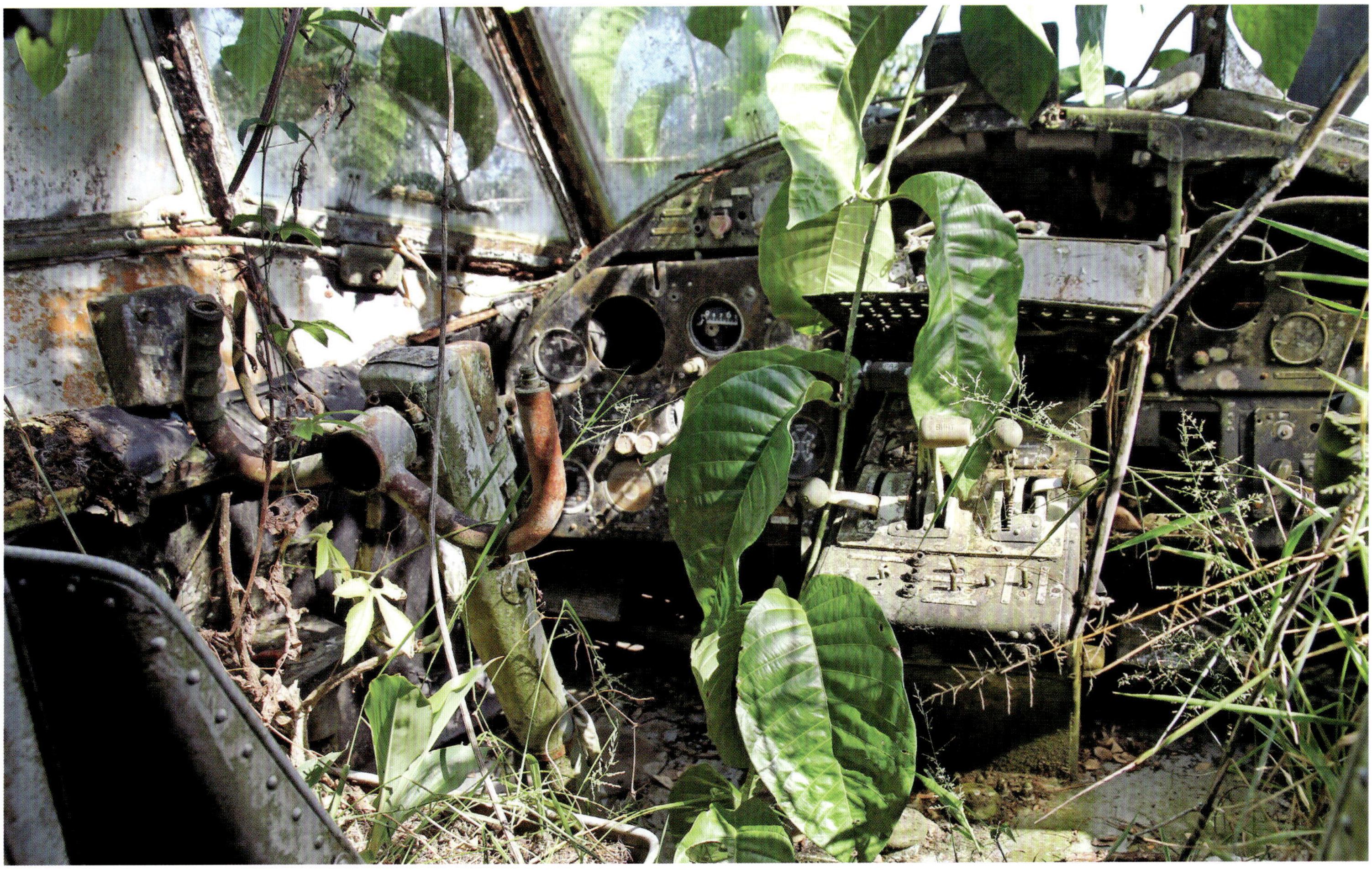

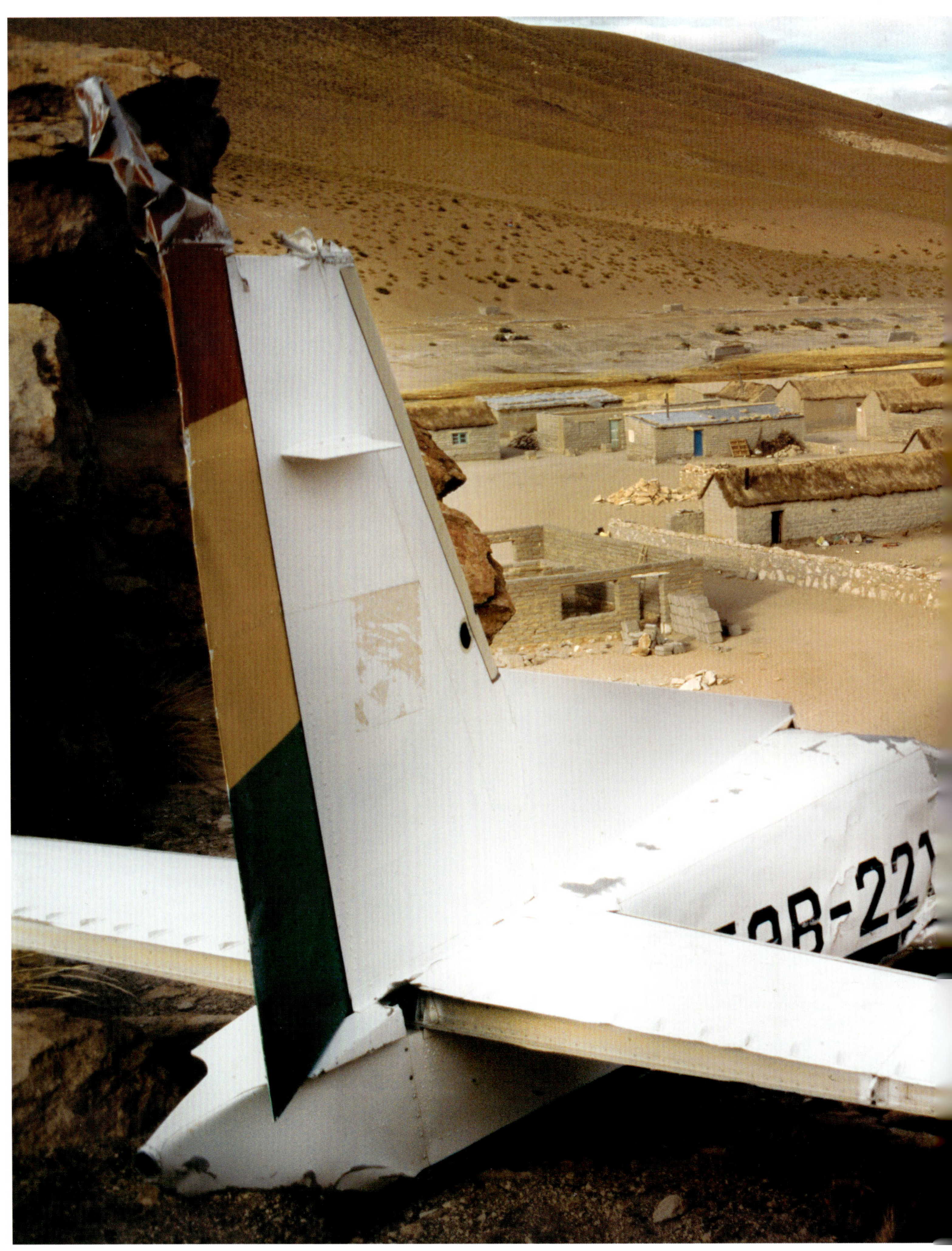

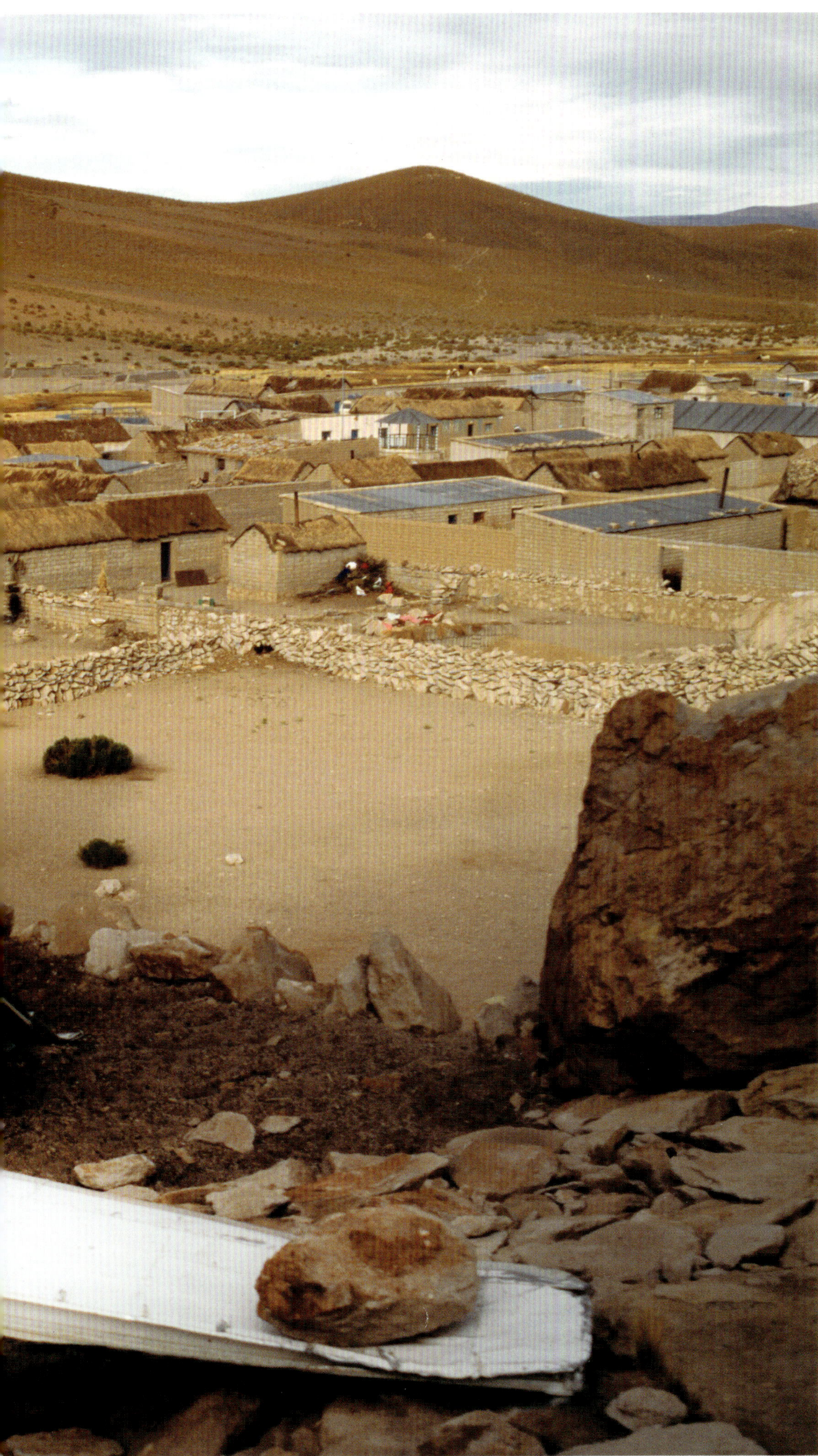

**Malko Village, southern
Altiplano, Bolivia**
Shorn from the rest of the aircraft,
the tailplane of a Bolivian Air
Force training aircraft that crashed
in 1992 sits above the village
of Malko. The dry climate has
ensured that the paintwork and
metal remain in good condition.

Picture Credits

Alamy: 7 (Redbrickstock.com), 8 (H Mark Weisman Photography), 10/11 (Martin Frank), 16/17 (McMaster Studio), 18/19 & 20/21 (Naturfoto-Online), 34 bottom (Andrey Nekrasov), 35 top (Entertainment Pictures), 35 bottom (Walt Disney Co./Everett Collection), 36/37 (Entertainment Pictures), 40/41 (Geoff Kirby), 44 top (Adam Burton), 46/47 (Robert Harding/Michael Nolan), 48/49 (Rolf Hicker Photography), 52 & 54/55 (Cultura Creative/Julian Ward), 56/57 (Scott Sim), 60 top & 61 (David Litschel), 62/63 (Jack Hinds – Travel), 64/65 (Jeffrey Blackler), 68/69 (Eleonora Saini), 70/71 (Cultura Creative/Julian Ward), 72/73 (George Phillipas), 74 top (John Crux), 74/75 bottom (Kevin Law), 75 top (Blickwinkel/Teister), 76/77 (Emilliano Rodriguez), 80/81 (George Oze), 84 top (Constantine Savvides), 84 bottom (Reuters/Andrew Biraj), 85 bottom (Martyn Williams), 86/87 (Felipe Guzman), 88/89 (Fillippo Ferrari), 90 (Eye Em/Markus Spiering), 91 top (Jordana Meilleur), 91 bottom (NH Collection), 92/93 & 94/95 (Findlay), 96/97 (Geophotos), 98 (Reuters/ Roger Bacon), 100/101 & 102/103 (US Army), 104 top (Theodore Kaye), 105 top (John Zada), 106/107 & 108/109 (Andrey Nekrasov), 110 top (Philip Game), 110 bottom (Shaktar Shabtai), 111 (Reuters/Roger Bacon), 112/113 (Johnny Saunderson), 114/115 (IML Image Group), 118 top (Fine Art), 118/119 bottom (Zute Lightfoot), 119 top (Nir Ben-Yosef), 120/121 (Reuters/Thomas Mukoya), 122 bottom (Chrisstockphotography), 123 top (DPA), 123 bottom (Agencja Fotograficzna Caro/Trappe), 126 top (Darren Bell), 126 bottom (Ryan Bonneau), 127 (Amanda Cotton), 128/129 (Reuters/Roger Bacon), 130 (David Wall), 132/133 (Amy Raedts), 134 top (Seppo Hinluka), 134 bottom (Graham Hardy), 135 (David Parker), 136/137 (Charles Harker), 138/139 top (Rob Crandall), 139 bottom (Michael Runkel), 140/141 (Brad Mitchell), 144/145 (Ivalyo Daskalov), 148 bottom (Nik Taylor), 149 (Allan Wright), 150 bottom (Frontline Photography), 151 bottom (David Forster), 152/153 (Jon Bilous), 154 top (Richard Bradley), 154 bottom (Media World Images), 155 top (Latitude Stock/Colin Weston), 156/157 (Johner Images), 158 top (James Schwabel), 158 bottom (Johner Images), 159 bottom (James Schwabel), 160/161 (Alexander Frolov), 164/165 (Phil Crean), 166 top (Ted Horowitz), 166 bottom (Alan Wilson), 167 (Jordan Fox), 168/169 (Octavio India), 172 (Waterframe), 174/175 (National Geographic Creative/Lola Akinmade Akerstrom), 176/177 (Richard Baker USA), 178/179 (Le Garsmeur American Collection), 180 top (Findlay), 181 top (John Zada), 184 top (Howard Chew), 184 bottom (F Jack Jackson), 188/189 (Joerg Boethling), 196/197 bottom (John van Rosendaal), 198/199 (Calavision), 200/201 (Andrey Nekrasov), 208/209 & 210/211(CTK/Lachnitt Julius), 212/213 & 214 bottom (Waterframe), 216/217 (National Geographic Creative/Pete Ryan), 218/219 (F1online Digitale Bildagentur/Tobias Friedrich), 220-221 all (Ryan M Bolton), 222/223 (Art Directors & TRIP/Mary Jeliffe)

Alamy/Imagebroker:12/13 & 22/23 (Norbert Probst), 26/27 (Daniel Kreher), 50/51 & 122 top (Michael Runkel), 180/181 bottom (Egmont Strigl)

Alamy/Stocktrek Images: 104/105 bottom & 116/117 & 124/125 (Andrew Chittock), 186/187 & 204/205 (Terry Moore), 214 top (Ethan Daniels), 215 (Steve Jones)

Depositphotos: 25 bottom (Dellfoto), 191 top (Docrob)

Dreamstime: 6 (James Mattil), 14 top (Serban Enache), 14 bottom (Vzmaze), 15 (Peter Lasovic), 24 top (Antonis Tsipropoulos), 24 bottom (Robin Valderman), 30 top (Kjuuurs), 30 bottom (Eg004713), 31 top (Wosabi), 32/33 & 34 top (Andrew Jalbert), 38/39 (Veronika Peskova), 42/43 (Benny Marty), 44/45 bottom (Gringos4), 45 top (Tony Campbell), 58/59 (Thomas Lusth), 60 bottom (Javaman), 66/67 (Chris Rb), 78/79 (Maxwell de Araujo Rodrigues), 138 bottom (Zhukovsky), 142 (Ragne Kabanova), 143 top (Michele Zuliani), 143 bottom (Neil Lockhart), 146/147 (Dmitry Vinogradov), 148 top (Cigdem Sean Cooper), 150 top (Darryl Brooks), 151 top (Maria Luisa Lopez Estivill), 155 bottom (Badahos), 159 top (Ron van Esch), 170/171 (Tatiana Morosava), 182/183 (Livshammond), 185 (Aleksei Kondraiuk), 190 top (Deymos), 190 bottom (James Mattil), 191 bottom (Alexandr Blinov), 192/193 (Simone Kesh), 202/203 (Mari1408), 206 top (Erectus), 206 bottom (Alexandr Blinov), 207 (Clive Magill)

Photoshot: 211 (London Aerial)

FEMA: 28/29 (Chris Ragazzo)

Fotolia: 82/83 (Vitaly Titov)

Getty Images: 25 top (Bloomberg), 31 bottom (Photoplus Magazine), 85 top (UIG/Insights), 196 top (Bryn Cotton), 197 top (Lonely Planet Images/Amos Chapple)

Frank C. Grace: 162/163

Ralph Mirebs: 194/195

Shutterstock: 142 (Muhammad Mughal)